DICTIONARY
of **Media** and
Communication
Studies
6th Edition

James Watson and Anne Hill

ARNOLD

First published in Great Britain in 1984
Second edition 1989
Third edition 1993
Fourth edition 1997
Fifth edition 2000
Sixth edition published in 2003 by
Arnold, a member of the Hodder Headline Group,
338 Euston Road, London NW1 3BH

http://www.arnoldpublishers.com

Distributed in the United States of America by
Oxford University Press Inc.
198 Madison Avenue, New York, NY 10016

British Library Cataloguing in Publication Data
A catalogue record for this book is available from the British Library

Library of Congress Cataloging-in-Publication Data
A catalog record for this book is available from the Library of Congress

ISBN 0 340 80829 2

1 2 3 4 5 6 7 8 9 10

Typeset in 9.5pt Baskerville by Dorchester Typesetting Group Ltd
Printed and bound in Malta.

What do you think about this book? Or any other Arnold title?
Please send your comments to feedback.arnold@hodder.co.uk

PREFACE TO 6TH EDITION

This edition reflects the advances in media globalization and the challenges to communication of multi-culturalism in the workplace and within societies generally (see, for example, INTERCULTURAL COMMUNICATION; M-TIME, P-TIME). Over 100 entries have been despatched, and over 50 new entries have taken their place. Survivors from previous editions have been extended, updated, pruned or generally toned up.

In addition, we have attempted to match the requirements of UK exam boards in Media and Communication Studies while at the same time keeping in mind the broader, more diverse expectations of undergraduate courses. We would also like to think the Dictionary provides a handy reference for the general reader curious to discover, for example, what DATA MINING, FLAK, GAGGING ORDERS, HISTORICAL ALLUSION or the REGULATION OF INVESTIGATORY POWERS ACT (UK) are all about.

Media literacy – the knowledge of media developments, awareness of and vigilance concerning the rights of the public with regard to media practices – has become a requirement of citizenship, hence our emphasis on the connection between people, media performance and the exercise of power in modern societies (see CULTURAL, OR CITIZEN RIGHTS AND THE MEDIA; GLOBAL MEDIA SYSTEM: THE MAIN PLAYERS; UNIVERSALITY).

We have tried to keep track of legislation concerning media, and the events and trends that affect regulation and deregulation of media ownership and control – still the chief issue, bone of contention and ground for debate, especially considering the globalization of such ownership and control (see MEDIA MOGULS: FOUR SOURCES OF CONCERN).

The Dictionary, as many of its entries indicate, is not altogether value-free. To have aimed at clinical objectivity might have lost some of the text's individuality and colour. We declare support for, though not an uncritical attitude towards, notions of public service in its ongoing relationship with private enterprise.

We acknowledge that the aims, objectives and achievements of public and private mass communication have much in common; that there are situations when public and private work amicably, productively and creatively, sometimes in partnership and sometimes in competition. At the same time, the media arena rings with the gladiatorial clash of interests, with governments often egging on the combatants and the combatants in turn pressurizing governments. May a fair fight continue (on level playing fields), with preferably an honourable draw being the target rather than defeat for one side or the other.

The study of communication has inexorably become more international in scope. Each new edition of the Dictionary has aimed to reflect and confirm the cosmopolite nature of the cultural contexts in which communication takes places, while at the same time respecting the critical value of localite experience and knowledge.

In the 5th edition, we introduced a Chronology of Media Events; in this edition we have created and placed before the alphabetic listing of entries, a *TOPIC GUIDE* on p. xvii. This is largely based on topic areas of required study published by exam boards in Media and Communication Studies. Most major entries in the Dictionary are listed in the Topic Guide.

It's our hope that this *TOPIC GUIDE* will assist the theme-based approach to study, facilitating research for assignments, by collectivizing most aspects of a given subject. Inevitably, as in all cross-referencing, there will be overlap. This in turn will affirm the essential interconnectivity of study.

James Watson and Anne Hill

☐ ABOUT THE AUTHORS

James Watson is now Visiting Lecturer in Media Studies on the BA in Media and Communication Studies offered by the University of Greenwich in partnership with the West Kent College in Tonbridge. He is also author of *Media Communication: An Introduction to Theory and Process* (UK: Palgrave Macmillan, 2nd edition, 2003) and a number of books for young readers, including *Talking in Whispers.*

Formerly Curriculum Coordinator in Media at West Kent College, and Communication Studies tutor on the West Kent/University of Greenwich BA, **Anne Hill** is now Senior Lecturer in Communication Studies at Southampton Institute.

A CHECKLIST FOR USE □

- Words in CAPITALS mean that there is a separate entry.

- Source references are usually included in the text of each entry rather than presented in an end-of-dictionary bibliography.

- Use is made of an asterisk (*) at the end of some entries: here books of special interest or value for further reading on the topic are recommended.

- Traditional practice of referring to the city or town where a book was first published has been modified in this dictionary, reference being made to the country of origin (US or UK).

- Where c. is used it is an abbreviation for century.

- Communication models are listed using the name of the persons who conceived them (e.g. SHANNON AND WEAVER'S MODEL OF COMMUNICATION, 1949), and commissions/committees on the media are referred to by the name of the chairpersons (e.g. PILKINGTON COMMISSION REPORT ON BROADCASTING (UK), 1962).

□ ACKNOWLEDGEMENTS

The publishers and authors would like to thank the following for permission to include copyright material.

Pearson Education for: 'Gerbner's model of communication, 1956', Page 117, from *Communication* by Denis McQuail, Longman (1993); 'Noelle-Neumann's spiral of silence model of public opinion, 1974', P.201, 'Newcomb's ABX model', P.191, McLeod and Chaffee's "Kite" model, 1973', P.168, 'Galtung and Ruge's model of selective gatekeeping', P.114 and 'McCombs and Shaw's agenda-setting model of media effects, 1976', P.165, from *Communication Models for the Study of Mass Communication,* Longman UK, 5th Impression (1998).

AEJMC for: 'White's gatekeeper model, 1950', P.311, from *Journalism Quarterly* 27 (1950); 'Wesley and MacLean's model of communication', P.309, from *Journalism Quarterly* 34 (1957); 'McNelly's model of news flow, 1959', P.169, from *Journalism Quarterly* 36 (1959); 'Bass's "double action" model, 1969', P.22, *Journalism Quarterly* 46 (1969).

Sage Publications Ltd for: 'Kepplinger and Habermeier model of events', P.100, from *European Journal of Communication,* September 1995; 'Ball-Rokeach and DeFleur's dependency model of communication effects, 1976', P.19, from *Communication Research* 3 (1976); 'Rogers and Dearing agenda setting model, 1987', P.253, from *Communication Yearbook* vol.11; 'McQuail's accountability of media model', P.170, from *European Journal of Communication,* (1997). 'McQuail's audience analysis', P.16, from *Audience Analysis* by Denis McQuail, Sage (1997). 'Westerståhl and Johansson model of news factors in foreign news, 1994' from *European Journal of Communication,* March 1994; 'Griswold cultural diamond model, 1994' from *Cultures and Societies in a Changing World,* Pine Forge Press, 1994.

Harcourt Publishers for: 'Andersch, Staats and Bostroom model of communication 1969', P.9, from *Communication in Everyday Use,* 3rd Edition, by Elizabeth G. Andersch, Lorin C. Staats and Robert N. Bostrom, CBS College Publishing (1969); 'Dance's helical model', P.77, from *Human Communication Theory,* edited by Frank Dance, Rinehart and Winston (1967); 'Berlo's SMCR model of communication, 1960', P.25, from *The Process of Communication: An Introduction to Theory and Practice,* by David K. Berlo, Holt, Rinehart & Winston (1960).

HarperCollins Publishers for: 'Barnlund's transactional models of communication, 1970', P.20, *Foundations of Communication Theory* edited by K.K. Sereno and C.D. Mortensen, Harper and Row (1970). Perseus Books Group for: 'Riley and Riley model of mass communication, 1959', P.252, from *Sociology Today: Problems and Prospects* edited by Robert K. Merton, Leonard Broom and Leonard S. Cottrell, Jr., Basic Books (1959). University of Minnesota Press for: 'Becker's mosaic of communication, 1968', P.24, from University of Minnesota's Spring Symposium in Speech Communication (1968). Hans-Bredow-Institut for: 'Maletzke's model of the mass communication process', from *The Psychology of Mass Communications,* Verlag Hans-Bredow-Institut (1963).

ABBREVIATIONS: A SELECTION ☐

AA	Advertising Association
AAP	Australian Associated Press
ABA	Australian Broadcasting Authority
ABE	Association of British Editors
ABS	Association of Broadcasting & Allied Staffs
ACTT	Association of Cinematography, Television & Allied Technicians
ADP	Association of Directors & Producers
ADP	Automatic Data Processing
ADSL	Asymmetrical Digital Subscriber Line
AFDC	Australian Film Development Corporation
AFP	Agence France-Presse
AIJ	Association of Investigative Journalists
ALCS	Author's Lending & Copyright Society
AP	Associated Press
AR	Audience Research
ASA	Advertising Standards Authority
ATV	Associated Television (Associated Broadcasting Company)
BAFTA	British Academy of Film & TV Arts
BAPLA	British Association of Picture Libraries & Agencies
BARB	Broadcasters Audience Research Board
BBC	British Broadcasting Corporation
BBFC	British Board of Film Classification
BBS	Bulletin Board System
BCC	Broadcasting Complaints Commission
BFI	British Film Institute
bit	binary digit
BJA	Black Journalists' Association
BLT	Bright, Light and Trite
BMIG	British Media Industry Group
BMWA	Black Media Workers Association
bps	bits per second
BSB	British Satellite Broadcasting
BSC	British Society of Cinematography
BSC	Broadcasting Standards Council
BT	British Telecom
CACI	Campaign Against Censorship of the Internet
CAM	Communications Advertising & Marketing Educational Foundation

CAP	Code of Advertising Practice; Campaign Against Pornography
CAR	Computer Assisted Reporting
CARM	Campaign Against Racism in the Media
CATV	Cable Antenna Television System
CCCS	Centre for Contemporary Culture Studies (University of Birmingham)
CCD	Charge-Coupled Device
CCN	Cable News Network
CD	Compact Disc
CDA	Critical Discourse Analysis
CDV	Compact Disc Video
CMCS	Computer Mediated Communication Systems
CNNI	Cable News Network International
COI	Central Office of Information
CPBF	Campaign for Press & Broadcasting Freedom
CPJ	Committee to Protect Journalists (US)
CRA	Community Radio Association
CRT	Cathode Ray Tube
DAB	Digital Audio Broadcasting
DBS	Direct Broadcasting Satellite
DIT	Digital Imaging Technology
DOS	Disc Operating System
DP	Data Processing
DTP	Desk Top Publishing
DTT	Digital Terrestrial Television
DVD	Digital Video Disc
EBU	European Broadcasting Union
EDP	Electronic Data Processing
ENG	Electronic News Gathering
ENS	Electronic Newsroom System
ESM	Experience Sampling Method
FAIR	Fairness and Accuracy in Reporting (US)
fax	facsimile
FFE	Fund for Free Expression (US)
FFE	Feminists for Free Expression
FM	Frequency Modulation
FOIA	Freedom of Information Act (US)
GAK	Government Access top Keys
GAMA	Global Alternative Media Association
GBNE	Guild of British Newspaper Editors
GCHQ	Government Communications Headquarters
GIGO	Garbage In, Garbage Out (computer operator's acronym)
GII	Global Information Infrastructure
HDTV	High-Definition Television
HDVS	High-Definition Video System

HF	High Frequency
HMD	Head Mounted Display
HMSO	Her Majesty's Stationery Office
IAD	Internet Addiction Disorder
IAMCR	International Association of Mass Communication Research
IARP	Independent Association of Radio Producers
IBA	Independent Broadcasting Authority (succeeded by the ITC in 1991)
IBM	International Business Machines
IBT	International Broadcasting Trust
ICF	Internet Crime Foundation
IFEX	International Freedom of Expression Exchange
IFFI	International Foundation for Freedom of Information
IFJ	International Federation of Journalists
IFVA	Independent Film & Video Makers Association
IGC	Institute for Global Communications
ILR	Independent Local Radio
INR	Independent National Radio
In-tel-sat	International Telecommunications Satellite (Consortium)
IOJ	International Organization of Journalists
IPA	Institute of Practitioners in Advertising
IPA	International Publishers' Association
IPC	International Publishing Corporation
IPDC	International Programme for the Development of Communication
IPI	International Press Institute
IPR	Institute of Public Relations
Iras	Infra-red astronomy satellite
IRL	In Real Life
ISBN	International Standard Book Number
ISDN	Integrated Services Digital Networks
ISN	International Services Digital Networks
ISOC	Internet Society
ISP	Internet Service Provider
IT	Information Technology
ITC	Independent Television Commission
ITCA	Independent TV Companies Association
ITU	International Telecommunications Union
ITV	Independent Television
IV	Interactive Video
IWF	Internet Watch Foundation
IWMF	International Women's Media Foundation
IWPR	Institute for War and Peace Reporting
JICNAR	Joint Industrial Council for Newspaper Audience Research
JICPAR	Joint Industrial Council for Poster Audience Research
JICRAR	Joint Industrial Committee for Radio Audience Research (succeeded by RAJAR in 1992)
JICTAR	Joint Independent Committee for TV Advertising Research

LAN	Local Area Network
laser	light amplification by stimulated emission radiation
LED	Light Emitting Diode
LOP	Least Objectionable Programme
MBS	Mutual Broadcasting System
MDC	More Developed Country
MIS	Management Information System
MO	Mass Observation
Modem	modulator-demodulator
MOMI	Museum of the Moving Image
MMX	Multi-Media Extensions
MPAA	Motion Picture Association of America
MR	Motivation Research
MUD	Multi-User Domain
NAHBO	National Association of Hospital Broadcasting Organizations
NANAP	Non-Aligned News Agencies Pool
NASB	National Association of Student Broadcasting
NBC	National Broadcasting Company (US)
NCIS	National Criminal Intelligence Service (UK)
NCU	National Communications Union
NFA	National Film Archive
NFT	National Film Theatre
NGO	Non-Government Agency
NIC	Newly Industrialized Country
NIIO	New International Information Order
NPA	Newspaper Proprietors Association (UK)
NUJ	National Union of Journalists
NVLA	National Viewers & Listeners Association
NWICO	New World Information & Communication Order
OB	Outside Broadcast
OCR	Optical Character Recognition
OFCOM	Office of Communications (UK)
OFTEL	Office of Telecommunications
PA	Press Association
PC	Politically Correct; Personal Computer
PCC	Press Complaints Commission
PEN	Poets/Playwrights/Editors/Essayists/Novelists: PEN International
PII	Public Interest Immunity
PKC	Public Key Cryptography
PLR	Public Lending Rights
PR	Public Relations
PSI	Para-Social Interaction
PSN	Public Switched Network

RA	Radio Authority
RAJAR	Radio Joint Audience Research (succeeded JICRAR in 1992)
RDS	Radio Data System
RI	Reaction Index
RIPA	Regulation of Investigatory Powers Act (UK)
RMB	Radio Marketing Bureau
RP	Received Pronunciation
rpm	revolutions per minute
RSF	Reporters Sans Frontières
RSI	Repetitive Strain Injury
RTS	Royal Television Society
SCA	Speech Communication Association (US)
SEFT	Society for Education in Film & Television
SIGINT	Signals Intelligence
STV	Straight-To-Video
SYNCOM	Synchronous Communication Satellite
TAM	Television Audience Measurement
T & SG	Television & Screen Writers Guild
TBDF	Trans-Border Data Flow
THESIS	Times Higher Education Supplement Internet Service
TNAUK	Talking Newspaper Association of the United Kingdom
TNC	Transnational Corporation
TTL	Through the Lens
UDHR	Universal Declaration of Human Rights
UHF	Ultra High Frequency
UNESCO	United Nations Educational Scientific and Cultural Organization
UPI	United Press International
USP	Unique Selling Point/Property
VDU	Visual Display Unit
VES	Video Encoding Standard
VHD	Video High Density
VHF	Very High Frequency
VHS	Video Home System
VLV	Voice of the Listener & Viewer
VR	Virtual Reality
WELL	Whole Earth Lectronic Link (US)
WPFC	World Press Freedom Committee
WSET	Writers & Scholars Educational Trust
WWW	World Wide Web

☐ TOPIC GUIDE

In this *TOPIC GUIDE*, entries are summarized under the following headings.

ADVERTISING/MARKETING

Advertising; Advertising: ambient advertising; Advertising: Code of Advertising Standards and Practice; Advertising: mainstreamers, aspirers, succeeders and reformers; Advertising: pester power; AIDA model; Attention model of mass communication; Attitudes; Audience; Audience: active audience; Audience appreciation; Audience: fragmentation of; Audience differentiation; Audience measurement; British Code of Advertising Practice; Campaign; Class; Code of Advertising Standards and Practice (ITC); Code of Programme Sponsorship; Commercial *laissez-faire* model of (media) communication; Commercial radio; Commercial television; Conglomerates; Congruence theory; Connotation; Consumerization; Consumer sovereignty; Consumption behaviour; Content analysis; Cultural capital; Culture; Culture:

consumer culture; Culture: globalization of; Culture: popular culture; Custom audience research; Decode; Deconstruction; Demographic analysis; Dissonance; Dominant, subordinate, radical; Effects of the mass media; Encode; Ethnographic (approach to audience measurement); Expectations, horizons of; Expectations; Focus groups; Franchises for Independent Television (UK); Franchises from 1993; Gender; Hegemony; Hidden Needs; Identification; Idents; Ideology; Image; Image, rhetoric of; Infomercials; Information blizzards; Infotainment; Interpretant; Intertextuality; Intervening variables (IV); iSociety; JICNARS scale; Latitudes of acceptance and rejection; Maslow's hierarchy of needs; Media imperialism; Metonymy; Motivation; Motivation research (MR); Niche audience; Nielsen ratings; Object language; One-step, two-step, multi-step flow model of communication; Opinion leader; Passivity; Perception; Play theory of mass communication; Polysemy; Pressure groups; Product placement; PR: Public relations; Reading; Reception studies; Reflexivity; Reinforcement; Representation; Resistive reading; Resonance; Salience; Sampling; Selective exposure; Self-concept; Self-identity; Self-presentation; Semantic differential; Semiology/semantics; Semiotic power; Sign; Signification; Smiling professions; Socialization; Sponsorship; Sponsorship: ITC Code of Programme Sponsorship; Status; Stereotype; Structuralism; Subliminal; Surveillance society; Tactics and strategies; Ten commandments for media consumers; Tertiary text; Text; Uses and gratifications theory; Validity effect; VALS typology; Values.

AUDIENCES/CONSUMPTION AND RECEPTION OF MEDIA

Accessed voices; Advertising: mainstreamers, aspirers, succeeders and reformers; Advertising: pester power; Attention model of mass communication; Audience; Audience: active audience; Audience appreciation; Audience: fragmentation of; Audience differentiation; Audience measurement; Boomerang response; Button apathy; Catharsis; Code of Advertising Standards and Practice (ITC); Commercial *laissez-faire* model of (media) communication; Compassion fatigue; Complicity of users; Consensus; Consistency; Constituency; Consumerization; Consumer sovereignty; Consumption behaviour; Cultivation differential; Cultural capital; Cultural, or citizen rights and the media; Culture; Culture: consumer culture; Culture: globalization of; Custom audience research; Decode; Dependency theory; Deregulation: five myths of; Disempowerment; Desensitization; Displacement effect; Dissonance; Dominant, subordinate, radical; Effects of the mass media; Emancipatory uses of the media; Empowerment; Ethnographic (approach to audience measurement); Expectations, horizons of; Expectations; Focus groups; Frankfurt school of theorists; Global scrutiny; Gossip networks; Hegemony; Historical allusion; HICT Project; Hidden Needs; Homophily; Hypodermic needle model of communication; Identification; Ideology of romance; Information blizzards; Information gaps; Interpretant; Intervening variables (IV); iSociety; J-Curve; JICNARS scale; Knowns, Unknowns; Kuleshov effect; Kuuki; Latitudes of acceptance and rejection; Maslow's hierarchy of needs; Misinformed society; Motivation; Mobilization; Motivation research (MR); Niche audience; News: audience evaluation, six dimensions of; One-step, two-step, multi-step flow model of communication; Opinion leader; Parasocial interaction, Passivity; Play theory of mass communication; Pleasure: active and reactive; Polysemy; Public opinion; Prejudice; Reading; Reception studies; Reflexivity; Reinforcement; Resistive reading; Resonance; Right of reply; Salience; Selective exposure; Self-fulfilling prophecy; Self-identity; Semiotic power; Socialization; Surveillance society; Tactics and strategies; Ten commandments for media consumers; Uses and gratifications theory; VALS typology; Values.

BROADCASTING

Annan Commission Report on Broadcasting (UK), 1977; Balanced programming; BARB; BBC digital; BBC, government white paper, 1994; BBC, origins; Beveridge Committee Report on Broadcasting (UK), 1950; British Media Industry Group (BMIG); Broadband; Broadcasting Act (UK), 1990; Broadcasting Act (UK), 1995; Broadcasting Act (UK), 1980; Broadcasting Complaints Commission (UK); Broadcasting legislation; Broadcasting Standards Council; Cable television; Campaign for Press & Broadcasting Freedom; Campaign for Quality Television Report (UK), 1999; CCTV: closed circuit television; Ceefax; Cellular radio; Channel 4; 'Clean-up TV Movement'; Colour TV; Commercial radio; Commercial television; Community radio; Cross-media ownership; Digital television; Digitization; Duopoly; Europe: cross-border TV channels; Fourteen-day rule (UK); Franchises for Independent Television (UK); Franchises from 1993; Hankey Committee Report on Television (UK), 1943; High-definition TV; Hunt Committee Report on Cable Expansion and Broadcasting Policy (UK), 1982; Independent producers; Interactive television; Internet: wireless Internet; KPFA Radio; Minority Report of Mr Selwyn Lloyd; Naturalistic illusion (of television); Paper Tiger TV; Pilkington Committee Report on Broadcasting (UK), 1962; Pirate radio; Programme flow; Public service broadcasting (PSB); Quotas; Radio Authority Programme codes 1 and 2; Radio broadcasting; Radio Northsea; RAJAR; Reality TV; Reflective-projective theory of broadcasting and mass communication; Reithian; Saniel Pedwar Cymru; Satellite transmission; Scheduling; Secondary viewing; Selsdon Committee Report on Television (UK), 1935; Sit-com; Soap opera; Social action broadcasting; Soundbite; Sound Broadcasting Act (UK), 1972; Telegenic; Teletext; Television: access television; Television broadcasting; Television drama; Television news; Time-shift viewing; Ullswater Committee Report on Broadcasting (UK), 1936; Universality; Video; *War of the Worlds*; Westminster view; Wireless Telegraphy Act (UK), 1904; World Trade Organization (WTO) telecommunications agreement, 1997.

COMMISSIONS, COMMITTEES, LEGISLATION

Annan Committee Report on Broadcasting, 1977; Broadcasting Act, 1980; Broadcasting Act, 1990; Broadcasting Act, 1995; Broadcasting legislation; Campaign for Quality Television report (UK), 1999; Commissions/committees on the media; Communications Bill (UK), 2002; Cross-media ownership; Communications Decency Act (US); Defamation; Fairness Doctrine (USA); Franchises for Independent Television (UK); Franchises from 1993; Freedom of information; Human Rights Act (UK), 2000; Hunt Committee Report on Cable Expansion and Broadcasting Policy, 1982; Libel; Paperwork Reduction Act (US), 1980; Pirate radio (UK); Prior Restraint; Radio Authority (UK) Programme Codes; Regulation of Investigatory Powers Act (RIPA) (UK), 2000; SLAPPS; Sponsorship: ITC Code of Programme Sponsorship; Terrorism: Terrorism, Crime and Security Act (UK), 2001; Text: integrity of the text; Video Recording Act (UK), 1984; Violence on TV: code of practice (UK); Wireless Telegraphy Act, 1904; World Trade Organization (WTO) Telecommunications Agreement, 1997.

COMMUNICATION MODELS

Alleyne's news revolution model, 1997; Andersch, Staats and Bostrom's model of communication, 1969; Attention model of mass communication; Ball-Rokeach and DeFleur's dependency model of mass communication effects, 1976; Barnlund's transactional model of communication, 1970; Bass's double action model of internal news flow, 1969; Becker's mosaic model of communication, 1968; Commercial *laissez-faire* model of (media) communication; Dance's helical model of communication, 1967; Galtung and Ruge's model of selective gatekeeping, 1965; Gerbner's model of communication, 1956; Griswold's cultural diamond model, 1994; Herman and Chomsky's propaganda model (see CONSENT, MANUFACTURE OF); Hypodermic needle model of communication; Jakobson's model of communication, 1958; Kepplinger and Habermeier's model of media events, 1995 (see EVENT); Lasswell's model of communication, 1948; Maletzke's model of the mass communication process, 1963; McCombs and Shaw's agenda-setting model of media effects, 1976; McLeod and Chaffey's 'kite' model, 1973; McNelly's model of news flow, 1959; McQuail's accountability of media model, 1997; McQuail's four stages of audience fragmentation (see AUDIENCE: FRAGMENTATION OF); Newcomb's ABX model of communication, 1953; Noelle-Neumann's spiral of silence model of public opinion, 1974; One-step, two-step, multi-step flow models of communication; Propaganda model (see CONSENT, MANUFACTURE OF); Riley and Riley's model of mass communication, 1959; Schramm's models of communication, 1954; Rogers and Dearing's agenda-setting model, 1987; Shannon and Weaver's model of communication, 1949; S-IV-R model of communication; Tripolar model of competing agendas (see ROGERS AND DEARING'S AGENDA-SETTING MODEL, 1987); Wesley and MacLean's model of communication, 1957; Westerstähl and Johansson's model of news factors in foreign news, 1994; White's gatekeeper model, 1950.

These and other models not included in the Dictionary – such as Comstock's Psychological Model of Television Effects on Individual Behaviour, 1978, DeFleur's Model of the American Mass Media System, 1979, and Gieber and Johnson's Model of Source-Reporter Relations, 1961 – may be read about in detail in *Communication Models for the Study of Mass Communications* (UK: Longman, 5th impression, 1998) by Denis McQuail and Sven Windahl.

COMMUNICATION THEORY

Allness attitude; Attribution theory; Audience; Codes; Codes of narrative; Communication; Communication: intercultural communication; Communication models; Communication, non-verbal (NVC); Communicative rationality; Congruence theory; Convergence; Cultural capital; Culture; Culture: globalization of; Cybernetics; Cyberspace; Decode; Deconstruction; Dependency theory; Discourse; Discourse analysis; Disempowerment; Encode; Ethnocentrism; Frankfurt school of theorists; Functionalist (mode of media analysis); Groups; Guard dog metaphor; Hegemony; Hot media, cold media; Hyperreality; Identification; Ideology; Interpersonal communication; Johari Window; Life positions; Linguistic determinism; Linguistics; Lookism; Market liberalism; Marxist (mode of media analysis) Maslow's hierarchy of needs; Meaning; Mediasphere; Medium; Message; Metamessage; Mobilization; M-time, p-time; Narrative; Narrative paradigm; Noise; Normative theories of mass media; Objectivity; Paradigm (paradigmatic) Paradigms of media; Play theory of mass communication; Postmodernism; Postulates of communication; Primacy, the law of; Proxemics; Reflective-projective theory of broadcasting and mass communication; Resonance; Roles; Sapir–Whorf linguistic relativity hypothesis; Scripts; Self-concept; Self-fulfilling prophecy; Self-identity; Semiology/semiotics; Semiotic power; Sign; Social action (mode of media analysis); Structuralism; Stereotype; Supervening social necessity; Symbolic convergence theory; Symbolic interactionalism; Technique: Ellul's theory of technique; Technological determinism; Television news: inherent limitations; Texts; Transactional analysis; Uses and gratifications theory; VALS typology.

CYBERCULTURE: THE NET, THE WEB

Communications Decency Act (US); Convergence; Culture: copyrighting culture; Cybernetics; Cyberspace; Globalization of media; Hacker, hacktivist; Mobilization; N-Gen; Pornography; Pretty Good Privacy; Regulation of Investigatory Powers Act (RIPA) UK, 2000; Teledemocracy; Text: integrity of the text; Transculturation; USA – Patriot Act, 2001; Virtual reality; Web: World Wide Web (www).

GENDER MATTERS

Empowerment; Enterprise fiction; Expectations; Feminism; *Film noir*; Gender; Gendered genre; Genderlects; He/man language; Ideology of romance; Intimization; Male-as-norm; News: the 'maleness' of news; Patriarchy; Pleasure: active and reactive; Profane language; Report-talk, rapport-talk; Representation; Semiotic power; Stereotype.

GLOBAL PERSPECTIVES

Al-Jazeer; Commanders of the social order; Commoditization of information; Communication: intercultural communication; Consumerization; Convergence; Core nations, peripheral nations; Culture: copyrighting culture; Culture: globalization of; Cyberspace; Empowerment; Ethnocentrism; Europe: cross-border TV channels; Globalization of media; Globalization: three engines of; Global media system: the main players; Hybridization; Internet; Localization and transnational TV; M-time, p-time; MacBride Commission; McDonaldization; McWorld vs Jihad; Media Imperialism; Media moguls: four sources of concern; Misinformed society; Mobilization; MTV; Murdoch effect; News: globalization of; New World Information Order; Organization cultures; Postmodernism; Press barons; Self-identity; Talloires Declaration, 1981; Teledemocracy; Transculturation; Universality; Yamousoukrou declaration; World Trade Organization (WTO) Telecommunications Agreement, 1997.

INTERPERSONAL COMMUNICATION

Accent; Anti-language; Apache silence; Assertiveness training; Attitudes; Attribution theory; Bad language; Civil inattention; Closure; Cocktail party problem; Communication; Communication: intercultural communication; Communication, non-verbal (NVC); Confirmation/disconfirmation; Congruence theory; Conversational styles; Defensive communication; Disqualifying communication; Dress; Elaborated and restricted codes; Empathy; Eye contact; Facial expression; First impressions; Framing: interpersonal; Gender; Gestural dance; Gesture; Gossip; Gossip networks; Groups; GSR; Guide signs; Halo effect; Head nods; Homophily; Identification; Impression management; Indicators; Influence; Insult signals; Integration; Interpersonal communication; Intervening variables (IV); Johari Window; Kineme; Kinesics; Latitudes of acceptance and rejection; Leadership; Life positions; Listening; Metamessage; Metasignals; M-time, p-time; Newcomb's ABX model of communication, 1953; Non-verbal behaviour: repertoire; Non-verbal vocalizations; Object language; Orientation; Other; Overhearing; Perception; Personal idiom; Personal space; Postural echo; Posture; Projection; Proxemics; Report-talk, rapport-talk; Roles; Scripts; Self-concept; Self-disclosure; Self-fulfilling prophecy; Self-identity; Self-monitoring; Self-presentation; Shortfall signals; Silence; Situational properties; Strategy; Tag questions; Territoriality; Tie-signs; Touch; Transactional analysis; Values; Zones.

LANGUAGE/DISCOURSE/NARRATIVE

Accent; Anecdote; Anti-language; Arbitrariness; Assertiveness training; Bad language; Climax order; Codes; Codes of narrative; Cognitive (and affective); Common sense;

Communication: intercultural communication; Communicative rationality; Connotation; Conversational styles; Corporate speech; Crime and the media; Crime: types of crime on screen; Cultural capital; Cultural memory; Cultural modes; Culture; Culture of deference; Deep structure; Determiner deletion; Diachronic linguistics; Dialect; Discourse; Discursive gap; Disqualifying communication; Dominant discourse; Elaborated and restricted codes; Emotive language; Fiction values; *Film noir*, Flashback; Framing: media; Gendered genre; Genderlects; Gossip; Graffiti; Hedges; He/man language; Iconic; Ideational functions of language; Idiolect; Journalese; Kineme; LAD (Language Acquisition Device); Lame; Language pollution; Langue and parole; Lexis; Linguistic determinism; Linguistics; Machinery of representation; Male-as-norm; Metaphor; Metonymy; Modality; Morphology; Narration; Narrative; Narrative: kernel and satellite; Narrative paradigm; Newspeak; News: the 'maleness of news'; Object language; Onomatopoeia; Open, closed texts; Paradigm; Performatives; Personal idiom; Phatic language; Phoneme; Phonetics; Phonology; Polarization; Postmodernism; Profane language; Projection; Propp's people; Proxemics; Radio Death; Reading; Received pronunciation (RP); Redundancy; Reflexivity; Register; Report-talk, rapport-talk; Rhetoric; Sapir–Whorf linguistic relativity hypothesis; Semantics; Semiology/semiotics; Sentence meaning, utterance meaning; Sign; Slang; Soaps; Style; Tag questions; Television drama (UK); Text; Text: integrity of text; Traditional transmission; Verbal devices in speech-making.

MEDIA ETHICS

Advertising: pester power; Code of Advertising Standards and Practice (ITC); Commercial confidentiality; Communications Decency Act (US); Cross-media ownership; Data protection; Democracy and the media; Flak; Human Rights Act (UK), 2000; Human Rights Watch; Index; Internet: monitoring of content; Journalism; McQuail's accountability of media model, 1997; Media: alternative (or radical) media; Normative theories of mass media; People's Communication Charter; Privacy; Radio Authority (UK) Programme Codes; Radio Death; Reality TV; Reithian; Supervening social necessity; Taste; Television: access television; Ten commandments for media consumers; Universality.

MEDIA: FREEDOM, CENSORSHIP

'Areopagitica'; Article 19; Clipper chip; Code of Advertising Standards and Practice (ITC); Commercial confidentiality; Communications Decency Act (US); Conspiracy of silence; Data protection; Democracy and the media; Defamation; D-Notices; Echelon; Gagging order; Hays Office; H-certificate; Historical allusion; HUAC: House Un-American Activities Committee; Human Rights Act (UK), 2000; Human Rights Watch; Index; Internet: monitoring of content; Lord Chamberlain; Milton's paradox; Music: censorship of music; Official Secrets Act (UK); Opera Omnia; *Oz* trial; Paperwork Reduction Act (US), 1980; Pool system; Pretty Good Privacy (PGP); Prior restraint; Privacy; Radio Authority (UK) Programme Codes; Regulation of Investigatory Powers Act (RIPA), UK, 2000; Re-regulation; SLAPPS, 'Somme, The Battle of the; *Spycatcher* case; Stamp duty; Supervening social necessity; Surveillance society; Taste; Terrorism: Anti-terrorism, Crime and Security Act (UK), 2001; USA – Patriot Act, 2001; Video nasties; War: four stages of war reporting; Williams Committee Report on Obscenity and Film Censorship, 1979; World Press Freedom Committee; World Trade Organization (WTO) telecommunications agreement, 1997; Zinoviev letter, 1924; Zircon affair.

MEDIA HISTORY

Agit-prop; Agora; Alexandra Palace; Animation; 'Areopagitica'; Audience measurement;

BBC, origins; Beveridge Committee Report on Broadcasting, 1950; Bribery; British Board of Film Censors; British Film Institute; Calotype; Camera; Celluloid; Cigarette cards; Cineclubs; Cinema legislation; Cinematography, origins; Cinéma Vérité; 'Clean up TV' movement; Colour TV; Comics; Commercial radio; Commercial television; Convergence; Cylinder or rotary press; Daguerrotype; *Death on the Rock*; Digitization; Facsimile; Federal Communications Commission (FCC); Federal Radio Commission; *Film noir*; Fourteen-Day Rule (UK); Fourth estate; Franchises for Independent Television; Franchises for 1993; Global jukebox; Gramophone; Hays Office; H-certificate; HUAC: House Un-American Activities Committee; Kinetoscope; Linotype printing; Lithography; Lord Chamberlain; March of Time; Mass Observation; McGregor Commission Report on the Press (UK), 1977; Minority Report of Mr Selwyn Lloyd; Miracle of Fleet Street; Monotype printing; Morse Code; Musical – film musical; Newspapers, origins; Newsreel; Nickelodeon; Northcliffe revolution; 'Pencil of Nature'; Persistence of vision; Phonodisc; Photography, origins; Photogravure; Photo-journalism; Picture postcards; Pilkington Committee Report on Broadcasting (UK), 1962; Pirate radio (UK); Poor Man's Guardian; Posters; Press barons; Printing; Privacy; Press Complaints Commission Code of Practice, 1977; Projection of pictures; Public service broadcasting (PSB); Radio broadcasting; Radio drama; Reithian; Roll film; Satellite transmission; Selsdon Committee Report on Television (UK), 1935; Shawcross Commission Report on the Press (UK), 1962; 'Somme, The Battle of the'; Sound Broadcasting Act (UK), 1972; Soviet Manifesto, 1928; Sovkino; Stamp duty; Stereoscopy; Synchronous sound; Telegraphy; Telephone; Telerecording; Television broadcasting; Thaumatrope; Typewriter; Ullswater Committee Report on Broadcasting (UK), 1936; V-discs; Victim funds; Video; Vitaphone; *War of the Worlds*; Watergate; Wireless telegraphy; Yellow Kid; Zinoviev letter, 1924; Zoopraxography.

MEDIA INSTITUTIONS

BBC, origins; British Board of Film Censors; British Film Institute; British Media Industry Group (BMIG); Broadcasting Standards Council; Casualization; Commanders of the Social Order; Commercial radio; Commercial television; Conglomerates; Core nations, peripheral nations; Deregulation; Deregulation: five myths of; Diversification; Europe: cross-border TV channels; Globalization of media; Guard dog metaphor; Independent producers; Institution; Media imperialism; Network; News agencies; News: globalization of; Newspapers, origins; Normative theories of mass media; Occupying powers; Organization cultures; Power; Press; Press barons; Press Complaints Commission; Public service broadcasting (PSB); Radio Broadcasting; Regulatory favours; Television; Underground press; World Trade Organization (WTO) Telecommunications Agreement, 1997.

MEDIA ISSUES AND DEBATES

Advertising; Audience: active audience; Censorship; Commanders of the social order; Commoditization of information; Computers in communication; Conglomerates; Consumerization; Core nations, peripheral nations; Crime and the media; Cultural, or citizen rights and the media; Culture: globalization of; Cyberspace; Data protection; Dependency theory; Deregulation; Deregulation: five myths of; Disempowerment; Effects of the mass media; Empowerment; Ethnocentrism; Feminism; Freedom of information; Gatekeeping; Globalization of media; Globalization: three engines of; Global media systems: the main players; Hegemony; Hyperreality; Ideological presumption; Ideological state apparatuses; Ideology; Ideology of romance; Impartiality; Independent producers; Information gaps; Journalism; Journalism: celebrity journalism; Localization and transnational TV; McDonaldization; McQuail's accountability of media model, 1997; Media: alternative (or radical) media; Media control; Media imperialism; Media moguls: four sources of concern; McWorld vs Jihad; Mobilization; Murdoch effect; News aid?; News: the 'maleness' of news; News values; New World Information Order; Objectivity; Other; People's Communication Charter; Pool System; Polysemy; Pornography; Power; Predatory pricing; Privacy; Privatization; Producer Choice; Public opinion; Public service broadcasting (PSB); Public sphere; Reality TV; Racism; Regulatory favours; Representation; Right of Reply; Self-identity; Showbusiness, age of; SLAPPS; Sponsorship; Supervening social necessity; Surveillance society; Tabloid, tabloidese, tabloidization; Text, integrity of the text; Virtual reality; Wedom, Theydom; Web: World Wide Web (www); World Trade Organization (WTO) Telecommunications Agreement, 1997.

MEDIA: OWNERSHIP AND CONTROL

Advertising; Agenda-setting; British Media Industry Group (BMIG); Berlusconi phenomenon; Casualization; Citizen Kane of the Global Village; Class; Commanders of the social order; Commercial confidentiality; Commoditization of information; Communications Bill (UK), 2002; Cross-media ownership; Conglomerates; Consumerization; Convergence; Cultural apparatus; Culture: copyrighting of culture; Culture: globalization of; Deregulation; Diversification; Elite; Europe: cross-border TV channels; Frankfurt school of theorists; Functionalist (mode of media analysis); Globalization of media; Globalization: the engines of; Global media system: the main players; Guard dog metaphor; Hegemony; Ideological state apparatuses; Ideology; Independent producers; Journalism; Leadership; Localization and transnational TV; Market liberalism; Marxist (mode of media analysis); McGregor Commission Report on the Press (UK), 1977; McLeod and Chaffee's 'kite' model, 1973; Media control; Media moguls: four sources of concern; Murdoch effect; News: globalization of; Northcliffe revolution; Occupying powers; Organization cultures; People's Communication Charter; Power; Power Elite; Press barons; Privatization; Producer choice; Public service broadcasting (PSB); Public sphere; Regulatory favours; Social action (mode of media analysis); Sponsorship; Synergy; World Trade Organization (WTO) Telecommunications Agreement, 1997.

MEDIA: POLITICS AND ECONOMICS

Accusatory studies; Advertising; Accessed voices; Alleyne's news revolution model, 1977; Audience; Berlusconi phenomenon; Commoditization of information; Consent, manufacture of; Conspiracy of silence; Core nations, peripheral nations; Class; Cultural apparatus; Cultural capital; Cultural, or citizen's rights and the media; Culture; Culture: globalization of; Democracy and the media; Deregulation, five myths of; Elite; Empowerment; Ethnocentrism; Fairness Doctrine (USA); Fatwa; Feminism; Flak; Frankfurt school of theorists; Functionalist (mode of media analysis); Fundamentalism; Gagging order; Guard dog metaphor; Hegemony; Human Rights Act (UK), 2000; Ideological state apparatuses; Ideology; Intervention; Leaks; Lobby practice; Legitimation/delegitimation; Machinery of representation; Market liberalism; Marxist (mode of media analysis); Media: alternative (or radical) media; Media control; Media imperialism; Media moguls: four sources of concern; Mediasphere; Mediatization; Misinformed Society; New World Information Order; Orientalism; Paradigms of media; Politics of accommodation; Polysemy; Power; Press barons; Privatization; Professionalization (of political communication); Public opinion; Public service broadcasting (PSB); Public sphere; Regulatory favours; Sponsorship; *Spycatcher* case; Surveillance society; Synergy; Television: access television;

Terrorism as communication; Terrorism, Crime and Security Act (UK), 2001; USA – Patriot Act, 2001; World Trade Organization (WTO) Telecommunications agreement, 1997; Zinoviev letter, 1924.

MEDIA: POWER, EFFECTS, INFLUENCE

Accessed voices; Agenda-setting; Anecdote; Anomie; Attitudes; Attribution theory; Audience; Ball-Rokeach and Defleur's dependency model of communication effects, 1976; Bigotry; Catalyst effect; Colonization; Commoditization of information; Compassion fatigue; Consensus; Consent, manufacture of; Consistency; Conspiracy theory; Consumerization; Contagion effect; Coups and earthquakes syndrome; Crime and the media; Crisis (definition); Cultivation; Cultural, or citizens rights and the media; Democracy and the media; Deviance amplification; Disempowerment; Displacement effect; Effects of the mass media; Frankfurt school of theorists; Global media system: the main players; Hypodermic needle model of communication; Ideological state apparatuses; Ideology; Information blizzards; Inheritance factor; Intervening variables (IV); Journalism; Kuleshov effect; Kuuki; Labelling process (and the media); Legitimation/delegitimation; Mainstreaming; McCombs and Shaw's agenda-setting model of media effects, 1976; Media imperialism; Media moguls: four sources of concern; Mediasphere; Mobilization; Moral panic; MTV; Multiplier effect; Narcotizing dysfunction; Noelle-Neumann's spiral of silence model of public opinion, 1974; Other; Pornography; Power; Primacy, law of; Public opinion; Radio Death; Resonance; Self-fulfilling prophecy; Showbusiness, age of; Significant spiral; Sleeper effect; Slow-drip; 'Somme, The Battle of the'; Survivors and the media; Television news: inherent limitations; VALS typology; Visions of order.

MEDIA: PROCESSES AND PRODUCTION

Advertising; Agenda-setting; Anchorage; Attention model of mass communication; Attitudes; Commoditization of information; Common sense; Compassion fatigue; Conglomerates; Convergence; Coups and earthquakes syndrome; Culture; Culture: globalization of; Demonization; Determiner deletion; Diffusion; Digitization; Ethnocentrism; Fly on the wall; Folk devils; Framing: Media; Gatekeeping; Gendered genre; Guard dog metaphor; Hammocking effect; Historical allusion; Hyphenized abridgement; Immediacy; Impartiality; Intensity; Intimization; Journalism; Label libel; Labelling process (and the media); Legitimation/delegitimation; Lookism; Loony leftism; Mainstreaming; Mediation; Mediatization; Moblilization; Multi-actuality; Myth; News; Structure of reassurance; One-step, two-step, multi-step models of communication; Other; Packaging; Performatives; Personalization; Personalizing Transformation; Power; Programme flow; Radio Death; Reality TV; Representation; Scheduling; Slow motion; Socialization; Special effects; Tabloid, tabliodese, tabloidization; Television news: inherent limitations; Voiceover; Vox popping; Wedom, Theydom.

MEDIA: TECHNOLOGIES

BBC digital; Bookmark (electronic); Broadband; CCTV: closed circuit television; Clipper chip; Colour TV; Computer graphics; Connectivity; Cyberspace; Cylinder or rotary press; Daguerrotype; Digitization; Digital retouching; Digital video disc (DVD); Electronic news-gathering; Fibre-optic technology; Flat-screen technology; Gramophone; Hacker, hacktivist; High-speed photography; Holography; Interactive television; Internet; Internet: wireless Internet; Kinetoscope; Kuleshov effect; Linotype printing; Lithography; Mobilization; Newsroom, The; Omnimax; Photography, origins; Photomontage; Phototypesetting; Pretty Good Privacy; Printing; Projection of pictures; Satellite transmission; Speech-recognition technology; Stereoscopy; Supervening social necessity; Technique: Ellul's theory of technique; Technological determinism; Telegraphy; Telematics; Telephone; Telerecording; Television broadcasting; Typewriter; Video; Vitaphone; Web: World Wide Web; Wireless telegraphy; World Trade Organization (WTO) Telecommunications Agreement, 1997; Xerography; Zoetrope; Zoopraxography.

MEDIA: VALUES AND IDEOLOGY

Accessed voices; Agenda-setting; Agenda-setting research; Audience; Balanced programming; Bias; Bigotry; British Board of Film Censors; British Code of Advertising Practice; Broadcasting Complaints Commission; Broadcasting Standards Council; Calcutt Committee Reports on Privacy and Related Matters, 1990 and 1993; Campaign for Press and Broadcasting Freedom; Celebrity; Censorship; Certification of films; Chapultepec, Declaration of, 1994; Chequebook journalism; 'Clean up TV' movement; Code of Advertising Standards and Practice (ITC); Communications Decency Act (US); Conglomerates; Consensus; Consent, manufacture of; Conspiracy of silence; Conspiracy theory; Consumerization; Convergence; Counter-culture; Coups and earthquakes syndrome; Cultivation; Cultural apparatus; Culture: consumer culture; Culture: copyright-ing culture; Culture: globalization of; Culture of deference; Culture: popular culture; Cyberspace; Defamation; Democracy and the media; Demonization; Deregulation, five myths of; Deviance; Deviance amplification; Discourse; Discourse analysis; Disempowerment; D-Notices; Dominant discourse; Effects of the mass media; Elite; Emancipatory use of the media; Emergent culture; Emotive language; Empowerment; Ethnocentrism; Exnomination; Feminism; Fiction values; Folk devils; Framing: media; Frankfurt school of theorists; Functionalist (mode of media analysis); Gatekeeping; Gender; Glasgow University Media Group; Globalization of media; Global scrutiny; Guard dog metaphor; Gultang and Ruge's model of selective gatekeeping, 1965; Hegemony; HUAC: House Un-American Activities Committee; Human Rights Act (UK), 2000; Ideological presumption; Ideological state apparatuses; Ideology; Ideology of romance; Image, rhetoric of; Immediacy; Impartiality; Implication; Information gaps; Infotainment; Institution; Intensity; International Federation of Journalists (IFJ); Intimization; Invisibility; iSociety; Issues; ITC Programme Code; Jingoism; Journalism; Journalism: celebrity journalism; Knowns, unknowns; Kuuki; Labelling process (and the media); Legitimation/delegitima-tion; Lobby Practice; MacBride Commission; Machinery of representation; Mainstreaming; Marginality, myth of; Market liberalism; Marxist (mode of media analysis); McCombs and Shaw's agenda setting model of media effects, 1976; McQuail's accounta-bility of media model, 1997; McWorld vs Jihad; Media: alternative (or radical) media; Media imperialism; Mediasphere; Moral entrepreneurs; Moral panic; Mr Gate; Myth; News; News Aid?; News frameworks; News: globalization of; News: the 'maleness' of news; News values; New World Information Order; Non-Aligned News Pool; Normative theories of the mass media; Objectivity; Orientalism; Other; Paper Tiger TV; Partisan; People's Communication Charter; Personalization; Photo-journalism; Pornography; Postmodernism; Power; Preferred reading; Prejudice; Press barons; Press Complaints Commission (UK); Privacy; Privacy: Press Complaints Commission Code of Practice, 1977; Propaganda; Public opinion; Public service broadcasting (PSB); Public sphere; Racism; Radio Authority Programme Codes; Realism; Reinforcement; Reithian; Representation; Rogers and Dearing's agenda-setting model, 1987; Self-identity; Sexism; Signification spiral; Silence: strategic silence; Small World Media; Soap opera; Social action (mode of media analysis); Socialization; Sociometrics (and media analysis); 'Somme, The Battle of the'; Sponsorship; Sponsorship: ITC Code of Programme Sponsorship; *Spycatcher* case;

Status quo; Stereotype; Structuralism; Subculture; Surveillance society; Tabloid, tabloidese, tabloidization; Technique: Ellul's theory of technique; Teledemocracy; Ten commandments for media consumers; Underground press; Values; Video nasties; Violence and the media; Violence on TV: codes of practice; Visions of order; Watchdogs; Watergate; Wedom, Theydom; Western; Westerstähl and Johansson's model of news factors in foreign news, 1994; Whistle-blowing; Youth culture; Zinoviev letter, 1924; Zircon affair.

NEWS MEDIA

Agenda-setting; Agenda-setting research; Alleyne's news revolution model, 1997; Al-Jazeer; Anchorage; Bass's 'double action' model of international news flow, 1969; Chronology; Compassion fatigue; Coups and earthquakes syndrome; Crimes of self-publicity; Critical news analysis; Determiner deletion; Event; Fiction values; Framing: media; Frequency; Gagging order; Galtung and Ruge's model of selective gatekeeping, 1965; Historical allusion; Horse-race story; Hyphenized abridgement; Ideological presumption; Immediacy; Impartiality; Implication; Intensity; Intimization; J-Curve; Journalism; Knowns, unknowns; Kuuki; Marginality, myth of; McLeod and Chaffee's 'kite' model, 1973; McNelly's model of news flow, 1959; News; News agencies; News: audience evaluation, six dimensions of; News elements: breaking, explanatory, deep background; News: globalization of; News: structure of reassurance; News: the 'maleness' of news; News values; Newsroom, The; One-step, two-step, multi-step flow models of communication; Performatives; Personalization; Photo-journalism; Pool system; Representation; Rogers and Dearing's agenda setting model, 1987; Significant spiral; Silence: strategic silence; Spot news; Television news: inherent limitations; Visions of order; War: four stages of war reporting; Westerstähl and Johansson's model of news factors in foreign news, 1994; White's gatekeeper model, 1950.

REPRESENTATION

Caricature; Chronology; Collective representations; Colonization; Coups and earthquakes syndrome; Crime and the media; Crime: types of crime on screen; Demonization; Determiner deletion; Deviance; Deviance amplification; Dominant, subordinate, radical; Enterprise fiction; Ethnocentrism; Folk devils; Gender; Hegemony; Invisibility: Label libel; Labelling process (and the media); Machinery of representation; Narrative; News; News: the 'maleness' of news; Orientalism; Other; Paraproxemics; Pornography; Power; Primary, secondary definers; Propaganda; Public opinion; Racism; Reality TV; Representation; Self-fulfilling prophecy; Self-identity; Sign; Soap operas; 'Somme, The Battle of the'; Stereotype; Style; Visions of order.

RESEARCH METHODS

Agenda-setting research; Audience measurement; Children, young people and the changing media environment; Communicology; Consumption behaviour; Content analysis; Control group; Crime: types of crime on screen; Critical news analysis; Cultivation differential; Custom audience research; Deconstruction; Demographic analysis; Discourse analysis; Empirical; Ethnographic (approach to audience measurement); Experimental group; First impressions; Focus groups; Functionalist (mode of media analysis); Glasgow University Media Group; Groups; HICT Project; Interviews; JICNARS scale; Marxist (mode of media analysis); Mass observation; Mean world syndrome; Motivation research (MR); Narrative paradigm; Nielsen ratings; Paradigms of media; Participant observation; People meter; Pleasure: active and reactive; Proxemics; Public opinion; Reception studies; Research centres (into the media); Sampling; Segmentation; Semantic differential; Social action (mode of media analysis); Sociometrics (and media analysis); Viewers: light, medium and heavy; Vox popping.

TEXTUAL ANALYSIS

Aberrant decoding; Anchorage; Androcentric rule; Audience; Audience: active audience; Audience, fragmentation of; Bad language; Berlo's SMCR model of communication, 1960; Bowdlerize; Bricolage; Celebrity; Chronology; Codes; Codes of narrative; Communication, Non-verbal (NVC); Connotation; Content analysis; Conventions; Cultural metaphor; Culture; Culture: consumer culture; Culture: copyrighting culture; Culture: globalization of; Culture: popular culture; Cyberspace; Decode; Deconstruction; Deep structure; Dialect; Discourse; Discourse analysis; Discursive gap; Dissolve; Dominant discourse; Dominant, subordinate, radical; Double exposure; Emotive language; Encode; Encrypt; Establishing shot; Ethnocentrism; Euphemism; Excorporation; Exnomination; Expectation, horizons of; Fade in; *Film noir*, Flashback; Framing: media; Frequency; Gendered genre; Gendered viewing; Genre; Hedges; Hegemony; He/man language; Hybridization; Hypertext; Iconic; Ideological state apparatuses; Ideology; Ideology of romance; Image; Image: rhetoric of; Insert shot; Interactive television; Interpretant; Intertextuality; Jargon; Journalese; Journalism: celebrity journalism; Jump-cut; Kineme; Kinesics; Kuleshov effect; Lexis; Linguistics; Lip-sync; Machinery of representation; Male-as-norm; McGuffin; Meaning; Media images; Mediation; Medium; Message; Metamessage; Metaphor; Metasignals; Metonymy; Mimetic/semiosic planes; Mix; Mixing; Monroe motivated sequence; Montage; Morphing; Morphology; Multi-actuality; Myth; Narration; Narrative; Narrative paradigm; Naturalistic illusion (of television); 'Niche' audience; Noise; Open, closed texts; Phoneme; Polysemy; Postmodernism; Post-synchronization; Preferred reading; Programme flow; Propp's people; Reaction shot; Referent; Representation; Resistive reading; Reterritorialization; Rhetoric; Segmentation; Semantic differential; Semantics; Semiology/semiotics; Sender/receiver; Shot; Sign; Signal; Signification; Signification spiral; Slow motion; Sound-bite; Special effects; Stereotype; Storyboard; Storyness; Structuralism; Symbol; Synchronous sound; Syntactics; Syntagm; Syntax; Tabloid, tabloidese, tabloidization; Tactics and strategies; Tag questions; Technique: Ellul's theory of techniques; Technology of the media; Tertiary text; Text; Text: integrity of the text; Voiceover.

A

AA-certificate, A-certificate See CERTIFICATION OF FILMS.

Aberrant decoding See DECODE.

Abstraction, ladder of See NARRATIVE.

ABX model of communication See NEWCOMB'S ABX MODEL OF COMMUNICATION, 1953.

Acceleration factor What results from the speed-up of forms of transportation, thus having far-reaching impact upon communities, nations and cultures. Marshall McLuhan preached that the combination of accelerated modes of transport communication and the rapid development of electric communication – telephone, TV – was having the effect of reducing the world to a 'global village'. 'All meaning,' says McLuhan in *Understanding Media* (UK: Routledge, latest edition, 2001), 'alters with acceleration, because all patterns of personal and political interdependence change with any acceleration of information.' See MOBILIZATION.

Accent The entire pattern of pronunciation typical of a particular region or social group. Accent is a feature of dialect. The use of most languages is marked by differing dialects and their accompanying accents. In Britain a range of regional accents still survive and are important signs of regional identity and affiliation. Though RECEIVED PRONUNCIATION (RP), may still be regarded as the prestige accent, more recently it has been argued that Estuary English, a slightly Cockneyfied accent, is starting to make in-roads into the traditional social territory of RP. Many individuals can use a range of accents and switch from one to another depending on the social situation. Accent is also an aspect of non-verbal communication.

A number of experiments have shown that reactions to speakers can be influenced by the accents they use. For example, in H. Giles and P.F. Powesland's study of responses to speakers using regional accents, *Speech Style and Social Evaluation* (UK: Academia Press, 1975), they found that speakers with Scottish or Yorkshire accents tend to be rated more favourably than received pronunciation speakers for qualities like personal integrity, good humour and good-naturedness by speakers with Scots or Yorkshire accents respectively.

In an article entitled, 'It's not what you say, it's the way that you say it', in the *Independent* (15 October 1997), Emma Haughton identifies RP, Refined Scots, Welsh and Irish, Yorkshire and Estuary English as being favourably received but Brummie, Belfast, Glaswegian and West Country accents as being viewed unfavourably. These findings are similar to those of Giles and Trudgill's study entitled 'Sociolinguistics and linguistic value judgments', in Peter Trudgill, *On Dialect* (UK: Blackwell, 1983).

Judgements will vary, though; an individual with a Brummie accent may not share the general view. Further there is evidence that among certain groups within society, a covert prestige can be attached to accents generally viewed as not prestigious, especially when they are part of 'non-standard' speech. Such accents and non-standard speech may also be used to convey an image of toughness and masculinity in certain situations, irrespective of the actual social status of the speaker. Differences in accents will often reflect differences in the social structure of a society, and in particular its patterns of social stratification.

Accessed voices Within any society, these are the people who have a ready and privileged access to the channels of mass communication: politicians, civil servants, industrialists, experts of various kinds, pundits, royals and celebrities; and it is their views and styles that are given voice. The term is used by John Hartley in his book *Understanding News* (UK: Methuen, 1982). Building on this idea in his *Language of News: Discourses and Ideology of the Press* (UK: Routledge, 1991), Roger Fowler writes, 'The political effect of this division between the accessed and unaccessed hardly needs stating: an imbalance between the representation of the already privileged, on the one hand, and the already unprivileged, on the other, with the views of the official, the powerful and the rich being constantly invoked to legitimate the status quo.' Imbalance of access results in partiality in both what is communicated and the way in which information is reported – the way it is shaped.

1

Access provider Or INTERNET service provider (ISP); company selling Internet connections, such as CompuServe, Demon, EasyNet and AOL (America On Line).

Access television See TELEVISION: ACCESS TELEVISION.

Accommodation, politics of See POLITICS OF ACCOMMODATION (IN THE MEDIA).

Accountability of media See McQUAIL'S ACCOUNTABILITY OF MEDIA MODEL, 1997.

Acculturation, deculturation The process by which a society or an individual adapts to the need for cultural change. The conditions for such change occur, for example, when encounters with other cultures continue on a prolonged basis such as in colonization, emigration and immigration. In analysing the process by which individuals adapt to life in a new country, Young Yun Kim in 'Adapting to a new culture', in Larry Samovar and Richard Porter, *Intercultural Communication: A Reader* (US: Wadsworth, 1997) comments, 'They are challenged to learn at least some new ways of thinking, feeling, and acting – an activity commonly called acculturation. … At the same time, they go through the process of deculturation … of unlearning some of their previously acquired cultural habits at least to the extent that new responses are adopted in situations that previously would have evoked old ones.' Such a process produces stress and anxiety, and it necessarily affects the communicative performance of those undergoing it. However, communication with those in the new culture is essential to adaptation.

Interestingly Kim argues that the mass media can be a useful source of information for those trying to acclimatize to a new culture as the messages they carry 'explicitly or implicitly convey the world views, myths, beliefs, values, mores and norms of the culture'. See COMMUNICATION: INTERCULTURAL COMMUNICATION.

Accusatory studies Jib Fowles in *The Case for Television Violence* (US: Sage, 1999) uses this term to describe the research studies that have focused on the effects of screen violence. They are 'accusatory' in the sense that they purport to prove the connection between screen and real violence, the one likely to instigate the other, or to desensitize audiences in their response to real violence. Such studies, in Fowles' view amplify the 'derogatory discourse' concerning violence in the cinema and on TV. See VIOLENCE ON TV: THE DEFENCE.

Action code See CODES OF NARRATIVE.

Action research Some social science research is motivated by the desire to alter and improve a social situation. Action research aims not only to collect and analyse information but also to bring about practical social change.

Active-audience thesis See AUDIENCE: ACTIVE AUDIENCE.

Active listening See LISTENING.

Active participation Occurs in situations where media interest in a news story becomes involvement, and the story takes on a media-induced direction. An appetite for stories of scandal and sensation, and the cut-throat competition for circulation, can lead newspapers into playing the role of *agent provocateur*, as handy with the chequebook as the reporter's notebook.

Actuality Material from real life – the presentation in a broadcast programme of real events and people to illustrate some current theme or practice. RADIO, in parallel with film documentary, pioneered actuality in the 1930s. Producers such as Olive Shapley and Harry Harding were early innovators in this field. The radio programme *Time to Spare*, made in 1934, documented unemployment, broadcasting the voices of the unemployed and their families, and creating an impact that was both moving and disturbing.

Actualization See MASLOW'S HIERARCHY OF NEEDS.

Adaptors See NON-VERBAL BEHAVIOUR: REPERTOIRE.

Advertising The extent of the *reliance* of all forms of mass media upon advertising can be gauged by glancing at any monthly edition of Brad, which comprises some 400 to 500 pages of information on where advertisements can be placed and how much they will cost. Everything is there – the national and local PRESS, TV and RADIO, CINEMA, POSTERS, bus shelters, parking meters, litter bins and transport advertising.

If advertising merely sold products, it would cause less critical concern than it does. But it also sells images, dreams, ideal ways of life, ideal images of self; it sells, then reinforces time and again, values – those of consumerism; and it trades in stereotypes. In *The Shocking History of Advertising* (UK: Penguin, revised edition, 1965), E.S. Turner states that 'Advertising is the whip which hustles humanity up the road to the Better Mousetrap.'

Advertising has speeded the introduction of useful inventions to a wide, as distinct from a select, circle of consumers; it has spread markets, reduced the price of goods, accelerated turnover and kept people in employment. For some analysts, advertising is a kind of magic. Raymond Williams in *Problems in Materialism and Culture* (UK: Verso, 1980), argues that it has the ability to 'associate consumption with human desires to which it has no real reference. The magic obscures the real sources of general satisfaction because their discovery would involve radical change in the whole common way of life.' Judith Williamson in *Decoding Advertisements* (UK: Marion Boyars, 1978; 1998) shares a similar concern: 'Advertisements obscure and avoid the real issues of society, those relating to work, to jobs and wages and who works for whom.

'The basic issues in the present state of society which do concern money and how it is earned, are sublimated into "meanings", "images", "lifestyles", to be bought with products not money.' Further, the magic of advertising means that we may believe commodities can convey messages about ourselves; this leads to us being 'alienated from ourselves, since we have allowed objects to "speak" for us and have become identified with them'. Such alienation may well lead to feelings of fragmentation and discomfort within the self, feelings that may fuel a desire to seek solace in further consumption.

A number of critics point to the danger that advertising messages and the consumption they partly fuel may undermine and distort self-development. Anthony Giddens writes in *Modernity and Self-Identity* (UK: Polity Press, 1991) that 'The consumption of ever-novel goods becomes a substitute for the genuine development of self: appearance replaces essence.' Self-actualization is 'packaged and distributed according to market criteria. Mediated experience is centrally involved here. The mass media routinely present modes of life to which, it is implied, everyone should aspire.' For Don Slater in *Consumer Culture and Modernity* (UK: Polity Press, 1997), 'Consumer culture "technicizes" the project of self by treating all problems as solvable through various commodities.'

Not all would agree with such criticisms. Those subscribing to the doctrines of nineteenth-century Liberalism, for example, would argue that consumer culture, of which advertising is an integral element, liberates rather than oppresses, in providing the individual with many opportunities to rationally pursue his/her self-interest. The range of choices offered by consumer culture and post-traditional society is to be celebrated rather than seen as a cause for concern: to be able to choose being seen as the essence of being human. It should also be borne in mind that the messages of advertising have to compete with a range of other influences on behaviour in their battle for hearts, minds and identities.

The many modes of advertising may be categorized as follows. (1) Commercial consumer advertising, with its target the mass audience and its channel the mass media. Latterly, of course, the new frontier for commercial advertising has become the INTERNET. (2) Trade and technical advertising, such as ads in specialist magazines. (3) Prestige advertising, particularly that of big business and large institutions, generally selling image and good name rather than specific products (see PR: PUBLIC RELATIONS). (4) Small ads, directly informational, which are the bedrock support of local periodicals and are the basis of the many giveaway papers that have been published in recent years. (5) Government advertising – health warnings, for example. (6) Charity advertising, seeking donations for worthwhile causes at home and abroad. (7) Advertising through sponsorship, mainly of sports, leisure and the arts. This indirect form of advertising has been a major development; its danger has been to make recipients of sponsorship come to rely more and more heavily on commercial support. Sponsors want quick publicity and prestige for their money, and their loyalties to recipients are very often short term.

The effect upon newspaper and broadcasting editorial and programme content is rarely overt; rather it is a process of media people 'internalizing' advertisers' demands. Ad-related newspaper features have grown enormously in the post-Second World War period, especially in the 'quality press', such as, in the UK, *The Times, Guardian, Independent* and *Daily Telegraph*, which derive over half their revenue from advertising. In press advertising, numbers count for less than the estimated purchasing power of the target readership. This explains why two major UK newspapers with big circulations – the *Daily Herald* (see MIRACLE OF FLEET STREET) and the *News Chronicle* – were closed down in the 1960s. They simply did not appeal to the advertisers.

Advertising has suffused our culture and our language, helping to form a consumer culture (see CULTURE: CONSUMER CULTURE). Its influence has been felt in modern art movements such as pop art; its snappy techniques as developed for TV have been widely adopted in the cinema. It has drawn into its service actors, celebrities, artists, photographers, writers, designers and film-makers. It is often said that on TV the adverts are better than the programmes; there is a grain of truth here as there is in the claim that it is because of the adverts, and the goals of those who commission and make them, that the programmes are not better, more original or more challenging. See AIDA MODEL; CODE OF ADVERTISING STANDARDS AND PRACTICE (ITC); GRAPHIC REVOLUTION; HARMONIOUS INTERACTION; PRODUCT PLACEMENT; SPONSORSHIP; SUBLIMINAL.

---

* Gillian Dyer, *Advertising as Communication* (UK: Methuen, 1982); Robert Goldman, *Reading Ads Socially* (UK: Routledge, 1992; reprinted 1995); Ien Ang, *Living Room Wars: Re-thinking Media Audiences for a Postmodern World* (UK: Routledge, 1995); Sean Brierley, *The Advertising Handbook* (UK: Routledge, 1995); Jib Fowles, *Advertising and Popular Culture* (UK: Sage, 1996); Angela Goddard, *The Language of Advertising: Written Texts* (US/UK: Routledge, 1998); Anne M. Cronin, *Advertising and Consumer Citizenship: Gender, Images and Rights* (UK: Routledge, 2000); John Tullock, *Watching Television Audiences: Cultural Theories and Methods* (UK: Arnold, 2000); Peter N. Stearns, *Consumerism in World History: The Global Transformation of Desire* (UK: Routledge, 2001).

Advertising: ambient advertising Advertisements that feature in contexts other than the printed page, on film or in broadcasting, which we encounter in everyday-life situations, designed to surround and to confront the prospective customer – in the street, on bus shelters, in underground stations and trains, in airports, public lavatories and latterly in places of education – indeed wherever there is space for the advertiser to press home image and message. On London's underground trains in 1997, for example, hang-straps were embellished with anti-perspirant ads; in a hot summer the perfect ambient reminder to consider Vaseline Intensive Care anti-perspirant deodorant.

An alternative term is 'captive audience' advertising. David Bollier of the Annenburg School of Communications, in an article entitled 'The grotesque, smirking gargoyle: the commercialization of America's consciousness', published on the tom.paine.com website (8 August 2002), writes of advertising 'ambushing people as they use public restrooms, gas pumps, elevators. ... By ones and twos, such actions generally are inconsequential. In aggregate, however, the sheer pervasiveness of commercialism in public spaces and contemporary life has the malodorous whiff of a Corporate Big Brother.'

Bollier believes that the 'sheer ubiquity of marketing in hundreds of nooks and crannies of daily life has become a defining framework of cultural values.'

Advertising boycotts The reliance of the press and of commercial television upon advertising for revenue indicates the important influence advertisers and their clients can wield over the media. Where a newspaper may be deemed to be publishing material or expressing views that might be detrimental to consumerist interest, companies pull out their expensive advertisement – or threaten to do so, and thus exercise censorship.

Advertising: Code of Advertising Standards and Practice See CODE OF ADVERTISING STANDARDS AND PRACTICE (ITC).

Advertising: mainstreamers, aspirers, succeeders and reformers Target audiences for advertising have traditionally been defined along the lines of social class. Research into consumer habits and tastes produced, in the 1980s, a classification entitled, in the UK, the Four Cs (cross-cultural consumer characterization), indicating the belief that these days we are all consumers and that class differences count for less than personal aspirations. A BBC QED programme, *It's Tough Being a Dolphin* (May 1988) gave currency to this new approach to discovering and satisfying consumer needs. Adman

John Banks described four categories of consumer. (1) Mainstreamers make up some 40 per cent of consumers; security is what characterizes them in terms of their central needs, thus they buy well-known, tried brand names. (2) Aspirers are those for whom personal status is of prime importance; they go for what is smart and fashionable, and is perceived to contribute towards the aspirer's image. (3) Succeeders have already arrived rather than being still on their way up; what characterizes them is their need for control – in their lives, their work, in their consumption. Advertisements that stress power and control are targeted at them. (4) Reformers are those who tend to put the quality of life before mere monetary acquisition.

A lifestyle report by Alex McKie for Barclay's bank in 1999 offered another of many variants of audience/consumer SEGMENTATION, using the term 'tribes'. Twenty-first-century tribes, suggested McKie, form into six clusters – New Hippies, Neo-Calvinists, Global Villagers, Post-Punk Outlaws, Barbie Babes and Ken Clones. The picturesqueness of the language is rather more arresting than the meaningfulness of the classification. Professor Laurie Taylor in his UK *Guardian* column, 'Off-cuts' (4 August 1999) deplores attempts at herding the public into categories. Referring to the tribes research in particular, he states that many of the definitions 'are so trivial and superficial that one suspects they were not so much based on research as dreamed up one night in a warm bath'. Even so, advertisers are only too keen to use any research that helps them target consumers more accurately. See HIDDEN NEEDS; MASLOW'S HIERARCHY OF NEEDS; MEDIA SPECIES; VALS TYPOLOGY.

Aesthetic code See CODES.

Affect displays See NON-VERBAL BEHAVIOUR; REPERTOIRE.

Affective See COGNITIVE (AND AFFECTIVE).

Agenda-setting Term used to describe the way the media set the order of importance of current issues, especially in the reportage of news. Closely linked with the process of gatekeeping, agenda-setting defines the context of transmission, establishes the terms of reference and the limits of debate. In BROADCASTING the agenda is more assertive than in newspapers where the reader can ignore the order of priorities set by the paper's editorial team and turn straight to the small ads or the sports page. Broadcasting is linear – one item following after another – and its agenda unavoidable (except by switching off). Interviewers in broadcasting are in *control* of pre-set agendas. They initiate and formulate the questions to be asked and have the chairperson's power of excluding areas of discussion. Very rarely does an interviewee break free from this form of control and succeed in widening the context of debate beyond what is 'on the agenda'.

G. Ray Funkhouser and Eugene F. Shaw in 'How synthetic experience shapes social reality', in *Journal of Communication*, spring 1990, subdivide agenda-setting into *micro-agenda-setting* and *macro-agenda-setting*. The first describes the way the mass media are able, through emphasis on content, to influence public perceptions of the relative importance of specific issues. The second they define as follows: 'The potential of electronic media to colour, distort, and perhaps even degrade an entire cultural world view, by presenting images of the world suited to the agenda of the media (in the US case, commercial interests), we might term "macro-agenda-setting".'

In recent years agenda-setting has been viewed as working from two levels, that of *subject* and that of *attribute*; and the theory is that the media's attention to the attributes of a subject is met with a corresponding image in the mind of the public. Level 1 of agenda-setting concerns the central theme or object of a public issue/news story; Level 2, the salient characteristics of the theme or object as emphasized by the media.

In an article, 'Agenda-setting in the 1996 Spanish General Election', published in the *Journal of Communication*, spring 2000, Maxwell McCombs, Esteban Lopez Escobar and Juan Pablo Llamas, refer to 'agendas of attributes, those characteristics and traits that fill out the picture of each object'. Some attributes are emphasized, given prominence, others de-emphasized, 'while many are ignored'. McCombs and his colleagues explain: 'Just as objects vary in salience, so do the attributes of each object. Just as there is an agenda of public issues, political candidates, or some other set of objects, there is also an agenda of attributes for each object. Both the selection by journalists of objects for attention and the selection of attributes for detailing the pictures of these objects are powerful agenda-setting roles.

The authors point out that 'Although object and attribute salience are conceptually distinct, they are integral and simultaneously present aspects of the agenda-setting process.' In their research into public attitudes to candidates at the 1996 election in Spain, the following attributes of the major contenders were measured: ideology/issues position of rival candidates, biographical details, perceived qualifications and integrity.

See McCOMBS AND SHAW'S AGENDA-SETTING MODEL OF MEDIA EFFECTS, 1976; PROTOTYPING CONCEPT; ROGERS AND DEARING'S AGENDA-SETTING MODEL, 1987.

---

* Maxwell E. McCombs and Donald L. Shaw, 'The evolution of agenda-setting research: twenty-five years in the marketplace of ideas' in *Journal of Communication*, spring 1993; James W. Dearing and Everett M. Rogers, *Agenda-Setting* (US/UK: Sage, 1996).

Agenda-setting research A key area of research into the relationship between mass communication and audience consumption of media, agenda-setting research generally takes two forms. James D. Dearing and Everett M. Rogers, in *Agenda-Setting* (UK: Sage, 1996), explain that research has traditionally taken a *hierarchical* form; this they describe as 'one-point-in-time correlation comparisons of media content with aggregated responses by the public to survey questions about issue salience', that is, their perceived importance. More recently the research approach has been through *longitudinal* studies. Such investigations 'include over-time participant observation in media organizations as well as the analysis of quantitative variables such as real world indicators'.

Longitudinal studies can detect trends and directions of influence, tease out whether media coverage prompts public awareness and interest or whether the media perch on the 'bandwagon' of public opinion. The over-time study can identify variants of events and issues, and thus, as Dearing and Rogers put it, 'illuminate the nature of media effects with special clarity. …'

A further focus of research into agenda-setting involves what Dearing and Rogers term 'trigger events'. These act as a 'cue-to-action that occurs at a point in time', each trigger event serving 'to crystallize attention and action'. A trigger event essentially 'simplifies the nature of a complex issue into a form that the public can more easily understand'.

Agitprop The Department of Agitation and Propaganda was created in 1920 as part of the Central Committee Secretariat of the Communist Party of the Soviet Union. Its responsibility was to use all available media – especially film – to disseminate information and ideas to the population of the world's first Communist state. The term agitprop has come to be used to describe any unashamedly political propagandizing.

Agora In the city states of Ancient Greece the agora was the place of assembly where the free citizens debated matters of public concern; where public *opinion* was formulated and asserted. Public spaces have long been surrendered to enclosure or to shopping malls, but the concept remains; its practice continues at second remove – the media speak for the people, purporting to articulate and defend public interest in their role as WATCHDOGS, guarding the public from the abuses of state. PUBLIC SERVICE BROADCASTING is perceived as an extension of the agora; hence the concern often expressed about the privatization of broadcast media, that it is turning the agora into a marketplace of commodities (including COMMODITIZATION OF INFORMATION and entertainment) rather than a marketplace of ideas and debate. However, it could be claimed that a modern, and expanding, form of the agora is the INTERNET. See INFORMATION COMMONS; MEDIASPHERE; PUBLIC OPINION; SALON DISCOURSE.

AIDA model Guide to the principal stages of advertising a product or service: A – create Awareness; I – create Interest; D – promote Desire; A – stimulate Action or response.

Alexandra Palace Birthplace of television in the United Kingdom. The first TV broadcasting took place from London's 'Ally Pally' on 2 November 1936. Initially the service reached only a few hundred privileged viewers in and around the capital. Some 400 TV sets, costing around £100 – the price of a small car – were in use. With the coming of the Second World War, TV broadcasts came to an abrupt end on 1 September 1939, by which time there were an estimated 20,000 TV sets in operation. The Alexandra Palace studios opened for business again on 7 June 1946 but had to briefly shut down transmission again in early 1947 because of the acute fuel crisis. The Alexandra Palace studios remained in service until 1955. See BROADCASTING; TELEVISION.

Alienation As a concept, derives largely from the work of Karl Marx (1818–83), who argued that the organization of industrial production robbed people of opportunities for meaningful and creative work, performed in cooperation with others and over which they had some control. Researchers have posed the question whether the mass character of the modern communications industry produces a sense of alienation in its own workers. Lewis Coser in *Men of Ideas* (US: Free Press, 1965) believes that the industrial mode of production within media organizations hamstrings the individual producer by denying his or her creativity in the quest for a mass culture and that this results in alienation.

The term has a wider application. Alienation is seen as a socio-psychological condition that affects certain individuals. William Kornhauser in *The Politics of Mass Society* (US: Free Press, 1959) argues that the breakdown and decline of community groups and the extended family in modern society produce feelings of isolation and increase the possibility that people will be influenced by the appeals of extremist political groups. Alienation might therefore be a significant variable in determining an individual's receptivity to certain types of communication. See ANOMIE; INTERVENING VARIABLES.

Alignment See FRAMING.

al-Jazeera Arab satellite TV channel, started up in 1996, which grabbed world headlines with its exclusive NEWS footage from Taliban-held areas during the war in Afghanistan, 2002, and the US pursuit of Osama bin Laden, thought to have masterminded the events of 11 September 2001. al-Jazeera scooped rival western channels with bin Laden's pre-recorded video messages. The channel's coverage of world affairs, including the Israeli–Palestinian conflict, has offered alternative perspectives and analysis, braving CENSORSHIP whenever it is threatened.

Often referred to as the Arab world's BBC, al-Jazeera is based in Qatar, and is substantially funded by its liberalizing emir. It was through al-Jazeera that viewers were able to witness the destruction by the Taliban of the giant Bamiyan Buddhas.

Alleyne's news revolution model, 1997 In *News Revolution: Political and Economic Decisions about Global Information* (UK: Macmillan, 1997), Mark D. Alleyne offers a model that 'is both a description of the international news system's political economy and a theory of the international relations of that system'. The Global News System located in the model's oval 'refers to the system of companies, organizations and people that produce the world's news'. Democratic necessity 'describes the body of reasons used to justify the existence of the news media' – the political justifications, and these Alleyne classifies as (1) watchdogs on government; (2) 'conduits for the two-way flow of information between people and their government'; and (3) 'as a source of information in the so-called marketplace of ideas'.

Along with political justification there is economic necessity: 'The press system and the economic system interact at a basic level whenever the media carry advertising. At a more sophisticated level, the media perform the information functions needed for trade, currency, equities, and bond markets to perform.' Not the least of the factors relating to economics is the capacity of the media to attract or deter capital: 'News of political instability scares away investment. More positive news attracts them.'

The model identifies a dynamic of interacting and sometimes conflicting claims, which often operate in a process of exchange, what Alleyne terms a 'trade in claims'. Claims at the top of the model are what the media want from structures of power and authority, while those at the bottom of the model are what the structures deem critical in the nature of information and its flow. Says Alleyne, 'Like the news media, these actors [states, companies, international organizations] like to manage what information the news media disseminate about them.

'They do this through censorship and propaganda. Like the news media, these actors seek self-preservation, and the actors operating in the market place are particularly concerned with getting information that will help them make efficient decisions.' Alleyne's own claim for his model is that it 'takes us from the stage of merely describing the wonders of new technologies and assuming positive political consequences from the so-called information revolution to a clear explanation and understanding of how the news media function in international relations'.

POWER/AUTHORITY STRUCTURES:

The News Revolution model

Allness attitude Gail and Michelle Myers in *The Dynamics of Human Communication* (US: McGraw-Hill, 1985), refer to what Alfred Korzybski termed 'allness', that is the attitude that you can know or say all there is about a person, group, issue and so on. As Myers and Myers point out, the allness attitude can constitute a considerable barrier in communication. It may mean that you communicate with certain people on the basis that you know all there is to know about them or the topic under discussion, and few people take kindly to such assumptions.

The attitude may also affect how you receive messages. For example, you may believe that you already know all that you are being told or you may reject a message that contradicts what you think you know. As Myers and Myers conclude, 'The allness attitude may do much to prevent you from developing satisfying relationships with others and from communicating effectively with them.'

Allusion See HISTORICAL ALLUSION.

Alternative (radical) media See MEDIA: ALTERNATIVE (OR RADICAL MEDIA).

Amplitude See NEWS VALUES.

Analysis – modes of media analysis See DISCOURSE ANALYSIS; ETHNOGRAPHIC (APPROACH TO AUDIENCE MEASUREMENT); FUNCTIONALIST; MARXIST; SOCIAL ACTION (MODES OF MEDIA ANALYSIS).

Anarchist cinema Epitomized in the work of French film-maker Jean Vigo (1905–34) who was 12 when his anarchist father, known as Miguel Almereyda, was found strangled in a French police cell in 1917. In *A propos de Nice* (1930), Vigo expressed the anarchist's views on inequality, contrasting the luxurious, suntanned life of wealthy holidaymakers with the underfed, deformed bodies of slum children. In his comic masterpiece *Zéro de de Conduite* (Nought for Conduct) produced in 1932, Vigo used anarchist friends as actors. His theme was the rebellion of schoolchildren against the rigidity of the school authorities. It was immediately banned by the French authorities. Vigo was a direct inspiration for the 'anarchistic' film of a modern, public school rebellion in Lindsay Anderson's *If*, made in 1968. (Anarchy: complete absence of law or government.)

Anchorage The part that captions play in helping to frame, or anchor, the meaning of photographic images, as reproduced in newspapers and magazines. French philosopher Roland Barthes used this term to describe the way captions help 'fix' or narrow down the choice of meanings of the published image. He defines the caption as a 'parasitic message designed to connote the image'.

Andersch, Staats and Bostrom's model of communication, 1969 Environmental or contextual factors are at the centre of the communication model devised by Elizabeth G. Andersch, Lorin C. Staats and Robert N. Bostrom, and presented in *Communication in Everyday Use* (US: Holt, Rinehart & Winston). Like BARNLUND'S TRANSACTIONAL MODEL this one stresses the transactional nature of the communication process, in which messages and their meanings are structured and evaluated by the Sender and subjected to reconstruction and evaluation on the part of the Receiver, all the while interacting with factors (or stimuli) in the environment. See *TOPIC GUIDE* under COMMUNICATION MODELS.

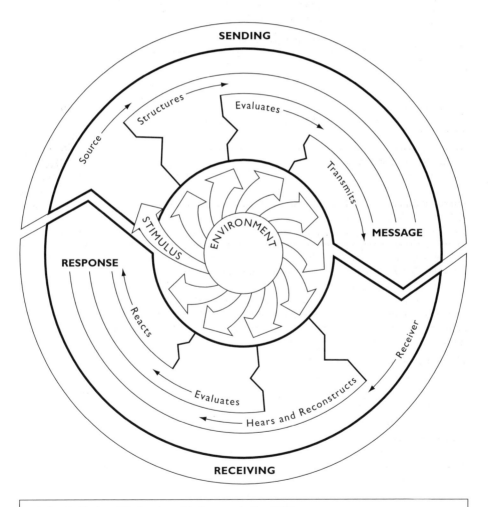

Andersch, Staats and Bostrom's model of communication, 1969

Androcentric rule Term used by Jennifer Coates in *Women, Men and Language* (UK: Longman, 1993, second edition) to describe the rule by which 'Men will be seen to behave linguistically in a way that fits the writer's view of what is desirable or admirable; women on the other hand will be blamed for any linguistic state or development which is regarded by the writer as negative or reprehensible.'

Anecdote A short narrative, usually of a personal nature, used to illustrate a general issue. Anecdotes are often used in media coverage to heighten the emotional aspect of an issue. Colin Seymour-Ure in *The Political Impact of the Mass Media* (UK: Constable, 1974) recounts the use made of one such anecdote by the politician Enoch Powell in his efforts to bring the immigration issue to public attention during 1967 and 1968. Powell claimed to have received a letter from a correspondent in Northumberland expressing concern about an elderly widow in Wolverhampton who feared harassment by newly arrived immigrants in the area. This anecdote was widely reported by the press, yet, despite strenuous efforts, no trace of the elderly widow could be found. The story did, however, do much to fuel the emotive manner in which the immigration issue was discussed in the popular press. See LOONY LEFTISM.

Animatic Sequence of drawings representing the story of a television advertisement, prior to filming. Another term for STORYBOARD.

Animation The process of filming still drawings, puppets, etc. in sequence to give the illusion of movement; also the actual direct drawing and painting on to positive or negative stock or on to clear celluloid itself. Long before CINEMATOGRAPHY was invented devices were in use that gave drawings the illusion of movement. By 1882 Emile Reynauld had combined his Praxinoscope with a projector and a decade later opened the Théâtre Optique in the Musée Grevin in Paris.

Live-action cinema became all-important once the Lumière brothers had shown its possibilities in 1895, but animation soon captured interest, from 1908 onwards, with the work of J. Stuart Blackton in the US and Emile Cohl in France. *New York Herald* cartoonist Winsor McCay made *Gertie the Dinosaur* in 1909, and in 1919 the first animated feature, *The Sinking of the Lusitania*.

In November 1928 Walt Disney (1901–66) presented Mortimer, later Mickey Mouse, to the world – using synchronous sound, in *Steamboat Willie*, along with his *Skeleton Dance* (1929) one of the true classics of animation film. The laboriousness of producing thousands of drawings for filming was dramatically altered in the 1980s by the introduction to animated film-making of computer graphics.

* Paul Wells, *Understanding Animation* (UK: Routledge, 1998).

Annan Commission Report on Broadcasting, 1977 Historian Lord Annan chaired the Royal Commission on the Future of Broadcasting, whose main task was to decide what should happen to the BROADCASTING industry once the right to broadcast of the RADIO and TELEVISION companies lapsed at the end of July 1979. Also, the Annan Commission was asked to make recommendations on a fourth television channel.

Annan favoured the continuance of much of the existing broadcasting system, though the Report suggested that both the BBC and IBA should lose their local radio stations to a new Local Broadcasting Authority. Annan also proposed a broadcasting complaints commission, empowered to award costs if a complaint were upheld, and a Public Enquiry Board for Broadcasting. The task of the Board would be to hold seven-yearly public audits of the way each authority had met its responsibilities and to conduct hearings on specific issues, particularly the award of franchises. A further recommendation was for an Open Broadcasting Authority to operate the fourth channel 'more as a publisher of material provided by others'.

What Annan wanted above all was a shift from duopoly to a more diverse system of broadcasting in Britain: 'We want the broadcasting industry to grow. But we do not want more of the same. ... What is needed now are programmes for the different minorities which add up to make the majority.' Annan also declared that there was 'a widely shared feeling that British broadcasting is run like a highly restricted club – managed exclusively by broadcasters according to their own criteria of what counts as good television and radio'.

The then Labour Government published a white paper, *Broadcasting* (July 1978), in response to Annan, declaring itself against the Local Broadcasting Authority and the Public Enquiry Board but in favour of the Complaints Commission and the Open Broadcasting Authority. Before there was time for legislation, the Conservatives came to power in May 1979. The Queen's Speech promised the fourth channel to commercial television and the proposal for an Open Broadcasting Authority was rejected. See CHANNEL 4. See also *TOPIC GUIDE* under COMMISSIONS, COMMITTEES, LEGISLATION.

Anomie It was Emile Durkheim (1858–1917), a French sociologist, who first used this term to describe a state of 'normlessness' in which the individual feels that there are no effective social rules governing behaviour or that those rules and VALUES to which he/she is exposed are conflicting and therefore confusing. The anomic state is most likely to occur when contact with others is limited. Durkheim linked anomie with the disturbance caused by social change and upheaval, and saw it as a temporary social phenomenon. Several contemporary observers consider it a more permanent feature of modern industrial society.

MASS SOCIETY theorists have tended to view those suffering from anomie as being particularly vulnerable to over-influence by mass communication. Observers have also found that some behaviour that was considered anomic was in fact subcultural. Another feature of anomie is that the individual may react to it by becoming ceaselessly ambitious, and this in some cases can lead to severe agitation and discontent. Dissatisfied ambition is a target for much advertising and is often seen as a desirable trait in modern capitalist societies – a perspective reinforced by some of the outpourings from the mass media. An area of concern is, then, the contribution of the mass media and in particular advertising to the condition of anomie. Anomie can lead to extensive personal as well as social breakdown, to suicide and mental illness as well as to crime, delinquency, drug addiction and alcoholism.

Anti-language Anti-languages, according to Martin Montgomery in *An Introduction to Language and Society* (UK: 1986, Methuen; Routledge, 1993) 'may be understood as extreme versions of social dialects'. Typically, anti-languages are developed by subcultures and groups that take an antagonistic stance towards mainstream society. This stance may be general or relate to a specific area of social activity. Further, the core activities of the group, those around which the anti-language often develops, may well be illegal.

The anti-language serves both to establish a boundary and a degree of separateness between the group and society, and to make its activities more difficult for outsiders to detect and follow. By their nature anti-languages are difficult to study but Montgomery discusses several types including those developed in Polish prisons, by the Calcutta underworld and CB radio slang – a weak form of anti-language even when the use of CB radio was illegal, but one with which many outsiders are now familiar.

Anti-languages are created by a process of *relexicalization* – that is, the substitution of new vocabulary for old, usually those words that refer to the activities that mark the group off from the wider community. The grammar of the parent language is often preserved. So, for example, in CB radio slang, the phrase 'bear in the air' was used for a police helicopter. Making up new words happens frequently in anti-languages, thus making them even more difficult to penetrate. *Overlexicalization* is often also a feature of anti-languages. Here a variety of new words may refer to an activity and may be used interchangeably in order to mislead or confuse 'outsiders'.

Anti-Terrorism, Crime and Security Act (UK), 2001 See TERRORISM: ANTI-TERRORISM, CRIME AND SECURITY ACT.

Apache silence The complex meanings of silence, as observed by the North American Apache tribes, have been tabulated by K.H. Basso in 'To give up words: silence in western Apache culture', in P. Giglioli (ed.), *Language and Social Context* (UK: Penguin, 1972). Basso describes Apache silence as 'a response to uncertainty and unpredictability in social relations'. Often baffling to the outsider, Apache silence was an important element in the courtship process; when meeting strangers; even when greeting children back from a long journey; and in the presence of other people's grief. See COMMUNICATION, NON-VERBAL.

---

* Adam Jaworski, *The Power of Silence: Social and Pragmatic Perspectives* (UK: Sage, 1993).

Apocryphal stories Those of doubtful origin, false or spurious. See DEMONIZATION; FOLK

DEVILS; LOONY LEFTISM; MYTH; RUMOUR.

Arbitrariness One of the characteristic features of human LANGUAGE is that between an object described and the word that describes it there is a connection that is purely arbitrary – that is, the speech sound does not reflect features of the object denoted. For example, the word chair describes the object chair, because the English have arbitrarily decided to name it thus as a matter of convention. In contrast, *onomatopoeic* expressions are representative rather than arbitrary in that they reflect properties of the non-linguistic world (for example, clatter, buzz, flap – and snap, crackle and pop).

'Areopagitica' Title of a tract or pamphlet by the English poet John Milton (1608–74) in defence of the freedom of the press, published in 1644. Milton spoke out, with eloquence and courage, following the revival of censorship by parliamentary ordinance in 1643 (traditional press censorship had broken down with the Long Parliament's abolition of the Star Chamber in 1641). The title was taken from the Greek *Areopagus* – the hill of Ares or Mars in Athens, where the highest judicial court held its sittings; a 'behind closed doors' court.

Milton celebrated the power and influence of the printed word: books 'do preserve, as in a vial, the purest efficacy and extraction of that living intellect that bred them. I know they are as lively, and as vigorously productive, as those fabulous dragon's teeth; and being sown up and down, may chance to spring up armed men. And yet, on the other hand, unless wariness be used, as good almost kill a man as kill a good book: who kills a man kills a reasonable creature, God's image; but he who destroys a good book, kills reason itself, kills the image of God, as it were, in the eye.' See MILTON'S PARADOX.

Artefacts Things made by human workmanship; in a communication sense, the adornments that are worn that 'say something' about the wearer: dress, hairstyles, jewellery, make-up; or objects that we possess – such as motor cars or media artefacts such as a newspaper, video or a DVD player – are indicators of our self-concept. See OBJECT LANGUAGE.

Article 19 This clause in the European Convention for the Protection of Human Rights and Fundamental Freedom states: '(1) Everyone has the right to freedom of expression. This right shall include freedom to hold opinions and to receive and impart information and ideas without interference by public authority and regardless of frontiers. (2) The exercise of these freedoms, since it carries with it duties and responsibilities, may be subject to such formalities, conditions, restrictions or penalties as are prescribed by law and are necessary in a democratic society, in the interests of national security, territorial integrity or public safety … for preventing the disclosure of information received in confidence, or for maintaining the authority and impartiality of the judiciary.' The upholding of the Convention is the task of the European Court of Human Rights, based in Strasbourg. The article gave birth to a pressure group, Article 19, centred in London, using electronic media to monitor state censorship around the world. See CENSORSHIP; PRIOR RESTRAINT; SPYCATCHER CASE.

Aspirers See ADVERTISING: MAINSTREAMERS, ASPIRERS, SUCCEEDERS AND REFORMERS.

Assertiveness To be assertive is to be able to communicate one's thoughts, feelings, beliefs, ATTITUDES, positions and so on in a clear, confident, honest and direct manner; it is in short to be able to stand up for oneself whilst also taking into consideration the needs and rights of other people. Being assertive differs from being aggressive in that aggressiveness involves a standing up for one's own rights and needs at the expense of others. In recent years there has been much interest in assertiveness training – that is, in enabling people to develop techniques and strategies, verbal and non-verbal, for INTERPERSONAL COMMUNICATION that will encourage them to assert themselves in social situations. The ability to be assertive is linked to self-esteem and self-confidence, and thus to a positive SELF-CONCEPT. Such training provides the opportunity for considerable exploration of the relationship between the self-concept and interpersonal behaviour.

Whilst assertiveness in communication may be encouraged in some individualistic cultures, such as those of the US or UK, collectivistic cultures, like that of Japan, tend to stress the importance of respect for others, tact, politeness and the maintenance of interpersonal harmony. In which case, assertiveness may be perceived as rudeness.

These different perspectives on assertiveness can be found within a culturally diverse society. Larry

Samovar and Richard Porter in *Communication Between Cultures* (US: Wadsworth/Thomson Learning, 2001) provide the following example from the US: 'In yet another experiment Caucasian mothers tended to interpret as positive those aspects of their children's speech and behaviour that reflected assertiveness, excitement and interest.

'Navajo mothers who observed the same behaviour in their children reported them as being mischievous and lacking discipline. To the Navajo mothers, assertive speech and behaviour reflected discourtesy, restlessness, self-centredness, and lack of discipline ...'. It would seem that assertiveness in communication is a potential barrier to successful intercultural communication. See COMMUNICATION: INTERCULTURAL COMMUNICATION; HIGH AND LOW CONTEXT COMMUNICATION.

Attention See PERCEPTION.

Attention model of mass communication Denis McQuail in *Mass Communication Theory: An Introduction* (UK: Sage, 1987), writes that 'the essence of any market is to bring goods and services to the attention of potential customers and keep their interest'.

Thus, in mass media terms, the attention model is about stimulus to buy: communication is considered to have succeeded as soon as AUDIENCE attention has been won, regardless of how that attention was won. This paradigm contrasts with the TRANSMISSION MODEL OF MASS COMMUNICATION, which essentially relates to notions of PUBLIC SERVICE BROADCASTING; that is, the function of communication is to deliver *messages*, to transmit information, knowledge, education and enlightenment as well as to entertain. Hence public *service*. See *audience-as-public* and *audience-as-market* in the entry on AUDIENCE.

Attitudes We all hold a range of attitudes on a variety of topics and issues. An attitude, according to Milton Rokeach in 'The nature of attitudes', *Encyclopaedia of the Social Sciences* (UK: Collier-Macmillan, 1965), is '... a relatively enduring organization of beliefs around an object or situation predisposing one to respond in some preferential manner'.

Attitudes are learned from direct experience or through socialization, and are capable of being changed. Attitudes may vary in their direction (that is, they may be positive, negative or neutral), their intensity and in the degree of importance attached to them. It is possible to discern three component elements of an attitude: the *cognitive* component, that is the knowledge one has, true or false, about a particular subject, which may have been gathered from a wide range of sources; the *affective* component, that is, one's emotional response or feelings towards a particular subject, which will be linked to one's beliefs and VALUES; and the *behaviour* component, that is, how one reacts with respect to a certain subject.

Attitudes cannot be seen. Their existence can only be inferred from what people say or do. It is for this reason that accurate attitude measurement is considered to be highly problematic: people may not be that willing to communicate what they really think or feel. It is basically through communicating with others that one develops attitudes. Attitudes, once developed, influence the way in which we perceive other people and thus how we behave towards them. The mass media may shape, reinforce or challenge attitudes. For example, in conveying STEREOTYPES, mass media messages may shape people's attitudes towards GROUPS with which they have had little, if any, contact. CAMPAIGNS, such as ADVERTISING campaigns, may be designed to change people's attitudes towards a certain product. See DISSONANCE; NOISE; REINFORCEMENT; SELECTIVE EXPOSURE.

Attribute dimensions See AGENDA-SETTING.

Attribute dimensions of agenda-setting See AGENDA-SETTING.

Attribution theory Concerned with the psychological processes by which individuals attribute causes to behaviour. Such attribution can be *dispositional* – behaviour attributed to such factors as personality and attitude – or *situational* – behaviour attributed to factors in the situation. We may, for example, blame a person's failure to gain employment on his/her laziness (dispositional attribution) or on the state of the economy (situational attribution). We tend to overestimate the influence of dispositional factors in the behaviour of other people and underestimate the influence of situational factors. Dispositional attribution can be difficult to change as evidence suggests that we are unwilling to discard dispositional attributions even when they are discredited.

This may help explain the persistence of STEREOTYPES and PREJUDICE. Carole Wade and Carol

Tavris, in *Psychology* (US: HarperCollins, 1993), note that 'When it comes to explaining their own behaviour, most Westerners tend to choose attributes that are favourable to them. ... This self-serving bias means that people like to take credit for their good actions and let the situation account for their bad ones.'

Audience Students of media communication recognize the term audience as overarching all the reception processes of message sending. Thus there is the audience for theatre, TELEVISION and cinema; there is the RADIO listener. There is the audience for a pop concert or at a public meeting. Communicators shape their messages to fit the perceived needs of their audience: they calculate the level of receptiveness, the degree of readiness to accept the message and the mode of delivery. Audience is readership too and the success in meeting audience/readership needs relies extensively on FEEDBACK.

Sometimes there is an extra factor in the communicator–audience situation. This might be the *client*. An advertising agency, for example, is employed by a client (a company wishing to have its products advertised) to create a commercial whose audience is the television-watching public.

Of course audience needs are not the only criterion for the communicator or the client but they are central to a process that is essentially interactive and subject to a wide range of social, cultural, economic, political and environmental influences. It might be argued that the advertiser's job is to *create* a need that his or her client's product or service will fulfil.

Increasingly during the 1980s and 1990s when deregulation and privatization became key ideas in the politics of BROADCASTING, and as TV has come to be seen as the most powerful means of mass communication, it has become necessary to discriminate between target audiences. Two current concepts of audience are the *audience-as-public* and the *audience-as-market*. The first stems from notions of PUBLIC SERVICE BROADCASTING (PSB), the other from COMMERCIAL (RADIO and TELEVISION) broadcasting.

Raymond Williams in *Communications* (UK: Penguin, 1976) spoke of the public service approach to broadcasting as being a 'paternal system' (see REITHIAN). Williams wrote of PSB as he knew it then as 'an authoritarian system with a conscience: that is to say, with values and purposes beyond the maintenance of its own power'. Though such a stance has long been open to accusations of elitism, in practical terms PSB – as represented by the BBC, for example – has been as sensitive to audience needs as its commercial rivals.

The audience-as-public relates to people as receivers of messages – information, knowledge, education, enlightenment as well as entertainment. The audience-as-market approach is less interested in the transmission of MEANING than in gaining audience attention: stimulate the customer, then sell him a product or service. Instead of a *transmission* model of communication here we have an *attention* model. In this case the purpose of broadcast communication is deemed effective once the audience's

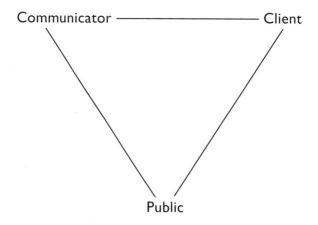

Communicator ———————— Client

Public

attention has been stimulated and held, no matter the quality of the stimulus.

The difference is simple but profound: broadcasting aimed at audience-as-public defines its function as being *to serve*, audience-as-market, *to sell*. The trend in recent times has been from one to the other, from audience-as-public to audience defined as consumers. Indeed, the 1990s saw a growing crisis in the audience-as-public paradigm as PSB was itself dragged into the 'market' for audiences. However, in *Desperately Seeking the Audience* (UK: Routledge, 1991), Ien Ang states that the rival paradigms 'are only relatively conflicting', for both commercial and public service institutions 'cannot with their specific goals and interests in mind stop struggling to conquer audience, no matter whether audience members are identified as consumers or citizens'.

In other words, commanding an audience is the prime function of both sets of institution.

John Ellis in an article 'Channel 4: Working notes', in *Screen* (24 (6), 1983), usefully discriminates between viewers, that is individuals, and audience, that is the aggregate of viewers. He writes ' "audience" is a profoundly ideological concept. ... Broadcasting institutions do not seek viewers, they seek audiences.' Ang adds weight to this view: ' "television audience" only exists as an imaginary entity, an abstraction constructed from the point of view of the institutions, in the interests of the institutions'. Increasingly the reality of audience as something that can be identified as well as defined and measured is problematic. With the fragmentation of audience brought about by new technologies that have considerably widened audience choice, the trend indicators suggest a shift away from *broadcast* transmission to *narrowcasting*, which in turn confirms a new emphasis on *consumption.*

Audiences have choice as never before: the power to switch from terrestrially produced media products to satellite, to decide when they will consume, thanks to video and DVD, or whether to direct attention to more lateral systems that cut out the major producers of media altogether – such as the Internet and World Wide Web. With the coming of DIGITIZATION, channel scarcity has rapidly given way to channel abundance. As Denis McQuail writes in *Audience Analysis* (US/UK: Sage, 1997), audience is a single word to describe a 'diverse and complex reality'. See *TOPIC GUIDE* under AUDIENCES/CONSUMPTION AND RECEPTION OF MEDIA.

---

* Pertti Alasuutari (ed.), *Rethinking the Media Audience: The New Agenda* (UK: Sage, 1999).

Audience: active audience An age-old media debate centres on the nature of audience reaction to media messages. The notion of the active audience considers audiences proactive and independent rather than docile and accepting. The active audience is seen to use the media rather than be used by it (see USES AND GRATIFICATIONS THEORY). This perception has come about substantially through findings of research which has observed members of audience consuming media in their own homes (see ETHNOGRAPHIC (APPROACH TO AUDIENCE MEASUREMENT)).

American media analyst Herbert Schiller takes issue with the optimistic view of the active or resistive audience. In *Culture Inc.: The Corporate Takeover of Public Expression* (US: Oxford University Press, 1989), Schiller argues that transnational corporations have colonized culture and cultural expression, in the US and globally. He writes of 'corporate pillaging of the national information supply' and the 'proprietary control of information'. Such manifest power, he believes, calls into question the active-audience paradigm: 'A great emphasis is given to the "resistance", "subversion", and "empowerment" of the viewer.'

'Where this resistance and subversion of the audience lead and what effects they have on the existing structure of power remain a mystery.' He goes on: 'It is not a matter of people being dupes, informational or cultural. It is that human beings are not equipped to deal with a pervasive disinformational system – administered from the command posts of social order – that assails the senses through all cultural forms and channels.'

In turn Schiller has been criticized for underestimating the potential resistance of audience to 'corporatization'. John B. Thompson in *The Media and Modernity: A Social Theory of Media* (UK: Polity, 1995) says that 'even if one sympathizes with Schiller's broad theoretical view and his critical perspectives, there are many respects in which the argument is deeply unsatisfactory'. In particular, Thompson counters Schiller's view that American cultural imperialism has wreaked havoc with indigenous cultures throughout the world, and that it is a seemingly unstoppable force. Thompson is of the opinion that 'Schiller … presents too uniform a view of American media culture … and of its global dominance.' See AUDIENCE: FRAGMENTATION OF; MEDIA IMPERIALISM; SELF-IDENTITY; SEMIOTIC POWER; TACTICS AND STRATEGIES.

Audience appreciation Term employed by RATINGS researchers, and to be differentiated from response measurement – to RADIO or TV programmes – concerned with numbers alone. Audience size, while being important, is considered by BBC radio as only one criterion for measurement; gauging audience interest (AI) and its judgment of quality is also crucial. In contrast, audience research into TV viewing focuses almost entirely on numbers watching. See BARB.

Audience: audience for news See NEWS: AUDIENCES FOR NEWS. See also *TOPIC GUIDE* under AUDIENCES/CONSUMPTION AND RECEPTION OF MEDIA; MEDIA ISSUES AND DEBATES; NEWS MEDIA.

Audience differentiation Like the 'mass', audiences – for RADIO, TELEVISION, the cinema or readers of the PRESS – are often simplistically regarded as a homogeneous lump. It is easier to make generalizations that way, but misleading. Audience differentiation works from the premise that analysis of audience response to media messages can only be purposeful if it recognizes that the mass is a complex of individuals, differentiated by gender, age, social class, profession, education and CULTURE. See ANALYSIS – MODES OF MEDIA ANALYSIS.

Audience: fragmentation of In *Audience Analysis* (UK: Sage, 1997), Denis McQuail publishes the following models, with acknowledgement to Jan van Cuilenburg, illustrating in four succeeding stages how audiences have become fragmented since the early years of TV. The Unitary Model 'implies a single audience that is more or less coextensive with the general public'. The texts of media – BROAD-CASTING in particular – were shared by all, and homogenous. With the expansion of provision and the increase in the number of channels, diversity is shown in the Pluralist Model, representing a 'pattern of limited internal diversification'. The Core–Periphery Model 'is one in which the multipli-

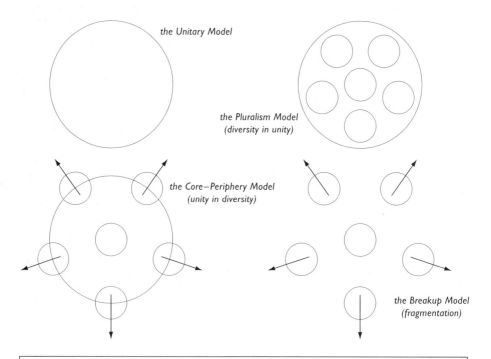

the Unitary Model

the Pluralism Model
(diversity in unity)

the Core–Periphery Model
(unity in diversity)

the Breakup Model
(fragmentation)

McQuail D., *Audience Analysis*, 1997, p. 138. Reproduced by permission of Sage Publications Inc.

cation of channels makes possible additional and competing alternatives outside this framework'.

At this stage, says McQuail, 'It becomes possible to enjoy a television diet that differs significantly from the majority or mainstream.' The Breakup Model is characterized by 'extensive fragmentation and the disintegration of the central core. The audience is distributed over many different channels in no fixed pattern, and there is only sporadically shared audience experiences.'

McQuail says that currently and for the most part, the 'core' still dominates audience use of TV: 'The reasons lie primarily in the near-universal appeal of mainstream content and the advantages to media organizations of continuing with mass provision, plus the continuing habits and patterns of social life.' The author believes that 'Media change is not enough on its own to disrupt established patterns of shared culture.' The breakup stage 'is certainly becoming more possible', but it is 'still a hypothetical pattern and has not been realised'. See DIGITIZATION.

Audience measurement Investigation of the size and constitution of mass media audiences has become one of the world's major service industries. Initially, audience measurement, or audience research (AR), is about number-crunching: how many readers? How many listeners or viewers? This data is then broken down along lines of class, gender, spending power, age, occupation etc. There are two categories of measurement – quantitative and qualitative – with pressure always to translate the one into the other.

In the UK, audience measurement of one kind or another has operated since the beginning of BROADCASTING. Once the monopoly of the airwaves held by the BBC gave way to competition with the advent of COMMERCIAL TELEVISION, audience preferences became increasingly significant, and audience measurement was quickly regarded as a duty and a lifeline for survival. In the UK the BBC and the ITCA (Independent TV Companies Association) share ownership of BARB (the Broadcasters' Audience Research Board) with Channel 5, BSkyB and the Institute of Practitioners in Advertising.

Two key terms (one might say dread terms, for programmes live or die by them) are *ratings* and *shares*. A rating is defined as the estimated percentage, in the case of television, of all the 'TV households' or of all the people within a demographic group who view a specific programme or station. A share refers to the percentage of the overall viewing figures a particular programme commands. Such figures were traditionally obtained through telephone research, the use of viewing diaries and the set meter.

In 1983, a British firm, Audit of Great Britain (AGB), entered the US audience measurement field with the so-called people meter (introduced into Europe as early as 1978 by Irish Television Audience Measurement and, in West Germany, by Telescopie). The people meter is designed to combine the personal element of the diary with the electronic objectivity of the set meter. The premier US ratings company, ACNielsen, responsible for the immensely influential *Nielsen ratings*, answered AGB's challenge with the *Homeunit*.

Of course, the problem with the people meter has turned out to be people: they forget to switch on or to switch off, and this human trait plays havoc with the accuracy of viewing figures. Also, the people meter has not proved very popular with the networks because an unexpected outcome of its use has been the registration of lower viewing figures than those denoted by traditional modes of measurement.

In *Inside Prime Time* (US: Pantheon, 1983), Todd Gitlin dubbed the obsession of the TV networks with ratings 'the fetish of immediate numerical gratification'. This fetish now extends to ways of measuring audience response using sensory devices that register viewing without buttons having to be pressed. The hunt for qualitative data arises essentially from the need of the sponsors and advertisers to have the question answered: is TV helping us to sell our products? Current research in the States is focusing on 'single-source' measurement by linking the viewing habits of specific families to their actual purchasing habits. Households are provided with an electronic 'wand' connected to the TV's people meter. With this, the household shopping is checked in, using the universal product code stamped on most packaged goods.

A major problem that has come to further haunt the already hypersensitive minds of measurers of audience is the fragmentation of audience through cable, video, DVD and satellite, not to mention the difficulties facing measurement with the zapping and zipping that goes on, facilitated by the remote control pad. In *Desperately Seeking the Audience* (UK: Routledge, 1991), Ien Ang argues that the obsession with measurement is ultimately self-defeating: 'There is no way,' she writes, 'to foretell the ratings performance of a new programme.' There is equally no way that the networks, faced with the pressures upon them to prove that someone out there is taking notice, are going to heed Ang's conclusion: the audience must be conquered and controlled. See CUSTOM AUDIENCE RESEARCH; ETHNO-GRAPHIC (APPROACH TO AUDIENCE MEASUREMENT).

---

* Shaun Moores, *Interpreting Audiences: The Ethnography of Media Consumption* (UK: Sage, 1993); James S. Ettema and D. Charles Whitney (eds), *Audiencemaking: How Media Create the Audience* (US: Sage, 1994); Raymond Kent (ed.), *Measuring Media Audiences* (UK: Routledge, 1994); Denis McQuail, *Audience Analysis* (UK: Sage, 1997).

Audience needs See USES AND GRATIFICATIONS THEORY. See also *TOPIC GUIDE* under AUDIENCES/CONSUMPTION AND RECEPTION OF MEDIA; MEDIA: POWER, EFFECTS, INFLUENCE.

Autocue Or teleprompt. A device that uses angled mirrors to project the words of a script on to a screen just below the lens of the TV camera. This enables a presenter to 'read' a script without looking down.

Autonomy The capacity to be self-governing, self-controlling and to be able to act in an independent manner. The term can be applied to individuals, groups or institutions. Debate normally centres on the degree of autonomy a particular individual, group or institution has; an example here would be debate about the degree to which the BBC can act independently of the government of the day. See IMPARTIALITY.

Avant-garde The innovative, advance guard in any art form; usually assaulting tradition and boundaries of acceptability. The phrase was used as early as 1845 by Gabriel-Désiré Laverdant, and the anarchist Michael Bakunin named a periodical *L'Avant-garde* in 1878.

B

Bad language Andersson and Trudgill in *Bad Language* (UK: Penguin, 1990), whilst acknowledging that the term bad language is far from clear and unambiguous, refer to bad language as 'all those things (sounds, words and phrases) that may be dangerous to use. Language contains explosive totems that should be handled with care' and argue that bad language can be usefully analysed by explaining the possible explosions that may be caused by certain words, pronunciations or uses of grammar. They also argue that ' "Badness" is not found in the language itself but in people's views of the language' and thus they highlight the importance of examining the values, attitudes and ideologies within societies that underpin the evaluation of some language as 'bad'.

When ordinary people are asked, Andersson and Trudgill argue, ' "What do you think of when you hear the phrase bad language?", most of them will certainly say "swearing".' Whilst swearing seems to be for most people what 'bad' language is, Andersson and Trudgill point out that the term is also used to refer to the use of slang and jargon, the incorrect or misuse of words, certain accents and dialects, and the use of 'non-standard' English. Several studies have shown that the evaluation of language as 'bad' in a particular instance will depend on a number of variables, which include the degree to which taboo words or words relating to taboo behaviour are used, the social context and the social roles, age and gender of the interactors.

Back region, front region See IMPRESSION MANAGEMENT.

Balanced programming The PILKINGTON REPORT, 1962, put forward three criteria for the creation of balance in TV programmes. Balance would be achieved, Pilkington stated, if channels provided the widest possible range of subject matter; if the fullest treatment was given to each subject within the range and if scheduling did not create imbalances by concentrating certain types of popular programmes at peak viewing times while relegating others, deemed less accessible, to inconvenient times. Balance has a more controversial, political connotation, when it is seen as a device to counter and control bias. More than any other medium, public broadcasting aspires to *equilibrium*. Being fair to all sides can have paradoxical results: if one programme, for example, condemns the destruction of Amazon rainforests, must the balance be sustained by allowing a programme which defends that destruction? It is questionable whether fairness is actually achieved by giving airtime to ideas that flout the very principle of fairness.

Balance might ultimately mean always sitting on the fence; it may indicate a position that considers all standpoints to be tenable. Yet the balanced position – the fulcrum, as it were – from which other viewpoints are presented, has to be decided by *someone*, whose IMPARTIALITY might in turn be questioned by others.

Ball-Rokeach and DeFleur's dependency model of mass communication effects, 1976 (See also, DEPENDENCY THEORY). Sandra Ball-Rokeach and Melvyn DeFleur's model poses the question, to what extent is contemporary society dependent, for information and for viewpoints, on the all-pervasive mass communication industry and, arising from this question, how far are we dependent on the media for our orientation towards the world beyond our immediate experience? In 'A dependency model of mass media effects', in *Communication Research* 3 (1976), the authors argue that the nature and degree of dependency relate closely first to the extent to which society is subject to change, conflict or instability and, second, to the functions of information provision and attitude shaping of the mass media within those social structures.

The model emphasizes the essentially interactive nature of the processes of media effect. The societal and media systems interact and influence audience responses, which in turn influence media and

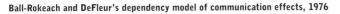
Ball-Rokeach and DeFleur's dependency model of communication effects, 1976

Barnlund's transactional models of communication, 1970

society. The cognitive effect is that which relates to matters of the intellect, and the affective to matters of emotion. In the cognitive area, the following areas of effect or influence are identified: creation and resolution of ambiguity; attitude formation; agenda-setting; expansion of people's belief systems; value clarification. Under the affective heading, the media may be perceived as creating fear or anxiety; increasing or decreasing morale and establishing a sense of alienation.

In terms of the third category, behaviour, the effects may be to activate or de-activate; formulate issues and influence their resolution. They may stimulate a range of behaviours from political demonstrations to altruistic acts such as donating money to good causes. The authors cite the model as avoiding 'a seemingly untenable all-or-nothing position of saying either that the media have no significant impact on people or society, or that the media have an unbounded capacity to manipulate people and society'.

Where the model is open to most serious criticism is in its assumption that the societal structure and the media structure are independent of one another and that these are in some sort of equilibrium with audience. In many cases the media are so interlinked with power structures that a free interaction is more likely in theory than in practice. See COGNITIVE (AND AFFECTIVE); CULTURAL APPARATUS; HEGEMONY; MEDIATION; POWER ELITE.

Band-wagon effect See NOELLE-NEUMANN'S SPIRAL OF SILENCE MODEL OF PUBLIC OPINION, 1974.

Bandwidth Range of frequencies available for carrying data and expressed in hertz (cycles per second). The amount of traffic a communication channel can carry is roughly proportional to its bandwidth. A telephone system, for example, requires a bandwidth of 4 Kilohertz while a 625-line TV channel requires around 8 Megahertz.

BARB Broadcasters' Audience Research Board, limited company jointly owned by the BBC and ITCA. (Independent TV, Channel 5, BSkyB and the Institute of Practitioners in Advertising.) See AUDIENCE MEASUREMENT.

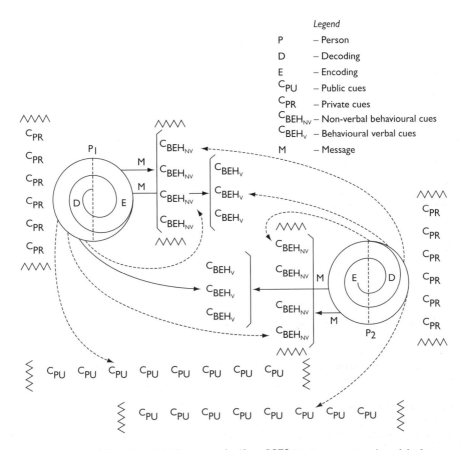

Barnlund's transactional model of communication, 1970 In 'A transactional model of communication', in K.K. Sereno and C.D. Mortensen (eds), *Foundations of Communication Theory* (US: Harper and Row, 1970), Dean C. Barnlund attempts to address the 'complexities of human communication', which present 'an unbelievably difficult challenge to the student of human affairs'. His model pays due respect to this complexity. For Barnlund, communication both describes the evolution of meaning and aims at the reduction of uncertainty. He stresses that meaning is something 'invented', 'assigned', 'given' rather than something 'received': 'Meanings may be generated while a man stands alone on a mountain trail or sits in the privacy of his study speculating about internal doubt.'

Within and around the communicant are *cues* of unlimited number, though some carrying more weight – or valence – than others at any given time. Barnlund's model indicates three sets of cues, each interacting upon one another. These are public cues, *private cues* and behavioural cues. DECODING and ENCODING are visualized as part of the same spiralling process – continuous, unrepeatable and irreversible.

Public cues Barnlund divides into *natural* – those supplied by the physical world without the intervention of people, such as atmospheric conditions, natural occurrences – and *artificial*, those resulting from people's modification and manipulation of their environment. For example, Barnlund places his communicant, Mr A, in a doctor's waiting room which contains many public artificial cues – a pile of magazines, a smell of antiseptic, a picture by Joan Miró on the wall. Private cues emanate from sources not automatically available to any other person who enters a communicative field: 'Public and private cues may be verbal or non-verbal in form, but the critical quality is that they were brought into existence and remain beyond the control of the communicants.' The third set of cues – *behavioural* –

are those initiated or controlled by the communicant him/herself and in response to public and private cues, coloured by the communicant's 'sensory-motor successes and failures in the past, combined with his current appetites and needs', which will establish 'his set towards the environment'.

In the second diagram, INTRAPERSONAL COMMUNICATION becomes INTERPERSONAL COMMUNICATION, with the multiplication of cues and the introduction of the message (M). Barnlund emphasizes the *transferability* of cues. Public cues can be transformed into private ones, private cues may be converted into public ones, while environmental and behavioural cues may merge. In short, the whole process is one of *transaction*, and few models have explored so impressively the inner dynamics of this process as Barnlund's, which also has useful application to the dynamics of MASS COMMUNICATION. See *TOPIC GUIDE* under COMMUNICATION MODELS.

Barrier signals Used as personal defence mechanisms in communication situations, gestures such as the placing of hands and arms across the body, or folding the arms. In the business world, the classic defensive barrier is the desk. On its role in the relationship between the executive and this modern version of the old moated castle and drawbridge, much has been written – about the size and dominance of the desk, its angle to the office door, the distance between the desk and the chair placed for those who approach the boss's territory. In *Manwatching: A Field Guide to Human Behaviour* (UK: Jonathan Cape, 1977), Desmond Morris would have us believe of the executive desk that 'many a businessman would feel naked without one and hides behind it gratefully every day, wearing it like a vast wooden chastity belt'.

Basic needs See MASLOW'S HIERARCHY OF NEEDS.

Bass's 'double action' model of internal news flow, 1969 A development of two earlier classic models addressing the processes of media news production – WHITE'S GATEKEEPER MODEL, 1950, and McNELLY'S MODEL OF NEWS FLOW, 1959. In his article, 'Refining the gatekeeper concept', in *Journalism Quarterly* 46 (1969), A.Z. Bass argues that the most important 'gates' in the exercise of GATEKEEPING are located within the news organization. Bass divides the operation into a newsgathering stage and a news processing stage.

Writers, reporters and local editors are closer to the 'raw' news, the event, than those involved in Stage II of the gatekeeping process, while those involved at Stage II are closer to the power centre of the organization and therefore more subject to the organization's norms and VALUES, and to pressures from competing stories. See MALETZKE'S MODEL OF THE MASS COMMUNICATION PROCESS, 1963.

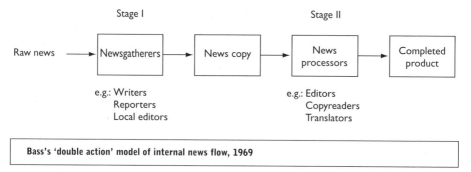

Bass's 'double action' model of internal news flow, 1969

Baton signal Chiefly manual gestures with which we beat time to the rhythm of spoken expression and which give emphasis and urgency. They are the stock-in-trade of declamatory communication, especially that of politicians. Not only the hands are employed in baton signals, but the head, shoulders and feet. See NON-VERBAL BEHAVIOUR: REPERTOIRE.

'Battle of the Somme, The' See 'SOMME, THE BATTLE OF THE'.

BBC See BBC DIGITAL; BBC, ORIGINS; BROADCASTING; BROADCASTING LEGISLATION; PUBLIC SERVICE BROADCASTING (PSB); RADIO BROADCASTING;

REITHIAN; SELSDON COMMITTEE REPORT ON TELEVISION, 1935; TELEVISION BROADCASTING; ULLSWATER COMMITTEE REPORT ON BROADCASTING, 1936. See also *TOPIC GUIDE* under BROADCASTING.

BBC America Launched in March 1998, BBC America comprises a broadcasting partnership between the BBC and the Discovery Channel of the US, issuing via cable and pay-TV channels worldwide, the 'best of the Beeb'.

BBC Digital The UK BBC anticipated, in 2001, the eventual shift from analogue to digital transmission of TV and RADIO, with a digital supplement to BBC1, giving viewers equipped with digital sets, or set-top conversion boxes, access to a broader range of programmes, including an interactive facility, than those available to viewers with analogue sets. The same extra provision became available to viewers of BBC2. On air shortly afterwards were the following new services: CBBC, a channel for children aged between six and thirteen; Cbeebies, for children under six; BBC4, an in-depth culture channel; BBC News 24 and BBC Choice aimed at a young adult audience, eventually to be retitled BBC3, and given the go-ahead by government in September 2002.

Interactive services across all digital channels come under the umbrella term BBCi. In addition, BBC Parliament covers all aspects of government, at home and in the European community. With the collapse in 2002 of ITV Digital, a pay service, the BBC was permitted by government to take up the shortfall in digital services, making these an impressive – and *free* – alternative to existing commercial digital channels.

Access to digital radio via the BBC has been available since 1995 on BBC Radio 1, 2, 3, 4 and 5 Live. From 2002 five new services came on stream – BBC 5 Live Sports Extra, 6 Music, aimed at rock and pop fans; 1Xtra, targeting young audiences interested in contemporary black music; Network Z (provisional working title), broadcasting comedy, book readings and drama for all ages, and BBC Asian Network. The long-standing BBC World Service became available in the UK digitally in 2002. The BBC's digital transmitters are planned to reach some 85 per cent of the UK population by 2004.

BBC: Government White Paper, 1994 The future of the BBC was guaranteed for another ten years by the White Paper, *The Future of the BBC: Serving the Nation, Competing Worldwide*. In renewing the corporation's charter, the White Paper confirmed that the BBC would continue as the main provider of PUBLIC SERVICE BROADCASTING (PSB). It should contribute to the growth of cable and satellite services; further develop commercial TV services worldwide; continue to provide a broad spectrum of TV and radio programmes; guarantee special support for news, current affairs and educational programmes, and cover cultural and sporting activities that 'bring the nation together'. As well as recommending giving more attention to the views of audience on matters of taste and decency, the White Paper proposed the merger of the BROADCASTING STANDARDS COUNCIL with the BROADCASTING COMPLAINTS COMMISSION, the function of the new council to be to monitor standards and provide guidance.

BBC, origins The BBC began life as the British Broadcasting Company, incorporated on 15 December 1922 and receiving its licence to broadcast on 18 January 1923. It was a private company made up chiefly of manufacturers of broadcasting equipment. The company was incorporated with 100,000 shares of stock worth £1 each. Any British wireless manufacturer could join by purchasing one or more shares, making a £50 deposit and agreeing to the terms that had been drawn up by the negotiating manufacturers and the Postmaster General.

The six largest manufacturers, in return for guaranteeing the continuing operation and financial solvency of the company, were given control. Although other manufacturers could buy stock and be admitted to membership, the principals could choose six of the company's nine directors and these in turn had the power to select its chairman. Each wireless set owner had to pay a 10-shilling (50p) licence fee to the Post Office annually and the government agreed to issue licences only to people using receivers made by members of the company. Thus the manufacturers were guaranteed protection against competition.

The company was to establish eight broadcasting stations in different parts of the British Isles. Only news originating from four established NEWS AGENCIES (such as the Press Association and Reuters) could be used in broadcasting, and there was to be no advertising. By April 1923 the Postmaster

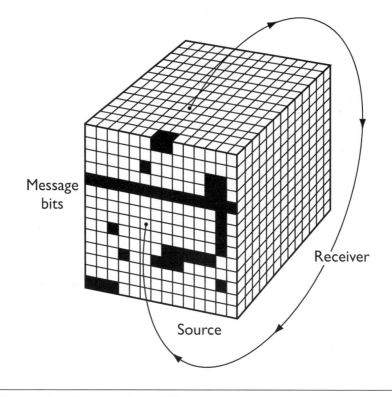

Message bits

Receiver

Source

Becker's mosaic model of communication, 1968

General had appointed a seven-man investigating committee to review the status of the British Broadcasting Company, headed by Sir Frederick Sykes, with a mandate to consider 'broadcasting in all its aspects'.

The Sykes Committee faced questions on widespread evasions of the equipment monopoly and condemnation by Beaverbrook newspapers of the control of the six. After 34 meetings, the Committee recommended – and the government accepted – a single receiver licence of 10 shillings to cover all types of radio, and the ban was raised on foreign receivers. Most importantly, Sykes forecast the eventual replacement of private by public operation: '... we consider that the control of such a potential power [of broadcasting] over public opinion and the life of the nation ought to remain with the State, and that the operation of so important a national service ought not to be allowed to become an unrestricted commercial monopoly'.

A new committee under the chairmanship of the Earl of Crawford and Balcarres, set up in 1925, led to the Charter and Licence, which created the British Broadcasting Corporation and authorized it to broadcast for ten years from 1 January 1927. It was established on three principles, which were to apply to British broadcasting until the coming of commercial television: broadcasting became a monopoly, financed by licence fees and administered by an independent public corporation.

---

* Asa Briggs, *The History of Broadcasting in the United Kingdom* (UK: Oxford, Vol. 1, 1961; Vol. 2, 1965; Vol. 3, 1979; Vol. 4, 1979); Andrew Crisell, *An Introductory History of British Broadcasting* (UK: Routledge, 1997).

BBC Written Archives In the words of Paddy Scannell, in *A Social History of British Broadcasting, Vol. 1 1922–1939: Serving the Nation* (UK: Blackwell, 1991) by Scannell and David Cardiff, the archives 'must surely be one of the most important historical depositories in Britain on all aspects of 20th century British life'. They are located in the grounds of the BBC Monitoring Service at Caversham Park, Reading, and contain at least 200,000 files on all aspects of broadcasting from the early 1920s to the early 1960s.

Beamwidth The angular width of a radio or radar beam.

Becker's mosaic model of communication, 1968 Messages are rarely single, coming along one line, so the concept of a mosaic as a model of the communication process is a useful variant on the linear theme. S.L. Becker in 'What rhetoric (communication theory) is relevant for contemporary speech communication?', a paper presented at the University of Minnesota Spring Symposium in Speech Communication, 1968, posed the theory of a 'communication mosaic', indicating that most communicative acts link message elements from more than the immediate social situation – from early impressions, previous conversations, from the media, from half-forgotten comments: a mosaic of source influences.

The layers of Becker's mosaic cube correspond to layers of information. Some elements of the mosaic assert themselves, others are blocked out. The model illustrates the complexity of the many layers of the communication process and the interaction between its 'cubes' or 'tesserae' of information, showing the internal as well as the external world of communication; that which is isolated or unique, that which is recurring in a dense and ever-changing pattern. See *TOPIC GUIDE* under COMMUNICATION MODELS.

Behavioural cues See BARNLUND'S TRANSACTION MODEL OF COMMUNICATION, 1970.

Behaviourism A school of psychological thought which maintains that a scientific understanding of human behaviour can only be attained from objective, observable action. Consciousness, feeling and other subjective aspects of human behaviour are not regarded as suitable bases for investigations.

Berlo's SMCR model of communication, 1960 David K. Berlo, who studied with Wilbur Schramm (see SCHRAMM'S MODELS OF COMMUNICATION, 1954) at the University of Illinois, produced the model shown in the accompanying figure in his *The Process of Communication: An Introduction to Theory and Practice* (US: Holt, Rinehart & Winston, 1960). It is a development in a sociological direction of SHANNON AND WEAVER'S MODEL OF COMMUNICATION, 1949. Features of the process have been made explicit, due acknowledgement being made of the significance to both Source and Receiver of the CULTURE and the social system in which the act of communication takes place. Berlo's model does not record the *flow* of communication, though the assumption must be that it is conceived as linear – in a line from Source to Receiver. Both FEEDBACK and the interaction of elements are implied rather than made explicit.

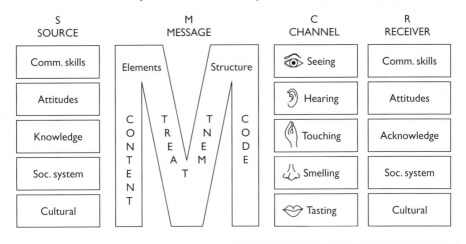

Berlo's SMCR model of communication, 1960

In a successful act of communication, Berlo's model suggests, the skills of Source and Receiver must, to a considerable extent, match each other. The same may be said for attitudes or values; and knowledge must be *acknowledged*. The model rewards analysis and testing out, especially its elegant portrayal of the message. See *TOPIC GUIDE* under COMMUNICATION MODELS.

Berlusconi phenomenon Term used by Gianpietro Mazzoleni in 'Towards a "Videocracy"? Italian Political Communication at a Turning Point', in the *European Journal of Communication*, September 1995, to describe the remarkable entry into politics, and election to prime minister of Italy in March 1994, of the media mogul Silvio Berlusconi. Mazzoleni identifies a number of interconnected factors that led to Berlusconi's success in forming a political party, Forza Italia, and in under 50 days' electioneering, displacing the traditional duopoly of political power in Italy (the Christian Democrats and the Communists). Forza was essentially the party of commercialization and it won popularity because Berlusconi, the media man, calculated the needs of the nation's electorate-as-audience. Because of his dominant control of commercial TV in Italy, Berlusconi was able to provide himself with the kind of 'tame press' every politician dreams of.

However, Mazzoleni is of the opinion that to attribute Berlusconi's electoral success solely to his media power is a short-sighted reading of the complexity of the Berlusconi phenomenon. Rather, his message, greatly aided by the power to communicate it across the nation, 'was successful because it found several ears ready to listen to it'. Further, Berlusconi understood, perhaps more clearly than any other media mogul, that today's elections are not only fought out on the television screen, they are about grabbing popular attention by combining the emotive with the entertaining.

Though Berlusconi's first premiership was short-lived – he resigned office within months – it set agendas for the future of political communication; and to prove that his electoral success was not a flash in the pan, Berlusconi was returned to office in the Italian elections of 2001. His position as prime minister has allowed him indirect control over state broadcasting, and a study by researchers at the University of Pavia in 2002 found that the time allocated on state broadcasting to the political opposition had been reduced by 10 per cent. Between May and July 2000 government airtime on RAI 2 news bulletins received 61 per cent of airtime compared with the opposition's 19 per cent.

As one opposition spokesman, Paoli Gentiloni, was quoted as saying, 'RAI news programmes are increasingly the voice of the government, while the space reserved for the opposition has been drastically reduced.' On Berlusconi's own channels the opposition received less than 5 per cent of political airtime on two channels and 23 per cent on the Channel 5 news programme. See *TOPIC GUIDE* under MEDIA: OWNERSHIP AND CONTROL.

Beveridge Committee Report on Broadcasting, 1950 Both from a theoretical and a practical point of view the Committee chaired by Lord Beveridge conducted the most thorough examination of broadcasting in Britain since its inception. Beveridge went to considerable lengths to identify and discuss the dangers of monopoly, as then held by the BBC. Nevertheless proposals for competitive broadcasting were rejected on the grounds that programmes would deteriorate in quality if there were rival corporations. Beveridge was equally firm in believing that broadcasting should be independent of government control, and declared against suggestions that the power of the BBC should be curbed through closer parliamentary supervision.

To prevent broadcasting becoming an uncontrolled bureaucracy, Beveridge recommended more active surveillance of output by the BBC's Board of Governors and a 'Public Representation Service' to bridge the gap between the BBC and the general public. Additionally, the Committee proposed regional and functional devolution of some of the corporation's activities, more comprehensive reports by the BBC on its work, and five-year reviews by small independent committees. A major recommendation, which made no headway, was that the monopoly of broadcasting be extended to local authorities and universities, allowing them to operate FM radio stations.

Commercial broadcasting in the US style was not approved of: 'Sponsoring ... puts the control of broadcasting ultimately in the hands of people whose interest is not broadcasting but the selling of some other goods or services or the propagation of particular ideas.' Interestingly, four of the eleven committee members (including Lord Beveridge) dissented from the majority verdict against any form of commercial advertising. See *TOPIC GUIDE* under COMMISSIONS, COMMITTEES, LEGISLATION.

Bias, biased From the French, *biais*, slant; a one-sided inclination of the mind. The student of communication approaches this term with extreme caution, for bias generally belongs to the realm of PERCEPTION, and other people's perceptions at that: like beauty, bias lies in the eye of the beholder, whose vision is coloured by VALUES and previous experience. The accusation of bias tends to be predicated on the assumption that there is an opposite – OBJECTIVITY; that there is an attainable ideal called IMPARTIALITY; that freedom from bias is not only possible but desirable. To speak, publish or broadcast without bias would imply the use of LANGUAGE that is value-free. Yet however careful we might be in what we say, we disclose something of ourselves, what shaped and formed us; what counts with us, what we value. When other people appear to call that value into question, we may be tempted to classify them as biased.

* Barrie Gunter, *Measuring Bias on Television* (UK: University of Luton Press, 1997).

Bibliotherapy Or 'book therapy'; help with human problems by means of books. Used chiefly with young people, bibliotherapy has also successfully been introduced to the elderly in long-stay hospital wards or other institutions.

Bifurcation of belief See IMPARTIALITY.

Bigotry An inability and/or unwillingness to consider views, beliefs, values and opinions other than the ones you already hold. The term refers to the rigid way in which an individual may hold his/her views, beliefs and so on. Bigotry is often allied with PREJUDICE. Clearly bigotry is a cause of NOISE within INTERPERSONAL COMMUNICATION. As regards the process of MASS COMMUNICATION one area of debate is whether or not television programmes designed to ridicule bigotry, particularly racial bigotry, succeed in doing this among all sections of the viewing audience. Two notable examples here are *Till Death Us Do Part*, a very popular comedy in the UK in the late 1960s and early 1970s on BBC1 and its American counterpart, *All in the Family*. *Till Death Us Do Part* focused on the bigotry of its central character, Alf Garnett. Johnny Speight, who devised the programme, intended to ridicule Alf Garnett's bigotry but as Angela Barry argues in 'Black mythologies: representations of black people on British television', in John Twitchin (ed.), *The Black and White Media Book* (UK: Trentham Books, 1990), the overall effect of the programme was the opposite.

The public airing of Alf Garnett's views gave them a real 'legitimacy'. Similar research was done on *All in the Family* (whose leading character, Archie Bunker, matched Alf Garnett for bigotry) by Neil Vidmar and Milton Rokeach. Their article 'Archie Bunker's bigotry: a study in selective perception and exposure', in the *Journal of Communication*, Winter 1974, concluded that the programme, whatever its intentions, often reinforced the bigotry of those viewers whose prejudice it most sought to challenge. See RACISM.

Binary opposition See POLARIZATION; SEMANTIC DIFFERENTIAL; WEDOM, THEYDOM.

Bit See COMPUTERS IN COMMUNICATION.

Black English See COMMUNICATION: INTERCULTURAL COMMUNICATION.

Blacklisting See HUAC: HOUSE UN-AMERICAN ACTIVITIES COMMITTEE.

Body language See COMMUNICATION, NON-VERBAL; GESTURE; INTERPERSONAL COMMUNICATION; NON-VERBAL BEHAVIOUR: REPERTOIRE; PROXEMICS; TOUCH. See also *TOPIC GUIDE* under INTERPERSONAL COMMUNICATION.

Bookmark (electronic) Just as a paper bookmark is used as a reminder of the page you have reached in a book, electronic bookmarks are used to bring you back to a website; and these can be saved for future use. For the same exercise, Internet Explorer prefers the term *favourites*.

Boom A movable trolley with a telescopic arm to which a microphone is attached during BROADCASTING or film-making, to allow positioning of the microphone.

Boomerang effect Term used by Gail and Michele Myers in *The Dynamics of Human Communication* (US: McGraw-Hill, 1985) to describe a situation in which a message falls within your latitude of rejection – that is, the known views on any given issue that you do not accept. It has the effect of then shrinking or narrowing your latitude of acceptance: positions on that issue which might have been acceptable or tolerated before will now be rejected. The authors argue that messages that are very threatening to your attitudes and views may produce this effect. See LATITUDES OF ACCEPTANCE AND REJECTION.

Boomerang response Effect of a mass media message which, in terms of audience reaction, proves to be the opposite of that which was intended.

Bowdlerize To extract from text what is deemed offensive; to expurgate. The word comes from the surname of Dr Thomas Bowdler who, in 1818, published *The Family Shakespeare*, which censored 'those words and expressions which cannot with propriety be read aloud in a family'. Not only 'bad language' is bowdlerized: harmful or subversive sentiments can be removed or toned down, very often when a wider audience for a work is being considered. In *Subculture: The Meaning of Style* (UK/US: Methuen, 1979; reissue, UK: Routledge, 2002), Dick Hebdige observes that the original messages conveyed by early jazz music – those of anger at the negro's position in US society, and sexual eroticism – were bowdlerized (or laundered) as jazz was fed into the mainstream popular culture of the country in the 1920s and 1930s.

B-Picture In the 1940s and 1950s it was cinema practice to put on two films, the main feature – the A-Picture – and a cheaply and quickly made supporting film – the B-Picture. The equivalent of the 'flip-side' of a popular record, the B-Picture, or B-Movie was invariably Budget and almost invariably Bad. Time, however, lends enchantment, and film enthusiasts often have a soft spot for a 'genre' the like of which just is not made any more. Examples are Joseph H. Lewis's *Gun Crazy* (1949), Nathan Juran's *Attack of the 50 Foot Woman* (1958) and Roger Corman's *Little Shop of Horrors* (1960), which the director claimed to have made in two days.

Brainwashing Concerted effort to change attitudes using a wide range of techniques; specifically refers to the 'washing out' of political beliefs and the attempt to replace these by the political beliefs of the group, party, movement or nation responsible for the brainwashing. A similar word is *indoctrination*. It is held that brainwashing works most effectively when the subject is isolated and when the treatment is intense; collaboration is induced through systems of rewards and punishments.

Breakup model of audience fragmentation See AUDIENCE: FRAGMENTATION OF.

Bribery 'Subsidies' by government to British newspapers in the late eighteenth and early nineteenth centuries were commonplace and extensive. Sir Robert Walpole, the first 'true prime minister', who held power from 1721 to 1742, made bribery a form of government. In the last decade of his administration £50,000 was paid out in bribes to newspapers and pamphleteers in return for giving his government a quiet and supportive press. Walpole's example set the tone for the future. In 1797, *The Times* with a circulation of 2000 received a government subsidy of £8112. At the same time, direct payments were made to journalists, and the government also spread its patronage by placing adverts in newspapers of which it approved. Today, bribery is a thing of the past. However, see REGULATORY FAVOURS.

Bricolage Term derived from anthropology, referring to the construction of meaning through an improvised combination of communicative elements originating prior to their current creative use. According to John Clarke in 'Style', published in *Resistance Through Rituals: Youth Subcultures in Post-War Britain* (UK: Hutchinson, 1976), edited by Stuart Hall and Tom Jefferson, bricolage is a 'reordering and recontextualization of objects to communicate fresh meanings'. Perhaps the most famous 'bricoleurs' were the Surrealists who took familiar images and objects out of their traditional contexts and rearranged them in juxtapositions that startled and initiated new discourses. As Dick Hebdige in *Subculture: The Meaning of Style* (UK: Methuen, 1979; reissue, UK: Routledge, 2002) states, 'the teddy boy's theft and transformation of the Edwardian style revived in the early 1950s by Savile Row for wealthy young men about town can be construed as an act of bricolage'.

British Board of Film Censors Set up in 1912 to approve films for public showing. The right of local authorities to ban films had been granted in the Cinematography Act of 1909. This had resulted in a chaos of contradictory judgements. The Cinematograph Exhibitors Association and the main production companies set up their own vetting office – the BBFC. The Board consists of a president and a secretary, both appointed by the film industry. Like most censorship bodies, the Board lagged behind public tastes for decades and was susceptible to influence by government. Under the more liberal regime of John Trevelyan (1958–71) the Board acquired a new image, casting off its earlier reputation for over-cautiousness. Since then the general trend of the Board's activity has been towards greater tolerance while at the same time maintaining a protective attitude towards children. See CERTIFICATION OF FILMS; WILLIAMS COMMITTEE REPORT.

British Broadcasting Company/British Broadcasting Corporation   See BBC; BBC, ORIGINS.

British Code of Advertising Practice   See CODE OF ADVERTISING STANDARDS AND PRACTICE (ITC).

British Film Institute   An outcome of the Report of the Commission on Educational and Cultural Films, financed chiefly by the Carnegie trustees (1929–32), the BFI was set up in 1933 to foster the use of film for educational purposes to preserve the cultural heritage of commercial film in the vaults of the National Film Library. Today the BFI's services to film in the UK are considerable. They include: the national film archive; the National Film Theatre on London's South Bank; the financing of films by British directors; widening commitments to film education and the publication of works on cinema.

British Media Industry Group (BMIG)   UK pressure group comprising Associated Newspapers, the Pearson Group, the *Guardian* Media Group and *Telegraph* newspapers, created in the summer of 1993 to urge an end to restrictions relating to CROSS-MEDIA OWNERSHIP; termed by Granville Williams of the CAMPAIGN FOR PRESS AND BROADCASTING FREEDOM (CPBF) 'an unholy alliance' (in 'Outraged onlookers or influential voices? The role of lobby and pressure groups in the UK and USA', published in *No News is Bad News: Radio Television and the Public*, UK: Longman, 2001, edited by Michael Bromley).

Williams asserts that 'The activities of the BMIG provide a telling example of the use of media power to shape favourable legislation.' He cites 'discreet lobbying, high-profile conferences aimed at opinion formers, and a stream of articles and reports promoting the case for the abandoning of media ownership restrictions'.

Through their contacts with key government departments, says Williams, and 'their broader political contacts with the government', media companies, and alliances such as the BMIG, 'are in a strong position … to dominate the arguments about media ownership and regulation'. Many of the aims of the BMIG came to fruition in the COMMUNICATIONS BILL (UK), 2002, which proposed abandoning regulations preventing cross-media ownership.

Broadband   High-speed electronic facility that allows for multiple informational and entertainment use – of films, computer games, music etc. – transmitted over airwaves, copper or fibre wires to a personal computer, telephone, television or electrical appliance. Some of the most substantial advances in the use of broadband are occurring in 3G (third generation) mobile handsets. See DIGITIZATION.

Broadcast and narrowcast codes   See CODES.

Broadcasting   See *TOPIC GUIDE* under BROADCASTING.

Broadcasting Act (UK), 1980   Receiving its Royal Assent on 13 November 1980, the Act extended the life of the IBA until the end of 1996; defined the Authority's responsibility for the new CHANNEL 4; set out special measures for the Fourth Channel in Wales, Saniel Pedwar Cymru (S4C); and contained a number of other important provisions relating to the future of broadcasting, including the establishment of a BROADCASTING COMPLAINTS COMMISSION.

Broadcasting Act (UK), 1990   Ushered in far-reaching and controversial changes to BROADCASTING in Britain. The Act constituted a further and substantial assault on the part of government upon the traditional duopoly (BBC/IBA) of broadcasting control, which had prevailed since the birth of commercial television in the UK in 1956. The Conservative government's White Paper, *Broadcasting in the '90s: Competition, Choice and Quality*, was published in 1988. The *Observer* (13 November 1988) called it 'the biggest bomb put under British TV in half-a-century'.

Announced in Parliament by the then Home Secretary, Douglas Hurd, the White Paper proposed a fifth TV channel, an expansion of Direct Satellite Broadcasting (DSB), more local TV stations, three new national radio networks and a growth in localized radio. The Act of 1990 wound up the Independent Broadcasting Authority (IBA) and replaced it with a 'light-touch' Independent Television Commission (ITC), whose most important first task was to select companies for the new commercial

TV franchises to operate from 1 January 1993 (see FRANCHISES FROM 1993).

Controversy raged over the manner in which the franchises were to be allocated – through secret auction. Would-be future franchise-holders were invited to put their case for selection and make a money bid, without any idea of what a reasonable bid might be. The result was regarded in many quarters as farcical: some companies bid vast amounts, others very little. The highest monetary bidder was not automatically selected, for there was an extra qualifier, a so-called 'Quality Threshold', though at no time were the criteria for quality ever spelt out.

Prior to the announcement of the franchises by the ITC (on 16 October 1991), existing franchise-holders had tightened their financial belts – cutting back on programme investment, laying off staff – in order to have enough cash to place a winning bid. Thus, it was argued by critics, 'quality' was already being sacrificed even before the quality threshold had been crossed. There were fears that promises of quality might not, once the franchises had been won, be translated into performance. The bids from the successful companies represented a windfall for the Treasury of over £350m a year, some £100m more than that provided by the outgoing system.

Ironically, TV-am, the company believed to be the favourite of Margaret Thatcher (her daughter Carol worked for it), the Prime Minister who had presided over the whole franchises enterprise, was consigned to the wilderness. The franchise was awarded to Sunrise TV. Decisions on the future of the BBC were not dealt with in the Act.

A study by the Third World and Environmental Broadcasting Project was to report that, following the 1990 Act, significant reductions occurred in DOCUMENTARY and current affairs programmes on all terrestrial TV services in the UK. On commercial channels there was a drop of 80 per cent in documentary programmes dealing with international issues. See DEREGULATION; PUBLIC SERVICE BROADCASTING (PSB); PRIVATIZATION.

Broadcasting Act (UK), 1995 A key piece of deregulatory legislation in the UK, the Act removed regulations preventing independent TV companies owning more than two licences, opening up the field for a new round of takeovers. However, no company would be permitted to own in excess of 15 per cent of total TV output.

Newspaper companies were permitted for the first time to control TV companies, though newspapers with more than 20 per cent of national circulation were barred from owning ITV licences – a ruling directly affecting Rupert Murdoch's News International and the Mirror Group. A central focus of the Act was the future of DIGITAL TELEVISION. Proposals for digitization of the airways offered a prospect of many more TV channels, with the BBC being awarded its own digital TV multiplex. In March 2002 the corporation's first digital channel, BBC4, began broadcasting along with 6 Music, a digital RADIO channel.

Broadcasting codes (UK) See RADIO AUTHORITY (UK) PROGRAMME CODES.

Broadcasting Complaints Commission In October 1971 an independent Programmes Complaints Commission was set up by the BBC, but disbanded in 1981 when the government-formed Broadcasting Complaints Commission began work under Part IV of the Broadcasting Act of 1980. Five commissioners appointed by the Secretary of State were empowered to consider and adjudicate on unjust or unfair treatment in sound or TV programmes and unwarranted infringements of privacy; consequently to oblige the offending broadcasting body to publicly acknowledge a proved complaint within a specified period. The Government White Paper of 1994, *The Future of the BBC: Serving the Nation, Competing Worldwide* decided on a merger of the Commission with the BROADCASTING STANDARDS COUNCIL.

Broadcasting legislation (UK) The first act of its kind in the world was the Wireless Telegraphy Act of 1904, in which the British government commanded substantial powers over the regulation of wireless telegraphy. The Act gave the Postmaster General the duty to license all wireless telegraphy apparatus. The British Broadcasting Company received its licence from the Post Office in 1923. The TELEVISION ACT, 1954, created COMMERCIAL TELEVISION in the UK with the formation of the Independent Television Authority (later the Independent Broadcasting Authority). ADVERTISING was to be kept separate from programming. Requirements were laid down to govern programming content.

The Copyright Act, 1956, initiated copyright protection of broadcast material. In 1972 the Sound Broadcasting Act inaugurated commercial radio and the ITA became the IBA. The Independent Broadcasting Authority Act, 1979, empowered the IBA to create CHANNEL 4, while the Broadcasting Act (1980), among other regulations, created the Broadcasting Complaints Commission. In 1984 came the Video Recording Act requiring the certification of all new video releases. The Cable and Broadcasting Act of the same year set up the Cable Authority whose task was to select operators for particular areas and to oversee organizational and programming stipulations. See COMMUNICA-TIONS BILL (UK), 2002.

Broadcasting research See AUDIENCE MEASUREMENT.

Broadcasting Standards Council (UK) Created in 1988 by the Conservative government in the UK to monitor sex and violence on British television screens. Under its first director, Roy Shaw, the BSC produced a Code of Practice in November 1989, and later used its modest funding to support research into broadcasting and its effects. The Council was merged with the Broadcasting Complaints Commission following the publication of the Government White Paper, *The Future of the BBC: Serving the Nation, Competing Worldwide* in 1994. The COMMUNICATIONS BILL (UK), 2002 makes provision for the transfer of the work of the BSC to OfCOM, a new body empowered to overview all aspects of broadcasting in the UK.

Browser Computer program facilitating, via the Internet, downloading and display of documents from the World Wide Web.

Button apathy When a TV viewer cannot be bothered to switch off a programme, or to switch from one channel to another, he/she is probably suffering from 'button apathy'. This is a challenge to programmers to trap audience interest rapidly and early. Very often, apathy – or lethargy – does the rest, and the viewer stays loyal. See SCHEDULING.

By-line Use of the journalist's/author's name on a report or article. These are very common now in the PRESS but at one time the granting of by-lines was a rare honour, to distinguish top writers or as a reward for outstanding reportage.

C

Cable and Broadcasting Act (UK), 1984 Drawn up by the Conservative government with the intention of facilitating the 'cabled society', the Act followed most of the recommendations of the HUNT COMMITTEE REPORT ON CABLE EXPANSION AND BROADCASTING POLICY (UK), 1982, which proposed a cable network for Britain with the minimum of rules and regulations. The Act set up a Cable Authority to select cable operators for particular areas and to maintain an overview on general matters of organization and programming.

Cable television Underground cable networks were established in the 1930s in the UK to relay radio broadcasts. These were later adapted to transmit TV to areas that received poor 'off-air' signals; reception problems were also the reason for the US 'cabling up' in the 1950s. Until the election of the Conservative government in 1979, the commercial potential of cable in developing information technology had stimulated only modest interest. In March 1982 the Tory cabinet's Information Technology Advisory Panel (ITAP), appointed in July 1981 by the Prime Minister Margaret Thatcher, recommended a rapid and substantial expansion of cable networks, to be established and operated by private companies, with a minimum capacity of 30 channels each. The operator of each network should, ITAP advised, be given monopoly control over the programmes transmitted. The Panel considered that it would cost some £2.5bn to wire up the homes of Britain's chief cities, the finance coming from private companies.

The Hunt Report (see HUNT COMMITTEE REPORT ON CABLE EXPANSION AND BROAD-CASTING POLICY (UK), 1982, made public in September 1982, also urged the 'wiring up' of the nation, with a minimum of rules and regulations. In 1983 the Home Secretary in Mrs Thatcher's newly elected government, Leon Brittan, issued special government licences prior to a full-scale spread of cable networks. See DIGITAL TELEVISION; FIBRE-OPTIC TECHNOLOGY

Cahiers du Cinéma French film magazine founded by André Bazin in 1951; associated with, and very often written by, the Nouvelle Vague, or New Wave, directors such as Claude Chabrol and François Truffaut. The young critics of *Cahiers* reacted against the current ideological conservatism in the film world, against its reluctance to face up to or to express the facts of contemporary life.

Calcutt Committee Reports on Privacy and Related Matters, 1990 and 1993 Lawyer and Master of Magdalene Còllege, Cambridge, David Calcutt was the government-appointed chairman in 1990 of a committee set up to examine British PRESS intrusions into personal privacy, after complaints from many quarters. Calcutt's chief recommendation was the creation of a non-statutory PRESS COMPLAINTS COMMISSION. The tenor of Calcutt's first report was a warning to the newspaper industry – either set your own house in order or it will be done for you by government legislation.

Subsequent high-profile press 'intrusions' into the 'private' lives of the royal family and of government ministers – stories that, incidentally, proved very popular with the newspaper-buying public – decided Calcutt that the voluntary route to better press behaviour had not worked. Calcutt's 1993 report, a solo effort, was greeted by Lord McGregor, the chairman of the Press Complaints Commission, child of Calcutt Mark 1, as potentially 'a disaster for democracy' and 'direct censorship for the first time in 300 years'.

Calcutt recommended: (1) a statutory code of practice for journalists and other press practitioners; (2) a press complaints tribunal comprising a judge and two lay assessors appointed by the Lord Chancellor; (3) new criminal offences to cover invasion of privacy, including bugging and the use of telephoto lenses. His report was highly critical of the performance of the Press Complaints Council, which had not been constituted, or evolved, in line with his 1990 recommendations. He dismissed the PCC as an ineffective regulator, too much in the hands of the newspaper owners.

The first government response to Calcutt Mark 2 was cool towards statutory enforcement through recommendations 1 and 2, but more persuaded concerning Calcutt's third recommendation – but not sufficiently persuaded to take any legislative action. See DEFAMATION. See also *TOPIC GUIDE* under COMMISSIONS, COMMITTEES, LEGISLATION.

Calotype Process of photographic print-making invented by William Henry Fox Talbot (1800–77). The Calotype method produced negatives on coated paper from which any number of paper prints could be made. Talbot celebrated his invention in his book *The Pencil of Light* (1844). See PHOTOGRAPHY, ORIGINS.

Camcorder A video camera and miniature sound recorder combined in a single unit.

Camera The first photographic camera on sale to the public was produced by London optician Francis West, for 'photogenic drawing' (1839). In the same year Baron Sèguier introduced a lightweight bellows camera with three 'firsts' in equipment – a darkroom tent, a photographic tripod and a ball-and-socket head. Binocular-type cameras were introduced as early as 1853, by John Benjamin Dancer of Manchester. In 1858 Thomas Skaife introduced his 'Pistolgraph': a spring shutter worked by rubber bands was released by a trigger. He once aimed his Pistolgraph at Queen Victoria and was nearly arrested for an attempt on her life. 1880 saw the first twin-reflex camera, a quarter plate with a roller-blind shutter attached to the taking lens, made by R. and J. Beck of London.

George Eastman produced the first camera incorporating roll film, calling it the Kodak (1888). The simplicity of this camera ('Pull the string – turn the key – press the button') made mass photography possible, especially as Eastman recommended the return of the camera to the factory for development and printing. Miniature cameras, as scientific precision instruments, were produced from 1924 (the Ermanox made by the Ernemann Works of Dresden). In 1912 George P. Smith of Missouri produced a 35mm camera taking one by one-and-a-half inch pictures on cine film, which was being mass produced at the time. The prototype of the Leica was constructed by Oskar Barnack in 1914; Rolleiflex was put on the market by Franke and Heidecke Braunschweig in 1947 and Voigtlander's zoom lens was introduced in 1959.

In the 1960s and 1970s the application of electronics revolutionized camera and lens design. The silicon chip allowed amazing feats of miniaturization. In 1963 Eastman Kodak introduced the 126 'instant loading' cartridge, a modernization of an old idea going back to the Expo Watch camera of 1905. In 1972 they produced the pocket 110, an ultraminiature cartridge-load camera. Polaroid, in the same year, launched the SX-70 instant photo system, which abandoned the method whereby a protective covering had to be peeled off the print. With SX-70, the photo image develops automatically in the light, protected by a plastic coating.

1976 saw Canon introduce its famous AE-1, a fully automatic SLR camera incorporating very advanced digital electronic technology, produced by automated methods. In the early 1980s Kodak launched its disc camera. Three-dimensional (3-D) cameras also came on to the market at this time. An offshoot of the 35mm camera is the Advanced Photo System (APS) offering smaller, lighter cameras into which 35mm film is inserted in cassette form. However, the digital camera system has fast become a market leader. This requires no film. Pictures are downloaded on to a computer. Generally the digital camera works using a small card, though cameras are available in which the electronic imaging device can be inserted into a 35mm camera, allowing traditional and modern uses. Digitally produced pictures can be reproduced and manipulated on-screen, issued as prints or e-mailed across the world. See PHOTOGRAPHY, ORIGINS; HIGH-SPEED PHOTOGRAPHY.

Camera cue Red light on a TV camera, which is illuminated when that camera is transmitting. Known also as a 'tally light'.

Camera obscura Latin for 'dark chamber'; an early means of projecting an image – a box or room with a lens at one end and at the other a reflector that throws an external image upon a screen or table. Antonio Canaletto (1697–1768) used the camera obscura to considerable effect in his paintings of Venice, though the device was referred to as early as Aristotle (384–322 BC).

It was French army officer Joseph Nicèphore Nièpce (1765–1833) in 1826 who first exposed a metal plate coated with a layer of bitumen to the image in a camera obscura. The light hardened the bitumen, which was washed away to reveal the fixed image. Photography, or as Nièpce termed it, 'heliography' – sun drawing – was born.

Where the camera obscura possessed a reflector, the camera lucida had a prism. When placed in front of an artist's eye the prism projects image on to paper, thus allowing accurate copying.

Campaign This term is most often used in the media studies context to refer to a conscious, structured and coordinated attempt at persuasion. The goals of such persuasion are varied. ADVERTISING campaigns, for example, aim to change people's choice of product or to persuade them to buy new products.

 Election campaigns aim to reinforce or change people's voting behaviour. PRESSURE GROUPS use campaigns to alert the public to a particular issue, to influence the public's opinion on that issue, to mobilize support and pressurize those in power to take some desired action. Access to the mass media is often crucial for a pressure group's successful campaign. Media personnel may also initiate campaigns to raise their audience's awareness of certain issues – child abuse, for example. Indeed such campaigns can be seen as part of the mass media's AGENDA-SETTING role. One focus for media research has been the measurement of how effective campaigns are.

Campaign for Press and Broadcasting Freedom UK organization founded by John Jennings in 1979 as a broad-based non-political party pressure group dedicated to making Britain's media more open, diverse and accountable. Specifically the Campaign has worked for the RIGHT OF REPLY, a Freedom of Information law and more community-based and 'alternative' newspapers. The Campaign publishes a bi-monthly bulletin, *Free Press.*

---

* www.cpbf.org.uk.

Campaign for Quality Television Report (UK), 1999 Written by Steven Barnett and Emily Seymour on behalf of the charity dedicated to promoting PUBLIC SERVICE BROADCASTING (PSB), *A Shrinking Iceberg Travelling South* highlighted the decline in serious drama and current affairs reporting in UK television. The authors' research found that the single or one-off play had been largely replaced by drama series dominated by police/detective stories; that homegrown TV drama had suffered relegation in face of American imports.

A *domestic* agenda was the key feature of NEWS and information services. As for investigative JOURNALISM, the report finds that there is scant room for 'speculative' investigations and very little programme innovation. 'Within the BBC,' comment Barnett and Seymour, referring to 30 confidential interviews with senior producers, 'there is concern that current affairs has lost its sense of direction and that internal structural changes have weakened its creative potential'. Formed in 1988, the Campaign for Quality Television was relaunched in 1995. See CASUALIZATION; TELEVISION DRAMA; TELEVISION: INDEPENDENT PRODUCERS.

Captive audience advertising See ADVERTISING: AMBIENT ADVERTISING.

Cards See CIGARETTE CARDS; PICTURE POSTCARDS.

Caricature A distorted REPRESENTATION of a person, type or action. Though we generally associate caricature with humorous cartoons, the process of distortion has played an important role in art. Known to the Egyptians and Greeks, caricature was revived by Italian artists of the Renaissance and developed throughout Europe in the eighteenth century. In England artists such as Rowlandson (1756–1827) combined high-quality draughtsmanship with trenchant social and political satire. Though the most famous, *Punch* was only one among many magazines carrying cartoons in the nineteenth century. In England, *Vanity Fair* (founded in 1868) proved a rival. In the US, *Puck* (1876), in France, *Le Rire* (1894), in Germany, *Simplicissimus* (1896), made the cartoon the most impactful form of printed illustration prior to the regular use of photography. Best known of all US magazines carrying cartoons, the *New Yorker*, was founded in 1925.

Carnivore Original title of computer software enabling the FBI in the US to 'spy' on global e-mailing by responding to the use of certain words; renamed DCS 1000 in order to conceal its teeth and its tracks. See HACKER, HACKTIVIST; REGULATION OF INVESTIGATORY POWERS ACT (RIPA) (UK), 2000; SURVEILLANCE SOCIETY.

Cartoons In fine art, a cartoon is the final preparatory drawing for a large-scale painting, tapestry or mosaic. The Leonardo cartoon in the National Gallery, London, is a notable example – ready for final working, but never completed by the artist. In modern terms, the cartoon is a humorous illustration or strip of illustrations. In 1841 a series of fine art cartoons was designed for paintings in the new Houses of Parliament in London. The satirical magazine *Punch*, founded in that year, poked fun at the drawings, with sketches entitled 'Punch's Cartoons'.

According to Alan Coren in his Foreword to W. Hewison's *The Cartoon Connection* (UK: Elm Tree Books, 1977), cartoons were born 'in the far Aurignacian days of 20,000 BC', when 'a squat, hirsute, browless man one morning dipped his stick in a dark rooty liquid, bent straight again, and, on the cave-wall of Lascaux, drew a joke about men running after buffalo'.

Hewison calls the cartoon 'drawn humour' and lists the following cartoon categories. (1) Recognition humour (where the viewer recognizes the workings of human nature); (2) Social comment (very often Recognition humour with a message); (3) Visual puns; (4) Zany (or screw-ball); (5) Black humour (or sick, or bad taste); (6) Geometric (where, for example, lines are made to fall in love with dots); (7) Faux Naif (pretended naivety) – 'When an ideas man can draw but cannot develop a satisfactory comic style of cartoon drawing, he quite often throws in the towel and adopts a deliberately childlike style' – and (8) the Strip cartoon the originator of which was Wilhelm Busch (1832–1904).

On the screen, Walt Disney has dominated the field of the animated cartoon but there have been many others: Paul Terry's *Terrytoons*, Pat Sulliven's *Felix the Cat*, Bob Cannon's *Gerald McBoing-Boing*, Ernest Pintoff's Human Rectangle, *Flebus*, Tex Avery's *Chilly Willy*, the endlessly warring Tom and Jerry created by William Hanna, Joe Barbera and Fred Quimby, along with countless others such as *Top Cat*, *Scooby Doo* and the *Flintstones*; Walter Lantz's *Woody Woodpecker* and Terry Gilliam's contributions to *Monty Python's Flying Circus*. Among those artists who have attempted to push the cartoon on film in an innovative direction are the Hungarian John Halas and his wife Joy Batchelor, Richard Williams and Bob Godfrey. In recent years Matt Groening's *The Simpsons* became arguably the world's most watched TV cartoon. A 1999 survey found that in the US 91 per cent of children and 84 per cent of adults could identify members of the Simpson family. Today's TV and movie cartoons (such as *Monsters, Inc.* 2002), benefit from computer generation.

Casualization In the UK in the late 1980s and 1990s, the casualization of jobs by shifting full-time to part-time appointments, and the offering of short-term work contracts has been particularly prevalent in the media. For example, BBC staffing dropped by 5000 from a total of 25,000 between 1989 and 1994. Jean Seaton writes in James Curran and Jean Seaton, *Power Without Responsibility* (UK: Routledge,

1997) that, 'By 1995 many staff were, in effect, pieceworkers or employed on short-term contracts.'

One estimate by Peter Law in N. Miller and R. Allen (eds), *Broadcasting Enters the Marketplace, Proceedings of the 24th University of Manchester Broadcasting Symposium* (UK: John Libbey, 1994) is that from 1987 to 1993, the BBC and ITV companies cut more than 14,000 jobs between them. A good many of those who left the various BROADCASTING organizations entered the freelance market or set up small independent production companies. More and more work traditionally done 'in house' has been offered on a freelance basis or to independent production companies, many of whom also employ a significant number of workers on short-term contracts or as freelances.

Fears continue to be expressed about the long-term impact of such structural changes within the TV industry in Britain, on quality and training. However, for the broadcasting organizations the casualization of a large section of the workforce was one of the key strategies for dealing with the development of a pluralist marketplace within the industry.

The argument that this opens the field to a free market in talent has to be balanced by questions concerning who will risk the expense of training such talent.

Catalyst effect Where a book, newspaper, film, TV or RADIO programme has the effect of modifying a situation, or taking a mediating role. The actual presence of TV cameras may, it is believed, influence the course of events. The debate continues as to whether such effects are substantial or marginal, for reliable proof is hard to come by. See MEDIATION.

Catharsis From the Greek, 'purging', catharsis is the effect upon an audience of tragedy in drama or the novel. The Greek philosopher Aristotle perceived the function of great tragedy to be the release of pent-up emotions in the audience. As a consequence, the mind is cleansed and purified. The so-termed *catharsis hypothesis* suggests that violence and aggression in films and on TV have a therapeutic effect. Exponents of this idea argue that the involvement in fantasy aggression may serve as a form of displacement, providing a harmless 'release' from hostile impulses that might otherwise be acted out. See EFFECTS OF THE MASS MEDIA.

CCTV: closed-circuit television One of the key means of public and private SURVEILLANCE contributing to what Bryan Appleyard in a UK *Sunday Times* article, 'No Hiding Place' (15 April 2001), describes as 'the final turn of the screw' in the transformation of Britain into a 'surveillance state' (see SURVEILLANCE SOCIETY). Appleyard's estimate at the time of writing is that over a million and a half CCTV cameras are in operation in the UK and some, 'as in the London borough of Newham, use facial recognition software that automatically identifies target individuals'.

The author worries that 'a police state with powers of control and surveillance beyond the wildest dreams of Hitler and Stalin could be established in Britain within 24 hours ... But the weirdest thing of all is that we really don't care.' It would seem that the public 'have such fear of crime, and such a mute acceptance of the seizure of power by the authorities, that we are actually comforted by the thought that we are being watched all the time'. See ECHELON; REGULATION OF INVESTIGATORY POWERS ACT (RIPA) (UK), 2000.

CD: compact disc See MP3.

Ceefax Trade name of the teletext service offered by the BBC since September 1974, giving viewers access to information on a wide range of services. The COMMERCIAL TELEVISION equivalent is Oracle.

Cellular radio Comprises RADIO frequencies divided up into 'cells' of air waves facilitating, in particular, personal communications systems. For example, anyone operating a car telephone will be switched automatically from one radio frequency to another as the operator passes through the airwave cells. See MEDIA TECHNOLOGY.

Celluloid A decisive technological breakthrough for still and movie photography came in 1865 with the creation by British metallurgist Alexander Parkes of a plastic substance from nitro-cellulose, camphor and alcohol, which he named Parkesite. The material, which provides an ideal medium for carrying images, was later modified by his associate Daniel Spill and called Xylonite. An improved version – celluloid – is credited to John W. Hyatt, a printer of Albany, New York State (1869).

Censorship Pre-emptive censorship is censorship before the event; punitive, after the event. They often work in tandem: one punishment serves as a warning to others. Censorship involves the curtailment, usually by or on behalf of those in authority, of the major freedoms – of belief, expression, movement, assembly and access to information. The most common form of censorship is that applied by the self. A thing is not expressed because of the risk of external censorship – from the law, from organizations and institutions, from PRESSURE GROUPS. Thus we have censorship by omission or evasion.

Few if any communities tolerate completely free expression. In the UK, for example, laws of DEFAMATION exist to protect persons against acts of communication that may offend or injure them, or their reputation in the community. Equally protective are restrictions upon material transmitted to children (see CERTIFICATION OF FILMS).

Such forms of censorship meet with general approval, but they represent only the tip of a large legal iceberg. The UK's Official Secrets Act is one of the most far-reaching weapons of legal censorship ever devised.

The Act (or Acts, 1911–91) makes it an offence for anyone to obtain and communicate documents and information that could be harmful to the safety and interest of the state. Such is the extent of the Official Secrets Act that, while protecting the state against the passing of crucial military secrets to the enemy, it could also prohibit the publication of the Prime Minister's lunchtime menu at Number 10 Downing Street. Employees in state services often have to sign a declaration agreeing not to disclose any information to which they have access (see LEAKS).

In addition, the state protects a commonality of interests with a wide range of laws. The UK's Public Order Act of 1936 restricted the way we behave, or what we say, in public. If an individual uses threatening or insulting words, likely to cause a breach of the peace, this is a punishable offence. The common law offence of Sedition, of long standing, protects the sovereign, the government and its institutions from individuals or groups causing intentional discontent and hatred, while the Incitement to Disaffection Act of 1934 made it an offence to try to persuade a member of the armed forces to commit an act of disloyalty. Equally, the Police Act of 1964 made it an offence to promote unfaithfulness by a police officer towards his duties.

It remains an offence to issue a blasphemy – this is, to speak or communicate in writing etc. matter that may cause hatred, contempt, insult or ridicule against the Church. It is a rarely used law but a law's potency lies in its existence, in the knowledge that it can always be used when free speech appears to be getting out of hand.

Obscenity too has occupied the minds of law-makers. Since the seventeenth century certain types of indecent expression or behaviour have been subject to punishment by the law. Material considered likely to 'deprave and corrupt' has often been subject to punitive legal censorship (see OZ TRIAL). Defining what is obscene and what is liable to deprave and corrupt has proved immensely difficult. The WILLIAMS COMMITTEE REPORT ON OBSCENITY AND FILM CENSORSHIP, 1979, is probably the most level-headed attempt to resolve this problem, and to suggest what to do about censorship generally in the UK.

The targets of censorship tend to be those actions or expressions that appear to endanger by subversion, ridicule, defiance or just plain disrespect, the VALUES and value systems of the dominant hierarchy of society – its establishment. In the UK 'sacred cows' have been the monarchy, the church, nationality, the family, defence, each a symbol in some way or other of law and order; of control. Censorship is a weapon to counter the ever-present threat – real or imagined – of social, and therefore political, destabilization.

To concentrate attention solely on the activities of the law in the process of censorship is to risk overlooking the immense pervasiveness of indirect censorship: 'back-door' censorship rather than crude, head-on tactics. Indeed a regularly identifiable characteristic of censorship is the difficulty of getting to the bottom of things – that is, who is responsible, why the censorship has taken place and what the motives behind the act of censorship are.

The INTERNET has become the most significant and controversial domain attracting censorship. In its early days perceived as free of controls by those in authority, the net has swiftly been reined in by legislation, in many countries, designed to facilitate SURVEILLANCE. Many commentators feel that the days of 'cyberfreedom' are fast becoming history; that Big Brother has tried surfing the net and found it to his liking. See CCTV: CLOSED-CIRCUIT TELEVISION; PRIVACY; REGULATION OF INVESTIGATORY POWERS ACT (RIPA) (UK), 2000; TERRORISM: ANTI-TERRORISM, CRIME AND SECURITY ACT (UK), 2001; USA – PATRIOT ACT, 2001. See also *TOPIC GUIDE* under MEDIA: FREEDOM, CENSORSHIP.

* Carl Jensen, *20 Years of Censored News* (US: Seven Stories Press, 1997); David Vincent, *The Culture of Secrecy in Britain 1832–1998* (UK: Oxford University Press, 1998).

Centrality Within the communication structure of any social group some members will derive certain advantages or disadvantages resulting from their position in that structure; in particular, from the FREQUENCY with which they communicate with other members of the group. By using a sociogram such as that illustrated here, the *centrality* of a person within the communication structure can be measured: the sociogram indicates that D's centrality index is highest; it is arrived at by taking the total number of communication links between group members and then dividing that by the total number of such links between one member and the other members of the group. In the diagram, D's centrality may arise because of his/her status, role, articulacy, personality, etc.

The concept of a centrality index enables observers to estimate quantitatively the degree of influence members of the group may have by virtue of their position in the group. The more central a member is in a communication network, the sooner he/she will be in possession of all the information at the disposal of the group. Influence is closely related to possession of information because the possessor has the power to choose what information to pass on, and to whom. Communication networks differ in the degree of centrality and the number of levels of centrality possible within them.

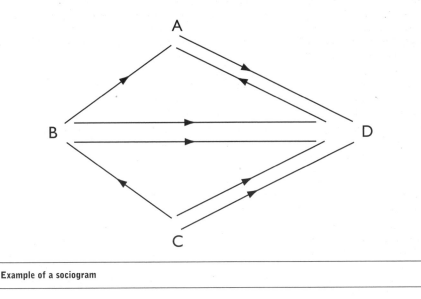

Example of a sociogram

Centres for research into the media See RESEARCH CENTRES (INTO THE MEDIA).

Certification of films (UK) For several years until December 1982, the BRITISH BOARD OF FILM CENSORS had the following system of certification: X, denoting films with high sex and violence content, or other disturbing subject matter to which those under 18 were not permitted; AA films, from which children under 14 were barred; A films, to which children were admitted if accompanied by an adult; and U-certificate films admitting all.

These were replaced in 1982 with: 18 (permitting admission for those 18 and over); 15 (replacing AA, and raising the admission age from 14 to 15); PG (Parental Guidance, a symbol used in the US, and intended to show that a film contains some scenes that individual parents may feel unsuitable for children); and U as before. A 12 certificate was introduced in 1989, mainly to target the first film in the *Batman* series.

In August 2002 the British Board of Film Classification, under pressure from a number of sources, including that of parents and children, made an adjustment to the 12 certification by adding a 12A rating, meaning that children could see formerly restricted films – such as *Spider-Man* – so long as they are accompanied by an adult over 18.

The 12A certificate marked the arrival of former civil servant Sir Quentin Thomas as chief censor. It brought Britain into line with other countries, including the US, Canada, Japan, Ireland, New Zealand and Spain. The first film to carry a UK 12A certificate was *The Bourne Identity* starring Matt Damon. 12A certification requires that posters advertising such films should carry warnings about scenes involving violence, sex and bad language. The 12 rating remains for film videos. See H-CERTIFICATE.

Chamberlain, Lord See LORD CHAMBERLAIN.

Channel Each MESSAGE-carrying signal requires a route along which it is transmitted from the sender to the receiver and along which feedback may be obtained. Channels may be physical (our voices or bodies), technical (the telephone) or social (our schools, media, etc.). In business organizations or institutions they may be vertical, hierarchical, formal and predominantly one-way – from the boss downwards; or horizontal, democratic, informal and two-way, as between workmates and groups with common tasks, interests and sympathies. Like country paths, channels need to be kept open and frequented – and sometimes repaired – if they are to continue to be recognized as viable. See COSMOPOLITE AND LOCALITE CHANNELS; JAKOBSON'S MODEL OF COMMUNICATION, 1958; PHATIC (LANGUAGE); SHANNON AND WEAVER'S MODEL OF COMMUNICATION, 1949.

Channel capacity C.E. Shannon and W.E. Weaver use this term to describe the upper limit of information that any communication system can handle at a given time. To discover this limit, it is first essential to know how much uncertainty – or *entropy* – a given signal will eliminate. See REDUNDANCY.

Channel 4 (UK) Under the direction of Jeremy Isaacs, in 1982, C4 became the UK's fourth TV channel; the 'quality' arm of commercial television. The new organization quickly became a major sponsor of independently made movies, drama series and documentaries. From the start the channel aimed to challenge set ways and attitudes. Much of its programming was international in theme, whether the subject was poverty in the developing world or American football. The new channel proved the argument for *broad*casting, mixing popular viewing with minority-interest programmes, and showing that the entertaining could be combined with the serious without sacrificing standards.

C4 became the first channel to provide a full hour of news daily. It was to create a high reputation for the funding of feature films, some of which, like *Four Weddings and a Funeral* (1994), proved worldwide cinema successes. The BROADCASTING ACT, 1990 cleared the way for C4 to negotiate directly its own advertising revenue. The Welsh fourth channel is called Saniel Pedwar Cymru (S4C).

Channel 5 (UK) The Independent Television Commission of the UK awarded Britain's fifth national terrestrial TV channel to Channel 5 Broadcasting in October 1995. Two other bidders, Canadian-backed UKTV and Virgin TV, were turned down on the grounds that, despite its lower bid, Channel 5 Broadcasting, led by Lord Hollick and Greg Dyke (later to be appointed Director General of the BBC), was offering more attractive and better-quality programming. Channel 5 began broadcasting in January 1997.

Chapultepec, Declaration of, 1994 Adopted, 11 March in Mexico City, by the Hemisphere Conference on Free Speech, organized by the Inter American Press Association (IAPA), the Declaration states that 'A free press enables societies to resolve their conflicts, promote their well-being and protect their liberty.' The defence of the freedom of the press is absolute and unqualified: 'No law or act of government may limit freedom of expression or of the press, whatever the medium.' Chapultepec rejects prior CENSORSHIP (Clause 5), licences for the importation of paper, newsgathering equipment and the assigning of RADIO frequencies (Clause 7), and asserts that no news medium nor journalist may be punished for publishing the truth, or for criticizing or denouncing government (Clause 10). See NEW WORLD INFORMATION ORDER; TALLOIRES DECLARATION, 1981.

Characteristics of mass communications   See MASS COMMUNICATION: SEVEN CHARACTERISTICS.

Chequebook journalism A euphemism for bribery – newspapers paying someone for exclusive rights on his or her story. The police pay their 'snouts' or 'grasses' for the common good; the press pay their informants for tomorrow's headline, to serve the public's 'right to know' and to boost sales in the war of circulation.

Children, Young People and the Changing Media Environment Title of a major research project carried out in 12 countries during 1997–8, involving a survey of almost 15,000 children and young people. Directed by Sonia Livingstone of the Media Research Group of the London School of Economics and Political Science, in collaboration with George Gaskell and Moira Bovill, the survey's ongoing findings about how young people use the media were published in a special issue of the *European Journal of Communication*, December 1998: 'Young People and the Changing Media Environment'.

Themes addressed in the research project and summarized in the *EJC* are Young People's Ownership and Uses of New and Old Forms of Media in Britain and The Netherlands; Patterns of Old and New Media Use among Young People in Flanders, Germany and Sweden; Family Lifestyles and Media Use Patterns; Media Use and the Relationships of Children and Teenagers with their Peer Groups; and Global Culture in Practice – a look at children and adolescents in Denmark, France and Israel.

The survey revealed valuable data for further investigation. For example, only 64 per cent of British children possessed a shelf of books compared to 95 per cent of the Dutch children questioned, and personal ownership of a computer in the UK was 48 per cent compared with 85 per cent in Holland. British children, however, watch more TV, the researchers explaining this as being in part due to the 'enviable reputation for producing qualilty programmes … in Britain'.

A research team led by Dafna Lemish reported on interesting initial perspectives concerning young people – French, Danish and Israeli – and their mediated relations with global CULTURE. They write that 'Media seem to connect young audiences to the social "centre" of humankind', while the Internet is seen as 'another type of transnational social space'. Young people seem at ease with the *hybridity* of modern culture: '…What we understand from our informants is that the meeting between the global and the local can be [that] of coexistence and conflation, rather than assimilation vs isolationism.'

Chronology News narratives on TV are often compared to those of fictional stories (see STORYNESS) but there are obvious differences, an important one being divergence over chronology. 'In news,' writes Allan Bell in *The Language of News Media* (UK: Blackwell, 1991), 'order is everything but chronology is nothing.' Indeed, in the news narrative the climax is reported first whereas in a story this usually comes at the end. Chronology has a low priority in the construction of news stories to the point where the AUDIENCE has to be highly news-literate to follow what is going on. Bell says, 'The time structure of news stories can make the shape of a difficult film or novel look straightforward in comparison.' See AGENDA-SETTING.

Cigarette cards: cultural indicators A US company, Allen Ginter, produced the forerunner of the first British cigarette card when it packed with its Richmond Gem brand a pair of oval cards held together by a stud, one section of which was a calendar for 1884, with UK parcel postage rates on the back. By the 1890s the larger British tobacco companies were issuing cards, beginning with advertisements then progressing to series on particular themes such as soldiers, ships, royalty, sport and famous beauties.

The first company to issue photographic cigarette cards on a large scale was Ogdens which, in 1894, began its Guinea Gold and Tabs cards covering, in the next 13 years, practically every facet of life of that period. In the early 1900s there were around 50 companies issuing cards in the UK and Ireland. Reflecting the dominance of the British Empire, the cards represented many military issues, along with major inventions of the time – the motor car and the aeroplane. Exploration and discovery, and the Edwardian craze for collecting things – bird's eggs, butterflies, porcelain – were prominently reflected in the choice of subject matter as were the music hall and the scouting movement.

Early in the First World War (1914–18) the Wills company actually issued cards as miniature recruiting posters, while Gallahers put out several series of Victoria Cross Heroes, in 1915 and 1916. Carreras issued Women on War Work and Raemaker's War Cartoons portraying the Germans as barbarians.

Later examples of these cultural ephemera were Gallahers' Boy Scouts, Fables and Their Morals; Wills' Cinema Stars and Radio Celebrities. Ogdens produced a series on Broadcasting. With the approach of the Second World War (1939–45) Carreras produced Britain's Defences (1938), Players issued Aircraft of the RAF in the same year and in 1939 Modern Naval Craft. The most ambitious cigarette card enterprise of the period was the Imperial Tobacco Company's Air Raid Precautions, made available in a variety of cigarette brands.

Cigarette card production remained popular in the post-war era, though the 1960s saw a marked decline. In the 1970s came the much sought-after series from Player, The Golden Age of Motoring, packed in Doncella cigars. The Golden Age continued with Steam (1976), Flying (1977) and Sail (1978). See PICTURE POSTCARDS.

Cine-clubs Played an important role in the development of cinema in many countries. Where, in the commercial film theatres, popular entertainment monopolized programmes, the cine-clubs showed new experimental and often non-fictional work. John Grierson (1898–1972) organized the first British showing of Sergei Eisenstein's *Battleship Potemkin* at the London Film Society (formed in 1925) in 1929, along with his own seminal documentary *Drifters*. Minister of Propaganda in Nazi Germany, Goebbels, outlawed all cine-clubs because of their 'subversive' nature and a similar fate befell the cine-club movement in pre-Second World War Japan.

The Depression and the failure of the media to meet head on the causes of depression, helped give belated birth to the US cine-club movement. The Workers' Film and Photo League, soon renamed the National Film and Photo League, was formed in New York in 1930. Members of the League made films as well as watched them, concentrating on filming the hunger marches and other mass protests of the time. Among their creations was a Workers' Newsreel, which the League persuaded some commercial cinemas to screen.

Cinema See CINEMATOGRAPHY, ORIGINS; FILM.

Cinema legislation The first legislation in the UK relating to cinema use was the Cinematograph Act of 1909. It concerned the licensing of exhibition premises and the safety of audiences. In 1922, the Celluloid and Cinematograph Film Act drew up safety rules for premises where raw celluloid or cinematograph film was stored and used. The Cinematograph Film Production (Special Loans) Act, 1949, established the National Film Finance Corporation and in the same year came the British Film Institute Act.

The Cinematograph Films Act, 1957, provided a statutory levy on exhibitors and exhibitions to be collected by Customs & Excise and paid to the British Film Fund Agency, which would use the monies to support film production in the UK and support the Children's Film Foundation. This made the formerly voluntary levy compulsory. The Cinematograph (Amendment) Acts of 1982 extended provision of the 1909 Act to include 'all exhibitions of moving pictures for private gain', bringing under regulation pornographic cinema and video 'clubs'. The Acts exclude from regulation bona fide film societies.

The Films Act, 1985, abolished the Cinematograph Films Council and the Eady Levy and dissolved the National Film Finance Corporation, replacing it with the British Screen Finance Consortium. The government provided a 'starter' of £1.5m for five years to the loan fund of the BSFC whose function would be to raise funds independently of state support. See BROADCASTING LEGISLATION.

CinemaScope Wide-screen process copyrighted by 20th Century Fox in 1953 but invented much earlier by Henri Chretien.

Cinematographie Word first used by G. Bouly in 1892 in a French patent specification for a movie camera.

Cinematography, origins Among the earliest moving-picture inventions was the *Thaumatropical Amusement* of Englishman Henry Fitton (1826). Exploiting the phenomenon of PERSISTENCE OF VISION the Thaumatrope consisted of a round box inside of which were a number of discs each with a design on it. When the discs were twirled round, the images merged and gave the impression of a single movement.

Joseph Plateau's *Phenakistoscope* (1833), a circular design opposite a mirror, worked the same little miracle. The ZOETROPE, or 'wheel of life', invented by Englishman W.G. Horner (1834) offered a revolving drum with strip sequences inside, enabling figures to jump, gallop or even do cartwheels. Emile Renauld's *Praxinoscope* of 1877 improved on the Zoetrope by removing the slots of the drum and using mirrors to reflect the images, thus avoiding the dizziness to viewers caused by the Zoetrope; and the wonder of this device was extended with the *Projecting Praxinoscope* using a revolving disc-blade shutter to project animated images on to a screen.

The main impetus in the development of cinematography came, however, from another direction. Working in the US, English photographer Edward Muybridge (1830–1904) in the 1870s took multiple photographs of animals, birds and humans in movement. His most famous experiment was the one in which a line of cameras, using exposures of less than one-thousandth of a second, 'filmed' a galloping horse. The horse triggered each camera as it passed – and proved, incidentally, that there are moments in a horse's movement when all its hooves are clear of the ground.

The next step was the projection of these in-sequence pictures. William Friese-Green (1855–1921), in 1890, revealed the potential of moving film when he set up a small slide projector in which the usual slide carrier had been replaced by a glass disc bearing a ring of pictures. Friese-Green's revolving disc was later demonstrated, to eager crowds, in the window of his studio in Piccadilly.

In France meanwhile Etienne Jules Marey (1830–1904) had invented a photographic 'gun' (1882) to take pictures of birds in flight, and soon followed this with a camera capable of snapping 60 pictures a second on a paper-based film. In the US Thomas Alva Edison (1847–1931) produced his *Kinetograph* to take moving pictures and his KINETOSCOPE to show them. The viewer looked through a peephole in the foot-high box. The 50 feet of film ran for about 13 seconds. 'Kinetoscope parlours' were set up in which people could view films by putting a coin in a slot.

The most important year in the development of cinematography was 1895, with the invention of projectors in the US by Thomas Armat and Woodville Latham, in France by the Lumière brothers – Auguste (1862–1954) and Louis (1864–1948) – and in the UK by Robert Paul. With the arrival of the Lumières on the scene, the cinema was truly born. Their vision and entrepreneurialism turned experiment into performance, private screenings into public, commercial profit. 'What did I do?' Louis Lumière is reported to have said. 'It was in the air.' Auguste Lumière was less modest than Louis: 'My brother,' he said, 'invented the cinema in one night.' On 28 December 1895, the Lumières, already highly successful in the photographic business, opened in the Salon Indien, in the Grand Café on the Boulevard des Capuchines. Seats were priced at one franc. Within weeks they were a worldwide success. Immediately the Lumières trained a brigade of cameramen-cum-projectionists and sent them abroad to several foreign countries; in quick time, some 1200 single-shot films were produced, including the Diamond Jubilee procession in London.

Cinéma vérité Or *Catalyst* cinema. In a 1961 DOCUMENTARY, *Chronique d'un Été* (Chronicle of a Summer), Jean Rouch, instead of simply recording the daily routines of Parisians, challenged them to face the camera and answer the question, 'Tell us, are you happy?' Rouch and co-producer Edgar Morin were suddenly on-camera participants. Their subjects, having been filmed, were invited to see the film rushes. Their discussion of these was filmed and recorded and used as part of the end product.

The style was named *cinéma vérité* in homage to the Russian movie pioneer Dziga Vertov, and translated from the term used by Vertov and his associates, *kino pravda*, film truth. Erik Barnouw in *Documentary* (UK: Oxford University Press, 1974), writes, 'The direct cinema documentarist took his camera to a situation of tension and waited hopefully for a crisis; the Rouch version of cinéma vérité tried to precipitate one. The direct cinema artist aspired to invisibility; the Rouch cinéma vérité was often an avowed participant.'

Cinerama Extra-wide screen system invented by Fred Waller and first demonstrated in *This is Cinerama* (1952). Three projectors, electronically synchronized, created a three-section picture on the screen, giving a disturbing visual wobble at the joins. The first film story using the process was *How the West Was Won* (1962). Shortly afterwards the three-camera system was abandoned in favour of 'single-lens Cinerama', practically identical to CINEMASCOPE, though with higher definition.

Citizen Kane of the global village Description of media mogul Rupert Murdoch by Alex Brummer and Victor Keegan in a *Guardian* article (13 May 1995) entitled 'Planet Rupert takes on the galaxy'. The authors examine the growth and growth of the Murdoch global empire. Kane was the fictional newspaper mogul in Orson Welles' film masterpiece *Citizen Kane* (1941), rather more than loosely based upon the life of the American newspaper baron William Randolph Hearst (1863–1951) – the Rupert Murdoch of his age. See MURDOCH EFFECT.

Civil inattention Phenomenon of INTERPERSONAL COMMUNICATION observed by Erving Goffman in *Behavior in Public Places* (US: Free Press, 1963), where, after initial EYE CONTACT, a person quickly withdraws visual attention from another to avoid any further recognition or need for further contact. As Goffman says, 'In performing this courtesy the eyes of the looker may pass over the eyes of the other, but no "recognition" is typically allowed.' The ritual of civil inattention, Goffman explains, is one that 'constantly regulates the social intercourse of persons in our society'. See INDICATORS.

Clapper board See SHOT.

Claptrap See VERBAL DEVICES OF SPEECH-MAKING.

Class A factor of vital importance in the analysis of interpersonal and mass communication is the concept of class; and the most significant impact on the development of that concept was made by the German philosopher Karl Marx (1818–83). For him, class denoted a relationship to the means of production in any given society. Marx identified two main classes: the owners of the *means of production* (land, factories), whom he called the *bourgeoisie,* and those who were obliged to sell their labour to the owners to make a living – the *proletariat.* Although aware of other classes, he considered them of minor importance.

Marx argued that as a result of their position in the economic order, members of each class shared common experiences, lifestyles and certain political and economic interests. He believed that there was and would remain, in a capitalist society, an inevitable conflict between the interests of the bourgeoisie and the proletariat. He further argued that GROUP identity, class-consciousness, and collective political and economic action would develop in the course of economic and political conflict. Proletarian class-consciousness was particularly likely to emerge as its members were thrown into serious difficulties and close daily associations at work.

The dominant class – the bourgeoisie – would, according to Marx, seek to impose its culture upon the rest of society. Its culture would become the *dominant* culture, its IDEOLOGY the dominant ideology. Consequently the communication systems of society would reflect the dominant culture of the bourgeoisie and also the conflict between the two classes. From a Marxist viewpoint, control of many facets of the mass media by the ownership of capital gives that class the opportunity to disseminate its own culture and ideology. Such control, in Marxist terms, plays a vital role in the maintenance of HEGEMONY.

The term is also commonly used when what is meant is *social* class. Social class membership is based, primarily, upon occupation rather than ownership or non-ownership of the means of production.

For the ADVERTISING industry and media management, social class is a significant factor in the profile of an audience. Market researchers are primarily interested in income and spending power. For those media organizations that are dependent on advertising revenue, the social class composition of its AUDIENCE is of obvious importance. The inter-relationships between the social class structure and the communication processes of society are complex, and research in this area is wide-ranged. Of particular concern is whether the narrowness of social class backgrounds of those who control and work in the media is reflected in its output. See *TOPIC GUIDE* under MEDIA: VALUES AND IDEOLOGIES.

Classic FM Commercial radio station broadcasting nationwide in the UK from the autumn of 1992. Its menu of popular classics presented in a lively and unpatronizing way, and a policy of winning audience loyalty through competitions and sponsored musical events has proved a notable success.

'Clean up TV' movement Brought together in Birmingham in 1963 by the late Mary Whitehouse and others; later called itself the National Viewers' and Listeners' Association (NVLA). Over the years the movement has succeeded in gaining access to practically every forum in which the issues of broadcasting are discussed; additionally, the NVLA has been active as a 'morality watchdog' in other arts, especially the theatre and publishing. The basis of NVLA thinking is that of traditional Christian ethics; the belief that the VALUES of chastity and the family underpin all that's best in western society, and that such values are constantly under threat and have to be protected. Of equal concern to the NVLA is the increase in the display, in film, on TV and in the theatre, of scenes of violence. See BROADCASTING STANDARDS COUNCIL (UK); CENSORSHIP; MORAL ENTREPRENEURS.

Climax order In the process of persuading others, the order in which arguments and evidence are placed is of considerable importance. Research has been conducted into the climax order and anti-climax order, that is when the best point of an argument is reserved until last (climax) or used at the outset (anti-climax). The two orders have varying advantages depending on the particular conditions under which the communication is presented, including the audience's predisposition and the type of matter being transmitted. Similar concepts are the Law of PRIMACY and the Law of RECENCY.

Clipper chip A microchip, called the spy in the computer, the 'sleeping policeman on the super-highway of information'. It was feared in the mid-1990s that it would become a compulsory element in US-made computers, allowing government agencies, by means of an electronic back door, to snoop on data into and out of computers. Such was the determination of users of the INTERNET and their campaign against the clipper chip that the Clinton government temporarily retreated from its plans.

 However, in February 1996 Clinton signed a Telecommunications Bill requiring that from 1998 all TV sets with a screen size of 13 inches or more should be fitted with a V (for violence)-chip. In the same month the European Parliament voted in favour of a similar measure – the insertion of V-chips into every new TV set sold in Europe under the Television Without Frontiers directive. See ENCRYPT; PRIVACY.

Clique A close-knit group of people within a social system whose communication is largely with each other. *Clique analysis* is used to determine communication groupings within a social system and its main tool is Sociometrics.

Closed text See OPEN, CLOSED TEXTS.

Closure Occurs in a communication situation when one participant, usually the receiver of information, closes down attention, and thus deflects the message or the messenger, or terminates an encounter. The reasons for closure may relate to the unacceptability of the MESSAGE: it may conflict with the attitudes, beliefs or VALUES of the receiver; it may be an 'uncomfortable truth' that causes the receiver a feeling of DISSONANCE. Also, it may have something to do with the messenger rather than the message – personal dislike of the sender on the part of the receiver or a simple unwillingness to receive this kind of message from this messenger, or it may simply reflect a wish to terminate the encounter and move on.

 The means of closure will involve NVC (non-verbal communication) as well as verbal strategies. The term is also used in relation to NARRATIVE, in the sense of *narrative closure*. This does not mean bringing the narrative to a close, but employing narrative devices to close down alternative readings or interpretations. See OPEN, CLOSED TEXTS; PREFERRED READING.

Cocktail party problem In *On Human Communication* (US: MIT Press, 1966), Colin Cherry writes, 'One of our most important faculties is the ability to listen to, and follow, one speaker in the presence of others. This is such a common experience that we may take it for granted; we may call it "the cocktail party problem". That is, how do we filter out a barrage of communication messages, selecting one to concentrate upon?' Cherry experimented with two different taped readings being played at once, with the instruction to the subject to concentrate on one and ignore the other.

Though the tapes produced a 'complete babel', and though very wide-ranging texts were used, considerable success in deciphering the message was demonstrated, illustrating the importance of 'our ingrained speech habits at the acoustic, syllabic, or syntactic levels'. Cherry and his colleagues also experimented to see what happened when a subject was asked to read a text out loud while simultaneously listening to another one. This process, of testing the subject's ability to select from competing message channels, they called 'shadowing'.

Code of Advertising Standards and Practice (ITC) The Independent Television Commission (ITC) of the UK was empowered by the BROADCASTING ACT, 1990, to draw up and enforce a code governing standards and practice in television advertising and the sponsorship of programmes (see SPONSORSHIP; ITC CODE OF PROGRAMME SPONSORSHIP). Modelled closely on the Code of Practice issued by the IBA (Independent Broadcasting Authority, which the ITC succeeded) and the Code of the Cable Authority, the ITC Code also had regard to the Code of Practice issued by the Broadcasting Standards Council as well as the need to fulfil requirements relating to TV advertising in the *European Community Directive on Television Broadcasting* (89/552/EEC) and the 1989 Council of Europe *Convention on Transfrontier Television.*

The ITC Code applies to all independent TV broadcasting, UK direct broadcast satellite (DBS) services and other satellite services operating out of the UK. The Code declares that television advertising 'should be legal, decent, honest and truthful'. Advertisements must at all times be distinguishable as such and recognizably separate from the programmes and they must not refer to themselves as 'programmes'.

Expressions such as the term 'news flash' are not acceptable. So-called 'subliminal' advertising is prohibited: 'No advertisement may include any technical device which, by using images of very brief duration or by any other means, exploits the possibility of conveying a message to, or otherwise influencing the minds of, members of the audience without their being aware, or fully aware, of what has been done.'

 No advertisement of a political nature is acceptable; and none may be used in relation to an industrial dispute. Prohibition is also extended to adverts that play upon the fears of the audience or attempt to exploit the superstitious, or that appear to discriminate on grounds of gender or race. The Code proscribes a range of products and services – breath-testing devices and products that purport to mask the effects of alcohol; the occult; betting tips and gaming, including the football pools.

The Code deals with a long list of requirements concerning health and safety, protection of the environment, the use of animals in advertisements, misleadingness, price claims, comparisons and denigration. There are seven sections in the Code relating to matrimonial and introduction agencies and thirteen on alcoholic drinks advertisement. Item (g) of Section 40, declares that advertisements 'must neither claim nor suggest that any drink can contribute towards sexual success or that drinking can enhance sexual attractiveness' and item (j) that no advertisement may suggest 'that drinking is an essential attribute of masculinity'.

Appendix 1 of the Code deals with advertising and children, and other appendices are: (2) financial advertising; (3) health claims, medicines and treatments; (4) charity advertising; and (5) religious advertising.

Code of Programme Sponsorship See SPONSORSHIP: ITC CODE OF PROGRAMME SPONSORSHIP.

Code of semes See CODES OF NARRATIVE.

Codes A code is generally defined as a system into which signs are organized, governed by consent. The study of codes – other than those *arbitrary* or fixed codes such as mathematics, chemical symbols, MORSE CODE, etc. – emphasizes the social dimension of communication. We have codes of conduct, ethical, aesthetic and LANGUAGE codes (see ELABORATED AND RESTRICTED CODES).

Non-verbal communication is carried on through what have been classified as *presentational codes*: gesture, movement of the eyes, expressions of the face, tone of voice. A *representation code* can be speech, writing, music, art, architecture, etc. Speech itself has non-verbal characteristics: *prosodic codes* affect the MEANING of the words used, through expression or pitch of voice.

The media are often referred to as employing *broadcast* and *narrowcast* codes in gearing content, level and style to expected audiences. In *Introducing Communication Studies* (UK: Methuen, 1982), John Fiske writes, 'Narrowcast codes have acquired the function in our mass society of stressing the difference between "us" (the users of the code) and "them" (the laymen, the lowbrows). Broadcast codes stress the similarities among "us" (the majority).' In the case of TV, *Coronation Street* would represent the broadcast code and a production of Shakespeare's *King Lear* a piece of narrowcasting, though eco-nomically speaking, in terms of advertising, narrowcast may simply indicate the target audience of the advertiser.

Aesthetic codes are crucially affected by their cultural context, some of it highly conventional, some AVANT-GARDE, subject to textual rather than commonly recognized cues to meaning. Much modern art, for example, has been encoded in visual languages accessible only to a small number of people. However, over time, innovative aesthetic encoding becomes conventionalized. The obscure code has become familiar. A case in point is Surrealism, whose intention was to shock cultural convention, yet whose dream symbols and often disturbing juxtapositions of objects have become a commonplace of mass advertising. What began as a code specific to itself has been transformed to one given its meaning by cultural convention. See CODES OF NARRATIVE; DECODE; DOMINANT, SUBORDINATE, RADICAL; ELITE; HIGHBROW; SEMIOLOGY/SEMIOTICS.

Codes of narrative Roland Barthes in *S/Z* (UK: Basil Blackwell, 1990; translated from the French by Richard Miller) applies a number of narrative codes in a book-length analysis, or deconstruction, of a 23-page short story, 'Sarrasine', written by Honoré de Balzac in 1830. Barthes describes 'five major codes under which all the textual signifiers can be grouped' in a narrative. The *Proiaretic* or *Action* code (the Voice of Empirics) tells us of events, of what happens, and thus is instrumental in the sequence of the story.

The code of the *seme* or sign ('semantically the unit of the signifier') refers to character and is categorized by Richard Howard in the Preface to *S/Z* as the *Semantic* code (though Barthes does not actually use this term in the text). Barthes speaks of this as the Voice of the Person. Under the *Hermeneutic* or *Enigma* code (the Voice of Truth) 'we list the various (formal) terms by which an enigma can be distinguished, suggested, formulated, held in suspense and finally disclosed'. *Cultural* or *Referential* codes 'are references to a science or a body of knowledge' – 'physical, physiological, medical, psychological, literary, historical, etc.'. These are the Voice of Science. Finally there is the *Symbolic* code, the Voice of Symbol.

Barthes writes of the codes that they 'create a kind of network, a *topos* [Greek: a place, location] through which the entire text passes (or rather, in passing, becomes text)'.

This taxonomy of codes is widely used in the analysis of texts of all kinds. Nowhere, however, does Barthes suggest that such coding is prescriptive, discrete or exact. He writes, 'The code is a perspective of quotations, a mirage of structures; we know only its departures and returns.' Barthes talks of a 'galaxy of signifiers, not a structure of signifieds'. For him the text 'is not unitary, architectonic, finite' and the approach to it is characterized by 'blanks and looseness of analysis'. The meaning of the 'readerly' as contrasted with the 'writerly' text is ultimately elusive. The 'blanks' and 'looseness of analysis' will be like 'footprints marking the escape of the text'.

Codes: programme codes See ITC PROGRAMME CODE; RADIO AUTHORITY PROGRAMME CODES; SPONSORSHIP: ITC CODE OF PROGRAMME SPONSORSHIP.

Cognitive (and affective) That area or domain of human behaviour that can be described as intel-lectual – knowing, understanding and reasoning – is often referred to as the *cognitive*. A substantial amount of media communication is aimed at producing cognitive responses in the receiver. That area that is involved with attitudes, emotions, VALUES and feelings is termed the *affective*. Obviously the two overlap and intertwine.

Whether the content of a MESSAGE is cognitive or affective in its orientations will greatly influence the mode chosen for its communication. If the content of a message is judged to be of cognitive intent, then LANGUAGE will generally be couched in neutral terms; presentation will strive after objectivity and balance. An affective message will be more likely to be framed in emotive language, its imagery directed towards emotional responses.

However, much recent media research has been directed towards a more critical analysis of the allegedly objective modes of cognitive messages. There is concern as to whether the dissemination of apparently neutral information – especially if that dissemination is of some FREQUENCY and CONSISTENCY of treatment – influences an audience's perception of national and world events. From the mass of available information, the media select and reject. They give emphasis – and legitimacy – to some issues rather than others, and they set the order of priorities (see AGENDA-

SETTING) as well as seeking to establish links between occurrences and their causes in the minds of the audience. See EFFECTS OF THE MASS MEDIA; GLASGOW UNIVERSITY MEDIA GROUP.

Cognitive capture See IMPARTIALITY.

Cognitive dissonance See CONGRUENCE THEORY; DISSONANCE.

Cold media, hot media See HOT MEDIA, COLD MEDIA.

Collective representations These describe the role played by the community in telling stories about itself, in particular those musical or dramatic forms, images and artefacts that speak for and about popular tastes, beliefs, VALUES and preoccupations. At the same time the term describes the way the community may adopt images and artefacts produced for it – works of art, for example – and assign to them significance rooted in popular needs and uses. The collective production of MEANING, says Wendy Griswold in *Cultures and Societies in a Changing World* (US: Pine Forge Press, 1994), 'tries to take away the mystery about the creation of art, ideas, beliefs, religion, and culture in general by revealing the many social activities, such as interaction, cooperation, organization, and contestation, involved in the formulation of what we designate as cultural objects'. See CULTURE; POPULAR CULTURE; EXPECTATION, HORIZONS OF.

Collocation The tendency of words to occur in regular association; words set together through customary usage such as 'fair' and 'play', 'auspicious' and 'occasion'.

Collodion or wet-plate process See PHOTOGRAPHY, ORIGINS.

Colloquialism An expression used in common, informal speech, but not as far removed from acceptable modes as SLANG. If your comments 'cut no ice' with somebody, that is a colloquialism; if you are told to 'keep yer 'air on', that is slang. It is a modest distinction, for as R. Ridout and C. Witting say in *The Facts of English* (UK: Pan Reference Books, 1973), 'the slang of yesterday becomes the colloquialism of today'. See DIALECT; JARGON; REGISTER.

Colonization Term used to describe the process by which assorted cultural material is acquired from a variety of contexts and then reassembled to construct particular messages. In this process the MEANING of the original signs is often changed, if not subverted; their use may appear to celebrate differences between people but the goal to which they are put may have as its purpose the REINFORCEMENT of the DOMINANT CULTURE, and the denial of differences and the conflict they bring.

Advertising messages contain many examples of colonization. For example, the signs and symbols widely associated with certain YOUTH CULTURES are often employed to sell goods and services to various audiences – whether young people themselves or older consumers who are presumed to identify with a particular youth culture. Ironically whilst youth cultures are often a site of resistance and challenge to the dominant culture, their signs and symbols are in this way used to draw them further into the dominant culture – for instance, through encouraging certain patterns of consumption and the use of financial services such as banking services.

Colour TV The first regular TV service in colour began in the US in 1954; 1960 saw the first colour service in Japan, seven years ahead of Britain. In 1969 there were 100,000 colour sets in use in the UK; by the same month in 1972 there were 1.6m and twice that 12 months later. Ferguson produced the first full-size colour receiver using transistors throughout, in 1967. Transistors consumed a quarter of the power of traditional valve receivers. They ran cooler and were more reliable.

Later came integrated circuits, doing away with many discrete components. The surface acoustic wave (SAW) filter further refined the accuracy of colour reception as did improved shadow-mask tubes. Here stripes of colour rather than dots achieved registration of the picture's red, green and blue components without the need for any of the many correction circuits previously required.

Comics The first newspaper comic strip is generally considered to be that which appeared on 16 February 1896 in the *New York Sunday World*. It was a three-quarter-page feature in colour called 'The Great Dog Show in M'Googan's Avenue'. Kids in the city's slum backyards were organizing their own dog show; the hero, dressed in a bright yellow nightgown, soon became the 'Yellow Kid' and 'Hogan's Alley' achieved immediate popularity as a long-running comic strip (see YELLOW KID).

The idea was not new. English cartoonist Thomas Rowlandson (1757–1827) created a comic character, Dr Syntax, who was popular with the public, and considerably earlier William Hogarth (1697–1764) included speech 'balloons' in his engravings satirizing London life. George Orwell took comics seriously enough to write about them. In 'Boys' weeklies' (1939), published in *Selected Essays* (UK: Penguin, 1957), Orwell analyses the social and political connotations of early publications in the genre. What seems to characterize comics, in Orwell's day or our own, is their social changelessness, deep down if not in the surface detail. Orwell did find differences between the older and the new generation of weeklies, however: in the new, 'better technique, more scientific interest, more bloodshed, more leaderworship'; in 'social outlook there is hardly any advance'.

As life appears to have become more complex, and society more complicated, the STEREOTYPE of the hero has had a sustaining appeal. Picture-strip heroes such as Clark Kent, alias Superman, who first made his appearance in *Action Comics* (1938) in the US, have not only led popular (and charmed) lives on the printed paper but have translated into immensely popular film heroes. The debate concerning comics, and comic books, centres around the extent to which they seem to legitimize dominant social values.

At the same time concern is expressed about the subversive potential of so-called *comix*, which offer a more pluralist, and sometimes radical, reading, as well as a more aesthetically conscious approach. This kind of comic also addresses adult audiences and is often anti-authority in essence. See CARTOONS.

Commanders of the social order Term used by Herbert I. Schiller in *Culture, Inc.: The Corporate Takeover of Public Expression* (UK: Oxford University Press, 1989), referring to the vast transnational corporations that, he argues, have come to dominate and shape CULTURE, establish prevailing discourses, set political, economic and cultural agendas and call the tune of mass media. Schiller talks of the PRIVATIZATION of public space: in a literal sense (public areas being transformed into privately owned and controlled shopping malls and pleasure domes); and in an intellectual sense, through the 'corporatization' of arts, literature and media. He cites the extent to which the entire world of information (libraries, museums, universities, mass communication); and of expression (architecture, music, art); and of public spectacle (sport), have been colonized by corporations, particularly in the US, but increasingly in the rest of the world. See AUDIENCE: ACTIVE AUDIENCE; BERLUSCONI PHENOMENON; CONSENSUS; ELITE; HEGEMONY; MANUFACTURE OF CONSENT; POWER ELITE; PRESS BARONS; PUBLIC SPHERE. See also *TOPIC GUIDE* under MEDIA: OWNERSHIP AND CONTROL.

Commercial confidentiality A CENSORSHIP device employed to prevent the media transmitting, or the general public receiving, information on the grounds that such information might be commercially damaging (regardless of whether that information might be in the public interest). One particularly sensitive area of commerce that is shrouded in mystery is the arms trade.

Britain is, for example, among the world's top arms-trading nations. Its government maintains an arms marketing and advisory service, the Defence Exports Services Organization (DECO), yet this organization is notoriously secretive whenever journalists seek to find out about its work, invariably answering that information cannot be supplied for reasons of 'commercial confidentiality'. Louis Blom-Cooper, chairman of the Press Council in 1990, expressed the view that 'Traditional English law places a higher value on commercial interests than on the public's right to know.'

Commercial laissez-faire model of (media) communication In their 'Introduction' to *The Manufacture of News* (UK: Constable, 1973) joint editors Stanley Cohen and Jock Young cite two general, and polarized, models that attempt to explain the intentions and impact of media on their audiences – the mass manipulative model and the commercial *laissez-faire* model. In the first, 'the public is seen as an atomized mass, passive receptacles of messages originating from a monolithic and powerful source'. From the perspective of the political Left it is big business – the hierarchy of capitalism – that is the seemingly all-powerful manipulator. From the perspective of the political Right, the media in this model are seen as manipulating 'standards' by lowering them.

Drawn from the *laissez-faire* (leave well alone) model of the economy, the commercial *laissez-faire* model mirrors the freedom of the marketplace where producers compete with one another to sell their products to consumers. Thus media corporations are seen as having to compete for the attention and loyalty of their consumers – the audience. Researchers using this model tend to argue that the consumer is sovereign and that media corporations have to tailor their products to suit consumer wishes, tastes and needs. The focus of their research is, therefore, often upon the mechanisms by which such tailoring is achieved.

The commercial *laissez-faire* model emerged as a critique of the mass manipulative model. It is generally the PREFERRED READING of journalists and media people themselves. Because there is competition, the argument goes, there is consequently 'variety and diversity in information and opinions presented in the mass media and … such variation minimizes the chances of manipulation'. This summary having been made in Cohen and Young's 'Introduction', the rest of the book's fascinating collection of reports and analyses is a remorseless exposé of fallacies perceived in the commercial *laissez-faire* model. See EFFECTS OF THE MASS MEDIA. See also *TOPIC GUIDE* under COMMUNICATION MODELS.

Commercial radio   Although PIRATE RADIO attempted to buck the BROADCASTING monopoly of the BBC during the 1960s, legitimate commercial broadcasting in the UK was not in operation until the 1970s, following the Conservative government's Sound Broadcasting Act of 1972. The IBA had, by 1983, 37 commercial RADIO stations operating under licence throughout the UK and plans for over 60 commercial stations.

In the US the first commercial radio station was KDKA of Pittsburgh, which went on the air on 2 November 1920 with a broadcast of the returns of the Harding–Cox presidential elections. In 1921 there were eight commercial radio stations and by 1922, 564. Development of radio in the US was spectacular and chaotic. In 1927 (the year that the BBC, by Royal Charter, was given a monopoly of radio broadcasting in the UK) Congress passed a Radio Act setting up the Federal Communications Commission to allocate wavelengths to broadcasters. Four radio networks were created as a hedge against monopoly – the National Broadcasting Commission (NBC), Columbia Broadcasting Service (CBS), Mutual Broadcasting System (MBS) and the American Broadcasting Company (ABC), while the FCC worked towards the growth of projects of educational interest.

Despite the BBC's monopoly in the UK, commercial broadcasts in English were transmitted from abroad as early as 1925. Radio Paris, broadcasting from the Eiffel Tower, presented a fashion talk in English, sponsored by Selfridges. Only three listeners wrote to the station to say they had heard the broadcast but the commercial lobby was undaunted. In the 1930s Captain L.F. Flugge, who had arranged the fashion talk, formed and ran the International Broadcasting Company. The IBC's Radio Normandy transmitted 15-minute shows for several hours a day from 1931 and, by the following year, 21 British firms were paying sponsorship money for commercial broadcasting, and the UK was being beamed at commercially from The Netherlands, Spain and Luxembourg.

The IBC actually set up offices in Portland Place, London, and had its own outside broadcasting vehicles, each painted black with 'Radio Normandy 274 metres' on the side. An important part of the company's operation was the International Broadcasting Club, formed in 1932, with free membership. By 1939, the IBC had 320,000 members.

Radio Luxembourg began broadcasting on 1191 metres long wave in 1933, its first two sponsors being Zam Buk and Bile Beans. Though the Post Office conducted a sustained campaign to close down these commercial stations, it was Adolf Hitler and the Second World War that did the trick: many transmitters were either destroyed by the Nazis or taken over. Radio Luxembourg became Hitler's major PROPAGANDA weapon against the British. The notorious Lord Haw-Haw (William Joyce), an Irishman committed to the German cause, broadcast daily recommendations to the British to lay down their arms, from the most powerful transmitter in Europe.

Of the commercial stations, Luxembourg was the only one to start up again after the war (finally closing down in 1992). The first accredited commercial radio station on British soil was Manx Radio, which began broadcasting in 1964. With the election of the Conservatives in 1970, the Minister of Posts and Telecommunications produced a White Paper, *An Alternative Service of Broadcasting*, proposing a network of about 60 commercial stations under the Independent Television Authority (to be renamed the Independent Broadcasting Authority). Opposition Spokesman Ivor Richards called it 'nothing more than the establishment of 60 pop stations'.

From the beginning, in 1972, local independent radio was to broadcast on stereo VHF as well as medium wave. The first FRANCHISES were awarded in 1973, to bring into existence the all-news London Broadcasting Company (LBC) and Capital Radio for London, with regional stations following soon afterwards. Additional franchises were granted by the IBA in 1981. By 1988 there were 40 independent local radio stations (compared to 27 BBC local stations).

The BROADCASTING ACT, 1990, separated out the statutory overseeing of radio and television, creating for TV (in place of the IBA) the INDEPENDENT TELEVISION COMMISSION (ITC) and for radio the Radio Authority. The Radio Authority was empowered to assign frequencies, appoint licensees, and to regulate programming and advertising. Also the Authority was required to draw up and periodically review codes of practice concerning programmes, advertising standards and other matters.

The Act, which came into force on 1 January 1991, with Lord Chalfont as chairman and Peter Baldwin as chief executive, substantially opened up the radio airwaves to independent, commercial stations. By 1992 well over 100 commercial stations were broadcasting throughout Britain, from Breeze-AM of Cheltenham to Xtra-AM of Birmingham/Coventry. For the first time three national radio (INR) licences were offered, INR1 going to Classic FM; 1992 saw the Authority seeking applications for INR2 (broadcasting on AM) and INR3 (a speech-based service). The cost of an application for an INR licence was £10,000 and the annual licence fee £645,000.

'Special event' licences, a Home Office remit prior to the Act, became the responsibility of the Radio Authority. Licences are usually granted for 28 days and for a localized coverage area. See COMMUNITY RADIO.

Commercial television Although TV in the US was commercial – relying on ADVERTISING for its revenues – from the beginning, TV in the UK was a PUBLIC SERVICE BROADCASTING (PSB) monopoly until the TELEVISION ACT, 1954, which gave birth to Independent Television. The ITA's first term ran from 1954 to 1964. It became the IBA (Independent Broadcasting Authority) from 1972, when the second term lasted until 1981. The third term, from 1982, was marked by the inauguration of CHANNEL 4. ITV programme companies were appointed for an eight-year contract period, serving modified areas and with two fresh dual regions. In its turn the IBA was succeeded by the Independent Television Commission (ITC) on 1 January 1992. Responsibility for RADIO became that of the new Radio Authority (see BROADCASTING ACT, 1990).

The passing of the IBA represented a significant watershed in the nature of BROADCASTING in the UK. A rigorously directive body, the IBA was very much a mirror image, in terms of regulation, of its opposite number in PSB (Public Service Broadcasting), the BBC. The Conservative government of the day was committed to PRIVATIZATION and DEREGULATION, and the duties of the new ITC represented a 'light-touch' approach to regulation.

The ITC is responsible for the licensing and regulating of all commercial television in the UK. In addition, it has responsibility for cable, satellite and such services as public TELETEXT. A core function of the ITC's work, as it was for the IBA, is the enforcement of a CODE OF ADVERTISING STANDARDS AND PRACTICE (ITC). This requires the Commission to set out advertising standards, ensure compliance with the Code and investigate complaints. It is empowered by the Control of Misleading Advertisements Regulations, 1988, to consider complaints about TV advertisements that are alleged to be misleading. The ITC's *Code of Programme Sponsorship* defines sponsorship in relation to commercial television and lays down guidelines. Rule 2 of the Code, for example, declares that 'No sponsor is permitted any influence on either the content or the scheduling of the programme he has sponsored', while Rule 7 states 'product placement is forbidden' (see PRODUCT PLACEMENT; SPONSORSHIP; SPONSORSHIP: ITC CODE OF PROGRAMME SPONSORSHIP).

The Broadcasting Act of 1990 also made it a statutory duty to draw up a *Programme Code* governing what the Foreword of the Code calls 'due impartiality and a general code governing the portrayal of violence, appeals for donations and such other matters concerning standards and practice for programmes as the ITC considers appropriate'. The Code also gives effect in the UK to a number of requirements relating to television programmes in the European Community Directive on Television Broadcasting on Transfrontier Television.

A significant stipulation arising from the new arrangements was that independents, that is independent programme-makers, must be allocated by the Channel 3 licensees a minimum of 25 per cent of broadcasting time, the quota being based upon programmes broadcast rather than programmes commissioned. Definition of a large as contrasted with a small licence area was specific under ITC terms. It was permitted for one body to hold a controlling interest in two regional Channel 3 licences as long as they were not both large (a limit that was raised by the BROADCASTING ACT, 1995). See COMMUNICATIONS BILL (UK), 2002; FRANCHISES FROM 1993.

Commissions/committees on the media See *TOPIC GUIDE* under COMMISSIONS, COMMITTEES, LEGISLATION.

Commoditization of information The notion that information is something upon which the possessor can put a price; thus information is bought and sold because it is a commodity rather than a public service. The process constitutes an important issue, and might also be termed the *privatization* of information. Herbert I. Schiller in 'Critical research in the information age', in *Journal of Communication*, Summer 1983, writes, 'The privatization of information is observable in all sectors of society ... A new international division of labour, no less inequitable than its predecessor, is being created practically before our eyes.'

Schiller refers to a 'gale of technological and industrial change whipping across the United States and other industrialized countries'. This has had far-reaching effects on the way we regard, and use, information: 'In sum, long-term, deep structural forces are making communication the central process in global, national and local social organization. At the same time, the most powerful national and transnational decision-making groups are initiating and deploying new information technologies to consolidate and extend their positions.' See CORPORATIONS AND MEDIA; HEGEMONY; INFORMATION GAPS; MEDIA IMPERIALISM; MOBILIZATION; POWER; POWER ELITE; TECHNOLOGICAL DETERMINISM.

Commonality In terms of language, beliefs, culture and, general outlook, that which is *shared* within a community; that which those who make up the community have in common.

Common sense In the study of media communication and its links with culture and politics, the term 'common sense' connotes an over-readiness to believe in the apparently obvious. The Italian philosopher Antonio Gramsci (1891–1937) defined common sense as being a composite of the attitudes, beliefs and assumptions of the mass of the people, and operating within a hierarchical social order.

Common sense tends towards conformism to the IDEOLOGY of the dominant social order, and in part is the product of that ideology. It accepts 'the way things are' – the *status quo* – as 'the way things should be'. Indeed such structures and circumstances are so obvious (so commonsensical) that they do not warrant being questioned. Gramsci believed that what he termed the 'chaotic aggregate of disparate conceptions' comprising common sense should be challenged by intellectuals, and the complacency of common sense explained and exposed. Many commentators have focused on the role the media play in nurturing and reinforcing rather than unpacking commonsensical visions of society. See EXNOMINATION; HEGEMONY.

Communication While the definitions of communication vary according to the theoretical frames of reference employed and the stress placed upon certain aspects of the total process, they all include five fundamental factors: an initiator; a recipient; a mode or vehicle; a message and an effect. Simply expressed, the communication process begins when a MESSAGE is conceived by a *sender*. It is then ENCODED – translated into a signal or sequence of signals – and *transmitted* via a particular MEDIUM or CHANNEL to a *receiver* who then decodes it and interprets the message, returning a signal in some way that the message has or has not been understood.

What has been termed NOISE, or interference, may impede the message. This may be internal (resistance to the message or to the sender, for example, on the part of the receiver) or external (actual noise, distraction, language level, etc.). During the communication process, sender, message and receiver are subject to a multitude of cues that influence the message, such as a person's appearance, his/her known status or the expression on his/her own face as the message is communicated or responded to (see BARNLUND'S TRANSACTIONAL MODEL, 1970).

While INTERPERSONAL COMMUNICATION is that which occurs between two or more people, INTRAPERSONAL COMMUNICATION is what you say within and to yourself. Inner thoughts, impressions, memories interact with external stimuli – the decor of a room, a painting on the wall, a beautiful landscape, a row of slum houses, a jostling crowd, a teacher at the front of the class, your friend's good or bad mood – to create a silent discourse, continuously changing and renewing itself, and influencing your perceptions of self and the world.

It is important to hold in mind, as Raymond Williams points out in *Keywords* (UK: Fontana, 1976), the 'unresolved range of the original noun of action, represented at its extremes by "transmit", a one-way process, and "share" … a common or mutual process'. This polarity of meaning – of the one-way process as against aspects of communion – is fundamental to the analysis of communication, hence the attempt to generalize the distinction in such phrases as *manipulative* communication and *participative* communication.

Frank Dance in 'Toward a theory of human communication', in the book he edited, *Human Communication Theory: Original Essays* (US: Holt, Rinehart & Winston, 1967), observes that communication is something that changes even while one is in the act of examining it; it is therefore an interaction and a *transaction*. Dance and C. Larson in *The Functions of Human Communication: A Theoretical Approach* (US: Holt, Rinehart & Winston, 1976), detail their examination of 126 definitions of communication. They specify notable differences but common agreement that communication is a *process*. The authors conclude with a definition of their own: 'The production of symbolic content by an individual, according to a code, with anticipated consumption by other(s) according to the same code.' Or as Colin Cherry succinctly puts it in *On Human Communication* (US: MIT Press, 1957), communication is 'essentially a social affair'.

Of course a painter or a poet may quarrel with this definition. He/she might claim that the process of communication is between artist–materials–subject-matter–artist's self or poet–words–feelings in an act of self-address, and that the eventual viewer of the painting or reader of the poem is of little account at the moment of encoding. It is open to debate whether, if the painting is stored in an attic or the poem burnt, any meaningful communication has taken place. Also, the painter or poet's work, once presented for consumption by others may be decoded – interpreted – in as many ways as there are people, each one reprocessing the work of art according to his/her own needs, norms, values, culture, expectations and SOCIALIZATION.

T.R. Nilson in 'On defining communication', in *Speech Trainer*, 1957, and reprinted in K.K. Sereno and C.D. Mortensen (eds), *Foundations of Communication Theory* (US: Harper & Row, 1970), distinguishes between communication that is *instrumental*, that is intended to stimulate a response, and *situational* in which there need not be any intention of evoking a response in the transmission of stimuli. As early as 1933, Edward Sapir differentiated between, *explicit* and *implicit* modes of communication, a perspective supported by Baker Brownell in *The Community: Its Philosophy and Practice for a Time of Crisis* (US: Harper & Bros, 1950) who speaks of *direct* and *indirect* communication. The latter Brownell defines as being a '… process wherein something converted into symbols is carried over from one person to another', while the former is a function of the '… identification of people with one another'.

A precept that few commentators would challenge is that it is *impossible not to communicate*. By saying nothing, by remaining blank-faced, by keeping our hands stiffly to our sides, we are still communicating, however negatively. We are still part of the interaction whether we like it or not. For Jurgen Ruesch, communication is 'all those processes by which people influence one another' (in 'Values, communication and culture', J. Ruesch and G. Bateson (eds), *The Social Matrix of Psychiatry* (US: W.W. Norton, 1951). At first we may resist the claim that whatever we do we are exerting an influence. Yet by trying not to influence we are arguably still affecting the patterns of communicative action, interaction and transaction. In our absence from the scene – from our family or work group, for example – as well as in our presence, we may still exert influence, however little, however unintended. See COMMUNICATION: INTERCULTURAL COMMUNICATION; COMMUNICATION, NON-VERBAL (NVC); SEMIOLOGY/SEMIOTICS.

Communication: intercultural communication Occurs between individuals from differing cultural backgrounds. Cultural differences are a potential source of much miscommunication and misunderstanding. According to Larry Samovar and Richard Porter in *Communication Between Cultures* (US: Wadsworth/Thomson Learning, 2001), 'intercultural communication will have two major points of contact: international and domestic. International contacts are those between people from different countries and cultures'. They point out that what also needs to be considered is 'that within each culture there are numerous co-cultures and specialized cultures. These provide the opportunity for domestic points of intercultural contact.' This is especially likely to be the case in multi-cultural societies such as those of Britain and the United States.

William B. Gudykunst and Young Yun Kim in *Communicating With Strangers: An Approach to Intercultural Communication* (US, McGraw-Hill, 1997) argue that intercultural communication is that 'between people from different societal cultures', but that rather than being a special case, 'the underlying process of communication between people from different cultures or subcultures is the same as the underlying process of communication between people from the same culture or subculture'. They suggest that an essential feature that may be found in such encounters is that people are communicating with strangers; that is, 'communicating with people who are unknown and unfamiliar, including people from another culture and people from our own culture or subculture who are in an environment new to them'.

To explore the dynamics of this process they propose a model that focuses on the influence of four categories of conceptual filter: *cultural, sociocultural, psychocultural* and *environmental*. They argue that 'Each of these types of filters influences how we will interpret messages encoded by strangers and what predictions we make about strangers' behaviour. Without understanding strangers' filters, we cannot accurately interpret or predict their behaviour.'

LANGUAGE and NON-VERBAL COMMUNICATION clearly vary across cultures but the impact of this variable arguably goes further than causing the obvious problems of translation in intercultural encounters. There are those who support the SAPIR–WHORF LINGUISTIC RELATIVITY HYPOTHESIS, which proposes that as language determines thought, people with different languages actually perceive the world differently rather than perceiving it in the same way but expressing their perceptions in different languages. This hypothesis remains controversial but a number of researchers would argue that whilst language may not determine thought, it does influence it. Richard Hudson, for example, in *Sociolinguistics* (UK: Cambridge University Press, 1996) comments, 'In short, language does affect thought in ways that go beyond the rather obvious effects of the specific lexical items. On the other hand, language is not the only kind of experience which does affect thought…'

There is also a range of other cultural variables to be considered. Geert Hofstede, for example, in *Culture's Consequences: International Differences in Work-Related Values* (US: Sage, 1980), identified four variables that he considered important: those of *individualism-collectivism* (see below); *uncertainty avoidance, power distance,* and *masculinity* and *femininity*. F. Kluckhohn and F. Strodtbeck earlier, in *Variations in Value Orientations* (US: Row Peterson, 1961), argued that five value orientations underpinned cultural differences: *human nature* orientation, *person–nature* orientation, *time* orientation, *activity* orientation and *relational* orientation.

One key cultural variable identified by a number of researchers, Triandis and Hofstede for example, is whether a culture is predominantly, though not exclusively, collectivistic or individualistic. Cultures in which collectivistic tendencies predominate stress the importance of the ties and obligations attached to membership of in-groups – people will tend to belong to a few in-groups and these will exercise considerable and general influence over members (for example, the family and workplace). The interests of the in-group are seen as more important than those of individual members; individuals are obliged to fit into the in-group. In-group identification is strong and there is an emphasis on cooperation, maintaining in-group harmony and avoiding conflict. There are often marked differences between the manner in which in-group members communicate with each other in comparison to communication with members of out-groups.

In contrast, cultures in which individualistic tendencies predominate stress the importance of the individual and the individual's aims, interests, achievements and self-development. Individuals are expected to be self-reliant and to take responsibility for themselves and their close family. Individuals may be members of a number of in-groups – most of which will have relatively limited and specific influence over their members. Individuals are encouraged to be competitive, to speak out and to stand out. There are likely to be fewer marked differences between the ways in which people communicate with in-group and out-group members.

It should be borne in mind, however, that people in any culture may have both collectivistic or individualistic orientations even though one will tend to be stronger. Further, not all people will necessarily identify strongly with the predominant tendency of the culture in which they live.

An important influence of the individualism-collectivism variable on communication lies in its relationship to the use of what Edward Hall in *Beyond Culture* (US, Doubleday, 1976), termed *high-* and *low-context* communication. High-context communication relies heavily on the aspects of the context – for example, the status differences between the communicators, to provide MEANING – and considerable use is made of non-verbal signs. Hall writes, 'When talking about something that they have on their minds, a high context individual will expect his interlocutor to know what's bothering him, so he doesn't have to be specific. The result is that he will talk around and around the point, in effect putting all the pieces in place except the crucial one. Placing it properly – this keystone – is the role of the interlocutor. To do this for him is an insult and a violation of his individuality.' As Gudykunst and Kim argue, 'High-context communication can be characterized as being indirect, ambiguous and understated with speakers being reserved and sensitive to listeners.' High-context communication is favoured by collectivistic cultures, such as that of Japan, in which the centrality of in-group membership ensures the degree of shared knowledge and understanding of contextual factors, essential for its effective use.

Individualistic cultures, such as that of European Americans, on the other hand, favour low-context communication. Here, such a degree of shared knowledge and understanding of contextual factors cannot be taken for granted so meaning is made obvious and less use is made of non-verbal signs – especially silence. As Gudykunst and Kim comment, 'Low-context communication … can be characterized as being direct, explicit, open, precise and consistent with one's feelings.'

Whilst the cultural variable of individualism/collectivism may predispose individuals to favour one pattern over another, they may in certain circumstances employ the contrasting pattern. So whilst those in individualistic cultures may generally employ low-context communication, in certain situations – for example, when talking to a longstanding friend – they may use high-context communication.

In cross-cultural encounters, some participants may be using high-context whilst others are using low-context communication patterns, and this will obviously be a source of confusion if not conflict. Those from collectivistic, high-context communication cultures, for example, may find the direct, open approach of those from individualistic, low-context cultures, socially inept and tactless; whilst those from individualistic, low-context cultures may get frustrated with the failure of those from collectivistic, high-context communication cultures, to 'get to the point'.

Individualism and collectivism also affect the coding and decoding of mass media artefacts such as advertisements. For example, Sang-Pil Han and Sharon Shavitt conducted a study entitled 'Persuasion and culture: advertising appeals in individualistic and collectivistic societies', *Journal of Experimental Social Psychology*, Vol. 30 (4), 1994, investigating the possible influence of individualism and collectivism on the encoding and decoding of a selection of magazine advertisements used in the US (individualistic culture) and Korea (collectivistic culture).

They concluded that in the United States advertisements were more likely to employ appeals to the individual whereas those in Korea focused on the benefits that a product or service could offer a group. Their study of the decoding of advertisements concluded that, 'in the U.S. advertisements emphasizing individualistic benefits were more persuasive, and ads. emphasizing family or ingroup benefits were less persuasive than they were in Korea. In both studies, however, product characteristics played a role in moderating these overall differences. Cultural differences emerged strongly … for advertised products that tend to be purchased and used with others, but were much less evident for products that are typically purchased and used individually.'

The influence of cultural variables will, however, interplay with other key variables. Social identities – for example, those of age, GENDER, social CLASS and ethnicity – constitute an important sociocultural influence. Thus, for example, the GENDERLECTS noted by Deborah Tannen in *You Just Don't*

Understand: Men and Women in Conversation (UK: Virago, 1992) could be expected to modify the degree to which, say, the cultural variable of individualism influences a person's communicative performance. Also part of the equation are psychocultural influences such as stereotyping, ETHNOCENTRISM and PREJUDICE, and environmental influences such as population density and terrain.

Encounters between people of different cultures can also be reflected in language; a pidgin, for example, may be generated. In trading and doing business with the English in the Far East, the Chinese and other peoples, such as the Malays, communicated in a very basic, utilitarian mode of half-English. Pidgin is a Chinese corruption of the word 'business' but the term is more widely used to to denote such basic means of communication. According to Elizabeth Closs Traugott and Mary Louise Pratt in *Linguistics* (US: Harcourt Brace Jovanovitch, 1980), a pidgin may be 'roughly defined as a language that is nobody's native language'.

Pidgins are developed in situations where people with differing native languages are brought together, some often in a relatively powerless position, and have to communicate. Pidgins, though, tend to meet only the basic needs of communication and are very reliant on the accompanying use of NON-VERBAL COMMUNICATION for their effectiveness. Creoles are normally developed by the children of pidgin speakers and these are more complex and more flexible languages. Over time, through the process of *decreolization*, a Creole often changes to resemble more closely the predominant or prestige language that was its base, if this language is still used in the area. This was the case with Jamaican Creole. In Britain, British Black English, derived largely from Jamaican Creole, is widely used by people with African-Caribbean origins as a linguistic marker of ETHNIC identity, and typically is part of a linguistic repertoire that also includes other varieties of English. See APACHE SILENCE, ASSERTIVENESS, M-TIME, P-TIME.

* Martin Montgomery, *An Introduction to Language and Society* (UK: Methuen, 1986; Routledge,1993); H.C. Triandis, *Individualism-collectivism* (US: Boulder: Westview, 1995).

Communication, functions Many and varied listings have been made by communications analysts. The following eight functions are usually quoted as being central: *instrumental* (to achieve or obtain something); *control* (to get someone to behave in a particular way); *information* (to find out or explain something); *expression* (to express one's feelings or put oneself over in a particular way); *social contact* (participating in company); *alleviation of anxiety* (to sort out a problem, ease a worry about something); *stimulation* (response to something of interest), and *role-related* (because the situation requires it). See JAKOBSON'S MODEL OF COMMUNICATION, 1958.

Communication integration See INTEGRATION.

Communication, interpersonal See INTERPERSONAL COMMUNICATION.

Communication, intrapersonal See INTRAPERSONAL COMMUNICATION.

Communication: mobile concept of See MOBILIZATION.

Communication models See *TOPIC GUIDE* under COMMUNICATION MODELS.

Communication, non-verbal (NVC) Michael Argyle in *Bodily Communication* (UK: Methuen, 1988) identifies the main codes of NVC: TOUCH and Bodily Contact; Spatial Behaviour (PROXEMICS and ORIENTATION); Appearance; FACIAL EXPRESSION; GESTURE and HEAD NODS; POSTURE; Gaze (eye movement and EYE CONTACT) and NON-VERBAL VOCALIZATIONS. Varyingly NVC conveys much of what we wish to say, and much of what we would wish to withhold. Common functions of non-verbal communication include: the conveying of interpersonal attitudes, the display of emotional states, self-presentation, the regulation of interaction, the giving of meaning to verbal communication, the maintenance of interest in a communicative encounter, the provision of advance warning of the kind of verbal communication to follow and, very importantly, the provision of FEEDBACK in communication.

Affiliation, sexual attraction, rejection, aggression, dominance, submission, appeasement, fear, grief, joy are often best expressed – and in some cases can only be expressed – through NVC. The amount of NVC in the repertoire of different peoples and nations varies considerably in range, emphasis, frequency and rules for use.

Some non-verbal signs appear to be universal – for example, the eyebrow flash used in greeting. There are also many cultural difference in non-verbal communication – for example, the rules regarding proximity, that is the amount of space or distance people should keep between them when communicating, are different for Middle Eastern countries when compared with our own (see PROXEMICS). The use of non-verbal communication may also be influenced by aspects of an individual's personality. Extroverts, for example, are thought to be more expansive in their use of gestures.

Some GENDER differences have also been noted in the use of NVC; for example, several studies have shown that women are more likely to touch each other in conversation than men are.

Certain mental illnesses may also influence a sufferer's non-verbal communicative behaviour; some people suffering schizophrenia, for example, prefer to keep a greater distance between themselves and others than is the norm for the situation.

Ambiguity often surrounds the interpretation of non-verbal signs, not least because quite a lot of body movement is not communicative in intent and it may be difficult for the receiver to know whether a particular sign was intended to communicate a message or not. Judy Gahagan in *Social Interaction and its Management* (UK: Methuen, 1984) argues that the ambiguity surrounding the interpretation of non-verbal signs is essential to one of their major functions in communication – dropping hints. People may wish such messages to be open to varied interpretation so that the hint can be retracted later, if necessary. Non-verbal signs thus provide what she calls 'diplomatic flexibility'. As Gahagan remarks, 'Non-verbal communication is a language adapted for hints and innuendo'. See ACCENT; FAST; NON-VERBAL BEHAVIOUR: REPERTOIRE; OBJECT LANGUAGE; SILENCE.

Communication postulates See POSTULATES OF COMMUNICATION.

Communication theory See *TOPIC GUIDE* under COMMUNICATION THEORY.

Communications Bill (UK), 2002 Legislation proposed by the Labour government to carry forward DEREGULATION of media controls, to abandon rules regulating CROSS-MEDIA OWNERSHIP and to further the 'light touch' approach to the supervision of BROADCASTING. Published jointly by the Department of Culture, Media and Sport and the Department of Trade and Industry, the Bill proposes the scrapping of the following regulatory rules: those (1) preventing single ownership of ITV; (2) preventing ownership of more than one national commercial radio licence; (3) preventing joint ownership of TV and radio stations; (4) obstructing large newspaper groups from acquiring Channel 5 TV or radio licences and (5) preventing non-European ownership.

OfCOM will be the new, all-encompassing regulatory body, its remit to include broadcasting and telecommunications generally, its prime function appearing to be the encouragement of broadcasting as a profit-making industry. In the words of a UK *Guardian* news report, 'Easing the reins on media moguls' (8 May 2002), by Matt Wells and Richard Wray, 'intense lobbying from Mr. Murdoch's acolytes has led to a significant relaxation of the cross-media ownership regulations'.

In the same issue media correspondent Emily Bell, in 'Murdoch must have done a deal', writes of the 'unexpected act of munificence' that 'has stunned the media industry, and judging by its reception in the Commons, half the Labour benches'. Bell believes the proposed legislation to be 'the most significant piece of media reform in the last 20 years'. She conjectures that '... someone in the Cabinet office checked the calendar and realized that they had missed Rupert's birthday ... and they just happened to have a spare channel kicking around in the cupboard'.

The view from across the Atlantic was similarly astonished. *Time* magazine (20 May) declared that the Bill 'threw open the airways to non-EU countries in a way not yet seen in Europe. The rules are a free-for-all: national newspapers and media giants like AOL Time Warner, Viacom and Disney can now buy commercial TV channels, while US concerns like Clear Channel are free to snap up radio stations.'

Granville Williams, writing in *Free Press*, journal of the CAMPAIGN FOR PRESS AND BROAD-CASTING FREEDOM, declares (in 'A market-driven bill', May–June 2002), that the Bill 'is a bonfire of all the rules that were there to protect diversity'. Williams goes on: 'By setting up a centralized Office of Communications (OfCOM), watering down public service broadcasting obligations and loosening ownership regulations, the Bill will sideline quality, accountability and diversity'.

In the same periodical (July–August 2002), American documentary film-maker and freelance writer Williams Rossa Cole, writes, in 'An American view of UK terrestrial TV', that 'the proposed further deregulation of UK terrestrial channels will change the unique content of broadcasting built on a public service ethos into a paltry shadow of itself'. Cole believes 'The key to sustaining consistency, quality and the all-important leashing-in of commercials is to be found in that one word: regulation'.

Pressure from various bodies, including many MPs and a media committee chaired by Lord Puttnam, brought about government modifications of the Bill, ear-marked to become law in the summer of 2003; though opening up UK broadcasting to foreign ownership (a situation now permitted in the US) remained government policy. See BRITISH MEDIA INDUSTRY GROUP (BMIG); COMMANDERS OF THE SOCIAL ORDER; REGULATORY FAVOURS.

Communications conglomerates See CONGLOMERATES: MEDIA CONGLOMERATES.

Communications Decency Act (US) Law passed overwhelmingly by the US Congress and signed by President Bill Clinton in February 1996, designed to ban porn on the Internet (see INTERNET: MONITORING OF CONTENT). The measure has faced a number of formidable and ongoing obstacles; first, the means of exercising censorship on the net; second, arriving at any definition of 'decency' (as compared, for example, with 'obscenity') that can win CONSENSUS in America; third, controlling indecency across frontiers (it is easy for American citizens to 'emigrate' across the net by transmitting under the guise of 'anonymous remailers') and, fourth, persuading other nations to introduce similar legislation. Perhaps the strongest impediment to the Communications Decency Act has been the United States' Constitution, the First Amendment of which prohibits Congress from 'abridging the freedom of speech'. See REGULATION OF INVESTIGATORY POWERS ACT (RIPA) (UK), 2000.

Communications gap Failure of understanding, usually as a result of a lack of information, especially between different age groups, economic classes, political factions or cultural groups. See INFORMATION GAPS.

Communicative rationality Jürgen Habermas in his vast and seminal work on communication and the public sphere, *The Theory of Communicative Action, Vol. 1: Reason and Rationalization* (US: Beacon, 1981), and *Vol. 2: The Critique of Functionalist Reason* (UK: Polity, 1983) poses the notion of commu-nicative rationality as being characterized by truth, appropriateness and sincerity. The operation of these criteria in public life rests upon the existence of free, open and egalitarian DISCOURSE – an 'ideal speech situation' – which in turn makes understanding between elements of society more likely. Communicative rationality rests essentially on an equality of opportunity to participate in communi-cation; still a dream aspiration as far as most societies are concerned.

Communicology The study of the nature, process and meanings sytems of all forms of communica-tion in what Dean C. Barnlund has described as 'the totality of time, space, personality and circum-stance' (in 'A transactional model of communication', K.K. Sereno and C.D. Mortensen (eds), *Foundations of Communication Theory*, US: Harper & Row, 1970).

Community radio Because RADIO BROADCASTING is the cheapest form of MASS COMMU-NICATION it lends itself to 'grass roots' use by communities of interest – geographical, cultural, political. Its potential is to be run by and for local communities, special interests and followings. The development of local radio in the UK has made some progress towards the community ideal, but full independence, in terms of appointments, policy, financing, programming, etc., remains at levels other than the local one.

Though the term community radio was probably first used in the UK by Rachel Powell in the pamphlet *Possibilities for Local Radio* (UK: Centre for Contemporary Cultural Studies, University of Birmingham, December 1965), the idea goes as far back as the BEVERIDGE REPORT, 1950, which proposed the use of VHF frequencies to 'establish local radio stations with independent programmes of their own. How large a scope there would be in Britain for local stations broadcasting programmes controlled by Universities or Local Authorities or public service organizations is not known, but the experiment of setting up some local stations should be tried without delay.'

In 1962 the PILKINGTON REPORT recommended that the BBC provide 'local sound broadcasting' on the basis of 'one service in some 250 localities', stations having a typical range of five miles. The 1971 government White Paper launched COMMERCIAL RADIO, but radio broadcasting through the next decades was to remain under the duopoly of the BBC and IBA.

Pressure to produce a 'third' force in broadcasting in the UK, to consist of highly individual and genuinely local stations, grew in the 1980s. Throughout the country groups dedicated to the furtherance of community radio multiplied, providing information, exerting pressure at national and local levels. The question that needs to be asked in identifying and characterizing community radio is whether, as well as aiming to serve the perceived interests of the community, that radio is also run *by* the community?

Though the most familiar model is generally associated with PUBLIC SERVICE BROADCASTING (PSB) initiatives, variations on community radio are to be found throughout the world, particularly in the United States. There, in January 2000, the Federal Communications Commission (FCC) approved the use of Low Power FM (LPFM), or micro-radio services that would be used for community-orientated programming, to serve schools, civic clubs, state and local governments, churches and other non-profit making organizations. However, the full-scale development of this *microcasting* met with the obstacle of vested interest as represented by corporate radio. The National Association of Broadcasters (NAB), working on behalf of the commercial sector, pressurized Congress for legislation that had the effect of eliminating the majority of the new voices, on the grounds of possible interference with high-power transmission.

As INTERNET services have expanded so has interest in, and development of, web radio, often referred to as 'webcasting'. Both public and private radio broadcasters already make available programmes on the web, but the opportunities for individuals, groups and communities to offer alternative broadcasting services through the net is strictly limited. Web radio draws benefit from low start-up costs and relatively cheap equipment, but, as Hans Ullrich Muhlenfeld points out in an article for the *European Journal of Communication*, March 2002, one of the main hazards in the way of the pro-fileration of web radio is *licensing*. In 'Research note: mass communication as participation. Web-radio in Germany: legal hazards and its contribution to an alternative way of mass communication', the author says that legal complexities, not helped by varying approaches to licensing in the different states within Germany, limit the contribution web radio can make to 'an alternative way of communication as much as the technological possibilities would allow'. Indeed, 'Quite the opposite is true. The legislature forces radio enthusiasts into an outlaw position or a difficult economic situation.' He regrets that currently 'the development of web-radios in Germany can be considered as just another way to transmit well-established ideas and ideologies'. See CONGLOMERATES: MEDIA CONGLOMER-ATES; PRIVATIZATION.

Commutation test A useful device for the analysis of the MEANING and impact of communication presentations such as photographs, paintings and advertisements. We may look at a newspaper picture of inner-city riots. By commuting elements – images or words – in the picture, removing them and replacing them by others, how is the meaning of the picture transformed?

Compassion fatigue The effect of world suffering upon mass media audiences may turn into what has been termed *compassion fatigue*, in which the exposure to suffering becomes too much to take in. In an article, 'Living in limbo', in the *Guardian* (21 April 1989), William Shawcross writes, 'Like Aids, Compassion Fatigue is a contemporary sickness. The symptoms are first a rush of concern for a distant and obviously suffering group, followed by tedium and a feeling of withdrawal that sometimes descends into disdain.'

Compassion fatigue is nurtured by the speed and plethora of communications that bewilder and disorient people everywhere. Shawcross finds this phenomenon a 'truly terrifying sickness. Those it afflicts do not waste away physically – it is their humanity that is harmed.' The compassion factor is further strained by the nature of NEWS itself, restlessly and hungrily switching its focus of attention from one disaster to another. A classic example is the way starvation in Africa was squeezed from news pages and news bulletins by the first Gulf War of 1991, only for the sufferings of the Iraqi people, including the Kurds, to be forgotten in their turn as attention focused on new issues and new tragedies.

The most thorough record of the causes and processes of compassion fatigue is to be found in Susan D. Moeller's book *Compassion Fatigue: How the Media Sell Disease, Famine, War and Death* (US/UK: Routledge, 1999). Defining it as a 'defence mechanism against the knowledge of horror', Moeller is highly critical of what she terms 'formulaic coverage' of world disasters which, in American reporting, suffers what she sees as *Americanization of events* (see EVENT: AMERICANIZATION OF).

Ultimately, Moeller argues the fault lies in piecemeal, often haphazard, selective and potentially hysterical media coverage of foreign news: 'Compassion fatigue, and even more clearly, compassion avoidance, are signals that the coverage of international affairs must change', and that, she asserts, means a need for 'great reporters, producers and editors' and a will 'to invest in such an un-sexy news beat as international affairs'. She urges that events beyond our shores should be reported 'day in day out, year in year out'; in short, 'to get back to the business of reporting all the news, all the time'. See COUPS AND EARTHQUAKES SYNDROME.

Competence In LINGUISTICS, a term used to describe a person's knowledge of his/her own language, its system of rules; his/her competence in understanding an unlimited number of sentences, in spotting grammatical errors, etc.

Compliance, identification and internalization See INTERNALIZATION.

Complicity of users Term employed by Cees J. Hamelink to describe the reluctance of audiences to be told the truth about crises, particularly war situations but also in cases concerning government and corporate matters. In 'Ethics for media users', published in the *European Journal of Communication*, December 1995, Hamelink cites findings that indicated nearly eight out of ten Americans supported restrictions on information imposed by the Pentagon while six out of ten said they believed the military should have exercised greater censorship. 'The [Gulf] war demonstrated that official censorship, jour-nalistic self-censorship and the users' refusal to be informed reinforced each other.' Hamelink goes on, 'The complicity of users was an essential component in the reduction of freedom of media performance.'

Compression technology A key science in the Age of Information, in particular the era of DIGITI-ZATION: the more data becomes available, the broader the available bandwidth, the greater the requirement to compress information, to compact data for transmission. See BROADBAND.

Computer graphics Truly one of the wonders of the modern world: art by numbers – computer numbers – capable of feats of design of astonishing virtuosity and potential. Computer capability in the field of graphics is vast, ranging from representation of three-dimensional technical design, complete with depth cueing, to simulations of space exploration and of nuclear conflict.

Computer graphics supply the visual wizardry of computer games and are also capable of producing animation in the manner of Walt Disney. In 1982, the Disney studios produced the first feature film using this technique, *Tron*. A quarter of the film is conventional live action; the rest is computer graphics or a mixture of computer-generated images with live action. Director of *Tron*, Steven Lisburger, said of animation by computer, 'It gives you a whole world, an entire geography, an entire physics, all from the mind of the computer.'

The implications of this technology do not apply merely to animation film: the computer can 'draw' backgrounds and figures so real, it can simulate everyday objects so accurately, and three-dimension-ally that the movie set of the future might exist only in an electronic console. In science and medicine computer graphics are applied microscopically, simulating, for example, molecular constructs and interaction, thus opening up possibilities in the development of new drugs.

Macroscopically, computer graphics have reconstructed in detail, in wire frame (line drawing), the entire city of Chicago and are serving an increasing role in space design testing. They are also opening up fresh areas of expression for artists as well as scientists.

The first-ever film entirely generated by computer was the highly popular *Toy Story* (1996), from the Disney studios.

Computers in communication Apart from chiefly military use during the Second World War (1939–45), computers did not begin to exert an impact upon society generally until the 1960s. An estimated 9000 computers were in operation in the world in 1960, mainly in the US. Since then the processing of information has been revolutionized.

Picture a vast library of books; the data it contains can now be placed on space-saving discs which, at the touch of a button, will summon up any item of information almost instantly. What in the past might have taken a researcher weeks can now be gathered immediately, not only from one library, but from libraries all over the world. If speed of access is remarkable, capacity is miraculous. The personal details of an entire nation can be recorded and recalled by courtesy of the computer. The implications here for PRIVACY constitute a major issue of our time.

Paradoxically, though the computer saves time it also makes work. It colonizes, and makes formal, information that in the past would have been deemed too complicated to gather; or simply unnecessary. Where, an organization might decide it wishes to know, is a worker at any given second of his or her day, and what exactly, to the minute, is that person doing? The computer can cope. It has enlarged the definition of verifiable fact: once a single item of information is gathered on an individual, a worker, a citizen, the only limit to data recording is infinity.

Every time we use a cash card to draw money from the bank, a credit card to purchase goods from a store or even pay cash for an electronically stamped ticket for the underground, we are leaving traces of ourselves. The convenience is considerable but the intrusion is worrying (see CCTV: CLOSED-CIRCUIT TELEVISION).

The computer has also given birth to a new global disease – the computer virus. Just as hurricanes are given picturesque titles, so are computer viruses whose effects are similarly devastating: 'Dark Avenger', the 'Maltese Amoeba', 'Christmas Tree Worm', 'Tequila' and 'Michelangelo'. In October 1990, for example, a Bulgarian-designed virus named 'Nomenklatura' turned the contents of computers in the UK House of Commons into a mass of jumbled characters. This was the work of Dark Avenger, a disgruntled computer-programmer.

A government-commissioned report in 1992 put the cost to British industry of computer viruses at £1bn. The incidence of computer fraud is probably incalculable. The ability of individuals, often using only the simplest computer equipment, to 'hack in' to sophisticated programs – even those controlling nuclear weapons – poses hair-raising questions concerning security (see HACKER).

The *displacement* of older technology by computers has been far-reaching. The newspaper industry in particular has undergone switches from mechanical, labour-intensive technology to computer-driven production, causing substantial cuts in the labour force. Also, traditional crafts were superseded by processes that were swifter and could be handled by unskilled or semi-skilled labour. At the same time, the computer has helped devolve the opportunity to publish, through the economies of desk-top publishing to communities, special interest groups and educational institutions. Computer literacy has become an essential ingredient of a basic education. Software for graphics and for industrial design has become increasingly sophisticated. Computer games are a worldwide industry. Computer conferencing draws together in discussion and debate business people from all over the world, without the need for plane tickets or the risk of airport hold-ups.

The issues remain: western dominance in computer technology and know-how sustains INFORMATION GAPS between them and developing nations; the dangers, globally, of computer error; the misuses of information, indeed the inaccuracy of information, which may be acted upon to the detriment of the individual; and secrecy – for while the library has its books open for all to see on the shelves, access to computer information requires access to computers, to passwords and the ability to operate the software. See CYBERSPACE; DATA PROTECTION; INTERNET; MEDIA IMPERIALISM; MOBILIZATION; PRIVACY; SURVEILLANCE SOCIETY; TECHNOLOGICAL DETERMINISM.

Conative function of communication See JAKOBSON'S MODEL OF COMMUNICATION, 1958.

Concurrence-seeking tendency In GROUPS, the cohesiveness of members may produce a tendency to agree at all costs, even when the decisions brought about by that unanimity may turn out to be disastrous. In *Groupthink. Psychological Studies of Policy Decisions and Fiascos* (US: Houghton Mifflin, 1972) Irving L. Janis identifies the concurrence-seeking tendency as being one that, developing unchecked in a group's decision-making processes, causes a 'deterioration of mental efficiency, reality testing, and moral judgment'.

Confederates See SLIDER.

Confirmation/disconfirmation Through communication with others we gain feedback on our

SELF-CONCEPT. Several authors, among them Gail Myers and Michele Myers in *The Dynamics of Human Communication* (US: McGraw-Hill, 1985), use the terms *confirmation* and *disconfirmation* to describe the kind of messages about yourself and your view of the world you may receive in feedback. Confirming responses tend to confirm or validate the view of yourself you have put forward and/or the views you have expressed in conversation. Examples of confirming responses include direct acknowledgement of your message, agreement with the content of your message and expression of positive feelings about you.

Disconfirming responses are likely to leave you feeling confused, dissatisfied, and maybe undermined. They are not clear expressions of either approval or rejection; they are ambiguous. Such responses include the *impervious response* when the receiver gives no acknowledgement of your message; the *interrupting response* when the receiver does not let you finish your message; and the *incongruous response* when the receiver's non-verbal response is clearly contrary to the verbal response he/she is making; for example, when a fixed smile accompanies words of praise.

Conglomerates: media conglomerates The increasing cost of entering the media market has, in part, fostered a concentration of ownership in the various sectors of the communications industry. Peter Golding and Graham Murdock in an article entitled, 'Culture, communications and political economy', in *Mass Media and Society* (UK: Arnold, 1996), edited by James Curran and Michael Gurevitch, write, 'The steadily increasing amount of cultural production accounted for by large corporations has long been a source of concern to theorists of democracy … these longstanding worries have been reinforced in recent years by the emergence of multi-media conglomerates with significant stakes across a range of central communications sectors …

'The rise of communications conglomerates adds a new element to the old debate about the potential abuses of owner power. It is no longer a simple case of proprietors intervening in editorial decisions or firing key personnel who fall foul of their political philosophies. Cultural production is also strongly influenced by commercial strategies built around "synergies" which exploit the overlaps between the company's different media interests.'

A communications conglomerate is an amalgam of corporations that operate mainly or wholly with communications or leisure interests – like the Granada group in the UK, which operates the Granada TV network, a large TV rental chain, and a paperback publishing company, and has interests in the cinema, music publishing and numerous other entertainment outlets. Significant sectors of the communications industry are, however, part of *general* conglomerates whose main business concerns are outside the communications field.

The mass media can be seen as related to the industrial system in two ways: first, they are part of it as large-scale buyers and sellers and makers of profit; second, they are preachers of its (industry's) messages. Much of the communications industry is in the control of multinational or transnational corporations – that is, companies that have large-scale investment in many different countries.

John B. Thompson in *The Media and Modernity* (UK: Polity Press, 1995) notes that a handful of multinational conglomerates such as Sony, Disney, Time Warner, Bertelsmann and News Corporation own and control large numbers of the myriad operations within the media industries. Thus the multinationals keep a substantial 'finger in the pie' of these countries' information systems (see MEDIA IMPERIALISM).

The power of such conglomerates is now being extended as a result of technological CONVERGENCE. As Golding and Murdock note, 'For the first time, all forms of communications – written text, statistical data, still and moving images, music and the human voice – can be coded, stored and relayed using the same basic digital array of zeros and ones, the language of computing. As a result, the boundaries that have separated different communications sectors up until now are being rubbed away.'

The concentration of ownership, the increased potential for power which it facilitates, and the interrelationship between the communications industry and other industrial and commercial interests constitute important areas of current media research. See BERLUSCONI PHENOMENON; GLOBALIZATION OF MEDIA; GLOBAL MEDIA SYSTEM: THE MAIN PLAYERS; WORLD TRADE ORGANIZATION (WTO) TELECOMMUNICATIONS AGREEMENT, 1997. See also

TOPIC GUIDE under MEDIA: OWNERSHIP AND CONTROL.

Congruence theory The basic premise of congruence or balance theory is that in the case of two people who like or dislike each other, some patterns of the relationship will be balanced – in congruence – and some will be unbalanced, as when a person dislikes the object which is liked by a liked person. You have congruence if a person you like approves of a cause or affirms a position with which you are in sympathy.

The principle of congruity as advanced by Charles Osgood and Percy Tannenbaum in 'The principle of congruity in the prediction of attitude change', *Psychological Review* 62 (1955) holds that when change in evaluation or attitude occurs, it always occurs in the direction of increased congruity with the prevailing frame of reference.

The opposite of cognitive balance is *cognitive dissonance*, a notion analysed by Leon Festinger in *A Theory of Cognitive Dissonance* (US: Row Peterson, 1957). The theory predicts that people will seek out information that confirms existing attitudes and views of the world or reinforces other aspects of behaviour. Similarly it predicts that people will avoid information that is likely to increase DISSONANCE. If you dislike a person, and you dislike his/her views, what he/she says is unlikely to cause cognitive dissonance, for there is a congruence here. Dissonance is acute when a liked person says something seemingly 'out of character' or fails to accord with expectations or the image held of him/her. See COGNITIVE (AND AFFECTIVE); DEFENSIVE COMMUNICATION; EFFECTS OF THE MASS MEDIA; NEWCOMB'S ABX MODEL OF COMMUNICATION, 1953; RESONANCE; SYMMETRY, STRAIN TOWARDS. See also *TOPIC GUIDE* under COMMUNICATION THEORY.

Connectivity Describes how the global web of computer information services interlink in a process of ever expanding diversification.

Connotation Roland Barthes' second order of SIGNIFICATION in the transmission of messages. The second order comprises connotation and myth. *Denotation*, the first order of signification, is simply a process of identification. The word 'green' represents a colour; but green, at a higher level, can connote the countryside, permission to go ahead, the Irish, etc. *Connotation* is the act of adding information, insight, angle, coloration, value – MEANING, in fact – to denotation.

---

* Roland Barthes, *Mythologies* (UK: Paladin, 1973).

Consensus That which is generally agreed; an area or basis of shared agreement among the majority. Three elements crucial to the function of consensus are: common acceptance of laws, rules and norms; attachment to the institutions that promulgate these laws, rules and norms; and a widespread sense of identity or unity, of similar or identical outlook.

The opposite term is *dissensus*. The elements obviously vary independently, yet the strength of any one helps to strengthen the others. Consensus, states the *International Encyclopaedia of Social Sciences* (ed. D.L. Sills; US: Macmillan and Free Press, 1968), 'operates to restrict the extension of dissensus and to limit conflict …'. Beliefs about consensus 'usually concern the rightness and the qualifications of those in authority to exercise it' and thus relate to the legitimacy of institutions, accepted standards and practices, and dominant principles. They tend to affirm existing patterns of the distribution of authority.

Consensus, therefore, is largely defined by those who have the power and the means to disseminate their definition; and the definition is employed as a means of acknowledging and reinforcing the legitimacy of the powerful. Equally important in this context is the close affinity of outlook of the central cultural system with the central institutional system. Stuart Hood in *Hood on Television* (UK: Pluto, 1980) says 'It is the essence of the idea of consensus that it attempts, at a conscious and unconscious level, to impose the view that there is only one "right" reading. This assumption derives from the view that we – that is the audience and the broadcaster – are united in one nation in spite of class or political definition.' See CULTURAL APPARATUS; DISCURSIVE GAP; IMPARTIALITY; NEWCOMB'S ABX MODEL OF COMMUNICATION, 1953.

Consent, manufacture of Noam Chomsky has defined the *manufacture of consent* as a complex process whereby powerful interests inside democracies such as the US and the UK create in the public mind patterns of acceptance. In an article written for *Index on Censorship* 1 (1987), entitled 'No anti-Israeli vendetta', Chomsky refers to 'devices of thought control' in democratic societies 'which are more pertinent for us than the crude methods of totalitarian states'.

The devices arise from such aspects of the media process as control over resources and the locus of decision-making in the state and private economy. Where state policy on an issue such as the Arab–Israeli conflict, or with regard to Central American politics, is rigorously committed to one side or the other, alternative options that the public might be interested in considering, are declared out of bounds – through what Chomsky describes as 'suppression, falsification, and Orwellian manipulation'.

The process of consent manufacture is most comprehensively analysed in *Manufacturing Consent: The Political Economy of the Mass Media* (US: Pantheon, 1988) by Edward S. Herman and Chomsky. They pose a model of propaganda, and that propaganda issues from the media on behalf of the interests of the POWER ELITE in any society. Essentially this is a GATEKEEPING model in the sense that the media select and shape material that aligns with the interests and VALUES of those who exercise control; in turn, the media censor material that may run counter to those interests and values.

Because the media are institutions often owned, controlled and run by institutions then it follows that the media 'toe the line' with the ideologies of those institutions and those who run them. Herman and Chomsky argue that the propaganda model describes 'the forces that cause the mass media to play a propaganda role' and assert that 'the workings of the media ... serve to mobilize support for the special interests that dominate the state and private activity'.

Leaders of the media 'claim that their news choices rest on unbiased professional and objective criteria, and they have support for the contention within the intellectual community. If, however, the powerful are able to fix the premises of discourse, to decide what the general populace is allowed, to see, hear, and think about, and to "manage" public opinion by regular propaganda campaigns, the standard view of how the system works is at serious odds with reality.'

Herman and Chomsky refer to five interconnecting *filters* in the processing of mass communication news, which serve to regulate and constrain. These are '(1) the size, concentrated ownership, owner wealth and profit orientation of the dominant media firms; (2) advertising as the primary income source of the mass media; (3) the reliance of the media on information provided by government, business, and "experts" funded and approved by these primary sources and agents of power; (4) "flak" as a means of disciplining the media [see FLAK]; and (5) "anti-communism" as a national religion and control mechanism.' Such filters 'interact and reinforce one another'.

The authors are of the view that the media constitute an ideological apparatus for the elite (see IDEOLOGICAL APPARATUSES), but their theory has incurred both criticism and the occasional academic cold shoulder – arguably for the reason that certain truths, while being self-evident, are too uncomfortable to accept.

The manufacture of consent becomes particularly imperative in times of crisis. Following the terrorist attacks on the Pentagon and New York's Twin Towers on 11 September 2001, public consent to the war in Afghanistan, while needing little coaxing from a shocked nation, nevertheless progressed in part as a result of the denial of opportunities for critics to suggest alternative responses.

William Blum points out in *Rogue State: A Guide to the World's Only Superpower* (UK: Zed Books, 2002), 'Many critics of the bombing campaign, who were in vulnerable positions, suffered consequences: a number of university teachers who had spoken out against the war lost their positions or were publicly rebuked by school officials ... the only members of Congress who voted against the "Authorization for Use of Military Force" received innumerable threats and hate mail ...'

Instilling fear in a community, often by exaggerating the threat to *us* from *them*, lies at the heart of large-scale persuasion. Blum poses a question that is high on the agenda of the study of mass communication and the public: 'How do they get away with it?'

In the view of Piers Robinson, in an article 'Theorizing the influence of media on world politics', published in *European Journal of Communication* (December 2001), the media are at their most potent, in aiding the manufacture of public consent, when there is *dissensus*, that is disagreement or uncertainty, within power elites, specifically within government itself. In such circumstances, believes Robinson, the media 'become an active participant in the field of decision-making and action', playing 'an important part in the formulation of government policy'. Robinson argues that 'the importance of the media regarding political outcomes is far greater than allowed for by existing manufacturing consent theory'.

For a detailed survey of Herman and Chomsky's propaganda model, see Jeffrey Klaehn's 'A critical review and assessment of Herman and Chomsky's "Propaganda Model"', in *European Journal of Communication* (June 2002). Klaehn concludes that the theory 'of media behaviour is forceful and convincing' and believes that 'If ever there was a time for the PM [propaganda model] to be included in scholarly debates on media performance, it is now.' See AGENDA-SETTING; DISCOURSE; HEGEMONY. See also *TOPIC GUIDE* under MEDIA: POLITICS AND ECONOMICS; MEDIA: VALUES AND IDEOLOGY.

Consistency There is general agreement among research analysts that the greater the degree of consistency in media coverage, the greater is the likelihood that audiences will absorb the projected version – adopt the PREFERRED READING of reported situations. See EFFECTS OF THE MASS MEDIA; FREQUENCY; INTENSITY.

Consonance, hypothesis of See NEWS VALUES.

Conspiracy of silence The tacit agreement among those with significant information to keep 'mum' about it – say nothing. An early use of the phrase, perhaps even the first as far as broadcasting was concerned, is ascribed to the head of BBC News in 1938 at the time of the Munich crisis, when the BBC failed to broadcast any close examination of Neville Chamberlain's policy of appeasement towards Nazi Germany. See CENSORSHIP; NOELLE-NEUMANN'S SPIRAL OF SILENCE MODEL OF PUBLIC OPINION, 1974.

Conspiracy theory Not so much a theory, more a hunch or suspicion. As far as the media are concerned, the 'conspiracy' relates – in the view of those who claim it exists – to the practice of manip-ulating messages in order to support those who own the means of communication, their social CLASS (i.e. middle and upper) and their interests. The conspiracy theorists argue that in a capitalist society where the media are owned or strongly influenced by the capitalist ESTABLISHMENT, information is shaped to underpin existing social, economic and political conditions (see CONSENT, MANUFACTURE OF).

In his 'Introduction' to the GLASGOW UNIVERSITY MEDIA GROUP publication *Bad News* (UK: Routledge & Kegan Paul, 1976), Richard Hoggart ventures to locate two levels or forms of conspiracy theory, high and low, the one aligning with the Marxist view of media operation, the other with the generality of people who at some time or another suspect that the media project the interests and the value systems of those who own, control or run them. See HEGEMONY.

Constituency Term generally applied to an electoral area that returns a parliamentary candidate; but it is also used by researchers to refer to the readership of a newspaper, and carries with it the implication that the reader's political views may be influenced by the paper's coverage of events. The notion of audience as constituency was particularly prevalent in the age of PRESS BARONS such as – in the UK – Lords Northcliffe, Rothermere and Beaverbrook, who claimed access to political decision-making on the strength of the constituency of their papers' readership.

Consumerization Describes a vision of contemporary life dominated by the marketplace and prompting fears that, with the global advance of transnational corporations, and their substantial buying-in to media and CULTURE generally, society has become one-dimensionalized – the consumer dimension.

Some commentators see consumption as being a modern substitute for religion, spending a substitute for praying, while the cathedrals of today are shopping malls. Big business sponsors art and thereby brings it under the wing of consumer criteria – is there a market for it and will it directly or indirectly make a profit? Big business sponsors schools and thus is in a position to appropriate education itself.

American writer Herbert J. Schiller, until his death in 2000, proved himself a scourge of corporate intrusions into the life of communities. In *Culture Inc.: The Corporate Takeover of Public Expression* (UK/US: Oxford University Press, 1989), Schiller believed, 'the Corporate voice, not surprisingly, is the loudest in the land' and it also rings around the world. He was of the view that consumerism 'as it is propagated by the transnational corporate system and carried to the four corners of the world by new information age technologies, now seems triumphant'. He talked of 'corporate pillaging of the national information supply' and the 'proprietory control of information'.

Even the museum has 'been enlisted as a corporate instrument': history is adopted for corporate use through sponsorship. Thus eventually museums become reliant on corporate 'approval' of the past. The pressure upon them is to choose to record the kind of history that suits the corporate purpose. Corporate power in the field of communication is so great, Schiller argued, that the active-audience paradigm is called into question: 'A great emphasis is given to the "resistance", "subversion", and "empowerment" of the viewer. Where this resistance and subversion of the audience lead and what effects they have on the existing structure of power remain a mystery.'

He expressed the view that 'It is not a matter of people being dupes, informational or cultural. It is that human beings are not equipped to deal with a pervasive disinformational system – administered from the command posts of social order – that assails the senses through all cultural forms and channels.'

Schiller's theme is echoed in the work of the French philosopher Jean Baudrillard whose *The Consumer Society: Myths and Structures* made its first appearance in English – translated by Chris Turner and published by Sage – in 1998. See McDONALDIZATION.

* Jeff Hearn and Sasha Roseneil (eds), *Consuming Cultures: Power and Resistance* (UK: Macmillan, 1999); Peter N. Stearns, *Consumerization in World History: The Global Transformation of Desire* (UK: Routledge, 2001).

Consumer sovereignty A phrase used in the Peacock Report, 1985, summarizing the attitude towards BROADCASTING of the Committee on Financing the BBC. The Committee took the marketplace view that the customer knows best and that consumer tastes should be the guiding principle of RADIO and TELEVISION programming. See PUBLIC SERVICE BROADCASTING.

Consumption behaviour Term used by researchers to describe the ways audiences respond to product marketing – attitudes towards ADVERTISING, knowledge of commercials and people's buying behaviour. At the nub of market research into consumption behaviour is motivation. Why do people watch a TV commercial, what makes them pay attention and heed the message?

Regularly cited are three major reasons for a positive audience response: (1) social utility – watching commercials in order to gain information about the 'social significance' of products or brands, and the association of advertising objects with social roles and lifestyles; (2) communication utility – watching in order to provide a basis for later interpersonal communication; (3) vicarious consumption – participating at second hand in desired lifestyles as a means of indirect association with those people possessing glamour or prestige. See ADVERTISING: MAINSTREAMERS, ASPIRERS, SUCCEEDERS AND REFORMERS; VALS TYPOLOGY.

Contagion effect Power of the media to create a craze or even an epidemic. Examples of this are the so-called Swastika Epidemic of 1959–60 where an outbreak of swastika daubing in the US was accelerated by media coverage, and the UK Mods vs Rockers seaside battles in the 1960s. Debate continues on whether media coverage 'worsens' or prompts street riots, often named copycat riots. Stanley Cohen in 'Sensitization: the case of the Mods and Rockers', in *The Manufacture of News* (UK: Constable, 1973), edited by Cohen and Jock Young, writes, 'Constant repetition of the warring gangs' image … had the effect of giving these loose collections a structure they never possessed and a mythology with which to justify the structure' and the court scenes at which those arrested by the police were tried were 'arenas for acting out society's morality plays'. See EMPOWERMENT; MEDIA IMAGES; MORAL PANIC.

Content analysis Research into mass media content identifies, categorizes, describes and quantifies short-term and long-term trends. An early and most valuable descriptive trend study was that of Ernst Kris and Nathan Leites in 1947. In 'Trends in 20th century propaganda', in B. Berelson and M. Janowitz (eds), *Reader in Public Opinion and Communication* (US: Free Press, 1947), the authors traced the trend in propaganda from the First World War (1914–18) to the Second (1939–45), identifying a changing style towards a less emotional, less moralistic and more truthful orientation.

Content analysis serves an important function by comparing the same material as presented in different media within a nation, or between different nations; or by comparing media content with some explicit set of standards or abstract categories. On the basis of the existing body of quantitative and qualitative research, several broad generalizations may be hazarded about the content of MASS COM-MUNICATION: what is communicated by the mass media is a highly selected sample of all that is available for communication; what is received and consumed by the potential AUDIENCE is a highly selected sample of all that is communicated; more of what is communicated is classifiable as enter-taining rather than informative or educative, and, because the mass media are aimed at the largest possible audience, most material is simple in form and uncomplicated in content. See AUDIENCE MEASUREMENT; ETHNOGRAPHIC (APPROACH TO AUDIENCE MEASUREMENT); GLASGOW UNIVERSITY MEDIA GROUP. See also *TOPIC GUIDE* under RESEARCH METHODS.

Control group In comparative research methods, the neutral body against which a test group is measured. Thus, in the case of AUDIENCE MEASUREMENT, the test group is exposed to a TV programme, for example, and their responses analysed against identical monitoring of the control group who have not seen the programme.

Control of the media See MEDIA CONTROL.

Conventions Established practices within a particular CULTURE or SUBCULTURE. Conventions are identifiable in every form of communication and behaviour – some strict, like rules of grammar, others open to wider application, such as dress. Conventions are largely culture-specific and context-specific. It is an accepted convention that a candidate dress smartly for a job interview yet it would be deemed unconventional if he or she appeared on the beach clad in the same manner.

Media practices have established many conventions that have become so familiar they appear 'the natural way to do things'. TELEVISION news holds to the convention of having on-screen news-readers; documentaries generally hold to the convention of having a voice-over narration. Innovators – for example, in the arts – break with convention. The shock of the new often stirs among the con-ventional a sense of affronted VALUES. The chances of the new becoming conventionalized will depend on various factors, such as opinion leaders, prevalent tastes and fashions, even newsworthiness. See LEADERSHIP; REDUNDANCY.

Convergence The coming together of communication devices and processes; a major feature of the development of media technology in the 1990s onwards. In *Of Media and People* (US: Sage, 1992), Everette E. Dennis writes of forms converging 'into a single electronically based, computer-driven mode that has been described as the nearly universal integration of systems that retrieve, process, and store text, data, sound, and image', in short, multi-media. Dennis points out that convergence is far more than 'the stuff of hardware and software: it is the driving force that has spurred major change in the media industries and almost everywhere else'.

Convergence has operated at the technical and operational level and at the level of ownership and control. Just as individual items of hard and software have been centralized into one multi-media outfit, so media production has been centralized into fewer corporate hands, most of these transnational. With convergence has come a blurring of media functions: with the aid of a modem, the telephone permits us to surf the INTERNET or, regulation permitting, to summon up channels of screen entertainment. We can work from home, shop from home, summon up the world from home (if we are lucky enough to be able to pay for the technology).

A further question is whether technical and operational convergence will lead to transcultural convergence and extend the reach of what some would see as the already well-established strategy of cultural and MEDIA IMPERIALISM. For those that support this thesis, GLOBALIZATION fosters homogeneity and works in the interests of the powerful producers of cultural artefacts often located in western countries – especially the US – whilst undermining the indigenous cultures of the less powerful receivers of such artefacts.

However, such a view is seen by others as underestimating the degree to which those who receive such artefacts adapt them in the process of absorbing them into the host culture. The resultant blend may limit the degree of convergence. It should also be noted that artefacts destined for a wide market are often tailored to take account of differentiation within the market and in this process characteristics of the differing host cultures may be considered in the construction of the artefact. Moreover the flow of cultural artefacts is arguably more complex than the cultural or media imperialism thesis suggests. A number of theorists point to the essential heterogeneity of culture(s) and argue consequently that it is unlikely that cultural convergence would occur. See CYBERSPACE; DIGITIZATION; MOBILIZA-TION. See also *TOPIC GUIDE* under MEDIA: PROCESSES AND PRODUCTION.

Conversational styles In a study of conversation among friends at dinner, entitled *Conversational Style: Analysing Talk Among Friends* (US: Ablex, 1984), Deborah Tannen identifies different conversational styles, which she terms 'High Considerateness' and 'High Involvement'. Each style has different priorities. The 'High Considerateness' style places a premium on being considerate of others in conversation, of not interrupting, of listening to what someone is saying. The 'High Involvement' style on the other hand is characterized by enthusiastic involvement in a conversation and this may be at the expense of giving sufficient space to others.

One style is not necessarily better than the other but often reflects cultural differences; for example, in her study, the Briton was the most considerate of all. However, this categorization can help explain problems in INTERPERSONAL COMMUNICATION. To the highly considerate speaker the highly involved speaker may seem an exhibitionist whilst the highly involved speaker may perceive the highly considerate speaker as aloof or distant.

Co-orientation approach See McCOMBS AND SHAW'S AGENDA-SETTING MODEL OF MEDIA EFFECTS, 1976.

Copycat effect See CONTAGION EFFECT.

Copyrighting culture See CULTURE: COPYRIGHTING CULTURE.

Core nations, peripheral nations Cees Hamelink makes this differentiation with regard to the distribution of information in and between nations in 'Information imbalance: core and periphery', in *Questioning The Media: A Critical Introduction* (UK: Sage, 1990), edited by John Downing, Ali Mohammadi and Annabelle Sreberny-Mohammadi. Hamelink argues that the transnational picture of information distribution is one of *imbalances* between core – usually industrial – nations such as the US, Canada, Western Europe, Japan and Australia, and the economic periphery, predominantly rural countries such as Africa, parts of Asia and Latin America.

Peripheral countries, in comparison with core nations, possess fewer newspapers, broadcasting stations, telephones and less computer hardware. Hamelink believes 'Information imbalance ... undermines cultural self-determination.' A number of critical questions arise from this situation. Might, for example, imbalances be resolved through greater integration – links – between core and peripheral nation systems? Should peripheral nations bargain for 'fairer schemes and terms of trade, for cheaper transfers of technology' by pooling resources and energy? Or, more radically, should the peripherals dissociate themselves – de-link – from international networks that hamper development?

Collective effort across the periphery, argues Hamelink, 'in itself requires the solving of many old and difficult conflicts among the poorer countries themselves'. In addition, it requires 'a visionary leadership willing to forego the immediate benefits of links with the core'. See INFORMATION GAPS; NEW WORLD INFORMATION ORDER; YAMOUSOUKROU DECLARATION.

Corporate commitment See IMPARTIALITY.

Corporate speech Best defined in a US context: that speech which is employed in the public domain by corporations, most obviously in terms of advertising, but applicable to a whole host of discourses in which industry and commerce address the public. Corporate speech in the US is classified as having the same right as the speech of individuals and is thus protected by the First Amendment of the US Constitution that guarantees freedom of speech. Thus, a tobacco company cannot be restrained from propagandizing, through public advertisement, its products. In such a case, corporate speech could be deemed life-threatening.

Even taxes on ADVERTISING have been fought against by corporations. An attempt to impose an advertising tax by the State of Florida in 1987 was repealed within six months, due to corporate pressure. According to Herbert I. Schiller in *Culture, Inc.: The Corporate Takeover of Public Expression* (UK: Oxford University Press, 1989), corporations use the First Amendment to do two things: protect their profits and duck social accountability. See CONGLOMERATES: MEDIA CONGLOMERATES.

Corporations and media See CONGLOMERATES: MEDIA CONGLOMERATES; CONSUMERIZATION; CULTURE: CONSUMER CULTURE; CULTURE: GLOBALIZATION OF; PRIVATIZATION. See also *TOPIC GUIDE* under MEDIA INSTITUTIONS.

Cosmopolite and localite channels The situation in which the sender and receiver of a message belong to different social systems or subsystems is referred to as *cosmopolite. Localite* channels are those in which both sender and receiver belong to the same social system or subsystem.

Cosmopoliteness In most social structures there are individuals who have considerable awareness of other social situations and frequent contact with those outside their own social structure. In general the more cosmopolite an individual is, the more receptive he/she is to messages containing new ideas.

Couch potato US term for confirmed and dedicated TV viewer. *20th Century Words* (UK: Oxford University Press, 1999), edited by John Ayto, says that the term was first used in 1979, its 'neat encapsulation of vacuous indolence' ensuring 'its success in the censorious 1980s'.

Counter-culture A type of SUBCULTURE firmly antagonistic to the dominant or prevailing CULTURE of a community. The term is generally used to describe the collection of mainly middle-class youth cultures that developed in the 1960s and whose central feature was the call for the adoption of alternative social structures and lifestyles. In 'Sub cultures, cultures and class', John Clarke and others in *Resistance Through Rituals* (UK: Hutchinson, 1976), edited by Stuart Hall and Tony Jefferson, explore some of the distinguishing features of such a counter-culture as compared with other types of youth subcultures. Its opposition to the dominant cultures took very open political and ideological forms and went beyond the registering of complaint and resistance to the elaborate construction of alternative institutions.

More recently examples of counter-cultural protests that have received significant media attention are those surrounding ecological issues, protests that challenge many of the environmental assumptions and values of western societies. 'Eco-warriors', as the more radical of the protesters are sometimes called, may adopt a radically different lifestyle based on the principles underpinning their protest. A favoured communications device of contemporary counter-cultures is the INTERNET, its global reach aiding the international nature of protests concerning corporate and state threats to the environment. Through the net the likeminded can bond, plan, organize, most famously focusing on organized protests wherever the nations of the World Trade Organization meet, such as in Seattle, London, Prague or Genoa; and by their collective protests commanding global media attention.

Countermodernization See CULTURE: GLOBALIZATION OF.

Coups and earthquakes syndrome Term coined by American journalist Mort Rosenblum to describe the western attitude to news emanating from 'Third World' developing nations in, for example, Africa and South America. For events in such countries to be deemed of NEWS VALUE they must come under the category of 'coups and earthquakes' – the overthrow of governments by force or natural disasters. Rosenblum wrote *Coups and Earthquakes* (US: Harper & Row) in 1979 but current practice seems not to have improved.

Mark D. Alleyne in *News Revolution: Political and Economic Decisions about Global Information* (UK: Macmillan, 1997), referring to the 'coups and earthquakes' syndrome, writes, 'It sometimes seems that there is a malicious attempt to stereotype these countries, and this attitude might be propelled by various factors, including racism, political ideology and ethnocentrism.' Alleyne believes that 'In this way, international news can be seen as a weapon of those with power in the international system, a tool to maintain the status quo, at least in regard to the inferior status of some peoples and nation-states.'

The key problem lies with prevailing news values, for the definition of news 'controls the way in which journalists decide what is important'. At the same time 'journalists often use vague, shorthand terms to describe complex issues and regions'. For example, the term 'Third World' is a 'woolly generalization'. See COMPASSION FATIGUE.

Crab and track See SHOT.

Creole See COMMUNICATION: INTERCULTURAL COMMUNICATION.

Crime and the media An issue of considerable and increasing concern is the televisualization of crime, invariably violent crime, as played out in the courts on both sides of the Atlantic. Most spectacular have been the trials of O.J. Simpson in the US and Rose West in the UK. In each case the media have been accused of, if not interfering with the course of justice, influencing it; taking it out of its legal framework and transforming proceedings into SOAP OPERA – titillating, often salaciously and obsessively interested in the minutae of violence.

Richard Osborn in an article 'Crime, media, violence', in *Free Press*, March–April 1996, argues that 'Crime and television are the two great cultural definers of our present era and when they are combined they are a lethal force.' Crime has NEWS VALUE aplenty: it is as Osborn puts it 'a seriously nasty business'. It is 'incredibly exciting, threatening, horrifying, fascinating and repellent all at once'. Consequently 'it makes bloody good television'. Thus TV 'wants a big slice of the action when it comes to real-life crime, and that means money, fame, news-doctoring and media trials in which the plodding business of the courts gets swamped by the video in the corner'. In Osborn's view, crime has become 'the staple diet of television' thus affecting the public's perception of crime, the 'way it thinks about crime' and the ways it responds to it. See CRIME: TYPES OF CRIME ON SCREEN; VIOLENCE AND THE MEDIA; VIOLENCE ON TV: THE DEFENCE.

Crime: types of crime on screen Five types of on-screen crime are identified by Jessica Allen, Sonia Livingstone and Robert Reiner in an article 'True lies: changing images of crime in British postwar cinema', in the *European Journal of Communication*, March 1998. The authors surveyed 1461 crime-related films released between 1945 and 1991, and popular with the public, reporting that 'contrary to general beliefs about increased crime content of the media … our data shows a constant rate of representation, at least in the cinema over 50 years'.

The authors discuss *primary, consequential, collateral* and *contextual* crimes. To the first, that which animates the NARRATIVE, they ascribe the term McGUFFIN, borrowed from film director Alfred Hitchcock, 'to refer to the object whose pursuit provides the driving force of the narrative'. Consequential crimes are those that are committed in the course of, or in order to cover up the McGuffin, while collateral crimes are not directly related to the McGuffin though they may be committed by the central criminals. Contextual crimes may also be unrelated to the McGuffin, the primary crime, 'but portray aspects of the wider society'.

Chief among McGuffins, say Allen, Livingstone and Reiner, is homicide, 48 per cent of their sample films having a homicide McGuffin – contrasting substantially with crime figures in the real world, where 90 per cent of recorded offences are property crimes. The authors noted an increase in contextual crimes during the 1960s: 'This is significant because it is contextual crime perhaps even more than the McGuffin which creates a sense of society as a whole being threatened by crime.'

This trend is linked to the 'increasing predominance of police heroes rather than amateur "sleuths"'; 'towards an increasingly graphic representation of violence in the portrayal of crime'; the degree to which crime traumatizes the victim, and the perception that crime has social origins. In their analysis, Allen, Livingstone and Reiner emphasize the complexity of the representation of crime in contexts of the 'collapse of moral certainties' in society, the dominance of Hollywood, the retreat from strict forms of CENSORSHIP and the demographic nature of AUDIENCE – largely made up of young people.

* Maggie Wykes, *News, Crime and Culture* (UK: Pluto, 1999).

Crimes of self-publicity See TERRORISM AS COMMUNICATION.

Crisis definition How do we know when a crisis is a crisis? One answer is – when the media tell us it is a crisis. Their capacity for AGENDA-SETTING, of selecting the front-page headlines or the lead stories, can not only crystallize the notion of crisis in the public mind but in some cases help precipitate one, at least in the sense that people in authority – such as governments – can be forced into a crisis response to a crisis stimulus.

Critical news analysis Generic term for a wide-ranging and complex approach to the analysis of the presentation of NEWS in the mass media. Perhaps the most influential starting point in the UK for this critical analysis is the book by Stanley Cohen and Jock Young (eds), *The Manufacture of News: Social*

Problems, Deviance and the Mass Media (UK: Constable, 1973). They, along with other commentators of the time, such as Professor Stuart Hall, and research teams such as the GLASGOW UNIVERSITY MEDIA GROUP, contributed to a developing awareness that the news is *socially constructed* and that it is both a social and an *ideological* construct. In other words, news isn't neutral. Critical news analysis focuses on content, presentation and language.

Emphasizing the importance of the linguistic assembly of messages in his book *Language in the News: Discourse and Ideology and the Press* (UK: Routledge, 1991), Roger Fowler says, 'There are different ways of saying the same thing, and they are not random, accidental alternatives'; thus there can never be 'a value-free reflection of "facts"'. Two processes occur: *selection* (see AGENDA-SETTING; GATEKEEPING; NEWS VALUES), followed by *transformation* according to the dictates of the MEDIUM and the influences upon all the encoders involved. Critical news analysis is essentially a process of *decoding*. For an excellent summary of the range of approaches developed through the 1980s and into the 1990s, see Chapter 12 of Fowler, 'Conclusion: prospects for critical analysis'. See HEGEMONY; IMPARTIALITY; JOURNALISM; SAPIR–WHORF LINGUISTIC RELATIVITY HYPOTHESIS.

Cropping Photographs for publication are rarely printed exactly as they emerge from the original negative or electronic transmission. They are very often 'cropped', that is cut to fulfil certain objectives: the space requirements of a page; to maximize impact; to serve aesthetic or ideological criteria. Generally pictures are cropped to get rid of redundant detail that might detract from the central thrust and drama of the picture's message. See ANCHORAGE; PREFERRED READING.

Cross-media ownership That is, where a PRESS BARON or corporation owns a range of media, newspapers, TV and RADIO stations. Resistance to cross-media ownership acts on the principle that to own the press and BROADCASTING in any particular area – city, district or region – constitutes a threat to media diversity and hence to the PLURALITY of the media; and such resistance has been incorporated in many countries in regulations designed to prevent monopoly.

In contrast, the corporate position is that regulation of cross-media ownership is an unnecessary inpediment to business practice and the making of profits. It follows that corporate owners of media seek DEREGULATION by pressurizing governments to abandon rules (generally made in the public interest) in favour of the free market (generally operating to the advantage of the corporations).

The issue of cross-media ownership has become a matter of profound concern, at least among media-watchers if not the public, because it trails other critical issues, such as the maintenance of quality, the integrity and independence of information; in short, the preservation of *public service* in the media. See COMMUNICATIONS BILL (UK), 2002; PRIVATIZATION; REGULATORY FAVOURS. See also *TOPIC GUIDE* under MEDIA: OWNERSHIP AND CONTROL.

Cryptography Secret LANGUAGE; the transfer of messages into secret codes. A cryptograph is anything written in *cypher*. See DATA PROTECTION.

Cues See BARNLUND'S TRANSACTIONAL MODEL OF COMMUNICATION, 1970.

Cultivation As used by US communication analyst George Gerbner, the term describes the way that the mass media system relates to the CULTURE from which it grows and which it addresses. The media 'cultivate' attitudes and VALUES in a culture. For example, audiences are cultivated into rejecting certain acts of violence while at the same time being cultivated into accepting or tolerating others. See MAINSTREAMING.

Cultivation differential The difference between the perceptions of heavy and light viewers on a particular aspect of social reality. Several researchers have focused on the influence of TV upon an individual's perception of social reality. George Gerbner and others in 'The demonstration of power: violence profile No. 10', in *Journal of Communication* 29 (1979), report on findings regarding the effect of TV portrayal of violence on certain viewer's perceptions of the incidence of real violence. They found that heavy viewers of TV were more likely to be influenced by, more likely to accept, the image of reality presented by TV programmes than light viewers. See EFFECTS OF THE MASS MEDIA; PORNOGRAPHY; VIOLENCE ON TV: THE DEFENCE.

Cultural apparatus 'Taken as a whole,' writes C. Wright Mills in *Power, Politics and People* (US:

Oxford University Press, 1963), 'the cultural apparatus is the lens of mankind through which men see; the medium by which they interpret and report what they see.' It is composed of 'all the organizations and *milieux* in which artistic, intellectual and scientific work goes on, and of the means by which such work is made available to circles, publics and masses'.

The cultural apparatus features large in the process of guiding experience, defining social truths, establishing standards of credibility, image making and opinion forming, and is 'used by dominant institutional orders'. It confers prestige and the 'prestige of culture is among the major means by which powers of decision are made to seem part of an unchallengeable authority'.

Wright Mills goes on to argue that, no matter how internally free the 'cultural workman', as he names the artist or intellectual, he/she is intrinsically part of the cultural apparatus that tends in every nation to become a 'close adjunct of national authority and a leading agency of nationalist propaganda'. CULTURE and authority overlap and this overlap 'may involve the ideological use of cultural products and of cultural workmen for the legitimation of power, and the justification of decisions and policies'. See CONSENSUS; HEGEMONY; IDEOLOGICAL STATE APPARATUSES.

Cultural capital French philosopher Pierre Bourdieu makes the distinction between economic capital and cultural capital – the latter being the knowledge, tastes, attitudes, VALUES and assumptions that individuals or groups possess with regard to various cultural artefacts and endeavours, in particular those of what might be termed legitimate culture – though definitions of such legitimacy are open to contest. An individual's cultural capital clearly may influence the way in which messages may be encoded or decoded. Advertisers, for example, often make assumptions about the cultural capital of the target consumer groups when constructing advertising messages.

A popular late 1960s' record may be used as the soundtrack in a television commercial not just because of its musical merits but because its location within a particular youth culture may be felt to give the product connotational and ideological meanings related to the desire for freedom and independence. The message may be read this way, though not necessarily accepted, by consumers familiar both with the song and the youth culture but is unlikely to be read as such by someone unfamiliar with either.

The notion of cultural capital is linked to CLASS, GENDER, ethnic identity and STATUS in that some cultural capital is more highly valued than others by the dominant groups within a society, and indeed possession of such cultural capital is often widely taken as a sign of membership of these groups. There is among these groups a tendency to denigrate popular cultural capital. Popular cultural capital on the other hand can be seen as a rich source of responses to, including resistance to, social subordination. See CULTURE; HIGHBROW; TASTE CULTURES; YOUTH CULTURE.

* Pierre Bourdieu, *Distinction* (UK: Routledge, 1984) and *The Field of Cultural Production* (UK: Polity Press, 1993).

Cultural diamond See GRISWOLD'S CULTURAL DIAMOND MODEL, 1994.

Cultural Indicators research project See MAINSTREAMING.

Cultural industry See FRANKFURT SCHOOL OF THEORISTS.

Cultural memory That which the community recalls, re-encodes in a process of making sense of the present. Cultural memory contrasts with what has been termed *instrumental* or *electronic* memory, that which can be numerically encoded and recorded, as on a computer. In *Communication, Culture and Hegemony: From the Media to Mediation* (UK: Sage, 1993), Jésus Martín-Barbero writes, 'In contrast to instrumental memory "cultural memory" does not work with pure information or as a process of linear accumulation'; rather, it is 'articulated through experience and events. Instead of simply accumulating, it filters and weighs.'

It is not, says Martín-Barbero, 'a memory we can use, but the memory of which we are made'. What threatens cultural memory inflicts damage on culture itself, particularly in cultures where tensions exist, dramatically, between tradition and progress. Says Martín-Barbero, a part of whose book focuses on media development in South American countries, 'In the dilemma of choice between underdevelopment and modernization, cultural memory does not count and has no place': a situation he and other scholars of cultural change view with dismay.

Cultural metaphor Generally an image, or a series of images, seen to represent a culture. The expression 'An Englishman's home is his castle' attempts to classify the English – perhaps even stereotype them – by means of a dominant image or practice. In this case a number of characteristics are drawn together in the image of home as something to be defended as though it were a castle – private, self-contained, constructed to be resistant to outside intrusions and influences.

According to Martin J. Gannon and associates in *Understanding Global Cultures: Metaphorical Journeys Through 17 Countries* (US: Sage, 1994), the use of identifying metaphors can assist us in grasping the nature of our own and other cultures. Gannon confirms the saying quoted above, arguing that the dominant cultural metaphor of Britain is the house, with its solid, firm foundations, rooted in the past; a place of privacy, walls and hedges. He and his associates take the view that 'the dynamics of the culture of a particular nation can be best understood through the use of one dominant metaphor that reflects the basic values that all or most of its members accept without question or conscious thought'.

The authors cite in detailed chapters of explanation the following metaphors that represent some of the cultures on their 'metaphorical journey': American football (USA), the dance of Shiva (India), the family altar (China), the opera (Italy), wine (France), lace (Belgium), ballet (Russia), the symphony orchestra (Germany), the bullfight (Spain), the kibbutz (Israel), the garden (Japan), the stuga or summer home (Sweden), the marketplace (Nigeria) and the coffee house (Turkey). For Ireland, home of the Blarney Stone, the authors perhaps appropriately select as the country's presiding metaphor, conversation.

Cultural modes The *literate* mode is rooted in the written word; the *oral* mode is spoken or visual. Traditionally they have been aligned to CLASS differences; that is, the upper, better-educated classes have lived by a literate mode of cultural interaction – the *dominant* CULTURE, while the more 'untutored' classes have relied upon oral modes. With the advent of electronic media the oral mode has become increasingly assertive. It is essentially the mode of film and television, though both media still tend to be run by a class educated in the literate mode and whose perceptions are conditioned by such a mode.

Cultural or citizen rights and the media In 'Rights and representations: public discourse and cultural citizenship', in *Television and Common Knowledge* (UK: Routledge, 1999), edited by J. Gripsrud, Graham Murdock poses the following citizen rights – what citizens have the right to expect from the mass media: (1) the right to information; (2) to have access to 'the greatest possible diversity of representations of personal and social experience'; (3) to knowledge, that is, access to 'frameworks of interpretation' that facilitate understanding of the links between issues, the causes that lead to effects, and the processes by which knowledge is assembled and represented to the public; and (4) to participation in a contemporary context where there is a demand from individuals and groups 'to speak about their own lives and aspirations in their own voice'.

The exercise of 'full citizenship', Murdock argues, depends upon the media's fulfilling these rights of information, experience, interpretation and participation. See *TOPIC GUIDE* under MEDIA ETHICS; MEDIA ISSUES AND DEBATES; MEDIA: VALUES AND IDEOLOGY; REPRESENTATION.

Cultural racism See RACISM.

Culture The sum of those characteristics that *identify* and *differentiate* human societies – a complex interweaving of many factors. The culture of a nation is made up of its LANGUAGE, history, traditions, climate, geography, arts, social, economic and political norms, and its system of VALUES; and such a nation's size, its neighbours and its current prosperity condition the nature of its culture.

There are cultures within cultures. Thus reference is made to working-class culture or middle-class culture. Organizations and institutions can have their own cultures (see ORGANIZATION CULTURES). We refer to cultural *epochs* resulting from developments – social, political, industrial, technological – that create cultural change.

Mass production and the mass media have contributed immensely to cultural change, giving rise to what critics have termed mass culture and disapprovingly portrayed as manufactured, manipulated, force-fed, marketed like soap powder and, because of its unique access to vast audiences, open to abuse of the mass by the powerful.

Alan Swingewood in *The Myth of Mass Culture* (UK: Macmillan, 1977) argues, however, that there 'is no mass culture, or mass society; but there is an ideology of mass culture and mass society'. The ideology is real enough, but the thing itself he describes as myth: 'If culture is the means whereby man affirms his humanity and his purposes and his aspirations to freedom and dignity then the concept and theory of mass culture are their denial and negation.'

Culture is transmitted through SOCIALIZATION to new members of a social group or society. The media play an important role in this process. A central concern of culturalist studies of the media is the degree to which the media's output may both reflect and communicate the culture of the more powerful social groups in that society at the expense of the less powerful. By asserting one culture against others, the media help to nurture a *dominant culture* and relegate rival cultures to the realms of deviance.

---

* Raymond Williams, *The Long Revolution* (UK: Chatto & Windus, 1961, and Penguin, 1965) and *Culture* (UK: Fontana, 1981); Richard Hoggart, *The Uses of Literacy* (UK: Penguin, 1958); James Curran and Michael Gurevitch, *Mass Media and Society* (UK: Edward Arnold, 1991 and subsequent editions); Nick Stevenson, *Understanding Media Cultures* (UK: Sage, 1995); Colleen Roach (ed.), *Communication and Culture in War and Peace* (UK: Sage, 1995); Peter Brooker, *Cultural Theory: A Glossary* (UK: Arnold, 1999); Andrew Tudor, *Decoding Culture: Theory and Method in Cultural Studies* (UK: Sage, 1999); Ben Highmore, *Everyday Life and Cultural Theory: An Introduction* (UK: Routledge, 2001); Brian McNair, *Striptease Culture* (UK: Routledge, 2002); David Hesmondhalgh, *The Cultural Industries: An Introduction* (UK: Sage, 2002).

Culture: consumer culture Arguably consumer culture is the prevailing culture of late modernity in western societies. Don Slater in *Consumer Culture & Modernity* (UK: Polity Press, 1997) argues that 'it is more generally bound up with central values, practices and institutions which define western modernity, such as choice, individualism and market relations'. For Slater its 'defining feature' is that it 'denotes a social arrangement in which the relation between lived culture and social resources, between meaningful ways of life and the symbolic and material resources on which they depend, is mediated through markets'. The media and cultural industries obviously play a pivotal role in the operation of consumer culture, and the nature of this relationship is the focus of much research.

Culture: copyrighting culture In the global context of communication, and in view of the open access properties of the INTERNET, a question of growing importance is – to whom does a TEXT or work belong? (see TEXT: INTEGRITY OF THE TEXT). R.V. Bettig, in *Copyrighting Culture: The Political Economy of Intellectual Property* (US/UK: Westview Press, 1996), addresses this concern, arguing that with information/knowledge becoming one of the chief commercial industries in the current age, the control of CULTURE has fallen to a number of transnational corporations (TNCs) through their ownership of copyright.

The fear of such TNCs is copyright piracy on a world scale, and their ambition is to extend, globally, measures to protect intellectual property from piracy. The Berne Convention laid initial guidelines on protection that eventually materialized in the Agreement on Trade-related Aspects of Intellectual Property Rights (TRIPS) of the World Trade Organization. This included the extension of protection to databases; computer programs being classified as literary works and therefore subject to copyright.

Texts are not only protected, their universal access – working within a global free market – is also protected; thus, for example, the attempts by one country to protect its own cultural products from cultural 'invasion' become an area of contention. The result, fears Bettig, threatens to be an economic domination of the information-rich nations over the information-poor.

Economic dominance brings with it ideological influence. Copyright becomes a device for the COM-MODITIZATION and PRIVATIZATION of knowledge where 'the views and accounts of the world held by the capitalist class and aligned class factions and groups are broadly disseminated and persist-ently publicized'.

Global agreements, however, in practice have a mother of all battles in the war against piracy. It has been estimated that in 1995 US trade lost over $14bn to piracy, approximately a half of this in computer software, while in 1996 the abuse of copyright on recorded music meant, according to the International Federation of the Photographic Industry, losses of $2bn. See INFORMATION COMMONS.

Culture: globalization of Considered by many commentators as a paramount trend in the late twentieth century, in which cultures and cultural practices of chiefly western nations, America in particular, spread through the world, dominating native, home-grown cultures. The media are seen to be the channels through which the globalizing torrent has poured; and those channels have been largely under the direction and control of transnational corporations (TNCs). Under the umbrella of globalization we encounter a couple of key, linked and interactive phenomena: CONSUMERIZA-TION and MEDIA IMPERIALISM.

With cultural dominance, fear some commentators, comes ideological dominance, and that IDEOLOGY centres around the processes of production and consumption, and the targeting of audiences in their role of consumers. Todd Gitlin in his chapter 'Prime time ideology: the hegemonic process in television entertainment', in *Television: The Critical View* (US/UK: Oxford University Press, 1994), edited by Horace Newcomb, believes, 'In the twentieth century, the dominant ideology has shifted toward sanctifying consumer satisfaction as the premium definition of "the pursuit of happiness".'

Corporate domination of the economy extends to corporate dominance – worldwide – of CULTURE, at least those cultures through which profits may be obtained. It is not happiness alone that global corporatization promises, says Gitlin, but liberty, equality and fraternity: all can 'be affirmed through the existing private commodity forms, under the benign, protective eye of the national security state'.

The vision of a world dominated by American cultural products (not to mention products of other kinds, such as Coca-Cola and McDonald's burgers – see McDONALDIZATION) is challenged by observers who see in localism a force of resistance, or if not resistance, assimilation. Roland Robinson offers us a useful term in this respect – *glocalization* (in 'Globalization or glocalization?' in the *Journal of International Communication* 1 (1994)), that is, the ability of people in their own cultures to deal with in their own way the cultural imports from the West, to absorb them, to adapt them – to glocalize them.

John B. Thompson in *The Media and Modernity: A Social Theory of Media* (UK: Polity, 1995) urges us to see trends of dominance within historical perspectives: 'Rather than assuming that prior to the importation of Western TV programmes etc. many Third World countries had indigenous traditions and cultural heritages which were largely unaffected by external pressures, we should see instead that the globalization of communication through electronic media is only the most recent of a series of cultural encounters, in some cases stretching back many centuries, through which values, beliefs and symbolic forms of different groups have been superimposed on one another, often in conjunction with the use of coercive, political and economic power.'

Thompson maintains that the media-imperialist position underestimates the power of audiences to make their own meanings from what they read, listen to or watch. 'Through the localized process of appropriation,' Thompson believes, 'media products are embedded in sets of practices which shape and alter their significance.'

Evidence for the process of glocalization is offered by Tamar Liebes and Elihu Katz in *The Export of Meaning: Cross Cultural Readings of 'Dallas'* (US: Oxford University Press, 1990; UK: Polity, 1993). Their research indicated that the American soap *Dallas* was read in quite different ways by people of different origins, cultures and outlooks. It was *Dallas* that was dominated, not the audience for *Dallas*.

Majid Tehranian in his chapter 'Ethnic discourse and the new world dysorder', in *Communication and Culture in War and Peace* (UK: Sage, 1993), edited by Colleen Roach, argues that the levelling out which is said to be a benefit of globalization is more apparent than real. In fact the 'levelling' has camouflaged 'a hegemonic project by a new modern, technocratic, internationalist elite' speaking 'the language of a new international, a new world order'. However, Tehranian perceives the 'periphery' reacting against the 'core' in a number of potentially conflictual, even explosive, ways.

He speaks of c*ountermodernization* as a significant contemporary trend, in which pressure GROUPS such as some traditional religions react against modern ideas and dominant ideologies – the resurgence, for example, of fundamentalist religion in the face of scientific and technological advances; while a contrary trend, *demodernization*, is expressed by the voices of environmentalists or feminists; and by those 'localites' (as contrasted with 'cosmopolites') whose advocacy is inspired by the notion that 'small is beautiful'.

The nature and degree of globalization of culture will continue to be fiercely debated and such debate will inevitably have to take into account inequalities of wealth, provision and media technology across nations. See NEWS: GLOBALIZATION OF; INFORMATION GAPS; SLAPPS. See also *TOPIC GUIDE* under GLOBAL PERSPECTIVES.

* Malcolm Waters, *Globalization* (UK: Routledge, 1995); Peter Golding and Phil Harris (eds), *Beyond Cultural Imperialism* (UK: Sage, 1996); Daya Kishan Thussu (ed.), *Electronic Empires: Global Media and Local Resistance* (UK: Arnold, 1998); Barry Smart (ed.), *Resisting McDonaldization* (UK: Sage, 1999); George Monbiot, *Captive State: The Corporate Takeover of Britain* (UK: Macmillan, 2001).

Culture: intercultural communication See COMMUNICATION: INTERCULTURAL COMMUNICATION.

Culture of deference Journalist Richard Norton-Taylor in an article 'Pressure behind the scenes' and subtitled 'A history of deference, and cosy relationships in Westminster, have made self-censorship acceptable' (UK: *Index on Censorship* 4 & 5, 1991), writes of a 'deep-seated culture of deference' existing between many British editors and journalists in their relationship with those in authority (see POWER ELITE) This, Norton-Taylor claims, arises out of an anxiety to be accepted by and be a part of the establishment. The deference has its 'origins in the centralization of the British state and in Britain's imperial past – where there was virtually unchallenged consensus about the Empire's "civilizing mission".'

Deference, says Norton-Taylor, continues to be applied to institutions of the state such as Whitehall, the monarchy, the courts and Parliament. This deference also helps create and supports CONSENSUS against 'enemies', against foreign rivals, in war or in business. See JOURNALISM.

Culture: popular culture Something of a redundant term in that all culture is to a degree 'popular'; otherwise if it is 'unpopular', that is, if it does not attract or involve an AUDIENCE, it vanishes. The term has come to mean the culture of 'ordinary people', of the working class, the non-elite majority as contrasted with so-termed *high* or *highbrow* culture. Popular culture generally signifies cohesion, high culture difference – difference, that is, from popular culture and those with whom it is associated.

Popular culture has traditionally been looked down on as something banal, trashy, unchallenging or even potentially harmful: an ELITE standpoint. In their time, theatricals, dancing, wassailing, 'pulp fiction', the PRESS, POSTERS, postcards, COMICS, SOAP OPERA, the hit parade and the cinema have varyingly been defined as the kind of culture that contains the potential for subversion – usually of 'standards'. Popular culture tends to be controlled where it emerges from or is generated by the populace itself; promoted when it falls into the category of *transmission*, that is, created by 'culture manufacturers' for profit.

According to the French philosopher Pierre Bourdieu, popular culture is basically associated with that section of the population who lack both economic and CULTURAL CAPITAL. Since at least the 1960s popular culture has become the focus of critical attention and re-evaluation: it is studied – analysed, measured, in short, taken seriously.

In *Cultures and Societies in a Changing World* (US: Pine Forge Press, 1994), Wendy Griswold writes that 'Scholars examining previously despised works, genres and systems of meaning found them to contain complexities and beauties; at the same time, deconstructing previously esteemed works, genres and systems of meaning, they found widespread representations of class, hegemony, patriarchy, and illegitimate canonization.'

Culture, whether popular or 'elitist', *cultivates*, hence its fascination for researchers, commentators and students of media. Television, it has been claimed, has appropriated popular culture and by doing so redefined the term to mean 'that which is popular on TV'. The nature of participation by the populace in generating and taking part in popular culture has not been lost on TV programme-makers: audience participation is the key to popular quiz and competition programmes and to so-termed REALITY TV series such as *Big Brother*, in many cases turning that which traditionally has been private and intimate into public display. See AUDIENCE: ACTIVE AUDIENCE; ETHNOGRAPHIC (APPROACH TO AUDIENCE MEASUREMENT); RESPONSE CODES.

* Dominic Strinati, *An Introduction to Studying Popular Culture* (UK: Routledge, 2000).

Cultures of organizations See ORGANIZATION CULTURES.

Custom audience research That which is commissioned or undertaken by a company or client into AUDIENCE response to the media marketing of its product or services, generally targeting specific media outlets. Such studies produce rich, focused data while at the same time incurring doubts concerning the objectivity of that data. In contrast, *syndicated* studies are grander in scope as, like the Nielsen ratings, they measure the audiences of multiple media outlets of audience response.

As Peter V. Miller says in 'Made-to-order and standardized audiences: forms of reality in audience measurement', published in *Audiencemaking: How the Media Create the Audience* (US: Sage, 1994) edited by James S. Ettema and D. Charles Whitney, 'The unique, made-to-order nature of the custom study is both its chief benefit and its major cost.' He goes on, 'The syndicated study offers comparative, longitudinal information about audiences that can be used to sell advertising space and time. Unlike the custom study, the syndicated effort provides the advertisers with a standard way to judge alternative vehicles for their messages.' See AUDIENCE MEASUREMENT.

Cut-off In INTERPERSONAL COMMUNICATION, actions that block – cut off – incoming visual signals when people are under stress: hands over eyes, deflected glance, glazed look, eyes shut, etc. See GESTURE.

Cybernetics The study of communication FEEDBACK systems in human, animal and machine. Taken from the Greek for 'steersman', the term was the invention of American Norbert Wiener, author of *Cybernetics: or Control and Communication in the Animal and the Machine* (US: Wiley, 1949). Essentially an interdisciplinary study, cybernetics ranges in its interest from control systems of the body to the monitoring and control of space missions. Cybernetics concerns itself with the analysis of 'whole' systems, their complexity of goals and hierarchies within contexts of perpetual change. The Greek steersman used the feedback of visual, aural and tactile indicators to chart his passage through rough seas. Today we have computers: the potential for accuracy and rapidity of feedback and control is vastly greater, and so is the potential for disaster should the feedback systems go wrong.

Cyberspace Term probably first used by William Gibson in his novel *Neuromancers* published in America by Ace Books in 1984. Gibson describes cyberspace as 'a consensual hallucination … [People are] creating a world. It's not really a place, it's not really space. It's notional space.' By pressing computer keys, and by grace of a modem and telephone line, the operator has access to potentially infinite information and endless exchanges with other users.

Network systems offer to the computer-explorer vast research possibilities all for a monthly rental equal to that of a TV set. We can write direct, through e-mail, to the President of the United States or to Bill Gates, president of Microsoft. We can call up information from the Library of Congress, check the strength of the market in Hong Kong or book a holiday in the Caribbean.

We can join pressure groups and 'globalize' the issues that concern us. The net alters for us both time and space. New York, Alaska or Alice Springs could be in the next room for all that distance counts in cyberspace; and national boundaries need no longer be barriers. Indeed, in cyberterms, national and geographical divisions are an out-of-date way of viewing the world.

According to Mark C. Taylor and Esa Saarinen in *Imagology: Media Philosophy* (UK: Routledge, 1994), itself a mercurial sortie into cybergraphics, chief among cyberspace's characteristics is speed. 'Power,' the authors declare, 'is speed' and the 'swift will inherit the earth'. Some commentators claim that control, traditionally exercised by governments and powerful groups such as the transnational corporations, is shifting away from centres to peripheries, from organizations to individuals forming their own, hierarchy-free associations. In a number of countries the electronic highway of information, knowledge and ideas is seen as a threat to hierarchy and authority.

The net is widely envisioned in terms of new-age exploration. A Boston software computer firm has claimed in its advertising, 'Sir Francis Drake was knighted for what we do every day … The spirit of exploration is alive at The Computer Merchant.' In the realm of virtual reality imagination knows no bounds. Henry Rheingold in the book he edited on the subject, *Virtual Reality* (US: Simon & Schuster, 1991) speaks of 'my own odyssey to the outposts of a new scientific frontier … and an advanced glimpse of a possible new world in which reality itself might become a manufactured and metered commodity'.

By the summer of 1994 there were over 32 million users of the Internet, and varyingly of the World Wide Web, Cix (Compulink Information Exchange), the Well (Whole Earth 'lectronic Link) and Compuserve with its 2000 different services. Information is but a part of cyberexchange. You have personal problems – illness, sexual abuse, stuttering; is your marriage heading for the rocks? Self-help groups on the net have proliferated as an antidote to the problems faced in the 'real' world.

Some commentators see cyberspace as a force for dismantling patriarchal structures in society and altering existing gender relations. Is cyberequality on its way? American academic Cheris Kramarae is not so sanguine. In 'A backstage critique of virtual reality', in *CyberSociety: Computer Mediated Communication and Community* (US: Sage, 1995) edited by Steven G. Jones, Kramarae argues that, 'Cyberspace, like earthspace, is not developed as a viable place for women.' She talks about 'malestream publications and other forums' and views 'cybersex' as something where game, play and match will continue to reflect sexist attitudes and behaviour. Also Kramarae fears for the real ecology when we spend so much time in cyberecology. She links those fears to gender roles: 'I worry about the programs that encourage us to leave for extended periods the dirt and water of the actual places we live in ... I can imagine the man of the house putting on his gloves and headset and visiting Costa Rica while the woman of the house stays in the real house, changing the diapers and fixing meals.' She asks whether all this means turning our backs on 'the messes we've made' in the real world.

Fears about the posting of paedophile information on the net, of information-exchange between extremist factions, of freely available information on how to make weapons of mass destruction have surfaced on to public agendas to the point where, in many countries, those in authority have sought to 'fence in' the open prairies of cyberspace by legislation. Such moves have prompted many expressions of concern about the CENSORSHIP of the net.

As Darin Barney says in *Prometheus Wired: The Hope for Democracy in the Age of Network Technology* (US: University of Chicago Press, 2000), 'The key to network systems is surveillance.' He quotes David Lyon in his book, *The Electronic Eye: The Rise of the Surveillance Society* (US: Minnesota University Press, 1994) who believes that to 'participate in modern society is to be under electronic surveillance'.

There are fears that the major CONGLOMERATES are set to 'colonize' cyberspace, with the intention of turning it into cybermalls. Linked with this is concern about the demography of usage. The net has been described as 'pale and male'. The first user survey of the World Wide Web, conducted by James E. Pitkow and Mimi Recker, found that of 4000 respondents to the survey, over 90 per cent of users were professional, Caucasian and male. Many analysts take the view that the net is unlikely to be a bridger of the gap between information-rich and information-poor, that it is failing to redress the balance between core and periphery; and some are of the opinion that cyberspace is largely off-limits to the poor, the ill-educated and the unemployed. See CORE NATIONS, PERIPHERAL NATIONS; INFORMATION GAPS; REGULATION OF INVESTIGATORY POWERS ACT (RIPA) (UK), 2000; SURVEILLANCE SOCIETY. See also *TOPIC GUIDE* under CYBERCULTURE: THE NET, THE WEB.

---

* David Bell, *An Introduction to Cybercultures* (UK: Routledge, 2001).

Cylinder or rotary press The most important technical development in PRINTING history following the invention of movable type was the steam-driven cylinder press invented by Friederich Koenig. Born in Saxony, Koenig moved to London in order to set up a works to manufacture the new machines (1812). He demonstrated that a cylinder press machine could take off impressions at the rate of over 1000 an hour. On 28 November 1814 one of the presses was used to print *The Times*. Its editor, John Walter, described the press as 'the greatest improvement connected with printing since the discovery of the art itself'. As a result of its advantage in using Koenig's press, *The Times* became the dominant and most influential newspaper of the nineteenth century in the UK. See *TOPIC GUIDE* under MEDIA: TECHNOLOGIES.

D

Daguerrotype Early photograph produced in the manner of Louis Daguerre (1789–1851) a French theatrical designer who teamed up with Joseph Nicèphore Nièpce (1765–1833), a founding father of photography, in 1830. Nièpce died three years later but Daguerre continued their work, fixing images

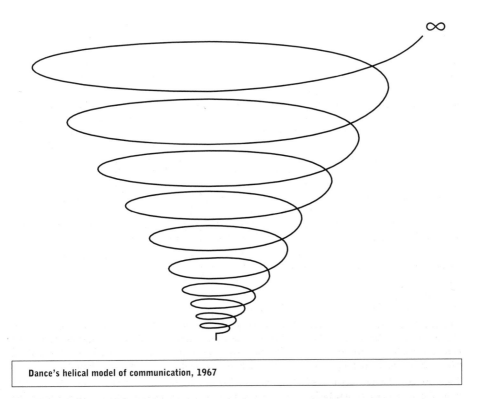

∞

Dance's helical model of communication, 1967

on metal plates coated with silver iodide, which he treated with mercury vapour in a darkroom. Daguerre was eventually able to reduce the exposure time of a photograph from eight hours to between 20 and 30 minutes. His Daguerrotype was taken up by the French government in July 1839 and revealed to the world at a meeting of the Académies des Sciences in August. No prints could be made from a Daguerrotype; thus Daguerre's method was a cul-de-sac in photography, though a vastly successful one at the time. See PHOTOGRAPHY, ORIGINS.

Dance's helical model of communication, 1967 The earliest communication models were linear; their successors were circular, emphasizing the crucial factor of FEEDBACK in the communication process. Frank E.X. Dance in 'A helical model of communication', in the book he edited, *Human Communication Theory* (US: Holt, Rinehart & Winston, 1967), commends the circular model as an advance upon the linear one but faults it on the grounds that it suggests that communication comes back full circle, to exactly the same point from which it started, an assumption which is 'manifestly erroneous'.

The helix or spiral, for Dance, 'combines the desirable features of the straight line and of the circle while avoiding the weaknesses of either'. He goes on, 'At any and all times, the helix gives geometric testimony to the concept that Communication while moving forward is at the same moment coming back upon itself and being affected by its past behaviour, for the coming curve of the helix is fundamentally affected by the curve from which it emerges.' Dance's helical model parallels theories of education put forward by Jerome Bruner, and generally referred to as the spiral curriculum. See *TOPIC GUIDE* under COMMUNICATION MODELS.

Data mining In a 1998 publication *Data Mining: Staking a Claim on Your Privacy*, Ann Cavoukian, Ontario (Canada) Information and Privacy Commissioner, defines data mining as 'a set of automated techniques used to extract buried or previously unknown pieces of information from large data bases'. The commissioner states that 'Successful data mining makes it possible to unearth patterns and relationships, and then use this "new" information to make proactive knowledge-driven business decisions.'

The process illustrates the penetrative power of surveillance (see SURVEILLANCE SOCIETY) made possible by computer networking. Extensively used by governments and business, data mining identifies patterns and trends in the seemingly disparate activities of citizens, such patterns and trends being used as indicators of future policy and promotion. See PRIVACY.

Data protection The increasing use of computers and sophisticated information technology has greatly magnified the harm to individual PRIVACY that can occur from any collection, storage or dissemination of personal information, and many countries have legislated against data abuse. Sweden, Denmark, Norway, Luxembourg, West Germany and France have all legislated to protect both the public and private sectors of society. In the US and Canada data protection legislation only applies to the public sector and compliance with it is voluntary.

In the UK, the report of the Lindop Committee (*Report of the Committee on Data Protection*, 1978) urged the need for individuals to have a right of veto on what information was passed on about them and how this would operate in the context of 'the interests of the rest of society, which include the efficient conduct of industry, commerce and administration'. In 1984, the DATA PROTECTION ACT entered the Statute Book, and began operation in 1987 (see the next entry).

CRYPTOGRAPHY, or what in modern parlance is termed *privacy transformation*, can be employed to 'scramble' data prior to storage in order to guard against accidental or deliberate disclosures of information. The problem here is how the key or code to the scrambling process is to be protected. In the US, the Hellman–Diffie method allowed for different keys for the scrambling and unscrambling processes. An alternative to this is the so-called *electronic signature*, which works by reversing the roles of scrambling and unscrambling keys. Another mode is PIN – personal identity number, where everybody is issued with a personal key. PIN is already in use for the authorization of electronic funds transfers. See ECHELON; PRETTY GOOD PRIVACY (PGP). See also *TOPIC GUIDE* under MEDIA: FREEDOM, CENSORSHIP.

Data Protection Act (UK), 1984 The purpose of the Act is 'to regulate the use of automatically processed information relating to individuals and the provision of services in respect of such information'. From November 1987 the public has been able to check if any organization holds information on them; to see a copy of that information, known as personal data; to complain to the Data Protection Registrar about the way the data were collected or are being used; to have inaccurate computer records corrected or deleted in certain circumstances, and to claim compensation through the courts if the 'data subject' has suffered damage by the loss or destruction of personal data, or through an unauthorized disclosure or because of inaccuracy.

Designed to bring Britain into line with the Council of Europe Convention for the Protection of Individuals with regard to Automatic Processing of Personal Data, the Act provides for the establishment of a data watchdog, the Data Protection Registrar, and outlines eight DATA PROTECTION PRINCIPLES.

The test of any act protecting the citizen is the size and scope of the exceptions. There are three unconditional exemptions from registration: personal data required to be exempt for the purpose of safeguarding national security; data which its user is required by law to make public; and personal data held by an individual and 'concerned with the management of his personal, family or household affairs or held by him only for recreational purposes'. Subject access is barred on matters of prevention or detection of crime, the apprehension or prosecution of offenders or the assessment or collection of any tax or duty.

Data protection principles Listed in the DATA PROTECTION ACT (UK), 1984, are the following eight principles governing data protection for computer users handling personal data: computer users must (1) obtain and process the information fairly and lawfully; (2) register the purposes for which they hold the data; (3) not use or disclose the information in a way contrary to those purposes; (4) hold only information that is adequate, relevant and not excessive for the purposes; (5) hold only accurate information and, where necessary, keep it up to date; (6) not keep any information longer than is necessary; (7) give the individual access to information about themselves and, where appropriate, correct or erase the information; (8) take appropriate security measures. Persons feeling that any computer user has broken one or more of the above principles may complain to the Data Protection Registrar. See PRIVACY; SECRECY.

Decency: Communications Decency Act, 1996 See COMMUNICATIONS DECENCY ACT (US).

Decisive moment French photographer Henri Cartier-Bresson used this term to describe the instant when pressing the shutter release button produced the desired image. Indeed some critics believe that Cartier-Bresson's timing, his ability to be at the ready when destiny appeared to be bringing highly photogenic elements together, this instinct for the decisive moment, qualifies him to be considered the finest of all twentieth-century photographers.

Declaration on the Mass Media (UNESCO General Council, 1978) See MEDIA IMPERIALISM.

Decode The process of interpreting, analysing and understanding the nature of messages – written, spoken, broadcast, etc. This requires not just an understanding of the words, signs or images used but also a sharing of the VALUES and assumptions that underpin their encoding into a message by the transmitter. A focus for research in communication studies is the extent to which the receiver decodes the message in the way the encoder or sender would prefer. This is an important element in the debate on the power and influence of the media.

If the message is received by an AUDIENCE that does not share the same codes or values as the sender, it will be interpreted in an 'aberrant' way – that is, a different meaning will be assumed than that which was intended, hence the term *aberrant decoding*. In short, it is a difference of 'reading' the message derived from a difference of experience, perception or evaluation. See PREFERRED READING. See also *TOPIC GUIDE* under COMMUNICATION THEORY; LANGUAGE/ DISCOURSE/NARRATIVE.

Deconstruction The process of deconstruction, as a mode of textual and intertextual analysis, is chiefly associated with the ideas of the French philosopher Jacques Derrida and his method of 'close-reading' of minute particulars in a text. The search is not for an ultimate MEANING; on the contrary, Derrida sees meaning as *undecidable*: signifiers within linguistic contexts refer to further signifiers, texts to further texts in an infinite web of INTERTEXTUALITY. Deconstructors such as Derrida seek to pry behind the dominant expressions of a TEXT, regarding these as serving to exclude subordinate terms. The technique is to *reverse* and *displace*, thus bring about an upending – an overthrow – of the hierarchies that rule all forms of expression.

In the words of Madan Sarup in *An Introductory Guide to Post-Structuralism and Postmodernism* (UK: Harvester Wheatsheaf, 1993), 'Deconstruction disarticulates traditional conceptions of the author and undermines conventional notions of reading and history ... It kills the author, turns history and tradition into textuality and' – we must gratefully note – 'celebrates the reader'. If *self* can be constructed as a text, then self is subject to deconstruction, which displaces the notion of a *stable* self. The only coherence, it would seem, is fragmentation, leading to the conclusion that there can be no meaning, only interpretation.

Sarup's phrase 'textual undecidability' usefully sums up the position of the deconstructors as does the term 'labyrinth of deconstruction', used by Christopher Norris in *Deconstruction: Theory and Practice* (UK: Methuen, 1982).

---

* Jacques Derrida, *Writing and Difference* (UK: Routledge & Kegan Paul, 1976); Christopher Norris, *Derrida* (UK: Collins, 1987).

Decreolization See COMMUNICATION: INTERCULTURAL COMMUNICATION.

Deep Dish TV See PAPER TIGER TV; TELEVISION: ACCESS TELEVISION.

Deep focus Film-making technique in which objects close to the camera and those far away are both in focus at the same time.

Deep structure Though the term was first used by Charles Hockett the concept was given widest currency by fellow US linguist Noam Chomsky in 'Current issues in linguistic theory', in J. Foder and

J. Katz (eds), *The Structure of Language: Readings in the Philosophy of Language* (US: Prentice-Hall, 1964). In its original form, deep structure is an underlying abstract level of sentence organization, which specifies the way a sentence should be interpreted. It is an abstract representation of syntax. Surface grammar is the final stage in the syntactical representation of a sentence – the nearest one gets to the actual spoken or written form of a sentence (arrived at via the phonological (sound component) or graphological (written component) of the grammar).

The deep structure is made manifest through a process of 'transformation'. A transformational grammar establishes the deep and surface structure of a sentence and then relates these through the process of transformation. For Chomsky the deep and surface structures, and the relationship between them, provide the essential bases of language which, far from being merely a sequence of words strung together, is rather a series of organized structures (see STRUCTURALISM). This deep structure, or level, supplies information that enables the reader or listener to distinguish between alternative inter-pretations of sentences that have the same surface form, or sentences that have different surface forms but have the same underlying meaning.

When, for example, a publisher replies to a budding author, 'I will waste no time in reading your manuscript', he presents a surface structure with alternative possible meanings. Yet by altering the surface structure of the sentence 'The dog chased the cat' to 'The cat was chased by the dog', the underlying idea is not altered. The transformations that might occur between deep and surface structure can be passive ('My father was warned by the doctor to give up smoking'), negative ('My father was not warned to give up smoking'), in question form ('Was my father warned to give up smoking?') or as an imperative ('Father was told – "Stop smoking!"'). See *TOPIC GUIDE* under LANGUAGE/DISCOURSE/NARRATIVE.

---

* Noam Chomsky, *Language and Mind* (UK: Harcourt Brace Jovanovitch, 1968).

Deep throat Journalists' parlance for 'anonymous sources'. Perhaps the most famous was the unknown telephone informant calling himself 'Deep throat' who set *Washington Post* reporters Bernstein and Woodward on the trail in the WATERGATE scandal that eventually led to the resignation of President Richard Nixon.

Defamation Any statement made by one person that is untrue and may be considered injurious to another's reputation, causing shame, resentment, ridicule or financial loss is regarded as defamation under the Defamation Act (UK) of 1952. In permanent form, such as expressed in print, records, films, tapes, photographs, images or effigies, defamation is classed as *libel*. In temporary form such as in spoken words or gestures, defamation is classified as *slander*.

No legal aid is granted to plaintiffs or defendants in defamation cases, thus persons even with the most genuine case for grievance at reports about them in the PRESS etc. must think twice before deciding to incur vast legal expenses in defending their reputation.

The 1996 Defamation Act is, in the words of the *Guardian* leader of 26 June, 'a generally sensitive attempt to impose practical rules upon the difficult relationship between the media and those who allege they have been defamed by them'. However, the late addition of the 'Hoffman clause' (brought by Lord Hoffman in the House of Lords and later approved by the House of Commons by a vote of 264 to 201) concerning defamation and MPs, meets with disapproval; raising 'issues of privilege which go much further than the draftsmen can ever have intended'. The clause devolves control over parliamentary privilege from the House as a whole to individual MPs, allowing them to waive parliamentary privilege in order to have the same rights as an ordinary citizen to take the media to court for alleged libel.

At first sight the amendment seems just: an MP has a right to make the media prove the truth of allegations. However, barrister Andrew Nicol, writing in the *Guardian* of 27 June 1996, states that the 'problem with such arguments is that they ignore the difference between journalistic evaluation of a story and the process of establishing the truth of a proposition in court'; in future mere doubt about whether truth can be proved in court may persuade nervous publishers to hold back on a story.

Nicol cites the 1963 decision by the US Supreme Court that if such conditions applied to public officials they would be an unconstitutional restriction on freedom of speech. Under the Hoffman clause, if an MP waived parliamentary privilege it would mean that no source material could be accepted as evidence unless the originator appeared in court to verify that information. This could destroy at a stroke the generally honourable tradition of the media protecting its sources. 'The information,' says Nicol, 'may, for instance, come from a reliable source but one who for good reason would not wish to testify in court.' See *TOPIC GUIDE* under MEDIA: FREEDOM, CENSORSHIP.

Defensive communication Occurs when people hear what they do not wish to hear. DISSONANCE arises when messages cut across, or contradict, VALUES and assumptions and the reaction varies from not concentrating on the MESSAGE to deliberately misrepresenting or misunderstanding the sender's motive as well as his/her message.

Climates of threat create defensive tactics just as supportive climates help reduce them. If we know that we are being tested or evaluated, for example, our communication response will be guarded. Equally we might resort to defensive tactics if we feel the communicator of the message is intent on winning control, exerting superiority. We are less defensive in situations in which spontaneity, empathy, equality and a sense of open-mindedness about the nature of the message are predominant.

Deference, culture of See CULTURE OF DEFERENCE.

Deliberative listening See LISTENING.

Democracy and the media Both the word democracy and the idea are of Greek origin. *Demos* means citizen body; thus democracy is rule by the citizens, suggesting the right of all to decide on what are matters of concern, and possessing the power to decide on those matters. Democracy implies a vote for every citizen of a certain age, regular elections, a genuine choice of parties to *represent* citizens; and a range of rights – free speech, security from arbitrary arrest, the freedoms of belief, movement and association.

The media can be seen – and they often see themselves – as WATCHDOGS of democracy; journalists as articulators and defenders of democracy, the eyes and ears of the public. In his analysis of whether new technologies – in particular, computer networks – enhance or diminish democracy, Darin Barney in *Prometheus Wired: The Hope for Democracy in the Age of Network Technology* (US: University of Chicago Press, 2000), identifies three elements he considers essential in *any* serious definition of democracy – equality, participation and 'a public sphere from which sovereignty emanates'.

Barney speaks of equality of *ability* as well as opportunity; and participation that is meaningful rather than 'frivolous or merely symbolic'. By this he suggests that 'Democratic participation must be clearly and decisively connected to the political decisions that direct the activity of the participants' community.'

Participation is not, he argues, confined to freedoms of 'consumer choice', the preferred interpretation of democracy by business. In Barney's view many self-proclaiming democracies would not pass the test of equality, participation and power through 'collective decisions'.

It has often been suggested that the media, through argument and advocacy, made democracy possible (see JOURNALISM). From Tom Paine's *The Rights of Man* (1891) through the age of the radical press during the nineteenth century, the cause of democracy was championed by journalists and editors, often risking life and liberty to make their case. Within a modern democracy, the media has an ongoing responsibility to exercise vigilance – to nurture, protect and celebrate a range of features that keep democracy healthy, protect it from corruption, manipulation, misuse and apathy. These might be described as *satellites* of democracy – facilitators – the absence of which threaten the democratic process; and they include full and fair transmission of information; PLURALITY of opinions and diversity of media provision. Their enemies are monopolization of media outlets by the few (see CONVERGENCE), the profits-generated insistence on treating people as consumers rather than citizens (see CONSUMERIZATION), and the consequent displacement or marginalization in media channels of information, critical analysis, debate and investigation. In this sense, considering the nature of media ownership (see *TOPIC GUIDE* under MEDIA: OWNERSHIP AND CONTROL), the media are as likely to subvert democracy, or at least relegate it in importance, as be its defender and its advocate. See AGORA; DISCURSIVE CONTESTATION; DISENFRANCHISEMENT (OF READERSHIP); FRAMING; PUBLIC OPINION; PUBLIC SERVICE BROADCASTING (PSB);

PUBLIC SPHERE. See also *TOPIC GUIDE* under MEDIA: POLITICS AND ECONOMICS; MEDIA: VALUES AND IDEOLOGIES.

Demographic analysis The collection and interpretation of data about the characteristics of people other than their beliefs, VALUES and attitudes. Specifically, *demography* is the study of population, while *demology* is the theory of the origin and nature of communities.

Demonization What the media do, particularly the popular PRESS, to those whose views they perceive to be dangerous, destabilizing, bad for business or subversive. The process of demonization begins with *personalization*, that is, focusing on the personal characteristics (invariably negative) of the leader or spokesperson advocating a cause or raising an issue, which the demonizers do not support. Having rendered the cause or issue a 'personal' matter associated with an individual, the aim of the media concerned is to destroy the credibility of the spokesperson and by doing so undermine, in the public mind, the cause for which he/she speaks. See FOLK DEVILS; LOONY LEFTISM.

Denotation See CONNOTATION.

Dependency theory The degree to which audiences are dependent upon the mass media constitutes one of the chief debates about the functions and effects of modern communication systems. In 'A dependency model of mass media effects', in G. Gumpert and R. Cathcart (eds), *Inter/Media: Interpersonal Communication in the Media* (US/UK: Oxford University Press, 1979), Sandra J. Ball-Rokeach and Melvyn DeFleur believe 'The potential for mass media messages to achieve a broad range of cognitive, affective, and behavioural effects will be increased when media systems serve many unique and central information systems.' The fewer the sources of information in a media world, the more likely the media will affect our minds and thoughts, our attitudes and how we behave. Further, that influence will have increased potential 'when there is a high degree of structural instability in the society due to conflict and change'.

However, just as the audience may be changed by the information/messages it receives, in turn the media systems themselves are changed according to AUDIENCE response. It is not one-way traffic. In the cognitive or intellectual sphere, the authors cite the following possible media roles: (1) resolution of ambiguity, and relatedly limiting the range of interpretations of situations which audiences are able to make; (2) attitude formation; (3) agenda-setting; (4) expansion of people's systems of beliefs (for example, the tremendous growth in awareness of ecological matters); (5) clarification of values, through the expression of value conflicts (see DEVIANCE).

The media play a significant role in the establishment and maintenance of 'we feeling', that is, communal solidarity and oneness; equally they may work towards the alienation of sections of the population who are traditionally discriminated against – women, blacks, etc.

At critical decision-making times, such as elections: people have become increasingly dependent on the media, especially TV, for election information and guidance. Ball-Rokeach and DeFleur argue that the greater the uncertainty in society, the less clear are people's frames of reference; consequently there is greater audience dependence on media communication. See BALL-ROKEACH AND DEFLEUR'S DEPENDENCY MODEL OF MASS COMMUNICATION EFFECTS, 1976; EFFECTS OF THE MASS MEDIA. See also *TOPIC GUIDE* under COMMUNICATION THEORY.

Deregulation Describes the process whereby channels of communication, specifically radio and TV, are opened up beyond the existing franchise holders. Another term in current use, 'privatization', emphasizes the practical nature of the shift, from public to commercial control, driven by the development of VIDEO, CABLE TELEVISION and SATELLITE, and accelerated by DIGITIZA-TION. Regulation is associated with public service communications, for example, PUBLIC SERVICE BROADCASTING (PSB), deregulation with the ambitions and practices of the practice sector of the communications industry. See COMMUNICATIONS BILL (UK), 2002; CONGLOMERATES: MEDIA CONGLOMERATES; CONSUMERIZATION.

Deregulation, five myths of In 'The mythology of telecommunications deregulation' (*Journal of Communication*, Winter, 1990), Vincent Mosco of Carleton University identifies five influential assumptions about the deregulation of telecommunications, which he describes as myths (see here Roland Barthes' definition of MYTH): that deregulation lessens the economic role of government, benefits consumers, diminishes economic concentration, is widely supported and is inevitable. Because deregulation is clearly in the interest of the non-public sector, particularly corporations profiting from the free market, it is in the sector's interest to establish the benefits of deregulation as a natural truth: unquestionably a good thing.

'Whatever their basis in fact,' writes Mosco, 'these myths continue to reflect significant political and economic interests. Moreover, they help to constitute those interests with a shared belief system ... promoting the dismantling of a public infrastructure and massive income redistribution up the social class ladder.' Mosco goes on, 'In the long run they want to advance the transformation of information from a public resource into a marketable commodity and a form of social management control. Deregulation is more than a policy instrument; it serves as a cohesive mythology around which those who would benefit from these short- and long-run interests might rally.'

Desensitization Process by which audiences are considered to be made immune, or less sensitive, to human suffering as a result of relentless exposure to such suffering in the media. A constant media diet of violence – real or fictional – is widely believed to 'harden up' people's tolerance of violence. See COMPASSION FATIGUE.

Detachment, ideology of See IMPARTIALITY.

Determiner deletion A common stylistic practice of journalists where the characteristics of a person and the name are linked without use of 'the' or 'a', in the interests of verbal economy while at the same time having the effect of *labelling* the named person. An example might be: 'Ex-jailbird six-times married Joe Bloggs yesterday told the press ...' or '"Kiss-and-tell" Minister's former live-in lover claims ...'. Allan Bell in *The Language of News Media* (UK: Blackwell, 1991) describes this practice as a form of *titleness* that gives instant NEWS VALUE to the person being reported. See HYPHENIZED ABRIDGEMENT; LABELLING PROCESS (AND THE MEDIA).

Determinism See TECHNOLOGICAL DETERMINISM.

Developmental news That which developing nations consider will help rather than harm their prospects. 'Western news' is seen by developing nations as essentially the pursuit of 'bad' news; and bad news hurts. The term implies government monopoly of information flow in the interests of giving a developing country a 'good name' and runs counter to western notions of free comment. The aspirations to a reporting tradition of social responsibility rather than sensation-seeking are honourable; and the dangers – of press subservience to government – obvious. See INFORMATION SOCIETY; MEDIA IMPERIALISM; NEW WORLD INFORMATION ORDER. See also *TOPIC GUIDE* under NEWS MEDIA.

Deviance Social behaviour that is considered unacceptable within a social community is deviant; and the defining of what constitutes deviance depends upon what norms of conduct prevail at any given time in a society. Of primary interest in the analysis of deviance is the question – who defines deviance and why? There are two main views on this: the first maintains that the definition of what is deviant behaviour stems from a general CONSENSUS within society; the second argues that it is the most powerful groups within a society that define as deviant behaviour that which may constitute a threat to themselves or their dominant position in society.

Particular interest has been focused on the role of the media in shaping definitions of deviance and then responding to those. While from a moral standpoint the media may disapprove of deviant behaviour, there is at the same time a reliance upon it: normative behaviour rarely makes a good headline. Deviant behaviour, on the other hand, is a NEWS VALUE and it might be argued that if deviance did not exist, it would be necessary for the media to invent it.

Several studies of deviance have been concerned with the role of the mass media in both the definition and amplification of deviance. Leslie Watkins first outlined the concept of *deviance amplification* in 'Some sociological factors in drug addiction control', in D. Wilner and G. Kassebaum (eds), *Narcotics* (US: McGraw-Hill, 1965). He argues that the way in which a society defines and reacts to deviance may in fact encourage those defined as deviant to act in a more deviant manner – this would be particularly true for deviants excluded from or restricted in participation in normal social activities.

If societal reaction to deviance is strong, it can lead to greater deviance which in turn may lead to stronger societal reaction and so on, establishing a deviance amplification *spiral* in which each increase in social control is met by an increase in the level of deviancy. The contribution of the mass media in precipitating and shaping such amplification spirals has proved a fruitful area of media research.

Deviant See SLIDER.

Diachronic linguistics The study of language through the course of its history. In contrast, *synchronic liguistics* takes a fixed instant as its point of observation (chiefly a contemporary one). The distinction was first posed by Swiss linguist Ferdinand de Saussure (1857–1913).

Dialect A dialect is usually regionally based and is a variation within a language as regards vocabulary, pronunciation and grammar. For this reason Suzanne Romaine in *Language and Society* (UK: Oxford University Press, 2000) argues, 'educated speakers of American English and British English can be regarded as using dialects of the same language'. In this case, she states, the differences are likely to be more evident in pronunciation and vocabulary than grammar; for example, the American English speaker using the word 'elevator' rather than 'lift'.

In post-war Britain (since 1945) regional dialects became increasingly accepted for their own inherent value. However, according to Martin Montgomery in *An Introduction to Language and Society* (UK/US: Routledge, 1995), 'within the British Isles many of the more fundamental differences of vocabulary and sentence structure between the English dialects have become eroded. ... Often, all that remains as a kind of historical residue of the original dialect is its distinctive mode of pronunciation – its accent.' He goes on to point out that, 'But the other kinds of dialect feature have not, of course, died out altogether.'

The study of dialect further illuminates connections between CLASS background and language usage in that until recently the use of standard English was associated with an individual of high social status. Suzanne Romaine comments that 'Boundaries are, however, often of a social nature, e.g. between different social class groups. In this case we may speak of "social dialects" ... Social dialects say who we are, and regional dialects where we came from.' Dialects, though they add richness and variety to a language, can also, of course, form a barrier to communication. See ACCENT; COLLOQUIAL-ISM; JARGON; REGISTER; SLANG. See also *TOPIC GUIDE* under LANGUAGE/DISCOURSE/NARRATIVE.

Diary stories See SPOT NEWS.

Diffusion The process by which innovations spread to the members of a social system. Diffusion studies are concerned with messages that convey new ideas, the processes by which those ideas are conveyed and received, and the extent to which those ideas are adopted or rejected. Appropriateness of CHANNEL to MESSAGE is particularly important. For example, mass media channels are often more useful at creating awareness – knowledge – of new ideas, but interpersonal channels are considered to be more important in changing attitudes towards innovations. The rate and success of diffusion is very much affected by the norms, VALUES and social structures in which the transmission of new ideas takes place. See EFFECTS OF MASS MEDIA.

Digitization The computer works digitally: information is broken down into a code of zeros and ones (*bits*). Today, all forms of electronic communication are converging through digital formats, and computer-mediated communication now applies to newspapers, telephone systems, BROADCAST-ING and film production, as well as the INTERNET. Digitization makes for *profusion* – of TELEVISION and RADIO channels and, in terms of use and reception, *fragmentation*. Such are the possibilities in the 'digital age' that each viewer or listener ceases to be, as in the past, part of a recognizable AUDIENCE. Specialized, more targeted provision comes at an extra price. Where once the annual licence fee was the only payment for radio and TV services, now reception depends more and more on subscriptions, smart-cards and digital conversion boxes. Viewing is becoming almost as expensive as a night at the opera.

Take up the new digital technology, and you pick up the cost of development and the rush for profits. Availability of what has been traditional screen fare for PUBLIC SERVICE BROADCASTING – that is, programmes available for the entire nation to watch – rapidly diminished in the last decade of the twentieth century. British digital broadcasting began in 1998, with two rivals in the field, Ondigital and Sky Digital (in which News International has a 40 per cent stake), with government insistence that they must produce compatible technology to minimize consumer confusion.

The cost to consumers of conversion or TV replacement has proved substantial enough to result in a less than wholehearted take-up on the part of the public, at least in the UK, of digital equipment (though digital video has fast become the norm across the nation). In March 2002 the massively invested ITV Digital went into liquidation, clearly indicating that government plans to switch completely from analogue to digital transmission and reception would have to be postponed.

Digitization is the ultimate form of CONVERGENCE, technically but also in terms of control. All texts converge in the bit, but the investment costs of turning the electronic world digital are enormous, meaning not only that the competition is to be between media giants but that even the major operators will be continually at risk from their competitors. At the same time there are serious worries that in terms of quality of programmes and schedules more may turn out to be more of the same. A key question is whether segments of the population will be left behind in the new age of subscription and pay-per-view. Many commentators fear that digitization favours the already *information-rich* and widens the INFORMATION GAP between them and the *information-poor*.

Linked to this are dark predictions about the impact of digitization on industries and jobs. It is feared that being able to do your banking and shopping from home threatens the structures and practices of commerce, and thus the future of those employed in the selling of goods and services.

Cees Hamelink in *World Communication: Disempowerment & Self-Empowerment* (UK/US: Zed Books, 1995) identifies four major trends in world communications, citing digitization as the first, and interacting and interlocking with the others – *consolidation, deregulation* and *globalization.* The cost of developing digitization leads to consolidation of ownership and control, which in turn demands the minimum of regulation in order to expand and traverse the boundaries of nation-states, and in particular regulations governing and protecting public interest communication.

Finally digitization provides the technological basis for globalization 'as it facilitates the global trading of services, worldwide financial networks, and the spreading of high-technology research and development across the globe'. Hamelink says that 'the digital age arrives with a monumental invasion of people's privacy' through the massive collection and sale of personal data, which he considers, referring to the proliferation of electronic monitoring by employers of their employees, to be 'a fundamental violation of human rights'. He believes that digital technology is creating 'transparent societies, "glass-house" countries that are very vulnerable to external forces and to the loss of their sovereign capacities'.

Hamelink registers concern about the unreliability of technology in an age of increasing technology-dependence. 'The magnitude of possible disruptions [to society through computer error, computer breakdown or computer fraud] is mind-boggling. Software bugs, systems malfunction, computer crime and hacking can cost millions of dollars and human lives.' He talks of 'dangerous levels of vulnerability' especially for less powerful users.

Digitization is seen to be both empowering (to the already powerful) and potentially disempowering (to those with less of it in the first place). In relation to the trend towards deregulation, Hamelink argues that 'tension between public good and private commodity is increasingly resolved to the latter's advantage'. Consequently the 'erosion of the public sphere by implication undermines diversity of information provision … everything that does not pass the market threshold because there is not a sufficiently large percentage of consumers, disappears. That may be good for markets, it may be suicidal for democratic politics and creative culture.' See DISEMPOWERMENT. See also *TOPIC GUIDE* under MEDIA: TECHNOLOGIES.

Digital retouching Or electronic retouching; process whereby laser and computer technology are combined to retouch or recreate photographs. A laser beam scans and measures images and pigmentations, then reduces them into a series of 'pixels', or minute segments. These are then recorded in digital form and stored in the computer's memory for eventual reproduction, which permits the rearrangement of the picture, a recreation – or just plain faking.

Digital television Traditionally TV has been brought to us using standard analogue waves, but the future for both terrestrial transmission and satellite transmission will lie with binary-coded digital signals. Digital TV uses less bandwidth than the analogue mode to transmit the same amount of information, thus it offers many more channels with improved visual and sound quality. Transmitting

TV digitally has incurred massive investment costs and involves ruthless competition. Ultimately, digital TV is only as good as the quality of its pictures and sound and, even more important, of its programmes. Squaring up to the might of Rupert Murdoch's BSkyB, Ondigital was eventually brought to its knees, having grossly overinvested in nationwide league football coverage. ITV Digital, funded by UK's Carlton and Granada companies, went into receivership in March 2002, while the major UK cable operator, ntl, made public its own acute cash problems.

Even so, as a UK *Guardian* leader put it, having led with the headline, 'The party is over: ITV's woes have big repercussions' (28 March 2002), 'the world is still going digital. Everyone will eventually have a digital set – and the country that gets there first may have an advantage in selling services to others.' See *TOPIC GUIDE* under MEDIA: TECHNOLOGIES.

Digital radio (UK) Though the initial cost of digital radios has been generally prohibitive, the future, for RADIO as well as TELEVISION, is seen to be digital. In March 2002 the BBC introduced 6 Music, the first national music radio station since the creation of BBC Radio 3 in 1970, and one of five new digital stations to serve audiences for sport, black and urban music, Asian life and culture – all of them broadcasting on the INTERNET, also on digital satellite television (Sky Digital channel 911 and Telewest 909), and most of them on cable. 6 Music aims for an audience of rock and pop fans aged between 25 and 44.

Digital video disc (DVD) Or digital *versatile*. One of a number of VIDEO compression systems, the size of a compact disc (CD) but holding up to 26 times more information. The DVD allows for four full feature-length films to be stored on a single disc, and permits wide-screen format. The cost of duplication is considerably less than that for VHS tape. DVDs can – unlike video tape – be encrypted, allowing the distributor to control viewing access, and in the case of parents to empower them, through the use of a program password, to restrict what their children view.

The Japanese company Sony, having pioneered the personal stereo, offered the world 'personal cinema'. The Glasstron, employing a pair of wrap-around spectacles with extra flaps, and using Dolby Surround Sound, is the first commuter-friendly cinema. It allows the viewer to watch movies on what to the brain appears to be a 52-inch screen. The DVD slots into a battery-driven, hand-held player. It provides facilities not available to the traditional film-goer, permitting its audience of one a choice of alternative endings, along with interviews with actors and directors, and supplementary film information.

Direct cinema Term used to describe the work of post-Second World War DOCUMENTARY filmmakers in the US, such as Albert Maysles (*Salesman*, 1969, and *Gimme Shelter*, 1970), who coined the phrase, Stephen Leacock (*Don't Look Back*, 1968) and Frederick Wiseman (*High School*, 1968). New, lightweight equipment and improved synchronous sound-recording facilities made the work of these observer-documentarists an inspiration for film-makers in many other countries. Direct cinema went out into the world and recorded life as it happened, in the 'raw'. An earlier, and British, link with this mode of film-making was free cinema, a short-lived 'collective' of directors in London, organized by Karel Reisz (*Momma Don't Allow*, 1956) and Lindsay Anderson (*O Dreamland*, 1953). Direct cinema filmmakers had the technical edge on free cinema because of the availability of superior sound recording. See CINÉMA VÉRITÉ.

Disconfirmation See CONFIRMATION/DISCOMFIRMATION.

Discourse A form, mode or GENRE of LANGUAGE use. Each person has in his/her repertoire a whole range of possible discourses – the language of love, of authority, of sport, of the domestic scene. In a media sense, an example of a discourse would be the NEWS, reflecting in its choice of language and style of presentation the social, economic, political and cultural context from which the discourse emanates.

Gunther Kress in *Linguistic Processes in Sociocultural Practice* (Australia: Deakin University Press, 1985) provides the following useful explanation of discourse: 'Institutions and social groupings have specific meanings and values which are articulated in language in systematic ways. Following the work particularly of Michel Foucault, I refer to these systematically-organized modes of talking as discourse. Discourses ... give expression to the meanings and values of an institution.

'Beyond that, they define, describe and delimit what is possible to say and not possible to say (and by extension what is possible to do or not to do) with respect to the area of concern of that institution, whether marginally or centrally. A discourse provides a set of possible statements about a given area, and organizes and gives structure to the manner in which a particular topic, object, process is to be talked about. In that it provides descriptions, rules, permissions and prohibitions of social and individual action.'

The analysis of discourses is central to the study of media, which is essentially about how TEXTS are encoded and how the MEANING of those texts, operating within and influenced by contexts, is decoded. Discourses are, in the words of John Fiske, 'socially produced' and a 'socially located way of making sense of an important area of experience'. Reality is a constant part of experience – how is it reconstructed into discourse? And how is it influenced by other discourses? (See INTERTEXTUALITY.)

All discourses are framed within *narratives* of one form or another. In news, or indeed in fiction, the story is what happens, the discourse how the story is told and the CONNOTATIONS or meanings embedded within it – the PREFERRED READINGS. Discourses struggle for attention, some are dominant and thus hold the public key to the definition of reality. They rigorously conform to *conventions* that work through mechanisms of information control (see AGENDA-SETTING; CONSENSUS; GATEKEEPING) and are IDEOLOGY-driven (see DEMONIZATION; PHOTO-GRAPHIC-NEGATIVIZATION; NEWS VALUES; WEDOM, THEYDOM).

Ultimately discourse is about ruling explanations and thus contributes to the nature of MYTH. Christopher P. Campbell in *Race, Myth and the News* (US: Sage, 1995) sees myth not as the 'grand storytelling tradition associated with ancient cultures' but in the 'sense of the stories that modern societies unwittingly create to reduce life's contradictions and complexities'. This is what the discourse of news does, it 'comprises continuing stories which uphold and consolidate myth which ultimately focuses on order and disorder'. Campbell argues that 'News is a way of creating order out of disorder, offering cultural meanings, resolutions and reassurances.'

Discourse serves (and services) myth and the desired end-product is COMMON SENSE; in other words a state of affairs in which that which is defined by discourses is so patently commonsensical that it cannot be seriously contradicted. Campbell identifies the *divisive* rather than *cohesive* potential of commonsensical discourse: 'The danger of the commonsense claim to truth is in its exclusion of those who live outside the familiar world it represents.' See DOMINANT DISCOURSE. See also *TOPIC GUIDE* under LANGUAGE/DISCOURSE/NARRATIVE.

Discourse analysis Form of MASS COMMUNICATION analysis that concentrates upon the ways in which the media convey information, focusing on the language of presentation – linguistic patterns, word and phrase selection (lexical choices), grammatical constructions and story coherence. In particular, discourse analysis sets out to account for the textual form in which the mass media present IDEOLOGY to readership or audience. See CONTENT ANALYSIS; MODES OF MEDIA ANALYSIS.

Discourse of power The French philosopher Michel Foucault wrote that *all* arguments as to the truth are driven by the will to power, that is to exert control. Clearly, in terms of the media, discourses are perceived as means of exerting influence and control over audiences. Foucault saw the field of a discourse in the same way that a physicist sees the electromagnetic field: it is defined not by its will to truth, but by its will to power. A discourse seeks power and that is what marks out its range. See HEGEMONY; IDEOLOGY.

Discursive communication Susanne Langer in *Philosophy in a New Key* (US: Harvard University Press, 1942) differentiated between what she named *discursive* communication – prose and logic – and *non-discursive* communication, such as poetry, music and ritual.

Discursive contestation Situation, usually occurring in the transmission of NEWS, where the AUDIENCE is permitted room to challenge or disagree; where news TEXTS passing through *frames* of production, are more open (to interpretation) than closed. News formats either facilitate discursive contestation or close down its potential.

Simon Cottle in 'Television news and citizenship: packaging the public sphere', published in *No News is Bad News: Radio, Television and the Public* (UK: Longman, 2001), edited by Michael Bromley, talks of how 'incredibly "restricted" some news formats are when reporting news stories'. Conventionalized TV news formats frame and discursively 'seal' the text from alternative interpretations. On the other hand, where 'words are spoken by accessed voices', that is by members of the public rather than media professionals, news texts are more open to discursive contestation.

Cottle argues that formats should work towards what he terms 'participatory control' or alternative frames where 'social actors are granted resources and news space to present in their own ways, and in their own words, their own frameworks of understanding'.

The author presents an analysis in tabular form of his studies of TV news formats (the result of a research project, UK News Access, funded by Bath Spa University College). He lists ten British TV news and presentational formats, varying from the 'tight' frame of newscaster only to the more discursive frame of live group interviews. He summarizes his findings by saying that 'Nearly half of all TV news items ... provide few if any opportunities for direct access and discursive engagement by non-news voices, and such voices that are referenced remain the discursive prisoners of the news presenters and their informing news frame.' See DISEMPOWERMENT; FRAMING: MEDIA.

Discursive gap Term used by Roger Fowler in *Language in the News: Discourse and Ideology in the Press* (UK: Routledge, 1991). The 'gap' is that which exists between the mode of address of the newspaper – formal, bureaucratic – and that of the perceived reception mode of the reader – informal and personal, especially readers of the popular press. Fowler argues that 'the fundamental device in narrowing the discursive gap is the promotion of oral models within the printed newspaper text, giving an illusion of conversation in which common sense is spoken about matters on which there is consensus'.

He believes 'the basic task for the writer is to word institutional statements (those of the newspaper, and those of its sources) in a style appropriate to interpersonal communication, because the reader is an individual and must be addressed as such. The task is not only stylistic, but also ideological: institutional concepts have to be translated into personal thought.' In brief, the press employs a range of devices to simulate a sense of 'orality' which has the writer sitting next to the reader around the kitchen table or in the pub and joining in a process of 'co-production'; the product being CONSENSUS, an apparently shared vision of the world.

Disempowerment The taking away, from individuals, GROUPS, communities or nations, of the power to have control over their lives. In *World Communication: Disempowerment & Self-Empowerment* (UK/US: Zed Books, 1995), Cees Hamelink describes disempowerment as 'the reduction of people's ability to define themselves and construct their own identities'. It can be the result of a deliberate strategy or the unintended outcome of developments locally, nationally or internationally. As a strategy, says Hamelink, disempowerment 'often employs the deceit of making people believe that existing conditions are desirable and preferred out of free will. The most perverse form of disempowerment makes people accept their own dependency and second rate position.'

A complicating factor in the assessment of the motives lying behind disempowerment 'is the real possibility of people inviting their own disempowerment'. In communication terms, disempowerment arises from the denial of access to, or the mediated access to, information and knowledge, for dominance 'does not only operate through imposition, but also through deprivation'.

The PRIVATIZATION of communications is seen as an agent of disempowerment: 'As knowledge is created and controlled as private property, knowledge as common good is destroyed.' For Hamelink the inherent meaning of privatization is *private = to deprive*.

It follows that if communication is a key tool in the process of empowerment, it can similarly be used as a tool of empowerment. Strategies of empowerment include regulation, the provision of power to people through human rights legislation (such as a FREEDOM OF INFORMATION act or laws facilitating a RIGHT OF REPLY) or public-interest regulation (such as the Charter of the BBC).

Regulation can also be seen in national press councils, usually voluntary arrangements, created to protect the public against abuses committed by newspapers and journals. The weaknesses of these forms of empowerment are many and varied: voluntary WATCHDOGS can so easily end up dogs without teeth, without the power to insist that media perform according to empowerment principles; and all of this presupposes that the law itself is a force for equality, of access and treatment.

Another key to empowerment is education, 'the need to make people critically aware of how media are organized, how they function, and how their contents can be analyzed', in other words, media education. Once again, problems abound, but the provision of media education is critical. Hamelink quotes Len Masterman in *Teaching the Media* (UK: Comedia, 1985) who believes that 'Media education is an essential step in the long march towards a truly participatory democracy, and the democratization of our institutions.' See PEOPLE'S COMMUNICATION CHARTER.

Disenfranchisement (of readership) Researchers have commented on the extent to which some newspapers reflect an assumption – possibly that of the owners and editors – that their readership is totally uninvolved and uninterested in the political processes and events of the country. It is as if the readers were politically disenfranchised, not able to participate in the political process, and thus news of political affairs is of no concern to them. Such papers aim to entertain, to concentrate on stories of human interest and drama rather than to inform.

Disinformation Derives from the Russian, *Dezinformatsiya*, a term especially associated with the former Soviet Union's secret service, the KGB. It applied to the use of forgery and other techniques to discredit targeted governments, persons or policies. The process of disinformation is, of course, as old as mankind, and sowing the seeds of disinformation is matched by accusing the opposition of spreading disinformation. See EFFECTS OF THE MASS MEDIA.

Displacement effect In psychological theory, *displacement* is one of the major mechanisms of ego-defence identified by Sigmund Freud. Displacement occurs when an individual chooses an alternative focus for the expression of feelings and emotions because he/she feels unable to express them towards their real target – the 'kick the cat' syndrome. In relation to the media, displacement *effect* refers to the reorganization of activities that takes place with the introduction of some new interest or attention-drawer, such as TV. Activities such as reading may be cut down, or stopped altogether, to make time for viewing. New media 'displace' or adjust the placement of other media. Cinema-going habits have been substantially affected by the introduction of TV, even more so with access to films on video and DVD.

The notion of *functional similarity* has often been applied as a yardstick to measure the extent and nature of displacement: if the new is functionally similar to the old, then the old is likely to be displaced. Functionally dissimilar activities are likely to hold their own. The difficulty is in establishing what functions a medium actually serves, which means that displacement is all the more difficult to assess.

As a result of TV, do people talk less, read less, go out with friends less, socialize less? Does TV mop up marginal activities, displace real with second-hand experience; does it displace 'day-dreaming'? Evidence concerning people's reactions to programmes is so open to influence from INTERVENING VARIABLES (IVs) that it is difficult to use it as a basis for reliable theory. That people stay in and watch TV more instead of dining out at a restaurant may have nothing to do with TV and everything to do with financial necessity. See EFFECTS OF THE MASS MEDIA; USES AND GRATIFICATIONS THEORY. See also *TOPIC GUIDE* under COMMUNICATION THEORY.

Disqualifying communication A form of self-protection, or DEFENSIVE COMMUNICATION when, in a situation causing embarrassment, anxiety or uneasiness, people talk aimlessly about, say, the weather, or go into a variety of non-verbal responses in order to avoid direct communication. The politician's version of this is 'No comment'. See INTERPERSONAL COMMUNICATION.

Dissolve A process in camerawork by which one picture fades out and the following scene fades in on top of it. Also called a 'mix'. See SHOT.

Dissonance Occurs when two COGNITIVE inputs to our mental processes are out of line. The result is a certain amount of psychological discomfort. Action is usually taken to resolve the dissonance and restore *balance*. Several strategies are commonly employed in order to achieve this: downgrading the source of dissonance; compliance with rather than acceptance of new expectations and ideas; changing one's previous ideas and attitudes; and avoidance of the source of dissonance.

All messages, particularly those conveyed to a mass AUDIENCE, are potentially a source of dissonance to someone. If they disturb the intended receiver(s), then they may well be ignored or rejected. The need for messages intended for a mass audience to be successful, however, ensures that such messages are often well 'laundered' in order to reduce their potential offensiveness. See CONGRUENCE THEORY; SELECTIVE EXPOSURE.

Distributed denial of service (DoS) Process by which computer hackers (see HACKER, HACKTIVIST) use special software to take control of other people's computers: a form of trespass or occupation in which endless – and spurious – requests for information block and disrupt the flow of genuine information exchange. This invariably malicious practice has affected the websites of individuals as well as those of corporate giants such as Amazon, Microsoft and Yahoo.

Diversification In media terms, the spread of ownership and control into a wide range of associated, and often unassociated, products and services. Thus newspapers have moved into TV share-holding; TV companies into set rentals, bingo and social clubs, and motorway catering services. In parallel, major corporations have moved into media ownership – oil companies buying up newspaper chains and investing in BROADCASTING interests, book publishing and record production. The result of diversification is often, paradoxically, concentration of control, and a real danger to a newspaper, film company or publishing house of being just another 'product' on the shelf of the multinational conglomerate whose objective is profit maximization above all other considerations. See CONGLOMERATES; DIGITIZATION.

D-Notices Defence notices; British government memoranda requesting newspapers not to publish specific items of information considered by authority to pose a security risk if widely disseminated. Notices are issued by the Services, Press and Broadcasting Committee. They have no binding force at law, even in wartime, but a newspaper or broadcasting station, by defying a D-Notice, may soon incur a harsher response from government.

At the beginning of the UK-supported US bombing of Afghanistan in October 2001, D-Notices were issued requesting the PRESS not to carry reports that speculated on possible troop movements. These followed accounts in the UK *Sunday Times* which stated that the SAS (Special Air Services) were already operating in Afghanistan. See CENSORSHIP; OFFICIAL SECRETS ACT (UK).

Documentary Any mode of communication which, in addressing an AUDIENCE, documents events or situations – books, radio, theatre, photography, film or TV. Usually based upon recorded or observable fact, the documentary may aim for objectivity or PROPAGANDA; it may, however, in terms of human documentation, be highly subjective. 'Even when temperate,' writes William Stott in *Documentary Expression and Thirties America* (US/UK: Oxford University Press, 1973), 'a human document carries and communicates feeling, the raw material of drama.'

British film director, producer and theorist John Grierson (1898–1972) is thought to have been first to use the word documentary, in a New York *Sun* review (1926) of Robert Flaherty's film *Moana*, a study of the way of life of the South Seas islanders. In fact, 'documentary' is as old as cinema itself. Louis Lumière's early short films of 1895, one showing the demolition of a wall, another of a train coming into a station, can be described as documentaries.

The founding father of documentary film-making in the UK and later in Canada, Grierson never claimed scientific objectivity for such films. For him the documentary was far more than a straightforward reconstruction on film of reality. He spoke of the 'creative use of actuality' in which the director re-formed fact in order to reach towards an inner truth. Indeed when documentarists have felt it necessary to get at the truth of a subject as they perceive it, they have not held back from fictionalization, often using actors, often turning the real-life person into an actor recreating a scene.

In the 1930s FILM documentary ran parallel with RADIO documentary – the BBC showed considerable innovative enterprise in this field, especially its Manchester studio – and, in the US, many impressive publications combined documentary evidence with outstanding photography. The themes were very often those of the Depression: concern at the plight of the poor, the unemployed, the alienated; and the mode was largely to have the people speak for themselves rather than distance the impact of their experience by using the mediation of a commentator.

The documentary approach has been a recurring feature in modern theatre, especially from the 1960s. Historical or contemporary events on stage are far from new: Aeschylus dramatized the victory of Marathon (490 BC) and Shakespeare reconstructed history, often to fit the perceptions of the Tudor monarchy, in a third of his output.

German dramatist Rolf Hochhuth won worldwide attention with his documentary drama *The Representative* in 1963, on the subject of the Papacy and the Jews during the Second World War

(1939–45). He followed this up with *Soldiers* (1967) based upon the alleged involvement of British Prime Minister Winston Churchill in the wartime death of the Polish General Sikorski. In the UK, Peter Brook's highly successful *US* (1966) was an indictment of American involvement in the Vietnam War.

On-stage documentaries – in the US often termed the Theatre of Fact – have frequently been presented with the aid of official and press reports, original diaries, projected photographs, tape recordings and newsreel films. In the case of the Royal Court production *Falkland Sound* (1983), a moving – and damning – recollection of the Falklands War (1982) was presented through the letters home of a young naval officer killed in action.

Faction or dramadoc are terms mainly associated with TV documentaries in which actors recreate historical lives, such as the BBC's *The Voyage of Charles Darwin* (1978) or play the part of famous people of the immediate past, such as Thames Television's *Edward and Mrs Simpson* (1978), Southern TV's *Winston Churchill – The Wilderness Years* (1981), and ITV's *Kennedy* (1983). To TV producers faction has come to represent an ideal synthesis of education, information and entertainment, albeit highly selective and deeply coloured by contemporary perspectives.

Just as documentary has borrowed from fictional narratives, fiction has taken on the 'guise' of documentary. Such works are described as 'mock' documentaries and they aim to examine the borderline between the real and the invented. A memorable example is Woody Allen's *Zelig* in which he achieved remarkable results by combining newsreels, stills and live footage (see Craig Hight and Jane Roscoe's *Faking It: Mock-Documentary and the Subversion of Factuality*, UK: Manchester University Press, 2001). See CINEMATOGRAPHY, ORIGINS; CINÉMA VÉRITÉ; DIRECT CINEMA; FLY-ON-THE-WALL; RADIO BALLADS; SOAPS: DOCU-SOAPS.

Dolly A trolley on which a camera unit can be soundlessly moved about during shooting; can usually be mounted on rails. A 'crab dolly' will move in any direction.

Domestication of the foreign See NEWS: GLOBALIZATION OF.

Dominant culture See CULTURE.

Dominant discourse In a general sense, DISCOURSE is talk; converse; holding forth in speech and writing on a subject. We are referring both to the content of communicative exchanges and to the level at which those exchanges take place, and in what mode or style as well as to whom the discourse is addressed. A dominant discourse is that which takes precedence over others, reducing alternative content, alternative approaches to 'holding forth' to subordinate discourses.

All public discourse is socially and culturally based, thus it follows that the dominant discourse is usually that which emanates from those dominant in the social and cultural order. See ELITE; IDEOLOGY; HEGEMONY; POWER ELITE.

Dominant, subordinate, radical Three categories of response in terms of the reading of media messages on the part of AUDIENCE are posed by Frank Parkin in *Class, Inequality and Political Order* (UK: Paladin, 1972). Do we accept what we are told, only half accept or substantially reject it? Parkin argues that it is our place in the social structure that conditions our response. Stuart Hall in 'The determination of news photographs', in Stanley Cohen and Jock Young (eds), *The Manufacture of News* (UK: Constable, 1973), supports Parkin's view, with the same categories but different terminology.

The dominant system of response (Hall calls it a *dominant code*) signifies that the dominant values and existing society are wholly accepted by the respondent; the subordinate response (Hall's *negotiated code*) indicates general acceptance of dominant VALUES and existing social structures, but the respondent is prepared to argue that a particular group – blacks, unemployed, women – within that structure may be unfairly dealt with and that something should be done about it. The radical response (Hall's *oppositional code*) rejects the PREFERRED READING of the dominant code and the social values that produced it.

David Morley's researches into audience response, published in *The Nationwide Audience* (UK: British Film Institute, 1980), give substance to Parkin and Hall's division of response, but also emphasize other response-conditioning factors such as education, occupation, political affiliation, geographical region, religion and family. More recent commentators have expanded on the response codes mentioned here; for example, a *popular* response may be characterized by *inattention* on the part of audience or the rejection of media messages because 'they have nothing to do with us'. See EFFECTS OF THE MASS MEDIA; ETHNOGRAPHIC (APPROACH TO AUDIENCE MEASUREMENT); POLYSEMY. See also *TOPIC GUIDE* under AUDIENCES/CONSUMPTION AND RECEPTION OF MEDIA.

Double exposure Two pictures superimposed upon one another on the same piece of film. Like reverse motion, double exposure in filming began by being a simple visual curiosity before it became a fully fledged means of artistic expression. It was first used in still photography, where double or multiple exposure images produced what was described as 'spirit photography'. Georges Méliès (1861–1938) used it in his films from 1908. It has been used dramatically to achieve many effects, chiefly that of suggesting the supernatural, and of conveying the process of thought and of spirituality.

Dramadoc See DOCUMENTARY.

Drama: television drama See TELEVISION DRAMA (UK).

Dress Dress is an important element of non-verbal communication and one that plays a significant role when people are forming first impressions of one another. Generally speaking, dress refers not only to clothes but also to hairstyle, jewellery, fashion accessories and make-up. Dress can communicate many messages about personality, cultural or group identity – gender, CLASS, status, wealth, age, roles, fashion-consciousness, STEREOTYPE, social context, historical context, to name but a few. A person may consciously or unconsciously convey messages through dress and, of course, receivers may decode these messages differently to what was intended by the sender; several receivers may decode the messages differently from each other. Dress, particularly uniforms, can though convey quite clear messages. See COMMUNICATION, NON-VERBAL; OBJECT LANGUAGE. See also *TOPIC GUIDE* under INTERPERSONAL COMMUNICATION.

---

* Dick Hebdige, *Sub-Culture: The Meaning of Style* (UK: Methuen, 1979; Routledge, 2002); Ken Gelder and Sarah Thornton (eds), *The Sub-Cultures Reader* (UK: Routledge, 1997); Angela McRobbie, *In the Culture Society: Art, Fashion and Popular Music* (UK: Sage, 1999); Stella Bruzzi and Pamela Church Gibson (eds), *Fashion Cultures: Theories, Explorations and Analysis* (UK: Sage, 2000).

Dry-run TV programme rehearsal in which action, lines, cues, etc. are tried out prior to the final rehearsal.

Dub, dubbing In film-making, to blend speech, music, incidental sound and sound-effects on to film or videotape. At a later stage, the language of the 'home' audience may be dubbed on to the sound track in preference to subtitles. See POST-SYNCHRONIZATION.

Dumping Worldwide practice, led by the US, of saturating foreign markets with broadcasting material, extremely cheap to hire in comparison with the cost of home companies making their own original programmes. See MEDIA IMPERIALISM.

Duopoly   A monopoly held by two organizations rather than one. In BROADCASTING, the term is used to refer to the duopoly once held in the UK, by the BBC and the IBA (Independent Broadcasting Authority; succeeded in 1991 by the ITC – Independent Television Commission). See MEDIA CONTROL.

DVD (Digital Video Disc)   See DIGITAL VIDEO DISC (DVD).

Dyad   A communication dyad consists of two persons interacting and is the elemental unit of INTER-PERSONAL COMMUNICATION.

Dynamic mediation   See IMPARTIALITY.

E

Echelon   An automated global computer intelligence-gathering network run in partnership between the UK Government Communication Headquarter Agency (GCHQ) and the US National Security; using the intelligence agencies' own network of satellite and listening bases and also operated in Canada, Australia and New Zealand. It has been estimated that Echelon intercepts up to three billion communications a day. So-termed Echelon Dictionaries search intercepted messages according to target lists of subjects and people. See SURVEILLANCE.

Effects of the mass media   Can be broadly defined as any change induced directly or indirectly by the recording, filming or reporting of events. Analysts of effects, or impact, are concerned with the modification of attitudes and of behaviour of individuals and GROUPS, and the process of measuring these effects is immensely complicated, as the ground upon which the measurements are taken is constantly shifting.

The actual effect of the media on audiences, so far as it can be ascertained, is arguably less significant than the *perceived* effect. In the nineteenth century those in authority were of the view that access by the mass of the population to the printed word might turn docility into uprising. The new mass medium of the cinema was similarly accused of a wide range of 'effects', while TV, in the eyes of some, is responsible for many of the ills of our time, as though such media could somehow be divorced from the social, political and cultural environment that produces them.

A few generalized hypotheses about effects can be tentatively posited: the media are probably more likely to modify and reinforce attitudes than change them; media impact will be greater among the uncommitted ('floating voters') than the committed; impact will be more influential if all the media are saying more or less the same thing at the same time (CONSISTENCY); equally, if the media are concentrating on a small rather than diverse number of stories (INTENSITY) and if they are repeating messages, images, viewpoints over and over again (FREQUENCY).

'The timing of communication processes,' writes Colin Seymour-Ure in *The Political Impact of Mass Media* (UK: Constable, 1974) 'is probably one of the most important determinants of mass media effects.' If the timing is right, the media can often be the arbiters of crisis, by being in the most prominent position to define it. Because of their AGENDA-SETTING capacity, the media have influence upon the criteria that, in the public domain, decide what is important and what is not, what is normal and what is deviant, what is CONSENSUS and what is *dissensus*, what is significant, or newsworthy, and what is marginal.

No summary of effects, however brief, should neglect the role played – some would say most powerfully – by the media in supporting, reinforcing and cementing patterns of social control, not the least by maintaining and sometimes fashioning the symbols of legitimate government. See *TOPIC GUIDE* under MEDIA: POWER, EFFECTS, INFLUENCE.

* Shearon A. Lowery and Melvyn L. DeFleur, *Milestones in Mass Media Research: Media Effects* (US: Longman, 1995).

Elaborated and Restricted Codes   In *Class, Codes and Control, Vol. 1* (UK: Paladin, 1971), Basil Bernstein posed a now-famous classification of language codes, the Elaborated and Restricted Codes based upon researches into the language use of children. Bernstein maintains that there are substantial differences in speech between middle-CLASS and working-class children, the former using the Elaborated Code, the latter the Restricted Code.

The determinant of the code in each case is the nature of the social relationships and influences to which the child is exposed. A close-knit, traditional working-class community, Bernstein argues, tends to use the Restricted Code because a high degree of shared MEANING is assumed. In the more typically loose-knit middle-class communities there are fewer grounds for making assumptions about shared meaning and therefore a more explicit, Elaborated, Code is used. This is not to say that the middle class does not possess its own Restricted Codes in particular social or professional situations. The important point is that the middle class can move with ease from a Restricted to an Elaborated Code.

The Restricted Code tends to be less complex than the Elaborated, with a small vocabulary and simpler sentence structure. It tends to be spoken rather than written. It is easy to predict (high in REDUNDANCY) whereas the Elaborated Code is less easy to predict (high in *entropy*). The Restricted Code is orientated towards social relations, towards COMMONALITY, while the Elaborated Code represents an emphasis on individuality and individual differences.

The one is the language of the street, the home, the playground, the pub; the other – very largely – the language of school, the language of formal education. Thus, Bernstein indicates, within the educational context, the user of the Restricted Code is placed at a disadvantage. He does not argue that the Elaborated Code is superior to the Restricted Code, only that it is different and more useful for upward social mobility.

Bernstein's claims prompted considerable debate, some of it critical, and a number of researchers would argue that his classification was inflexible. Martin Montgomery, for instance, in *An Introduction to Language and Society* (UK/US: Routledge, 1995) argues that 'There is, for example, in the final analysis hardly any linguistic evidence to support the division of speech into two mutually exclusive codes or speech variants. And by the same token, Bernstein's treatment of the social structure looks with hindsight somewhat rigid and schematic.' See *TOPIC GUIDE* under LANGUAGE/DISCOURSE/NARRATIVE; REPRESENTATION.

* Basil Bernstein, 'Social class, language and socialization', an extract from his major work, in J. Corner and J. Hawthorn (eds), *Communication Studies* (UK: Arnold, 1993).

Electreotactile illusion By means of virtual reality technology the feel of something is stimulated and simulated: the touch of (virtual) sandpaper, of (virtual) skin, hair, marble, leather; usually created by data gloves installed with a tactile feedback system.

Electronic democracy See TELEVISION: INTERACTIVE TELEVISION.

Electronic mail: e-mail The sending and receiving of e-mails – letters and memos through the 'postal' system of the computer – has become the fastest-growing means of communication in business, within institutions and between friends, families and total strangers across the world. It has proved a useful tool in the exchange of knowledge, the provision of advice, the two-way transmission of research data, and the sharing across social and national boundaries of a myriad of problems. It serves as a link between GROUPS and communities of like interest – all for the cost of a local phone call.

In 1992 only 2 per cent of the American population used the e-mail service. This rose in 1998 to 15 per cent. The rise in what has been referred to as 'computer babble' – both for business and leisure use – is such that e-mails now constitute a problem as much as an opportunity. The *Wall Street Journal* has gauged that a typical worker in a European company deals with an average 150 e-mails a day. Allowing time to read these and reply, it would take some four to five hours to process – a dramatic case of information overload. The *Journal* reported that an executive returning to the States from a business trip in Europe found 2000 e-mails waiting to be dealt with.

E-mails are also very public statements, open to the scrutiny of those not intended to read them. Then there is the growth of junk e-mails (known as 'spam'), as a UK *Guardian* leader of 19 January 1999 puts it: 'unsolicited e-mails from companies advertising their wares, or net nuts who believe that the whole world hangs on their thoughts'. As for ENCRYPTING messages in and out, the *Guardian* believes that 'the remedy may be worse than the disease'. As the INTERNET grows in popularity, e-mails will become INFORMATION BLIZZARDS. 'Soon,' the paper fears, 'it may be ripe to re-invent the envelope.' See *TOPIC GUIDE* under CYBERCULTURE: THE NET, THE WEB; MEDIA: TECHNOLOGIES.

Electronic newsgathering Referred to as ENG, the gathering of sound and vision NEWS reports electronically, usually transmitted via telephone links or from transmitter vans. Much lighter and more compact than traditional film or TV cameras, electronic equipment records on to cassette, bypassing the film processing stage: pictures from the scene of action can be transmitted directly or stored electronically. EFP (Electronic Field Production) is an advance on ENG, making location programmes of all kinds possible without having the cameras tied to an outside broadcasting (OB) vehicle.

Elite A small group within a society who may be socially acknowledged as superior in some sense and who influence or control some or all sectors of the society. Several definitions of the term elite exist and these influence the precise focus of research into the relationship between the media, elites and society.

Early writers generally see the elite as a ruling elite or oligarchy whose power is general and affects most aspects of society. Writers such as Vilfredo Pareto (1848–1923) and Gaetano Mosca (1848–1941) regarded elites as being inevitable, whatever the political system. C. Wright Mills in a study of elites in US society entitled *The Power Elite* (US: Oxford University Press, 1956) points to the similarity of backgrounds, attitudes and VALUES, and power skills of the members of the three elites which, he argues, dominate American society: the *military*, the *economic* and the *political*. He also comments on the degree of personal and family contacts between elite members and the interchangeability of personnel between top posts in the military, economic and political elites from which the 'power elite' is recruited.

This concept of *elite cohesion* has been of interest to several media researchers who have sought to investigate links between members of economic and political elites and those who own or control the media, and the effect such links might have on media output.

The notion of a ruling elite or oligarchy contrasts with the Marxist concept of a ruling CLASS. Whilst elite theorists point out the necessity for the elite to recruit from outside itself, to remain accessible to the influence of the non-elite and to maintain a CONSENSUS among the non-elite, which legitimates the elite's right to rule, Marxist analysis stresses the continuing and increasing polarization or separation of the ruling from the ruled class. Marxist analysis of the media therefore concentrates upon the role of the media in propagating the ideas of the dominant class in order to create a false consciousness, or to create HEGEMONY, which is instrumental in subjugating the rest.

The liberalist-PLURALIST school of analysis sees the media as a kind of FOURTH ESTATE pressuring governing elites and reminding them of their dependency on majority opinion. Other commentators have pointed to the role social elites play in media *coverage*. Stuart Hall in 'The determination of news photographs', in Stanley Cohen and Jock Young (eds), *The Manufacture of News: Deviance, Social Problems and the Mass Media* (UK: Constable, 1973), comments that 'Newspapers are full of the actions, situations and attributes of elite persons.' See COMMANDERS OF THE SOCIAL ORDER; DOMINANT DISCOURSE; ESTABLISHMENT; GUARD DOG METAPHOR; NEWS VALUES; POWER ELITE.

Ellipsis jump-cut See SOUND-BITE.

Ellul's theory of technique See TECHNIQUE: ELLUL'S THEORY OF TECHNIQUE.

E-mail See ELECTRONIC MAIL: E-MAIL.

Emancipatory use of the media Term employed by Hans Magnus Enzensberger in 'Constituents of a theory of the media', in *Sociology of Mass Communication* (UK: Penguin, 1972), edited by Denis McQuail, to contrast with what he defines as the *repressive* use of the media. He characterizes the emancipatory use of the media as follows: decentralized programme (as opposed to the repressive mode of a centrally controlled programme); each receiver a potential transmitter (as opposed to one transmitter, many receivers); mobilization of the masses (as opposed to immobilization of isolated individuals); interaction of those involved, and FEEDBACK (as opposed to passive consumer behaviour); a political learning process (as opposed to *depoliticization*); and collective production, social control by self-organization (as opposed to production by specialists, control by property owners or bureaucracy). See DEMOCRACY; DOMINANT, SUBORDINATE, RADICAL.

Embargo Restriction set upon a news item, indicating when that item can be published or broadcast. A PRESS release from government or industry, for example, will be headed 'Not for publication/broadcasting until ...' and give a specific date.

Emblem See NON-VERBAL BEHAVIOUR: REPERTOIRE.

Emergent culture Raymond Williams uses this term in *Marxism and Literature* (UK: Oxford University Press, 1977) when he argues that HEGEMONY, the state of cultural dominance of a POWER ELITE over the population, is never complete; that the dominant discourses that operate in the hegemonic process are countered by alternative ways of seeing, reading and believing. Each emergent culture enters into debate or conflict with the dominant culture and is an agent for the mobilization of opposition to hegemonic control.

'No mode of production and therefore no dominant social order,' Williams writes, 'ever in reality includes or exhausts all human practice, human energy, and human intention.' There are residual VALUES and meanings that represent 'areas of human experience, aspiration, and achievement which the dominant culture neglects, undervalues, opposes, represses or even cannot recognize'.

Emotional dynamization Russian film director Sergei Eisenstein (1898–1948) used this expression to describe the collision of different images and actions brought about by the editing of film to detonate emotional response, both in relation to the theme of the film and its cinematic or aesthetic intent. See MONTAGE.

Emotive language To describe a crowd as a 'mob' or a 'rabble' is to be emotive, to convey not only information but one's own attitude towards the crowd and one's intention of influencing the receiver's attitude towards it. Emotive language tells as much about the communicator as the message. It reveals what he/she thinks and very often how he/she thinks. IDEOLOGY is the root and inspiration of the media use of emotive language. Newspapers often use it on those they disagree with, who appear somehow to threaten what the newspapers wish to preserve. In times of national emergency such as a war, emotive language is used to whip up support and fervour for the cause and to forge a sense of national unity.

Empathetic listening See LISTENING.

Empathy The ability to put oneself into another person's position, into another person's shoes, and to attempt to understand his/her behaviour and perspectives without filtering them through one's own value system. It is not possible totally to avoid such filtering but to be empathetic requires that an individual makes an effort to avoid judging others on the basis of his/her own subjective experiences and perspectives, and makes an attempt to see things from the other person's point of view, whilst retaining his/her own perspectives, values and so on. Clearly empathy has an important role to play in effective interpersonal communication and in reducing barriers to communication.

Empirical Based upon experience. Empirical research in the social sciences centres upon fieldwork – the collection of evidence about observable human behaviour. Such enquiry usually lacks or does not make explicit the theory guiding its procedures. Its evidence may be used to establish an isolated proposition, to test certain theoretical analyses against observable behaviour, or to gain insight into certain behaviours. Such evidence may itself generate hypotheses, concepts, models and theories.

Empowerment Giving to people, individually, as GROUPS or communities, power over their lives, of choice and decision. The role of the media in advocating, assisting, blocking or subverting empowerment is the subject of keen debate as the media increasingly operate on a global scale. Empowerment also refers to the ways in which AUDIENCE respond to media message, the degree to which it is capable of resistive reading (see DOMINANT, SUBORDINATE, RADICAL). Those who are 'empowered' are, first, capable of interpreting for themselves the agendas and meanings of media communication. They are able to 'make use' of these agendas and meanings to further individual or communal needs, ultimately with a political purpose: the power is to change things.

In *Soap Opera and Women's Talk: The Pleasure of Resistance* (US: Sage, 1994), Mary Ellen Brown suggests that soap opera viewing 'generally considered not only apolitical but also antipolitical, can, in fact, be political and the basis for a kind of empowerment'. She argues that for women in particular, soap operas are terrain in which women's GOSSIP NETWORKS can operate in a resistive way. The very notion of empowerment in relation to the media seems to be underpinned by the idea that, without media, people are 'without power' and that with it they are in danger of being 'disempowered' by the distractions offered by entertainment.

Yet some of the most notable examples of people asserting their own power by challenging that of the authorities indicate not only the power of values *collectively* expressed, but that of protesters in using the media to gain footholds on public agendas. See EMANCIPATORY USE OF THE MEDIA; PEOPLE'S COMMUNICATION CHARTER. See also *TOPIC GUIDE* under AUDIENCES/CONSUMPTION AND RECEPTION OF MEDIA; GENDER MATTERS; MEDIA ISSUES AND DEBATES.

Encode We communicate by means of a variety of visual and aural signals, which are assembled according to certain rules or codes. If Person A wishes to convey to Person B a MESSAGE that Person B is likely to understand, then the MESSAGE has to be encoded with Person B's ability to DECODE the message-carrying signals well in mind. The MEANING of a message is something the receiver assigns in the act of decoding, which is itself a part of an interaction with the encoder.

A glance at ANDERSCH, STAATS AND BOSTROM'S MODEL OF COMMUNICATION, 1969, helps here. This emphasizes the stages through which the act of encoding passes. There is a stimulus to a message, which is structured – put together – and evaluated for its possible effect on the receiver before it is transmitted. The same process occurs on the part of the receiver: the message is registered; it is reconstructed according to the decoder's perception of the message and of the encoder who has delivered the message; then the response is evaluated prior to transmission.

This is only the beginning of a continuing circle of sending and receiving, encoding and decoding. Contributory to the perceptions of encoder and decoder in the process of communication are such factors as previous experience, the current and future context of the interaction and the feelings, opinions, assumptions and values of the encoder and decoder. The terms *encipher* and *decipher* are sometimes used instead of encode and decode. See DEEP STRUCTURE; ELABORATED AND RESTRICTED CODES.

Encompassing situation Term coined by W.E. Brockriede in 'Demonstrations of the concept of rhetoric', *Quarterly Journal* 54 (1968) to describe the context of each and every act of communication, specifically the elaborate set of conventions and rules imposed upon an individual's behaviour in social situations.

Encrypt To 'scramble' signals – for satellite TV, for example, so that non-subscribers cannot tune into programmes.

Enculturation The process by which an individual acquires the VALUES, language, skills, ways of thinking and behavioural patterns of a particular CULTURE that enable them to function effectively within it. See ACCULTURATION, DECULTURATION; INTERCULTURAL COMMUNICATION; M-TIME, P-TIME; SAPIR–WHORF LINGUISTIC RELATIVITY HYPOTHESIS.

Enigma code See CODES OF NARRATIVE.

Enterprise fiction Term used by Estella Tincknell in an article entitled, 'Enterprise fictions: women of substance', in *Off-Centre: Feminism and Cultural Studies*, edited by Sarah Franklin, Celia Lury and Jackie Stacey (UK: HarperCollins Academic, 1991), to describe those works of fiction, written predominantly by and for women, whose central character is a woman who by dint of enterprise, energy, good looks and determination succeeds despite humble roots and early hardships in 'having it all' – wealth, power, lovers and a family.

Significantly the central female characters succeed through individual endeavour working *within* the patriarchal status quo, not by challenging it. These fictions, whilst celebrating certain aspects of femininity, can be charged with undermining the feminist cause by denying the need for the collective action and structural change necessary to advance the opportunities and rights of the *majority* of real-life women. See FEMINISM; GENDER.

Entropy See REDUNDANCY.

Ephemera In communications terms, publications such as cigarette cards, PICTURE POSTCARDS, and POSTERS produced for the moment, conveying information for immediate use. Ironically such ephemera are now collectors' items and illuminating records of our past. See CIGARETTE CARDS: CULTURAL INDICATORS.

Establishing shot Opening shot or sequence showing the location of a film scene or a juxtaposition of characters who will be involved in the subsequent NARRATIVE.

Establishment The ELITE in society, comprising people who because of wealth, birth or position in government are able to exercise considerable power and influence. Generally the term is applied to those who are not directly democratically answerable in their positions of power. See HEGEMONY; POWER ELITE.

Ethnic Term used in the social sciences to refer to a community of people possessing its own CULTURE. The characteristics that identify an ethnic group may include a common language, common customs and beliefs, and a cultural tradition. A society may contain several ethnic groups some of whom, but not all, may also be racial groups. One focus of current research is an exploration of the role the media play in the construction of ethnic identities.

Ethnocentrism The use of one's own CULTURE, its norms and VALUES, as a yardstick by which to measure, to judge, the attributes and activities of other cultures. Such judgement bears the implicit or explicit assumption that one's own culture is superior. Robert Levine and Donald Campbell in *Ethnocentrism: Theories of Conflict, Ethnic Attitudes and Group Behaviour* (US: Wiley, 1972) argue that there is a tendency for all social groups and societies to be ethnocentric. If this is the case, then such a tendency could be expected to have considerable impact upon the way in which messages about other cultures are interpreted and the way in which other cultures are discussed in any one culture.

According to H. Ehrlich in *The Social Psychology of Prejudice* (US: Wiley, 1973) *Ethnophaulisms*, for example, may be employed to convey a negative attitude towards those from another culture. Ehrlich identifies three categories of ethnophaulisms: 'First are the disparaging group nicknames. Second are words or expressions that explicitly devaluate the ethnic group. Third are words or expressions that have no explicit disparagement, but that function as mild derogations by using ethnic names irrelevantly. According to Ehrlich, ethnophaulisms serve as 'a linguistic indicator of past and present intergroup relations' and as 'an indicator of the user's attitude'. Their use can be seen as an indicator of PREJUDICE.

Ethnocentrism is seen by many commentators on media performance to influence the coverage of NEWS. We see, and thus report, the world through the lens of our ethnocentric perception, often falling into the trap of envisioning that world in terms of *us* and *them* (see WEDOM, THEYDOM). It follows that OBJECTIVITY is often at the mercy of how we see the world rather than how it actually is. See AGENDA-SETTING; EVENT: AMERICANIZING OF; MEDIA IMPERIALISM; NEWS VALUES.

Ethnographic (approach to audience measurement) An important body of cultural research into the relationship and interaction between TV texts and audience has been described as *ethnographic* – that is, describing a culture, emphasizing the native point of view. Researchers such as David Morley (see *The 'Nationwide' Audience: Structure and Decoding*, UK: British Film Institute, 1980) have set out to discover how audiences make active use of TELEVISION as part of their own CULTURE; as John Fiske puts it in 'British cultural studies', in *Channels of Discourse: Television and Contemporary Criticism*, edited by Robert C. Allen (UK: Methuen, 1987, reprinted by Routledge, 1990), to use television 'to make meanings that are useful to them in making sense of their own social experience and therefore themselves'.

Morley and other scholars such as Dorothy Hobson (see *'Crossroads': The Drama of a Soap Opera*, UK: Methuen, 1982), went to the people, kept a low profile in terms of shaping responses – so as to avoid what has been termed 'colonial representation' – and listened, at length and over fairly extended periods, to what audience groups thought of certain programmes, their characters, their narratives, their PREFERRED READINGS.

Ethnographic studies have revealed the fact that people respond to programmes much less along lines of social CLASS and in a much more varied way than some commentators have believed. Morley's findings indicated, for example, that the categories of textual reading by Frank Parkin (see DOMINANT, SUBORDINATE, RADICAL) and the similar reception code posed by Professor Stuart Hall, were simplistic: indeed the wide range of differing readings resisted categorization. See *TOPIC GUIDE* under RESEARCH METHODS.

* Shaun Moores, *Interpreting Audiences: The Ethnography of Media Consumption* (UK: Sage, 1993); Jennifer Mason, *Qualitative Researching* (UK: Sage, 1996); Stephen Taylor (ed.), *Ethnographic Research: A Reader* (UK/US: Sage 2001). See also from Sage two journals established in 2001: *Ethnography* and *Qualitative Research.*

Ethnophaulisms See ETHNOCENTRISM.

Ethos In communication terms, the ethos of a communicator determines the image one has of him or her at any given time – either one person or a GROUP. In their paper 'A summary of experimental research in ethos', *Speech Monographs* 30 (1963) Kenneth Anderson and Theodore Clevenger Jr refer to research findings that point to two general categories of ethos: *extrinsic* and *intrinsic*. The first is the image, say, of a speaker as it exists prior to a given speech; the second is the image derived from elements during the presentation of a speech, consciously or unconsciously provided by the speaker. The final impression is a mixture of extrinsic and intrinsic factors.

The prestige of a speaker, his/her appearance, likeableness, credibility, social CLASS, voice, etc. contribute to his/her ethos. Anderson and Clevenger assert that evidence from research proves 'that the ethos of the source is related in some way to the impact of the message' and that this applies 'not only to political, social, religious and economic issues but also to matters of aesthetic judgment and personal taste'.

Euphemism In polite circles, 'belly' is not referred to, but 'stomach' is acceptable. That is a euphemism, the rendering of blunt, harsh or unpleasant terms in mild, inoffensive or quaint LANGUAGE. Thus 'to die' may be rendered euphemistically as 'to pass away'; a 'bookie' may prefer to seek more status by calling him/herself a 'turf accountant'. In advertising 'budget items' are preferred to 'cheap goods'. In business, people are not 'sacked' but 'the labour force is slimmed' or 'downsized'.

Some euphemism is justifiable in INTERPERSONAL COMMUNICATION, for example at times of grief and tragedy; some are insulting to language and to human intelligence and dignity, such as the terminology of armed conflict where 'demographic targeting' means the destruction of cities by nuclear weapons; 'support structure' is civilians and 'collateral damage' is dead civilians. A recent euphemism in the UK has been the term 'entitlement card' broached by the Home Office to disguise its true intention, of being an ID card; euphemism in this case being used as a form of political *spin.*

Euronet A consortium of national computer interests in a number of European countries, working towards the creation of a mutually compatible interconnection of European databases. Euronet is designed for reasons as much political as economical, as a method of ensuring that in the long term the economic control of Europe remains in European hands, and thus, inextricably, the control of information.

European Community and media: Television Without Frontiers Title of a Council of Europe directive, October 1989, the first attempt by the European Community to regulate and institutionalize BROADCASTING between member nations. The directive requires EC members to guarantee unrestricted reception for audiences across Europe and to avoid any strategies likely to limit retransmission in their territory of any EC broadcasts that meet Community conditions. The directive lays down a policy of minimum regulation, granting equal rights to commercial operators and public service broadcasters while at the same time requiring no legal obligations to enhance public discourse. See DEREGULATION; FAIRNESS DOCTRINE (USA); PRIVATIZATION.

Europe: cross-border TV channels Since the 1980s the number of cross-border TV channels has risen to over 100, some 80 of these holding a licence from the UK Independent Television Commission (ITC), whose licences are cheap and easy to obtain, the prime criterion being that such stations are based in the UK.

Among the major cross border players are Arte, BBC Prime, BBC World, Bloomberg, Cartoon Network, CNN International, Discovery, Eurosport, Fox Kids, MTV, National Geographical and Sky News, most of which are registered with the ITC.

The expansion of cross-border transmission was made possible and encouraged by, three key factors: (1) DEREGULATION, which occurred through Europe (and elsewhere) during the 1980s and 1990s; (2) the European Community's Television Without Frontiers directive (see above), Article 2 of which prevents member states barring broadcasting emanating from other member states and (3) the possibilities brought about by SATELLITE TRANSMISSION. See LOCALIZATION.

---

* Jean K. Chalaby, 'Transnational television in Europe: the role of pan-European channels', *European Journal of Communication* (June 2002).

Event The occurrence that gives rise to media coverage will have fulfilled one or more, or an amalgam of, NEWS VALUES. In the analysis of media, different forms of event can be identified. Primarily there is the *key event* triggering media and subsequently public attention. Such an event may – as in the case of the terrorist attacks on the US Pentagon and New York's Twin Towers of the World Trade Center on 11 September 2001 – in turn trigger a worldwide sense of crisis.

In 'The impact of key events on the presentation of reality', in the *European Journal of Communication*, September 1995, Hans Mathias Kepplinger and Johanna Habermeier suggest a useful typology of the causes and communicative functions of events (see diagram). The coverage of events, especially if they give grounds for concern about causes and consequences, stimulates the 'activities of pressure groups who see an opportunity of gaining media attention, since their concerns fit in with the established topic. The consequence is an increased number of mediated and staged events.'

Equally, such coverage tends to exert 'pressure upon decision-makers in politics, business, administration, etc.'. The authors give the example of how safety rules for petrol tankers may be changed as a result of media conjecture about possible, rather than actual, accidents. Coverage of key events will, say Kepplinger and Habermeier, enhance the coverage of similar or related events, and add interest and urgency to events thematically linked.

		Causes	
Communicative functions	Genuine (independent of the media)	Mediated (influenced by the media)	Staged (for the media)
Key events			
Similar events			
Thematically related events			

Kepplinger and Habermeier's model of media events, 1995

Of course, the nature of coverage will vary between media – for example, between daily and weekly newspapers or between broadsheets and tabloids. The authors note a tendency in the reporting of key events to give the impression of an *accumulation* of such events (hence the sense of crisis) whereas what is actually happening is an accumulation of another kind: similar stories, being gathered together from the past as well as the present, are being reinvigorated and intensified as they compound information about the new key event.

Key events thus trigger apparent waves of such events when in reality only one has occurred: 'Here one has to take into account that the news coverage creates a false impression that events accumulate and problems become more urgent.' See EVENT: AMERICANIZING OF.

Event: Americanizing of Practice, in the US, of reporting world events in relation to American interest or interests. As Susan D. Moeller points out in *Compassion Fatigue: How the Media Sell Disease, Famine, War and Death* (US/UK: Routledge, 1999), 'The American filter, the notion of relevance to the United States, is very important.' Speaking of the American public, Moeller says, 'Since our knowledge about the lands outside our borders is minimal, even the abbreviated version of events which makes it into news has to be translated for us' (see ETHNOCENTRISM).

In the conclusion to her analysis of compassion fatigue and how the media can strive to avoid creating or reinforcing it, Moeller believes that the Americanizing of events '(once called the "Coca-Colonization" of events) can be a positive force to attract the public's attention to a far-off event, but it should not be the defining characterization of that event' for 'once in play, the Americanization can become a crutch, simplifying a crisis beyond recognition, and certainly beyond understanding'.

The author concedes that 'Americans are already too self-involved' and she blames the media's 'entrenched news net and news priorities' as the cause 'of their neglect of certain events or countries'. See HISTORICAL ALLUSION.

Excorporation The process by which those who are not members of the dominant group(s) within society – for example, members of YOUTH CULTURES and SUBCULTURES utilize the material resources provided by the prevailing system to fashion cultural statements that communicate their difference from or opposition to the dominant culture. See BRICOLAGE; COUNTER-CULTURE; STYLE.

Exnomination Roland Barthes uses this term in *Mythologies* (UK: Paladin, 1973) to describe the assumption on the part of the communicator, usually the mass media, that certain VALUES are so basic and so widely shared, indeed so natural, that they are beyond question and need not be referred to or justified. Exnomination is integral to the working of IDEOLOGY, representing the dominant code of a society. See COMMON SENSE; HEGEMONY; MYTH.

Exotica Interest in, and commodification of, ethnic differences; most strikingly demonstrated in fashion.

Expectation, horizons of Describes the 'readiness factor' of AUDIENCE in terms of what its expectations are concerning a communicative TEXT: is the audience well primed for what is to come or likely to be resistant out of unawareness, ignorance, prejudice; and is audience likely to conform to the PREFERRED READING or *aberrantly decode* the text? (See DECODE.) The German literary critic Hans Robert Jans uses the phrase in *Towards an Aesthetic of Reception* (US: University of Minneapolis Press, 1982), referring to each reader of a text as approaching it with horizons of expectation shaped by previous literary, cultural and social experience. A text is interpreted on a basis of how it accords with or challenges expectations. Such expectations need to be seen in relation to, and generally arising from and interactive with COLLECTIVE REPRESENTATIONS.

Expectations People come to have a collection of ideas about what is expected of them in terms of their behaviour in certain social situations and, in turn, of what they should expect concerning the behaviour of others and of their treatment in society generally. Research into human PERCEPTION has highlighted the important influence expectations have on an individual's perception of new information.

Expectations are formed from personal experience and by information received from various other sources. Information received from these other sources may modify previous expectations or play a particularly crucial role in shaping expectations about persons or social situations of which the individual has no direct experience.

An item of information will be more readily accepted if it is compatible with existing ideas and expectations; if it is not then DISSONANCE may occur and the information may be rejected or ignored.

The media are an important source of information about many social and political events of which the individual has little or no first-hand experience. Several researchers have therefore sought to investigate the role played by the media in shaping the audience's expectations about certain persons, social GROUPS or social situations – those related to social unrest for example – of which the audience has little or no direct experience against which to test the validity of the media's presentation.

The matter of concern here is that in such cases individuals are more than usually vulnerable to PROPAGANDA. Also of interest is the role of the media in creating STEREOTYPES by engendering a set of expectations and beliefs about particular individuals, social groups or social situations.

Experimental group A research term for the group within an experiment to whom the experimental treatment is applied (for example, the group may be asked to conform to a particularly rigorous procedure of communication whilst performing a set task). The results from this group are then compared to those from a comparable *control group* that was not subjected to the experimental treatment. The control group provides the base-line against which the effectiveness of the treatment can be judged. Changes that take place in the behaviour of the experimental group but not the control group are likely to be seen as resulting from the treatment. See *TOPIC GUIDE* under RESEARCH METHODS.

Extracted information See KUUKI.

Extrapersonal communication That which takes place without human involvement: machine-to-machine communication, for example; a major growth industry of communications with the coming of computers, increased automation and the development of robotics.

Eye contact Perhaps the most subtle and significant feature of non-verbal communication (see COMMUNICATION, NON-VERBAL). 'So complex is mutual eye contact,' writes C. David Mortensen in *Communication: The Study of Human Interaction* (US: McGraw-Hill, 1972), 'that a whole vocabulary is necessary to distinguish among the ways people look at each other.' We stare, glower, peep, pierce, glance, watch, gaze and scan; and we do it directly or indirectly, provocatively or furtively, confidently or nervously.

Centring is when we fix our gaze upon the eyes or face of another centrally, as an initiator of relationship. The impression of being looked at depends not simply on the directness of the eyeline but upon the relation between eye movements and that of head, facial and bodily orientation to others.

Eye contact is rarely constant, nor is it necessarily mutual. It may be maintained longer when relationships are close or where there is a sustaining activity between participants. When innocuous subjects are discussed, eye contact is likely to be more prolonged than when conversation turns upon personal matters. Women, it is held, engage in more mutual glancing than men do.

Factors of psychological dominance and submissiveness are reflected in the extent and nature of eye contact. A single glance may be all that is required for an individual to assert him/herself over others, take initiative or leadership. Eye contact indicates awareness and signals interest in further contact: it can open a relationship, further it, or, by avoidance, close that relationship down.

Looking behaviour provides a valuable means of eliciting information from another person. As Mortensen says, 'While virtually any non-verbal cue may serve as an indicator of individual response to message cues, the fact is ... that the area of the human eye is the most visible and richly revealing of all sources of expressive meaning.' See CIVIL INATTENTION; INDICATORS; PROXEMICS; REGULATORS. See also *TOPIC GUIDE* under INTERPERSONAL COMMUNICATION.

F

Facial expression The face's main role in providing non-verbal communication lies in the expression of emotions. Michael Argyle in *Bodily Communication* (UK: Methuen, 1988) argues that the main facial expressions used to display emotion are those for happiness, surprise, fear, sadness, anger, disgust, contempt and interest. Further, several studies have suggested that the facial expressions used to display such emotions are, to quite a large extent, universal – that is, the same across different cultures.

Facial expressions play a key role in providing FEEDBACK during conversations. However, there are difficulties in accurately judging emotions from facial expressions because people often take care to conceal negative feelings and the face is thought to be more carefully controlled than other sources of non-verbal signal.

In some cultures, the Japanese for example, this is particularly the case. Despite attempts to conceal one's reactions *leakage* may occur, that is some other part of the body, often in the lower half, might reveal one's true reaction. For example, whilst the face might be passive, a tapping foot might indicate that one is agitated by the message being received. See COMMUNICATION, NON-VERBAL; FAST.

Facsimile Exact copy; today, facsimile (or fax) is the transmission of a printed or handwritten page or image by electronic means. As early as 1842 Scotsman Alexander Bain proposed the first facsimile system, though it was not until the 1920s that the process was generally employed for the transmission of news, photographs, weather maps and maps for military purposes.

Newspaper editions can be transmitted across continents for simultaneous publication; the pictures of wanted criminals can be relayed instantly to practically every police force in the world while the facsimile machine can combine with the domestic TV receiver to provide a permanent record of news and other items appearing on the screen.

Faction See DOCUMENTARY.

Fade in Gradual emergence of a scene from blackness to clear, full definition. The term is used in RADIO as well as film and TV.

Fairness Doctrine (USA) A BROADCASTING regulation in the US until 1987 when the Federal Communications Commission (FCC), responsible for the observation of the regulation, abolished it. The doctrine required broadcasters to devote time to controversial issues and to air varied opposed viewpoints. In the 1980s expansion in RADIO and TELEVISION channels and a dominant ideology that prized the private above the public, led to pressures to *deregulate* broadcasting. The FCC was persuaded that the broader and more diverse marketplace would ensure plurality of opinion without regulation.

In *Democracy Without Citizens: Media and the Decay of American Politics* (US: Oxford University Press, 1989), Robert M. Entman voices deep scepticism about the idea of leaving controversial matters in the hands of market forces. He writes of the 'dangers of basing public policy on the assumption that the economic market inevitably nourishes journalism's contribution to democratic citizenship'; indeed, 'decisions rooted in this premise, as the FCC's elimination of the Fairness Doctrine, might actually retard progress towards a freer press and citizenship'. See DEREGULATION; PRIVATIZATION.

Family Viewing Policy See ITC PROGRAMME CODE; VIOLENCE ON TV.

FAST Facial Affect Scoring Technique that divides the face into three areas for analysis: the brows and forehead; eyes and lids; and the lower face. See FACIAL EXPRESSION; EYE CONTACT; COM-MUNICATION, NON-VERBAL.

Fatwa On St Valentine's Day 1989, Iran's Ayatollah Khomeini issued a 'fatwa', or edict, against the British novelist Salman Rushdie for his novel *The Satanic Verses* (1988). The book was deemed blasphemous, guilty of containing scenes so insulting to the Islamic faith that every true Muslim had a bounden duty to kill the author. To carry out the fatwa would guarantee a place in heaven. Rushdie went into hiding, with police protection. He became a Middle Eastern hostage, only in his own country. The fatwa applied to all those involved in the publication of the novel. Bookshops were fire-bombed. The Japanese translator of the novel was attacked, beaten up and stabbed to death, and an Italian translator stabbed.

The case illustrates the profound differences in cultural expectations and practices between western and Islamic nations. The Iranian government distanced itself from the fatwa death sentence in 1998, without actually withdrawing it officially. See CENSORSHIP.

In November 2002, a fatwa was issued against UK-educated Nigerian journalist, Isioma Daniel, following her article, published in the *ThisDay* newspaper, on the Miss World Competition due to take place in Nigeria – and subsequently relocated to Europe, having provoked religious rioting in which over 200 were killed. Daniel argued in her article that such a competition might benefit Nigeria's economy and expressed the view that Mohammed might 'in all honesty probably have chosen a wife' from among the contestants.

The fatwa was issued by the deputy governor of the Islamist state government of Zamfera. Miss Daniel's profuse apologies, and resignation as a feature editor on *ThisDay*, cut no ice. She fled to America.

Fax See FACSIMILE.

Federal Communications Commission (FCC) Set up by the US federal government in 1934; a body empowered to regulate interstate and foreign communications such as radio and TV. Its effectiveness in the role of protector of public-sector broadcasting against the ambitions and predatory intentions of the private sector in the US has long been questioned. In 'An American view of UK terrestrial TV', published in *Free Press*, journal of the Campaign for Press & Broadcasting Freedom (CPBF), July–August 2002 edition, American documentary-maker and journalist Willams Rossa Cole states that US government 'regulation of content for the public interest has diminished consistently over the last decades'. He is of the view that the FCC 'is so passive in the realm of television content and ownership that it might as well shut its doors to save the taxpayer some money'.

Cole quotes the FCC chairman, Michael Powell (son of the then secretary of state, Colin Powell) – 'thoroughly pro-deregulation and pro-market' – as stating on his first day in office, that he 'had waited for a visit from the angel of public interest ... but she did not come'. See COMMUNICATIONS BILL (UK), 2002; DEREGULATION; REGULATORY FAVOURS.

Feedback According to *Chambers Twentieth Century Dictionary* (edited by A.M. Macdonald, UK, 1972), feedback is the 'return of part of the output of a system to the input as a means towards improved quality or self-correction of error'; in *A Dictionary of New English, 1963–1972* (edited by C.L. Barnhart, S. Steinmetz and R.K. Barnhart, US/UK: Longman, 1973), feedback is 'a reciprocal effect of one person or thing upon another; a reaction or response that modifies, corrects, etc., the behaviour of that which produced the reaction or response'. Without feedback – the signal that is stimulated by an act of communication, biological, mechanical, human or animal – meaningful contact halts and cannot make progress.

Feedback is the regenerative circuit, or loop, of communication. A student who submits his/her essay to the teacher expects feedback in terms of comments and a mark. Unless this feedback occurs, the student lacks guidance for the future; more, he/she is likely to be demotivated and draw back from further communicative interaction.

When the student's essay is returned it may contain *positive* or *negative* feedback: harsh comments, without encouragement, and a low mark might well be more demotivating than not receiving any feedback at all. Praise and supportive criticism on the other hand are likely to produce a positive response – of greater effort and motivation.

Central to the purpose of feedback is *control*; that is, feedback enables the communicator to adjust his/her message, or response, to that of the sender, and to the context in which the communicative activity takes place. At the interpersonal level feedback is transmitted by voice, expression, GESTURE, sight, hearing, TOUCH, smell, etc.

The greater the distance between communicators, the fewer of the 'senses' being employed to 'read' and return feedback, the more difficult it is to arrange and control, and the more difficult it is to assess its nature and meaning. See AUDIENCE MEASUREMENT; CYBERNETICS. See also *TOPIC GUIDE* under COMMUNICATION THEORY.

Feminism Though embracing different perspectives and schools of thought, fundamentally feminism is concerned with the advancement and achievement of equal social and political rights for women, and the fight against SEXISM. Feminism challenges many traditional, patriarchal, assumptions about the behavioural difference expected of men and women, and the assignment of social roles and STATUS that rests on them; and what it perceives as a widespread devaluing of women's attributes, experiences and perspectives.

One focus of current research is the exploration of the role that the media play both in fostering and reinforcing sexism, and more generally notions of femininity and masculinity, and media coverage of women's rights issues and the feminist movement and its ideas. Another important research interest is the degree to which language and its use reflect and perpetuate sexism and assumptions about differences between masculine and feminine behaviour. See ANDROCENTRIC RULE; GENDER. See also *TOPIC GUIDE* under GENDER MATTERS.

* Jennifer Coates, *Women, Men and Language* (UK: Longman, 1993); Liesbet van Zoonen, 'Feminist perspectives', in James Curran and Michael Gurevitch (eds), *Mass Media and Society* (UK: Arnold, 1996); Charlotte Brunsden, Julie D'Acci and Lyn Spigel (eds), *Feminist Television Criticism* (US/UK: Clarendon Press, 1997); Caroline Ramazanoglu and Janet Holland (eds), *Feminist Methodology: Challenges and Choices* (UK: Sage, 2002).

Fibre-optic technology One of the wonder-products of the Information Age, fibre-optic cable is fine-spun glass, a mixture of silicon and oxygen, through which digital codes are passed in pulsing light. Its impact on telephone technology has been immense and its potential for this, cable television, and many other purposes, turns so rapidly into achievement and new possibilities that even the experts find it difficult to plan for fibre's accelerating capacity.

Fibre-optic cable can carry ten times further than coaxial without requiring a booster. Over 7500 different channels can operate along a single pair of optical fibres, though the potential number lies in millions. Because fibre-optic transmission is free from electrical interference, cable can be laid cheaply along existing railway lines; it can follow existing electricity pylons, enclosed in the earth wire. Fibre-optic cable has crossed the English Channel and the Atlantic (1989).

All forms of cable are limited in terms of the span of the networks by the number of cable terminals. In contrast, satellite transmission has a global reception capacity: the extension of one is the opportunity of the other – the harnessing of cable and satellite within the same transmission systems. See *TOPIC GUIDE* under MEDIA: TECHNOLOGIES.

Fiction values These work with and as NEWS VALUES. Milly Buonanno in an article 'News-values and fiction-values: news as serial device and criteria of "fictionworthiness" in Italian fiction', published in the *European Journal of Communication,* June 1993, argues that the criteria for modern TV and film fiction parallel news values. She cites, for example, the high social STATUS of the protagonists (the ELITE value of news) and the emphasis on *proximity*, that which is 'happening in our own backyards' (an *ethnocentric* news value). Buonanno quotes Giuseppe Ferrara, Italian film and TV director, who incorporates real news dramas into his fictions, referring to these as *news pills.* See NARRATIVE.

Film See ANARCHIST CINEMA; ANIMATION; BRITISH BOARD OF FILM CENSORS; BRITISH FILM INSTITUTE; BRITISH FILM PRODUCTION FUND; CATALYST EFFECT; CELLULOID; CERTIFICATION OF FILMS; CINEMATOGRAPHY, ORIGINS; CINÉMA VÉRITÉ; DIGITAL VIDEO DISC (DVD); DIRECT CINEMA; DOCUMENTARY; DOUBLE EXPOSURE; EMOTIONAL DYNAMIZATION; FILM NOIR; FLASHBACK; FLY ON THE WALL; HAYS OFFICE; HIGH-SPEED PHOTOGRAPHY; HOLLYWOOD; IMAX; KINETOSCOPE; KULESHOV EFFECT; MARCH OF TIME; McGUFFIN; MONTAGE; MULTIPLE IMAGE; MUSICAL: FILM MUSICAL; NATIONAL FILM ARCHIVE; NEWSREEL; NEW WAVE; OMNIMAX; PERSISTENCE OF VISION; RUSHES; SHOT; SLOW MOTION; 'SOMME, THE BATTLE OF THE'; SOVIET MANIFESTO, 1928; SPECIAL EFFECTS; SYNCHRONOUS SOUND; VAMP; VIDEO; WESTERN; WILLIAMS COMMITTEE REPORT ON OBSCENITY AND FILM CENSORSHIP (UK), 1979; ZOOM LENS; ZOOPRAXOGRAPHY.

Film censorship See CENSORSHIP; CERTIFICATION OF FILMS.

Filmless camera Launched by the Japanese in 1987, the all-electronic camera is instant, avoids the need for chemical processing, can project its pictures from a standard television monitor and permits its images to be transmitted down a TELEPHONE line or fed into a computer for further processing. Paper pictures can be swiftly produced from VIDEO printers.

Film noir Term used by French film critics, notably Nino Frank, to describe a particular kind of dark, suspenseful thriller. A classic of the GENRE is French director Marcel Carné's *Le Jour se Lève* (1939)

(Day Arises), starring Jean Gabin. We see the last doomed hours of a man wanted by the police for murder. He has barred himself in his attic bedroom in an apartment block. He is totally surrounded. He has no chance; but then, Carné makes clear, the man never did have a chance. At dawn he shoots himself and, as he lies dying, his alarm clock goes off, reminding him of his otherwise intolerable life as a worker.

Described as 'symbolism with a three o'clock in the morning mood', *film noir* gained substantial currency in the US, generally thriving between the early years of the Second World War and the late 1950s, and ranging from John Huston's *Maltese Falcon* (1941) to Orson Welles' *Touch of Evil* (1958). Hollywood *film noir*, says Michael Walker in the 'Introduction' to *The Movie Book of Film Noir* (UK: Studio Vista, 1992), edited by Ian Cameron, features 'heroes who are frequently victims of a hostile world'. Such movies are characterized by a 'distinctive and exciting visual style, an unusual narrative complexity' and 'a generally more critical and subversive view of American ideology than the norm'.

Women in *film noir*, writes E. Ann Kaplan in *Women in Film Noir* (UK: British Film Institute, 1980), edited by Kaplan, are 'presented as desirable but dangerous to men'. They 'function as the obstacle to the male quest. The hero's success or not depends on the degree to which he can extricate himself from the woman's manipulations.' Billy Wilder's *Double Indemnity* (1941), with Fred MacMurray as the (willingly) manipulated male victim and Barbara Stanwick as the alluring manipulator, is a classic example of the genre.

---

* Foster Hirsch, *Film Noir: The Dark Side of the Screen* (US: Da Capo Press, paperback, 1983).

First impressions There is evidence that we tend to give too much attention to the initial information we may receive about an individual, and relatively less to later information that may be contradictory; that is, we are biased towards primacy effects. (see PRIMACY, THE LAW OF). There is some evidence that negative first impressions in particular can be resistant to change.

First impressions can clearly count in situations where most of the information is received about a person in a fairly short, discrete period of time, as in an interview. In this instance there might be little opportunity for first impressions to be modified.

In some circumstances – as when a considerable time gap intervenes between sets of information received about an individual or when there is regular, close contact with that individual – first impressions can be modified. Here the later information received may have greater impact. This is known as the *recency* effect, because it is the more recent information that is the more influential. See *TOPIC GUIDE* under COMMUNICATION THEORY.

Five filters of the news process See CONSENT: MANUFACTURE OF.

Five myths of deregulation See DEREGULATION, FIVE MYTHS OF.

Flak Term used by Edward Herman and Noam Chomsky in *Manufacturing Consent: The Political Economy of the Media* (US: Pantheon, 1988), to describe a 'negative response to a media statement or programme', and this may resemble flak in its wartime sense: a blitz taking the form 'of letters, telegrams, phone calls, petitions, lawsuits, speeches and bills before Congress, and other modes of complain, threat, and punitive action'.

The authors argue that 'If flak is produced on a large scale, or by individuals or groups with substantial resources, it can be both uncomfortable and costly to the media.' Used by the powerful, such as the major corporations, flak is intended to inhibit media activity, or bring about the cessation of that activity. Flak can be aimed at media activity indirectly as well as directly 'by [in the case of corporations] complaining to their own constituencies (stockholders, employees) about the media, by generating institutional advertising that does the same, and by funding right-wing monitoring or think-tank operations designed to attack the media'. See CONSENT: MANUFACTURE OF.

Flashback A break in the chronology of a NARRATIVE in which events from the past are disclosed to the reader, listener or viewer, and which have a bearing on the present situation. Flashback was a device used very early in the history of the cinema. D.W. Griffith's epic *Intolerance* (1916) is made up of four flashbacks. Used with a narrator, the form achieved its greatest popularity in the cinema in the 1930s and 1940s. Orson Welles' *Citizen Kane* (1941) is made up entirely of a dazzling series of flashbacks. Equally inventive is the flashback narrative of the Ealing comedy, Robert Hamer's *Kind Hearts and Coronets* (1949).

Flat-screen technology Called 'roll-up TV'; the late 1990s saw a race to develop flexible liquid crystal display (LCD) technology that would replace bulky TV sets reliant on the cathode-ray tube, with light, high-definition screens that could be hung like paintings on a wall. Flat screens made their first appearance in early laptop computers, but these lacked colour fidelity and image resolution. The so-termed Malvern screen, developed at the Worcestershire headquarters of the imaging department of the UK's Defence Evaluation and Research Agency (DERA) employs, as later laptop computers have done, ferroelectric crystals, but operating at different voltages and alignments. When not in use the screen can be used to display works of art or photographs. DERA's prime motive in developing the Malvern screen has been to produce roll-up, animated electronic maps, or miniature screen displays built into a pilot's helmet.

Fleet Street Until the 1980s, the home of most of Britain's major national newspapers; indeed the name had become the generic term for the nation's PRESS; a figure of speech (see METONYMY). The advent of new technology linked with the cost-cutting ambitions of newspaper owners, both of which led to bitter conflict with the print unions, caused an exodus from 'The Street' of all the major titles.

* Laura Melvern, *The End of the Street* (UK: Methuen, 1986).

Flow See PROGRAMME FLOW.

Fly on the wall Popular title given to a GENRE of DOCUMENTARY film-making, for the cinema or TV, in which the camera remains concealed, or is handled so discreetly that the subjects forget they are being filmed. Richard Denton, producer of the BBC documentary series *Kingswood: A Comprehensive School* (1982), describes the approach in 'Fly on the wall – designed to invade privacy', *Listener* (13 January 1983), as attempting 'to remove the process of filming so far from the consciousness of the contributors that they will, in theory, forget its existence and so behave in a markedly more natural, truthful and realistic manner'.

Denton speaks of two distinct problems: 'The first concerns the question of accuracy and context ... The second, and probably most important, problem concerns privacy.' Outstanding examples of the fly-on-the-wall approach were the BBC's *Police* series (1982), the work of Roger Graef and Charles Stewart, and Channel 4's *Murder Squad* (1992). Of particular interest for fly-on-the-wall documentarists has been *family interaction*. First in the UK to win fame by exposing their lives to the eye of the camera was the Wilkins family of Reading, featured in the BBC series, *The Family* (1974). In 1999 Granada Television screened the lives of a mixed-race family from Leeds, in *Family Life*. See CINÉMA VÉRITÉ; DIRECT CINEMA.

Focus groups Focus groups are frequently employed in market research. Members of a group are brought together by a researcher to discuss aspects of a product, be it soap powder, a political party or a television programme. The group is often chosen to be a representative SAMPLE of all those who are thought to be the actual or potential consumers of the product. As a qualitative research method, use of focus groups allows for in-depth discussion and exploration of consumers' orientations towards and evaluations of a product. See *TOPIC GUIDE* under RESEARCH METHODS.

Foe creation See WEDOM, THEYDOM.

Folk culture Term generally applied to the CULTURE of pre-industrial societies. Such societies have certain distinguishing features that are thought to affect the elements of their culture: work and leisure are undifferentiated; there is relatively little division of labour; the communities are small and social action is normally collectivist as opposed to individualist. Thus folk songs, for example, are usually firmly rooted in the everyday experience and beliefs of both the AUDIENCE and the performer.

Folk devils Stanley Cohen in *Folk Devils and Moral Panics* (UK: MacGibbon & Kee, 1972), argues that societies are subject to periods of moral panic in which certain groups are picked out as being a special threat to the VALUES and interests of society. The media and in particular the press play an important role in transmitting this sense of outrage to the general public.

These groups or individuals are usually those transgressing the values of the dominant hierarchy. It is further argued by Cohen and others that the castigation of such groups, such folk devils, by the media is a mechanism by which adherence to dominant social norms is strengthened, along with support for the forces of law and order and an extension of their powers. See LOONY LEFTISM; MORAL PANICS.

* Stanley Cohen and Jock Young (eds), *The Manufacture of News: Deviance, Social Problems and the Mass Media* (UK: Constable, 1973).

Footage Length of film expressed in feet.

Footprint Term used to describe the area in which a signal from a communications satellite can be received. See SATELLITE TRANSMISSION.

Four stages in audience fragmentation See AUDIENCE: FRAGMENTATION OF.

Fourteen-Day Rule (UK) In the period after the Second World War (1939–45) the BBC entered into an agreement with government whereby it would not try to usurp the functions of the House of Commons as the supreme forum of the nation by BROADCASTING on issues due to be debated in Parliament. An embargo was placed upon all such issues until 14 days after Parliament had debated them. It was a crippling intrusion upon the editorial rights of the corporation, and the BEVERIDGE COMMITTEE REPORT ON BROADCASTING (UK), 1950, called for the abandonment of the Rule. Nevertheless, successive governments held tenaciously to it.

In 1956 the House of Commons set up a Select Committee to investigate the workings and effects of the Rule: it recommended a reduction to seven days. Pressure from broadcasters and the press continued unabated and within a year the Rule was abandoned altogether (1957). See *TOPIC GUIDE* under MEDIA: FREEDOM, CENSORSHIP; MEDIA HISTORY.

Four theories of the press See PRESS, FOUR THEORIES OF.

Fourth estate The eighteenth-century parliamentarian Edmund Burke (1729–97) is thought to have been the originator of this phrase describing the press and its role in society. According to Burke's definition, the other three 'estates' were the Lords Spiritual (the church), the Lords Temporal (the judiciary) and the Commons. 'And yonder,' he is believed to have said in Parliament, 'sits the Fourth Estate, more important than them all.'

The implication is that the press, like the other estates, serves the state, as differentiable from government, and thus functions as a force for social, cultural and national cohesion. Underlying this argument is the assumption that while governments might be in error, the state is benign if not sacrosanct. A glance at states ancient and modern would suggest otherwise. The classifying of the press as the fourth estate points up the ambivalent role of media in society: does it tell the truth, the whole truth and nothing but the truth; or because the priorities of state seem to require it, manipulate, conceal or deny that truth? See ELITE; GUARD DOG METAPHOR; MEDIA CONTROL; POWER ELITE; WATCHDOGS. See *TOPIC GUIDE* under MEDIA HISTORY.

Fragmentation of audience See AUDIENCE: FRAGMENTATION OF.

Framing: interpersonal Conversations are often framed by METASIGNALS that let observers and participants know what kind of activity is going on so that they are better able to interpret the conversation. For example, is the conversation a serious argument or horseplay?

Such signals also allow people to recognize what Erving Goffman in *Frame Analysis* (US: Harper & Row, 1974) terms the *alignment*, that is the relative positions with regard to STATUS, intimacy and so on, being taken by the participants; themselves included. If A, for instance, explains something to B in a condescending manner, A is taking a superior alignment with regard to B.

In *You Just Don't Understand: Men and Women in Conversation* (UK: Virago, 1992), Deborah Tannen argues that protective comments and gestures from men towards women 'reinforce the traditional alignment by which men protect women'. She goes on to argue that 'the act of protecting frames the protector as dominant and the protected as subordinate'. However, arguably because men and women are fundamentally tuned to interpret some aspects of conversation differently, the difference in relative status signalled by such comments may be more apparent to men than women. Women may simply interpret them as indicating a desire to protect or be supportive rather than as indicative of women's traditionally subordinate status in society. See GENDER; GENDERLECTS.

Framing: media The process by which the media place reality into frame; and the study of the process of framing is at the core of media analysis, hence the length of this entry. Framing constitutes a NARRATIVE device. What is *not* on the page of a newspaper is 'out of frame'; what does not appear within the frame of the TV is off the public agenda. For the NEWS, there is the world – and 20 minutes to put it in the frame. *Time*, then – the shortness of it – is an important deciding factor. For a soap opera, time also poses problems of framing. There are 30-minute slots to be filled, each to conclude with unfinished business, preferably dramatic and suspenseful, while not being so dramatically 'final' that the series cannot continue day by day, week by week. Presented with such a time-frame, soaps require many characters and many plots. To facilitate this requirement (and to capture and retain AUDIENCE attention) scriptwriters divide up the frame into quick-bite scenes – framing within frames.

What happens outside the creative frame – audience measurement, for example – influences the nature of the frame and what goes on inside it. Robert Entman, in 'Framing: toward clarification of a fractured paradigm', in the *Journal of Communication* 4 (1992), says that a crucial task of analysis is to show 'exactly how framing influences thinking' for 'the concept of framing consistently offers a way to describe the power of a communicating text'.

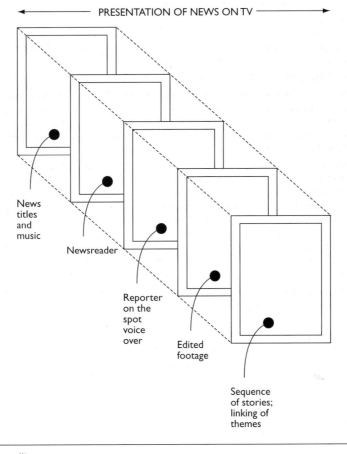

PRESENTATION OF NEWS ON TV

News titles and music

Newsreader

Reporter on the spot voice over

Edited footage

Sequence of stories; linking of themes

Framing reality

He argues, 'Analysis of frames illuminates the precise way in which influence over a human consciousness is exerted by the transfer (or communication) of information from one location such as speech, utterance, news report, or novel – to the consciousness.' Essentially, framing constitutes *selection* and *salience* – what is perceived to be most meaningful, the one serving the other. Entman suggests that framing serves four main purposes: (1) to define problems; (2) to diagnose causes; (3) to make moral judgments; and (4) to suggest remedies.

These will function varyingly according to the text, but they operate in four locations in the communication process: the *communicator*, the *text*, the *receiver* and the *culture*. Communicators 'make conscious or unconscious framing judgments in deciding what to say, guided by frames (often called schemata) that organize their belief systems'.

Before we frame, we are in a frame. The text will not only be framed by the framer within a frame, it will be shaped by a number of factors – requirements concerning format and presentation, aesthetic considerations, notions of professionalism and pressures to meet the expectations of convention.

When the text comes to be 'read', the frames as presented may be at variance with the frames that guide the receiver's thinking. For Entman the culture is 'the stock of commonly invoked frames … exhibited in the discourse and thinking of most people in a social grouping'. 'Framing in all four locations includes similar functions: selection and highlighting, and use of the highlighting elements to construct an argument about problems and their causation, evaluation and/or solution.' This approach is useful in analysing the encoding of messages and gauging their effectiveness. It emphasizes the subjective nature of encoding by recognizing the 'invisible' schemata – psychological templates – which, however hard we try to be objective and impartial, deeply influence our actions.

For successful communication – that is, winning the interest and attention of the audience, and perhaps even going beyond that in terms of gaining the audience's assent or approval – there seems to be a need for a meeting of schemata: a common ground. The communicator selects, then attempts to give salience to those parts of the story that may fit with the existing schemata in a receiver's belief system.

Much of what we know about the past, about history, is itself in frames – in ancient palaces and tombs, on triumphal arches, the walls and ceilings of great monasteries and cathedrals. These artefacts do not necessarily tell us what life was like in those days, rather, they tell us what was considered salient by those with the power to make decisions. In *The Nature and Origins of Public Opinion* (US: Cambridge University Press, 1992), J.R. Zaller says that framing is a central power in the democratic process: it is political elites that control the framing of issues. Such framing, Zaller believes, not only influences public opinion but is capable of defining it.

At a practical level, framing is governed by professional conventions, indeed by ritual: newspapers are framed by deadlines and publication times. TV news is framed with music, graphics, headlines and newsreaders; each ritual presence reinforcing and increasing the salience of the frame, its dominance over alternative frames. The study of media is an example of what Entman calls *counterframing* in that it attempts to call the ritual frames into question by analysing them in the light of possible alternative frames.

In 'Framing European politics: a content analysis of press and television news', in the *Journal of Communication*, Spring 2000, Holli A. Semetko and Patti M. Valkenburg identify five key frames in which the media present the news – *attribution of responsibility, conflict, economic consequences, human interest* and *morality*. In their researches, the authors found less divergence between press and TV and more between serious and sensationalist press; the first operating within the attribution of responsibility frame, the second in the human interest frame. See *TOPIC GUIDE* under MEDIA: PROCESSES AND PRODUCTION.

---

* Dietram A. Scheufele, 'Framing as a theory of media effects', *Journal of Communication*, Winter 1999.

Franchise Contractual agreement; most commonly associated with the licensing to broadcast, for fixed periods, of commercial TELEVISION and commercial RADIO companies.

Franchises for Independent Television (UK) Royal Assent to the TELEVISION ACT, 1954, was received on 30 July, and on 4 August the Independent Television Authority (later to become the

Independent Broadcasting Authority) was set up by the Postmaster-General under the chairmanship of Sir Kenneth Clark, and the first COMMERCIAL TELEVISION franchises were issued in 1955, with the Associated Broadcasting Company (ATV) beginning its first London transmission on 24 September 1955, and its first Midlands transmission on 17 February 1956.

The other original franchise holders were: Associated Rediffusion (broadcasting weekdays in London); Granada Television Network (weekdays, north of England); Associated British Picture Corporation (Midlands and north of England; Scottish Television (central Scotland), TWW, Television Wales and West (South Wales and the west of England); Southern Television (south of England); Tyne-Tees Television (north-east England); Anglia Television (east of England); Ulster Television (Northern Ireland); Westward Television (south-west England); Border Television (borders and Isle of Man); Channel Television (Channel Islands); Grampian Television (south-east Scotland) and Wales (west and north). A subsidiary of ABC (Associated British Corporation), Associated British Cinemas (Television) became that franchise-holders' programme contractor; in January 1964 Wales (west and north) became a subsidiary of TWW.

On 30 July 1964 all the contracts were renewed to run until 1967. Then, on 27 January 1966, it was announced that the contracts would be extended to 31 July 1968. From July 1968 some franchise areas were altered. Wales and west England – the Harlech Consortium (HTV) – took in TWW. Harlech began transmissions in March 1968 using TWW's schedules and eventually introduced its own programmes in May 1968. New areas in 1968 were the Midlands (Associated Television Network – ATV), Lancashire (Granada Television), Yorkshire (Yorkshire Television, originally Telefusion Yorkshire and Yorkshire Independent Television; first transmission date 29 July 1968) and two London franchises: London weekends (London Weekend Television) and London weekdays (Thames Television, including ABC Television and Rediffusion). All of these contracts were extended to run to 31 December 1981.

The IBA publicly announced its decision on new franchises on Sunday 28 December 1980, the contracts to run from 1 January 1982, for eight years. The authority, under the chairmanship of Lady Plowden, announced that Southern Television and Westward Television would lose their franchises and be replaced respectively by South and South Eastern Communications Ltd (TVS – Television South) and Television South West Ltd – TSW. Major share changes or other restructuring was insisted upon for Yorkshire Television and ATV Midlands (subsequently called Central Independent Television).

The franchise-holders from 1982 were: Border Television, Scottish Television, Channel Islands Communications (Television), Central (East and West Midlands), Anglia, London Weekend, Thames, Grampian, Tyne-Tees, Granada, TVS, Television South West, Harlech, Yorkshire and Ulster.

Following the UK government's White Paper, *Broadcasting in the 90s*, a radical shake-up in the system of franchise allocation – by auction – was proposed, under the supervision of a new 'light touch' regulatory body, the INDEPENDENT TELEVISION COMMISSION (ITC).

Franchises from 1993 (UK) What the *Guardian* called 'the biggest shake-up in television's 36-year history', with an estimated loss of some 2500 jobs, occurred in October 1991. The Independent Television Commission (ITC) chaired by George Russell announced the winners of the 'auction' for 16 regional commercial TV franchises, including a breakfast TV licence, to extend over ten years and commencing 1 January 1993.

Four existing stations lost their renewal bids: Thames Television (replaced by Carlton Communications), Television South (Meridian Broadcasting), Television South West (Westcountry Television) and the breakfast station TV-am (Sunrise Television). The stations empowered to continued broadcasting through the 1990s were: Granada Television (for the north-west), London Weekend, Yorkshire, Anglia Television, Tyne-Tees (north-east), Harlech Television (Wales), Ulster Television, Channel Television (Channel Islands), Central Television (Midlands) and the Scottish channels Grampian, Border and Scottish Television. Russell declared that though the process had caused 'undoubted turmoil' within ITV, 'the quality and the viewers will win out'. This point of view was not shared by George Walden in an article 'Is this merely a lottery, or is it a serious business?' (*Daily Telegraph*, 17 October 1991). 'Sadly,' he wrote, 'what has been at stake in this lottery is the quality of British television.'

The Times leader of 17 October called the whole affair an 'ITV auction fiasco' and said, 'The government should never ask such a task again … auctioning terrestrial commercial television was always intended to benefit the Treasury not the television viewer. The result must be fewer resources available for programme-making and thus for competing with the cheap products on offer from the American television industry.'

The original plan of the Conservative government was to auction off the franchises to the highest bidder in a blind sale. This was later modified by the introduction of a so-called 'quality threshold'. Eight of the 16 licences did not go to the highest bidder and 13 applications were judged not to have passed the quality threshold. One notable characteristic of the new franchise winners was the declared policy of running lightly staffed publisher–broadcaster stations, on the lines of Channel 4, buying in programmes from independent producers rather than the companies originating most of their own material.

Frankfurt school of theorists Founded in 1923, the Institute for Social Research in Frankfurt became the meeting point of several young Marxist intellectuals, among whom were Theodor Adorno, Herbert Marcuse and Max Horkheimer. The members of the 'school' placed at the forefront of their thinking and analysis the centrality of the role of IDEOLOGY in mass communication. When Hitler came to power in 1933, the Institute moved to New York and until 1942 it was affiliated to the Sociology Department of the University of Columbia. In 1949, Horkheimer led the Institute back to Frankfurt, though Marcuse remained in America.

The Frankfurt school posed the questions: why had the prospect of radical change in society so little popular or natural support? Why was there so little consciousness of the need for politically radical change – indeed how had that sense of need been apparently eliminated from popular consciousness? Marcuse, in *One Dimensional Man* (UK: Sphere Books, 1968), contends that in advanced societies capitalism appears to have proved its worth; by 'producing the goods' it is deemed a successful system and therefore one that has rendered itself immune to criticism.

The Frankfurt school believed that culture – traditionally transcendent of capitalist ethic and thus in many ways potentially subversive of it – had been harnessed by the mass media (see HEGEMONY). Classical art had been popularized, yes; but in the process of media-adoption, it had been deprived of its *oppositional* values (see DOMINANT, SUBORDINATE, RADICAL). The Frankfurt school has had considerable influence upon thinking about the media and its power to shape cultures, but has been criticized for condemning existing reality without proposing how it might be changed for the better. See AUDIENCE: ACTIVE AUDIENCE; CULTIVATION; CULTURAL APPARATUS; DOMINANT DISCOURSE. See also *TOPIC GUIDE* under COMMUNICATION THEORY.

* Rolf Wiggershaus, *The Frankfurt School: Its History, Theories and Political Significance* (UK: Polity Press, paperback, 1995).

Freedom of information The right of access by citizens to information of public interest is enshrined in legislation in many countries, in particular the United States. In the UK in 1994 the Conservative government under John Major took a tentative step towards creating a degree of open government with its Code of Practice on Access to Government Information. In opposition, the Labour government made no secret of its intention to end secret government, the future Labour Prime Minister Tony Blair promising that a Freedom of Information Act, should Labour be elected, would 'signal a new relationship between government and people; a relationship which sees the public as legitimate stakeholders in the running of the country'. The basis of this relationship was to be freedom of information.

Not long after the massive election victory of Labour in 1997, the minister entrusted with navigating a freedom of information bill through Parliament, David Clark, was sacked and responsibility for the legislation passed to the Home Office. The draft White Paper, *Your Right to Know*, was put on hold. No mention of a Freedom of Information Act was made in the Queen's Speech at the opening of Parliament, 1998, but in May 1999 Home Secretary Jack Straw broke the government's silence on FOL (freedom of information legislation). According to the Home Office's website Freedom of Information Unit, the draft Bill was 'a major step towards implementing the Government's commitment to increasing openness in the public sector; a significant step towards involving people more in decisions which affect their lives'. The sting came in the tail: 'subject to clearly defined exemptions and conditions'.

The Bill raised the number of exemptions listed in the White Paper from 7 to 21 and was generally condemned, throughout the UK press, as representing a retreat, even from Major's Code of Practice. A key element of the White Paper is that restriction of access would only occur if an independent commissioner was satisfied that 'substantial harm' would, by revelation, be done to public interest. This condition was removed from the Bill.

While signalling the appointment of a freedom of information commissioner, the Bill denies him or her independent powers, subjecting his actions to the will of government ministers. In 2000 the European Convention on Human Rights (ECHR) became part of British law. This contains rights of access to information. However, with the re-election of Labour in 2001, the Freedom of Information Act was put on the back-burner until 2005. In contrast, legislation that curtails access to information and free expression was high on the new government's agenda. See CENSORSHIP; HUMAN RIGHTS ACT (UK), 2000; REGULATION OF INVESTIGATORY POWERS ACT (RIPA) (UK), 2000; SURVEILLANCE; TERRORISM: ANTI-TERRORISM, CRIME AND SECURITY ACT (UK), 2001. See also *TOPIC GUIDE* under MEDIA: FREEDOM, CENSORSHIP.

Frequency In a non-technical sense, and as used in relation to the media, frequency is the degree of repetition of topics of NEWS or information in the press, on RADIO or TV. The more frequently a topic inhabits news headlines and news stories, the more likely it is to continue to do so; to be defined and accepted as 'important', and to have media impact.

Negative frequency operates when stories are overlooked, or edged to the margins of attention. Consequently they rarely have the chance either to improve their status as news or impart the full weight of their argument. The term may also be used to refer to the way in which news items fit the frequency – the *time-scale* – of the mode of communication. See CONSISTENCY; EFFECTS OF THE MASS MEDIA; IMMEDIACY; INTENSITY; NEWS VALUES.

Front See SELF-PRESENTATION.

Front region, back region See IMPRESSION MANAGEMENT.

Functionalist (mode of media analysis) Interprets social behaviour in terms of its contribution to the assumed overall goals of society, recognizing a CONSENSUS within society of common norms and VALUES. The main focus of functionalist analysis is upon the ways in which social systems maintain *equilibrium*. A functionalist would consider any social or cultural element in relation to its contribution to the survival, integration or stability of society. The communication process features as a major component in the 'servicing' of equilibrium.

Structural functionalism, a mode of analysis developed by US sociologist Talcott Parsons, identifies common features of a complex industrial society that are central to its survival. These include the delineation and maintenance of boundaries (social, cultural, etc.), the definition of major structural units of society and the connections between them, and an overriding concern with system maintenance. This school of analysis has been particularly strong in the US.

Within the functionalist perspective, activities that contribute to the survival of a system are known as *eufunctions*; those that contribute to disturbance are known as *dysfunctions*. A distinction is also made between manifest and latent functions, the one intended and recognized by the participants, the other neither intended nor recognized.

The functionalist approach makes challengeable assumptions about consensus over the goals of society, leaving untouched important questions about the source of these goals and the degree to which an identified source may influence the nature of the social structure and social action. Its tendency is to legitimize the status quo and to emphasize the predominance of the whole over the parts, overlooking alternative means of achieving the same or similar functions. See MARXIST (MODE OF MEDIA ANALYSIS).

Functions of communication See COMMUNICATION, FUNCTIONS.

Functions of mass media See NORMATIVE THEORIES OF MASS MEDIA.

G

Gagging order Issued by judges to restrain the publication or broadcast of information where it is considered that such information breaches the law. Companies in the UK may seek gagging orders to prevent communication to the public that seems a threat to *commercial confidentiality*; individuals may seek the imposition of such orders to protect their personal PRIVACY.

The HUMAN RIGHTS ACT (UK), 2000, emanating from the European Convention of Human Rights forbids, for example, publication of details of a person's health. Deemed a 'private matter' this nevertheless raises difficult questions when a person's individual 'health – say if he or she is a health worker suffering from HIV – may have implications for the public. See *TOPIC GUIDE* under MEDIA: FREEDOM, CENSORSHIP.

Galtung and Ruge's model of selective gatekeeping, 1965 Whenever 'newsworthiness' is discussed and analysed the names of Johan Galtung and Mari Ruge are likely to be mentioned before all others. Their article, 'The structure of foreign news: the presentation of the Congo, Cuba and Cyprus crises in four foreign newspapers', in the *Journal of International Peace Research* 1 (1965) and reprinted in *The Manufacture of News* (UK: Constable, 1973), edited by Stanley Cohen and Jock Young, has proved a focal point for those who ask the questions: what qualifies as news and what makes one item of news predominate over another?

The model represents the way in which events pass through the GATEKEEPING processes of the media – initially the perceptions of media people as to whether the event qualifies as news, then the selection according to a set of news criteria (I to IX) alone or in combination. For details of the criteria identified by Galtung and Ruge, see NEWS VALUES. See also *TOPIC GUIDE* under COMMUNI-CATION MODELS.

Galtung and Ruge's model of selective gatekeeping, 1965

Games See TRANSACTIONAL ANALYSIS.

Gatekeeping To reach its intended target, every MESSAGE has to pass through many 'gates'; some will be wide open, some ajar, some tightly closed. At work, the boss's secretary is the archetypal gatekeeper. She may be under instruction to welcome callers or delay them, by letter, by telephone or physically by 'guarding' the boss's door. Writing about gatekeepers in the media, Stuart Hood in 'The politics of television', in Denis McQuail (ed.), *Sociology of Mass Communications* (UK: Penguin, 1972) says 'A news bulletin is the result of a number of choices by a variety of "gatekeepers".

'They include the editor who decides on the day's coverage, or the organizer who briefs the camera crews and reporters and allocates assignments, the film editor who selects the film to be included in the bulletin, the copy-taster who chooses the stories from the tape to accompany the film, the sub-editor who writes the story and the duty editor who supervises the compilation of the bulletin, fixes the running order of the stories and gives it its final shape.'

The selection or rejection of material is made according to a set of criteria determined by a number of factors – the gatekeeper's class background, upbringing and education and his/her attitudes to the world (VALUES); plus the values, norms and traditional wisdom of the organization for which the gatekeeper works.

The process and effect of gatekeeping in the media have undergone substantial modification in the age of electronic transmission. The age of scarcity of channels has been transformed to an age of BANDWIDTH abundance. Consumers of communication now have at their fingertips the power to evade traditional modes of gatekeeping. Text, pictures, the latest movies and pop tunes have become available online; and if gatekeeping has always been a process of manipulation by the communicators as well as selection, the consumer can do this too with the images and texts that he or she can summon up.

As populations access the net in increasing numbers, there is the potential for a shift of control from producer to consumer. This, at the same time, threatens to lessen the ability of governments to exercise intervention in the form of regulation and censorship. The very freedom of expression that electronic data exchange offers people worldwide will prompt governments to seek to curb this freedom – a possibility that will be made more viable once all transmission forms share the same digital network. See AGENDA-SETTING; CONSENSUS; DIGITIZATION; GALTUNG AND RUGE'S MODEL OF SELECTIVE GATEKEEPING, 1965; MR GATE; NEWS VALUES; WHITE'S GATEKEEPING MODEL, 1950. See also *TOPIC GUIDE* under MEDIA: PROCESSES AND PRODUCTION; NEWS MEDIA.

Gender Our gender or gender identity refers to our categorization, and that of others, of ourselves as either male or female. According to Richard D. Gross in *Psychology: The Science of Mind and Behaviour* (UK: Hodder & Stoughton, 1987), gender is a cultural term and one's gender role 'refers to the behaviours, attitudes, values, beliefs and so on which a particular society expects from, or considers appropriate to, males and females on the basis of their biological sex'.

Definitions of appropriate behaviour for males and females can vary from one CULTURE to another and, over time, within a particular culture or society. Conflict also exists within our own society regarding the precise definition of what should constitute appropriate behaviour for the different gender roles. One area of research within media studies focuses on the role that the media may play in forming or reinforcing gender STEREOTYPES and certain EXPECTATIONS about gender roles. Another current focus of research interest is the degree to which a society's language and its use shape and reflect notions of gender identity and gender roles.

Gendered genre Term used in cultural analysis to denote GENRES of film or television that are seen to appeal to one GENDER rather than another. For example, SOAP OPERAS have traditionally been seen to be primarily directed at a female audience whilst crime series are perceived to appeal more to male audiences. The TEXT and its NARRATIVE patterns typically reflect such differences in AUDIENCE and in part, though not uncritically, assumptions about gender roles and typical masculine and feminine behaviour.

Soap operas, for instance, concentrate on the family and local neighbourhood, and the interplay of interpersonal relationships within these contexts; whereas the crime series focuses on action, heroic deeds and male bonding. Some researchers have argued that the concept of gendered genre over-simplifies the potentially complex relationship between the text, its narrative form, its authors and its audience.

The term *gendered viewing* describes the different perspectives, ways of seeing, *between* genders in relation to cultural, social and historical contexts. This is not simply a matter of the ways men look, or perceive, compared with the way women perceive, for as Mary Ellen Brown asserts in *Soap Opera and Women's Talk: The Pleasure of Resistance* (US: Sage, 1994), 'gender role characteristics of the one sex can be displayed by people of either sex'. Indeed, the 'simple delineations of masculine and feminine are also somewhat inappropriate because they imply masculinity as central and femininity as marginal'.

Brown's book explores the ways in which women view – and use – soaps to assemble DISCOURSES of resistance through what she terms GOSSIP NETWORKS. Brown writes, 'Both soap operas and gossip claim for women a space and time in which there is freedom to play with dialogue – dialogue that does not necessarily advance the plot but is simply there for pleasure. All of these aspects fly in the face of dominant conventions.' See FEMINISM; GENRE; SEXISM. See also *TOPIC GUIDE* under GENDER MATTERS.

Genderlects In *You Just Don't Understand: Men and Women in Conversation* (UK: Virago, 1992), Deborah Tannen argues that in conversation while men 'speak and hear a language of status and independence', women 'speak' and hear a language of 'connection and intimacy'. These fundamentally different orientations and their influence on perception are, she argues, important factors in creating confusion and misunderstanding in conversations between men and women.

These differences have led Tannen to conclude that men and women speak different *genderlects* and her book examines examples of how male and female differences in orientation and consequently in interpretation can be observed in many different contexts. See REPORT-TALK, RAPPORT-TALK.

---

* Mary Crawford, *Talking Difference: On Gender and Language* (UK: Sage, 1995).

Gender signals Male and female signals in interpersonal conduct and appearance that label or place emphasis upon the sex of the signaller. See GESTURE; PROXEMICS.

Generalized other As contrasted with SIGNIFICANT OTHERS; representing society at large – the organized community or social group which, in the words of George Herbert Mead *in Mind, Self and Society From the Standpoint of a Social Behaviourist* (US: University of Chicago Press, 1934), 'gives the individual his unity of self'. Mead argues that 'it is in the form of the generalized other that the social process influences the behaviour of individuals involved in it and carrying it on'. Thus the generalized other exercises a degree of control over the conduct of its members; and its norms and VALUES are important determining factors in the individual's thinking. The *significant other* – a parent, friend, group leader or public figure – may varyingly reinforce, modify, challenge or counteract the influence of the generalized other. See SYMBOLIC INTERACTIONISM.

Genre Term deriving from the French, meaning type or classification. In literature the major classic genres were epic, tragedy, lyric, comedy and satire, eventually to be followed by the novel and short story. Genres, working at least approximately to basic ground rules of form and style, are categories to be found in all modes of artistic expression. In films there are genres of the WESTERN, gangster movies, FILM NOIR, science fiction, romantic comedy, horror, disaster, costume drama, etc. In TELEVISION there are SIT-COMS, SOAPS, detective and police series. Genres are rarely discrete or singular entities. They are subject to influence by other genres, and are often a mixture of genre elements. Indeed part of the pleasure audiences derive from genre TEXTS is their inventiveness, the way the CODES of different genres have been knowingly manipulated, sometimes to satirical effect. In short, what attracts and fascinates is their INTERTEXTUALITY. Writing in *Acts of Literature* (UK: Routledge, 1992), French philosopher Jacques Derrida is of the opinion that there is 'no genreless text'; thus the way is open to classify TV news, party political broadcasts, weather reports, quiz shows, chat shows and consumer programmes as genres. See NARRATIVE. See also *TOPIC GUIDE* under LANGUAGE/DISCOURSE/NARRATIVE.

Gerbner's model of communication, 1956 This is described by Denis McQuail in *Communication*, (UK: Longman, 2nd edition, 1993) as perhaps 'the most comprehensive attempt yet to specify all the component stages and activities of communication'. Below is a modified version of George Gerbner's model as presented in 'Towards a general model of communication', in *Audio Visual Communication Review* 4. M is responder to E (event) and may be human or machine (such as a microphone or camera). Gerbner's emphasis is upon the considerable variability in the perception of an EVENT by a communicating agent and also in the way the MESSAGE is perceived by a receiver. He speaks of the essential 'creative, interactional nature of the perceptual process'. Equally important is the stress placed upon the importance of context to the 'reading' of messages, and of the open nature of human communication.

For Gerbner the relationship between form and context in the communication process (S = Signal) is dynamic and interactive. It is also concerned with access and control, dimensions that inevitably affect the nature and content of communication messages – their selection, shaping and distortion. At the level of the mass media this is obvious, but access and control also operate at the level of interperson-

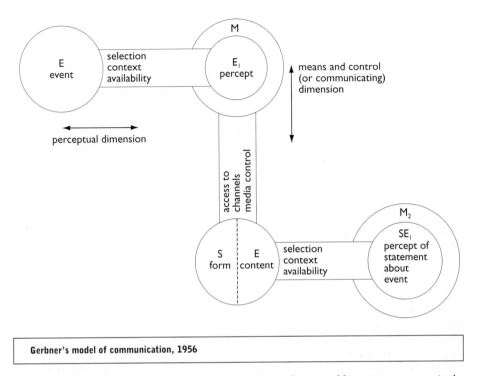

Gerbner's model of communication, 1956

al communication – teachers in classrooms, for example, speakers at public meetings, parents in the home situation.

Back on the horizontal axis, Gerbner stresses the importance of *availability*. A literate electorate may have the capacity to read all the facts about a political situation, all the pros and cons of an industrial dispute but that capacity can only operate, and the pros and cons be properly weighed, if the necessary facts are made available. What Gerbner's model does not do is address itself fully to the problems of how MEANING is generated. The form or code of the message (S) is taken for granted, whereas the advocate of SEMIOLOGY/SEMIOTICS would argue that meaning is of the essence. See *TOPIC GUIDE* under COMMUNICATION MODELS.

Gestural dance A term that has been used to describe the way in which gestures are employed to achieve interactional synchrony between participants in an encounter. For example, the smooth handing over of the conversational floor from speaker to listener is achieved by a combination of prolonged gaze, falling intonation, returning of the hands to a rest position and possibly the use of a gesture towards the listener to invite a contribution. The listener may have indicated a wish to speak by the use of rapid HEAD NODS.

Gestural echo See POSTURAL ECHO.

Gesture Michael Argyle in *Bodily Communication* (UK: Methuen, 1988) divides gestures and bodily movements into three main categories: *Emblems, Illustrators* and *Self-touching*. Emblems are movements, often hand movements, that can easily be translated into speech in terms of their MEANING (they may often stand in for speech) within a particular GROUP or CULTURE. The use, in Britain, of the thumbs-up gesture to mean OK would be an example. Illustrators are those gestures used to illustrate or accompany speech often to aid explanation; for example, gestures used when giving directions. Self-touching normally indicates information about an individual's emotional state, such as the scratching of the face when anxious.

In *Manwatching: A Field Guide to Human Behaviour* (UK: Jonathan Cape, 1977), Desmond Morris defines a gesture as 'any action that sends a visual signal to an onlooker'. Incidental gestures may be unintentional, accidental, but they still communicate messages – such as mood information. Primary gestures are those that are intended – a wave, a nod, a wink. Morris offers six categories of gesture. (1) *Expressive*, shared by other animals as well as humans, and including facial expression and manual ges- ticulations. (2) *Mimic gestures*, exclusively human, 'The essential quality of a Mimic Gesture is that it attempts to copy the thing it is trying to portray.' This category Morris subdivides into *social* mimicry (or 'putting on a good face'); *theatrical* mimicry; *partial* mimicry (pretending your hand is a gun, for example); and what he terms *vacuum* mimicry – gestures to indicate hunger or thirst. (3) *Schematic* gestures are those in which imitations become abbreviated or abridged; a gestural shorthand. (4) *Symbolic* gestures represent moods and ideas – such as the SIGN to indicate that you consider someone is 'round the twist'. (5) *Technical* gestures constitute specialized signal systems recognized only by those in the trade or profession, such as those employed by a TV studio manager or a fireman to his colleagues. (6) *Coded* gestures are based upon formal systems, such as deaf-and-dumb sign language, semaphore and the tic-tac signalling of the race-course.

Many gestures carry universal meaning but in general the gesture is critically dependent upon the cultural context in which it is made and specific contexts of timing and situation, as well as the combination of gestures, for rarely do they exist alone, or without vocal accompaniment. See BARRIER SIGNALS; BATON SIGNAL; COMMUNICATION, NON-VERBAL; CUT-OFF; METASIGNALS; NON-VERBAL BEHAVIOUR: REPERTOIRE; PROXEMICS; SALUTATION DISPLAY; SHORTFALL SIGNALS; TIE-SIGNS. See also *TOPIC GUIDE* under INTERPERSON- AL COMMUNICATION.

Ghost-writer One who does literary work for someone else – usually a celebrity – who takes the credit.

Glasgow University Media Group Set up with a grant from the UK Social Science Research Council, the Group has published research findings that have won considerable attention and not unexpected- ly drawn fire from the media under investigation. By 1982, the Group had published three major works tabulating its exhaustive research into the way TV handles the NEWS. First came *Bad News* (UK: Routledge & Kegan Paul, 1976), which exploded the generally held image of broadcasters being sub- stantially more objective and reliable in news reporting than the PRESS. 'Our study,' wrote the eight authors of the original study, 'does not support a received view that television news is "the news as it happens".' The Group had monitored all TV news broadcasts over a six-month period, from January to June 1975. Notable among the Group's findings was evidence of a bias in TV against the activities of organized labour and a relentless emphasis upon effects rather than causes.

Later publications by the Glasgow University Media Group have been *More Bad News* (UK: Routledge & Kegan Paul, 1980), *Really Bad News* (UK: Writers and Readers' Publishing Co-operative, 1982) and *War and Peace News* (UK: Open University Press, 1985) about media coverage of the Falklands War, the Miners' Strike and the situation in Northern Ireland. The theoretical base from which the Group works may be summarized by a quotation from *More Bad News*: 'news is not a neutral and not a natural phenomenon: it is rather the manufactured production of ideology'.

The GUMG was back in the news again in 2002 with research findings suggesting that TV news has failed to inform young people about the Israeli–Palestinian conflict. Reporting the findings of the Group in a UK *Guardian* article (16 April), 'Missing in action', Greg Philo writes, 'If you don't understand the Middle East crisis it might be because you are watching it on TV news.' The research group interviewed 12 small audience groups involving 85 people with a cross-section of ages. These were asked a series of questions on the Middle East situation, and then the same questions were posed to 300 young people between the ages of 17 and 22. It was found that 'many of those questioned had little understanding of the reasons for the conflict and its origins'.

The conclusions drawn from this research were that the failure to place events into a historical *context* occurred as a result of TV news existing 'in a very competitive market' subject to anxiety about audience ratings: 'In this respect it is better to have great pictures of being in the middle of a riot with journalists ducking stones than to explain what the conflict is about.' The reluctance to contextualize, says Philo, also lies in the political roots of the conflict in which 'Israel is closely allied to the United States and there are very strong pro-Israeli lobbies in the US and to some extent in Britain.' See

RESEARCH CENTRES IN THE MEDIA (UK). See also *TOPIC GUIDE* under RESEARCH METHODS.

* Greg Philo, *Developments in Sociology* (UK: Causeway Press, 2002).

Glasnost Openness; Russian term for greater freedom of expression and less state secrecy. The word became universal currency with the election to leadership in the Soviet Union of Mikhail Gorbachev, who welcomed rather than shunned world publicity and demonstrated an openness within the Russian nation and in communication with other countries not experienced since the early days of the Russian Revolution (and only fitfully experienced since). Linked with *glasnost* has been *perestroika*, meaning reconstruction, reform in relation to government practices and expectations.

Global culture and young people See CHILDREN, YOUNG PEOPLE AND THE CHANGING MEDIA ENVIRONMENT.

Globalization of culture See CULTURE: GLOBALIZATION OF.

Globalization of media As early as the 1960s Marshall McLuhan was describing the world as an electronic village and his phrase 'global village' is now part of the language of mass communication. Certainly electronic transmission of information has become global and the institutions, the transnational corporations (TNCs) responsible for that transmission, are global in scale and intention. The similarity with village life is more obscure. Thanks to global transmission we are theoretically capable of knowing what is happening in backyards, or back gardens, worldwide. It is feared that what we may be permitted to see there will come to look more and more like what is happening in our own backyards, as familiar as American apple pie.

Globalization is also a process of CONVERGENCE, of hardware and software, of systems of ownership and control. Globalization brings the world to our TV screens, and through the INTERNET to our computers. Information in and out converges; services (computer shopping, for example), converge with the capacity to summon up data for our individual needs. With the DIGITIZATION of information, turning every element of data – words, pictures, sound – into digits that can be transmitted terrestrially, through the telephone line and cable, via satellite, or all of them together, the possibilities of the control of multi-media services falling into fewer and fewer corporate hands deserves to stimulate global concern.

Just as the technology of media converges, so do operation systems. Traditional regulations preventing cross-media ownership were modified or dismantled throughout the 1990s. News International, the flagship of the Murdoch dynasty (see CITIZEN KANE OF THE GLOBAL VILLAGE; MURDOCH EFFECT) operates globally in every conceivable field of mass communication, and where it does not operate alone, it is a decisive part of other conglomerate activities in the media field. For example, in May 1995 News International formed a $2bn link with the American telecommunications giant, MCI, rival of the all-powerful US company AT&T. The deal put Murdoch's empire directly on to the carrier system of the superhighway, establishing Murdoch as a galactic superstar.

An observer from outer space might survey the current media scene – in which Murdoch feasts the globe with his vast library of films from the Fox archives, with American football, UK Premier League soccer and Rugby League; dominates European satellite transmission with Britain's BSkyB satellite and Asian satellite services with Star TV (not to mention his control of Australia's Channel 7 and the Delphi On-Line Internet Service) – and conclude that a synonym for globalization is 'Murdochization' and that the true name of McLuhan's global village is Rupertsville. However, the Murdoch empire is not the world's biggest media-corp; that distinction falls to AOL Time Warner. See EUROPE: CROSS-BORDER TV CHANNELS; GLOBAL MEDIA SYSTEM: THE MAIN PLAYERS; LOCALIZATION; MOBILIZATION. See also *TOPIC GUIDE* under GLOBAL PERSPECTIVES; MEDIA TECHNOLOGIES.

Globalization of news See NEWS: GLOBALIZATION OF.

Globalization: three engines of According to the Group of Lisbon publication *Limits to Competition* (US: MIT Press, 1995), the three engines driving globalization are *liberalization, deregulation* and *privatization*, the first permitting companies to move capital and operations to locations offering competitive terms (such as low wages). DEREGULATION allows liberalization and, as a consequence, leads to PRIVATIZATION of public utilities. Ultimately, many commentators fear, these three engines of global financial and industrial activity undermine, if not dismantle altogether, the welfare state of individual nations. The authors of *Limits to Competition* argue that at the core of the dismantling process is the conviction that the more labour costs are cut and related social benefits reduced, the better will be the country's competitiveness.

As the media are so substantially a part of the portfolios of TNCs (transnational corporations) the danger is that they will either advocate these trends or hold back from the public responsibility of subjecting them to critical scrutiny.

Global jukebox Name given to the *Live Aid* for Africa rock concert held jointly at Wembley Stadium, UK, and the John F. Kennedy Stadium, Philadelphia, US, on 13 July 1985. This, the first worldwide rock concert of its kind, was the brainchild of its principal organizer, rock musician Bob Geldof, and it was held to raise money for famine victims in the Sudan, Ethiopia and the Sub-Sahara.

The concert, lasting 16 hours, was transmitted by 11 satellites to an estimated television audience of between 1.5 and 2 billion people in 160 different countries – some of whom also contributed live performances and messages of support, via satellite, which were slotted into the programme. The event, featuring some of the best-known names from two generations of rock stars, vividly demonstrated the potential offered by developments in communications technology and gripped the public's imagination; it broke the largest live television audience record over 16 hours. The concert had raised more than US$100 million for famine relief by mid-1986.

Global media system: the main players Fewer than 15 transnational corporations (TNCs) dominate world media ownership. The ranking of these is subject to rapid shifts resulting from mergers, but the current players at the top of the media tree are: AOL Time Warner, Vivendi, Viacom, Disney, Sony, Bertelsmann, News Corporation, Segram (snapped up by Vivendi in 2000), PolyGram and General Electric.

The giant of giants is AOL Time Warner (owning *Time* magazine, Time Life Books, Warner Music Group, America On Line, Warner Brothers films, HBO cable channel, CNN etc. etc.). A close challenger is Disney (ABC, film studios, theme parks, record production, book publication, global cable TV channels etc.). Vivendi, headquartered in France, leapt to second in the world rankings when it obtained Segram. In addition to its massive media holdings, Vivendi is in to transport, energy, water supply and waste management. The company controls Universal Music Group, the largest music company in the world, operating in 59 countries, Universal Pictures, Canal+ in France, and theme parks in Hollywood and Barcelona.

Close business links between the media giants is a key feature of operations, alliances between them being more common than direct competition. Rupert Murdoch's News Corp has equity joint ventures in long-term alliances with AOL Time Warner, Viacom, EMI, Granada TV and Globo of Brazil. Disney is involved in joint ventures with Bertelsmann, NBC and Hearst Newspapers (not to mention Coca-Cola and McDonald's). Bertelsmann of Germany is in joint enterprises with (in addition to Disney) AOL Time Warner, Sony, Pearson Publications (UK) and the BBC. The US Comedy Central channel is jointly owned by AOL Time Warner and Viacom.

The objective of the great media corporations is expansion worldwide linked with a policy of *customizing* or tailoring the media product to local needs, tastes and expectations; thus Disney's ESPN 24-hour-a-day sports channel broadcasts in over 20 languages to over 160 countries (see EUROPE: CROSS-BORDER TV CHANNELS).

The bigger the giant, the more it is capable of *cross-promotion* to improve sales. MTV, for example, promotes Viacom's Paramount film productions, which naturally feature prominently on the shelves of Viacom-owned Blockbuster video outlets.

What applies to electronic communication applies in equal measure to publishing, now dominated by six major players, the largest, HarperCollins, being part of the Murdoch stable, while Random House belongs to Bertelsmann. Orion belongs to Hachette, which in turn is owned by Lagadère Media, linked with Vivendi.

It would be a mistake to regard these behemoths, as they have been described, as so massive and powerful that they are impervious to the tide of events. The AOL Time Warner merger, for example, has not turned out to be the unparalleled success story that the marriage promised; and Vivendi has also experienced turbulent times, its shares plummeting on world stock markets.

In order to update information on the merry-go-round of global media ownership, readers are recommended to consult the Corpwatch website (www.corpwatch.org) and for an analysis of global trends, *The Global Media: The New Missionaries of Corporate Capitalism* (UK/US: Continuum, 1997) by Edward S. Herman and Robert W. McChesney. See MEDIA MAGNATES: FOUR SOURCES OF CONCERN. See also *TOPIC GUIDE* under MEDIA: OWNERSHIP AND CONTROL.

Global scrutiny Describes the vastly increased *visibility* of people and events on a global scale, largely as a result of TELEVISION. John B. Thompson in *The Media and Modernity: A Social Theory of the Media* (UK: Polity, 1995) speaks of a 'regime of visibility created by an increasingly globalized system of communication'; and, however structured (see FRAMING), this power to scrutinize represents a 'significant historical development. For it means not only that political leaders must now act in an arena which is in principle open to view on a global scale, but also that recipients are able to see and experience distant individuals and events in a way that was simply not possible before'.

Global village See GLOBALIZATION OF MEDIA; McLUHANISM.

Glocalization See McWORLD VS JIHAD.

Golden pen of freedom Annual award by the International Federation of Newspaper Publishers (FIEJ), based in Paris.

Gossip Traditionally gossip has been ranked as 'women's talk' and, within DISCOURSES and social structures that are male-dominated, given low status in the order of exchange, or even disparaged. Gossip, to outsiders, usually male, appears to be 'going nowhere', 'undirected' and ultimately pointless if not damaging. Such judgements are essentially made from ideological positions that view communication as less an exchange of experience (a cultural exchange) and more a transmission of information: in short, 'men's talk'.

Gossip deserves more serious attention than is usually given to it. In 'Gossip: notes on women's oral culture', in *Women's Studies International Quarterly* 3 (1980), Deborah Jones defines gossip as 'a way of talking between women in their roles as women, intimate in style, personal and domestic in topic and setting, a female cultural event which springs from and perpetuates the restrictions of the female role, but also gives the comfort of validation'. Jones lists four functions of gossip: *house-talk, scandal, bitching* and *chatting*. Such talk establishes and confirms the pleasures of interaction while at the same time working to give them value and validity. As such, it is potentially empowering.

Gossip networks A mode of resistance, by women, to male-dominated DISCOURSES. The term is used by Mary Ellen Brown in *Soap Opera and Women's Talk: The Pleasure of Resistance* (UK: Sage, 1994). Brown discusses how gossip networks arise out of viewing SOAP OPERA, and the use of such entertainment as a means of constructing alternative meanings. The author asks how 'can such a trivial or even exploitative genre as soap opera be associated with the notion of empowerment for its viewers?' She responds to the question by arguing that the answer 'lies in the invisible discourse networks it plugs into and helps solidify. Such discourse networks, or gossip networks, are important for women's resistive pleasure.'

Graffiti The poor man or woman's tilt at literary immortality; writings in public but forbidden places attempting crudely or pithily, or both, to summarize some of life's basic truths, such as 'Suicide is the most sincere form of self-criticism', or pertinent advice, such as 'let's keep incest in the family' or even historical analysis, such as 'Emmanuel Kant but Ghengis Khan'. Ultimately, of course, 'Graffiti should be obscene and not heard', and specially provided blank walls for graffiti writers such as Sweden has provided rob the 'art' of the thrill of doing something illegal.

Today, in the age of the image, we associate graffiti with spray-can 'doodles' or personal 'signatures', but occasionally graffiti can stir the interest of cultural ELITES. An example is that of the New York graffiti artist Jean-Michel Basquiat, whose work was physically appropriated and transformed from 'public nuisance' to cultural commodity, making him potentially a wealthy artist – that is, from the forbidden wall to the status-ensuring art gallery. Sadly Basquiat died aged 27 in 1988, of a drug overdose. See the film documentary, *Basquiat* by his artist friend, Julian Schnabel.

Gramophone   Originally the phonograph, invented by Thomas Alva Edison (1847–1931), his first sketch of which was published in the *Scientific American*, 22 December 1877. His 'talking tinfoil' led to the creation in 1878 of the Edison Speaking Phonograph Company, and soon a single exhibition phonograph could earn as much as US$1800 a week. Concurrently, Edison designed different models, including a disc machine with a volute spiral that anticipated later developments.

Commercial recordings began in 1890, though sound reproduction remained poor, the wax cylinders could only play for two minutes and there was no way of mass producing the cylinders. Machines were driven by cumbersome, heavy-duty batteries and were very expensive to purchase – that is until Thomas Hood Macdonald, a manager of Graphophone, rival company to Edison's, put on sale the first mechanical phonograph (1894), retailing at US$75.

The Columbia company was the first to manufacture double-sided discs (1908), though the next major innovation was electrical recording, initiated by Lionel Guest and H.O. Merrimen in 1920 when they recorded, by electrical process, the Unknown Warrior burial service in Westminster Abbey. Bell Laboratories in the US proved substantial pioneers in this area, which they termed *orthophonic* recording.

The miraculous rise of the gramophone was eventually hit by the more popular mass appeal of RADIO and the 1930s were lean years, though the record industry in Europe did not plumb the depths to the extent it did in the US where, by January 1933, the record business was practically extinct. However, in September 1934, the RCA Victor sales department offered the Duo Junior, consisting of an electrically powered turntable and a magnetic pickup, primitive but popular, and by 1935 the notion of 'high-fidelity' was born. Station W2XR (later WQXR) in New York began 'high-fidelity broadcast-ing' in 1934, in truth, as much high publicity as hi-fi.

The Second World War (1939–45) cut non-military use of shellac – the material used to make the discs – principally imported from India, and record production was severely curtailed. 1944 saw the first examples of Decca's 'ffrr' sound reaching British ears. This was 'full frequency range reproduction' achieving standards of reproduction never previously heard.

In 1941, 127 million discs were sold; in 1947, 400 million – a year before Columbia Records in the US launched the unbreakable microgroove disc, with a playing time of 23 minutes per side. The LP (long playing) record had arrived. It bore between 224 and 300 grooves per inch compared to 85 grooves on the ordinary disc; and it moved on the turntable at 33⅓rpm instead of the traditional 78. Not to be outdone, RCA Victor hit back with the 45rpm record, thus beginning the so-called Battle of the Speeds, diminishing trade in what turned out to be a period of consumer uncertainty. It was the period too when recording by magnetic tape was rapidly expanding. Neither ousted the other: in fact they proved complementary and expanded together in the dynamic growth period of rock 'n' roll and the radio disc jockey.

Stereophonic sound, or 'two-eared listening', had been possible since the Bell Laboratories had put on binaural demonstrations at the Chicago World's Fair of 1933, and Walt Disney's film *Fantasia* (1940) showed the possibilities of multi-source music reproduction in a cinema. The stereo effect was caught first on high-quality magnetic tape; then in 1957 the Westrex Company devised a successful method of putting two stereo channels into a single groove. By September of the following year every major record company in the US was offering stereo discs for sale.

The tape cassette emerged from Philips, which demonstrated its potential at the 1963 Berlin Radio Show. The company improved it substantially and in 1970 along came the Dolby system just at the time when tape machines were becoming popular as in-car entertainment.

An innovation in gramophone technology that never quite caught on was quadrophony, using four speakers rather than two, the additional channels intended to convey 'ambient' sound – fractionally delayed impulses reflected from the rear of the recording hall. Digital recording is now standard. The trusty stylus has been eased into history by the laser, and discs as we have known them face banishment by new developments in miniaturization. See *TOPIC GUIDE* under MEDIA HISTORY.

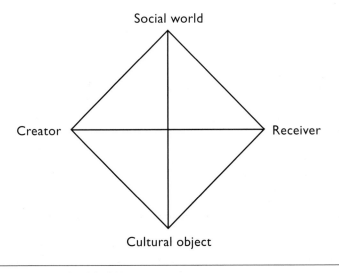

Social world

Creator

Receiver

Cultural object

Griswold's cultural diamond model, 1994

Grip Person in a film crew responsible for laying tracks, portable 'railway lines' for the smooth movement of the camera mounted on a DOLLY.

Griswold's cultural diamond model, 1994 In *Cultures and Societies in a Changing World* (US: Pine Forge Press, 1994), Wendy Griswold offers readers the accompanying diagram as an aid to the analysis of the cultural process. Each of the four points is linked and thus seen as interactive. Griswold admits, 'We cannot call it a theory of culture because it says nothing about how the points are related' and it is not a model 'in the strict sense because it does not indicate cause and effect'. Rather, she sees the diamond as 'an accounting device intended to encourage a fuller understanding of any cultural object's relationships to the social world'.

Groups A good deal of communication takes place within groups of one type or another. Charles H. Cooley, one of the initiators of research into group behaviour and communication, in his work, *Social Organization* (US: Scribner, 1909), classifies groups into two main types. *Primary* groups such as the family are defined as groups in which there is face-to-face communication; in which norms and mores are produced; in which roles are allocated and in which a feeling of solidarity is enjoyed.

Secondary groups, such as social class groups, are much larger aggregates. Several researchers have sought to determine the communication processes that take place within groups and in particular the inter-relationship between a group's CULTURE, ROLES, STATUS structure, cohesiveness, size and type, and its communication processes.

The performance of individuals is often affected by group membership. Being in a group can enhance or inhibit individual performance depending on such factors as the nature of the task, the degree of effective leadership, the cohesiveness of the group and the flexibility of its communication networks. These factors also determine the quality of group decision-making.

In certain circumstances individuals may feel they need to make less effort in a group situation and become social *loafers*; alternatively they may be motivated to work harder and become social *labourers*. At times individuals may be prepared to work harder to make up for their less energetic group members and contribute to social *compensation*.

Certain dynamics also appear to come into play when groups make decisions. Robert A. Baron and Donn Byrne provide some examples, in *Social Psychology* (US: Allyn & Bacon, 1994 edition), noting that 'groups often demonstrate group polarization, a tendency to shift toward more extreme views. Two other potential difficulties faced by decision-making groups are *groupthink* ... and an inability to pool unshared information.'

A small primary group particularly has the potential to influence the perceptions of its individual members and thus the way in which they interpret and respond to communication from sources both within and outside the group. Secondary groups are not without influence either, in the communication process. Basil Bernstein argues, in 'Social class, language and socialization', in *Communication Studies: An Introductory Reader* (UK: Arnold, 1993), edited by John Corner and Jeremy Hawthorn, that a relationship exists between membership of a social class group and the LANGUAGE code adopted. See CONCURRENCE-SEEKING TENDENCY.

Grub Street Description of any form of literary or journalistic drudgery. According to Dr Johnson (1709–84) Grub Street was 'originally the name of a street near Moorfields in London, much inhabited by writers of small histories, dictionaries and temporary poems, whence any mean production is called grub street'.

GSR Galvanic skin response: a measure of stress and emotion caused to individuals by others, especially when spatial territories have been invaded – that is, someone coming too close for psychological comfort. See PROXEMICS; SPATIAL ZONES.

Guard dog metaphor A variation of (and in contrast to) the WATCHDOG metaphor; representing one of the traditional functions of mass media. The term suggests that the media perform as a *sentry* – not for the community but for special interest GROUPS that have the power and influence to establish and maintain their own security systems (see POWER ELITE). In 'A guard dog perspective on the role of media', in the *Journal of Communication*, Spring, 1995, George A. Donohue, Phillip J. Tichenor and Clarise N. Olien of the University of Minnesota argue that the guard dog media 'are conditioned to be suspicious of all potential intruders, and they occasionally sound the alarm for reasons that individuals in the master households, that is, the authority structure, can neither understand nor prevent. These occasions occur primarily when authority within the structure is divided.' In communities where there is no apparent conflict within power structures 'the media are sleeping guard dogs'.

The guiding principle appears to be: support the powerful unless the powerful are intruders. 'Where different local groups have conflicting interests,' say Donohue *et al.*, 'the media are more likely to reflect the views of the more powerful groups.' Consequently the guard dog role works towards internal cohesion. The metaphor contrasts with that of the media's perceived role as *watchdog*. The role in this case is one of surveillance of the powerful on behalf of and in the interests of the public. The media serve as freedom-seekers and defenders, hence the titles of so many early newspapers – *Sentinel, Voice of the People, Champion, Justice, Poor Man's Guardian, Observer, Enquirer* and *Advocate*.

A third 'dog' in the repertoire of the media is the lapdog. As Donohue *et al.* point out, 'A lapdog perspective is a total rejection of the Fourth Estate view on all counts.' The lapdog is submissive to authority and oblivious 'to all interests except those of powerful groups' and serves to frame all 'issues according to the perspectives of the highest powers in the system'.

While the guard dog is characterized by deference as contrasted with submissiveness, at least it recognizes the existence of, and gives attention to, conflict. The greater the social differentiation within a community or nation, the more extensive is the reporting of conflict. Where there is 'power uncertainty' the media are likely to 'display a tendency to concentrate on individuals while accepting the structure. In doing so, the media are reinforcing the tendency within the culture to emphasize great men and personalities rather than individuals as actors in the system who are subject to the influence of social forces and processes.' See AGENDA-SETTING; NEWS VALUES.

Guide signs Actions indicating direction, sometimes called *deictic signals*: finger pointing, head pointing, eye pointing. Thumbs down and thumbs up come into this category, and all the gestures of beckoning as well as repelling. See NON-VERBAL BEHAVIOUR: REPERTOIRE.

Gum print Nineteenth-century mode of photograph printing that made the pictures resemble oil painting.

H

Hacker, hacktivist Just as the tomb robbers of ancient Egypt broke into seemingly impregnable pyramids and underground tombs, so the 'hacker' breaks into computer codes and computer systems. All the hacker needs is a personal micro, know-how and persistence, and some of the world's most closely guarded information banks can be penetrated. What has been termed a *hacktivist* is a hacker with a social or political agenda, and hacking becomes a form of protest. Chief among the targets of hacktivists is the corporation, intent on occupying and then controlling CYBERSPACE.

In an article 'Net tightens around the hacktivists', in the UK *Guardian* (2 January 2001), Tania Branijan writes, 'Rocketing numbers of political campaigners are embracing the internet with the fervour their parents showed for sitins as they try to claw back its independence and make online actions a standard form of modern protests.'

The hacktivist pursues a range of tactics, from simple e-mail protests to causing websites to crash and diverting visitors to other sites. Then there are 'bombs' – e-mails by the thousand directed at offending sites; and, of course, the spread of viruses. See REGULATION OF INVESTIGATORY POWERS ACT (RIPA) (UK), 2001.

Halo effect In initial encounters we tend to pick out one or two characteristics of a person and let these influence our general impression of him or her. For example, at an interview, it may be assumed that someone who is well qualified, neatly dressed and pleasant in manner will necessarily perform well in the job and work hard. Such generalizations from one or two characteristics are based on our implicit personality theory – that is, our basic assumptions about which characteristics go together, and how people are likely to behave.

Hammocking Strategy used by TV schedulers to boost the viewing figures of a programme by placing it between two popular programmes.

Hankey Committee Report on Television, 1943 Set up under the Coalition War Government in the UK, chaired by Lord Hankey, the committee was requested to 'prepare plans for the reinstatement and development of the television service after the War'. Hankey recommended a reopening on the 1939 basis of the 405-line system rather than wait for the development of any new, improved version. The Report was of the view that 'it is in the televising of actual events, the ability to give the viewer a front-row seat at almost every possible kind of exciting or memorable spectacle, that Television will perform its greatest service'. Hankey's general conclusion was 'that Television has come to stay …'. See *TOPIC GUIDE* under COMMISSIONS, COMMITTEES, LEGISLATION.

Hard times scenario See VALS TYPOLOGY.

Harmonious interaction Fred Inglis uses this phrase in *The Imagery of Power: A Critique of Advertising* (UK: Heinemann, 1972) to describe the friendly and mutually supportive relationship between the media and the forces of advertising. This 'harmonious interaction' of ADVERTISING and editorial styles consistently reproduces and endorses the consumer's way of life, argues Inglis.

Hays Office In the US for three decades the Hays Office meant CENSORSHIP. In 1922 leading figures in the film industry formed Motion Picture Producers and Distributors of America Incorporated (MPPDA) to protect their interests against a range of would-be film censors in a climate that had produced Prohibition (Volstead Act, 1919). Will H. Hays, Postmaster-General to the Harding administration, was invited to become president.

In 1930 Martin Quigley, a Chicago publisher, and Father Lord, Society of Jesus, reframed the Hays Office studio recommendations of 1927, into a Production Code (the Hays Office Code) to meet the even more restrictive demands emanating from the recently formed Legion of Decency made up of leaders of the Roman Catholic Church and other religious denominations. A Production Code Administration was prised out of the MPPDA under the direction of Roman Catholic Joseph I. Breen who, between 1934 and the anti-trust decree of 1948, supervised 95 per cent of films made in the US. Any film released without Breen's approval was liable to a $25,000 fine and condemnation by the Legion.

Political as well as moral attitudes and behaviour were subject to severe censorship. The Legion, for example, supported the Fascists in the Spanish Civil War and generally opposed any production with Leftish leanings. The Hays Office Code remained operative until 1966. See HUAC: HOUSE UN-AMERICAN ACTIVITIES COMMITTEE. See also *TOPIC GUIDE* under MEDIA: FREEDOM, CENSORSHIP.

H-certificate Category introduced by the BRITISH BOARD OF FILM CENSORS in 1930 to describe films dealing with the horrific or the supernatural, and considered unsuitable for children. From 1951 the certificate was discontinued and films of this nature were included under the new X-certificate. See CERTIFICATION OF FILMS.

Head nods Head nods are an element of non-verbal communication and can be used to communicate a range of messages. They are, for example, commonly used to give positive FEEDBACK to the sender of a message by indicating both interest and/or approval on the part of the receiver; to indicate *floor appointment*, that is to signal whose turn it is to speak next; and to give emphasis to speech. See COMMUNICATION: NON-VERBAL.

Hearsay See RUMOUR.

Hedges According to Jennifer Coates in *Women, Men and Language* (UK: Longman, second edition, 1993) hedges are 'linguistic forms such as *I think, I'm sure, you know, sort of* and *perhaps* which express the speaker's certainty or uncertainty about the proposition under discussion'. The precise function of hedges varies with the social context and the relationship of the interactors. Coates discusses the range of uses to which hedges may be put: such as expressing confidence, suggesting uncertainty and enabling face-saving to occur when sensitive topics are being discussed. Women appear to use more hedges than men do in conversation but the precise interpretation to be placed on this is a matter for debate.

Hegemony The concept of hegemony owes much to the work of Italian political thinker Antonio Gramsci (1891–1937). A state of hegemony is achieved when a provisional alliance of certain social groups exerts a CONSENSUS that makes the power of the dominant group appear both natural and legitimate.

Hegemony can, however, only be maintained by the *won consent* of the dominated. It is therefore, like consensus, subject to re-negotiation and ongoing redefinition. Also, the consensus may be broken as the ideologies of the *subordinate* cannot always be accommodated.

Institutions such as the mass media, the family, the education system and religion, play a key role in the shaping of people's awareness and consciousness, and thus can be agents through which hegemony is constructed, exercised and maintained. The definition and workings of hegemony have obviously undergone adaptation since Gramsci's day. The power, reach and global penetration of the media as instruments of hegemony have intensified issues of control and influence.

Todd Gitlin in his chapter 'Prime time television: the hegemonic process in television entertainment', in *Television: The Critical View* (US/UK: Oxford University Press, 1994), edited by Horace Newcomb, speaks of the survival of hegemony resulting from the flexibility of its IDEOLOGY: 'In the twentieth century, the dominant ideology has shifted toward sanctifying consumer satisfaction as the premium definition of "the pursuit of happiness", in this way justifying corporate domination of the economy. What is hegemonic in consumer capitalist ideology is precisely the notion that happiness, or liberty, or equality, or fraternity can be affirmed through the existing private commodity forms, under the benign, protective eye of the national security state.'

A further strand of modern hegemony, one Gramsci would have found difficult to envisage, is the stress in modern life upon technology and the consequent socio-cultural emphasis on efficiency and consequently of uniformity. If, as Jacques Ellul and a number of other commentators believe, efficiency has fast become the key determinant of human affairs in modern society (See TECHNIQUE: ELLUL'S THEORY OF TECHNIQUE), then hegemonic power, in the hands of the state and the corporate system, is likely to increase rather than diminish. See ELITE; IDEOLOGICAL STATE APPARATUSES; McDONALDIZATION. See also *TOPIC GUIDE* under MEDIA: VALUES AND IDEOLOGY.

---

* Jacques Ellul, *The Technological Society* (US: Knopf, 1964); Antonio Gramsci, *Selections from the Prison Notebooks* (UK: Lawrence & Wishart, 1971).

Helical model of communication See DANCE'S HELICAL MODEL OF COMMUNICATION, 1967.

Helical scan See TELERECORDING.

Heliological metaphor See VISIONS OF ORDER.

He/man language Dale Spender in her book *Man Made Language* (UK: HarperCollins, 1990 edition) refers to the principle by which for several centuries the terms *he* and *man* have been used to include women, for example, *man*kind. This principle has, according to Spender, not only the effect of contributing to the perspective of MALE-AS-NORM, of males as more worthy, but also helps to construct the invisibility of women in language, thought and reality. Not everyone, of course, either agrees with or employs this principle, and it has become the focus of some critical scrutiny in recent decades.

Herman and Chomsky's propaganda model See CONSENT, MANUFACTURE OF.

Hermeneutic code See CODES OF NARRATIVE.

Hermeneutics The science of interpretations or understanding. The word is taken from the Greek, *hermeneuein*, and derives from Hermes, messenger of the gods; it means to make things clear, to announce or unveil a MESSAGE. In film study, a hermeneutic code, or 'code of enigma', explains by one device or another the mysteries of the plot – the situation or predicament characters find themselves in, and indicates the process of resolution.

Heterophily See HOMOPHILY.

HICT project Household Uses of Information and Communication Technology: a major research project funded by the UK's Economic and Social Research Council. Its task has been to investigate the domestic use of TV, VCR, home computer and telephone technology. It was initially carried out by a team including Andrea Dahlberg, Eric Hirsch, Sonia Livingstone, David Morley and Roger Silverstone, with the Centre for Research into Innovation, Culture and Technology at Brunel University. The researchers studied 20 families living in the south-east of England, using ethnographic/participant observation methods followed up by a diversity of other approaches – time-use diaries, mental maps or brain patterns illustrating the perceived spatial location and significance of various technologies; and even scrutinizing family photo albums.

The notion of the household as a 'moral economy' is posed by the Brunel team. Are the location and use of such communication technology a reflection of the 'ordering' of the household, of relative degrees of power and status, of priorities; does it enhance or pose barriers to family interactivity; and how are differences over the uses of such technology resolved within the community of the household?

In *Consuming Technologies: Media and Information in Domestic Spaces* (UK, Routledge, 1992), edited by Silverstone, Hirsch and Morley, the authors write, 'To understand the household as a moral economy … is to understand the household as part of a transactional system, dynamically involved in … the production and exchange of commodities and meanings.' See *TOPIC GUIDE* under RESEARCH METHODS.

Hidden agenda When the underlying objective of an act of communication is different from that which is stated. See IMPRESSION MANAGEMENT.

Hidden needs Vance Packard in *The Hidden Persuaders* (UK: Penguin, 1960, with updated editions) cites eight 'hidden needs' the adman can cater for. These are: emotional security; reassurance of worth; ego-gratification; creative outlets; love objects; a sense of power; a sense of roots; and immortality. See ADVERTISING; MASLOW'S HIERARCHY OF NEEDS; VALS TYPOLOGY.

Hierarchy Classification in graded subdivisions. The hierarchy of a company starts at the top with the chairperson or managing director; a social hierarchy is dominated by the ELITE classes who varyingly influence those CLASS divisions below them. In the media, the dominant hierarchy are the owners, top executives, major shareholders, boards of directors, etc. See ORGANIZATION CULTURES.

High and low context communication See COMMUNICATION: INTERCULTURAL COMMUNICATION.

Highbrow Someone considered to be a member of the intellectual and cultural ELITE, whose tastes are, by definition, considered to be aesthetically superior to those of the majority, is deemed a highbrow. Highbrow tastes are limited to the few. The terms middlebrow and lowbrow are used to indicate a level of intellectual capacity of cultural appreciation judged against the standards of the highbrow elite. See CULTURAL CAPITAL.

High-fidelity See GRAMOPHONE.

High-speed photography One of the wonders of modern technology, but a preoccupation of photographers from the earliest pioneering days, the high-speed flash process slows down, or magnifies time: the splash of a drop of water, the trajectory of a bullet, can be reduced to slow motion that permits astonishing revelations. Foremost among developers of ultra-high-speed electronic flash photography as a tool of scientific analysis was the American Harold Edgerton, inventor of the stroboscope.

The term *stroboscopic photography*, or strobe photography, refers to pictures of single or multiple exposure taken by flashes of light from electrical discharges, permitting objects moving at their natural speeds to be observed in slow motion, the rate of the slow motion depending on the frequency of the strobe and object. When the flash frequency exactly equals that of the rotation or vibration, the object is illuminated in the same position during each cycle, and appears stationary.

Mechanical cameras such as the register-pin intermittent action camera are capable of 500 frames a second; for faster objects, there is the rotating prism camera at 1500 frames a second, slowing time down between 200 and 400 times. Even faster is the rotating mirror camera, capable of 10,000 pictures a second – a capacity that, however, is dwarfed by the image tube electronic camera, which can take a million-million pictures a second.

In contrast to high-speed photography, *time-lapse photography*, by taking pictures at timed intervals of seconds, minutes, hours or days, speeds up or telescopes time. In a few moments of film we can see the germination of a seed, the hatching of an egg or blow-fly maggots consuming a dead mouse. Audiences in the 1930s delighted in the time-lapse spectacle in *Four Minutes to Brighton*, of travelling, via film, at 760mph on the Brighton Belle. Apollo astronauts on the moon used time-lapse photography. Both high-speed and time-lapse photography are employed most widely to answer two questions: how is it done, and what went wrong? See PHOTOGRAPHY, ORIGINS.

Historical allusion The practice in NEWS reporting of making reference – alluding to – events in the past perceived as being similar to current events, recognized by AUDIENCE as such, and potentially capable of adding to the NEWS VALUE of a story. For example, a convenient (and often all-too-easy) way to DEMONIZE an 'enemy' leader is to compare him to Hitler, the activities of 'enemy' peoples to Nazis, and to use past terminology such 'holocaust' and 'death camps'.

Such language was prominently used by the western media to describe events in Serbia, Bosnia and Croatia during the 'ethnic cleansing' of the 1990s. For example, a *New York Times* editorial of 4 August 1992 declared that 'The chilling reports from Bosnia evoke this century's greatest nightmare, Hitler's genocide against Jews, Gypsies and Slavs.' Two days later, the *Chicago Tribune* asked, 'Are the Nazi era death camps being reprised in the Balkans? Unthinkable, you say? Think again … The ghost of World War II genocide is abroad in Bosnia …'.

Following the terrorist assaults on the US Pentagon and the World Trade Center in New York on 11 September 2001, and the subsequent build-up to war by the US and UK, the British Prime Minister Tony Blair was compared in the media – varyingly and queryingly – with the pugnacious war-leader Winston Churchill, the nineteenth-century Prime Minister William Gladstone (whose mission was to 'pacify Ireland') and the gunboat-happy British Foreign Secretary Lord Palmerston.

Such use of analogies and metaphors is seen generally to serve to place events into contexts familiar to the public. However, in *Compassion Fatigue: How the Media Sell Disease, Famine, War and Death* (US/UK: Routledge, 1999), Susan D. Moeller issues a cautionary note on this practice. 'The effect … ,' she believes, has been 'that readers and viewers' have come to 'overlook the complexity' of reported conflicts, and 'to believe in the simplicity of comparisons'.

Historical revisionism Term addressed specifically to attempts in the US and Europe to write out of history the genocide of the Third Reich of Adolph Hitler; to deny that the atrocities ever took place.

Hits The number of times a website is logged on to by INTERNET visitors.

Hollywood Centre of the US film industry, located in California, providing maximum sunshine for outdoor shooting and some magnificent scenery. In 1908 *The Count of Monte Cristo*, begun in Chicago, was completed in California and the first Hollywood studio was established in 1911. Within a year another 15 film companies had set up in business. The Hollywood studio system reached its peak in the 1930s. Its fortunes have since fluctuated, at first knocked sideways by the advent of TV, then restored by a simple philosophy of 'if you can't beat them, join them'. Today Hollywood plays a key role in the US television industries, while its film enterprises are profitably supplemented by global sales of movies on video and DVD.

---

* Janet Wasko, *Hollywood in the Information Age: Beyond the Silver Screen* (UK: Polity Press, 1994).

Holography With the invention of the laser in 1960 an intriguing new form of three-dimensional photography, holography, became possible. Though the theory originated with Dennis Gabor as early as 1947, development was not possible until an intense source of 'coherent' light became available, which the laser supplied. Coherent light is light of 'pure' colour containing waves of a single frequency whose wave fronts all move in perfect step.

Derived from the Greek, *holos*, or whole, and *gram*, message, the hologram is made without a lens by splitting a laser beam so that part of it is directed at the subject and part becomes a reference beam. When light reflected from the subject and light from the reference beam meet on the photographic plate, the wave fronts create interference patterns that contain all the visual information needed to construct a three-dimensional image of the subject, amazingly lifelike, and viewable from different angles. Recent developments have enabled holograms to be made for viewing by ordinary white light.

Holography has proved a boon to the world of business. Machine-readable reflection holograms store digital information in hundreds of layers within the emulsion of a film or plastic card. The holographed data on a credit card, passport, security access card or ticket to a high-priced event, forming a three-dimensional pattern, can be read electronically, thus providing a formidable obstacle to counterfeiting.

Home page The primary website document for a person, group or organization.

Home Service Name of the BBC's prime talk RADIO channel, founded in 1939. The name was changed to BBC Radio 4 in 1967. See BBC DIGITAL; RADIO 1, RADIO 2, RADIO 3, RADIO 4, RADIO 5 LIVE.

Homo narrans See NARRATIVE PARADIGM.

Homophily Interacting individuals who share certain attributes – beliefs, VALUES, educational background, social status – are said to be *homophilous*. Communication is commonly believed to be closer when between people who are homophilous as they are more likely to share a common language level and pattern of MEANING. On the other hand, *heterophily* refers to the degree to which interacting individuals differ in these attributes. Generally, heterophilic interaction is likely to cause some disturbance and confusion to the individuals concerned and thus more effort is required to make communication effective. See CONGRUENCE THEORY.

Horizons of expectation See EXPECTATION, HORIZONS OF.

Horizontal integration See INTEGRATION: VERTICAL AND HORIZONTAL.

Horse-race story Approach to NEWS coverage of elections anchored in the metaphor of horse-racing (or any other competitive sport), in which the political party ahead in the opinion polls is 'winning at a canter' or is losing ground to the opposition, which is coming up fast on the outside. Todd Gitlin in 'Bites and blips: chunk news, savvy talk and the bifurcation of American politics', in *Communication and Citizenship: Journalism and the Public Sphere* (UK: Routledge, 1991) edited by Peter Dahlgren and Colin Sparks, calls this mode of campaign journalism an 'enchantment – with means characteristic of a society which is competitive, bureaucratic, professional and technological all in one … This is a success culture bedazzled by sports statistics and empty of criteria for value other than numbers to answer the question, "How am I doing?" Journalists compete, news organizations compete, the channel aggression of the race is what makes their blood run.' See *TOPIC GUIDE* under NEWS MEDIA.

Hot media, cold media Terms coined by Marshall McLuhan, author of *The Gutenberg Galaxy* (Canada: University of Toronto Press, 1962) and *Understanding Media* (UK: Routledge & Kegan Paul, 1964), and forming a basic tool of his analysis of the media. For McLuhan, 'hot' media extend one sense-mode with high-definition data. Examples of 'hot' media are RADIO and FILM. 'Cold' media provide, in contrast, low-definition data, requiring much more participation by the individual. Examples are TV, telephone and cartoons. As Ralph Berry queries in *Communication through the Mass Media* (UK: Edward Arnold, 1971), 'All this is highly controversial ... for example, the "hot–cold" metaphor runs speedily into difficulties (is the living theatre significantly different in the front or the rear stalls?).'

Hotspot Or flashpoint; where activity on the INTERNET becomes so busy it resembles a major traffic jam.

Household Uses of Information and Communication Technology See HICT PROJECT.

HUAC: House Un-American Activities Committee Inspiration for Arthur Miller's play, *The Crucible*, which explored the nature of community hysteria leading to the persecution of 'suspected witches'. In the case of HUAC, set up by the US Congress in 1938 (and not wound up until February 1969), the witches were Communists, alleged Communists or Communist sympathizers. Among the witch-finders were Richard Nixon, later Republican President, and the notorious Senator Joseph McCarthy.

Every section of society was scrutinized for suspects, not the least the entertainment industry. One committee member, John Rankin, a 'virulent bigot who equated Jews with Communists and Negroes with monkeys', as Godfrey Ryan describes him in his three-part series of articles, 'Un-American activities' (UK: *Index on Censorship* 1, 2 and 3, 1973), declared 'one of the most dangerous plots ever instigated for the overthrow of this government has its headquarters in Hollywood ... The information we get is that this is the greatest hot-bed of subversive activities in the United States.'

HUAC's pursuit of 'subversives' thrived in the years of the Second World War and flourished even more in the years of the so-called Cold War. In *Joe McCarthy and McCarthyism: The Hate That Haunts America* (US: McGraw-Hill, 1972), Roberta Fauerlicht writes, 'Since the government had to find subversives before they could subvert, people were punished not for what they did but for what they might do. Men and women found their loyalty questioned because they liked Russian music, because they had books on Communism in their libraries, or because they believed in equality for blacks or civil liberties for Communists.' A total of 139 government employees were fired as a result of HUAC investigations, although not a single one was found guilty of subversive acts. Hearst newspapers were prominent in applauding the work of the HUAC.

Perhaps the most insidious result of HUAC activities was *blacklisting*, whereby 'suspects' – often mysteriously – failed to gain employment or were laid off from work for specious reasons. Blacklisting was keenly felt in the movie industry and in broadcasting. It is a cruel irony that where accusations were publicly proved to be fraudulent, blacklisting increased rather than decreased.

Prominent victims of HUAC scrutiny were Arthur Miller himself (he was refused a passport by the State Department in 1956), the black singer Paul Robeson, Hollywood scriptwriters Ring Lardner and Dalton Trumbo, film directors Elia Kazan and Martin Ritt (see Ritt's movie of 1976, *The Front*, on the theme of blacklisting), writers Clifford Odets and Lillian Hellman, and actors Zero Mostel (star of *The Front*) and Edward G. Robinson. During the 1960s HUAC's dominance of the hearts and minds of the American nationals was repeatedly challenged. Indeed its momentum had been seriously checked by TV commentator Edward R. Murrow who produced a *See It Now* documentary (1954) in which he suggested that McCarthy had repeatedly stepped over the fine line between investigating and persecuting.

The nightmare spell which McCarthy cast over a nation was mercifully broken when he died of liver failure in May 1957. In 1969 HUAC was reincarnated as the House Internal Security Committee which, learning the lessons of the past, opted for low-key activities, holding fewer sessions and avoiding unpleasant confrontations by not subpoenaing unfriendly witnesses. See *TOPIC GUIDE* under MEDIA ETHICS; MEDIA: FREEDOM, CENSORSHIP; MEDIA HISTORY.

Human Rights Act (UK), 2000 Incorporating into British law the European Convention on Human Rights, the Act has been described as the biggest change in UK law since the Bill of Rights of 1688.

The Act guarantees freedom of thought, conscience and religion; freedom of expression, and this right 'shall include freedom to hold opinions and to receive and impart information and ideas without interference by public authority and regardless of frontiers'.

Freedom of expression is deemed to be subject to 'duties and responsibilities' and conditional upon 'restrictions and penalties as are prescribed by law and are necessary in a democratic society, in the interests of national security, territorial integrity or public safety'. That freedom is equally subject to criteria concerning 'the prevention of disorder or crime, for the protection of health and morals, for the protection of the rights of others, for the preventing the disclosure of information received in confidence or for maintaining the authority and impartiality of the judiciary'.

Discrimination 'on any ground such as sex, race, colour, language, religion, political or other opinion, national or social origin, association with a national minority, property, birth or other status' is prohibited. The right to life, to a fair trial, to respect for private and family life, freedom of assembly, the right to marry are all confirmed. See *TOPIC GUIDE* under COMMISSIONS, COMMITTEES, LEGISLATION.

Human Rights Watch An independent, non-governmental organization funded by private individuals and foundations worldwide, with offices in New York, Washington, Rio de Janeiro and Hong Kong. Formed in 1978, Human Rights Watch investigates and reports on the state of human rights in Africa, the Americas, Asia, the Middle East and the signatories of the Helsinki Accord on Human Rights, scrutinizing such matters as arms transfers, women's and children's rights, and prison conditions. The organization also makes grants to writers who have suffered from political persecution.

Hunt Committee Report on Cable Expansion and Broadcasting Policy (UK), 1982 Set up by the Conservative government, the three-man committee chaired by Lord Hunt, a former top civil servant, was required to report and make recommendations on the future of cable systems in the UK, in order to 'secure the benefits for the United Kingdom which cable technology can offer … in a way consistent with the wider public interest, in particular the safeguarding of public service broadcasting …'. In brief, the report, the result of a hurried investigation begun in March 1982 and finalized by September, recommended a future pattern of cable transmission systems marked by few regulations, many channels and as much ADVERTISING as operators could attract. The committee urged immediate expansion even before the proposed body for the supervision of franchises was created.

Pay-per-view TV was not given the green light by Hunt on the grounds that major national events, such as the Cup Final or Wimbledon, might be siphoned off from national access and be seen only by those on cable and able to pay. 'Cherry picking' – cabling just for the well-off suburbs of a city, for example – was also to be barred. See CABLE TELEVISION.

Hybridization Described by James Lull in *Media, Communication, Culture* (UK: Polity Press, 1995) as the 'fusing of cultural forms'. Travel and the global nature of much of the media and music industries enable a cultural form that originates in one culture to be disseminated quite quickly and easily to other cultures, where it may well be influenced by and merge with local cultural forms, thus producing a cultural hybrid. Lull gives the example of rap music that has travelled widely from its roots in US inner-city ghettos and has become incorporated into other kinds of popular music in a number of other countries. See GLOBAL VILLAGE.

In particular, TV is seen as a prime agency of hybridization (or *hybridity*). It represents a site of travel in which people draw images, IDEOLOGY and visions of lifestyles other than their own. Arguments over hybridity centre on whether TV as a travelling medium creates cultural *diversity* or results in cultural *homogeneity*, or sameness. In addition to TV (and perhaps more importantly), the INTERNET can be seen as an agency of hybridization.

Hyperreality Just as hyperactivity is enhanced, or beyond-the-normal activity, hyperreality, in the age of mass production and reproduction, offers us reality-plus. Images, simulations of reality, serve to extend, to heighten the realities they represent, to the point, in the view of some commentators, that they are more real than and preferable to actual realities. Both the French philosopher Jean Baudrillard and the Italian semiologist Umberto Eco cite Disneyland as having taken realities to a point when they achieve hyperreality, a substitute that supplants, even erases, the original and replaces it with the 'reality' of simulation. In short, that which is imitating is more real, more significant, than that which is imitated.

Baudrillard, in *Selected Writings* (UK: Polity Press, 1988), edited by Mark Poster, refers to the 'society of the image' in which the real is subsumed by 'all the entangled orders of simulation'. Eco does not go so far as to say that the hyperreal supplants the real, but, in *Travels in Hyperreality* (UK: Picador, 1986), states that imitations are indeed coming to be preferred – by those who create them and those who consume them – to the original. He refers to such fakes as deriving from 'a present without depth'. He classifies Disneyland as the home of the 'total fake'. However, the real, he believes, can be reasserted through a sense of history that 'allows an escape from the temptations of hyperreality'.

Hypertext Electronic text on computer, interfaced with links or pathways to other, related texts. For example, the text of a novel might be the primary text while a web of supplementary texts – background notes, critiques, biographies – will be instantly available for consultation and use.

Hyphenized abridgement Herbert Marcuse uses this term in *One-Dimensional Man* (UK: Sphere Books, 1968) to describe the practice of the PRESS of concentrating information by bringing two or more descriptive facts together by using a hyphen. Thus: 'Georgia's high-handed-lowbrowed governor ... had the stage set for one of his wild political rallies last week.' Marcuse argues, 'The governor, his function, his physical features and his political practices are fused together into one indivisible and immutable structure' by the press employing this device 'which in its natural innocence and immediacy, overwhelms the reader's mind. The structure leaves no space for distinction ... it moves and lives only as a whole.'

Hyphenized abridgement, used repeatedly and assertively, 'imposes images while discouraging on the part of the reader, conceptualization; that is, it beats him/her with images, but impedes thinking; and thus the media define for us the terms in which we are permitted to think'. See DETERMINER DELETION; EFFECTS OF MASS MEDIA; FRANKFURT SCHOOL OF THEORISTS; PSEUDO-CONTEXT; TABLOID, TABLOIDESE, TABLOIDIZATION.

Hypodermic needle model of communication More a METAPHOR representing a view of the effects of the mass media, the Hypodermic needle 'model' has formed a point of general reference in crediting the media with power over audiences. The basic assumption is that the mass media have a direct, immediate and influential effect upon audiences by 'injecting' information into the conscious-ness of the masses.

The AUDIENCE is seen as impressionable and open to manipulation. Like other early models of communication flow from the media, it overlooks the possible effects of INTERVENING VARIABLES (IVs) in the communication process and presents the masses as being unquestioning receptacles of media messages. This sense of the all-powerfulness of the media is a central feature of early mass society research. It is now regarded as crude and simplistic. See AUDIENCE: ACTIVE AUDIENCE; COMMERCIAL LAISSEZ-FAIRE MODEL OF (MEDIA) COMMUNICATION.

Hypothesis The first step of the research cycle is the formulation of a hypothesis. This will usually be based on an idea or hunch gained by the researcher from his/her own reading of earlier studies and/or from his/her own observations of society. Starting with this basic idea the researcher usually proposes a working hypothesis that will guide the research. The hypothesis proposes a relationship between certain social phenomena: for example, that people from a higher-education background are more likely to read what is regarded as the quality press.

Not all hypotheses are expressed as formal statements. Some can be a general collection of ideas about particular social phenomena. All hypotheses, though, must be capable of EMPIRICAL testing; that is, they must be capable of being proved or disproved by facts and argument. The hypothesis will determine the nature of the research design – the method of collecting the information that will prove or disprove the hypothesis.

Once this information has been collected and analysed the hypothesis is reviewed. It may be proved, disproved or amended. Indeed in many cases the original hypothesis may have been modified during the data collection stage of the research. Alternatively it may be decided that further evidence is required before any conclusion is reached.

Hypothesis of consonance See NEWS VALUES.

I

Iconic Describes a SIGN that, in some way, resembles its object, looks like it, or sounds like it. Picture-writing is iconic, as is a map. ONOMATOPOEIA (word sounds that resemble real sounds) is iconic. In SEMIOLOGY/SEMIOTICS the iconic is one of three categories of sign defined by American philosopher C.S. Peirce (1834–1914). Where the *iconic* describes or resembles, an *index* is connected with its object, like smoke to fire, while the *symbol* has no resemblance or connection, and communicates MEANING only because people agree that it shall stand for what it does. A word is a symbol. The categories are not separate and distinct. One sign may be made up of all three categories. See *TOPIC GUIDE* under LANGUAGE/DISCOURSE/NARRATIVE.

Ideational functions of language The use of language to explore, interpret, construct and express views about ourselves and the world. Another major function of language, the interpersonal function, is that of establishing and maintaining relationships with others. Clearly both functions are often present in communicative encounters and the two are often related.

Identification The degree to which people identify with and are influenced by characters, fictional or otherwise, in books, radio, films and TV has fascinated media analysts, especially in areas of behaviour where that identification might lead to anti-social activity such as violence. 'To identify with' has two common meanings: to participate in the situation of someone whose plight has caught one's sympathy; and to incorporate characteristics of an admired person into one's own identity by adopting that person's system of values.

Identification is used in a more specific sense when we discuss the degree of influence persons, institutions and the media may have on others. In 'Processes of opinion change', *Public Opinion Quarterly* 25 (1965), Herbert Kelman explores three basic processes of social influence with reference to opinion change and to communication. These are *compliance, identification* and *internalization*. The first position, compliance, in this 'social influence theory' refers to the acceptance of influence in the hope of either receiving a reward or avoiding punishment. Identification occurs 'when an individual adopts behaviour derived from another person or a group because this behaviour is associated with a satisfying self-defining relationship to this person or group'.

As with compliance, change or influence is reliant upon the external source and 'dependent on social support'. Internalization occurs when the proposed change, the influence, is fully believed in, accepted, taken fully on board, because the influenced person 'finds it useful for the solution of a problem or because it is congenial to his own orientation, or because it is demanded of his own values'.

Linked to the analysis of the extent to which identification takes place is the interest in how we identify along lines of age, CLASS or GENDER.

Identity See SELF-IDENTITY.

Idents TV channel identities; snapshot films, reminding viewers in graphic, computer-generated form which channel they are tuned to. Idents are designed to establish an image of the channel, a channel branding. The generic ident is basically suitable for any programme introduction while specific idents create images closely reflecting the nature of particular programmes or series.

Ideological presumption Describes the view that journalists and the NEWS media are necessarily and unavoidably ideologically implicated in the MESSAGE systems and DISCOURSES to which they contribute. In *The Foucault Reader* (US: Random House, 1984) the French philosopher Michel Foucault states that the social relations of power produce and constitute knowledge, and that socio-economic power lies at the root of what we are, what we believe and what we are shown – through the media. The position locates journalists as *cultural workers*, in the service of those with power and authority.

The view is challenged by Matthew Kieron in 'News reporting and the ideological presumption', published in the *Journal of Communication*, Spring 1997. He declares that the 'presumption' is 'either false, incoherent or trivial'; it is 'overextended, misplaced and distortive'. Kieron argues that we should, in our scrutiny of journalism, acknowledge that in broadly free societies there are sufficient variables in interpretation and approach to escape the grip of the voice of authority.

Ideological state apparatuses   This term derives from the work of the French philosopher Louis Althusser. Ideological state apparatuses (ISAs) are those social institutions that, according to Althusser, help shape people's consciousness in a way that secures support for the IDEOLOGY of those who control the state – that is, the dominant ideology. Such institutions include education, the family, religion, the legal system, the party-political system and the mass media. The dominant ideology is thus represented as both natural and neutral. As a result it becomes almost unseen, taken-for-granted.

In contrast there is what Althusser calls the RSA (*Repressive State Apparatus*), the law, police, military; brought into operation – using coercion – when the RSA is failing, through persuasion, to secure its objectives of social control. Authority relies on the media to serve as an ISA and to support situations when the RSA is brought into action. See COMMON SENSE; DISCOURSE; ELITE; HEGEMONY; MYTH; POWER ELITE. See also *TOPIC GUIDE* under MEDIA: POLITICS AND PRODUCTION; MEDIA: VALUES AND IDEOLOGY.

Ideology   An ideology is a system of ideas and beliefs about human conduct that has normally been simplified and manipulated in order to obtain popular support for certain actions, and that is usually emotive in its reference to social action. Karl Marx (1818–83) used the term to apply to any form of thought that underpins the social structure of a society and that consequently upholds the position of the ruling class. Twentieth-century French philosopher Louis Althusser, drawing on the work of Marx, saw ideology as being an unconscious set of VALUES and beliefs that provides frames for our thinking and helps us make sense of the world.

Ideology can often be found to be hiding (or hidden) under terms such as 'common sense', or 'common sense view', which Marx would claim was merely the view of the ruling CLASS translated by repeated usage through channels of communication into wisdom as apparently natural as fresh air – a process sometimes referred to as *mystification*. Within society there may be a variety of contending ideologies at play, representing different sets of social interests, each seeking to extend recognition and acceptance of its way of making sense of the world, its own capacity to give order and explain social existence.

Language itself may be seen not as a neutral medium but as ideological, thus in its use ensuring that ideology is present in all discourses. Each may seek to become the dominant ideology and it can be argued that the capacity to make use of the channels of mass communication is crucial to either achieving or maintaining this position.

The use of the media in this respect is the focus of much media research and analysis. German-British sociologist Karl Mannheim (1893–1947) in *Ideology and Utopia* (1936) distinguishes between ideas that defend existing interests, the status quo, which he terms *ideologies,* and ideas that seek to change the social order, which he terms *utopias*. See CONSENSUS; CULTURAL APPARATUS; DISCOURSE; DOMINANT DISCOURSE; HEGEMONY; IDEOLOGICAL STATE APPARATUSES; MALE-AS-NORM. See also *TOPIC GUIDE* under MEDIA: VALUES AND IDEOLOGY.

---

* Mike Cormack, *Ideology* (UK: Batsford, 1992); Tuen A. van Dijk, *Ideology: A Multidisciplinary Approach* (UK: Sage, 1998).

Ideology of detachment   See IMPARTIALITY.

Ideology of romance   An aspect of HEGEMONY in which the perceptions and attitudes of women, in particular teenage girls, are 'shaped' by DOMINANT DISCOURSES into accepting the roles of wife and mother within an essentially patriarchal social structure. Wendy Halloway in 'Gender difference and the production of subjectivity', in *Changing the Subject: Psychology, Social Regulation and Subjectivity* (UK: Methuen, 1984), edited by J. Henriques *et al.*, calls this mode of communicative conditioning a *'to have and to hold'* discourse, which links acceptable behaviour with monogamous relationships.

The ideology of romance can be found expressed and reinforced in magazines, films, pop songs, ADVERTISING and SOAP OPERAS. It is, in the view of Mary Ellen Brown, author of *Soap Operas and Women's Talk: The Pleasures of Resistance* (UK: Sage, 1994), an ideology that 'can leave young women few options'. At the same time the ideology of romance can be seen as a rational response to, and a means of coping with, material and economic subordination, encapsulated in the song *Diamonds are a*

Girl's Best Friend. Says Brown, 'Such romantic ideology positions young women in such a way that they can easily decide to buy into the system.' Most feminist writers would argue that the ideology of romance is coterminous with the notion of the *ideology of dependence.*

Ideology of silence The belief, held chiefly by governments, that the best way of 'getting things done' in, for example, attempts to win the release of political prisoners or hostages, is by secret, behind-the-scenes diplomacy. The same rule would apply in cases where one government may feel obliged, perhaps through public pressure, to protest to another country. The problem in such cases is that there is no real proof that a protest has been made and consequently no evidence as to the nature of that proof.

In an article, 'Against silence', in *Index on Censorship* (February 1987), Jacob Timerman, formerly a political prisoner in Argentina, expands on the notion of the ideology of silence and concludes that 'the only way to solve problems of decency and civilization is to speak out'.

Idiolect An individual's personal dialect, which incorporates the individual variations that exist between people in their use of punctuation, grammar, vocabulary and style. No two people are likely to express themselves in exactly the same way.

Idiot salutations See PHATIC (LANGUAGE).

Image A likeness; a representation; a visualization. The term can have several meanings depending on the context in which it is used. It may refer to a visual representation of reality such as is seen in a photograph; it can also refer to a mental, imaginative conception of an individual, event, location or object as, for example, one conjures up an image of a character in a novel. The image does not merely reproduce, it interprets; it has added to it certain meanings. The writer, artist, architect, photographer and advertising image-maker all use assemblies of signs in order to represent or suggest states of mind, or abstractions. Van Dyck's equestrian portrait of Charles I portrays the monarch on a noble steed against a background suffused with dramatic light. All the details of this painting converge to create an image of kingship, thus a process of *symbolization* has taken place.

The purpose of image creation obviously varies, but all images are devised in order to evoke responses of one kind or another, usually emotional. Images often serve as psychological triggers effecting responses that are not always easy to articulate. Advertisements regale us with images of the good life; they play upon our perceived needs (see HIDDEN NEEDS; MASLOW'S HIERARCHY OF NEEDS). Image is also something we present of ourselves – our best face, the way we want the world to perceive us. Politicians work at their images more than most, and these are portrayed to fit in with the image appropriate to a public figure whose aim is to impress voters by his or her qualities of leadership and trustworthiness.

Sometimes we talk of a person whose image 'has slipped', which seems to indicate the connection between image and *performance* (see IMPRESSION MANAGEMENT) and that it relates to an ideal. For the artist, whatever his or her medium, imagery is central to expression. It is a part of STYLE and a key to the construction of MEANING. See METAPHOR. See also *TOPIC GUIDE* under REPRESENTATION.

Image, rhetoric of In its contemporary use, the word *rhetoric* is interchangeable for persuasion or PROPAGANDA; thus the rhetoric of the image indicates the use of images as a means of persuasion; of inculcation or reinforcement of ideological positions. The power of the image is employed, particularly in the NEWS, to *empower* the overt or covert MESSAGE. Such images have the effect of closing off, by their dramatic and emotional nature, alternative ways of reporting and interpreting realities.

IMAX Canadian film projection system developed in the 1970s, notable for the vastness of its screen for 70mm film; installed in the UK in 1983 at the National Museum of Photography, Film and Television in Bradford; and later in London. See OMNIMAX.

Immediacy A prime NEWS VALUE in western newspaper, radio and television newsgathering and presentation. At the centre of decision-making and of news control is the time factor, usually related to the daily cycle. In his article 'Newsmen and their time machine', in the *British Journal of Sociology* (September 1977), Philip Schlesinger points out that in industrialized societies an exceptional degree of precision of timing is necessary in our working lives. 'Especially noteworthy are those who operate communication and transport systems … Newsmen … are members of a stopwatch culture.'

Immediacy shapes and structures the approach to newsgathering. The report of an event must be as close to the event as possible, and ideally the event should be reported as it happens. The pure type of immediacy would be the live broadcast. News, says Schlesinger, is 'hot' when it is most immediate. 'It is "cold", and old, when it can no longer be used during the newsday in question.' Immediacy is not only a vital factor in the selection of a story for treatment; it also helps fashion that treatment. Pace is what counts in presentation, especially in TV news where the priority is to keep the audience 'hooked'.

The danger with such emphasis on immediacy is that news tends to be all foreground and little background, all events and too little context, all current happenings and too little concentration on historical and cultural frameworks. Schlesinger rounds off his article by saying that it is plausible to argue 'that the more we take note of news, the less we can be aware of what lies behind it'. See EFFECTS OF MASS MEDIA. See also *TOPIC GUIDE* under NEWS MEDIA.

Immersion The degree to which the virtual, the invented – as in VIRTUAL REALITY (VR) – submerges the real perception system of the user. The more that VR works to the exclusion of contact with the real, physical world, the more it is classified as being immersive. The prospect of near-total immersion, on the part of some users, is a matter of interest and concern. As Frank Biocca says in 'Communication within virtual reality: creating a space for research', in *Journal of Communication*, Autumn 1992, 'If people eventually use VR technology for the same amount of time that they spend watching television and using computers, some users could spend 20 or more years "inside" virtual reality.'

Impact of the mass media See EFFECTS OF THE MASS MEDIA.

Impartiality Just as Professor Stuart Hall doubts the existence, in media terms, of OBJECTIVITY, so Philip Schlesinger, in a remarkable study of the workings of BBC news, has cast doubt on the possibility of impartiality. Between 1972 and 1976, Schlesinger had a unique research opportunity to conduct in the newsrooms of Broadcasting House and the Television Centre, London, fieldwork that attempted 'to grasp how the world looks from the point of view of those studied': the reporters, correspondents, editors and managing editors in the most prestigious media organization in the world. He interviewed over 120 BBC news staff and spent 90 days in observation. His findings were published in *Putting 'Reality' Together. BBC News* (UK: Constable, 1978; Methuen/University Paperback, with new Preface, 1987).

Several key words framed the basic principles of news production: *balance, objectivity, responsibility, fairness, freedom* from bias; and these were, in the 'ordinary discourse of newsmen' for the most part 'interchangeable'. They could be gathered under one banner, that of impartiality, what Schlesinger refers to as the central mediating factor in news processing at the BBC, 'the linchpin of the BBC's ideology'. Schlesinger found this a notion 'saturated' with political and philosophical implications' and classifies the 'ideology of detachment' as in essence an example of 'latter-day Mannheimianism'. In *Ideology and Utopia* (UK: Routledge & Kegan Paul, 1936), Karl Mannheim explained how a 'socially unattached intelligentsia' could play a role in society that was above all conflict, capable of representing to society all relevant views.

It is a theory that has regularly been condemned as an unrealistic dream but the doctrine has remained persistently attractive: by virtue of their education, argued Mannheim, the intellectuals, *déclassées*, are exposed to the 'influence of opposing tendencies in social reality'; thus theirs is the potential to improve social integration, to produce a new CONSENSUS by means of 'dynamic mediation'.

The theory implies that it is possible to view the world in a value-free way, and act accordingly. Schlesinger calls value-freedom 'a myth', yet one that in terms of the BBC's aspiration to impartiality, to being above the fray, 'is believed by those who propagate it' as well as being 'essential for public consumption'. Such beliefs, Schlesinger argues, 'anchor news production in the status quo'. What the BBC produces as news is 'structurally limited by the organization's place in Britain's social order' and the main consequence of that position is that 'the outputs of broadcasting are, in general, supportive of the existing social order'. See *TOPIC GUIDE* under MEDIA ISSUES AND DEBATES.

Imperialism in information systems See MEDIA IMPERIALISM.

Implication In the production of TEXTS, particularly the NEWS, much is left implicit: assumptions about prior knowledge, expectations about response, are implied rather than made manifest and this implication is generally if not always *ideological.* As Tuen van Dijk says in 'Media contents: the inter-disciplinary study of news as discourse', in *A Handbook of Qualitative Methodologies for Mass Communication* Research (UK: Routledge, 1991), edited by Klaus Bruhn Jensen and Nicholas W. Jakowsky, 'The analysis of the "unsaid" is sometimes more revealing than the study of what is actually expressed in the text.' This would suggest a key aspect of the study of media – a focus on what is omitted, or *absent,* as well as what is included and present.

Impression management   Technique of self-presentation defined by Erving Goffman in *The Presentation of Self in Everyday Life* (US: Anchor, 1959; UK: Penguin, 1971). Because most social interaction requires instant judgements, alignments and behaviour, the individual must be able rapidly to convey impressions of him/herself to others, highlighting favourable aspects, concealing others. Goffman argues that impression management has the character of drama: all social ROLES, he believes, are, in a sense, performances in which it is important to set a scene and rehearse a role, and this means coordinating activities with others in the 'drama'. Thus we put up a front, 'that part of the individual's performance which regularly functions in a general and fixed fashion to define the situation for those who observe the performance'.

Our formal, public selves Goffman calls *front region* and our more informal, relaxed selves, *back region.* Indeed Goffman believes that all our roles depend upon the performer having a back region; equally all front-region roles rely upon keeping the audience out of the back regions.

Teams as well as individuals operate in front and back regions: in a restaurant, for example, the front-stage conduct of the team of waiters and other staff subscribes to formal rules and rituals, even a mystique. Behind the scenes, however, the performers relax. The need to unify in sustaining an expected version of reality – of smartness, politeness, professionalism – gives way to a back-stage reality where individual differences can freely be aired without letting the team, or the performance, down. See SELF-PRESENTATION.

Independent producers See TELEVISION: INDEPENDENT PRODUCERS.

Independent Television Commission (ITC) See COMMERCIAL TELEVISION.

Independent Television Commission: Code of Advertising Standards and Practice See CODE OF ADVERTISING PRACTICE (ITC).

Independent Television franchises See FRANCHISES FOR INDEPENDENT TELEVISION (UK).

Index Short for *Index librorum prohibitorum,* a list of proscribed books. The Council of Trent, in attempting to turn the tide against the Protestant Reformation, drew up a set of rules about what Roman Catholics should, or rather should not, read. In accordance with these rules the Index was published by authority of Pope Paul IV in 1559. In its current form, the Index is a list not only of works prohibited in their entirety to the faithful but also of works not to be read unless or until they are corrected.

The *Index expurgatorius* or Expurgatory Index (1571), specifies passages to be expurgated in works otherwise permitted. Appropriately, the word has been used in the title of the UK magazine whose chief aim is to counter such repressions of information and expression: *Index of Censorship.*

Index as a sign See SIGN.

Indicators In INTERPERSONAL COMMUNICATION the means by which one communicator conveys his/her attitude and response to another – feelings of attraction or rejection, of evaluation or esteem of the other person. Proximity, for example, is an ideal indicator of liking (unless, of course, it becomes a GESTURE of threat or intimidation). Also important as indicators are frequent eye contact, body orientations and spontaneous gestures. See PROXEMICS.

Indies See TELEVISION: INDEPENDENT PRODUCERS.

Inductive reasoning Involves the drawing of conclusions from collected observations and data – from evidence. The acceptability of the conclusions drawn depends upon whether or not the type and quantity of evidence can reasonably be said to support them. It is important to recognize how limited such conclusions may be. Someone unfamiliar with traffic observing the flow of traffic between 10a.m.

and 2p.m. for one week, in a busy street, for example, may note that when the red traffic light is illuminated, cars in front of the light stop. He/she may conclude that the illumination of the red traffic light caused the cars to stop, certainly at the times at which he/she was observing the traffic. The observer, however, could not reasonably draw conclusions about, for example, why this was the case or whether or not this occurred at times when he/she was not observing the traffic; that would require further investigation.

Deductive reasoning involves the application of an already accepted generalization or generalizations to an individual case. It is the reverse of inductive reasoning. Someone who has accepted, for example, that drinking too much alcohol before driving is dangerous might as a consequence regulate their intake of alcohol at a party if he/she were driving home – a decision based upon deductive reasoning. See EMPIRICAL; HYPOTHESIS.

Inference According to Gail Myers and Michele Myers in *The Dynamics of Human Communication* (US: McGraw-Hill, 1985), 'A statement of inference is a guess about the unknown based on the known.' We often infer, that is make assumptions, about people, events, behaviour and so on. In doing so we add these inferences to our observations. For example, if we saw a young man running away from an elderly woman we might infer that he had stolen her purse, but we might be quite wrong and he might be running for a bus.

We automatically make inferences and in doing so rely on a range of factors such as past experiences, stereotyping, VALUES, attitudes and beliefs. Yet inferences can mislead both ourselves and others if they stray too far from our actual observations or accepted facts. Clearly, in communication we need to be careful to distinguish between statements of fact and statements of inference.

Inflection The patterns of alteration or modulation in the pitch of a person's voice.

Influence of the mass media See EFFECTS OF THE MASS MEDIA.

Infomercials Television commercials presented as programmes in their own right. A channel dedicated entirely to advertisements, Infonet, beamed to viewers by satellite, was available to American viewers in 1991. The aim of infomercials is to develop the informational and entertainment potential of traditional commercials, and extend them considerably in length. The first infomercials promoted magazines and reference books using documentary techniques.

Info-rich, info-poor See INFORMATION GAPS.

Information blizzards Traditionally, a nation's citizens have been granted too little information on which to base decisions and choices; yet by the late twentieth century that position appeared to have been reversed: nowadays there is too much information, blizzards of it, and the result is not under-nourishment but confusion. John Keane in *The Media and Democracy* (UK: Polity, 1991), writes, 'The world seems so full of information that what is scarce is citizens' capacities to make sense of it. The release of new opinions through the media rarely shatters unaccountable power. Publicity better resembles the throwing of snowballs into a blizzard – or the blowing of bubbles into warm summer's air.'

The term 'blizzard' has also been used to describe the multiple and interacting images we encounter daily, brought to us with ever-new associations by the media (see TEXT). For the French cultural critic Jean Baudrillard the sheer volume of signifiers in the contemporary world of mass communication, so readily and regularly detached from their original SIGNIFICATION, meaning is too lost in the blizzard to be worth the trouble of attempting to define it. Consequently in this cultural blizzard anything can be made to mean anything. See Chapter 5, 'Baudrillard's blizzards', in Nick Stephenson's *Culture, Social Theory and Mass Communication* (UK: Sage, 1995) in which Baudrillard's 'irrationalism' is challenged.

Information commons Equivalent to 'common land', that is space or territory accessible, by right, to the public, without charge; thus information commons relates to public space, or the public *domain*, with regard to information and expression. Some commentators fear that the public domain as typified by our shared culture, has long been subject to a process of *enclosure*, or PRIVATIZATION, in which cultural artefacts and practices, once part of the information commons have been turned into private property accessible only as commodity.

A particular area of concern is copyrighting, which has extended far beyond the protection of the works of writers, artists, musicians etc. into images, sounds, acronyms and names. In a tom.paine.com online article (1 August 2002), entitled 'Stopping the privatization of public knowledge: the endangered public domain', David Bollier of the Annenberg School of Communications, Philadelphia, talks of 'content autocrats' dedicated to copyright enforcement operating in an atmosphere of 'fully fledged cultural pathology'.

Enclosed through privatization, the enforcement of copyright in the courts has proved a serious intrusion upon the freedoms of cultural expression. He cites McDonald's threatening 'every food business that uses "Mc" in their names' or Mattel threatening 'legal action against art photographers who use images of Barbie dolls to comment on American beauty ideals'. See CULTURE: COPY-RIGHTING CULTURE.

Information gaps   Many have focused their studies on the inequality in the distribution of information among different groups in societies. Such inequalities are mostly the result of educational or social CLASS differences with the advantage being enjoyed by the better-educated and those in the higher-status groups. The role of the mass media in creating, widening or narrowing information gaps has prompted widespread concern.

There are differing kinds of gap depending on the nature of the information. Gaps – between *information-rich* and *information-poor* – may close or widen with time. It had been thought that the increasing flow of information from the mass media might help to decrease such gaps, but the evidence here is mixed. Whilst the media may have the potential to close gaps it seems that an advantage remains with those with most communication potential and new gaps open as old ones are closed.

Whilst information gaps may exist between groups within societies, the greatest inequalities seem to be those between more developed and the less developed societies. Most of the channels of global communication are controlled by the former. This means that not only have they the potential to acquire and disseminate more information, but they also have the potential for considerable control of the flow and content of the information going to the less developed countries. Thus the majority of information flowing from info-disadvantaged countries is *raw*, compared with the *mediated* information that flows in the other direction.

Information gaps can also be generated, reinforced or modified through patterns of interpersonal communication. See DIFFUSION; DISCURSIVE GAP; J-CURVE; MEDIA IMPERIALISM; MISINFORMED SOCIETY.

Information society   The Japanese were the first to apply the tag to this stage in the growth of the industrial era in which information has become the central and most significant 'commodity'. Through the development of computers and associated electronic systems, such aspects of national and international life as class relationships, government, economics and diplomacy are being visualized as functions of information transfer. Indeed, we are at the point when information and wealth are practically one and the same thing.

With the development of satellite surveillance it is now possible for a country highly advanced in informatics to know more about the topography of, say, a developing nation than that country's own government does. And information is power that crosses national boundaries with greater ease than invading armies.

Information is not only a commodity but a social and cultural resource, raising questions of social allocation and control, with such associated problems as PRIVACY, access, commercial privilege and public interest. See COMMODITIZATION OF INFORMATION; MEDIA IMPERIALISM; MISINFORMED SOCIETY; MOBILIZATION.

Information suburbs   See TECHNOLOGICAL DETERMINISM.

Information technology (IT)   Microelectronics plus computing plus telecommunications equals IT. Its formal definition is framed as follows in a UK Department of Industry publication (1981) for Information Technology Year (1982): 'The acquisition, processing, storage and dissemination of vocal, pictorial, textual and numerical information by a micro-electronics-based combination of computing and telecommunications.'

Information Technology Advisory Panel (ITAP) Report on Cable Systems See CABLE TELEVISION.

Infotainment Term used to describe the trend towards enhancing the entertainment value of factual programmes in order to increase their popularity with audiences. There are concerns, expressed by a number of analysts, that NEWS and current affairs coverage may become trivialized by such an approach. See DOCUMENTARY.

Inheritance factor The TV programme that captures a viewer's attention paves the way for those that follow it. Some commentators have complained that because certain types of programme enjoy greater popularity than others, there is a danger of SCHEDULING similar programmes at times of popular viewing, thus lessening opportunities for diversity. See BUTTON APATHY.

Inner-outer directed See VALS TYPOLOGY.

Inoculation effect In the processes of persuasion, a relative immunity in an AUDIENCE may be induced by 'inoculation' prior to a concerted exercise in persuasion: if an audience is forewarned about an attempt to persuade it, when that attempt occurs, the audience is more capable of defence against influence.

Insert shot In film, close-up inserted into a dramatic scene, usually for the purpose of giving the AUDIENCE a view of what the character on the screen is seeing, such as a newspaper headline, the title of a book, a cigarette, a letter, etc. See SHOT.

Institution The term institution is generally applied to patterns of behaviour that are established, approved and usually of some permanence. Such patterns of behaviour are normally rational and conscious. The term can be applied to both the *abstract* – for example, religion – and the *concrete* concept of an institution, such as a media organization. The patterns of behaviour to which this term is applied can vary, from simple routine acts to large complexes of standardized procedures governing social relationships in a large section of the population.

All institutions embody a particular complex of norms, VALUES, ROLES and role structures. They also, often, evolve relationships with other institutions.

FUNCTIONALIST analysis tends to represent institutions as performing the functions essential to the maintenance of society, and views them as being mutually sustaining. Some research has, however, indicated the relative *autonomy* of most institutions and the often conflicting goals to be found within them. Much research into the mass media has concentrated upon their *corporate* role as major social institutions, upon their norms, VALUES and relationships with other major social institutions.

Insult signals Generally defined as those signals that are always insulting, no matter what the context in which the signal has been made; though these do vary substantially between nationality and nationality. Such signals may communicate lack of interest, boredom, superiority, contempt, impatience, rejection and mockery. *Dirt signals* appear to be universal and refer to human and animal waste products on the basis, presumably, of: cleanliness = good; filth = bad. Picking the nose with forefinger and thumb in Syria means 'Go to blazes' while in the UK a gesture of derision is to pull an imaginary lavatory chain at the same time as holding the nose. In Greece, pushing the flat of the palm towards another's face is the ultimate insult signal. Called the *moutza*, the signal represents a thrusting of filth into the opponent's face, and has ancient roots (see RELIC GESTURES).

Beyond the insult signal is the *threat signal*, an attempt to intimidate without, necessarily, recourse to blows. Threat signals are mostly violence substitutes rather than prologues to violence, because such signals are checked, held back and distance maintained between threatener and threatened. Also, such signals are often redirected – to the insulter's own body, such as mock strangulation.

Of *obscene signals*, the phallic-displaying gesture is as old as civilized man. The Romans, for example, referred to the middle finger as the impudent and obscene finger. The more expressive forearm jerk is common throughout the western world and is employed particularly in France, Italy and Spain as a threatening insult by one male towards another; however, in the UK, the signal tends to be more a crude sexual comment than a direct insult. The V-sign, with palm facing the communicator, is the most potent gestural insult in Britain along with its single-finger variant. See COMMUNICATION, NON-VERBAL (NVC); NON-VERBAL BEHAVIOUR: REPERTOIRE.

Integrateds See VALS TYPOLOGY.

Integration New ideas and behaviour vary in the degree to which they are incorporated into the continuing operations and way of life of members of a SOCIAL SYSTEM or sub-system. The term *communication integration* is used to describe the degree to which the members/units of a social system are interconnected by INTERPERSONAL COMMUNICATION CHANNELS.

Integration: vertical and horizontal Vertical integration occurs when an enterprise owns and controls all the processes and stages involved in production. An example is where a film company initiates ideas and facilitates all aspects of production, marketing and ADVERTISING, and has direct or associate interest in product dissemination and consumption, including related promotional merchandise. In contrast, horizontal integration indicates concentration of ownership across rather than within products and producers – in media terms, CROSS-MEDIA OWNERSHIP and control.

Integrity of the text See TEXT: INTEGRITY OF THE TEXT.

Intellectual property See CULTURE: COPYRIGHTING CULTURE; TEXT: INTEGRITY OF THE TEXT.

In-tel-sat Acronym for International Telecommunications Satellite (Consortium), an organization of over 70 member nations formed to control and promote work in global communications by means of satellites. See SATELLITE TRANSMISSION.

Intensity Some NEWS stories receive much more concentrated, more intense, coverage by the media than others, and tend to dominate or stifle competing stories. Intensity, if appropriate in terms of timing, and if given the promise of frequency, abetted by consistency of coverage, equals *influence*, at least in the sense of making audiences aware.

General elections provide useful illustrations of the intensity of media coverage. National attention is focused on the event (usually more on personalities than issues) and the legitimacy of the event is given substance and flavour. In contrast, local elections derive neither substance nor flavour from the media, who largely ignore them. See DISPLACEMENT EFFECT; EFFECTS OF THE MASS MEDIA; NEWS VALUES.

Interaction The reciprocal action and communication, verbal or non-verbal, between two or more individuals, or two or more social groups. Successful negotiation of social interaction requires considerable mastery of the verbal and non-verbal communication deemed appropriate to the social situation and the social ROLES being performed. As Judy Gahagan comments in *Social Interaction and its Management* (UK: Methuen, 1984), 'The mere presence of others introduces a degree of control over our demeanour that we do not display when we are alone … This control over demeanour suggests we follow quite strict sets of rules of conduct.' Most of these rules, however, are unwritten and learned, often unconsciously, through the process of SOCIALIZATION. There are arguably more rituals and rules involved in our everyday social interaction than we realize. Gahagan notes that, 'We are in fact quite unaware of their existence until someone does something "odd".' See IMPRESSION MANAGEMENT; INTERPERSONAL COMMUNICATION; SELF-MONITORING; SELF-PRESENTATION.

Interactive television Process by which TV viewers are enabled, through telephone link or cable and computer terminal, to respond to programmes and to questions put to them by programme companies. This mode of instant FEEDBACK has considerable potential and the social, political and cultural issues are far-reaching. First, only those able to afford the necessary press-button equipment will be able to register a 'vote' or opinion. Unlike the absolute secrecy of the ballot box, that vote is recordable; that is, computers will be able to bank the response patterns of individuals and GROUPS.

The potential of – and enthusiasm for – interactive TV have diminished in the face of INTERNET use. As Edward Herman and Robert McChesney write in *The Global Media: The New Missionaries of Corporate Capitalism* (US/UK: Continuum, 1997), 'If consumers with computers and modems could have access to countless websites at no admission price, they were not going to be especially enthralled by interactive TV or expensive private computer services.' See *TOPIC GUIDE* under BROADCASTING.

Interactivity In the simulation of VIRTUAL REALITY (VR), interactivity describes the process by which the user exerts control over the form and content of the mediated environment.

Intercultural communication See COMMUNICATION: INTERCULTURAL COMMUNICATION.

Internalization See IDENTIFICATION.

International Commission for the Study of Communication Problems Report, 1980 See MACBRIDE COMMISSION.

International Federation of Journalists (IFJ) Organization whose testament is that 'the promotion of a new world order of information is first and foremost the business of journalists and the trade unions and not of states, governments or any pressure group of whatever kind'. The IFJ is chiefly made up of western journalists and was formed to monitor and counteract moves through the United Nations Educational, Scientific and Cultural Organization (UNESCO) to 'impose', through government legislation, a NEW WORLD INFORMATION ORDER. See MACBRIDE COMMISSION; MEDIA IMPERIALISM; WORLD PRESS FREEDOM COMMITTEE.

International Law Enforcement Telecommunications Seminar (ILETS) See INTERNET: MONITORING OF CONTENT.

International Programme for the Development of Communication (IPDC) See MACBRIDE COMMISSION; MEDIA IMPERIALISM; NEW WORLD INFORMATION ORDER.

Internet (see also CYBERSPACE) Worldwide network of interlinked computer systems exchange of digital information – texts, sounds, pictures or video. One of the few global communication systems *not* owned by the transnationals; in fact, the Internet is not 'owned' by anyone (yet). The net was first established in the 1960s as an American military project, ARPANet, to link computers at research establishments and to form a network of information distribution which could survive a nuclear attack.

The information available on the Internet via websites, along with the use of the net, has grown exponentially in recent years, but the take-up has, in global terms, been uneven. In 1998 four trillion e-mails were sent in the US, and that was still only representative of 15 per cent of the population. The *Wall Street Journal* has calculated that a typical worker in a European company deals with some 150 e-mails a day.

Few businesses can have grown as fast as the industry in websites. In western nations every self-respecting company, local authority, educational establishment, human rights agency or pressure group now has its own growing website. This applies also to the media organizations such as the BBC which, according to Fletcher Research, became in 1999 the second largest among the UK's top ten websites, beaten to pole position only by Yahoo, which is essentially an Internet 'gateway' to other services, while the BBC is a content provider. Thus RADIO and TELEVISION, the BBC's market specialisms, are joined to a PRESS function: the BBC puts into print, pictures and sound its vast archives of material (see CONVERGENCE). Additionally the BBC's commitment to Internet use is nurturing interest that in turn will encourage growth in the numbers of people coming online.

It has been claimed for the net – with some justification – that it is today's version of the AGORA, the open space in which public DISCOURSE can be conducted without the MEDIATION of those in authority and without the GATEKEEPING and AGENDA-SETTING of the mass media. Citizens speak to citizens across geographical and political boundaries; and certainly governments are worried about the freedom of access to and use of information which computer-mediated communication allows. Lin Hai, a Chinese Internet user who distributed 30,000 e-mail addresses to a democracy magazine published in the US, was jailed in 1999 for crimes against the state. His imprisonment can only be seen as a warning to others for China is estimated to have over two million net surfers and rising.

Another key question concerning Internet use is how far it is a *leveller* that is, through the ease of exchange, helping to level up opportunities for peoples of different economic, cultural and political status. Does the net help the poor – individuals, communities and nations, or does it somehow threaten to increase the INFORMATION GAP between them and better-off individuals, communities and nations? In 'The Internet and knowledge gaps: a theoretical and empirical investigation' (*European Journal of Communication*, March 2002), Heinz Bonfadelli focuses on the *digital divide*, identifying four barriers preventing people benefiting fully from the information society. These are (1) a continuing lack of basic computer skills 'and connected fears and negative attitudes especially among older and less educated people'; (2) restrictions on *access* to the necessary hardware and software – in short, expense; (3) the lack of user friendliness; and (4) the actual use of the net. Bonfadelli quotes research that suggests the 'higher the educational background [of the user], the more people use the Internet in an instrumental way, and the lower the educational background, the more people seem to use the Internet only for entertainment purposes'. See MOBILIZATION.

Internet: monitoring of content   The 'freedom' of the net has long been a matter of public concern, on the one hand for those in authority anxious about websites preaching political and racial hatred or providing PORNOGRAPHY, and on the other hand for those fearful of ambitions held chiefly by governments, to censor network exchange. Some commentators have argued that the key to network systems is not freedom but SURVEILLANCE. As Darin Barney points out in *Prometheus Wired: The Hope for Democracy in the Age of Network Technology* (US: University of Chicago Press, 2000), 'networked computers have emerged as surveillance technology par excellence'.

In May 1999 it was reported that European Commission ministers were planning to require manufacturers and operators to build in 'interception interfaces' to the Internet and all future digital communication systems. Details are set out in Enfopol 19, a restricted document leaked to the Foundation for Information Policy research, based in London. In an article 'Intercepting the Internet', in the UK *Guardian* (29 April 1999), freelance writer Duncan Campbell reports on plans requiring 'the installation of a network of tapping centres throughout Europe, operating almost instantly across all national boundaries, providing access to every kind of communications including the net and satellites'.

According to Campbell, the plans were formulated by an organization founded in 1993 by the American FBI and the International Law Enforcement Telecommunications Seminar (ILETS), made up of police and security agents from some 20 countries. ILETS has had success in persuading the European Community to adopt its recommendations contained in a document drawn up in Bonn in 1994, the International Requirements For Interception. These have become law in the US.

At meetings in subsequent years, ILETS has tightened further its monitoring requirements. So far, the major obstacle to the fulfilment of the demands listed in Enfopol 19 has been the cost of enforcement. However, the ease with which governments introduce laws of restriction, and the determination of those governments to spy on the net, promise a serious reining in of Internet freedoms. See REGULATION OF INVESTIGATORY POWERS ACT (RIPA) (UK), 2000. See also *TOPIC GUIDE* under MEDIA: FREEDOM, CENSORSHIP.

Internet: wireless internet   The use of the net without cables or wires; transmission of Internet messages by wireless technology. Developed in the late 1990s, wi-fi, as it is termed, employs a technical standard known as 802.11b, using the radio spectrum 2.4GHz, and operating through 'data clouds' between multi-directional antennae.

Originally used in rural areas where cabling up proved too costly, wi-fi has moved into cities. Essentially, it is a local operation, its reach, though restricted, offering opportunities for community interactivity. It remains, in the UK, illegal to use wi-fi for public access networks, but the likelihood is that regulation will be changed and satellite BROADBAND – expensive for individuals but a real possibility when access is shared by groups of users – might obviate the cost of cabling: no more trench digging, perhaps, for the Internet future might just lie in the 'clouds'. See MOBILIZATION.

Interpersonal communication   Describes any mode of communication, verbal or non-verbal, between two or more people. While the term MEDIO COMMUNICATION has often been used to specify interpersonal communication at a greater than face-to-face distance, such as when the communication is by letter, e-mail or telephone, it is most useful to keep the definition as wide and unprescriptive as possible.

Michele Gail Myers in *The Dynamics of Human Communication* (US: McGraw-Hill, 1985) writes, 'Interpersonal communication can be defined ... in relation to what you do with it. First, you can use communication to have an effect on your "environment", a term which means not only your immediate physical surroundings but also the psychological climate you live in, the people around you, the social interchanges you have, the information you want to get or give in order to control the questions and answers of your living. Second, you use communication to improve the predictability of your relations with all environmental forces, which act on you and on which you act to make things happen.'

A great many factors affect the sending and receiving of MESSAGES within the process of interpersonal communication, only some of which can be mentioned here. In constructing a message the sender may be influenced by his/her SELF-CONCEPT and perception of the receiver(s), and the knowledge, beliefs, attitudes, VALUES, assumptions and experiences on which they rest; his/her personality; the role he/she is playing at the time; the state of his/her MOTIVATION; his/her communicative competence and the context in which the communicative encounter takes place. All of these factors and others affect decisions about SELF-PRESENTATION. They also influence the receiver(s) and how he/she will interpret messages sent.

Barriers often arise in interpersonal communication and these are categorized by Richard Dimbleby and Graeme Burton in *More Than Words: An Introduction to Communication* (UK: Routledge, 3rd impression, 1997) into three main types: *technical* (physical barriers such as a noisy environment); *semantic* (barriers arising from an inability to understand the signs, verbal or non-verbal, being used by one or more of the persons involved in the transaction); and *psychological* (barriers caused by a range of psychological factors – for example, the message may be perceived as a threat to one's values). Common errors made in the process of social perception, such as stereotyping, also constitute psychological barriers to effective communication.

Speech and non-verbal communication are the main means by which messages are sent in interpersonal communication, non-verbal communication being particularly important in providing FEEDBACK and in regulating interaction. Interpersonal communication is also affected by the context in which it takes place – in GROUPS or organizations, for example – and factors found there such as norms, MORES, power relationships and so on. Good interpersonal communication skills are valued and many techniques have been developed to try to improve them, ASSERTIVENESS training and TRANSACTIONAL ANALYSIS being but two examples. There is of course a rich interplay between the messages received in interpersonal and MASS COMMUNICATION and our reflection on them in the process of INTRAPERSONAL COMMUNICATION. To complicate matters further, most of the factors influencing the process of interpersonal communication are formed and shaped through that process. See *TOPIC GUIDE* under INTERPERSONAL COMMUNICATION.

---

* Michael Argyle, *The Psychology of Interpersonal Behaviour* (UK: Penguin, 1994) and *Bodily Communication* (UK: Methuen, 1988); Richard Ellis and Ann McClintock, *If You Take My Meaning: Theory into Practice in Human Communication* (UK: Edward Arnold, 1990); John Corner and Jeremy Hawthorn (eds), *Communication Studies: An Introductory Reader* (UK: Arnold, 1993); Michael Burgoon, Frank G. Hansaker and Edward Edwin J. Dawson (eds), *Human Communication* (UK: Sage, 1994); J. Devito, *Human Communication: The Basic Course* (UK: Addison-Wesley/Longman, 2000).

Interpretant C.S. Peirce (1839–1914), generally regarded as the founder of the American strand of SEMIOLOGY/SEMIOTICS, used the word interpretant in his model defining the nature of a SIGN, which 'addresses somebody, that is, it creates in the mind of that person an equivalent sign, or perhaps a more developed sign. The sign which it creates I call the interpretant of the first sign. The sign stands for something, its object'. (from J. Zeman, 'Pierce's theory of signs', in T. Sebeok (ed.), *A Perfusion of Signs*, US: Indiana University Press, 1977). The interpretant, then, is a mental concept produced both by the sign itself and by the user's experience of the object. Peirce's sign and interpretant find a parallel in the *signifier* and *signified* of the father of the European strand of semiology, Swiss linguist, Ferdinand de Saussure (1857–1913).

Intertextuality See TEXT.

Intervening variables (IVs) Those influences that come between the encoder, the message and the decoder are referred to as *intervening variables*, mediating factors that influence the way a MESSAGE is perceived, and the nature and degree of its impact. Time of day, mood, state of health can all constitute intervening variables. More importantly family, friends, peer groups, respected persons, opinion leaders, etc. are capable of significant mediation between what we are told and what we accept, believe or reject.

Whilst people may act as intervening variables between media messages and audience, the media may also be intervening variables between people: the TV socializes the child as do parents. It also 'comes between them' in the sense that it can stop interaction, modify it, improve it, re-channelize it (not to mention the DISSONANCE it might cause in a family when, for example, it provokes controversy). See S-IV-R MODEL OF COMMUNICATION. See also *TOPIC GUIDE* under COMMUNICATION MODELS.

Intervention Chiefly describes the policy and practice of governments to 'intervene' in, and attempt to control, the nature and flow of information. Intervention operates through laws, regulations and SURVEILLANCE. From earliest times governments have, with justification, believed that communication is power – that it is an agent of change – and that such power is a threat to existing power structures. Intervention remains high on the agenda of contemporary governments apprehensive about the freedoms of access and expression brought about by online services. See ENCRYPT; CENSORSHIP; CLIPPER CHIP; INTERNET: INTERNET: MONITORING OF CONTENT; NEWS MANAGEMENT.

Interviews Though there are many forms of interview and many different reasons for conducting them, the common goal is that of gaining more information from and understanding of other people, through a planned process of questions and answers. PRESS and television journalists use interviews as a means of collecting information and opinions. Interviews can be used to provide entertainment as in chat shows; they are the most common means of selecting people for jobs or students for courses; they are a major method of data collection in the social sciences.

The kinds of question widely used in interviews are: (1) open questions; these are broad, usually unstructured and often simply introduce the topic under discussion in a way that allows the interviewee a good deal of freedom in answering; (2) closed questions; these are restrictive, offering a fairly narrow range of answers from which the interviewee must choose; (3) primary questions; these introduce the subject or each new aspect of the subject under discussion; (4) subsidiary or secondary questions; these follow up the answers to primary questions; (5) neutral questions; these do not suggest any preferred response; and (6) leading questions, which suggest a preferred response and are not normally used in research interviews. See *TOPIC GUIDE* under RESEARCH METHODS.

Intimacy at a distance See PARASOCIAL INTERACTION.

Intimization Mode of dealing with information, especially NEWS, and focusing on human interest; presented in a manner that is intimate and personal, termed 'matters of personality' by Liesbet van Zoonen in 'A tyranny of intimacy? Women, femininity and television news', in *Communication and Citizenship: Journalism and the Public Sphere* (UK: Routledge, 1991) edited by Peter Dahlgren and Colin Sparks. Van Zoonen is referring specifically to Dutch TV and argues that the increasing use of women presenters in the media is 'part and parcel of the intimization that seems to permeate most news' and risks being 'yet another articulation of traditional femininity' and what she calls 'the gendered nature of private sphere values'.

Intrapersonal communication That which takes place within ourselves: our inner monologues; our reflection upon ourselves, upon our relationships with others and with our environment. What goes on inside our heads (or hearts) is conditioned and controlled by our *self-view* and that self-view has emerged from a vast complex of past and present influences – on the view we perceive others holding about us, on our past achievements and failures, on memory banks of good, bad and neutral actions and impressions.

Our concept of self interacts with our view of the world. Having been formed by experience, it is shaped and modified by subsequent experience, though rarely straightforwardly. The psychologist, for example, speaks of the *extrovert* personality and the *introvert* personality. On the face of it, the extrovert is characterized by a confidence in public performance that may indicate inner assurance, while the introvert may demonstrate a public shyness or guardedness reflective of inner uncertainty. However, the outer confidence may well be a role, as in a play or performance, which may conceal an altogether different inner image or performance. The so-called introvert, on the other hand, may, through the richness or assurance of inner resources, have opted out of public role playing, or selected the role of introvert as a public defence mechanism.

Arising from both inner and outer stimuli, intrapersonal communication is a convergence, a coming-together, of both. A piece of music stirs in us, perhaps, previous memories; these memories of people or places may join with immediate impressions of events to create an ongoing DISCOURSE, between ourselves in the past, our former selves and our selves, perceiving and perceived, in the present.

Through intrapersonal communication we come to terms (or fail to come to terms) with ourselves and with others. Through it we create bridges or battlements; we make connections or we sever them; we open ourselves up or we establish self-defences. Most of us, it is important to note, are, as it were, on our own side. We use intrapersonal communication as a means of self-assurance, of confidence-building or confidence-maintenance as well as self-discovery (or indeed self-delusion). It is what makes us unique.

Investigatory Powers Act (RIPA) (UK), 2000   See REGULATION OF INVESTIGATORY POWERS ACT (RIPA) (UK), 2000.

Invisibility   That is, invisible to the public as represented by media. The case is put by many commentators that certain sections of the population are overlooked, neglected, denied rightful attention by media, as though they did not exist. Ethnic minorities are seen to be 'invisible' or 'absent' in mainstream representations, except when they are viewed as a 'problem' in which case the spotlight of attention is trained upon them. Nations as well as individuals and groups are cloaked in invisibility, fulfilling NEWS VALUES only when there is trouble, conflict, a perceived threat to order. Visibility, then, comes at the price of STEREOTYPING and the nurturing of 'us and them' (or WEDOM, THEYDOM attitudes). Tuen van Dijk in *Racism and the Press* (UK: Routledge, 1991) writes that 'minorities continue to be associated with a restricted number of stereotypical topics, such as immigration problems, crime, violence (especially "riots"), and ethnic relations (especially discrimination), whereas other topics, such as those in the realm of politics, social affairs and culture are under-reported'. See *TOPIC GUIDE* under MEDIA ISSUES AND DEBATES.

iSociety   Term describing the dominant VALUES and desired lifestyles characteristic of people in the UK in the late 1990s. In place of the 'I'm all right' CULTURE of the 1980s are attitudes guided by notions of individuality, independence and interactivity. In a major survey conducted by the Future Foundation it was found that the 'me culture' identified with Conservatism under Prime Minister Margaret Thatcher had given way to a more ethical, tolerant and less competitive way of life, with fairer relationships between men and women.

Author of the Foundation's report, Melanie Howard, told *Observer* reporter Richard Thomas ('The iSociety', 4 April 1999), 'People in the iSociety are interested in the wider impact of what they do and what they buy', and attitudes have changed in relation to jobs and careers, people defining themselves by what they do rather than by their income, prizing more and more the quality of life. Howard believes that the iGeneration in the iSociety is leaving behind the binary certainties of the past, 'Left and Right, work and home, women and men's roles'.

Readers may recognize in the criteria of the iSociety some familiar old landmarks – MASLOW'S HIERARCHY OF NEEDS, for example; in particular Maslow's idea of *self-actualizing* needs. An encouraging dimension of iSociety thinking is the desire to extend ethical principles governing interpersonal relationships to the workplace, both in terms of the ways employers treat those who work for them and in the social responsibility of their operations. See VALS TYPOLOGY.

Issue proponents   GROUPS or individuals, often SIGNIFICANT OTHERS, who promote, or help determine, the ranking of an issue on the media agenda. See AGENDA-SETTING.

Issues   Those social, cultural, economic or political concerns or ideas that are, at any given time, considered important, and that are the source of debate, controversy or conflict. What is an issue for one social group may not be considered such by another. Environmental issues have arguably grown out of middle-class concern, in particular among the younger, often college-educated members of that class.

Of vital interest to the student of communications are such questions as: how are issues disseminated? Why do some issues 'make it' to the national forum of debate while others fall by the wayside? What are the characteristics of a 'successful' issue? What prolongs an issue? What factors, other than the resolution of the issue, are involved in the decline of an issue? And, running through all these questions, what role do the processes of communication play in the definition, shaping and promoting of issues?

The media are, of course, themselves an issue, like all institutions wielding power and influence, and the issues involving the role of the media in society are meat and drink for the student of communication. This has been given due acknowledgment in communication and media study syllabuses. Among the many issues of current interest involving the media are: censorship; media ownership and control, including the role of conglomerates in worldwide media activity; the part played by the media in the REINFORCEMENT of the STATUS QUO in society; in SOCIALIZATION; in their claim to act as the so-called FOURTH ESTATE; in policing the boundaries of social and political dissent and in being largely unquestioning advocates of the capitalist consumer-orientated society. See EFFECTS OF THE MASS MEDIA; LABELLING PROCESS (AND THE MEDIA); McCOMBS AND SHAW'S AGENDA-SETTING MODEL OF MEDIA EFFECTS, 1976; MEDIA CONTROL; MAINSTREAMING; MEDIA IMPERIALISM; NEWS VALUES. See also *TOPIC GUIDE* under MEDIA ISSUES AND DEBATES.

ITC: Code of Advertising Standards and Practice   See CODE OF ADVERTISING STANDARDS AND PRACTICE (ITC).

ITC Programme Code   The Independent Television Commission succeeded the Independent Broadcasting Authority (IBA) in January 1991, consequent upon the BROADCASTING ACT (UK), 1990 (responsibility for COMMERCIAL RADIO was transferred to the Radio Authority). The Broadcasting Act required of both authorities the drawing up of codes of practice that would regulate all commercial broadcasting in the UK. The ITC was required to draw up and enforce a code 'governing due impartiality and a general code governing the portrayal of violence, appeals for donations and such other matters concerning standards and practice for programmes as the ITC considers appropriate'.

The Code deals with bad language, sex and nudity ('Representation of sexual intercourse should be reserved until after 9 pm'), bad taste in humour (that is, jokes about personal disability and racial jokes), the portrayal of violence, scenes of extreme suffering and distress, coverage of terrorism, crime and anti-social behaviour. Much of the Code is identical to the regulations laid out in the RADIO AUTHORITY (UK) PROGRAMME CODES.

The Family Viewing Policy warns that material 'unsuitable for children must not be broadcast at times when the largest numbers of children are viewing … After 9 pm and until 5.30 am, progressively less suitable (i.e. more adult) material may be shown and it may be that a programme will be acceptable, for example, at 10.30 pm which would not be suitable at 9 pm.'

J

J-Curve   One focus of communications research has been the part played by personal contact in the diffusion of information about NEWS events featured in the mass media. The assassination of President Kennedy in 1963 and the speedy diffusion of the news of the EVENT gave an impetus to this research.

The J-Curve arose from the conclusions of B.S. Greenberg and stems mainly from his work on the Kennedy assassination, when he investigated the first sources of knowledge about 18 different news events. It represents the relationship between the overall extent of awareness people have of such an event and the proportion of those learning of it through interpersonal sources.

Greenberg argues that news events can be divided into three groups as regards the manner of their diffusion and the involvement of personal contact in it. Type 1 events are important to the few people who may be affected by them but are of little concern to the general public. Such events, though reported in the media, will be most generally diffused by personal contact – the announcement of an engagement, for example. Type 2 events such as those in typical main news stories are generally regarded as important and command the attention of a large number of people.

News of such events is not likely to be passed on as information through personal contact, although they may be discussed as it will be taken for granted that most people will either know of such news or that it is not of vital interest to them. An example here might be an earthquake in another country. Type 3 events are dramatic, important and of very wide interest. Such events, like the assassination of President Kennedy, the death of Diana, Princess of Wales, or the destruction of New York's World Trade Center by passenger planes hijacked by terrorists, get speedy and all-enveloping coverage from

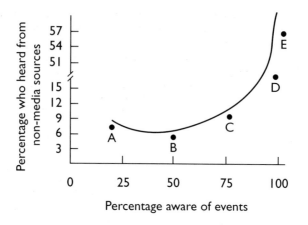

the media. They also mobilize interpersonal sources and the proportion of those who learn of the events from personal sources will be considerably higher than for Type 2 news items.

Such events are, however, rare and are usually related to crisis situations. In the case of the Kennedy assassination, Greenberg and Parker found that the extent and speed of diffusion was amazing: 99.85 per cent of the US population knew of the event within five hours of its occurrence. About 50 per cent of people first heard about it through personal sources and of these a fairly high proportion were strangers – revealing the degree to which people departed from established communication patterns.

By plotting the proportion of people eventually aware of all types of event against the proportion who heard about them first from personal contacts, it was possible to group them into five categories, and the line joining these five categories was J-shaped as shown in the diagram. A is in Type 1, B, C, D are in Type 2 and E is in Type 3. It can be seen that the size of the total audience increases progressively but the proportion of those receiving information from interpersonal sources does not; the proportion is higher for some of Type 1 than for Type 2 but highest for Type 3. See *TOPIC GUIDE* under COMMUNICATION THEORY.

Jakobson's model of communication, 1958 A linguist, Roman Jakobson was concerned with notions of meaning and of the internal structure of messages. His model is a double one, involving the *constitutive factors* in an act of communication; each of these factors is then locked on to the *function* it performs.

Thus the constitutive factors are:

	Context	
Addresser	*Message*	*Addressee*
	Contact	
	Code	

The functions form an identically structured model:

	Referential	
	(Reality orientation of message)	
Emotive	*Poetic*	*Conative*
(Expressive)	*Phatic*	(Effect of a message on addressee)
	Metalingual	

Phatic here refers to the function of keeping the channels of communication open and Metalingual is the function of actually identifying the communication code that is being used. See REDUNDANCY. See also *TOPIC GUIDE* under COMMUNICATION MODELS.

Jargon The specialist speech of groups of people with common identity – of religion, science, medicine, art, trade, profession, political party, etc. We can have educational jargon, cricket jargon, sociological jargon – that is, the in-language of people with specialist knowledge or interest. For those creating and operating jargon, it is a useful and vital means of communicating quickly between expert and expert. For those outside, jargon appears to be an unnecessarily complicated alternative to plain speaking, and a barrier to good communication. Without the growth of jargon words and expressions in Communication and Media Studies, this Dictionary would not have been deemed necessary.

JICNARS scale Administered by the Joint Industrial Committee for National Readership Surveys in the UK, JICNARS measures AUDIENCE according to social CLASS, occupation and perceived economic status: *Category A* (upper middle class; business and professional people, considerable private means); *Category B* (middle class, senior people of reasonable affluence; respectable rather than luxurious lifestyle); *Category C1* (white-collar workers, tradespeople, supervisory and clerical jobs), *C2* (blue-collar skilled workers); *D* (semi-skilled or unskilled members of the 'blue-collar' class); and *E* (those at the lowest level of subsistence, casual workers, those unemployed and/or dependent on social security schemes).

This classification has come under increasing criticism over the years, especially the emphasis upon targeting the occupation of the head of a household, traditionally male. More 'with it' methods of gauging patterns of consumption have concentrated on the notion of lifestyle as reflected in people's aspirations. The best known of these is VALS (Values and Lifestyles). See HICT PROJECT.

Jingoism Extreme and uncritical form of national patriotism. The word derives from G.W. Hunt's song, written at the time of the Russo-Turkish War (1877–78) when anti-Russian feeling in the UK was running high and the Prime Minister, Benjamin Disraeli, ordered the Mediterranean fleet to Constantinople: *We don't want to fight, but by Jingo if we do/We've got the ships, we've got the men, and got the money too.* 'The Falklands War of 1982 stirred up similar sentiments in Britain's popular press, which used language as declamatory and as sensational as anything employed during the Boer War, the two world wars or the British invasion of Suez (1956).

From the *Sun* ('The paper that supports our boys'): '74 Days That Shook the World!', 'Lions Who Did the Impossible – By land, sea and air, our boys never faltered in their fight against tyranny' and, on the front page, in three-inch high type, 'We've Won!' (15 July 1982). With the NATO bombing of Serbia in 1999, the *Sun* showed that it had not lost its jingoist panache. Under the resounding headline 'Clobba Slobba' (referring to the Yugoslav leader Slobodan Milosevic), the paper trumpeted 'Our boys batter Serb butcher in Nato bomb blitz'. And at the foot of the page, 'We go in: See pages 2, 3, 4, 5, 6, 7 and 8'.

Jingoism is at its most familiar in the reporting of sport between nations as a trawl of the UK tabloids at the time of the 2002 World Cup would prove. In England in particular the heady mix of flag-waving nationalism and royalty mania over the Queen's 50th jubilee made for headlines and editorials doused in self-congratulation. However, while urging the nation to 'ROAR OUR BOYS ON' the *Daily Star* of 3 June 2002 remembered the old enemy, Germany, with a leader headlined 'JUST MORE KRAUT', a riposte to a *Der Spiegel* article that had described the Queen as 'a nondescript little housewife' and her children of being interested only in 'sex and horses'. The *Star's* explanation for such an attack was that 'Germany is still smarting over the 5-1 thrashing [by England] they took on their own soil in last year's soccer international.' See *TOPIC GUIDE* under MEDIA: VALUES AND IDEOLOGY.

Johari Window The term Johari Window is derived from the first names of those who devised the model, Joseph Luft and Harrington Ingram. Effective interaction depends largely on the degree of and growth of understanding between the individuals concerned. Luft's theory of the Johari Window, expounded in his work entitled *Of Human Interaction* (US: National Press Books, 1969), is a useful way in which to look at such factors of INTERPERSONAL COMMUNICATION as SELF-DISCLOSURE and FEEDBACK, and the way these may influence our SELF-CONCEPT. The model, shown in the accompanying figure, represents a way of analysing the self.

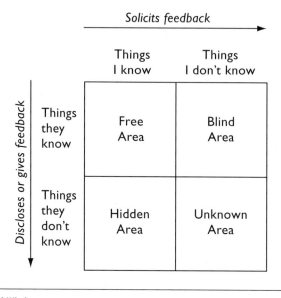

The Johari Window

The *free area* represents the public self: information about yourself that is known to you and to others, such as your GENDER or race. There is a free and open exchange of information in this area. The *blind area* contains information about yourself that is not known to you but that is known to others, such as any irritating mannerisms you might have. The *hidden area* contains things you know about yourself but wish to keep hidden from others, such as your lack of confidence in certain situations. You normally take action to protect this area from the scrutiny of others. The *unknown area* contains information that neither you nor others are fully conscious of, but that might still be influencing your behaviour – unconscious fears, for example.

The model can be used to analyse many aspects of interpersonal behaviour. Through interpersonal communication we can come to understand ourselves better, increase the size of the free area, and decrease the size of the other three. For example, self-disclosure can reduce the hidden area and increase the free area, and thus enhance communication with others. Feedback from others has the potential to reduce the blind area, although possibly at some cost to self-esteem, and further increase the free area. The degree to which we may be willing to make such changes to the relative size of the areas will of course vary with the situation and relationship. Generally speaking, the greater the free area in any given situation, the easier the interaction.

Journalese A manner of writing that employs ready-made phrases and formulas, and that breeds its own short-cut language and cliches, rarely without some catchy word-rhythm: 'Tory, Tory, Hallelujah' proclaimed the UK *Daily Express* in 1982; in 1900, the paper's headlines were equally ringing: 'The Boers' Last Grip Loosened'. The aim is to squeeze out the most dramatic expression with the minimum use of words. The higher the pressure on space, the more pronounced the journalese. See TABLOID, TABLOIDESE, TABLOIDIZATION.

Journalism While many professions feature in the public eye, journalism can be said to *be* the public eye. Journalism reports to the public, conveying to it information, analysis, comment and entertainment while equally purporting to represent the public; to speak for it in the public arena.

At the same time journalism is in the business of representing to the public 'the reality out there'. It is only at first sight a curiosity that journalists refer to the reports they write, edit or present, as 'stories', yet many commentators have drawn close comparisons between journalism and fiction. In an article

'The nature of aesthetic experience', published in the *International Journal of Ethics* 36 (1926), George Herbert Mead defined two models of journalism, the *information model* and the *story model*, stating that 'the reporter is generally sent out to get a story not the facts'. Of course journalists are not always happy to be described as storytellers; after all, the job of the serious journalist is to provide information and analysis, and not to turn news into entertainment.

Yet subsequent commentators have confirmed Mead's definition. John Langer in 'Truly awful news on television', published in *Journalism and Popular Culture* (UK: Sage, 1992), edited by Peter Dahlgren and Colin Sparks, argues that 'serious news is also based around the story model'. However, 'it pretends that it is not – it declares that it is concerned with imparting the important information of the day'. Langer is of the view that 'the world of fact and the world of fiction are bound more closely together than broadcasters are prepared to have us believe'.

The implication here is that journalism has a storytelling function that has much to do with VALUES, telling stories about who we are, how we have become what we are and should become. The journalist to a degree is a maker, or at least an upholder, of *myth* in the sense that the French philosopher Roland Barthes has used the word: mythologizing is essentially a mode of explaining things, a giver of meaning albeit simplified and clarified. As Barthes puts it in *Mythologies* (UK: Paladin, 1973), myth 'abolishes the complexity of human acts'.

By a process of elimination and emphasis, the journalist *frames* meaning (see FRAMING). In the study of media we are as interested in what does not appear in the frame as what does appear; what is *absent*. The frame can also be seen as a set of boundaries that journalism defines and patrols. Cultural, social or political DEVIANCE is defined and labelled by the journalist. There are those – people, movements, ideas – that are DEMONIZED, defined as dangerous to the security of the community (see LOONY LEFTISM). It might even be suggested that the media have a policing role in society and that journalists, at least some of them, carry out the part of 'copper's nark'.

The relationship between the role of the journalist and the exercise of power and control has been a keen focus of study. In *Visualizing Deviance: A Study of News Organizations* (UK: Open University, 1987), Richard Ericson, Patricia Baranak and Janet Chan speak of news journalists as a 'deviance-defining elite' who 'provide on-going articulation of the proper bounds to behaviour in all organized spheres of life'. American media analyst David Barsamian refers to journalists as 'stenographers of power' in *Stenographers of Power: Media and Propaganda* (US: Common Courage, 1992), meaning basically that journalists are largely servants of the state, taking down verbatim their script from the POWER ELITE. This could be described as the 'Poodle to the Powerful' model.

While not being so dismissive, Allan Bell in *The Language of News Media* (UK: Blackwell, 1991) acknowledges that 'News is what an authoritative source tells a journalist … The more elite the source, the more newsworthy the story.' In contrast, believes Bell, 'alternative sources tend to be ignored: individuals, opposition parties, unions, minorities, fringe groups, the disadvantaged'. In certain situations, particularly of national crisis such as wartime, the editors of *Media, Crisis and Democracy: Mass Communication and the Disruption of Social Order* (UK: Sage, 1992), Marc Raboy and Bernard Dagenais, argue that the media become an 'extension of the state'. They quote Anthony Lewis of the *New York Times* describing the press during the first Gulf War (1991) as 'a claque applauding the American generals and politicians in charge'; while television behaved as the 'most egregious official lapdog during the war'.

The contrasting model to the Poodle is that of the Watchdog, where journalism stands guard over the public interest, a tireless terrier that snaps and snarls at injustice, corruption and abuse. Since the birth of the printed word in 1450 (in the West, that is – the Chinese had developed printing much earlier) there have been ample cases of conformity and rebellion (if not revolution) in journalism. In the nineteenth century the courageous editors of the radical press, such as Richard Carlile and Henry Hetherington, spent many years of their lives in prison for writing about and publishing beliefs that ran counter to those of the ruling elite. In the twentieth century hundreds of journalists and news photographers have been killed while reporting events throughout the world and the twenty-first century has seen no diminution in the death-toll of the bringers-of-news.

In journalism there will always be the biased and the spurious; there will continue to be invasion of PRIVACY, nationalist hype, shameless and malicious STEREOTYPING, wallowing in scandal – all 'examples' of contemporary journalism in action. There will also continue to be high-quality investigative journalism that, in the words of John Keane in 'The crisis of the sovereign state' (in Raboy and Dagenais) 'seeks to counteract the secretive and noisy arrogance of the democratic Leviathan'; that 'involves the patient investigation and exposure of political corruption and misconduct'; that sets out to 'sting political power, to tame its arrogance by extending the limits of public controversy and widening citizens' involvement in the public spheres of civil society'. See DEMOCRACY AND THE MEDIA; MEDIASPHERE; PUBLIC SPHERE; WATCHDOGS. See also *TOPIC GUIDE* under MEDIA ETHICS; MEDIA: FREEDOM, CENSORSHIP; MEDIA: ISSUES AND DEBATES; NEWS MEDIA.

Journalism: celebrity journalism The preoccupation in modern print journalism with recording the activities, sayings, scandals of celebrities; described by Peter Hamill in *News is a Verb* (US: Ballentine, 1998) as a virus, and 'the most widespread phenomena [sic] of the times'. Hamill is of the view that 'True accomplishment is marginal to the recognition factor. There is seldom any attention paid to scientists, poets, educators or archeologists.'

Big names are the constant focus of attention to the exclusion of other subjects. The obsession with celebrity worries many media-watchers for coverage of celebrity *displaces* the reporting of events, the analysis of ISSUES that are *in* the public interest as contrasted with being *of* interest to the public; the issue here being the swamping of important information by populist entertainment.

Jump-cut Where two scenes in a TV news report are of the same subject, taken from the same angle and distance, the 'jump-cut' is to be avoided; to get round this 'jump' from one shot to virtually the same, usually of someone being interviewed, a 'cutaway' shot is inserted – that is, a reaction shot from the interviewer.

Juxtaposition jump-cut See SOUND-BITE.

K

Katz and Lazarsfeld's two-step flow model of mass communication and personal influence See ONE-STEP, TWO-STEP, MULTI-STEP FLOW MODELS OF COMMUNICATION.

Kepplinger and Habermeier's Events Typology See EVENT.

Kernel and satellite See NARRATIVE: KERNEL AND SATELLITE.

KPFA Radio In the US, the first listener-supported independent RADIO station, founded by Lewis Hill in 1949, broadcasting from Berkeley, California. Sister stations were later introduced: KFPK in Los Angeles (1959) and WBA1 in New York (1960). Working under the umbrella link of the Pacific Foundation the outspokenness of the stations proved a thorn in the side of government and the establishment in America. In 1970 KFPT went on air in Houston, Texas. It was fire-bombed twice by the Ku Klux Klan, but broadcasts continued.

Kineme A segment or fraction of a whole communicative GESTURE; a kinetic parallel to a phoneme (element of verbal language). The term was invented by Ray Birdwhistell. In *Kinesics and Context* (US: University of Philadelphia, 1970), Birdwhistell draws up a vocabulary of 60 kinemes, which he found in the gestural/postural/expressive movements of American subjects. He maintains that these kinemes combine to form large units (*kinemorphs*) on the analogy of *morphemes* (or words). An example would be waving a fist or prodding the air with a finger while at the same time smiling or looking angry. See KINESICS.

Kinesics The study of communication through GESTURE, posture and body movement. In *Communication* (UK: Open University, Block 3, Units 7–10, 1975), the OU course team loosely classify kinesics under five headings: (1) information (indicating, for example, welcome or 'keep away'); (2) communication markers (head and body movements to give emphasis to a spoken message); (3) emotional state (as expression of feeling); (4) expression of self (in the way you sit or walk or hold yourself); and (5) expression of relationship (revealing attitude to others by how close you stand to someone, how you angle, tilt, shift your body in relationship to others or by the way hair or clothes are touched, a tie adjusted). See COMMUNICATION, NON-VERBAL; NON-VERBAL BEHAVIOUR: REPERTOIRE; PROXEMICS; TOUCH.

Kinetoscope Early form of film projection invented in 1887 by Thomas Alva Edison (1847–1931) and his assistant K.L. Dickson. On 14 April 1894, the first Kinetoscope Parlor was opened on Broadway, New York. The Kinetoscope was a wooden cabinet furnished with a peep-slit and an inspection lens through which a single person could view the endless loop of celluloid film that passed below it. It was driven by a small electric motor and illuminated by an electric lamp. Edison's lasting contribution to cinematography was his use of celluloid film 35mm wide, with four perforations for each picture. See CINEMATOGRAPHY, ORIGINS.

'Kite' co-orientation approach See McLEOD AND CHAFFEY'S 'KITE' MODEL, 1973.

Knowns, unknowns In *Deciding What's News* (US: Pantheon, 1979) Herbert Gans says that those who are famous in society, *knowns*, appear at least four times more frequently in TV news bulletins than *unknowns*. The POWER ELITE and celebrities generally tend to be both the source and subject matter of news stories; and by being so they further qualify themselves to appear on the news as knowns. Gans states that fewer than 50 individuals regularly appear on US news. It is not only the actions of knowns that qualify as newsworthy, but their speech. As Allan Bell says in *The Language of News Media* (UK: Blackwell, 1991), 'Talk is news only if the right person is talking.' Meanwhile the dominance of the headlines by knowns, by the elite, leads to other actors, other talk, being ignored. See NEWS VALUES.

Kuleshov effect Lev Kuleshov (1899–1970) was in at the sunrise of Russian cinema. He was film designer, film-maker and film theorist. In 1920 he was given a workshop to study film methods with a group of students. His Kuleshov effect, demonstrated in 1922, proved how, by altering the juxtaposition of film images, their significance for the audience could be changed.

In 1929 he wrote 'The content of the shot in itself is not so important as the joining of two shots of different content and the method of their connection and their alternation.' An experiment, aimed at proving his theory, showed a close-up of an actor playing a prisoner. This is linked to two different shots representing what the prisoner sees: first a bowl of soup, then the open door of freedom. Audiences were convinced that the expression on the man's face was different in each instance, though it was the same piece of film. See MONTAGE; SHOT.

Kuuki Japanese term, shared by the Chinese and Koreans, meaning a climate of opinion requiring compliance. In an article entitled 'The future of political communication research: a Japanese perspective', published in the *Journal of Communication*, Autumn 1993, Youichi Ito explains how kuuki may be nurtured by the media or by those in government or by the production of what he calls *extracted information* – that which the public draws from sources other than the mass media, for example from personal experience and observation, and talking to others. The more people talk to each other, argues Ito, the less dependent they are on the mass media. Conversely, the less they talk among themselves the more media agendas dominate the public's way of thinking and perceiving.

'If people depend heavily upon mass media for information,' writes Ito, 'and if personal influence in political communication is weak, then the political influence of mass media may be overwhelming.' The kuuki, the climate of opinion requiring compliance, has been shaped by the media: the more meagre the extracted information, the weaker is the response to dominant definitions and therefore the more ready the compliance.

It is important to recognize that, at least in non-totalitarian states, the public arena is witness to competing agendas and that the agenda-setters (government, big business, the media) are often in alliance, and occasionally in competition or even conflict. Where for instance there is an alliance between the agenda of state and the public agenda, against that of big business, or the media, then we might discern kuuki in operation, that is a climate of opinion that may force big business or the media into line; and where the media agenda allies with public agendas against the agendas of state, government may move into line.

Youichi Ito sees the media at one point of a triangle, with government and the public making up the other two points. He concludes that, 'Mass media have effects only when they stand on the majority side of the mainstream in a triadic relationship that creates and supports the kuuki that functions as a social pressure on the minority side.' See AGENDA-SETTING; ROGERS AND DEARING'S AGENDA-SETTING MODEL, 1987; NOELLE-NEUMANN'S SPIRIAL OF SILENCE MODEL OF PUBLIC OPINION.

L

Label libel A McLUHANISM. Marshall McLuhan (1911–80), media guru of the 1960s, wrote of the way that the mass media stick labels on people, trap them in STEREOTYPES, typecast them, pigeon-hole them to the point that such generalizations become invidious and thus a mode of DEFAMATION.

Labelling process (and the media) Howard Becker in a classic study, *The Outsiders; Studies in the Sociology of Deviancy* (US: Free Press, 1963), analyses the process by which certain social actions or ideas, and those who perform or express them, come to be defined as DEVIANT; and which he calls 'the labelling process': 'The deviant is one to whom the label has successfully been applied; deviant behaviour is behaviour that people so label.'

Becker's work highlights the role that powerful social groups and individuals play in defining the limits of acceptable and unacceptable behaviour, through the labelling process. He argues that certain groups within society, moral entrepreneurs, are particularly able to shape, via the mass media, new images of deviancy and new definitions of social problems. See CRISIS DEFINITION; ISSUES.

LAD (Language Acquisition Device) According to linguists such as Noam Chomsky, LAD is an innate device within the human mind that allows us to acquire language. The LAD is a hypothetical model of this process and is grounded in the theory that human beings are programmed to acquire and create language, and thus can develop competence in any language that they are exposed to, over a period of time. See DEEP STRUCTURE.

Lame A term used by William Labov in *Language in the Inner City* (US: University of Pennsylvania Press, 1972) to describe individuals who are relatively isolated, on the margins of a group and its culture. This relatively isolated position often shows itself linguistically in that such individuals will use fewer of the significant linguistic features of the group or culture in question.

Language See *TOPIC GUIDE* under LANGUAGE/DISCOURSE/NARRATIVE.

Language pollution According to Gail and Michele Meyers in *The Dynamics of Human Communication* (US: McGraw-Hill, 1985), this occurs 'When language is used by people to say what in fact they do not believe, when words are used, sometimes unwittingly, sometimes deliberately, to cover up rather than to explain reality, our symbolic world becomes polluted. This means that language becomes an unreliable instrument for adapting to the environment and for communicating.'

The authors identify three main types of language pollution and their common characteristics: *confusion* (unknown meanings), characterized by the use of foreign languages, unfamiliar words, technical jargon and misused terminology; *ambiguity* (too many meanings), characterized by vagueness, the use of words with multiple definitions and the use of very general imprecise statements, or terms; and *deception* (obscured meanings), characterized by outright lies, distortion, and giving incomplete information or non-answers to questions.

Langue and parole In his *Cours de Linguistique Générale* (1916), published after his death, Ferdinand de Saussure (1857–1914) defined *La langue*, or language, as a system, while *La parole* represented the actual manifestations of language in speech and writing. The former he conceived as an 'institution', a set of interpersonal rules and norms; the latter, events or instances, taking their MEANING from, or giving meaning to, the system.

---

* F. De Saussure, *Course in General Linguistics* (English translation; UK: Fontana/Collins, 1974).

Lasswell's model of communication, 1948 A questioning device rather than an actual model of the communication process, Harold Lasswell's five-point approach to the analysis of the mass media has nevertheless given enduring service. It remains a useful first step in interpreting the transmission and reception of messages.

In 'The structure and function of communication in society', in Lymon Bryson (ed.), *The Communication of Ideas* (US: Harper & Row, 1948) Lasswell suggests that in order to arrive at a due understanding of the MEANING systems of MASS COMMUNICATION the following sequence of questions might be put:

Who

Says *What*

In which *channel*

To *whom*

With what *effect?*

Assuming that the last question would include the notion of FEEDBACK, Lasswell's model could still do with an additional question: 'In what *context* (social, economic, cultural, political, aesthetic) is the communication process taking place?' Also Lasswell makes no provision for INTERVENING VARIABLES (IVs), those mediating factors that impact on the ways in which messages are received and responded to. It is useful to compare Lasswell's list to the verbal version of GERBNER'S MODEL OF COMMUNICATION, 1956. In 'Towards a general model of communication', in *Audio-Visual Communication Review* 4 (1956), George Gerbner offers the following formula:

1   Someone

2   perceives an event

3   and reacts

4   in a situation

5   through some means

6   to make available materials

7   in some form

8   and context

9   conveying content

10   with some consequence.

See *TOPIC GUIDE* under COMMUNICATION MODELS.

Latitudes of acceptance and rejection The greater the gap between an attitude a person already holds and that which another wants to persuade him/her to adopt, the less likely it is that any shift in attitude will occur. C.W. Sherif in *Attitudes and Attitude Change* (US: Greenwood Press, 1982) argues that our responses to attempts to challenge or change our attitudes are divided into three main types. (1) An individual's *latitude of acceptance* contains the opinions, ideas and so on about an issue that a person is ready to agree with or accept. (2) The *latitude of non-commitment* contains the range of opinions and ideas on the same issue that the individual is neutral about. (3) The *latitude of rejection* contains those ideas and opinions about an ISSUE that the individual finds unacceptable. Further, unacceptable statements tend to be interpreted as even more hostile and unfavourable than they really are – the *contrast effect* – whilst those that are not far removed from the latitude of acceptance may gradually be incorporated into it – the *assimilation effect.* See BOOMERANG EFFECT.

Law of minimal effects Point of view that the media have little or no effect in forming or modifying the attitude of audiences. See EFFECTS OF THE MASS MEDIA.

LBC: London Broadcasting Corporation The first COMMERCIAL RADIO station to come on air in the UK, in October 1973, followed a few days later by Capital Radio.

Leadership Leaders can generally be defined as individuals within GROUPS or organizations who have influence, who provide focus, coordination and direction for the activities of the group. It may be argued that the purpose of leadership is to enable the group to function effectively and achieve its goals, although in practice leadership may not always have this effect. Leadership may be and often is invested in one person but it can also be shared.

Leaders may be emergent or appointed. An emergent leader is one who comes to acquire the role of leader through the process of group INTERACTION. He or she may, for example, be the person with the best ideas or communication skills. An appointed leader is one who is formally selected; leaders in work situations are often appointed to their position.

A considerable amount of research has been conducted with the aim of trying to ascertain the qualities and interpersonal skills required for effective leadership, and the type of leadership needed for the optimum performance of groups or organizations. An early perspective was the *trait* approach to leadership, which argues that individuals who become leaders have certain personality traits or characteristics that enable them to cope well with leadership. The suggestion is that leaders are born, not made. However, this approach has been widely criticized for being simplistic and lacking in any hard evidence to substantiate its claims.

Another approach examines the varying *styles* of leadership that may be adopted and the characteristics of each style. An example here would be represented by the work of Robert Likert. In *The Human Organization* (US: McGraw-Hill, 1967), Likert identifies four main styles of leadership: *Automatic, Persuasive, Consultative* and *Democratic*. Research into leadership styles tends to point towards the democratic leadership style as being superior to the others. However, the *situational* approach to leadership argues that different styles of leadership will be appropriate to different situations.

Examples of key situational factors identified as determining suitable leadership styles include the nature of the task, the characteristics of the group and the organizational CULTURE. The *functional* approach to leadership focuses on identifying the behaviour needed from leaders so that particular groups and organizations may achieve their goals. The implication here is that individuals can improve their leadership abilities. One point all approaches are agreed on is that a good leader has to be a good communicator.

Leakage See FACIAL EXPRESSION.

Leaks A time-honoured way in which governments disseminate information, often through 'sources close to' the president or the prime minister; a way of authority manipulating the media. Leaks can always be denied. Sometimes, of course, leaks are genuine – that is, they are true divulgences of information that those in authority would wish to be withheld. Here, those close to the centres of power, perhaps disagreeing with decisions about to be made or affronted at the potential mismanagement of power, disclose information with the intention of causing embarrassment and, through publicity, a change of policy. See DEEP THROAT; SECRECY.

Learned journals on communication See PERIODICALS FOR THE STUDY OF MEDIA.

Legislation See *TOPIC GUIDE* under COMMISSIONS, COMMITTEES, LEGISLATION.

Legitimation/delegitimation In *Ideology: A Multicultural Approach* (UK: Sage, 1998) Tuen A. Van Dijk states that 'Legitimation is one of the main social functions of ideologies.' It is the process whereby a group, society or nation gives a status of acceptance – legitimizes – ways of doing or saying things. By the same token, a process of delegitimation occurs in which the 'We' or 'Us' of a situation seek overtly, or convertly, to deny acceptance to *other,* or what Van Dijk refers to as 'outgroups'. Reference, for example, to 'illegal' immigrants has the effect of delegitimating a host of different 'others' and, in the public mind, creates antipathy, fear (of the 'foreigner') and rejection.

Legitimation is very much about being a member of a group, and relies in some part upon a recognition of what differentiates Us from Them (those who are not part of the group). Van Dijk speaks of an 'ideological square' in which four main positions are taken in relation to legitimation/delegitimation. The square serves as (a) a positive SELF-PRESENTATION and (b) a negative 'other' presentation. The positions are as follows: (1) express/emphasize information that is positive about Us; (2) express/emphasize negative points about Them; (3) suppress/de-emphasize information that is positive about Them; and (4) suppress/de-emphasize information that is positive about Us.

Communicative strategies employed in legitimation/delegitimation DISCOURSES are numerous, depending on the nature of the communication and the contexts in which it takes place. They work through the *implicit,* by assumption; by implication, presupposition, assertion and manipulation; their aim is the maintenance of power through the creation of compliance and consent. See HEGEMONY; IDEOLOGY.

Lexis Linguist's term to describe the vocabulary of a language: a unit of vocabulary is generally referred to as a *lexical* item or *lexeme*. A complete inventory of the lexical items of a language constitutes a dictionary, a lexicon. Lexicography is the overall study of the vocabulary of language, including its history.

Libel A written accusation; any malicious, defamatory publication or statement. The spoken equivalent of libel is *slander*. Both constitute DEFAMATION and the law in the UK may impose heavy fines on those proved to have injured someone's good name. However, it is not possible to obtain legal aid in order to take, for example, a newspaper to court for libel in order to protect that good name.

Life positions In his book, *I'm O.K. You're O.K.* (US: Harper & Row, 1969), Thomas Harris identifies four life positions that can be used in TRANSACTIONAL ANALYSIS for exploring and examining people's feelings, attitudes or positions towards themselves and others, and the way in which these influence their social interaction.

The I'm OK–You're OK position is one in which an individual believes in his/her own worth and that of others. It is a position in which we accept ourselves and others, and base our transactions on this orientation. Harris argues that to reach this position requires conscious decision and effort.

Harris believes many people hold an I'm not OK–You're OK position as a result of early socialization which, in attempting to shape an individual's behaviour into a pattern that is socially acceptable, contains a lot of messages critical of the individual: not OK messages. This position may lead to a feeling of inferiority that shows itself in defensive communication such as game playing.

Experiences in early childhood, especially abuse and neglect, may result in the individual forming the perspective that whilst he/she is OK, other people are not, hence the I'm OK–You're not OK position, which may show itself in a characteristically hostile, or aggressive communicative style. I'm not OK–You're not OK is the position of those who feel neither themselves nor others are OK. This negative perspective may show itself through a despairing and resigned attitude when communicating with others. Life positions influence the kinds of life SCRIPTS, individuals write for themselves. See TOPIC GUIDE under INTERPERSONAL COMMUNICATION.

* Ian Stewart and Vann Joines, *TA Today* (UK: Lifespace, 1987); Amy and Thomas Harris, *Staying OK* (UK: Arrow Books, 1995).

Lifestyle See STYLE; VALS TYPOLOGY.

Lighting cameraman In a film crew, the lighting cameraman or camerawoman is responsible for the pictorial composition of the film image as well as the arrangements for lighting.

Light Programme One of three BBC radio channels until the introduction of Radio 1 in 1967, and a change of names for the rest: Light became Radio 2, Home Service became Radio 4 and the Third Programme Radio 3. The Light Programme, for general entertainment RADIO, was created in the year the Second World War ended, 1945.

Lindup Committee Report on Data Protection, 1978 See DATA PROTECTION.

Linguistic determinism The proposition that the language of a culture determines the way in which the world is perceived and thought about. Thus in acquiring a language an individual is also acquiring a particular way of thinking about the world, a particular worldview. The two linguists closely associated with this position are Benjamin Lee Whorf and Edward Sapir whose Linguistic Relativity Hypothesis helped to establish this particular view on the relationship between language and thought. Though their proposition that language actually determines thought has been much questioned, many would accept that the language at an individual's disposal influences the way he/she thinks about the world. See SAPIR–WHORF LINGUISTIC RELATIVITY HYPOTHESIS.

Linguistics The scientific study of language. *Diachronic* or *historical* linguistics investigates how language use has changed over time; *synchronic* linguistics is concerned with the state of language at any given point in time; *general* linguistics seeks to establish principles for the study of all languages; *descriptive* linguistics is concerned with the analysis of the characteristics of specific language; *contrastive* linguistics explores the contrasts between different languages or families of languages, while *comparative* linguistics concentrates on common characteristics. Among a profusion of other linguistics-related studies are *anthropological linguistics, biolinguistics, psycholinguistics* and *sociolinguistics.* See PARADIGM; SEMIOLOGY/SEMIOTICS; STRUCTURALISM.

Linotype printing Patented in 1894 by German immigrant to Baltimore, US, Ottmar Mergenthaler. The operator uses a keyboard similar to that of a typewriter. As each key is depressed a brass matrix for that particular letter drops into place. When the line is complete, the row of matrices is placed over a mould and the line of type is cast, the molten lead alloy setting almost at once. See MONOTYPE PRINTING; PRINTING.

Lip-sync Synchronization between mouth movement and the words on the film soundtrack.

Listening Though often taken for granted, listening is a crucial element in human communication. Gail Myers and Michele Myers in *The Dynamics of Human Communication* (US: McGraw-Hill, 1985) point out that 'Listening is often not the natural process that it is often believed to be.' Poor listening can be the cause of many breakdowns in communication. Myers and Myers go on to identify ways in which listening can be improved and communication thereby made more effective.

Active listening reflects a certain attitude towards others, recognizing that what they say is worth listening to and that one should attempt to imagine how what is being said makes sense to the person saying it and the feelings involved. The receiver needs to listen to the sender without initially passing judgement on what is being said and then mirror back to the sender what was said in order to show and to check that he/she understands the message and the feelings that lie within it. This helps to build a supportive situation in which communication can take place. Active listening is also known as *empathetic listening*, whereas *deliberative listening* involves trying to determine, accurately, the content of the message.

Lithography Printing from stone, slate or a substitute such as zinc or aluminium, with greasy ink; invented in 1798 by Alois Senefelder.

Lloyd's List The oldest international daily newspaper, founded in 1734; perhaps most noted for its role as almanac of world shipping movements and casualty reports.

Lobbying A process in which individuals or GROUPS seek to influence those in power. In the UK Parliament, the lobby is the passage through which MPs pass to record their votes. Lobbying includes any device – postal and electronic mailing through to financial contributions – to persuade other people, usually those in authority, to give an issue their support. Most major vested interests – such as the so-termed Gun Lobby in the US – see lobbying as an essential part of their strategies of persuasion or dissuasion.

Lobby Practice A book of rules of conduct written by, and abided by, UK parliamentary lobby correspondents who operate from offices in the House of Commons and whose access to the centres of power is highly prized. The lobby system in the British House of Commons goes as far back as 1886. Correspondents meet daily at Downing Street, the home of the Prime Minister, and weekly on Thursdays in the Commons for a briefing by the PM's press secretary.

The system has been subjected to considerable criticism on the grounds of its secrecy, alleged cosiness and the danger of collusion between government and privileged lobby correspondents. It has been varyingly called 'an instrument of closed government' and the 'real cancer of British journalism'. At the heart of the criticism is the fact that the lobby correspondents receive no more information than government wishes them to know; if they break the rules of Lobby Practice they know their privileges will be withdrawn. In 2002, the Labour government announced a liberalization of lobby practices in which briefings by government to the media would be unrestricted.

Localization The process by which global media tailor their products for local markets and local audiences. The 1980s and 1990s saw a dramatic expansion of TV channels crossing national borders, and this trend was nowhere more manifest than in Europe. Companies such as MTV, CNN, Sky News, BBC Prime, BBC World and National Geographic have been reaching out for pan-European audiences.

Initially, channels such as MTV (launched in the US in 1981 and in Europe in 1987) operated in a global capacity, that is in the sense of an increasingly homogenous culture, offering a single brand regardless of national and regional differences. They were swiftly to recognize the importance of catering to local tastes.

Jean K. Chalaby in 'Transnational television in Europe: the role of pan-European channels', in the *European Journal of Communication* (June 2002) writes that 'these cross-border players awoke to the reality of national boundaries and cultural and linguistic markers and realized that there were limits to the exportability of their programmes'.

Localization became an imperative, at first by opening local ADVERTISING windows, then by adapting programming itself, especially of entertainment, to local needs. Chalaby is of the view that localization is a practical and convenient step on the way towards further GLOBALIZATION rather than a force working against it. While the 'necessity for localization can be interpreted as evidence of the limits of cultural globalization', it nevertheless 'accelerates the process of globalization, notably because it allows global players to operate in a multinational environment'. True, the 'music may become local' but the 'expansion plan remains global'.

Localization is less evident in NEWS services such as CNN and BBC World. For them the reporting of international events is their key function. In contrast, channels dedicated to children's entertainment, such as Fox Kids or the Cartoon Network, demand localization, the originating language being converted to the 'home' language directly or through dubbing or subtitling.

Chalaby believes 'Localized channels are not so much a "hybrid" cultural form incorporating the local – as is sometimes suggested – than a bridge that helps the global reach the local.' See EUROPE: CROSS-BORDER TV CHANNELS.

Looking behaviour See CIVIL INATTENTION; EYE CONTACT.

Lookism Theory that the better-looking you are, the more successful you will be in life. The term was first used as early as 1978, in the *Washington Post Magazine*, but more recently has been written about at length by American psychologist Nancy Etcoff in *Survival of the Prettiest: The Science of Beauty* (US: Little, Brown, 1999). In an age of images, the image dominates our perceptions, our thoughts and our judgements. According to Etcoff even mothers love their offspring just a little bit less if they are less than handsome. In the world of work, says Dr Etcoff, 'Good looking men are more likely to get hired, at a higher salary than unattractive men.' She compares 'looking' with sexism and racism. However, these are conscious, easily recognized attitudes, while Lookism works at a subconscious level. We are largely unaware of favouring the beautiful.

Loony Leftism In the 1980s in the UK a mythology was created by local and national newspapers about the policies of Labour-led councils, particularly those in Greater London. 'Loony' became the catchword whenever councils such as Hackney, Haringey or Islington were mentioned: and the accusation arose from rumours that were simply untrue. For example, the *Daily Star* printed a headline story declaring that Hackney council, in its attempt to stamp out racism and racist language in the borough, had banned the singing of 'Baa, Baa, Black Sheep' in playschools.

Hackney had never considered banning the nursery rhyme; however, newspapers throughout the country and in the rest of the world picked on this example of 'Loony Leftism'. Once in print, the story gained momentum and credence. Even Labour MPs took on board the Loony Left slogan. See *TOPIC GUIDE* under MEDIA ISSUES AND DEBATES.

Lord Chamberlain (UK) Until they were abolished in 1968 the powers of the Lord Chamberlain to censor plays in the British theatre went as far back as the reign of James I, though such powers were not defined by statute until 1737. All plays, except those performed by theatre clubs, were obliged to obtain a licence from the Lord Chamberlain's office. Each script was vetted for bad language, subversive ideas and any criticism of monarchy, parliament, the Church, etc.

In 1967 a Joint Committee on Censorship of the Theatre was set up by government. This recommended freedom for the stage 'subject to the overriding requirements of the criminal law' and that managements and dramatists should be protected from 'frivolous or arbitrary' prosecutions. These recommendations formed the basis of Labour MP George Strauss's private member's bill, which became law, liberating the theatre from the Lord Chamberlain in the Theatres Act of September 1968.

Lowbrow See HIGHBROW.

LP See GRAMOPHONE.

M

MacBride Commission International Commission for the Study of Communication Problems under the chairmanship of Sean MacBride, former secretary general of the International Commission of Jurists, to hear, distil and report on evidence submitted with regard to media information interaction between western and 'Third World' countries. In particular, the Commission was to report on the impact of western media technology, and the subsequent flow of western-orientated information, upon developing nations. Set up by the United Nations Educational, Scientific and Cultural Organization (UNESCO) in 1978 with a committee of 'fifteen wise men and one woman', including Colombian novelist Gabriel Garcia Marquez and Canadian media guru Marshall McLuhan, the Commission produced a 484-page report in 1980.

This urged a strengthening of Third World independence in the field of information gathering and transmission, and measures to defend national cultures against the formidable one-way flow of information and entertainment from western capitalist nations, chiefly the US. Faced with the antipathy and resistance of such nations, the Commission's recommendations, and their vision of a NEW WORLD INFORMATION ORDER were left dead in the water. See CHAPULTEPEC, DECLARATION OF, 1994; INFORMATION GAPS; MEDIA IMPERIALISM; TALLOIRES DECLARATION, 1981; YAMOUSOUKROU DECLARATION. See also *TOPIC GUIDE* under GLOBAL PERSPECTIVES.

Machinery of representation In modern societies, the various forms of mass media have been named the 'machinery of representation' by Professor Stuart Hall in his chapter on media power and class power in *Bending Reality: The State of the Media* (UK: Pluto Press, 1986), edited by James Curran, Jake Ecclestone, Giles Oakley and Alan Richardson. Hall writes of the 'whole process of reporting and construction' through which reality is translated into media forms – forms that the AUDIENCE is expected to recognize as reality.

Yet reality, argues Hall, is not simply transcribed in 'great unassimilated lumps through our daily dose of newspapers or our nightly diet of television': 'They all work using language, words, text, pictures, still or moving; combining in different ways through the practices and techniques of selection, editing, montage, design, layout, format, linkage, narrative, openings, closures – to represent the world to us.' The media exercise 'the power to represent the world in certain ways. And because there are many different and conflicting ways in which meaning about the world can be constructed, it matters profoundly what and who gets represented, what and who regularly and routinely gets left out; and how things, people, events, relationships are represented.' See DISCURSIVE GAP; HEGEMONY; LEGITIMATION/DELEGIT-IMATION; POWER ELITE; PREFERRED READING.

Magnum International cooperative agency of photo-journalists, formed in 1947. Among its early members were Henri Cartier-Bresson, Robert Capa, Marc Bresson and Inge Morath. Magnum's objectives have been: top-quality photography, independence, objectivity and control – by the members – over the use of their pictures.

* William Manchester, *In Our Time: The World as Seen by Magnum Photographers* (UK: Andre Deutsch, 1989).

Mainstreamers See ADVERTISING: MAINSTREAMERS, ASPIRERS, SUCCEEDERS AND REFORMERS.

Mainstreaming Professor George Gerbner and a team of researchers at the Annenberg School of Communications, University of Pennsylvania, conducted a massive and ongoing research project throughout the 1980s on the impact of television on cultural attitudes and attitude formation. A process is identified that Gerbner calls *mainstreaming*, whereby television creates a coming-together, a CONVERGENCE, of attitude among viewers. In their article, 'The "mainstreaming" of America: violence profile No. 11', in *Journal of Communication* (Summer 1980), Gerbner, Larry Gross, Michael Morgan and Nancy Signorielli write, 'In particular, heavy viewing may serve to cultivate beliefs of otherwise disparate and divergent groups towards a more homogeneous "mainstream" view.'

The authors' opinion is that TV's images 'cultivate the dominant tendencies of our culture's beliefs, ideologies, and world views' and that the 'size' of an 'effect' is far less critical 'than the direction of its steady contribution'. The light viewer is more likely to hold divergent views and the heavy viewer more convergent views: 'For heavy viewers, television virtually monopolizes and subsumes other sources of information, ideas and consciousness.' Convergence in this sense is to the world as shown on television.

Returning to this theme in an article for the American magazine *Et cetera* (Spring 1987), Gerbner writes, in 'Television's populist brew: the three Bs', 'The most striking political difference between light and heavy viewers in most groups is the collapse of the liberal position as the one most likely to diverge from and challenge traditional assumptions.' The three *Bs* referred to in Gerbner's article are the processes by which television brings about mainstreaming. First, television *blurs* traditional social distinctions; second, it *blends* otherwise divergent groups into the mainstream and, third, *bends* 'the mainstream in the direction of the medium's interests in profit, populist politics, and power'.

In a study conducted in the UK in 1987, researchers from the Portsmouth Media Research Group, Anthony Piepe, Peter Charlton and Judy Morey (see their article 'Politics and television viewing in England: hegemony or pluralism?',· in *Journal of Communication* (Winter 1990)), found that British television 'does not cultivate a single mainstream around which a heterogenous audience converges', as in the US, but that it contains two message systems and constructs two audiences: that for essentially news-related programmes, which keep pluralist options open, and that for soaps which do, the researchers confirm, hasten a mainstreaming tendency, particularly when heavy viewing is involved.

In 1994 a study of TV influence on political attitudes in Italy was published by Luca Ricolfi of the University of Turin. According to his findings, summarized in 'Elections and mass media. How many votes has television moved?' (*Il Mulino* 356), TV, public and commercial, had influenced 10 per cent of the Italian electorate and the commercial channels had significantly assisted the shift of voters from the Left and Centre to the Right. See CULTIVATION; CULTIVATION DIFFERENTIAL; EFFECTS OF THE MASS MEDIA; GLASGOW UNVERSITY MEDIA GROUP; MACHINERY OF REPRESENTATION; MEAN WORLD SYNDROME; RESONANCE; SHOWBUSINESS, AGE OF; VIOLENCE ON TV: THE DEFENCE.

Male-as-norm   In her introduction to *Man Made Language* (UK: Routledge & Kegan Paul, 1980) Dale Spender says, 'One semantic rule which we can see in operation in the language is that of the male-as-norm. At the onset it may appear to be a relatively innocuous rule for classifying the objects and events of the world, but closer examination exposes it as one of the most pervasive and pernicious rules that has been encoded.' The rules of society are man-made and so, Spender argues, is the language we use – the 'edification of male supremacy'. Thus women are allotted a *negative semantic space*, illustrated by the way women are often referred to when they occupy a role traditionally the preserve of men. Suzanne Romaine in *Language and Society: An Introduction to Sociolinguistics* (UK: Oxford University Press, 2000) comments that in the British National Census of 1995 'I found the following usages: *lady* doctor (125 times), *woman* doctor (20 times), *female* doctor (10 times), compared to *male* doctor (14 times).' *Other* terms used for male-as-norm in relation to language are *androcentralism* (male centred) and *masculist*, as well as *patriarchal*. See *TOPIC GUIDE* under GENDER MATTERS.

Maletzke's model of the mass communication process, 1963   What is so useful about the model constructed by German Maletzke and presented in *The Psychology of Mass Communications* (West Germany: Verlag Hans Bredow-Institut, 1963) is the comprehensiveness of the factors operating upon the participants in the mass communication process and at the same time of the complex interaction of such factors.

The SELF-IMAGE of the communicator corresponds with that of the receiver: both act upon and are influenced by the message, which is itself constrained by the dictates of the medium chosen. To add to the complexity, the message is influenced by the communicator's image of the receiver and the receiver's image of the communicator. Maletzke's is a model suggesting that in the communication process many shoulders are being looked over: the more shoulders, the more compromises, the more adjustments.

Thus not only is the communicator taking into due regard the medium and the nature of AUDIENCE, and perceiving these things through the filter of self-image and personality structure, he or she is also keenly responsive to other factors – the communication team, with its own special set of values (see NEWS VALUES) and professional practices. Beyond the team, there is the organization, which in turn has to look over its shoulder towards government or the general public (see IMPARTIALITY).

Just as the communicator is a member of a team within an organizational environment, so the receiver is part of a larger context of reception: he or she is subject to influences other than the media message. Those influences may start in the living room of a family home, and the influencers might be the viewer's or reader's family, but there are contextual influences beyond that in the pub, at work, in the community.

Maletzke's model provides students of the media with a structure for analysis. By its complexity, by suggesting an almost limitless interaction of variables, it also indicates the enormous difficulty faced by

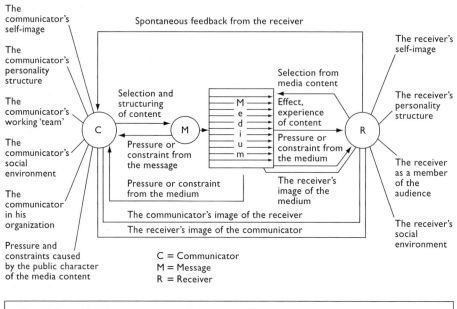

The communicator's self-image

Spontaneous feedback from the receiver

The receiver's self-image

The communicator's personality structure

Selection from media content

The receiver's personality structure

The communicator's working 'team'

Selection and structuring of content

M
e
d
i
u
m

Effect, experience of content

Pressure or constraint from the medium

The communicator's social environment

Pressure or constraint from the message

The receiver as a member of the audience

The communicator in his organization

Pressure or constraint from the medium

The receiver's image of the medium

The communicator's image of the receiver

The receiver's image of the communicator

The receiver's social environment

Pressure and constraints caused by the public character of the media content

C = Communicator
M = Message
R = Receiver

Maletzke's model of the mass communication process, 1963

research into the EFFECTS OF THE MASS MEDIA. As Denis McQuail and Sven Windahl say in *Communication Models for the Study of Mass Communication* (UK: Longman, 5th impression, 1998), 'This complexity is, no doubt, an important reason why mass communication research has been fairly unsuccessful in explaining and predicting outcomes of the mass communication process.' See *TOPIC GUIDE* under COMMUNICATION MODELS.

Manufacture of consent See CONSENT, MANUFACTURE OF.

March of Time Famous US newsreel series of the 1930s, and a classic example of media interaction. Roy Larsen, one of Henry Luce's aides on *Time* magazine, had arranged to have items from the magazine broadcast on RADIO, and these newscasts became so popular among listeners that they were developed into a network programme, *The March of Time*. One attraction was that the programme dramatized the news; actors played 'memorable scenes from the news of the week'.

In 1934, Louis de Rochement, under Larsen's supervision, adapted the radio format to film which, after early uncertainties, made a notable impact. The monthly film panoramas of American and international events alerted the public to the growing menace of Fascism. They carried an Academy Award-winning report on life inside Nazi Germany (1938) and an even more powerful one on refugees. In 1935, 432 US cinemas were showing the *March of Time*, with its famous end-of-programme words, 'Time … marches on!' and by 1939 the number had trebled. The series continued until 1953. See DOCUMENTARY. See also *TOPIC GUIDE* under MEDIA HISTORY.

Marginality See DISPLACEMENT EFFECT.

Market liberalism IDEOLOGY dominant in western countries, adopted worldwide after the fall of Soviet Communism as a normative way of state, industrial and commercial governance; its key principle – *leave to market forces*. It is essentially the same as *capitalism* where all attempts to restrict free enterprise by state control or regulation are generally perceived to be ill-judged, an interference with the 'natural order of things'. Ownership of the means of production is essentially private: the 'public' denomination of private corporations has nothing to do with the public – rather, it denotes shareholding by other 'public' bodies and private individuals. Out of market liberalism has sprung the concept of the free press; policies urging PRIVATIZATION of all mass communication; and DEREGULATION.

John Keane in *The Media and Democracy* (UK: Polity Press, 1991) says that many market liberals 'love to talk of the need for a free communications market without censorship'. However, 'they are ... unsympathetic or hostile to citizens' attempts to extend the role of law, to reduce the arbitrariness and secrecy of political power'. Thus two competing principles are at work. The 'free market' process coexists within 'a powerful, authoritative state which acts as an overlord of the market'. This amounts to a position where there is liberty for some but not necessarily for all.

Keane believes market liberalism 'succours the old doctrine of sovereignty of the state – permission for the state to defend itself by any means should it feel threatened, including controlling and regulating the liberties of the public'. Should there at the same time appear to be a threat to the free market, then the free market will collude with the state in seeking out and identifying 'enemies of the state'. Private-sector media, in particular the PRESS, will have taken on the role of GUARD DOG. See COMMERCIAL LAISSEZ-FAIRE MODEL OF (MEDIA) COMMUNICATION; HEGEMONY.

Market threshold Decisions on media production – whether to initiate, go ahead or continue with media enterprises – depend more and more on whether there is a sufficiently large percentage of consumers to warrant investment. The market threshold is the critical point at which a media artefact justifies, financially, its existence; and the greater the competition within the market, the more critical that threshold becomes. See PRODUCER CHOICE.

Marxist (mode of media analysis) Focuses on social conflict, which is seen as being essentially derived from the mode of production in capitalist societies. Karl Marx argued that the CULTURE – and communication process – of a capitalist society reflects the NORMS and VALUES of that section of the community, which owns the means of production: out of the dominant CLASS springs the dominant IDEOLOGY, which the media serve to disseminate and reinforce in the 'disguise' of CONSENSUS.

Marxist analysts have employed three main strategies of research (also used by other, non-Marxist commentators): *structuralist, political/economic* and *culturalist.* The structuralist approach examines the ideology embodied in media content, concentrating on 'text' and the source of the ideology. The political/economic approach investigates the location of media power within economic processes, and the structure of media production. The culturalist approach commences from the standpoint that all societies are made up of a rich variety of group cultures, but seeks to indicate that some groups – therefore some cultures – receive a disproportionate representation in the media in the process of shaping and defining consensus and obscuring the roots of genuine conflict. See FUNCTIONAL-IST/SOCIAL ACTION (MODES OF MEDIA ANALYSIS). See also *TOPIC GUIDE* under RESEARCH METHODS.

Maslow's hierarchy of needs According to Abraham Maslow in his highly influential book, *Motivation and Personality* (US: Harper & Row, 1954), human behaviour reflects a range of basic needs that form a hierarchy. 'For the man who is extremely and dangerously hungry,' writes Maslow, 'no other interests exist but food.' When that need is satisfied, 'new (and still higher) needs emerge'. In what he terms a holistic-dynamic theory of MOTIVATION, Maslow cites the following basic needs: *physiological, safety* needs; *belongingness* and *loving* needs; *esteem* needs and the need for *self-actualization.* Among the physiological needs are food, water, sleep and sex. Safety needs include security, stability, protection, freedom from fear, from anxiety and from chaos; the need for structure, order, law, limits; the preference for the familiar over the unfamiliar, the known rather than the unknown; for religion.

Maslow writes that the threat of chaos or humiliation can be expected in most human beings 'to produce a regression from any higher needs to the prepotent safety needs, so that a common, almost expectable reaction, is the easier acceptance of dictatorship or of military rule' and this is 'most true of those living near the safety line'. Such people are 'particularly disturbed by threats to authority, to legality, and to the representatives of the law' (see MAINSTREAMING). Belongingness and loving needs include the 'deeply animal tendency to herd, to flock, to join, to belong'.

Maslow's highest-order need is self-actualization, where a person seeks and finds fulfilment: 'A musician must make music, an artist must paint if they are ultimately to be at peace with themselves.' 'What a man can be, he must be.' The term itself was coined by Kurt Goldstein in *The Organism* (US: American Book, 1939), and means in Maslow's words, 'to become everything that one is capable of becoming'. Maslow argues that the fulfilment of needs depends on essential preconditions, obviously, at the physiological level, the availability of food and water, but at the higher levels such conditions as 'freedom to speak, freedom to do what one wishes so long as no harm is done to others, freedom to express oneself, freedom to investigate and seek for information, freedom to defend oneself'. In Maslow's view, 'Secrecy, censorship, dishonesty, blocking of communication threatens all the basis needs.'

An essential part of the process of self-actualization is the desire to know and to understand, 'to systematize, to organize, to analyze, to look for relations and meanings, to construct a system of values' and these aspects too tend towards a hierarchy: to know leads us to want to understand. Within this frame too are aesthetic needs. Maslow speaks of some individuals who 'get sick (in special ways) from ugliness, and are cured by beautiful surroundings'.

The hierarchy as cited by Maslow is dynamic and capable of reversal. Some people, for example, may go for esteem before love (though at the same time these may 'seek self-assertion for the sake of love rather than self-esteem itself'). There are artists who put creation before all else; there is the psychopathic personality suffering from a permanent loss of the love needs; and there is the potential reversal caused by the undervaluing of a long-satisfied need: 'Thus a man who has given up his job rather than lose his self-respect, and who then starves for six months or so, may be willing to take his job back even at the price of losing his self-respect.'

The hierarchy is at its most reversible in situations involving 'ideals, high social standards, high values, and the like. With such values people become martyrs.' Torture victims who defy their oppressors also confound Maslow's hierarchy. It is also acknowledged by Maslow that human behaviour is prompted by multiple motivations. It would be theoretically possible, he says, 'to analyze a single act of an individual and see in it the expression of his physiological needs, his safety needs, his love needs, his esteem needs, and self-actualization'. Equally, not all behaviour is motivated; and motivation must also be considered in the light of the 'external field', the pressures placed upon people to react in certain ways. See iSOCIETY; SELF-CONCEPT; VALS TYPOLOGY. See also *TOPIC GUIDE* under COMMUNICATION THEORY.

Mass communication Describes institutionalized forms of public message production and dissemination, operating on a large scale, involving a considerable division of labour in their production processes and functioning through complex mediations of print, film, recording tape and photography. John Corner and Jeremy Hawthorn point out in *Communication Studies: An Introductory Reader* (UK: Edward Arnold, 1980) that 'mass communications are industrial activities, produced within large organizations whose policies and professional routines are located within the political, economic and legal structures of the societies in which they operate'. Mass communication systems are deeply involved in the process of *culture production*. See CULTIVATION; CULTURAL APPARATUS; MASS COMMUNICATIONS: SEVEN CHARACTERISTICS; NORMATIVE THEORIES OF MASS MEDIA.

* Marsha and Emma Jones, *Mass Media* (UK: Macmillan, 1999).

Mass communications: seven characteristics In *Towards a Sociology of Mass Communications* (UK: Collier-Macmillan, 1969), Denis McQuail poses the following features of mass communications. (1) They normally require complex formal organizations. (2) They are directed towards large audiences. (3) They are public – the content is open to all and the distribution is relatively unstructured and informal. (4) Audiences are heterogeneous – of many different kinds – in composition; people living under widely different conditions in widely differing cultures. (5) The mass media can establish simultaneous contact with very large numbers of people at a distance from the source, and widely separated from one another. (6) The relationship between communicator and audience is addressed by persons known only in their public role as communicators. (7) The audience for mass communications is 'collectively unique to modern society'. It is an 'aggregate of individuals united by a common focus of interest, engaging in an identical form of behaviour, and open to activation towards common ends', yet the individuals involved 'are unknown to each other, have only a restricted amount of interaction, do not orient their actions to each other and are only loosely organized or lacking in organization'.

Massification However large the population, it is made up of individuals. Massification – a US term – is the process by which the population is regarded as, and treated as, a lumpen mass with similar if not identical tastes and attitudes. Massification serves as an excuse by society's privileged and ELITE to regard the mass as 'only capable' of benefiting from art, education, information, entertainment if it is presented in its simplest, most unchallenging form. Massification only makes headway when large numbers of people accept the image of themselves as projected by the purveyors of mass culture. See ADVERTISING; PUBLIC SERVICE BROADCASTING (PSB).

Mass manipulative model of (media) communication See COMMERCIAL LAISSEZ-FAIRE MODEL OF (MEDIA) COMMUNICATION.

Mass media See MASS COMMUNICATION.

Mass media effects See EFFECTS OF THE MASS MEDIA.

Mass Observation An organization founded in 1937 by Charles Madge and Tom Harrisson, with the purpose of furthering the scientific study of human behaviour in the UK. Large numbers of volunteer observers were used, recruited through advertisements in the national press. At one time it is estimated that there were over 1000 such volunteers. The object of Mass Observation was ultimately the 'observation of everyone by everyone, including themselves'.

Data that has been collected is to be found in the Tom Harrisson Mass Observation Archives in the University of Sussex. See MEDIA ANALYSIS.

Mathematical theory of communication See SHANNON AND WEAVER'S MODEL OF COMMUNICATION, 1949.

Max Headroom The first male computer-generated television personality; followed by Roxscene, the first female. The *Max Headroom Show* on the UK's CHANNEL 4 won the Royal Television Society's Original Programme Award in 1986.

McCombs and Shaw's agenda-setting model of media effects, 1976 The process and effects of agenda-setting have been a central interest for media research and study. Two important contributions to our understanding of agenda-setting theory have been articles by Maxwell E. McCombs and

McCombs and Shaw's agenda-setting model of media effects, 1976

Donald L. Shaw – 'The agenda-setting function of mass media', in *Public Opinion Quarterly*, 36 (1972) and 'Structuring the "unseen environment"', in the *Journal of Communication* (Spring 1976). Shaw followed these up with 'Agenda-setting and mass communication theory', in the *Gazette* XXV (2) (1979).

In their 1976 publication, the authors write, 'Audiences not only learn about public issues and other matters through the media, they also learn how much importance to attach to an issue or topic from the emphasis the mass media place upon it. For example, in reflecting what candidates are saying during a campaign, the mass media apparently determine the important issues. In other words, the mass media set the "agenda" of the campaign.' Thus in the view of McCombs and Shaw, the media are highly influential in shaping our perceptions of the world: 'This ability to affect cognitive change among individuals is one of the most important aspects of the power of mass communication' (see EFFECTS OF THE MASS MEDIA).

As the model indicates, there is a direct correlation between the amount of media exposure of X (the issue) and the degree to which the public sees X as being important. Some writers have been critical of this model for oversimplifying the process of media influence. It takes no account of influences other than the media in setting personal agendas in relation to public issues (see INTERVENING VARIABLES (IVs); ONE-STEP, TWO-STEP, MULTI-STEP FLOW MODELS OF COMMUNI-CATION; SIGNIFICANT OTHERS).

Another problem with the McCombs and Shaw model is highlighted by Denis McQuail and Sven Windahl in *Communication Models for the Study of Mass Communications* (UK: Longman, 5th impression, 1998). They identify not one but a range of agendas: 'We can speak of the agendas of individuals and groups or we can speak of the agendas of institutions – political parties and governments. There is an important distinction between the notion of setting personal agendas by communication directly to the public and setting an institutional agenda by influencing the politicians and decision makers.' McQuail and Windahl perceive here a dual role for the media, influencing public opinion and influencing the ELITE: 'In reality there is a continuous interaction between elite proposals and public views, with the media acting as carrier as well as source.'

A third criticism of McCombs and Shaw's model relates to the actual intentions of the media: do they initiate and select the issues they go on to amplify, climb aboard a 'bandwagon' of nascent public interest or respond chiefly to the promptings of the power elite? See CONSENT, MANUFACTURE OF; GUARD DOG METAPHOR; MAINSTREAMING; MEAN WORLD SYNDROME; NOELLE-NEUMANN'S SPIRAL OF SILENCE MODEL OF PUBLIC OPINION, 1974. See also *TOPIC GUIDE* under COMMUNICATION MODELS.

---

* McCombs and Shaw, 'The evolution of agenda-setting research: twenty-five years in the marketplace of ideas', *Journal of Communication*, Spring 1993.

McDonaldization Term formulated, and introduced in his book *The McDonaldization of Society* (US: Pine Forge Press, 1992; revised edition, 1996) by George Ritzer, and with the subtitle 'An investigation into the changing character of contemporary social life'. As Ritzer points out, the book is not about the fast-food business but serves as a major 'paradigm' of a 'wide-ranging process I call McDonaldization', the 'process by which the principles of the fast-food restaurants are coming to dominate more and more sectors of American society as well as of the rest of the world', and these effects are felt throughout CULTURE, in 'education, work, health care, travel, leisure, dieting, politics, the family, and virtually every other aspect of society'.

Ritzer sees McDonaldization as showing every sign 'of being an inexorable process by sweeping through seemingly impervious institutions and parts of the world'. McDonald's *is* America, and wherever Big Mac and fries are consumed, so is the American way of life, the American dream. The author analyses his subject through the frame of ideas posed by the German social theorist, Max Weber (1864–1920), on the workings of bureaucracy in the creation of an 'iron cage' of rationality, that is a bureaucratic sameness of normative behaviour from which it is impossible to escape.

In Ritzer's view, the universalization, the rationalization of eating and other behaviours, as represented and driven by the McDonald's empire are based upon four 'alluring dimensions' of irresistibility:

efficiency ('the optimum method for getting from one point to another'); *calculability* ('Quantity has become the equivalent to quality'); *predictability* ('There is great comfort in knowing that McDonald's offers no surprises'); and *control*, a production/service discipline that applies equally to customers as to those who serve them.

Crucial in the exercise of control is the use of technology, 'the soft-drink dispenser that shuts itself off when the glass is full, the french fries machine that rings and lifts itself out of the oil when the fries are crisp'. This technology, says Ritzer, 'increases the corporation's control over workers'.

Ritzer acknowledges that McDonaldization has 'powerful advantages' but he argues that the foundations of its success mentioned above 'can be thought of as the basic components of a rational system' and his view is that 'rational systems inevitably spawn irrationalities' and 'irrational consequences', not the least of them matters of ecological concern. Ritzer's book focuses on the 'great costs and enormous risks of McDonaldization' and its purpose is to help alert the public to them and 'to stem its tide', while fearing that 'the future will bring with it more rather than less McDonaldization'. By 2001 the 'McTide' had reached over 120 countries, served by nearly 24,000 restaurants. See SLAPPS. See also *TOPIC GUIDE* under GLOBAL PERSPECTIVES.

---

* Barry Smart (ed.), *Resisting McDonaldization* (UK: Sage, 1999).

McGregor Commission Report on the Press (UK), 1977 Under the chairmanship of Professor O.R. McGregor, the Royal Commission produced an interim report in 1976. Concerned about the shaky finances of newspapers, the Commission proposed that the state should give interest relief on loans which papers would need if they were to modernize their printing methods and cut costs. Like so many inspired ideas emerging from royal commissions, the proposal got nowhere.

In its final report (1977), the Commission recognized the anti-Labour bias in most of the nation's press: 'We have no doubt that over most of this century, the press had treated the beliefs and activities of the Labour movement with hostility.' The Commission recommended that the Press Council be strengthened, its influence increased; that, for example, its lay members be equal in number to its press representation. This recommendation was accepted, though the Council demurred at other advice. See COMMISSIONS/COMMITTEES ON THE MEDIA.

McGuffin Film director Alfred Hitchcock (1899–1980) was fond of using this expression to describe any device or element of plot that captures the attention and interest of the audience, but which is intended to be, and acknowledged to be, merely a means to an end: an amiable red herring. Hitch himself described the McGuffin as 'that which spies are after (in films) but the audience don't care'. See NARRATIVE.

McLeod and Chaffee's 'kite' model, 1973 This is best studied in conjunction with NEWCOMB'S ABX MODEL OF COMMUNICATION, 1953. Newcomb focuses on interpersonal links in relation to ISSUES, believing that each element (Person A and Person B) is *co-orientated* towards the other and towards X, the issue in a triangular relationship. McLeod and Chaffee take this model and apply it to mass communication. In 'Interpersonal approaches to communication research', in the *American Behavioural Scientist* 16 (1973), they too refer to a 'co-orientational approach'. In their model there are three major 'players' – the ELITE, the public and, in a MEDIATING role, the media.

The tail of the kite is current NEWS, and issues in the news – an endless stream of new matter, which the media process with the elite and public in mind, serving, as it were, both. Such a balanced, symmetrical arrangement is closer to the ideal than a reflection of realities, for quite clearly the elite (see POWER ELITE) have considerably more influence over media performance than the public; indeed ownership and control of media lie largely with the elite in one form or another.

To obtain a more accurate representation of the co-orientational nature of the relationship between the key players in the drama of media, it would be necessary to shift the axis a little, with the media being in much closer proximity to the elite than to the public. However, the kite metaphor remains a useful one in that the situation all the players find themselves in is unstable, and it is the stream of Xs – EVENTS, innovations, developments, changes – that causes that instability. This model should also be looked at in relation to AGENDA-SETTING models (see ROGERS AND DEARING'S

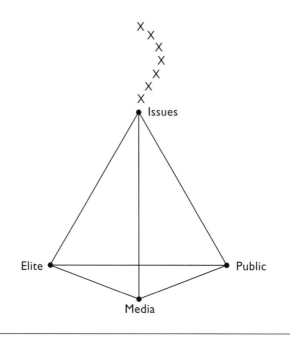

AGENDA-SETTING MODEL, 1987). See also *TOPIC GUIDE* under COMMUNICATION MODELS; COMMUNICATION THEORY.

McLuhanism The archpriest of media analysis in the late 1960s was the Canadian professor Marshall McLuhan (1911–80), creator of the Centre for Media Studies in Toronto. His headline-catching assertions and prophesies about the effect of the new media, particularly TV, on society as we know it were aided and abetted by inspired phrase-making. Described by Northrop Fry as a 'manic depressive roller-coaster of publicity', McLuhan foretold the annihilation of the printed word by the electronic media, yet his books sold (and were read) in thousands.

The most quoted McLuhanism is his phrase *the medium is the message*, used as the heading of Chapter 1 in *Understanding the Media* (UK: Routledge & Kegan Paul, 1964; Routledge, 2002). McLuhan was convinced that with electronic transmission, especially TV, content was everywhere swamped by *process*. Equally he was concerned at the irresistible cultural spread that RADIO, TELEVISION and FILM made possible throughout the world, turning it into a *global village*. Radio he called the Tribal Drum, photography was the Brothel-without-walls, TV the Timid Giant, the motor car the Mechanical Bride.

Perhaps McLuhan's most valuable analysis is to be found in his examination of the impact of printing on civilization in *The Gutenberg Galaxy: The Making of Typographic Man* (UK: Routledge & Kegan Paul, 1962). See HOT MEDIA, COLD MEDIA.

McNelly's model of news flow, 1959 An improvement upon WHITE'S GATEKEEPER MODEL, 1950. In 'Intermediary communicators in the international news', in *Journalism Quarterly* 36 (1959), J.T. McNelly identifies several intermediary stages through which a NEWS item passes from EVENT to presentation in mass communication form. The author follows the progress of a newsworthy event (E) taken up by a foreign correspondent (CI) and then passed through several agencies where the report of E is shaped and shortened (rather like the game of Chinese whispers, though, hopefully, not with the same hilarious results).

McNelly illustrates a very complex process of MEDIATION, which continues beyond the

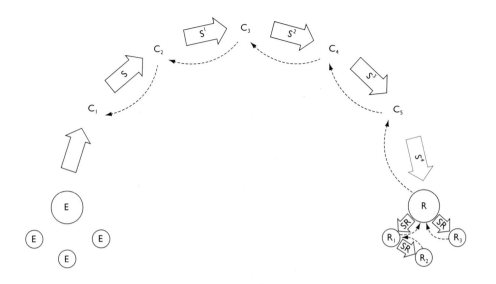

McNelly's model of intermediary communicators in news flow, showing news passing different 'gatekeepers' (after McNelly, 1959)

Key to symbols in diagram:

E = Newsworthy event

C_1 = Foreign agency correspondent

C_2 = Regional bureau editor

C_3 = Agency central bureau or deskman

C_4 = National or regional home bureau editor

C_5 = Telegraph editor or radio or TV news editor

S, S^1, S^2, etc. = The report in a succession of altered (shortened) forms

R = Receiver

R_1, R_2, etc. = Family members, friends, associates, etc.

S – R = Story as modified by word of mouth transmission

Dotted line = Feedback

production/presentation stage when readers or viewers pass on the news to others by word of mouth. What the model does not do is address the criteria for news selection, the NEWS VALUES that operate the operators of the GATEKEEPING process. See GALTUNG AND RUGE'S MODEL OF SELECTIVE GATEKEEPING, 1965.

McQuail's accountability of media model, 1997 In a number of books and periodical articles Denis McQuail has written searchingly on the responsibilities of media to society. His model illustrating the relationship between media freedom, responsibility and accountability is published in the *European Journal of Communication*, December 1997, and analysed in the article 'Accountability of media and society: principles and means'.

The model is underpinned by principles of public service – that is, the 'best interests' of society in its broadest sense – and this framework includes people as voters and citizens as well as consumers. Assigned obligations may be discerned, for example, in the broadcasting charters of PUBLIC

FREE MEDIA
have
RESPONSIBILITIES
in the form of
OBLIGATIONS
which are either:

ASSIGNED   CONTRACTED   SELF-IMPOSED

for which they are held
ACCOUNTABLE
(legally, socially or morally)
either in the sense of:

LIABILITY   or   ANSWERABILITY
for harm caused   for quality of performance

McQuail's accountability of media model. McQuail, D., *European Journal of Communication,* **December 1977, p. 518.** © **Reprinted by permission of Sage Publications Inc.**

SERVICE BROADCASTING (PSB) while contracted obligations may relate to those bodies that commission and pay for media services.

Media have responsibilities to source, to AUDIENCE, to the public at large, to minorities and obligations in relation to community and nation. Liability for harm caused can be seen to operate when the media are brought to court on charges of DEFAMATION, though ensuring answerability in relation to quality of performance is obviously more problematic.

McQuail believes 'we face a major dilemma in reconciling the interests of society with current trends of media development'. More than ever, control over the media has become difficult to exercise, partly because of media's proliferation into many modes – brought about by new technology – and because of the *transnationalization* of media ownership: 'Modern mass media are less inclined to make voluntary commitments to society, less able to have any meaningful relationship with their audiences and those whom they affect, less ready to enter into dialogue.' He sees accountability as being in a state of crisis. His article examines possible ways of achieving accountability, and suggests how principles and practice might cope with present and future developments.

Concluding his analysis, McQuail cautions against overstating the 'crisis of accountability'. After all, 'The performance of media reflects the imperfections of society as much as their own failings.' We must realize that 'free media have the right to be "irresponsible" and that some perceived "misuses" of autonomy will be a necessary price for potential benefits of invention, creativity, opposition, deviation and change'.

---

* Denis McQuail, *Media Performance: Mass Communication in the Public Interest* (UK: Sage, 1992).

McQuail's four stages of audience fragmentation, 1997 See AUDIENCE, FRAGMENTATION OF.

McWorld vs Jihad A global conflict in cultures, represented by the transnational corporation bringing to the world 'sameness' and the counter-forces of localism. Benjamin R. Barber in *Jihad vs McWorld* (US: Times Books, 1995) investigates the dynamic scenario of *localite* resistance to the burgeoning power of all-encompassing cultures emanating chiefly from the United States (and sometimes referred to as 'Americanization'). McWorld is characterized by 'fast music, fast computers and fast food – MTV, Macintosh and McDonald's – pressing nations into one homogenous global theme park ...'.

Jihad on the other hand celebrates tribalism. The resistance is seen to take the form of adoption and assimilation of dominant imported cultures, what Roland Robinson has called *glocalization*, turning the global into the local. See his 'Globalization or glocalization?', in *Journal of International Communication* 1 (1994).

With the terrorist destruction of the Twin Towers of the World Trade Center in New York on 11 September 2001, what had been perceived as essentially a *cultural* conflict passed into a new sphere of crisis, in which the government of the US, aided by that of the UK, declared a jihad (holy war) ostensibly on terrorism but in the view of many commentators effectively deepening cultural and political divisions globally, in particular along fault-lines between western and Muslim nations.

Meaning In communication terms, a dynamic interaction between reader/viewer/listener etc. and the MESSAGE. As John Fiske put it in *Introducing Communication Studies* (UK: Methuen, 1982 and subsequent editions), 'A reader is constituted by his socio-cultural experience and thus he is the channel through which message and culture interact. This is meaning.'

When we say something is 'a question of semantics', we are referring to the hazardous nature of actually pinning down, with any exactitude, the meaning of what a person says or has written. The word 'freedom' on some lips has quite a different CONNOTATION than if expressed by others.

There is a ready tendency to consider words as actually the embodiment of the meaning they attempt to describe; in fact they are approximations. Just as paper money has no intrinsic value, words have no intrinsic meaning: rather they are accredited with value or meaning by common consent. Like currency, word meanings are subject to devaluation and manipulation. Ultimately you can paper the walls with debased currency; debased language becomes a weapon against meaning.

A prevalent – and understandable – assumption is that an act or work of communication has to mean *something*. Thus a bemused spectator in front of, say, a work of abstract art, might declare, 'But what does it mean?' The short answer is that our spectator is unfamiliar with (or resistant to) the nature of the DISCOURSE that has, in the first instance, taken place between the artist, his/her medium and his/her environment (in place and time). Unless the spectator can 'tune in' to the signals – the CODES – operated by the artist, unless the spectator can recognize that a discourse is actually taking place, then the art he or she witnesses – for him or her, not necessarily anyone else – is meaningless.

On the other hand, the spectator might instinctively warm to a work of art – be attracted by its colour, shape, texture – and still be at a loss to grasp its meaning. In this case, common ground between artist, work of art and spectator has been found. Communication has begun, and so, arguably, has meaning.

Meaning, obviously, has to be worked at. The codes or practices of specific communicative discourses have to be recognized and eventually understood; the relationship between speaker/writer/artist/musician actor/dancer, etc., and the forms and conventions of the chosen medium of communication responded to preferably sympathetically and with EMPATHY.

Meaning can be said to be in a perpetual state of re-working or re-negotiation. The artist's meaning may never be the spectator's meaning; but meaning is the property of neither. Indeed, to regard meaning as something universally determinable and fixed is to create MYTH and to deal in PROPAGANDA. See DECONSTRUCTION; DEEP STRUCTURE; PARADIGM; POLYSEMY; SEMIOLOGY/SEMIOTICS.

Meaning systems See DOMINANT, SUBORDINATE, RADICAL.

Mean world syndrome It is argued by commentators such as the American media analyst George Gerbner that the more people watch television, the more likely they will consider that out there is a 'mean world'. On the small screen, content analysis tells us, crime rages about ten times more often than in real life. Heavy viewers, according to Gerbner in a series of published analyses since 1980, overestimate the statistical chance of violence in their own lives (see RESONANCE) and consequently harbour a heightened mistrust of strangers. However, Gerbner's conclusions have been challenged – in terms of reliable proof – by recent researchers.

While granting that Gerbner's scenario of TV *cultivating* in viewers a fear of crime is interesting, Guy Cumberbatch and Dennis Howitt in *A Measure of Uncertainty. The Effects of the Mass Media* (UK: Broadcasting Standards Council/John Libbey, 1989) write, 'All in all, few empirical studies lend full support to the original Gerbner hypothesis, while there are many failures to replicate.' This position is reinforced by Jib Fowles in *The Case for Television Violence* (US: Sage, 1999) who refers to 'substantial studies done outside laboratories and with large numbers of respondents that could find no evidence of a relationship between television violence and real-world aggression'; further, such evidence indicated that 'exposure on a large scale to violence was linked to reduced aggressiveness and criminality'. The debate continues. See EFFECTS OF THE MASS MEDIA; MAINSTREAMING.

Media accountability See McQUAIL'S ACCOUNTABILITY OF MEDIA MODEL, 1997.

Media: alternative (or radical) media Essentially counter-hegemonic, that is challenging established, hierarchical systems of politics, economics and CULTURE, alternative media take many forms. These can operate at individual or group level, like GRAFFITI, through DRESS, song, or even bumper stickers; they have expressed themselves through pamphlets, newspapers, novels, comics, street theatre, performance art and – not least in impact – PORNOGRAPHY.

Protesting at the disappearances of their loved ones in Argentina, the Mothers of the Plaza De Mayo communicated their message through *assembly*, wearing diapers as headscarves and carrying placards bearing the dates on which their loved ones were last seen alive: eventually images of their courage and resolution were transmitted around the world.

The INTERNET has been seen as potentially the most effective mode of alternative media, by its reach and accessibility, and its interactive power. However, the risk of being colonized by the 'usual suspects', big business and government, through commercialization and legal restraint, has diminished optimism that struggles for justice and equality can be fought online. See UNDERGROUND PRESS.

---

* John D.H. Downing, *Radical Media: Rebellious Communication and Social Movements* (US/UK: Sage, 2001).

Media control Four categories of media control are generally recognized: *Authoritarian*; *Paternal*; *Commercial* and *Democratic*. They can apply to an individual communications system, such as ownership of a newspaper, or to a state pattern of control. The first indicates a total monopoly of the means of communication and control over what is expressed. The second is what Raymond Williams in *Communication* (UK: Pelican, 1966) terms 'authoritarianism with a conscience', that is, authority with VALUES and purposes beyond those concerning the maintenance of its own power. The third relates to control by market forces: anything can be said provided that you can afford to say it and that you can say it profitably.

Democratic control is the rarest category, implying active involvement in decisions by the workforce and, indeed, the readership or audience. Control works at different levels – at the *operational* level (editors, producers, etc.), at the *allocative* level (of funds, personnel, etc.) and at the *external* level (government, advertisers, consumers).

Trends in media control have been towards greater concentration of ownership; towards ownership by CONGLOMERATE organizations and subsequently a series of over-diversifying control NETWORKS in which international finance has fingers in practically every communications pie, from newspapers to cinema, from records to satellites. Running parallel with these trends has been the development of multi-marketing of media products – books, films, TV series, DVDs, etc. with such products being packaged for worldwide consumption; audience maximization, and therefore profit maximization being the most important driving force. See GLOBAL MEDIA SYSTEM: THE MAIN PLAYERS; NORMATIVE THEORIES OF MASS MEDIA; WORLD TRADE ORGANIZATION (WTO) TELECOMMUNICATIONS AGREEMENT, 1997. See also *TOPIC GUIDE* under MEDIA: OWNERSHIP AND CONTROL.

Mediacy Term first given public prominence at the 1983 British Association conference by Michael Weiss and Carol Lorac of the Communication and Social Skills Project at Brighton Polytechnic. Deemed as important, in the education curriculum of the future, as literacy and numeracy are today, mediacy is defined by Weiss and Lorac as 'the ability to understand and manipulate recorded sound and vision. Information technology and video are the machinery of mediacy: its pen and paper'.

Media effects See EFFECTS OF THE MASS MEDIA.

Media: hot and cold See HOT MEDIA, COLD MEDIA.

Media images These are the 'truths', or some would say STEREOTYPES – most certainly conventions – which the media operate in the definition and redefinition of CONSENSUS and by which they define, and sometimes police, the normative contours of society. As a considerable amount of our knowledge of others comes to us at second hand, through the media, the images the media use provide us with benchmarks or points of reference.

Consensus is regularly defined by the media's concentration on *deviation* from consensus (see DEVIANCE). Equally, the media stand forth as sentinels of the 'moral constituency' of society as Howard S. Becker puts it in *Outsiders: Studies in the Sociology of Deviance* (US: Free Press, 1963); and it is their images, repeated, dramatized, often expressed in panic terms, that provide the major source of current information in society. See EFFECTS OF THE MASS MEDIA; FOLK DEVILS; GUARD DOGS; MORAL ENTREPRENEURS; WATCHDOGS.

Media imperialism Term used to describe the role western capitalist media play in dominating 'Third World' developing countries through communication systems. Crucial to the notion of media or *cultural* imperialism is the understanding of the relationship between economic, territorial, cultural and informational factors. In the age of western economic colonialism in the nineteenth century the flow of information was a vital process of growth and reinforcement. Where the trade went, so followed developing media practice and technology, reflecting the VALUES and assumptions of those who owned and manned the service.

As developing countries reached independence much concern was felt at the degree of penetration by western media. In 1972, the General Conference of the United Nations Educational, Scientific and Cultural Organization (UNESCO) drew attention to the way the media of the richer sections of the world were a means towards 'the domination of world public opinion or a source of moral and cultural pollution'. Since then the movement towards a NEW WORLD INFORMATION ORDER has grown in vigour and strength.

In 1973, in Algiers, a meeting of heads of state of non-aligned countries agreed to take concerted action to promote a fairer, more balanced exchange of information among themselves and release themselves from dependence upon the experts of the richer nations, demanding the 'reorganization of existing communication channels which are the legacy of the colonial past …'. By 1978, the UNESCO General Council agreed its new Declaration on Mass Media emphasizing the 'balanced' aspect of a concept of information based on the principle of 'free and balanced flow'.

Developing countries have long held a heart-felt belief that western agencies only report the bad news of what happens in their countries and that this bad news – based upon what Anthony Smith in his book *The Geopolitics of Information* (UK: Faber, 1980) terms 'aberrational' criteria for news selection – causes serious harm, especially when such countries are in need of western financial support and investment.

One proponent of the imperialist thesis, Herbert Schiller, writing in the late 1960s, saw American television exports as part of an attempt by the American military industrial complex 'to subjugate the world'. He argued that the declining European empires had been replaced by an emergent US empire; one arm of this empire being the US-based, transnational communications industries, which Schiller saw as working in collaboration with western (predominantly US) political and military interests.

These communications industries were for the most part funded privately by advertising revenue and were thus extensively tied to commercial interests. The cultural artefacts exported, mainly from the US, to other countries were seen as promoting the values of consumer capitalism.

As such they could be seen as either reinforcing these values where they already existed, as for example in western European countries, or as undermining traditional values and supplanting them with those of consumer capitalism in countries, such as Third World countries, where capitalist modes of production were non-existent or less developed. It was, for Schiller, a means by which the US could encourage, among other things, demand for its own products.

Schiller's thesis has met with some criticism. John B. Thompson in *The Media and Modernity* (UK: Polity Press, 1995), for example, argues that it overlooks the *multipolar* nature of the global economy in which Europe, Japan and Southeast Asia have played an increasingly important role; the growing foreign investment in US communications such as that of Sony in Columbia, Tristar and CBS records; and the importance of other exporters of cultural artefacts such as Britain, Australia, Mexico, Brazil and India as regional producers.

Thompson believes that, 'It would be quite implausible to suggest that this complex and shifting field of global power relations could be analyzed in terms of the thesis of cultural imperialism. The thesis is simply too rigid and one-dimensional to do justice to a global situation which is in considerable flux.'

Further, argues Thompson, the thesis tends to overlook the fact that whilst messages may be diffused on a global scale, many factors within the locale of their reception can affect the way in which they are *appropriated* by the audience. Both senders and receivers contribute to the construction of their meaning. Tamar Liebes and Elihu Katz, for example, in their classic study of audience reception of episodes of *Dallas*, the American SOAP OPERA, *The Export of Meaning: Cross-cultural Readings of 'Dallas'* (UK: Polity Press, 1993), demonstrate the impact cultural variables can have on the reading of television texts.

Schiller, in later writings, acknowledged these criticisms yet maintained that global domination by US culture has not significantly declined. Whatever the criticisms of the media imperialism thesis, the concentration of symbolic power mainly in the US as a result of the ongoing process of GLOBALIZA-TION of ownership within the media and cultural industries cannot be denied. (See in particular Schiller's *Culture Inc.: The Corporate Takeover of Public Expression* (US: Oxford University Press, 1989).)

Not in dispute are inequalities of wealth – and therefore of cultural and media provision between so-called core nations and peripheral nations (see CORE NATIONS, PERIPHERAL NATIONS) and the serious and ongoing INFORMATION GAPS between them; gaps that are unlikely to be bridged until the *structures* of deprivation are removed.

It is not only the inequalities in the distribution of information that cause concern but the *flow* of that communication. Cees Hamelink in *World Communication: Disempowerment and Self Empowerment* (UK: Zed Books, 1995) says: 'Information flows across the globe are imbalanced, since most of the world's information moves among the countries in the North, less between the North and the South, and very little flows among the countries of the South' and this 'differential access to the management of information has put the developing countries at a serious disadvantage in the world political-economy'.

This situation 'compromises their national sovereignty' and in so far as developing nations have increased 'their import capacity for communication technology, they have become more dependent upon the economic forces of the North'. See CONVERGENCE; GLOBAL MEDIA SYSTEM: THE MAIN PLAYERS; INTERNATIONAL FEDERATION OF JOURNALISTS (IFJ); MACBRIDE COMMISSION; NEWS AGENCIES; NEWS AID?; NEWS VALUES; NON-ALIGNED NEWS POOL; TALLOIRES DECLARATION; WORLD PRESS FREEDOM COMMITTEE. See also *TOPIC GUIDE* under GLOBAL PERSPECTIVES; MEDIA ISSUES AND DEBATES; MEDIA: OWNERSHIP AND CONTROL.

---

* Jonathan Benthall, *Disasters, Relief and the Media* (US: I.B. Tauris, 1995); James Lull, *Media, Communication, Culture: A Global Approach* (UK: Polity Press, 1995); Edward S. Herman and R.W. Chesney, *The Global Media: The New Missionaries of Corporate Capitalization* (UK/US: Cassell, 1997); George Monbiot, *The Capitalist State: The Corporate Takeover of Britain* (UK: Macmillan, 2001).

Media moguls: four sources of concern The issue of global media ambitions on the part of transnational corporations (TNCs) prompts debate between those alarmed by the CONVERGENCE of ownership across the world, and others who accept its inevitability while at the same time arguing that 'media moguls' are not as all-powerful, or their progress as inevitable, as some commentators feel.

Such a debate was conducted on the openDemocracy website (www.opendemocracy.net) by analysts on both sides of the Atlantic. One contributor to this debate is James Curran who, in an online article, 'Global media concentration: shifting the argument' (23 May 2002), discussed what he perceives as four sources of concern in relation to what he sees as a 'pattern of domination'. First, Curran believes that 'the private concentration of symbolic power potentially distorts the democratic process'. He cites the example of Italian media mogul Silvio Berlusconi whose media empire helped catapult him 'into the premiership of Italy without having any experience of democratic office … Berlusconi would not be ruling Italy now if he did not dominate a massive media empire that enabled him to manufacture a political party.'

The second concern 'is that the power potentially at the disposal of media moguls tends to be exerted in a one-sided way' usually rightist and consumerist-orientated. Curran refers to Rupert Murdoch who 'may have presided over the subversive *Simpsons* but he is also the man who bullied his British journalists to follow a right-wing agenda … part of a more general pattern in which shareholder interventions sometimes advance conservative or market-friendly positions, but more rarely their antithesis'.

Curran's third concern is that 'the concentration of market power can stifle competition'. He believes that a 'fundamental reason for the long-standing deficiencies of the British national press … is that it has been controlled so long by an oligopoly'. Leading on from this is the fourth concern, a 'one-sided protection of our freedoms'; on the one hand 'a state of constant alert against the abuse of state power over media, reflected in the development of numerous safeguards', yet on the other hand 'not matched by an equivalent vigilance and set of safeguards directed against the abuse of shareholder power over the media'.

In other words, in the conflict between media power and public interest the latter is likely to lose out. One consequence of what Curran describes as 'the current quiescence' (in the face of the media's assertion of its own freedoms) 'is that media conglomerates have been able to persuade governments around the world to ease monopoly controls'. See BERLUSCONI PHENOMENON; CROSS-MEDIA OWNERSHIP; GLOBALIZATION OF MEDIA; GLOBAL MEDIA SYSTEM: THE MAIN PLAYERS; MURDOCH EFFECT; REGULATORY FAVOURS. See also *TOPIC GUIDE* under MEDIA: OWNERSHIP AND CONTROL.

Media research centres See RESEARCH CENTRES.

Media technology See *TOPIC GUIDE* under MEDIA: TECHNOLOGIES.

Mediation Between an EVENT and the reporting or broadcasting of it to an AUDIENCE, mediation occurs, that is, a process of interpretation – shaping, selecting, editing, emphasizing, de-emphasizing – according to the perceptions, expectations and previous experience of those involved in the reporting of the event; and in accordance with the requirements and characteristics of the means of reporting. Between the event of a car accident or a murder and the report of such an event a whole series of inter-mediating actions take place. The event is translated into words or pictures; it is processed according to the demands of the MEDIUM – for headlines, for good pictures – and pressures such as time, space and contending messages.

Even when, in INTERPERSONAL COMMUNICATION, A communicates a message to B, which B conveys to C, a process of mediation inevitably takes place: B may rephrase the message, give parts of it prominence and understate other parts, supplement or distort the information. Mediation is inescapable: much of our knowledge of life and the world comes to us at second hand, through the mediation of PRESS and TV; our perceptions of events are coloured by the perceptions, preoccupations, VALUES, of the mediators.

However, the *construct* of events is far from a monopoly of the mass media; it is further mediated, and the process modified or altered altogether, by those around us who exert influence – friends, relatives, work colleagues etc. – and other so-called intervening variables such as personal mood, time of day or state of health. See S-IV-R MODEL OF COMMUNICATION.

Media species Classification of the public in terms of their attitudes to ADVERTISING. A 1997 report drawn from research by CIA Medialab in the UK defines the following public 'species': *cynics, acquiescents, enthusiasts* and *ambivalents*. The research arm of CIA Medianetwork, Medialab conducted an 18-month survey using nationally representative focus groups; 25 per cent of these, named cynics, resent the intrusion of national ads and feel strongly about the capacity of advertisements to subvert. Acquiescents are better news for adworld. Comprising 21 per cent of the survey findings, they are easy-going, and they approve of ads that are funny, colourful and vivid. They do not care for national newspaper ads, or direct mail, which makes acquiescents feel vulnerable. Enthusiasts make up 35 per cent of respondents. They too seem unimpressed by national newspaper ads, but they enjoy TV commercials, often more than the programmes they accompany. The ambivalents are seen to be a rather inert band, resistant through being uninterested, and they take a fatalistic attitude to the effects/dangers of advertising. See ADVERTISING: MAINSTREAMERS, ASPIRERS,

SUCCEEDERS AND REFORMERS; VALS TYPOLOGY. See also *TOPIC GUIDE* under ADVERTISING/MARKETING.

Mediasphere Term posed and defined by John Hartley in *Popular Reality: Journalism, Modernity, Popular Culture* (UK: Arnold, 1996) to describe the positioning of media, its range and breadth of influence, in relationship to the PUBLIC SPHERE, and the notion of the *Semiosphere* put forward by Yuri Lotman in *The Universe of the Mind: A Semiotic Theory of Culture* (US: University of Indiana Press, 1990). Hartley sees the semiosphere – the sphere of cultural expression and cultural MEANING – as being in a constant process of interaction with the mediasphere and public sphere. He images the relationship as resembling Russian dolls: the public sphere fits within the mediasphere, which in turn, fits within the semiosphere.

The most salient feature of these interlocking spheres, argues Hartley, is JOURNALISM. It was journalism that originated and nurtured concepts of freedom, of human rights, within societies. It served a key function in, and in turn was served by, the success of the American and French revolutions. The public sphere of the nineteenth century was created by journalism. Hartley believes 'there would be no public' and consequently no progress towards the sovereignty of the people without the aid of journalistic writing, which has served, and continues to serve, as a counterforce to subordination. Indeed, it is 'the mechanism for making these [democratic] discourses generally available, and also for articulating the different forms of resistance'.

Ultimately, though, journalism's power to define and further the public sphere depends on readership. The changing nature of readership also alters the nature of the public and private spheres. Hartley believes that we have moved from the traditional *adversarial* mode of journalism, with its public, political and masculine bias to a POSTMODERNIST phase, driven in particular by popular journalism (described by Hartley as 'the textual system of modernity').

This gives emphasis not to public life 'but to private meaning'. He identifies the following shifts in the nature of readership: from male to female, from old to young, from militant to meditative, from public to private, from governmental to consumerist and from law-making to identity-forming. Hartley describes the mediasphere as 'suffused with images and issues which connect popular readerships and popular meanings together ... the mainstream of contemporary journalism is fashion, gossip, lifestyle, consumerism and celebrity, and "news" is private, visual, narrativized and personalized'. It follows that the icon of the contemporary mediasphere is 'not the superpower but the supermodel'.

The shifts mentioned here are not, however, to be seen as having become disengaged from the past of journalism/readership: modern journalism is, yes, populist. Yet it remains in the tradition of the radical journalism that helped give birth to the American and French revolutions. See DEMOCRACY AND THE MEDIA.

Mediatization Process whereby political or indeed any public activity, having become reliant for its audience/electorate upon the media for its messages to be communicated, adopts the principles and methods of media communication. In particular TV has become the medium and channel of political communication. Consequently political communication pays greater attention to entertainment value as practised by TV, for example PERSONALIZATION, simplification and an emphasis on using 'media-*genic*' players (see LOOKISM).

In 'Towards a "videocracy"?: Italian political communication at a turning point', in the *European Journal of Communication*, September 1995, Gianpietro Mazzoleni said of the situation in Italy at the time of the 1994 elections, 'The parties are increasingly unable to bring their message to the voters and have to do it by relying on the channels of mass communication. The toll that the parties must pay is the mediatization of their communication activities.' In consequence, media ceases to be the servant to and observer of political parties; and political parties become in thrall to the media, in their grip. Mazzoleni considers this a significant and far-reaching 'metamorphosis', in which the media take on the role of *kingmaker* – a case specifically illustrated when media mogul Silvio Berlusconi, using the power of his own media empire, was, in 2001, elected prime minister of Italy for the second time. See BERLUSCONI PHENOMENON.

Media user ethics See TEN COMMANDMENTS FOR MEDIA CONSUMERS.

Media: uses of media by the young See CHILDREN, YOUNG PEOPLE AND THE CHANGING MEDIA ENVIRONMENT.

Medio communication That mode of communication between direct, face-to-face address and MASS COMMUNICATION; into this classification comes communication by letter, e-mail or telephone.

Medium The physical or technical means of converting a communication message into a signal capable of being transmitted along a given channel. TV, for example, is a medium that employs the channels of vision and sound. John Fiske in *Introduction to Communication Studies* (UK: Methuen, 1982 and subsequent editions), divides media into three categories. (1) *Presentational* media: the voice, face, body; the spoken word, GESTURE; where the medium is actually the communicator. (2) *Representational* media: books, paintings, photographs, etc., using cultural and aesthetic conventions 'to create a "text" of some sort'; they become independent of the communicator, being *works* of communication (whereas presentational media are *acts* of communication). (3) *Mechanical* media: telephone, radio, TV, film, etc., and they are *transmitters* of 1 and 2. The properties of the medium determine the range of CODES it can transmit; and considerably affect the nature of the message and its reception.

Medium is the message One of the classic quotes of media literature and perhaps the best known of Marshall McLuhan (1911–80). The medium is the message is the first chapter heading in *Understanding Media: The Extensions of Man* (UK: Routledge & Kegan Paul, 1964; Routledge, 2002). What is said, McLuhan believes, is deeply conditioned by the MEDIUM through which it said. The particular attributes of any medium help to determine the MEANING of the communication, and no medium is neutral. See McLUHANISM.

Message That which an act, or work, of communication is *about*. For purposes of definition and analysis it is sometimes necessary to treat the message as something separable from the *process* of communication; but ultimately a message can only meaningfully be examined in the context of other elements, all of which are interlinked and interacting.

It is important to distinguish between the actual signal that carries the message and the message itself: a wink is a signal but what is its message? The answer depends on many factors – for example, who is winking, to whom and in what context? (see SIGN). While message-signals, in the form of visual or aural CODES may be sent, the message may well not be understood. Thus an ambiguous smile may represent the signal that a message is being conveyed, but the receiver may fail to understand the message while recognizing the signal.

The message may draw its initial shape or purpose from the Sender or Communicator: it will be similarly influenced by the nature of the medium in which it is sent. The Receiver of a message may be close at hand, in sight of the Communicator, or some distance away. If the message involves INTRAPERSONAL COMMUNICATION, the Communicator and the Receiver may be one and the same. Both the signal and the intended message may encounter NOISE – that is, physical or psychological interference that will affect its meaningfulness. The message may elicit FEEDBACK, which will further modify the message and indeed create a new communication situation and new signals and messages.

Denis McQuail in *Communication* (UK: Longman, 1975) writes that the simplest way of regarding human communication is 'to consider it as the sending from one person to another of meaningful messages'. We can rarely if ever be certain of how other people will interpret our signals, or whether we will 'get our message across'. Thus the message sent may be quite different from the message received, and while we think we are communicating a single message we may, unconsciously, be putting across all sorts of other messages, too.

We are selecting in and selecting out a barrage of message-carrying signals all the time. We give attention to them if we are motivated to do so. The effectiveness of a message depends, at a basic, instrumental level, on the weight it carries in competition with other signals and messages, but equally it depends upon the significance attached to it by the receivers.

This in turn depends upon the 'set' or preparedness, of the receivers for the Sender/Message/Medium. The message of a satirical cartoon, for example, might be completely lost if the reader knows nothing about the particular circumstances to which the cartoon refers. Even a knowledge of the facts may not be enough to facilitate the intended interpretation, because this may only occur if the reader shares the social, political or cultural values of the cartoonist. In short, whether we 'get our message across' depends partly upon the context in which it is received; and the VALUES, attitudes, perceptions and knowledge of the receiver are a crucial part of that context. See DOMINANT, SUBORDINATE, RADICAL; INTERVENING VARIABLES (IVs); METAMESSAGE; POLYSEMY; PREFERRED READING.

Metamessage The underlying message in a communicative act. This may differ from what on the surface appears to be the message. The metamessage is conveyed both verbally and, often more crucially, non-verbally. The metamessage carries information about the relationships of those involved in an encounter and the attitudes they have towards each other and the topic in question.

The interpretation of the metamessage is usually influenced by the way in which the message is communicated and non-verbal communication thus plays a vital role in the sending and receiving of metamessages. A simple question such as 'May I help you?' asked by someone in a higher-status ROLE, for example, can be interpreted as a friendly gesture or as an accusation of incompetence depending, in part, on the tone of voice adopted.

Metamessages can also help to frame a conversation as they help to define the nature of the encounter by, for example, defining the seriousness of the conversation and the relationships of those taking part.

Metaphor A figure of speech or a visual device that works by transporting qualities from one plane of reality to another: 'the camel is the ship of the desert'; 'life for Mary was a bed of roses'. Without metaphor there would be no scope for the development of either visual or verbal language; it would remain clinical and colourless.

Metaphor is not merely an expressive device but an integral part of the function of language as a *definer* as well as a reflector of reality. As a rhetorical device metaphor is central to the way media define reality, structure, maintain and monitor DISCOURSE, uphold (and sometimes challenge) hierarchies, service (and sometimes undermine) HEGEMONY. Metaphor provides us with the pictures by which we envision the world: we define time by metaphor ('time is money'); we view the public as inhabiting a 'space' (see AGORA); we define public argument and debate using metaphors of conflict, and the notion of argument as 'war' is built into the CULTURE we inhabit.

Even where peace is being referred to, the media are more than likely to express it in military terms: 'War breaks out over classroom peace plans'. Press language is riddled with the bombast of conflict – things are axed, chopped, smashed, slashed; knives are constantly out; prime ministers stick to their guns, oppositions are routed.

We use metaphor to define the nature of communication: communication as *transmission* or communication as *ritual*. We talk of *homo narrans* (see NARRATIVE PARADIGM), casting the human being as the storytelling animal; or, with Erving Goffman, we may use the *dramaturgical* model, the metaphor of life as a stage.

In *An Introductory Guide to Post-Structuralism and Postmodernism* (UK: Harvester Wheatsheaf, 1993), Madan Sarap states 'that metaphors determine to a large extent what we think in any field. Metaphors are not idle flourishes – they shape what we do. They can help make, and defend a world view.' As well as being 'productive of insights and fresh illuminations', metaphors, according to Sarap, 'can encapsulate and put forward proposals for another way of looking at things'. They can serve as agents of change as well as weapons of reinforcement (see STEREOTYPE).

'Through metaphor,' says Sarap, 'we can have increased awareness of alternative possible worlds.' Few contemporary media phenomena have prompted so many, and varied metaphors as the INTERNET. Early in its history it was described as an open prairie or a superhighway; in more recent terms, its SURVEILLANCE capacity has earned it the metaphor of *electronic eye*.

The so-called *mixed metaphor*, beloved of politicians seeking by their RHETORIC to attract media attention, contains in a statement two or more ineptly linked images: 'Lame ducks will be barking up the wrong tree if they think government is going to bail them out every time profits take a hammering.' Though the metaphorical allusions may be all over the place, the statement's underlying IDEOLOGY is, however, crystal clear. See EUPHEMISM; METONYMY; VISIONS OF ORDER. See also *TOPIC GUIDE* under LANGUAGE/DISCOURSE/NARRATIVE.

Metasignal A signal that makes a comment about a signal, or a set of signals: it directs us to the accurate meaning of the signals. For example, two people appear to exchange blows: is the fight real or make-believe? Their smiling faces form the metasignal which indicates that, at least on the surface, what we are seeing is a play-fight.

Body posture is among the chief metasignals. Equally, *uniform* serves effectively in this capacity. We react differently to the policeman in uniform than we might to the same person in off-duty jeans and T-shirt. Desmond Morris in *Manwatching: A Field Guide to Human Behaviour* (UK: Jonathan Cape, 1977) says that 'In a sense the whole world of entertainment presents a non-stop Metasignal, in the form of the proscenium arch around the stage of a theatre, or the edge of the cinema or TV screen.' Audiences, he believes, can tolerate – and gain entertainment from – films and plays featuring dollops of death and mayhem because of the metasignals that indicate 'this isn't real'. Morris argues that though the actors may aim at maximum reality in their dark deeds, 'no matter how convincing they are, we still carry at the back of our minds (even as we gasp when the knife plunges home) the Metasignal of the "edge" of their stage'.

Metonymy A figure of speech in which the thing meant is represented by something that is an attribute of the original. When we talk of the newspaper business, we refer to the press – something that stands for the whole.

As far as images are concerned, the metonym is a selection of one of those available to represent the whole; and from that selection flows our interpretation or understanding of the whole. Thus the selection of a piece of film of young people lounging at a street corner, or strike pickets in combat with the police, acts as the 'trigger of meaning' for the way the teenager or the striker is defined. For this reason, metonyms are powerful conveyors of reality, indeed so powerful that they can come to be accepted as actually being reality, the way things really are.

Micro-myth, macro-myth Philip Schlesinger in *Putting 'Reality' Together. BBC News* (UK: Constable, 1978; Methuen/University Paperback, 1987) examines the BBC news machine at work, and identifies what in his view are two myths entertained by those who work in BBC news: the *micro-myth* that production staff are permitted autonomy within the organization; the *macro-myth*, that the BBC is an independent organization, largely socially unattached. See IMPARTIALITY.

Milieu The social environment of the individual, group, CULTURE or nation.

Milton's paradox On the one hand the English poet John Milton (1608–74) is famous for his stalwart defence of the freedom of expression (see AREOPAGITICA); on the other Milton did not entirely practise what he preached. Dominant in Milton's own life was anti-Catholicism. The paradox arises from the difference between principle and practice: during the period of the Interregnum, 1649–60 (the Commonwealth of Oliver Cromwell) Milton was an official censor, though apologists argue that the poet was less involved in CENSORSHIP than in editing and supervision.

In 'Milton's paradox: the market-place of ideas in post-Communist Bulgaria', in the *European Journal of Communication*, September 1997, Ekaterina Ognianova and Byron Scott believe that 'in a simplistic way at least, Milton represents a perennial conflict between general beliefs and specific behaviour, between concepts and practice when it comes to the question of how much freedom to permit'.

Mimetic/semiosic planes In NARRATIVE, the mimetic is the plane of *representation*, the semiosic the plane of *meaning* production. See CODES OF NARRATIVE; CONNOTATION; NARRATIVE PARADIGM; PROPP'S PEOPLE; SEMIOLOGY/SEMIOTICS.

Minneapolis City Council enquiry into pornography See PORNOGRAPHY.

Minority Report of Mr Selwyn Lloyd This was attached to the majority BEVERIDGE COMMITTEE REPORT ON BROADCASTING, 1950, and, contrary to Beveridge who supported a continued monopoly of broadcasting for the BBC, argued that independent – and commercial – competition would be a good thing. Author of the Minority Report was Conservative MP Selwyn Lloyd, who produced a scheme for a Commission for British Broadcasting to be set up, which would license a number of rival broadcasting stations.

Lloyd wrote, 'Having considered these arguments put forward by the BBC on behalf of monopoly, I am of the opinion that independent competition will be healthy for broadcasting.' His view had considerable support in the Tory Party and in the business world: commercial broadcasting in the UK was on the horizon. See COMMERCIAL RADIO; COMMERCIAL TELEVISION. See also *TOPIC GUIDE* under BROADCASTING.

Miracle of Fleet Street Description by Lord Northcliffe (1865–1922) of the redoubtable UK *Daily Herald* (1912–64), a sometimes swashbuckling radical paper that, despite having a substantial circulation and vast readership, received little ADVERTISING as a result partly of its left-wing views but perhaps more importantly because of its insistence on thorough reporting of political issues, considered at that time to appeal more to male readers. When other national popular papers were priced at one penny, the *Daily Herald* was forced to charge two pence. Yet it lost very little in circulation, due to the energy and leadership of its greatest editor, George Lansbury, MP (1859–1940).

The *Herald* was the first newspaper in the world to reach a circulation of 2 million – in mid-1933 – though it was soon overtaken by Beaverbrook's *Daily Express*. By the time the *Herald* had reached its peak circulation of 2.1 million in 1947, the *Daily Mirror* and *Daily Express* were pushing 4 million and, by 1960, sales had tumbled to 1.6 million. The *Herald* struggled on until 14 September 1964. See *TOPIC GUIDE* under MEDIA HISTORY.

Misinformed society As the means of communication expand, the assumption that more and diverse information equates with better-informed citizens has been challenged by many commentators. In asking the question 'How far have media succeeded/failed to provide information for citizenship?', Peter Golding argues that the so-termed information society 'is a myth'. In 'Telling stories: sociology, journalism and the informed citizen', in the *European Journal of Communication* (December 1994), Golding believes, 'We live in a media society, in which information is available at a price, or not at all' and that a more accurate term for today would be the misinformed society: 'Wherever we look, in coverage of race, industrial relations, welfare, foreign relations, or electoral politics, the media have failed democracy. We live in a society in blinkers.'

For Golding the 'information age' constitutes not a devolution of the message systems reaching ever wider into every part of society but a scene made up of media monoliths and a society that has become increasingly centralized in terms of decision-making and the 'reach' of vital information (see GLOBALIZATION OF MEDIA; INFORMATION BLIZZARDS; PRIVATIZATION; SURVEILLANCE SOCIETY). Golding's misinformed society is marked by a diminishing range of media ownership and the casualization of labour in the media industry – BBC staff dropped by 5000 from 25,000 between 1989 and 1994.

In terms of programming, Golding warns of the marginalization of serious information programmes on TV and an obsession with maximizing ratings, both of which threaten the range and diversity of broadcasting. He sees the current flow and quality of information as fragmenting rather than unifying society, furthering not equality but inequality. The media of today render a 'flawed account of social reality' and shirk the abiding principle of a self-respecting media, 'to tell the truth and make things better'.

---

* Danny Schechter, *The More You Watch, The Less You Know* (US: Seven Stories Press, 1996).

Mix, mixing In film-making a *mix* is a gradual transition between two shots where one dissolves into another. It is a soft fade, often used to denote the passage of time (see MONTAGE; SHOT). *Mixing* is the process of re-recording all original dialogue, music and sound effects on to a single master soundtrack. See SYNCHRONOUS SOUND.

Mobile concept of communication See MOBILIZATION.

Mobile phone See MOBILIZATION.

Mobilization An important capacity of the media is to mobilize public opinion, that is to arouse sympathy or concern about certain issues to the point where *action* is taken by the public themselves, or by those in authority. The classic example is the role played by the media in the preparation of a nation for war. In such a case, the media are instrumental in both informing the public about the situation, arguing the case for action and then, when the action takes place, reporting it – usually – from a strictly partisan point of view. Their role becomes that of propagandist.

A twenty-first-century alternative, but nicely linked, definition of mobilization refers to the remarkable expansion, until it has become a cultural phenomenon, of the use of the mobile phone. Few technological advances have become so much part of modern communication at every level of society so rapidly as the mobile, to the point where reference is made to the *m-generation*, to *m-commerce* and to the *m-future* in which the dominance of the computer as the hub of network transactions is seen to be giving way to the mobile with all its manifold functions.

Thus the term mobilization refers to the process by which people's activities, in particular their communicative exchanges, are increasingly 'mobilized'. According to an Orange press release of July 2000, the 'whole concept of communication is being changed'. The mobile is operated by individuals in any location, its characteristics brevity and speed; but it is a process essentially part of electronic systems operated through network institutions.

George Myerson in *Heidegger, Habermas and the Mobile Phone* (UK: Icon Books, 2001), part of a series entitled Postmodernist Encounters, writes of a paradox: 'Countless – but counted – individuals are seeking their desires separately, yet unknowingly they are caught up in a huge system.' Myerson talks about the 'mobile concept of communication' and sees it – as he images the philosophers Martin Heidegger and Jürgen Habermas would – as being essentially instrumental (he calls it the *Principle of Want*) rather than a communicative process that, in the pursuit of understanding, requires the exercise of the critical faculty. It follows, in Myerson's view, that in mobile communication 'Meaning is bypassed, as being too slow a medium for the ideal interaction.'

The author acknowledges that the mobile is 'the most rich of technological developments' but regards it as being 'packaged in such an impoverishing vision', a vision which for most intents and purposes is one framed within the dictates of commerce, of money: 'Communication is being increasingly measured in terms of money, becoming "metered".' He fears that in future, 'To communicate will mean the same thing as to exchange money. The two activities will simply be merged ... where the ideal conversation aspires to the condition of a credit card transaction.'

Myerson believes that 'More and more of our life will be lived in systems space, where efficient and minimal messaging will replace the slow and messy process of dialogue.'

Modality The use of the words 'may' or 'might' are referred to by linguists as *modal auxiliaries*, part of the modal system of language. Modality serves to insert 'yes but' into definitions, for example of truth or reality. Modality can be confirming or disconfirming by means of its degree of affinity with that which is described, within the system or contexts in which it is described. Thus affinity between a speaker and a listener will condition the degree of modality: they may agree, 'This is true' or 'This is real,' and agreement gives both a sense of security and status.

Robert Hodge and Gunther Kress in *Social Semiotics* (UK: Polity Press, 1988) write that 'A high degree of affinity indicates the expression of solidarity between participants.' The authors define affinity as 'an indicator of relations of solidarity or of power: that is, relations orientated towards the expression of solidarity or of power (difference)'. Thus 'Modality points to the social construction or contestation of knowledge-systems'. Agreement confirms the status of 'truth' and 'reality', disagreement disconfirms or undermines that status. 'Modality is consequently one of the crucial indicators of political struggle. It is a central means of contestations, and the site of the working out, whether by negotiation or imposition, of ideological systems.'

Model In social science research, a model is a tentative description of what a social process, say the communication process, or system might be like. It is a tool of explanation and analysis – very often in diagrammatic form – that attempts to show how the various elements of a situation being studied relate to each other. Models are not statements of reality; only after much further research and testing would the model be considered viable. It could then develop into a theory.

The term can also refer to a familiar process or object that is used as a point of reference when an attempt to explain the unknown is being made. An analogy is made showing the similarities between the phenomenon to be explained and one that is well known, i.e. the model.

Additionally, a model can be a person whose behaviour others wish to imitate, on whom they wish to model themselves – a ROLE model. The desire to model oneself on other persons is particularly strong in one's teenage years; the mass media play a significant part in presenting teenagers with a variety of such models. See HYPOTHESIS; IDENTIFICATION. See also *TOPIC GUIDE* under COMMUNICATION MODELS.

Modem Device for converting *analogue* signals to *digital* signals and from digital to analogue. Modem is short for modulator/demodulator.

Modes of media analysis See FUNCTIONALIST (MODE OF MEDIA ANALYSIS); MARXIST (MODE OF MEDIA ANALYSIS); SOCIAL ACTION (MODE OF MEDIA ANALYSIS). See also *TOPIC GUIDE* under RESEARCH METHODS.

Monofunctional In a media sense, the term ascribing to a work – of literature, RADIO, film, TV – a single function; for example, to entertain. Research findings over the years have seriously challenged assumptions that particular forms of content are monofunctional. Adults declare a considerable interest in NEWS programmes, yet functional studies have shown that for many viewers, the primary function of news is not informational. The news broadcast is, apparently, more closely related to habit; and it also affords the individual feelings of security and of social contact. See EFFECTS OF THE MASS MEDIA; SURVEILLANCE.

Monopoly, four scandals of According to the BEVERIDGE COMMITTEE REPORT ON BROADCASTING (UK), 1950, these were 'bureacracy, complacency, favouritism and inefficiency', indicators that the Committee saw in the performance of the BBC as monopoly-holder of British airwaves. Nevertheless, Beveridge recommended the Corporation's licence be renewed because the alternative, US-style commercial TV, promised a system that was considered to be much worse.

Monotype printing Invented in 1889 by American Tolbert Lanston. The machine is in two parts. The first, operated by the keyboard, punches coded holes into a paper tape; the second has the tape fed into it and the code controls the casting operation. In monotype casting, unlike linotype printing, every letter and space is cast separately.

Monroe motivated sequence Five-step sequence advocated by American Professor Alan Monroe in *Principles of Speech Communication* by Douglas Ehninger, Bruce E. Cronbach and Monroe (US: Scott, Foresman, 1984) for use in organizing speeches, especially those with an intent to persuade. The first step is to command, and maintain, audience *attention* by some eye- or ear-catching device (such as a lively story, anecdote or dramatic set of statistics). The second step is to fulfil an audience *need,* achieved through making the speech relevant. What follows is *satisfaction,* where possible solutions are proposed and examined. The speaker then proceeds to *visualization,* where the audience is persuaded to see more clearly how the speaker's information or ideas will help them. Step five is *action,* a plea for response, for the taking-up of the speaker's points.

Montage From the French, *monter,* to assemble; the process of cutting up film and arranging – editing – it into the screened sequence. Sergei Eisenstein (1898–1948) explained montage as putting together camera shots which, in combination, made a greater impact than did the sum of the parts – a creative juxtaposition. Separate elements combine to produce a new MEANING. Montage is the *synthesis* that gives film its unique character.

Montage is used as a *narrative* device and an *expressive* device, the one concerned with sequencing, ensuring the smooth continuity of action, the other with the intention of producing a particular effect by the clash, comparison or contrast of two or more images, often symbolic or metaphoric in meaning. This use of montage is often compared with *collage* in art in that it draws attention to itself as an exercise in construction: it says, 'Look at me as film, not reality.' See ALIENATION EFFECT; KULESHOV EFFECT; SHOT.

Moral economy See HICT PROJECT.

Moral entrepreneurs Howard Becker first used this term in *Outsiders: Studies in the Sociology of Deviance* (US: Free Press, 1963) to describe those members of the community who take upon themselves the role of guard dog (see GUARD DOG METAPHOR), vigilant against alleged attempts to subvert public morals. Such individuals often try, sometimes with success, to use the media to gain public support for their views. The letters columns of newspapers can be a particular vehicle for the expression of their views. Such entrepreneurs can play an important role in the development of a MORAL PANIC.

Moral panic Individuals and social GROUPS can by their activities emerge as a focus for outrage expressed by influential members of society who perceive these activities as seriously subverting the MORES and interests of the dominant CULTURE. Such reactions are, says Stanley Cohen in *Folk*

Devils and Moral Panics (UK: MacGibbon & Kee, 1972 and subsequent editions), disseminated by the mass media usually in a hysterical, stylized and stereotypical manner, thus engendering a sense of moral panic. Generally such panics occur in relation to the OTHER, for example when immigrants or asylum-seekers are perceived, via media coverage, and the repetition of that coverage over time and by agencies with political motivation, as a threat; a problem about which those in authority seem to be doing nothing, or too little. See DEVIANCE; LABELLING PROCESS (AND THE MEDIA); PREJUDICE.

Moral rights (in a text) See TEXT: INTEGRITY OF THE TEXT.

Mores Those social rules concerning acceptable behaviour that it is considered wrong to break. Such rules play an important part in the maintenance of social order and cohesion; consequently breaches of mores usually meet with the imposition of sanctions by society – formally through laws, informally through, for example, social rejection.

Some mores are particular to a specific society, others can be found in most societies. A majority of societies respects the sanctity of human life, though this is varyingly weighed against the sanctity of social order. Also, within a society, different social GROUPS may have different mores. Traditionally it is against the unwritten law of school life for pupils to tell tales to teacher. The sanction against those who do may be their temporary isolation or ejection from the group – or reprisals after school. Mores may often prescribe both the tone and content of communication. Differences in sexual mores, for example, underpin many of the arguments about the dissemination of PORNOGRAPHY.

Morphing In film-making, seamlessly joining together different images; special effects most notably used in horror movies, when images – faces, for example – 'metamorphose' into one another or change dramatically in appearance. Also employed in popular music videos such as Michael Jackson's *Black or White.*

Morphology Study of the structure or forms of words, traditionally distinguished from SYNTAX, which deals with the rules governing the combination of words in sentences. Generally morphology divides into two fields: the study of inflections and of word formation.

Morse Code Devised by Samuel Morse (1791–1872), American artist and sculptor, and one of the great pioneers of TELEGRAPHY, the Morse Code is a binary code made up of dots and dashes to represent letters of the alphabet, numbers 0 to 9 and punctuation marks. By 1838 Morse had developed his code using from one to four bits (binary digits) to encode letters of the alphabet, five bits for each number and six bits for punctuation. Thus A equals dot-dash; the number one, dot-dash-dash-dash-dash; a question mark equals dot-dot-dash-dash-dot-dot, while the vital SOS (Save Our Souls) equals dot-dot-dot-dash-dash-dash-dot-dot-dot. Subsequently modified to suit newer operations, the Morse Code – now the International Morse Code – continues in use. See *TOPIC GUIDE* under MEDIA HISTORY.

Motivation Ernest R. Hilgard, Richard C. Atkinson and Rita L. Atkinson in *Introduction to Psychology* (US: Harcourt Brace Jovanovich, 1975) define motivation as 'a general term referring to the regulation of need-satisfying and goal-seeking behaviour'. The sources of motivation are varied and complex. There is general agreement that motivation arises from the desire to satisfy many needs, but there are different theories about the nature of such needs and the relative importance attached by different individuals to them (see MASLOW'S HIERARCHY OF NEEDS).

The concept of motivation is relevant to several areas of communication and media studies. Motivation theories, for example, can help to provide a range of ideas about why people want to communicate. Of relevance here is William Schutz's theory of interpersonal needs. Schutz, in *The Interpersonal World* (US: Science and Behaviour Books, 1966), identifies three basic interpersonal needs, which, he argues, underlie most interpersonal behaviour: the need for *inclusion*, the need for *control* and the need for *affection*. These, then, are the needs one might wish to have satisfied in INTERPERSONAL COMMUNICATION. Situations in which others satisfy one or more of your needs are likely to be valued; those situations in which your needs are not met may well be avoided.

Another example of the use made of the concept of motivation is in the consideration of why and how people might be influenced or persuaded to act in certain ways, by certain messages. Much effort is expended in the ADVERTISING and public relations industries trying to devise strategies for selling products, services or people, by appealing to what are thought to be the motivations of the general public. See HIDDEN NEEDS; MOTIVATION RESEARCH (MR); VALS TYPOLOGY. See also *TOPIC GUIDE* under COMMUNICATION THEORY.

Motivation research (MR) The key question in MR is: what motivates people to buy, or in media terms, what motivates them to tune in, to read, to watch – in short, to respond; and how might that motivation be influenced in order for them to continue responding? MR's traditional mechanisms of questionnaires, interviews, focus groups have long been supplemented by electronic devices such as the pupilometer to measure respondents' eye movements and the degree of 'stopping power' of, for example, an audience member's response to a TV advertisement.

There are machines that offer voice-pitch analysis; machines to tabulate brainwaves. Not only is psychology wheeled into action in the service of MR but so are the findings of psycholinguists, who study the mental processes governing the learning and use of language. MR is involved in an ever-restless process of seeking more and more sophisticated ways of 'reading' consumption, whether it is of sports trainers or TV series, but it is seen by some commentators as being more and more into the business of *shaping* or manipulating responses, not the least in the arena of politics. See *TOPIC GUIDE* under ADVERTISING/MARKETING.

MP3 Digitized music file with the potential to revolutionize the music industry, and in the words of David Edwards in a UK *Daily Mirror* article, 'CD R.I.P. Why your shiny new album collection is being made obsolete by the march of MP3', promises to change for ever 'the way people buy and listen to music'. The initial reaction by the music industry to the MP3 file, which allows music to be downloaded from the INTERNET, free of charge, was to resist it. Napster, a company offering free music on the net was shut down following legal action by the Recording Industry Association of the US.

The industry, having attempted to outlaw such facilities, has begun to switch to a policy of commandeering them. HMV, the UK's largest music retailer, announced in 2002 the creation of a website from which *subscribers* will be able to download from nearly 100,000 tracks for a fee of £4.99 per month. EMI soon followed suit.

Delivery may be to personal computers in the traditional way, but new avenues in reception hardware are opening up – MP3 players in various forms. Edwards notes in his article that over a million MP3 players were sold in the UK between 2000 and 2002. By contrast, sales of CD players have dropped substantially. As Edwards points out, MP3 'has great benefits, very few overheads, no production costs, no packaging and potentially, no need for record shops'.

Mr Gate American media analyst David Manning White in 1950 investigated the process of GATEKEEPING by studying the editing selections by a copy-editor – 'Mr Gate' – from the (then) three major American news agencies on a 30,000-circulation daily newspaper in the midwest. 'Mr Gate' in one week used 1297 column inches – about one-tenth of the 11,910 column inches supplied. 'Mr Gate' confessed to a few prejudices, which might well cause him to put items on the spike (reject them), and to a preference: 'I go for human interest stories in a big way'; but White also perceived how important the pressure of time was on the selection process. The nearer the next edition of the newspaper came, the stronger in NEWS VALUE a story had to be not to be rejected. See WHITE'S GATEKEEPER MODEL, 1950.

M-time, P-time Edward Hall in *The Dance of Life: Other Dimensions of Time* (US: Doubleday, 1983) contends that cultures tend to adopt either a *monochronic* (M-time) or *polychronic* (P-time) perspective to managing time. The M-time perspective focuses on the clock: time is measured into units; time should be used productively; punctuality and meeting deadlines are viewed as important; time is represented as having a linear pattern and the focus is on doing one thing at a time. In contrast, the P-time perspective focuses on people and events, not the clock: time is fluid and flexible; activities have an evolving timescale; deadlines and appointments are not rigidly adhered to; several activities may be undertaken at the same time, and tasks and conversations are likely to be interrupted. There is a tendency for individualistic cultures to be driven by M-time and for collectivistic cultures to embrace the P-time perspective (see COMMUNICATION: INTERCULTURAL COMMUNICATION).

Such differences can be the cause of misunderstanding and friction in intercultural encounters. Stella

Ting-Toomey in *Communication Across Cultures* (US: Guilford Press, 1999) discusses the problems differences in time rhythms can cause; to take one example from conflict management situations: 'M-time people want to establish a clear timetable to achieve specific conflict goals and objectives; P-time people want to spend more time building up trust and commitment between the conflict parties. Different M-time and P-time rhythms … can further polarize individualists and collectivists …'.

MTV Music Television; worldwide popular music video-broadcasting service created by Robert Pittman in the US, to take advantage of initially free programming provided by popular VIDEO. Transmitted via satellite and cable television, MTV (now part of the Viacom media empire) is financed by advertising (90 per cent) and sponsorship. The launch of MTV took place in August 1981. From 1.5m North American subscribers the reach of MTV has become global. Over 103 million households in over 40 territories see MTV on cable, satellite, digital and terrestrial TV.

It is difficult to exaggerate the cultural impact of MTV broadcasting popular music, in English, to practically every corner of the world. Corinna Sturmer in 'MTV Europe. An imaginary continent?', in *Channels of Resistance: Global Television and Local Empowerment* (UK: British Film Institute/Channel 4 TV, 1993), edited by Tony Dowmunt, refers to an 'MTV generation'. At first sight it would seem that 'national culture is ruptured along the age faultline' with the teenage-plus age group having, through the enculturalizing impact of MTV, more in common with teenage-plus in other countries than with their own older generations.

However, as Sturmer says, 'The key problem for MTV E [Europe] is that European youth is not a homogeneous entity, and its aim must therefore be to combine global marketing with targeted regional consumers.' MTV's burgeoning success raises a number of questions about cultural dominance. For example, is American pop about to rule the world (if it does not do so already) and by doing so, demolish all locally created rivals? There are anomalies too, as Corinna Sturmer points out: 'In the political climate of the post-communist world, MTV's Janus-faced nature comes to light. While constructing its appeal around the rebellious image and anti-authoritarian values of rock-'n'-roll, at the same time it typifies and exists to serve the interests of advanced consumer capital.'

Multi-actuality The meaning of communication signs – language – is not fixed but subject to differing interpretations according to context. The term originated with Valentin Volosinov in *Marxism and the Philosophy of Language* (US: Seminar Press, 1973; first published in Russian, 1929–30) who argued that the prevailing MEANING of a word or expression – such as democracy or freedom, for example – works towards the suppression of multi-actuality, except in terms of 'social crises or revolutionary changes'. In other words, the dominant hierarchy will strive to impose its own meaning – one meaning as opposed to many. Signs, therefore, Volosinov believes, may become the 'arena for the class struggle' as the dominant group of interpreters of meaning strive to eradicate alternative meanings. See HEGEMONY; IDEOLOGY; METAPHOR.

Multiplane Walt Disney (1901–66) used this word to explain an innovation in the process of ANIMATION, illustrated in *Fantasia* (1940). Instead of building up a drawing by laying 'cells' one directly on top of the other, an illusion of depth was achieved by a space being left between the celluloid images of foreground, background and principal figures.

Multiple image A number of images printed beside each other on the same film frame, often showing different camera angles of the same action, or separate actions. Abel Gance (1889–1981) used this device with stunning effect in his masterpiece of 1926, *Napoleon*.

Multiplier effect Where CULTURE as a commodity – usually in the form of films and TV programmes – exported to other countries, opens up markets for other goods. James Monaco in 'Images and sounds as cultural commodities', in *Sight & Sound*, Autumn 1980, quotes American professor Dallas Smythe: 'The distribution of television programmes around the world from the United States … has the double purpose of making money for itself and serving as the front runner for the industry of the country which produced it. It is a form of advertisement; it is like the battleships, gunboats, which used to show the flag.' See MEDIA IMPERIALISM.

Murdoch effect Arising from the dominance of the media by Rupert Murdoch and his global organization MediaCorp in several countries, the term relates to the connection between JOURNALISM and money. Quoted in John Pilger's *Hidden Agenda* (UK: Vintage, 1998), prize-winning journalist Reiner

Luyken believes that 'Whether you read the *Daily Mirror* or the *Telegraph* or turn on the BBC, you get the feeling that the purpose of the enterprise of journalism has been turned on its head and the new ethic is that journalism is a commodity, purely to generate money. This is the Murdoch effect.'

Musical: film musical Essentially the invention and hallmark of the US, and of Broadway, New York, in particular. Though *The Jazz Singer* (1927) was not by any means the first film to be accompanied by music, it is nevertheless classified as the first film musical as well as the 'talkie' that made the break-through for SYNCHRONOUS SOUND. The first all-talking, all-singing, all-dancing film was *The Broadway Melody* (1929).

Colour in musicals was used with earliest success in *The Wizard of Oz* (1939). The heyday of the musical stretched glitteringly from the 1930s to the end of the 1950s when vastly increased production costs and the decline in mass audiences made musicals uneconomical. They were replaced in their extrava-gance with musical stories such as *Oklahoma!* (1955), *West Side Story* (1961) and *My Fair Lady* (1965), with *The Sound of Music* (1965) capping all at the box office. Imitations failed, though *Cabaret* (1972) proved that old forms and old patterns could be creatively extended; while, against the odds, *Moulin Rouge* (2000) and *Chicago* (2003) proved critical and box office successes.

Music: censorship of music The entire edition of *Index on Censorship* 6, 1998, was given over to a survey, worldwide, of the CENSORSHIP of music. In an editorial, Ursula Owen, Marie Korpe and Ole Reitov state that 'Music is probably the most censored art form' and that its subversive nature 'has long been recognized by rulers, religions and moralists'. Banning the performance of music, or its broadcast-ing, is only one mode of censorship. When the generals seized power in Chile in 1976, the popular folk singer Victor Jara was 'silenced' forever by being tortured and beaten to death. In Somalia in the 1980s, opera star Maryam Mursal was arrested, sacked from the National Opera, forbidden to perform and eventually forced into exile for her song 'Ulimada', a critique of the regime of General Mohammed Siyed Barre. In Algeria in 1998, the singer Lounès Matoub, outspoken defender of Berber culture, was murdered.

In the UK the BBC has long exercised music censorship. Events in Northern Ireland prompted the Corporation to refuse airtime to Wings' *Give Ireland Back to the Irish* and, during the first Gulf War (1991), the BBC Radio Training Unit compiled a list of records it considered should be treated with caution during the war.

---

* Martin Cloonan, *Banned! – Censorship of Popular Music in Britain: 1967–92* (UK: Arena, 1996).

Music Television See MTV.

Mystification See HEGEMONY.

Myth The generally accepted meaning of myth is of a fictitious (primitive) tale usually involving super-natural characters embodying some popular idea concerning natural or historical phenomena, often symbolizing virtues or other timeless qualities. In everyday parlance, a myth is something invented, not true. For analysts of the communication process, myth has more specific connotations. Myth is an inter-pretation of the way things are; a justification, a 'charter' as Bronislaw Malinowski (1884–1942) put it. For Claude Lévi-Strauss myth is a force generated to overcome *contradictions*. Either way, at the heart of myth is IDEOLOGY, chiefly the value system of those at the top of society.

The French philosopher Roland Barthes (1915–80) ascribes myth to the second order of SIGNIFICA-TION, that is, CONNOTATION, but connotation with a very special task – to distort, to become a charter, yes, but also an alibi. For Barthes, myth is a weapon of the bourgeoisie, which it uses to regenerate its cultural dominance.

In *Mythologies* (UK: Paladin, 1973), Barthes writes, 'Myth does not deny things, on the contrary, its function is to talk about them; simply, it purifies them, it makes them innocent, it gives them a natural and eternal justification, it gives them a clarity which is not that of an explanation but that of a statement of fact.' Myth defines 'eternal verities' that may neither be eternal nor verities. And myth acts economically, 'it abolishes the complexity of human acts, it gives them the simplicity of essences, it does away with all the dialectics, without any going back beyond what is immediately visible, it organizes a world which is without contradictions because it is without depth, a world wide open and wallowing in the evident, it establishes a blissful clarity: things appear to mean something by themselves'.

Myth succours and supports the status quo; its chief inspiration is *order* and its communication mode is RHETORIC. See SEMIOLOGY/SEMIOTICS. See also *TOPIC GUIDE* under MEDIA: POWER, EFFECTS, INFLUENCE; MEDIA: POLITICS AND ECONOMICS; MEDIA: PROCESSES AND PRODUCTION: MEDIA: VALUES AND IDEOLOGIES; REPRESENTATION.

---

* Jonathan Cuffer, *Barthes* (UK: Fontana, 1983).

Myths of deregulation See DEREGULATION, FIVE MYTHS OF.

N

Narcotizing dysfunction One of the chief social consequences of AUDIENCE exposure over time to the mass media, in the view of P.H. Lazarsfeld and R. Merton in 'Communication, taste and social action', in L. Bryson (ed.), *The Communication of Ideas* (US: Harper & Row, 1948). This rather awful-sounding affliction, of first being subdued, or 'drugged', and then put out of action, comes about, believe the authors, because audiences are reduced to 'mass apathy' by a heroic effort to keep up with the vast amount of information placed before them.

'Mass communications may be included among the most respectable and efficient of social narcotics … increasing dosages of mass communications may be inadvertently transforming the energies of men from active participation into passive knowledge.' See COMPASSION FATIGUE; EFFECTS OF THE MASS MEDIA; USES AND GRATIFICATIONS THEORY; MAINSTREAMING.

Narration In, for example, a TV documentary, what the narrator or the voiceover tells the AUDIENCE helps structure both programme and response. Narration is the intermediary between 'raw information' and the ordered DISCOURSE or TEXT. In his monograph *Television Discourse and History* (UK: British Film Institute, 1980), Colin McArthur argues that the 'central ideological function of narration is to confer authority on, and to elide contradictions in, the discourse'. Narration, therefore, serves to identify and help further an ideological base.

Narration is as much a technical convenience as an ideological mechanism. It is a time-saver; permits summary; allows for efficient transition; it is custom-built for an expensive, time-conscious medium. Given creative independence, many programme producers have reduced the dominance of narrative or done away with it altogether, as much as possible letting the world 'speak for itself' by using sound and vision without comment; allowing camera and microphone to eavesdrop on activities free from a FRAMING narrative.

Of course the process of MEDIATION is ultimately unavoidable – cameras have to be set up in one place or another; pointed in one direction rather than another; decisions have to be made about long-shot and close-up and, finally, the film has to be edited: even without a narrator, a *story* has been told; reality has been reconstructed. See CODES OF NARRATIVE; NARRATIVE; NARRATIVE PARADIGM; SYMBOLIC CONVERGENCE THEORY.

Narrative In *Narratives in Popular Culture, Media, and Everyday Life* (UK: Sage, 1997) Arthur Asa Berger defines narrative as 'a story, and stories tell about things that have happened or are happening, to people, animals, aliens from outer space, insects – whatever. That is, a story contains a sequence of events, which means that narratives take place within or over, to be more precise, some kind of time period. This time period can be very short, as in a nursery tale, or very long, as in some novels and epics.'

As Berger picturesquely puts it, our lives are 'immersed in narratives. Every day we swim in a sea of stories and tales … from our earliest days to our deaths.' Inevitably, then, the study of communication is very much concerned with the study of narratives – how they are put together, what their functions are and what uses are made of them by those who read, listen to or watch stories. In the view of Michel de Certeau in *The Practice of Everyday Life* (US: University of California, 1984), narratives 'articulate our existences'; indeed, we as social, communal animals, are 'defined by stories'.

At the level of denotation narratives tell us what happened to whom and in what circumstances; at the CONNOTATIONAL level we enter the realm of MEANING, of signification: what is the story really about? This applies as much to NEWS stories as to fictional stories; indeed the news can be classified as a GENRE, that is, a mode of narrative that conforms (for the most part) to a particular set of rules.

In 1926 George Herbert Mead (in 'The nature of aesthetic experience', in the *International Journal of Ethics* 36) defined two models of JOURNALISM – the information model and the story model – stating that 'the reporter is generally sent out to get a story not the facts'. The storyness theme is taken up by Peter Dahlgren in his *Introduction to Journalism and Popular Culture* (UK: Sage, 1992, edited by Dahlgren and Colin Sparks). He writes that 'Storytelling ... is a key link which unites journalism and popular culture ... narrative is a way of knowing the world.' He goes on: 'Journalism officially aims to inform about events in the world – analytical mode – and does this most often in the story mode', which both 'enhances and delimits the likely range of meanings'.

Above all, like social rituals generally, the story mode has the power to bring about a sense of shared experience and of shared VALUES. This, it might be said, is the 'story' of news, its connotational function: it is about cohesion-making as much as it is about information-transmission (see STRUCTURE OF NEWS: REASSURANCE).

In this multi-media age narratives more than ever before interact and overlap but for convenience – of analysis and study – they continue to be classified under the heading of genres, each with its own narrative rules and traditions, each with recognizable FRAMING devices. In some genres the frame is tight, highly restrictive to the point of being ritualistic. Other genres have 'flexible' framing and offer the potential for change and development. SOAP OPERAS have this potential, situation comedies (SIT-COMS) less so, contends Jasper Rees in the UK *Independent*, reviewing the second festival of sit-coms run by the UK's Channel 4. In his article 'Slap 'n' Tickle', 30 July 1996, Rees says, 'In a play, events take place which irrepressibly alter the relationship between the characters. Whatever happens in a sitcom, you always go back to square one at the start of a fresh episode; the idea of stasis is built into the design. No doubt sooner or later a writer will come along and create a sitcom which breaks new ground, though this will depend as much upon external framing mechanisms such as programming and popularity as the nature of the genre itself.'

Each genre contains a range of signifiers, of conventions that audiences recognize and come to expect while at the same time readily accepting experiment with those conventions. Knowledge of the conventions on the part of audience, and recognition when convention is flouted, suggests an active 'union' between the encoder and the decoder. Audience, as it were, is 'let in on the act'; and this 'knowingness' is an important part of the enjoyment of narrative genres. When the hero in a western chooses not to wear a gun (a great rarity), audience (because we are familiar with tradition) recognizes the salience of this decision. Such recognition could be said to constitute a form of participation.

We use our familiarity with old 'routines' as a frame for reading this new twist of narrative. We wonder whether convention will be flouted altogether as the story proceeds or whether the rules of the genre will be reasserted by the hero taking up the gun to bring about a resolution to the story. For a soap opera, *time* is a key element in the framing process. There are 30-minute slots to be filled, each to conclude with unfinished business, preferably dramatic and suspenseful, while not being so dramatically 'final' that the series cannot continue into an indefinite future.

Soap narratives need time to bed down, unfold, and in their own time they reflect the time-scales of audience. In some cases, the time-frame of the soap is as important as the time-frames within it. The soap 'frame', thus amply provided with time, requires many characters and many plots. The narrative template or mould out of which soaps emerge is, give or take an adjustment, the same or similar to that which produces popular narratives of all kinds, including the news. They must attract and hold attention. They must gratify both COGNITIVE (intellectual) and affective (emotional) needs. They must facilitate IDENTIFICATION, personal reference as well as diversion (see USES AND GRATI-FICATIONS THEORY). They must meet the needs of a certain type of audience at a certain time of day while at the same time fulfilling such criteria as commercial viability which in turn is conditional upon ratings and audience share.

Another key element of narratives is what is termed *binary* framing, that is the story being structured in terms of opposites: heroes–villains; good–evil; kind–cruel; tolerant–intolerant; beautiful–ugly. In *Narratives … Asa Berger* talks of 'central oppositions'. Stories are built around protagonists who are archetypal, with character traits that are readily recognized – heroes, heroines, villains and victims (see PROPP'S PEOPLE). Something happens, an event producing a state of *disequilibrium*, of imbalance, that has to be corrected or resolved; and in the resolution we may read a MESSAGE, a moral – about valour or self-sacrifice.

Robert C. Allen, writing in *Channels of Discourse: Television and Contemporary Criticism* (UK: Routledge, 1987, edited by Allen), differentiates between what he calls the *Hollywood narrative mode* and the *rhetorical mode*. The first hides the *means* by which the text is created. It invites audience to believe that what they are seeing is real: one is absorbed into the text without being, as it were, addressed by it. In contrast, the rhetorical mode directly addresses the viewer. The news, Allen sees presented in this way: the newsreader looks directly out at us; and similar formats can be recognized in cooking, sports and gardening programmes on TV: 'The texts are not only presented for us, but directed out at us.'

Asa Berger concludes his book by affirming the importance of narrative analysis in the study of communication: 'We used to think of the stories we read, listen to, and watch as little more than trivial amusements to "kill time". Now we know that people learn from stories, are emotionally affected by them, and actually need stories to lend colour and interest to their everyday lives.' See CODES OF NARRATIVE; NARRATIVE PARADIGM. See also *TOPIC GUIDE* under LANGUAGE/DISCOURSE/NARRATIVE.

Narrative codes See CODES OF NARRATIVE.

Narrative: kernel and satellite Terms defined by Seymour Chatman in *Story and Discourse: Narrative Structure in Fiction and Film* (US: Cornell University Press, 1978) to describe structural elements in narrative. The *kernel* is an event or decision crucial to the advance of the plot, serving to direct the story's progress and development.

A *satellite* is a minor feature of the story that embellishes the plot, adding detail, fleshing out the narrative. Chatman writes of kernels as 'narrative moments that give rise to cruxes in the direction taken by events. They are nodes or hinges in the structure, branching points which force a movement into one of two (or more) possible paths'. Satellites are secondary elements that feed in to the kernal. Their loss would not seriously hinder the plot development. Without kernels, however, there would be no story.

Narrative paradigm Theory that sees people as essentially storytellers, defining humankind as *homo narrans*. A substantial section of the Autumn 1985 edition of the *Journal of Communication* was devoted to an analysis, by a variety of contributors, of the notion that if storytelling is central to human DISCOURSE and interaction, then the paradigm provides an important METAPHOR for communications research, which has its own story – its own narrative base – rooted in beliefs about truth and falsehood, fact and fiction, and the nature of reason.

Walter R. Fisher, Professor of Communication Arts and Sciences at the University of Southern California, in 'The narrative paradigm: in the beginning', believes that rationality in humans is determined by the nature of persons as narrative beings, by 'their inherent awareness of narrative probability, what constitutes a coherent story, and their constant habit of testing narrative fidelity, whether the stories they experience ring true with stories they know in their lives'. He goes on, 'the world is a set of stories which must be chosen among to live the good life in a process of continual recreation'.

Narratives: grand narratives See POSTMODERNISM.

Narrowcasting As contrasted with *broad*casting; the term describes the process whereby programme-makers and advertisers aim at 'special-interest' audiences, from gardening to golf, from astronomy to cookery; or at special levels of AUDIENCE distinguished by, for example, social CLASS, education or spending power.

National Film Archive (UK) Founded in May 1935, the NFA is the largest division of the BRITISH FILM INSTITUTE. Its role is to acquire, preserve and make available for study a collection of films and TV programmes of all kinds exhibited or transmitted in the UK from any source and of any nationality. Particular emphasis is placed on British productions, which may have lasting value as works of art, examples of film or TV history or as valuable records of past and present contemporary behaviour.

National Viewers' and Listeners' Association (NVLA) See 'CLEAN UP TV' MOVEMENT.

Naturalistic illusion (of television) The visual qualities of TV can lead to the assumption that it is merely a window on the world, showing life as it really is. Stuart Hall in 'The rediscovery of "ideology"', in M. Gurevitch, T. Bennett, J. Curran and J. Woollacott (eds), *Culture, Society and the Media* (UK: Methuen, 1982), refers to this phenomenon as the 'naturalistic illusion'. TV programmes are in fact the result of considerable planning and research.

Elaborate procedures of FRAMING, editing and the matching of images with dialogue have to be undertaken in order to present an exposition. During these procedures decisions are taken that may significantly affect the finished presentation. Different impressions can be given, for example, of a demonstration depending upon when or where the film is taken and how it is edited. In short, what TV produces is a *construct* of reality as perceived by those with the power to represent it, and transmit it to the public. See IDEOLOGY.

Necessity, supervening social necessity (technology) See SUPERVENING SOCIAL NECESSITY.

Needs See MASLOW'S HIERARCHY OF NEEDS.

Negative news values See NEW VALUES.

Negative semantic space See MALE-AS-NORM.

Negativization See VISIONS OF ORDER.

Negotiated code See DOMINANT, SUBORDINATE, RADICAL.

Neologism The invention or usage of a new word, or giving an old word a new MEANING, such as 'viewer' from the French 'voyeur' to indicate someone who views other people's, sometimes illicit, activities. One of the most picturesque neologisms in the area of media is COUCH POTATO.

Net See INTERNET.

Network Channels of communication that are interconnected are termed networks, to be found in all communication in which numbers of people are involved, such as GROUPS and organizations. Basically a communication network consists of linked dyads in which the *receiver* in one DYAD is the source in the next. Such networks will vary in size, and not all members of the network will necessarily

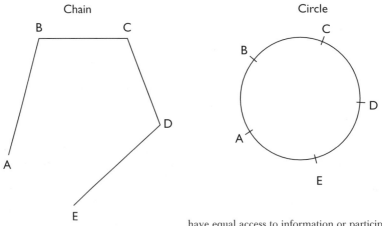

have equal access to information or participation.

Examples of communication networks

A communication structure is a network in which some channels are systematically neglected. Generally speaking the greater the number of links between members, and the closer the distance between them, the more likely it is that information is distributed equally; assuming all members communicate through all the links at their disposal.

In a network with a high level of centrality it is likely that some members will possess more information than others. Communication networks may take several forms, such as the two illustrated here. Networks may vary as to the ease with which individual members can be isolated from fellow members, and some networks will suffer more than others from the removal of a member or a link. If a member or link is missing from a chain network, for example, the effect is likely to be more serious than if either were missing from a circle network.

A network may also spawn a sub-network: a sub-network can be said to exist when the number of links between certain members is greater than the number of links between these members and others.

The term network is used in BROADCASTING to describe the pattern of connection of the broadcasting stations of a broadcasting company or companies. Such a connection allows the simultaneous broadcast of the same programme. To network a programme means to broadcast it to the widest number of TV/radio stations both within one network and in other networks. In the US, the term is used more specifically: the networks are those companies that commission programmes and programme series.

Perhaps the most familiar use of the term network applies to those established *electronically*. Computer networks (see INTERNET) are key to practically every aspect of modern life, at the personal, national and global levels. See DIGITIZATION; SURVEILLANCE SOCIETY.

Newcomb's ABX model of communication, 1953 In contrast to the linear structure of SHANNON AND WEAVER'S MODEL OF COMMUNICATION, 1949, Theodore H. Newcomb's model is triangular in shape, and is the first to introduce as a factor the role of communication in a society or a social relationship. A and B are communicators and X is the situation or social context in which the communication takes place. Both the individuals are orientated to each other and to X, and communication is conceived of as the process that supports this *orientational* structure. Symmetry or balance is maintained between the three elements by the transmission of information about any change in circumstance or relationship, thus allowing adjustment to take place.

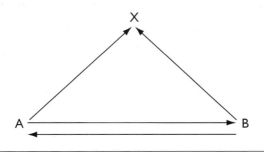

Newcomb's ABX model

For Newcomb, the process of communication is one of the interdependent factors maintaining *equilibrium*, or as Newcomb himself puts it in 'An approach to the study of communicative acts', in *Psychological Review* 60 (1953) 'communication among human beings performs the essential functions of enabling two or more individuals to maintain simultaneous orientation to each other and towards objects of an external environment'. See CONGRUENCE THEORY; McCOMBS AND SHAW'S AGENDA-SETTING MODEL OF MEDIA EFFECTS, 1976; McLEOD AND CHAFFEE'S 'KITE' MODEL, 1973; WESLEY AND MACLEAN'S MODEL OF COMMUNICATION, 1957.

New International Information Order See NEW WORLD INFORMATION ORDER.

News The study of news is central to most if not all courses in communication and media studies. Like information itself, the news is a vital component of the life of individuals, GROUPS, communities and nations. News brings us information, several times daily, often on the hour.

Whether it is in print or broadcast form, the news re-presents to us the world – reality; and every student soon learns that the news is a process, or rather an amalgam of many processes that mediate information: select it, edit it, emphasize some parts of it, distort it, even manipulate it. News – that is, the raw information that is eventually constructed as news – is turned into NARRATIVE, a mode of storytelling, which by the application of certain professional practices – conventions – establishes what has come to be termed news DISCOURSE.

In this sense, news can actually be described as 'olds': what has by precedent been counted as news continues to be classified and used as news. We become acutely aware of the *selective* nature of news, of the fact that, for example, the ELITE – persons, societies, nations – appear more often in the news than ordinary people or less prestigious societies and nations. And there is a reciprocal nature about inclusion in the news: if you are important, the news covers what you do or say; if the news covers what you do or say, what you do or say becomes better known. You become a Known instead of an Unknown.

The focus of study will shift from the analysis of news *sources*, to the predisposition, reportorial approach, and the constraints upon that approach, of the *practitioners* of news; and their activities will be examined in micro and macro situations. At the micro level we would scrutinize the relationship of a practitioner to the organization that employs him/her, and thus directs and influences his or her professional activities.

At the macro level we would study the influences from outside the organization, from society itself: what part in shaping news content and presentation does big business have, or government, or the law? What social, cultural, economic or political pressures are brought to bear on news production that will influence the shape and tenor of it as it reaches the audience?

We would be equally interested in how the news was put together, how decisions are made about what is considered important or less important. This might lead us into an investigation of AGENDA-SETTING, in turn providing us with a useful guide to the processes of GATEKEEPING. The agenda controls the gate; but what controls the agenda? We would need to explore the basic principles of what information, at any given time, is considered *newsworthy*. We would focus on the NEWS VALUES that both practitioners and media analysts have identified as influencing decision-making.

Very importantly, we would be interested in investigating how news is *received* by AUDIENCE. We would attempt to discover how audiences actually *use* the news; how far it actually does inform them, and whether it influences them. We soon understand that news reconstructs the world according to the *perceptions* of those who produce the news, and those who employ or influence the news producers; and we would be interested in discovering to what extent audiences take on board the 'reality' presented by news.

In examining the approaches to news production and presentation we would be alert to the capacity of audience to choose *alternative* readings to the realities with which they are being presented. We will most certainly have noted how news presentation has developed over the years: that it is more lively than ever before in style and content; that it is more entertaining. We might need to ask whether such developments have increased or decreased audience comprehension of the matters being presented: how much of what is read or seen on TV news is fully grasped, *contextualized*; indeed, how much of it has been retained as meaningful information?

No form of public communication has a higher profile than news production, and management and issues relating to this concern a number of high aspirations – *objectivity*, *balance* and *impartiality* – each difficult to define both in theory and practice. Many commentators would argue that a more pressing issue is the nature of ownership and control and whether, in any given society, there is a *plurality* in the ways information and opinion are presented.

Finally, news and news production have to be seen in relation to trends – the impact of new media technologies, the *transnationalization* of media ownership, the *privatization* of public media services and the *globalization* of message/meaning systems. See NEWS: AUDIENCE EVALUATION, SIX DIMENSIONS OF; NEWS: AUDIENCES FOR NEWS; NEWS: STRUCTURE OF

REASSURANCE; NEWS: THE 'MALENESS' OF NEWS. For a full listing, see *TOPIC GUIDE* under NEWS MEDIA.

News agencies 'The invention of the news agency,' writes Anthony Smith in *The Geopolitics of Information* (UK: Faber, 1980), 'was the most important single development in the newspaper industry in the early 1800s, apart from the rotary press.' The early agencies – Reuters, Havas and Wolff – carved up the world into spheres of activity in much the same way as imperialist nations parcelled out 'Third World' territories between them.

In 1869 the major agencies signed an Agency Alliance Treaty. Reuters was 'granted' the British Empire and the whole of the Far East; Havas – a French agency – was granted Italy, Spain, France and the Portuguese empires and the Germany-based Wolff received Austria, Scandinavia and Russia. America was awarded jointly to Havas and Reuters.

Today, the biggest agencies are the Associated Press (AP), the Press Association (PA, created as early as 1868), Reuters and United Press International. Out of the traditional, print-centred news agencies have developed international television news agencies such as Visnews (owned by Reuters, the BBC and NBC), WTN and Worldwide Television News (owned by Independent Television News and United Press International) distributing TV news material around the clock, both 'raw' footage and complete news stories ready for transmission.

Concern has focused on the role of international news agencies in giving world news a *western* 'slant' through the operation of NEWS VALUES reflecting the IDEOLOGY of western nations' news flow. Jeremy Tunstall in *The Media Are American* (UK: Constable, 1994) argues that the British and two US agencies '… have acquired special international legitimacy' due to the widespread perception that their news is more *neutral* and accurate than alternatives.

According to Tunstall, 'These agencies have largely shaped the presentation of international news in all countries around the world; these agencies do not merely play a major part in establishing the international political agenda, but they have done so now for a hundred years. And for a hundred years they have been the main definers of world "news values", of what sort of things have become news'.

Of special interest to researchers has been the nature of the *flow* of information for which the agencies are responsible, and the degree to which that flow is *mediated*. What has been termed *raw* news flows from the periphery to the centre, but on the way it becomes *cooked* news – constructed according to western production values; while the flow of information from the centre is almost invariably cooked – shaped, that is, according to western news values. See EVENT; MEDIA IMPERIALISM; NEW WORLD INFORMATION ORDER; NON-ALIGNED NEWS POOL.

News Aid? Paul Harrison and Robin Palmer use this term in their book *News Out of Africa: Biafra to Band Aid* (UK: Hilary Shipman, 1986), to illustrate the ambivalent relationship between the media's coverage of the dramatic and distressing effects of famine in the so-called 'Third World', particularly Africa. The authors note the media's long-term reticence, in news or current affairs programmes, to participate in a DISCOURSE about the underlying causes of such famine and ways in which famines might be prevented. Such reticence begs the question of whether or not coverage of the effects of famine, however galvanizing of public opinion and action in the short term, really aids finding a solution to the problem.

Indeed, some commentators argue that the media's tendency to concentrate reporting of Third World countries, like Africa, around issues of natural disasters or conflict leads to the perpetuation of negative and stereotypical images of Third World citizens. Liam Kane in 'Media Studies and images of the "Third World"', in the Spring 1994 edition of *Media Education*, comments that '"Third World" people tend to be portrayed very negatively, as passive victims of an unexplained poverty.' The consequence, he goes on to argue, is that we can 'easily blame poverty on a combination of "natural disasters" and the supposed ignorance, laziness or backwardness of Asians, Africans, and Latin Americans'.

What are often overlooked are the structural causes of these problems that lie in both national and international inequalities in the distribution of resources and power and the resilience and achievement of Third World citizens despite their often formidably adverse circumstances. Another fear is of course that concentration on the symptoms rather than the causes of disasters, like famine, may lead ultimately to a dulling of the audience's sensibility to them. See COMPASSION FATIGUE.

News: audience evaluation, six dimensions of In 'Research note: the effects of live television reporting on recall and appreciation of political news', in *European Journal of Communication*, March 2000, Roland Snoeijer, Claes H. de Vreese and Holli A. Semetoko examine 'the evaluative judgment that viewers make of television news'. They pose six *evaluative dimensions*: Credibility, Importance, Involvement, Attractiveness, Immediacy and Comprehensibility.

TV news scores highly in terms of audience belief in its credibility, in part because viewers not only see what is happening, but, as a result of SATELLITE TRANSMISSION, they can see events as they are actually happening. 'The concept of importance,' write the authors, 'refers to the implications or impact that a story is believed to have for society as a whole', viewers taking their cue from 'the importance of a story defined by newsmakers' (see AGENDA-SETTING). Involvement relates to NEWS VALUES, and centres around personal likes and dislikes, interests and geographical proximity.

'Information,' consider the authors, 'is found to be attractive if it is vivid, lively and attention grabbing' though perceptions and responses vary in impact, some GROUPS of people 'finding it very attractive, others disturbing', and this dimension, as with credibility, applies to both the content and presentation of the news.

The speed at which TV news can report events – its immediacy – is highly appreciated by the audience for news. Finally, viewers need to believe that 'that they have received the information in a comprehensible way' and the success in this relates to the way news stories are structured and the way they tackle the complexity of events. See FRAMING: NEWS.

News: audience for news The Pew Research Center of the US, in a phone survey conducted between April and May 1998, identified six groups of news consumers in America. The results, stated the Center's research report, indicated 'how differently the generations are responding to the information explosion'. The news-consuming groups identified were: (1) the *Mainstream news* audience, deemed to have 'middle-of-the-road' preferences; newspaper readers who also regularly tune in to local and networked TV news shows; (2) the *Basically broadcast* audience, relying primarily for its news on TV; (3) the *Very occasional* audience, which 'only follows the news when something major is happening'; (4) the *Constant* audience 'that watches, reads and listens to just about everything – seemingly indiscriminately'; (5) the *Serious news* audience, equally committed but more selective; and (6) the *Tabloid* audience, which 'rejects broadcast news and favours the *National Enquirer*, tabloid TV and the tell-all talk show ...'.

'Ironically,' the Pew report states, 'the daily newspaper, the oldest format, is the only news source used regularly by a majority of all groups.' See *TOPIC GUIDE* under AUDIENCES/CONSUMPTION AND RECEPTION OF MEDIA.

News consensus See CONSISTENCY.

News elements: breaking, explanatory, deep background In an article, 'Public broadcasting: imperfect but essential', posted on the openDemocracy website (www.openDemocracy.net), 26 June 2001, Jean Seaton identifies three central elements of news provision: (1) *Breaking news*, what she describes as 'attention-grabbing top stories that are often visually dramatic ... that attract audiences by virtue of their drama'; (2) *Explanatory* or 'understanding' news – longer-format news programmes such as the UK's Channel 4 early evening news, 'which provides some context to understand headlines and breaking news'; and (3) *Deep background* news formats 'that track issues to the root'.

In Seaton's view, examples of the third element 'are rare – that's part of the problem', for she sees, in the light of new technologies, of digital CONVERGENCE and remorseless pressures of competition, the threat of cost-cutting and the undermining of deep background, investigatory JOURNALISM. She considers that 'mainstream broadcast news is wilting under the pressure of the market and is losing intelligence, style, authority and audience'. She argues that 'In a world of globalized corporate power, full scale detailed investigation is essential to provide the public with the truth about what is going on.' See DEREGULATION; NEWS, GLOBALIZATION OF.

News frameworks Consist of a shared set of assumptions by reporters and editors about what is newsworthy. These assumptions influence the selection of items for investigation and reporting, and to some extent how they will be presented. This set of assumptions also enables journalists and editors to relate news items to an image of society in order to give them MEANING. Thus the framework can provide a 'ready reckoner' for constructing as well as selecting news, which allows deadlines to be met. See FRAMING: MEDIA; NEWS VALUES.

News, globalization of Satellite technology coupled with trends in transnational media ownership and control have created global patterns of information transmission characterized by both CONVERGENCE and diversity. TV news services worldwide show marked similarities of content and narrative approach when stories of international dimensions are being reported. In contrast, diversity is maintained when national and local stories are dealt with.

In 'The global newsroom: convergences and diversities in the globalization of television news', in *Communication and Citizenship: Journalism and the Public Sphere* (UK: Routledge, 1991) edited by Peter Dahlgren and Colin Sparks, Michael Gurevitch, Mark R. Levy and Itzhak Roeh write that convergence is in part predicated by the availability, worldwide, of pictures, and reinforces what the authors term a measure of 'shared professional culture', a certain 'commonality in news values and news judgments, across all services'.

However, diversity asserts itself in 'lesser items' suggesting 'that this sharing of news values is not complete and that national social and political differences, as well as journalistic norms between nations, also play a part in shaping patterns of news coverage'.

Examples are cited of how globally available film footage is actually harnessed to national meanings – same pictures, different reading. This in the opinion of the authors is a practice offering 'an important antidote to "naive universalism" – that is, to the assumption that events reported in the news carry their own meanings, and that the meanings embedded in news stories produced in one country can therefore be generalized to news stories told in other societies'.

Gurevitch *et al.* identify what they call the 'domestication of the foreign', that is, foreign stories are 'told in ways which render them more familiar, more comprehensive and more compatible for consumption by different national audiences'. TV news, then, anchored as it generally tends to be 'in narrative frameworks that are already familiar to and recognizable by news men as well as by audiences situated in particular cultures', 'simultaneously maintains both global and culturally specific orientations'. The domestication of the foreign serves as a 'countervailing force to the pull of globalization'. See AUDIENCE: ACTIVE AUDIENCE.

News-literate Term used by John Hartley in *Understanding News* (UK: Methuen, 1982) to describe the ability of a reader, listener or viewer to comprehend the norms, codes and conventions of news programmes; to intelligently scan the news, 'recognize its familiar cast of characters and events', and to be able to spontaneously 'interpret the world at large in terms of the codes we have learnt from the news'. See NEWS VALUES.

News management Refers to the tactics employed by those – usually in government or important positions in society – who wish to shape the news to their own advantage, or to control events in such a way as to win favourable publicity. In recent years the operative word to describe news management is *spin*. The so-termed spin doctors, drawn almost invariably from the ranks of professional JOURNALISM, are essentially in the business of PROPAGANDA, that is talking up the good news and concealing as far as possible the bad.

Where the communication of bad news is unavoidable, a favourite ploy of the spin doctors is to issue that bad news when other events are attracting media and public attention. The danger here is that such spin, instead of distracting attention, achieves the opposite, while at the same time incurring accusations of deceit. See PREFERRED READING.

Newspaper price wars See PREDATORY PRICING.

Newspapers, origins The earliest newspapers in Britain were far more internationalist in outlook and interest than they tend to be today. The reason for this was the extensive CENSORSHIP of home news by monarch and council. As early as the seventeenth century there was the so-called *Relation*, the publication of a single news story, usually related long after the events. The *Coranto* served to join individual Relations into a continuity, though still not appearing regularly. The *Diurnall* was a step forward, providing a weekly account of occurrences over several days. Like the others before it, the *Mercury* appeared in book-like form, but bore more prominently the individual stamp of writers, and tended to be more immediate and more diverse. During the English Civil War (1642–49) *Mercuries* appeared in great abundance, even on Sundays.

Contemporaneous with the *Mercury* was the *Intelligencer*, usually more formal, aspiring to be 'official'. A notable example was *The Publick Intelligencer* published with the blessing of Protector Oliver Cromwell. Indeed, the street journalism of all kinds that emerged in the heady days of the Civil War laid the basis for the popular journalism we recognize today. In the 20 years between 1640 and the restoration of the monarchy under Charles II, 30,000 news publications and pamphlets emerged in London alone.

The date usually cited for London's first regular daily paper is 1702. The intention of Samuel Buckley's *Daily Courant* was 'to give news, give it daily and impartially', and it continued for 6000 editions. By 1750 London had five daily papers, six thrice-weeklies, five weeklies and several other periodicals, all amounting to a circulation of 100,000 copies a week.

The Stamp Act of 1712 heralded over a century of increasing concern on the part of the authorities about the proliferation and influence of newspapers. Government agents reported on the contents of newspapers and there was a bristling array of laws to use against the press, such as seditious libel and profanation.

Of dubious legality but considerable effectiveness was the general warrant enabling arrests and seizures of unnamed persons to be made by the King's Messengers, practically at their discretion. Though several warrants were no longer legal after 1766, the stamp duty and other taxes on knowledge were burgeoning until the middle of the nineteenth century when massive and sustained press and popular pressure led to the reduction and eventual abolition of the duties.

New technology, the growth of ADVERTISING and a more literate general public contributed to a massive expansion of newspapers in the latter half of the nineteenth century. In 1821 there had been 267 newspapers, including weeklies, in the UK and by 1861, 1102. Newspaper trains, which began running in 1876, meant that the London papers could reach all parts of the country, while TELEGRAPHY speeded news, increasingly provided by the NEWS AGENCIES (Paul Julius Reuter opened his London office in 1851). By 1880 London had 18 dailies; in the English provinces there were 96 dailies, four in Wales, 21 in Scotland and 17 in Ireland.

The most dramatic example of the rise in the popularity of newspapers was the boom in Sunday papers, whose audience, writes Anthony Smith in *The Newspaper: An International History* (UK: Thames & Hudson, 1979), 'came increasingly to consist of the newly literate who could not afford six papers a week and were interested in non-political news. The Sunday journals traded in horrible murders, ghastly seductions and lurid rapes, but they were combined with a distinct brand of radicalism.' Edward Lloyd's *Weekly News*, founded in 1842, was the first periodical to reach a circulation of a million, leaving the highest-selling daily paper, the *Daily Telegraph*, with a 200,000 circulation, well behind.

The pattern for the future was set: new technology facilitated (and made economically necessary) massive print runs; journalism aimed for vast readerships; advertising became more and more the staple financial support of the press; ownership rested with very rich individuals or joint stock companies; readership patterns hardened along lines of social CLASS – and competition became increasingly desperate. See DEMOCRACY AND THE MEDIA; JOURNALISM; NORTHCLIFFE REVOLUTION; PHOTO-JOURNALISM; PRESS BARONS. See also *TOPIC GUIDE* under MEDIA HISTORY.

Newspeak As opposed to Oldspeak in George Orwell's novel *Nineteen Eighty-Four* (1949), where private thought and individual language were crimes against the totalitarian state of Oceania, and where the TV screen could actually hear what viewers were saying and see whether they were indulging in one of the worst of all crimes: private reading. Guardian of Newspeak – the official language divested of all superfluities by the meaning defined by the State – was the Ministry of Truth (which, incidentally, had a sub-section called Pornsoc).

Orwell's Appendix to the novel, 'The Principles of Newspeak', explains that Newspeak was 'not only to provide a medium of expression for the world-view and mental habits proper to the devotees of Ingsoc (English Socialism), but to make all other modes of thought impossible'. Though the word 'free' would be retained in Newspeak, its meaning applied in the sense of 'This dog is free from lice.'

Newsreel The Lumière brothers fathered newsreel film at the birth of the cinema, from 1895, but the first regular newsreel, *Pathé Journal*, began in 1908, and French influence upon news on film was considerable for many years.

The First World War (1914–18) gave impetus to newsreel, especially in Germany, and with the Revolution in Russia (1917) propaganda-newsreel (see AGITPROP) was regarded by the Communist government as being of vital importance in the war for hearts and minds. Dziga Vertov's *Kino-Pravda* newsreel series ran from 1922 to 1925. Companies in the US were the first to add sound to newsreels, and in the UK British Movietone was the first to adopt sound (1928). In the 1930s the outstanding newsreel in the US was the MARCH OF TIME series. News on TV eventually put an end to cinema newsreels. See CINEMATOGRAPHY, ORIGINS; DOCUMENTARY.

Newsroom, The Museum, research and educational centre set up in Farringdon Road, London, in 2002 by the Scott Trust, telling the story of the Trust's sister papers, the *Observer* (the world's oldest Sunday newspaper, over 200 years old) and the *Guardian*.

The Newsroom contains exhibitions of photo-journalism, documents, diaries etc. kept by some of the most distinguished of the papers' writers, features a permanent interactive exhibition telling the history of the two papers, an oral history recording staff recollections going back several decades, and a 90-seat lecture theatre. Students have the opportunity to use the archive's resources and student groups are encouraged to produce their own newspapers using the latest technology.

News selection See AGENDA-SETTING; GALTUNG AND RUGE'S MODEL OF SELECTIVE GATEKEEPING, 1965; NEWS VALUES; PROTOTYING CONCEPT; ROGERS AND DEARING'S AGENDA-SETTING MODEL, 1987.

News: structure of reassurance In *Representing Order: Crime, Law and Justice in the News Media* (UK: Open University Press, 1991), Richard Ericson, Patricia M. Barnek and Janet B.L. Chan argue that in the construction of reality in news production a guiding function of the journalist and editor is to render things 'plausible' and thus 'provide a familiar discourse, based in common sense and precedent'. This plausibility 'in turn provides a structure of reassurance, a tool of acknowledging the familiar': by asserting the plausible-become-familiar the news construction process silences alternative definitions.

News: the 'maleness' of news If the news is to be ascribed a gender classification, some commentators argue that it is essentially 'male': male-orientated in terms of decisions over content, over NEWS VALUES and in the practical matter of who gathers, reports, edits and presents the news.

In *Feminist Media Studies* (UK: Sage, 1994; new edition, 2000), Lisbet van Zoonen argues that women journalists are often expected, by male colleagues and by the organizations employing them, to perform professionally in a manner different from men; to subscribe to expectations of 'femininity': 'Women,' writes van Zoonen, 'are confronted by social and cultural expectations of femininity and at the same time are expected to meet criteria of professionalism', yet there is no evidence that women constitute a different group of professionals from their male counterparts and there was no difference 'in the actual selection of topics or issues'.

Sue Curry Jansen in 'Beaches without bases: the gender order', published in *Invisible Crises: What Conglomerate Control of the Media Means for America and the World* (US: Westview Press, 1996), edited by George Gerbner, Hamid Mowlana and Herbert I. Schiller, states that conditions and prospects for women are equally disadvantaged in the United States. For Jansen, the news generally, and international news in particular, needs to be viewed through the 'prism of gender'.

She talks of an institutionalized bias towards maleness: 'In the United States men write most of the front-page newspaper stories. They are the subject of most of those stories – 85 per cent of the references and 66 per cent of the photos in 1993. They also dominate electronic media, accounting for 86 per cent of the correspondents and 75 per cent of the sources for US network television evening programmes.'

In international news coverage, 'women not only are marginal but also normally absent'. Jansen says, 'Under the present global gender order, policymakers and journalists find it more manly to deal with guns, missiles, and violent conflicts than with matters like female infanticide in China' or 'the increased trade in children in the sex markets of Manila and Bangkok in the wake of the AIDS epidemic …'.

Jansen's views received support from data published in April 1997 by the UK Fawcett Society. During a week's monitoring of election coverage during main news bulletins on the BBC, ITN and Channel 4, it was found that 80 per cent of newsgathering and presentation was carried out by male journalists; and the number of women featured as spokespersons in the news was similarly in a minority. Of 26 government officials asked for their views, none was a woman.

The picture in the twenty-first century so far has arguably improved, at least in terms of the number of women journalists who work in the most dangerous places on earth to report war, atrocity, famine and persecution. The Chechnyan war in Russia, the post-11 September war in Afghanistan, the horrific events in Israel–Palestine in 2002–3 were ably and bravely reported by women, almost to the point when war reporting might be considered a female preserve. Among the UK women journalists proving themselves equals in a traditionally male world are the BBC's Kate Adie and Orla Guerin, and the UK *Guardian's* Maggie O'Kane and Suzanne Goldberg. When, following the rout of the Taliban in Afghanistan, the *Independent Kabul Weekly* was re-born in January 2002, there were three women journalists on the staff.

---

* Penny Colman, *Where the Action Was: Women War Correspondents in World War II* (US: Random House, 2002).

News values According to the former editor of the UK *Sunday Times* and *The Times*, Harold Evans, in his book *The Practice of Journalism* (UK: Heinemann, 1963), 'News is people.' Long-time journalist Denis MacShane in *Using the Media* (UK: Pluto Press, 1979) sums up what journalists are on the lookout for with five tenets: *conflict, hardship* and *danger* to the community; the *unusual* (oddity, novelty); *scandal*; and *individualism*.

He quotes Lord Northcliffe (1869–1922), one of the original PRESS BARONS, who once declared, 'News is what somebody somewhere wants to suppress; all the rest is advertising.' Stuart Hood in *Hood on Television* (UK: Pluto Press, 1980), refers to news sense as 'the ability to judge the language and attitudes permissible within the opinion-forming organization of our society'; well within CONSENSUS thinking.

One of the most succinct explanations of news values is that of Johan Galtung and Mari Ruge in 'Structuring and selecting news', in Stanley Cohen and Jock Young (eds), *The Manufacture of News* (UK: Constable, 1973). Events will be more likely to be reported if they fulfil any, some or several of the following criteria. (1) *Frequency*: if the event takes a time approximate to the frequency of the medium. A murder, for example, is more newsworthy than the slow progress of a 'Third World' country. (2) *Amplitude*: the bigger, the better, the more dramatic – the greater is the likelihood of the story achieving what the authors call 'threshold value'. (3) *Unambiguity*: the more clear-cut, uncomplicated, the events, the more they will be noticed and reported. (4) *Familiarity*: that which is ethnocentric, of cultural proximity, and that which is relevant; so things close to home matter most, unless things close to home are affected by far-away events. (5) *Correspondence*: that is, the degree to which the events meet with our expectations, our predictions, even. In this case, say Galtung and Ruge, 'news' is actually 'olds'. They term this the 'hypothesis of consonance' – that which is familiar is registered, that which is unfamiliar is less likely to be registered. (6) *Surprise* 'this forms an antidote in terms of criteria to (4) and (5), and works to the benefit of good news: 'Events have to be unexpected or rare, or preferably both, to become good news.' (7) *Continuity*: that which has been defined as news – which has hit the headlines – will continue to be newsworthy even if amplitude is reduced. (8) *Composition*: the need for a 'balance' in a news spread leads the producer or editor to feed in contrasting elements – some home news if the predominant stories have been foreign; a little good news if the news has generally been gloomy.

Galtung and Ruge draw the following generalizations: the more events concern elite nations or elite people, the more events can be seen in personal terms and the more negative the event is in its consequences, the greater is the likelihood of selection. Consequently, once a news item has been selected, what makes it newsworthy will be accentuated (the authors call this stage 'Distortion'). Selection and distortion will, it is argued, take place at all steps in the chain from event to reader ('Replication').

Although Galtung and Ruge's study deals only with newspaper content, Jeremy Tunstall in *Journalists at Work* (UK: Constable, 1971), referring to the Galtung and Ruge article that had first been published in the *Journal of International Peace Research* (1965), adapts the scheme to TV news values. He itemizes four points of difference. (1) In TV the *visual* is given pre-eminence. The possession of new film will often increase the prominence given to a news story. (2) News items that include film of 'our own reporters' interviewing or commentating on a story are preferred. (3) TV makes use of a small fraction of the number of stories the newspapers carry, and even major TV items are short compared with newspaper coverage. (4) There is preference for 'hard' stories or ACTUALITY on TV news.

In 'The global newsroom: convergences and diversities in the globalization of television news', published in *Communication and Citizenship: Journalism and the Public Sphere* (UK: Routledge, 1991), edited by Peter Dahlgren and Colin Sparks, Michael Gurevitch, Mark R. Levy and Itzhak Roeh write that 'in a pictures-driven medium, the availability of dramatic pictures competes with, and often supersedes, other news considerations'.

They also argue that for an event to be judged newsworthy 'it must be anchored in narrative frameworks that are already familiar to and recognizable by news men as well as by audiences situated in particular cultures'; for 'different societies tell themselves – on television and elsewhere – different stories'.

The operation of such news values can be seen in the initial difficulties that can be encountered in getting airtime for stories about famine; some of which were documented by Paul Harrison and Robert Palmer in their book, *News Out of Africa: Biafra to Band Aid* (UK: Hilary Shipman, 1986). According to Harrison and Palmer even the world-famous, harrowing 1984 footage from Korem in Ethiopia by Mohammed Amin of Visnews and Michael Buerk of the BBC was turned down for transmission by Eurovision and met initial resistance at the US network NBC, on the grounds that there was a more important domestic crisis to cover. Even the BBC ran the item as the fourth story on its 9 o'clock edition of the television news on the day the story broke.

However, the BBC did keep the story running in the following weeks and months to keep concern focused. Once shown, the film galvanized worldwide support to aid Ethiopia. One result of the widespread shocked reaction to this footage was the formation of Band Aid and the Live Aid global music event, which ultimately demonstrated the power of television in raising funds.

Harrison and Palmer comment that there were no major news stories in Europe at the time and that had there been, the famine footage might never have been screened at all. Indeed, the build-up to a more recent crisis in Ethiopia, Sudan, Somalia and Mozambique received little media attention because of the preoccupation with the Gulf War (1991). Conspicuous in the reporting of the military intervention of the US in Afghanistan (2001–02) was the media focus on *action* to the neglect of the effect of the war on the civilian population.

Underscoring the application of news values is a *condition* that favours novelty and reacts to staleness. If, like fruit, a story is fresh, it might attract media attention so long as it stays fresh and as long as the media are prepared to 'freshen it up'. However, media attention is eternally subject to new attractions. Stories of human tragedy are so commonplace that unless they appear to have special news values they are likely to be overlooked or, if reported, covered and then forgotten.

The media are all too aware of COMPASSION FATIGUE on the part of the public, an issue thoroughly examined by Susan D. Moeller in *Compassion Fatigue: How the Media Sell Disease, Famine, War and Death* (US/UK: Routledge, 1999). As Moeller points out, it is not always fatigue that makes the media hold back on stories of tragedy, but *compassion avoidance,* resulting in switch-off, however dramatically a story fulfils the values identified here. See GALTUNG AND RUGE'S MODEL OF SELECTIVE GATEKEEPING, 1965; GLOBAL JUKEBOX; IMMEDIACY; IMPARTIALITY. See also *TOPIC GUIDE* under COMMUNICATION THEORY.

New Wave In the year 1959–60 an astonishing 67 new directors made their film debuts in France: this was the *nouvelle vague* as Françoise Giroud described it. At the crest of the wave were critics writing for the film magazine *Cahiers du Cinéma*, including François Truffaut (1932–84), Jean-Luc Godard (b. 1930) and Claude Chabrol (b. 1930). Their films were made cheaply, often with unknown actors, improvisation, hand-held cameras, location shooting and without huge teams of technicians.

The New Wave was always a loose-knit grouping of individual directors, and it was individualism – the belief in the film director as auteur – that was the common characteristic. The New Wave reacted against the studio product, and produced films of extraordinary richness and variety. Others in the Wave have been Alain Resnais, Chris Marker, Eric Rohmer, Jacques Rivette, Louis Malle, Roger Vadim and Agnès Varda.

New World Information Order Campaign sponsored by the United Nations Educational, Scientific and Cultural Organization (UNESCO) to counter MEDIA IMPERIALISM by creating an information order that gives a more balanced view of developing countries than has been generally presented by western capitalist press coverage. The intentions of UNESCO, with its International Programme for the Development of Communication (IPDC), have been interpreted as a means of exerting greater national control over access to and use of information. This, allege the critics of the Programme, would constitute a dangerous form of censorship. For details of the principles and aims of this proposed new order, see MACBRIDE COMMISSION.

In 1981 the US Congress directed the Reagan administration to withdraw its contribution to UNESCO – a quarter of its budget – if measures were taken to restrict the free flow of information. The US withdrew effectively from the organization on 31 December 1984, and was joined in its move by the UK. See INTERNATIONAL FEDERATION OF JOURNALISTS (IFJ); NON-ALIGNED NEWS POOL; TALLOIRES DECLARATION; WORLD PRESS FREEDOM COMMITTEE. See also *TOPIC GUIDE* under GLOBAL PERSPECTIVES.

N-Gen Short for Net-Generation, a term describing young people familiar with, and users of, the INTERNET and digital technology in general. The 'N-Geners' are characterized by a level of MEDIACY that marks them out from their parents' generation. See CHILDREN, YOUNG PEOPLE AND THE CHANGING MEDIA ENVIRONMENT; VIDEO GAMES.

'Niche' audiences With the growth of SATELLITE TRANSMISSION, audiences have become more fragmented and consequently advertisers have to target them more precisely. Not only have they to reach the right 'niche' in terms of the age, social CLASS, spending power, cultural attitudes and education of the TV viewer, but they have to identify the best times of day or night when the appropriate niche audience might be tuning in.

Nickelodeon An early and primitive form of cinema, of immense popularity in the US by 1905, usually consisting of a long, narrow room furnished with wooden bench seats and very basic equipment for film projection; frequently converted from a shop or store.

The term is thought to have been used by showman John P. Harris, combining the Greek for theatre with the slang expression for the five cents charged for admission. The English equivalent was the *penny gaf.*

Soon the Nickelodeon gave way to the more stately film-houses. In 1913, Mitchell L. Mark bought the Strand Theatre, a 3000-seater on Broadway, New York, and set in motion a fashion for neo-Baroque splendour. The movies had moved up market. Much later, the jukebox got referred to as the nickelodeon; a translation in meaning testified in the post-Second World War hit song, 'Put another nickel in/In the Nickelodeon …'.

Nielsen ratings Audience measurement figures produced by the US company AC Nielsen, the best-known and most influential ratings information business. See AUDIENCE MEASUREMENT.

Nine American lifestyles See VALS TYPOLOGY.

Noelle-Neumann's spiral of silence model of public opinion, 1974 In her paper, 'The spiral of silence: a theory of public opinion', published in the *Journal of Communication* 24 (1974), German professor of communications research Elisabeth Noelle-Neumann examines the interplay between three communicative factors: the mass media, INTERPERSONAL COMMUNICATION and an individual's PERCEPTION of his or her own standpoint in relation to others in society.

The model is based upon the belief that people are uneasy – suffer DISSONANCE – if they feel themselves to be *isolates* with regard to general opinion and attitude: that they are the odd one out. In response to a situation, we tend to ask, what do other people think; what is the majority or dominant opinion? A person may find 'that the views he holds are losing ground; the more this appears to be so, the more uncertain he will become of himself, and the less he will be inclined to express his opinion'. This is the spiral of silence.

The dominant view, which the mass media express (see ELITE; HEGEMONY; POWER ELITE),

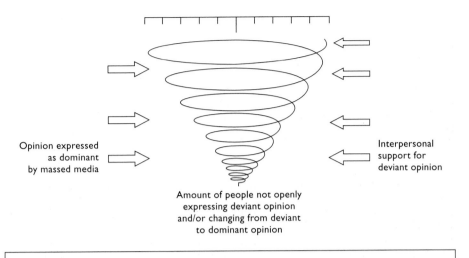

Opinion expressed
as dominant
by massed media

Interpersonal
support for
deviant opinion

Amount of people not openly
expressing deviant opinion
and/or changing from deviant
to dominant opinion

Noelle-Neumann's spiral of silence model of public opinion, 1974

exerts pressure to conform, to step into line; and the more this view is expressed, the more the dominant view is reinforced; the more dominant it appears, the more difficult it becomes to hold a contrary view. In a sense, Noelle-Neumann's model is a spiral within a spiral, the one an assertion, the other a withdrawal into a silence as the assertion grows stronger.

In particular, note the arrows at the right-hand side of the model. In relation to others around them, those holding 'different' opinions and attitudes grow more and more isolated. Thus a spiral of silence on the part of individual members of the public reflects the spiral of dominance represented by the media.

Professor Noelle-Neumann's definition of public opinion is that 'which can be voiced in public without fear of sanctions and upon which action in public can be based ... voicing opposite opinions, or acting in public accordingly, incurs the danger of isolation'. The model prompts the query whether the public merely holds back from expressing diverging or contrary views, but continues to hold them, or whether attitudes have actually been changed as a result of dominant media voices. See *TOPIC GUIDE* under COMMUNICATION MODELS.

Noise Impedance or barrier between the sending and receiving of communication signals. C.E. Shannon and W. Weaver in *The Mathematical Theory of Communication* (US: University of Illinois Press, 1949) posit two levels of noise problem: level A, *engineering noise* and, at the higher level B, *semantic noise*. Level A is physical and technical, and is defined as any distortion of MEANING occurring in the communication process that is not intended by the source, but that affects the reception of the MESSAGE-carrying signals and their clarity. The semantic level is 'noise' or impedance in terms of CODES – linguistic, personal, psychological, cultural, etc. Later writers have identified *psychological noise* as a category in its own right.

Non-Aligned News Pool Worldwide, non-profitmaking NEWS agency brought into existence by a decision of the Fifth Non-Aligned Summit Conference in Colombo, August 1976. A total of 85 nations undertook to share information from their respective newsgathering agencies with the aim of achieving greater balance in the reporting of events and development in non-aligned countries.

The News Pool has been useful, but its potential has been limited by the competition offered by major NEWS AGENCIES and by the political situation in many countries where governments censor the free flow of information. See MEDIA IMPERIALISM.

Non-verbal behaviour: repertoire A useful classification scheme for the repertoire of non-verbal behaviour is suggested by American authors Paul Ekman and Wallace V. Friesen in 'The repertoire of nonverbal behaviour: categories, origins, usage and coding', in *Semiotica* 1 (1969). Their five categories of non-verbal movement are: emblem, illustrators, affect displays, regulators and adaptors.

Emblems are non-verbal behaviours that directly suggest specific words or phrases, usually without vocal accompaniment. Thus the beckoning first finger is the emblem for 'Come here'. Emblems are short-cut communication signals useful in many ways, especially where verbal communication is difficult or inappropriate, for example when a person is thumbing a lift.

Illustrators accompany and reinforce verbal messages – the nod of the head, a supportive smile, leaning forward to show interest, sketching something in the air with finger or hand, to give a point emphasis or clarity. Illustrators tend to be less culture-specific than emblems.

Affect displays are movements of the face and body that hold emotional meaning: disappointment, rage, happiness, hopefulness, shock, etc.; indeed our whole body language constitutes affect displays.

For Ekman and Friesen, *regulators* are non-verbal actions that monitor and control the communication of another individual. These can take the form of encouragement of the other person to go on speaking, to explain more fully, to quicken up, slow down, or get to the point. Here we use nods, smiles, grunts, 'ah-ha's; we shake our heads, we glance away, blink, pucker our lips. Equally we can employ regulators in a negative sense by using non-verbal behaviours to discourage the other person from talking.

Adaptors are generally habitual behaviours used to make a person feel more at ease in communication interactions: twisting a lock of hair, scratching, stroking (the hair, the chin, etc.), wringing hands, turning a ring around the finger, fiddling with jewellery, playing with matches – actions that are more private than public and are likely to undergo some modification when the private actions extend into a public domain. See COMMUNICATION, NON-VERBAL; GESTURE; PROXEMICS. See also *TOPIC GUIDE* under INTERPERSONAL COMMUNICATION.

Non-verbal communication See COMMUNICATION, NON-VERBAL.

Non-verbal vocalizations In communication a number of sounds are used that are not speech but that convey important information contributing to the overall MEANING of the message being conveyed. At times these sounds communicate a message without the need for accompanying speech.

Michael Argyle in *Bodily Communication* (UK: Methuen, 1988) identifies some of the main non-verbal vocalizations. There are those that aid the understanding and regulating of speech. These include *prosodic signals*, like the raising of pitch to indicate that what is being said is a question; *synchronizing signals*, such as the lowering of pitch to indicate that one has finished speaking for the time being; and *speech disturbances* such as stutters and repetitions.

Some are more independent of speech but communicate emotions, attitudes or other social information that may affect the encoding and decoding of the message. These include emotional noises such as cries and laughter; paralinguistic noises that convey emotional information by such means as pitch, volume and speed; and aspects of the personal voice quality and accent.

Normative theories of mass media Building on an early work by American media analysts G.F. Siebert, T. Peterson and Wilbur Schramm, *Four Theories of the Press* (US: University of Illinois Press, 1956), Denis McQuail posits six normative theories of the mass media. In *Mass Communication Theory: An Introduction* (UK: Sage, 1983), McQuail lists: (1) Authoritarian Theory; (2) Free Press Theory; (3) Social Responsibility Theory; (4) Soviet Media Theory; (5) Development Media Theory; and (6) Democratic-Participant Theory.

By normative, we mean how the media should be, what is to be expected of them rather than what necessarily happens in practice; and it is out of the political, cultural and economic context that the normative principles arise. Central to the normative theory is the way the media 'behave' in relation to the state, and the dominant expectations that the state has of the role of the media.

The *Authoritarian Theory* thus appertains in a state in which press or BROADCASTING freedoms not only do not exist but are not considered – by those in power, or those who support them in power – desirable even as ideals. What Siebert *et al.* call 'Libertarian theory' McQuail terms the *Free Press Theory*, which is considered the chief legitimating principle for the print media in liberal democracies. Free and public expression is, implies this theory, the best way to arrive at the truth and expose error. It is a principle enshrined in the First Amendment of the American Constitution. This states that 'Congress shall make no law ... abridging the freedom of speech of the press.'

McQuail's analysis of this principle in practice is well worth noting, for he asks searching questions about whose freedom; about monopoly tendencies; about the close identification of notions of freedom with profit and private ownership.

The *Social Responsibility Theory* believes in freedom so long as it is harnessed to responsibility. Independence is desirable only so long as it is reconcilable with an obligation to society. In this sense, the media are perceived as fulfilling a role of public stewardship. They are the WATCHDOGS of the common good against government or private abuse of power or corruption. There is an emphasis on neutrality and balance – most of all, a belief in media accountability to society.

Soviet Media Theory (worth noting even though the Soviet system has passed away) derives from the postulates of Marx, Engels and Lenin. Here, the media serve the interests of the socialist state, the state being an embodiment of all the members of a classless society. Because the media are of the people, they belong to the people. In practice, of course, they belonged to the people's leadership. The tasks of media are to socialize the people into desirable NORMS as defined in Marxist doctrine; to educate, inform, motivate and *mobilize* in the aims and aspirations of a socialist society.

Development Media Theory has arisen out of special needs in the 'Third World' developing nations (see MACBRIDE COMMISSION; MEDIA IMPERIALISM; NEW WORLD INFORMATION ORDER). This theory eschews bad news theory and favours positive reporting on the grounds that for developing nations, often struggling for economic survival in competition with western industrialized countries, reporting of disasters and setbacks can substantially injure the process of nation building.

The *Democratic-Participant Media Theory* emphasizes the individual rights of access, of citizen and minority GROUPS, to the media, in fact the right to *communicate*, to be served by the media according to a more democratic determination of need (see DEMOCRACY AND THE MEDIA). Thus the theory opposes the concentration of ownership and rejects the role of AUDIENCE as tame receiver. Media should be answerable, free of government or big-business intervention, small-scale, interactive and participative (see CAMPAIGN FOR PRESS AND BROADCASTING FREEDOM; COMMUNITY RADIO; RIGHT OF REPLY).

In a later publication, 'Mass media in the public interest: towards a framework of norms for media performance', in *Mass Media and Society*, edited by James Curran and Michael Gurevitch (UK: Edward Arnold, 1991), McQuail re-examines the validity of normative models because 'attempts to formulate consistent "theories" of the press' become increasingly difficult to sustain 'when media technologies and distribution systems are multiplying and when there is less consensus about basic values than in the past'. The dissolution of the Soviet Union is a case in point, though it is arguable that the 'Marxist' media theory continues to apply in China and Cuba.

McQuail proffers a set of defining principles by which media performance can be judged, and these relate to community values. He cites the following as Public Communication Values: (1) *Freedom*, acquiring its public definition through the independent status of the media, public access to channels and diversity of supply; (2) *Equality*, which concerns openness, access and OBJECTIVITY (characterized by neutrality, fairness and truth); and (3) *Order*, a classification relating both to order in the sense of solidarity and in the sense of control (the one operating bottom upwards, as it were, the other top downwards).

The principles interrelate, interact and are obviously in constant conflict with one another. McQuail acknowledges 'deep fissures and inconsistencies, depending on how they [the principles] are interpreted'. However, the application of these principles to the changing patterns of media operation provides 'the essential building blocks for a quite comprehensive, flexible and changing "social theory of media", relevant to our times and of practical value in the ever widening circle of public discussion of the role of mass media in society'. See McQUAIL'S ACCOUNTABILITY OF MEDIA MODEL, 1997.

Norms Shared expectations or standards of behaviour within a particular social group or society. Any type of established group will have norms, both peculiar to itself and shared with the wider community. Of those norms widely accepted in a society, some will operate on a high, some on a low

CONSENSUS. Any individual's PERCEPTION and interpretation of experience will be influenced by the norms of the social groups and society to which he/she belongs. Individuals generally take such norms for granted.

Communication between individuals likewise reflects certain norms, such as those of grammar and style of writing or norms of conduct that guide social INTERACTION.

Norms arise from such interaction between various individuals and social groups. Once developed, they are passed on through SOCIALIZATION to new members. Norms are not static: they are subject to renegotiation. They play a significant part in maintaining the social position of particular groups and individuals, and constitute an influential agent of informal social control.

The media, as agents of communication and socialization, are in a position to both reinforce general societal norms and express the norms of certain social groups. In addition, the media have the potential *to shape* expectations of behaviour, particularly with regard to individuals or groups with whom the viewer, listener or reader is unfamiliar. It is this potential that has aroused considerable research interest. See CULTURE; MALE-AS-NORM; VALUES.

Northcliffe revolution New schooling in the late nineteenth century in the UK following the Foster Education Act of 1870 created a rapidly expanding readership of literature and NEWS. Alfred Charles William Harmsworth (1865–1922), later Lord Northcliffe, perhaps the most dynamic and extraordinary of the PRESS BARONS, built a press empire on the new flood-tide of literacy. Creator of the *Daily Mail* (1896) and the *Daily Mirror* (1903), Northcliffe combined a 'popular-educator' emphasis with a marketing sense that was energetic, imaginative, daring and ruthless. Northcliffe represents the fundamental shift towards the exploitation of, and increasing dependence upon, ADVERTISING as a means of newspaper finance.

Publicity was everything. Rivalry between papers, in terms of sensation-seeking and attention-grabbing stunts resembled – as it continues to do today – the Battle of the Titans. Raymond Williams in *The Long Revolution* (UK: Chatto & Windus, 1961) says, 'The true "Northcliffe Revolution" is less an innovation in actual journalism than a radical change in the economic basis of newspapers, tied to the new kind of advertising.'

By 1908 Northcliffe's press empire included the *Mail*, the *Mirror*, *The Times*, two Sunday papers (*Observer* and *Dispatch*) and an evening paper (*News*) plus a host of periodicals such as *Tit-Bits* and *Answers* (whose circulation had leapt from 12,000 at its inception to 352,000 two years later).

Though the so-called Northcliffe revolution was chiefly characterized by the employment of new technology, the drive for mass circulations and the wholesale reliance on advertising as the prime source of press revenue, the 'flavour' of that revolution must not be overlooked – that is, the style and content emanating from the press barons themselves. James Curran and Jean Seaton in *Power Without Responsibility: The Press and Broadcasting in Britain* (UK: Routledge, 5th edition, 1997), write 'Northcliffe and Beaverbrook shaped the entire content of their favourite papers, including their lay-out.'

When *The Times* changed the position in the paper of its weather report, Northcliffe raged '… if it's moved again, whoever does it is fired'. Curran and Seaton speak of how the personal tastes of the barons influenced the popular journalism of the time: 'Northcliffe had a lifelong obsession with torture and death: he even kept an aquarium containing a goldfish and a pike, with a dividing partition, which he would lift up when he was in need of diversion.' He told staff of the *Daily Mail* to find 'one murder a day'.

Meddling with the content by newspaper proprietors was not, of course, new. It had gone on throughout the nineteenth century, but then interference had focused mainly upon political matters. What was different with Northcliffe and his ilk was that the new proprietors meddled in everything. See NEWSPAPERS, ORIGINS. See also *TOPIC GUIDE* under MEDIA HISTORY.

* Kevin Williams, *Get Me A Murder a Day! A History of Mass Communication in Britain* (UK: Arnold, 1997).

NVC See COMMUNICATION, NON-VERBAL (NVC).

O

Object See SIGN.

Objectivity Professor Stuart Hall has expressed the view that objectivity, 'like impartiality, is an operational fiction' (in 'Media power: the double bind', *Journal of Communication*, Autumn 1984). In examining the media, analysts encounter the Famous Four: balance, CONSENSUS, IMPARTIALI-TY and objectivity, upon which all good reporting is said to be based. The questions arising from this precept are as follows. Balance between what and what? Consensus among whom? Impartiality in what sense? Objectivity in whose eyes? Considering the complex processes of MEDIATION between an event and its report in media form, is it possible to have value-free information?

'All edited or manipulated symbolic reality,' says Hall, 'is impregnated with values, viewpoints, implicit theorizings, common-sense assumptions.' When there are differences between what is objective and what is not, whose opinion wins the day? Hall says of consensus that it is 'structured dominance', that is, the prevailing definition usually rests with the POWER ELITE, the 'power-ideology complex' in any society whose control of and influence upon the media gives them a greater say in the definitions of objectivity. See CULTURAL APPARATUS; ELITE; HEGEMONY; MACHINERY OF REPRE-SENTATION.

Object language According to Gail Myers and Michele Myers in *The Dynamics of Human Communication* (US: McGraw-Hill, 1985) this term refers to 'the meanings you attribute to objects with which you surround yourself'. These objects might be items of dress – for example, clothes, hairstyle, fashion accessories – your house, your furniture and so on.

These and many other objects may say something about you to others: they can all be part of your SELF-PRESENTATION. These objects may not of course always convey to others the MESSAGE you wish them to. Others may not be aware of the symbolic value of the objects or simply read into them different meanings than the ones intended. You may of course be unaware yourself of messages that you may be sending to others through the objects you have. Object language may be particularly important when people are forming first impressions of one another. A great deal of ADVERTISING certainly works on the assumption that consumer objects have as their main appeal a *symbolic* rather than a purely functional value.

In their book *Understanding and Sharing: An Introduction to Speech Communication* (US: Brown, 1979, reprinted 1985), authors Judy Cornelia Pearson, Paul Edward Nelson and Donald Yoder use the term *objectics*, the study of 'clothing, adornments, hairstyles, cosmetics and other artefacts that we carry with us or possess'. Object language conveys information about our age, sex, status, role, personality, rela-tionships with groups and with other people, psychological and emotional state, self-concept, and the 'physical climate in which we live'. See COMMUNICATION, NON-VERBAL (NVC); SELF-CONCEPT.

Obscene signals See INSULT SIGNALS.

Obscenity and film censorship See WILLIAMS COMMITTEE REPORT ON OBSCENITY AND FILM CENSORSHIP (UK), 1979.

Obsolescence Generally, anything passing out of date or out of use. In a communications sense, it refers to the link between social habits and media-using habits. Obsolescence can be defined as the abandoning of formerly institutionalized modes of conduct related to some established cultural activity.

Œuvre French for 'work', generally the complete works of an artist, writer, composer, etc. The word refers to the work of the mind as well as of hand and eye. Thus we may refer to the *œuvre* of Pablo Picasso (1891–1973) and mean not only the items of his work – paintings, sculpture, pottery – but, by implication, the nature or character of that work. See OPUS.

OfCOM See COMMUNICATIONS BILL (UK), 2002.

Official Secrets Act (UK) Born in a spy scare during the Agadir crisis of 1911, reinforced in 1920 during the 'Troubles' in Ireland, given further power as war broke out in 1939, the Act censors information – access to it, and expression of it – which might be of use to the nation's enemies. It is easier to define what the Act does not cover rather than what it does. Without question, it is the single most comprehensive weapon of CENSORSHIP with regard to the activities of government in the UK, and has few parallels in the 'free' world.

For a time, the saving grace of the Act was the possibility of defending individual, group or media breaches of secrecy on the grounds that such breaches were in the *public interest*. This was excised from the Act by the Conservative government in 1990 and to date Labour administrations have made no move to put it back. Even in cases where information covered by the Act concerns corruption or other forms of criminality, the dead hand of secrecy remains. Brian Raymond, solicitor to the civil servant Clive Ponting, who was unsuccessfully prosecuted under the Act for revealing information about the sinking of the *Belgrano* during the Falklands War (1982), said: 'The obliteration of the public interest defence ... amounts to a licence to cover up Government wrong-doing.' See D-NOTICES; REGULATION OF INVESTI-GATORY POWERS ACT (RIPA) (UK), 2000; SECRECY; FREEDOM OF INFORMATION; SPYCATCHER CASE. See also *TOPIC GUIDE* under MEDIA: FREEDOM, CENSORSHIP.

Oligopolization Oligarchy is government by a small exclusive CLASS or group; in media terms, oligopolization is the process of communication systems falling into the hands of a small exclusive group of owners or corporations.

Omnimax Spectator-surrounding film projection technique developed, like IMAX, in Canada from a system invented by an Australian, Ron James. Though there are several Omnimax screens in North America, the first in Europe – and the largest screen in the world – operates at the 55-hectare Paris exhibition complex, Cité des Sciences et de L'Industrie at Porte La Villette, which opened in 1986.

La Gèode offers a projection screen covering 10,000 square feet and surrounds spectators with a complete hemisphere, exceeding the normal field of vision. Like Imax, Omnimax uses 70mm film, which passes through the camera horizontally producing a 5 x 7cm film image – approximately nine times the image area of ordinary cinema film. Camera and projector use a 25mm fish-eye lens with a scope of 172 degrees. A massive light source is required to project such a gigantic picture and Omnimax has a 15kW water-cooled xenon lamp.

One-step, two-step, multi-step flow models of communication Basically these are refinements of the HYPODERMIC NEEDLE MODEL OF COMMUNICATION. The one-step model ignores the role of the OPINION LEADER in the flow of communication and presents the view that the mass media communicate directly to a mass AUDIENCE. There is no suggestion, however, that the messages reach all receivers equally or that they have the same effect on each individual in the audience. The model takes into account the influence of an individual's PERCEPTION, memory and SELECTIVE EXPOSURE on his/her particular interpretation of a MESSAGE. SALIENCE – or the factor of prominence – is also considered to be an important variable in the model.

A study conducted by Paul Lazarsfeld and others of the 1940 presidential election in the US threw doubt on the validity of the one-step theory. Reporting in *The People's Choice* (US: Duell, Sloan & Pearce, 1944), the authors found little evidence of the direct influence of the media; indeed people seemed more influenced by face-to-face contact with others. Lazarsfeld and his fellow researchers suggested that the flow of communication to the individual is often directed through an opinion leader who plays a vital role in both spreading and interpreting the information.

They thus proposed a *two-step model* of communication flow, which later research has found to be generally useful. In highlighting the importance of the social context of the receiver in the process of the interpretation of mass communication messages this model differs significantly from earlier ones. It presents the mass audience as being composed of interacting and responsive individuals rather than of the socially isolated, passive atoms of earlier theories.

The *multi-step model* is a development of the other two, allowing for the sequential relaying of a message. It is not specific about the number of steps there will be in the relaying process nor does it specify that messages must originate from a source and then pass straight through the agencies of the mass media. The model suggests a variable number of relays in the communication process and that the receivers may receive the message at various stages along the relay network. The exact number of steps in the process depends upon the following: (1) the intentions of the source; (2) the availability of the mass media; (3) the extent of audience exposure to agencies of communication; (4) the nature of the message; and (5) the importance of the message to the audience.

The model has often been used in recent research. Its advantage is that it allows the researcher to account for different variables in different communication situations. See *TOPIC GUIDE* under COMMUNICATION MODELS.

Onomatopoeia Words that imitate actual sounds are onomatopoeic, such as bang, thud, crackle, hiss, quack and twitter. They are mostly invented words. The first ever attempts at spoken language were very probably onomatopoeic and such words continue to be invented, not a few of them (zap, for example) starting life in comics and cartoons.

Open, closed texts Italian semiologist Umberto Eco has made this useful separation between TEXTS that are varyingly shaped – to permit little interpretation on the part of AUDIENCE (*closed texts*) or to allow plenty of room for interpretation (*open texts*). A work of art – a poem, a painting, a piece of sculpture, for example – would represent an open text in that the intention of the writer, painter or sculptor is to express ideas or feelings that may be interpreted in different ways and at different levels.

The open text invites a sense of participation in the reader or viewer, and the interaction that occurs between creator, creation and audience is one in which 'right answers' are less important than the possibility of a proactive response; and this may be subject to flux in differing instances and at varying times. PROPAGANDA would constitute closed text in that there is a rigorously PREFERRED READING: the decoder is expected to receive the message and register its MEANING as intended by the communicator. Any divergence from acceptance would, to quote another term of Eco's, represent *aberrant decoding*. See ANCHORAGE; DECODE.

'Open source' creed Belief in the free availability of data online; put into practice by public-spirited computer programmers encouraging people to freely adapt software rather than allowing it to be patented by big companies. An example is Freenet, developed by Ian Clarke at the University of Edinburgh. This is a decentralized information system designed to bypass government-approved and/or commercially based ISPs (Internet Service Providers). In the UK the potential for this free and anonymous exchange and interactivity stands at risk in face of invasive legislation, in particular the REGULATION OF INVESTIGATORY POWERS ACT (RIPA) (UK), 2000 (its reach substantially increased in 2002, its principles and practices also extended to other countries in the European Community).

Opera omnia Latin for 'all his works', the term denotes a total ban on an author's writings imposed by the Roman Catholic *Index Librorum Prohibitorum*, first issued in 1559. A few such prohibited writers have been David Hume, Emile Zola, Jean-Paul Sartre and Alberto Moravia. See CENSORSHIP; INDEX.

Opinion leader Someone able to influence informally other individuals' attitudes and/or behaviour in a desired way with relative frequency. He/she is a type of informal leader. Opinion leadership is earned and maintained by the individual's technical competence, sociability and conformity to the NORMS of the social system. When such leaders are compared to their followers several characteristics are of note: opinion leaders are more exposed to all forms of external communication; more *cosmopolite*; of a higher social status; and more innovative. Opinion leaders are widely thought to play a vital role in the spreading of new ideas, VALUES and beliefs.

An opinion leader whose range of influence is limited to one specific topic exercises *monomorphic* opinion leadership. This type of leadership is thought to be typical of modern, industrial societies as the complex technological base of such societies results in a sophisticated division of labour and considerable specialization of roles. An opinion leader whose influence covers a wide range of topics exercises *polymorphic* opinion leadership. This is generally thought to be more common in traditional societies. A respected, elderly member of a village, for example, might be consulted on a variety of matters ranging from marriage problems to methods of harvesting.

Opinion poll The process or processes by which public opinion is researched, the findings of which are widely and regularly published and broadcast, and are seen not only as evidence upon which governments, oppositions, public bodies etc. might act, but as an influence in their own right. For example, in election campaigns poll results are seen as vital indicators of the way the public intends to vote, but the headlines such opinion polls produce are also seen to influence the electorate, particularly if the findings suggest a CONSENSUS of opinion. For this reason, some countries ban the publishing of poll results in the immediate run-up to elections.

Oppositional code See DOMINANT, SUBORDINATE, RADICAL; POLYSEMY.

Optical fibre cable See FIBRE-OPTIC TECHNOLOGY.

Opus Latin for 'work', a term most often applied to musical compositions in order of their creation; for example, Beethoven's Ninth Symphony is Opus 125.

Oral culture An oral CULTURE or SUBCULTURE is one in which essentially most communication is by word of mouth. Pictures may also be used as a supplement but reading and writing play a minor role in the communication process.

Orality: primary and secondary In *Orality and the Technology of the Word* (US: Cornell University Press, 1982) Walter Ong in investigating the nature of the shift between oral and literate cultures differentiates between 'primary' and 'secondary' orality. The first refers to and describes *preliterate* societies, the second results from the introduction of electronic media into *literate* societies.

Order, visions of See VISIONS OF ORDER.

Organization cultures In examining the NORMS, VALUES and practices of business organizations in his *Understanding Organizations* (UK: Penguin, 1993 edition). Charles B. Handy identifies four forms of organizational CULTURE that affect the nature or 'profile' of the organization and its patterns of communication. Each culture has, according to Handy, its own presiding deity. These are as follows. (1) The *power culture*, depending upon a central power source, with 'rays of power and influence' (and communication) spreading out from a central figure. Zeus, the chief of the gods of Ancient Greece, who ruled by 'whim and impulse, by thunderbolt and shower of gold' is seen as the patron god of this culture. An example of such a culture is the self-made business person running his/her own company (see BERLUSCONI PHENOMENON; MURDOCH EFFECT). Without such a 'spider', the web structure of the culture would collapse.

(2) The *role culture* is the classic bureaucracy, its model like a Greek temple, with the leadership – directors, governors, etc. – represented by the pediment, the various organizational departments, the pillars of the temple and the workers at the base. Here, plainly, the communication process, following lines of authority, is vertical and chiefly one-way. Apollo, the god of reason, is seen as the patron god of this organization whose culture values logic and rationality. In media terms, the BBC would be a good example of a role culture.

(3) The *task culture*. This is a skills- or ability-orientated culture in which what an employee is capable of doing is more important than who he/she is in terms of position or role. The model is net-shaped, made up of interdependent strands; LEADERSHIP is exchangeable according to the task in hand. This culture, centred on task completion, is not seen by Handy as having any one overall presiding deity but Athena, the warrior goddess, and Odysseus, the champion of commando leaders, would best reflect its ethos. This so-called *matrix structure* is characterized by very flexible channels of communication, horizontal rather than vertical in direction, and is responsive to change. Examples from the media of a task culture would be a creative ADVERTISING agency or small companies producing film or VIDEO, or designing and operating websites.

(4) The *person culture* is, in terms of business organizations, the rarest of the four. Here the organization exists only to serve the individuals within it. The model is of a cluster, a galaxy of individual stars, without hierarchical structures, constantly interchanging in form. Dionysus, the god of the 'self-orientated individual' is its ruling deity.

As Handy says, 'Clearly not many organizations can exist with this sort of culture, since organizations tend to have objectives over and above the collective objectives of those who comprise them.' In its purest form, the kibbutz (small egalitarian Israeli community) is an example of the person culture. Cooperatives in the arts are examples of the people culture (see MAGNUM). The factors Handy cites as influencing organization cultures are: history and ownership; size; technology; goals and objectives; the environment and the people.

In *The Empty Raincoat* (UK: Arrow Books, 1995) Handy discusses a new model for organizations, based on what he terms the *doughnut* principle. This, he argues, reflects the way in which the traditional models and cultures have changed and will continue to change in order to survive shifts in the technological and economic environment.

The doughnut consists of a *core* surrounded by *bounded space*. It is 'an inside-out doughnut, one with the hole on the outside and the dough in the middle'. It is a 'conceptual doughnut, one for thinking with, not eating'. The core contains 'necessary jobs and necessary people'. These full-time employees often organize the activities of the bounded space that contains many other people working for the organization as flexible workers tied to the organization by flexible and often short-term contracts.

Thus organizations will become much smaller in terms of the number of people they directly employ; consequently it is likely that more people will be self-employed or freelance workers. Within the television industry, for example, this method of working is now well established. See CASUALIZATION; PRODUCER CHOICE.

Orientalism Concept posed by Edward Said describing the STEREOTYPICAL image of Asia held by those in European cultures. Representation of the Orient arises from ETHNOCENTRIC attitudes with an imperialist ancestry, and results in a projected image of Asia and Asians as being exotic ('the lure of the Orient'), indolent, untrustworthy and devious; in short, a misrepresentation by western commentators and analysts, of OTHER. In *Orientalism* (UK: Routledge, 1978), Said raises the question whether anything can be truly or objectively represented. See also Said's *Culture and Imperialism* (UK: Chatto & Windus, 1993).

The potency of the term has been reinforced by new millennium events such as the war on ('Arab') terrorism conducted by the US in Afghanistan and other alleged terrorist enclaves following the destruction of New York's World Trade Center on 11 September 2001, and the military invasion by Israel of territories occupied by Palestinians; some research findings indicating on the part of the reactions of western politicians and western media a pro-Israeli bias. See GLASGOW UNIVERSITY MEDIA GROUP.

Orientation An element of non-verbal communication referring to the angle at which people sit or stand in relation to one another. Orientation can be used to convey a range of messages about relationships, mood, personality and social context. For example, if people are in a potentially hostile or competitive situation they usually face each other head on. See COMMUNICATION, NON-VERBAL (NVC).

Other A person, persons, group, social CLASS, community, race or nation who are not 'us' and who are defined by their difference from us; yet who by that difference contribute to our concept of self, as individuals, members of groups etc. There is the ranking of *generalized* Other, as illustrated by the statement, 'Other people might like to shop on a Sunday, but for me it is still a day of rest.' Also, there are SIGNIFICANT OTHERS. These may be people, or types of people, whom we respect and whose opinions carry weight with us. They count in our lives, and they may be real or fictitious. They are often, or have the potential to be, ROLE models.

'Other' in general media use represents, by and large, those whom we disapprove of, dislike, fear; and the popular media use of Other works in *binary* fashion (see WEDOM, THEYDOM). In everyday communication, Other plays a key role in jokes – Irish jokes, Scottish jokes, etc. – each one relying for its effect upon a CONSENSUS about the negative qualities of the butt of that joke.

In TABLOID press headlines name-calling is a favourite device to put down Other and consequently boost the sense of superiority of Us over Them. When Other is perceived as a threat, the demarcation lines become more forcible; and of course in sport, Other is always the opposition – at which point Germans become 'Krauts' and the French become 'Frogs'. Other, then, is almost invariably those in opposition, those who are different in appearance or CULTURE and are seen in some way as a challenge to 'our' ways.

Outer-inner directed See VALS TYPOLOGY.

Out-take Piece of film that is not actually used in the completed version.

Overhearing Kurt H. Wolff in *The Sociology of Georg Simmel* (US: Free Press, 1950) uses this expression to describe how recipients of messages may proceed, usually below the level of awareness, to select certain parts for special attention, often distorting them, while at the same time overlooking ('overhearing') other parts entirely. In short, the human organism perceives to a considerable degree what it wants to perceive. See COCKTAIL PARTY PROBLEM; PERCEPTION; SELECTIVE EXPOSURE.

209

Overkill signals See SHORTFALL SIGNALS.

Ownership and control of mass media See BERLUSCONI PHENOMENON; GLOBALIZA-TION: THREE ENGINES OF; GLOBAL MEDIA SYSTEM: THE MAIN PLAYERS; MEDIA CONTROL; MURDOCH EFFECT; PRESS BARONS. See also *TOPIC GUIDE* under MEDIA: OWNERSHIP AND CONTROL.

Oz Trial The longest-ever obscenity trial in the UK, lasting 26 days in the summer of 1971, centred on the *Oz School Kids Issue* (*Oz* 28). The three editors, Richard Neville, Felix Dennis and Jim Anderson, were eventually acquitted on the most serious charge – that of conspiring to corrupt the morals of children but a majority of ten to one of the trial jury found *Oz* guilty of publishing an obscene article, sending such articles through the post and having such articles for profit and gain.

Oz Publications Ink Ltd. received a total fine of £1000 with £1250 costs. Neville got a 15-month jail sentence and a recommendation that he be deported (he was Australian). Anderson received twelve months and Dennis nine. See CENSORSHIP; SPYCATCHER CASE. See also *TOPIC GUIDE* under MEDIA: FREEDOM, CENSORSHIP.

P

Packaging The style and the framework within which TV programmes are presented on our screens: good-looking announcers or interviewers, titling, music, the tailoring of programmes to suitable lengths, indeed any form of image-making for a media product. The word gives emphasis to the connection between the manufacture and sale of goods, and the making and presentation of media products. Stuart Hood in *Hood on Television* (UK: Pluto Press, 1980) refers to TV announcers as the 'sales people of the air'. See LOOKISM.

Panopticon See SURVEILLANCE SOCIETY.

Paparazzo Aggressive, prying and often unscrupulous freelance photographer who specializes in taking pictures of celebrities; pursuing them wherever they go, armed with thick skin and zoom lenses. The word is an Italian – Calabrian – surname. It was suggested by writer Ennio Flaiano as a name for a character in Federico Fellini's film *La Dolce Vita* (The Sweet Life), made in 1960. Paparazzi were accused of hounding Diana, Princess of Wales, to her death in 1997 and the press at that time made a number of resolutions to curb the use of 'intrusive' pictures.

Paper Tiger TV Media collective based in New York from 1981; an example of 'action' or 'alternative' media. A networking system of access and production, generally run on a volunteer basis, it aims to encourage grassroots resistance to the dominance of the media industry. In 1995 Paper Tiger received a grant to distribute programming by satellite to public access centres around the US. Its Deep Dish TV has become a nationwide organization with a steering committee and small full-time staff. Among programmes transmitted by Deep Dish TV are *Green Screen: Grassroots Views of the Environmental Crisis*, *Behind Censorship: The Assault on Civil Liberties* and *Water, Oil and Power*.

Paperwork Reduction Act (US), 1980 On the face of it, a welcome onslaught on the overproduc-tion of bureaucratic paperwork; yet critics of this piece of American legislation view it with a degree of cynicism. In 'The tug-of-war over the First Amendment', published in *Questioning the Media: A Critical Introduction* (UK: Sage, 1990), edited by John Downing, Ali Mohammadi and Annabelle Sreberny-Mohammadi, Donna A. Demac and John Downing write that the Act was 'promptly used to curtail public access to government information'; in short, backdoor CENSORSHIP. Supervised and guided by the Office of Management and Budget, government agencies have used the Act to transfer the management of key information programmes to the private sector, thus furthering the retreat from public to private of information services.

Demac and Downing say that by 1985 'one-fourth of all government information was made available only in computer tapes, which put its utilization out of the financial and technical reach of the vast majority of citizens'.

Paradigm (paradigmic) Commonly used in the social sciences, the term refers to a framework of explanation within which theories from various schools of thought in a discipline are located and from which research operates. In *linguistics*, paradigm describes the set of relationships a linguistic unit – such as a letter or a word – has with other units in a specific context. The word is applicable in all SIGN systems, verbal, numerical, musical, etc. The alphabet is a paradigm, or set of signs, from which a choice is made to formulate the message. A *syntagm* is a combination of the chosen signs, a chain that amounts to MEANING. In language we can describe the vocabulary we use as *paradigmic*, and the sentence that vocabulary is formed into, *syntagmic.*

All messages, therefore, involve selection from a paradigm and combination into a syntagm. All the units in a paradigm must share characteristics that determine the membership of that paradigm, thus letters in the alphabetic paradigm, numbers in the numerical paradigm, notes in the musical paradigm.

Each unit within the paradigm must be clearly differentiable from other units; it must be characterized by distinctive features. Just as the paradigm is governed by shared characteristics and distinctive features, the syntagm is determined by rules or conventions by which the combination of paradigms is made – rules of grammar and syntax or, in music, rules of harmony. See PARADIGMS OF THE MEDIA; SEMIOLOGY/SEMIOTICS.

Paradigms of the media James Curran in 'Rethinking the media as a public sphere', in *Communication and Citizenship* (UK: Routledge, 1991), edited by Peter Dahlgren and Colin Sparks, has identified three paradigms that seek to explain the relationship between the mass media and the POWER structure of societies in which they operate: the *Marxist* or *Neo-Marxist*, the *Liberal-Pluralist* and the *Radical Democratic* paradigms.

The Marxist or Neo-Marxist school argue that it is those who own and control economic capital who are at the heart of a society's power structure and that such a position allows them to exercise power over cultural institutions, such as the mass media, in order to better pursue their economic goals. Media professionals may view themselves as autonomous but, it is argued, they have been socialized into and have *internalized* the NORMS and VALUES of the dominant CLASS.

Thus from this perspective, a key ideological contribution made by the mass media is that it provides the audience with frameworks for interpreting messages, which encourage it to construct readings that are consistent with the interests of the dominant class. Critics of this tradition have argued, though, that it overlooks the degree of leeway that does exist for journalists to ask awkward questions, and the need to consider the AUDIENCE and the audience's role in constructing the MEANING of mass media messages.

A competing paradigm is that offered by the Liberal-Pluralist tradition of media research, which argues that the mass media is and should be composed of a number of competing groups operating within a free market, though subject to state intervention when this is deemed in the public interest. Groups within the mass media tend to be seen as in competition for power and influence within society.

Media professionals, such as journalists, are seen to enjoy a considerable degree of *autonomy* over the production of media artefacts. Within this tradition some perceive the media to have a responsibility within society to behave as a WATCHDOG whose role it is to provide an arena for wide public debate about civil issues, facilitating the articulation of a *plurality* of views and values, and in so doing to allow private individuals to exercise a form of informal control over the state.

This tradition has, however, been subject to much criticism for its failure to address the narrow social base from which media professionals are often drawn resulting in women and those from working-class and/or ethnic backgrounds being under-represented; and the degree to which the political economy of media ownership, the CULTURE of media organizations and the place of these organizations in the political economy of a society, influence the content and reading of media artefacts.

The Radical Democratic paradigm, according to James Curran, offers a synthesis between the other two paradigms. Whilst this paradigm acknowledges the links between the ownership and control of media institutions, and that of other key institutions, and that the free market tends to be skewed in favour of the dominant class, it does not perceive the links to be so close that the media could be conceived as an arm of the ruling class. Rather the media is seen as 'caught in the crossfire', providing 'a battleground between contending forces. The way in which the media responds to and mediates this conflict affects the balance of social forces and, ultimately, the distribution of rewards within society.'

Journalists and media professionals are viewed as having day-to-day autonomy that allows them to make a difference and opens up the possibility for the committed radical journalism that would allow the media to act as a countervailing force and to further the cause of the less powerful. It also recognizes that not all journalists and media professionals work in media organizations that have one dominant owner, and argues that those working in BROADCASTING and in commercial media where ownership is dispersed among a number of shareholders may enjoy considerable freedom to criticize the powerful. The structure of the media, however, is seen as being in need of reform if it is to achieve its potential for providing diverse debate within a democratic society. See DEMOCRACY AND THE MEDIA. See also *TOPIC GUIDE* under MEDIA INSTITUTIONS.

Paralanguage See NON-VERBAL VOCALIZATIONS.

Parallel processing Our visual capacity allows us to process many images simultaneously – in parallel; to record both foreground and background actions. In contrast, speech capacity depends upon *serial* processing: we hear one word or phrase at a time and process it before proceeding to subsequent data.

Paraproxemics Term used to classify the way TV handles the space between people in its programmes, echoing and simulating the real-life use of space (see PROXEMICS) by individuals – for example, the close-up, medium range and distance camera shots paralleling the spatial zones of intimate, personal and social space. Joshua Meyrowitz in 'Television and interpersonal behaviour: codes of perception and response', in G. Gumpert and R. Cathcart (eds), *Inter/Media: Interpersonal Communication in a Media World* (US/UK: Oxford University Press, 1979) writes, 'the way in which a person is framed [by the TV camera] may suggest an interpersonal distance between that person and the viewer'. Distance, in fact, shapes viewer response, with the TV screen becoming 'a kind of "extended retina" for the viewer'.

Parasocial interaction The illusion, contributed to both by the performer and the AUDIENCE in mass media communication, especially RADIO, TV and film, of an interpersonal relationship existing between them, free of MEDIATION. Characters (or *persona*) on air or film, actual or fictional, are often cited as being more 'real' to audiences than the real people they know.

In 'Mass communication and parasocial interaction: observation on intimacy at a distance', *Journal of Psychiatry* 19 (1956), D. Horton and R.R. Wohl write, 'The persona offers, above all, a continuing relationship. His appearance is a regular and dependable event, to be counted on, planned for, and integrated into the routines of daily life' and may be considered by his audience as 'a friend, counsellor, comforter, and model', but unlike all those real people around him, the persona is changeless. 'Typically, there are no challenges to a spectator's self … that cannot be met comfortably.' Arguably the strongest relationship or interaction is that between audiences and fictitious characters, especially those in long-running series such as SOAP OPERAS.

Parental Guidance (PG) See CERTIFICATION OF FILMS.

Participant observation Some research evidence is collected by the researcher becoming a member of the group or social situation under observation. The researcher participates fully in the situation and those being observed may be unaware that he/she is a researcher. The advantage of this method of data collection is that the greater involvement of the researcher may facilitate an increased insight into and greater understanding of the behaviour being investigated. See ETHNOGRAPHIC (APPROACH TO AUDIENCE MEASUREMENT). See also *TOPIC GUIDE* under RESEARCH METHODS.

Partisan An adherent of a particular party or cause. The term is also used to describe actions as well as allegiances. Within media studies, much research has focused upon the political partisanship of the press and TV companies, that is, upon the degree to which they may support one or other political party or faction, and colour their political coverage accordingly. If such coverage gives space to the views of two factions or parties it is generally described as being *bi-partisan*; if its tone is one of general disinterest, of being above party politics, it is described as being *anti-partisan*. Partisan perspectives may not, though, permeate political coverage only; they may pervade media presentations generally. See EFFECTS OF THE MASS MEDIA.

Passivity One influential and widely held PERCEPTION of the mass AUDIENCE is that it is largely passive and unreflective. There is little evidence for this, though assumptions carry weight, and are reflected in content selection and approach, regardless of evidence. Modern media commentators insist on the diversity of response of audiences. James Curran and Jean Seaton in *Power Without Responsibility* (UK: Routledge, 5th edition, 1997) believe 'The public is not a passive empty box merely waiting to be filled with the injunctions of advertisers. How people react to what they see is determined by their class, age and the beliefs they already hold.' See AUDIENCE: ACTIVE AUDIENCE; AUDIENCE MEASUREMENT; EFFECTS OF THE MASS MEDIA; EMPOWERMENT; INTERACTIVITY; PLEASURE: ACTIVE AND REACTIVE; RESISTIVE READING.

Paternity of the text See TEXT: INTEGRITY OF THE TEXT.

Patriarchy Society ruled by or dominated by men; patriarch means father, thus patriarchal relates to a CULTURE shaped and governed in the interests of men, with women in a subordinate and, in some cases, subject, role. Patriarchy is reflected in customs, NORMS and VALUES, the law, education, commerce, industry, the arts, sport and, not least, language. Many commentators have also identified patriarchy as being assertively alive in the media, though at least at the *operative* (rather than *managerial*) level substantial advances have been made by women in JOURNALISM and BROADCASTING. See NEWS: THE 'MALENESS' OF NEWS.

Patriot Act (US), 2001 See USA – PATRIOT ACT (2001).

Pauper press See UNDERGROUND PRESS.

PeaceNet See TELEDEMOCRACY.

'Pencil of Nature, The' Title of the first book ever illustrated with photographs, published in England in 1844, the work of William Henry Fox Talbot (1800–77), inventor of the CALOTYPE process of photo-printing. The range of photographs pasted into *The Pencil of Nature* was extraordinary and included intimate, informal studies of Talbot's household at his home, Laycock Abbey. See PHOTOGRAPHY, ORIGINS.

People meter Electronic recording device used to measure individual TV viewing habits. Each member of a family has a portable keypad very like the TV's remote control device. Linked to the home by telephone lines, the system's central computer correlates each viewer's number with demographical data already on record.

People's Communication Charter Proposed by Cees Hamelink in *World Communication: Disempowerment and Self-Empowerment* (UK: Zed Books, 1995) in light of his vision that the GLOBALIZATION of communication threatens to further divide the information-rich from the information-poor, at the personal, community and national levels. The Charter provides a valuable text in which issues are highlighted, rights and responsibilities spelt out.

The preamble to the Charter opens with the affirmation that 'communication is basic to the life of individuals and peoples and that communication is crucial in the issues and crises which affect all members of the world community'. It is mindful 'that communication can be used to support the powerful and to victimize the powerless and that communication is fundamental to the shaping of the cultural environment of every society'.

Disempowerment is seen as a major trend; and it occurs through the 'withholding of information, by distorting information, by overwhelming people with overloads of information, or by obstructing people's access to communication channels'. In consequence the Charter urges support to enable people to develop their own communication channels through which they can speak for themselves. Under General Standards, Article 1 declares the 'conviction that all people are entitled to the respect of their dignity, integrity, equality, and liberty'. Article 2 asserts freedom of expression but aligned with that 'there should be free and independent channels of communication' on the basis that 'Free media are pluralist media.'

Article 3 speaks of the right to receive information 'about matters of public interest' and 'This includes the right to receive information which is independent of commercial and political interests.' Article 7 concerns the RIGHT OF REPLY, Article 8 speaks of the need to nurture a 'diversity of languages' and the need to 'create provisions for minority languages in the media'. Article 9 argues for the protection of people's cultural identity.

In an annexe to the fourth draft of the Charter Hamelink acknowledges contributions made by Howard Frederick, George Gerbner, David Goldberg, Wolfgang Kleinwachter, Kaarle Nordenstreng and students from Ohio State University, the American University at Washington, the University of Amsterdam and the Institute of Social Studies at the Hague. The author invites all further contributions via e-mail (hamelink@antenna.nl). See *TOPIC GUIDE* under MEDIA ETHICS.

Perception The process of becoming aware and making sense of the stimuli received from our environment by the senses: sight, hearing, smell, taste and TOUCH. *Social perception* refers to the application of this process to our attempts to explain, understand, make judgements about and predict the behaviour of other people.

Perception is selective. We are surrounded by many sensations but we tend to direct our attention to only a few of these. Our decision as to what to attend to can be influenced by environmental and personal factors: for example, environmental factors can include the intensity, size, motion or novelty of the stimuli whilst personal factors can include present needs and drives, physiological features, past experiences and learning – *perceptual set* – and personality.

The influence of personal factors explains why individuals may pay attention to different stimuli, to different messages or parts of a message. See ATTITUDES; CULTURE; EMPATHY; EXPECTA-TIONS; FIRST IMPRESSIONS; HALO EFFECT; LABELLING PROCESS (AND THE MEDIA); MALE-AS-NORM; MORES; MOTIVATION; NORMS; PROJECTION; SAPIR–WHORF HYPOTHESIS; SELECTIVE EXPOSURE; SELF-CONCEPT; SELF-FULFILLING PROPHECY; STEREOTYPE; SUBCULTURE; VALUES.

Performance See SELF-PRESENTATION.

Performatives Action words that indicate the nature of action through talk: *announce, insist, declare* or *denounce*. In the reporting of speech in NEWS, performatives often embody evaluative connotations, indicating approval on the part of the encoder, or disapproval. 'The Minister declined to comment' carries with it marginally less disapproval than the statement 'The Prime Minister refused to comment.' The word *say* may be classified as a *neutral performative* unless it is contrasted with a performative used disapprovingly; thus 'The Management say their pay offer is final, while the unions claim their actions will bring about further concessions.'

Periodicals for the study of media For the serious study of communication, students have a right to expect college or university libraries to stock the US-based, but international, publication, the *Journal of Communication* and the *European Journal of Communication*, both essential for the latest thinking and findings on all aspects of communication. The best-funded libraries will also stock *Communication Research, Discourse Studies, Discourse & Society, Ethnography, European Journal of Cultural Studies, Feminist Theory, International Journal of Cultural Studies, Journalism, Media, Culture & Society* and *New Media & Society*, all from the Sage Publications stable; and, from Routledge, *Continuum: Journal of Media and Cultural Studies, Feminist Media Studies* and *Historical Journal of Film, Radio and Television.*

Periodicity Describes the time-scale of the schedules of NEWS organizations; thus a daily newspaper has a 24-hour periodicity. The more the time-scale of a potential item of news coincides with the periodicity of the news organization, the more likely it is that the story will 'make the headlines'. Information that can be gathered, processed and dramatized within a 24-hour cycle (such as assassi-nations, clashes with the police, the speeches of politicians), stands a better chance of breaking through the news threshold than news that is gradual and undramatic. See NEWS VALUES.

Persistence of vision The realization that the eye retains an image for a split second after the object has passed gave birth to the cinema. The principle was first illustrated, and proved marketable, with toys of the nineteenth century such as the THAUMATROPE – a disc with images on each side; when the disc was spun round the images merged into a single action. The ZOETROPE was a drum with illustrations of figures inside which, when spun round, conveyed the impression of movement. See CINEMATOGRAPHY, ORIGINS.

Persona See PARASOCIAL INTERACTION; SELF-PRESENTATION.

Personal idiom Or idiosyncratic language; occurring in interpersonal relationships; serves the function of building relationship cohesiveness. Results of research into the use of personal idiom were published in an article 'Couples' personal idioms: exploring intimate talk', in the *Journal of Communication* (Winter, 1981) by Robert Hopper, Mark L. Knapp and Lorel Scott. Such idioms, they found, take the form of a range of idiomatic exchanges: partner nicknames; expressions of affection; labels for others outside the relationship; for use in confrontations; to deal with requests and routines; sexual references and euphemisms; sexual invitations and teasing insults (or 'kidding').

Personalization One of the chief conventions of media reportage. Where a potential NEWS item can be personalized it has a greater chance of being included than if it is difficult to translate into personality terms. The preference is for elite personalities (see NEWS VALUES).

John Lloyd in an article entitled 'The death of privacy: J'accuse!' (*New Statesman*, 5 March 1999) argues that this emphasis on the personal has been at the expense of an exploration of policy and ISSUES. He acknowledges that within TV news and current affairs it is 'a received wisdom that only by personalizing a story can it be given meaning for a mass audience. Thus a story about public spending must find someone in pain on a hospital waiting list.' Lloyd warns 'the hazard of such stories is that the feeling swamps the understanding'.

Personalizing transformation Stuart Hall in 'The determination of news photographs', in *The Manufacture of News: Social Problems, Deviance and the Mass Media* (UK: Constable, 1981), edited by Stanley Cohen and Jock Young, discusses the way TV news is skewed by the search for an angle from which to cover a story on the basis of available footage. One effect of this process is that television news tends to be person-orientated at the cost of giving focus to the underlying structural content of the news item, through what Hall termed a picture's 'personalizing transformation'. That is, the audience are deflected from considering the issues involved by their responses to the people they see in the coverage of the item on screen.

Personal space That which every individual feels easy in and which, if encroached upon, causes anxiety, tension or resistance. Personal space is fluid and mobile, whereas *territorial space* tends to be stationary. S. Lyman and M. Scott in 'Territoriality: a neglected social dimension', in *Social Problems* 15 (1967) refer to personal space as 'the most private and inviolate of territories belonging to an individual'. See PROXEMICS.

Phatic (language) Derives from the Greek, 'phasis', *utterance*; a term finding its modern connotation in the phrase 'phatic communion' coined by anthropologist Bronislaw Malinowski (1884–1942), meaning that part of communication which is used for establishing an atmosphere or maintaining social contact rather than for exchanging information or ideas. Phatic words and phrases have been called 'idiot salutations' and, when they comprise dialogue, 'two-stroke conversations'. Comments about the weather, enquiries about health, everyday exchanges, including nods, smiles, waves, are part of the phatic communion essential for 'oiling' or maintaining channels of communication.

Phatic language is central to human relationships; its significance can best be noted by its absence: you give a cheery 'hello' to a friend passing in the street to be greeted by stony silence; you halt your car to permit another motorist to go ahead of you, and he/she does not acknowledge your gesture. From such phatic neglect might spring responses out of all proportion to the MEANING of the exchange, or lack of it. See JAKOBSON'S MODEL OF COMMUNICATION, 1958.

Phoneme The smallest unit in the sound system of a language. Each language can be shown to operate with a relatively small number of phonemes, some having as few as 15, others as many as 50. Phonemics is the study of the basic sounds of language.

Phone-tapping See PRIVACY.

Phonetics The science of human sound-making, especially sounds used in speech. Phonetics includes the study of articulation, acoustics or perception of speech, and the properties of specific languages.

Phonodisc First-ever VIDEO recording, developed by John Logie Baird (1888–1946) in 1928. This was a 10-inch 78rpm record, in every way similar to the acoustic discs already being produced for conventional sound recording. Despite its novelty, the Phonodisc, coming so early in the age of the development of TV, failed to succeed commercially.

Phonograph See GRAMOPHONE.

Phonology A branch of LINGUISTICS that studies the sound systems of languages. Its aim is to demonstrate the patterns of distinctive sound in spoken language and to make as general statements as possible about the nature of sound systems in languages throughout the world.

Photographic negativization See VISIONS OF ORDER.

Photography, origins Joseph Nicèphore Nièpce (1765–1833) and his brother Claude were the first to fix images of the CAMERA OBSCURA by chemical means in 1793, though the light sensitivity of silver nitrate had been known and written about as early as 1727 when Johann Heinrich Schulze, Professor of Anatomy at the University of Altdorf, published a paper indicating that the darkening of silver salts was due not to heat but to light.

1826 is generally recognized as the year in which the first photographic image was captured. Joseph Nièpce's reproduction of a roof-top scene, on a pewter plate, he called Heliographie – sun drawing. In 1830 he teamed up with Louis Daguerre (1789–1851), theatrical designer and co-inventor of the diorama. The death of Nièpce three years later left Daguerre to lead the field in France. He discovered that an almost invisible latent image could be developed using mercury vapour, thus reducing exposure time from around eight hours to between 20 and 30 minutes.

His DAGUERROTYPE was taken up by the French government in 1839, and elicited from Paul Delaroche the immortal line, 'from today, painting is dead!' In the UK astronomer Sir John Herschel (1792–1871) read a paper 'On the art of photography' to the Royal Society, accompanied by 23 photographs. He was the first to use the verb *to photograph* and the adjective *photographic*, in 1840 to identify *negative* and *positive,* and 20 years later to use the term *snapshot.*

William Henry Fox Talbot (1800–77) won fame and fortune with his CALOTYPE (1841), the true technical base of photography because, unlike the Daguerrotype, its negative/positive principle made possible the making of prints from the original photographs. The inventions and discoveries that followed helped to improve the effectiveness of the photographic process. Frederick Scott Archer's *collodion* or wet-plate process, details of which were published in 1851, greatly increased sensitivity; the use of gelatine silver bromide emulsion, invented in 1871 by Dr Richard Leach Maddox, and later improved upon by John Burgess, Richard Kennett and Charles Bennett, proved a considerable advance on the collodion method, and ushered in the modern era of factory-produced photographic material, freeing the photographer from the necessity of preparing his/her own plates.

CELLULOID was invented by Alexander Parkes in 1861 and roll film made from celluloid was produced by the Eastman Company in the US from 1889. By 1902, Eastman, manufacturers of Kodak, were producing between 80 and 90 per cent of the world's output. Very swiftly, photography became the hobby of the man in the street. Every tenth person in the UK – 4 million people – was estimated to own a camera by 1900.

Colour film photography hit many technical snags in its development. A colour screen process was patented as early as 1904 by the Lumière brothers. They commercially introduced their Autochrome plates in 1907 when good panchromatic emulsion was available. However, exposure was about 40 times longer than that for black and white film.

Modern methods based on multiple-layer film and coupling components were simultaneously introduced by Kodak and Agfa. In 1935, Kodachrome, created by two American amateurs, Leopold Godowsky and Leopold Mannes, was marketed, a year ahead of Agfacolor. In both, transparencies were obtained suitable for projection as well as reproduction. Electronic flash was invented in 1931 by Harold E. Egerton. See CAMERA, ORIGINS; FILMLESS CAMERA; HIGH-SPEED PHOTOGRAPHY; PHOTO-JOURNALISM; PHOTOMONTAGE; TIME-LAPSE PHOTO-GRAPHY. See also *TOPIC GUIDE* under MEDIA HISTORY.

Photogravure Engraving by photography, for purposes of printing, was invented by Englishman William Henry Fox Talbot (1800–77) in 1852. It was not until 1947 that the first machine to do a complete typesetting job by means of photography was invented.

Photo-journalism Despite the popularity of photography among the general public, the press were curiously slow to realize the possibilities of photographs. The *Daily Mirror* was first in the field in the UK at the turn of the twentieth century, but the use of photographs did not become commonplace until the end of the First World War (1914–18). In June 1919, the New York *Illustrated Daily News* at last fully acknowledged a vital means of communication – 39 years after the feasibility of printing a half-tone block (reproducing light and shade by dots of different sizes and densities) alongside type had been demonstrated by Stephen H. Horgan in the New York *Daily Graphic.* It was not until the 1920s that photo-journalism in the modern sense began, with the introduction of the Ermanox camera and ultra-rapid plates.

Among the fathers of photo-journalism were Erich Saloman (1886–1944), Felix H. Man and Wolfgang Weber. With a camera hidden in his top hat, Arthur Barrett secretly took court photographs of the suffragettes, and, in February 1928, Saloman took sensational pictures of a Coburg murder trial. Man pioneered the picture story in, for example, *A Day in the Life of Mussolini*, 1934, and it was Man who founded *Weekly Illustrated* in the same year. He became chief photographer for *Picture Post*, founded in 1938, a position he held until 1945.

Photo-journalism was given increasing status over the years by many outstanding photographers. Henri Cartier-Bresson (b. 1908) photo-reported visits to Spain (1933) and Mexico (1934); Robert Capa (1913–54) won undying fame with his war photography, especially his pictures taken during the Spanish Civil War; Bill Brandt (1905–83) photographed the *English at Home* (1936) while Margaret Bowke-White, in *You Have Seen Their Faces* (1937) portrayed the conditions in the south of the US, in particular the negro chain-gangs. Suppression of the photo-reportage of Bert Hardy from the Korean War by the proprietors of *Picture Post* led to the resignation of the magazine's outstanding editor, Tom Hopkinson.

Talented, fearless and concerned photo-journalists continue to the present, even in the age of TV and with the closure of photo-papers. Don McCullin has photo-reported war, oppression, hardship and carnage all over the world in a vast array of unforgettable images. He was, incidentally, one of the photographers not given permission by the Ministry of Defence to cover the Falklands War (1982).

In *A Concise History of Photography* (UK: Thames & Hudson, 1965; 3rd edition by Helmet, 1986), Helmet and Alison Gernsheim write, 'No other medium can bring life and reality so close as does photography and it is in the fields of reportage and documentation that photography's most important contribution lies in modern times.' Not the least of its achievements, photography and photo-journalism have proved powerful agents in the awakening of social conscience.

A cautionary word about the present status of photo-journalism is expressed by John Pilger in his introduction to *Reporting the World: John Pilger's Great Eye Witness Photographers* (UK: 21 Publishing, 2001), a publication accompanying a photo-exhibition of the same name at London's Barbican galleries. Pilger writes: 'As media technology has advanced and become "global", so journalism, especially photo-journalism, has become increasingly parochial, prurient and politically safe. The great documentary form, the still photograph, has become largely a fashion and fame vehicle, answering to the incessant demands of the "market", serving what *Time* magazine calls "the eternal present". As for people's true lives, these are deemed unprofitable and of minimal interest.'

However, Pilger concedes there 'remain outstanding exceptions to this'. The exhibition celebrated the work of several outstanding photo-journalists, ranging from Keith Bernstein to Paul Weinberg and including four women photographers – Marion Kaplan, Susan Meiselas, Penny Tweedy and Anastasia Vrachnos. See DOCUMENTARY; MEDIASPHERE.

---

* John Hartley, *The Politics of Pictures: The Creation of the Public in the Age of Popular Media* (UK: Routledge, 1992).

Photomontage Process of mounting, superimposing, one photograph on top of another; a method almost as old as photography itself. The Dadaists and Surrealists experimented with photomontage to produce visionary pictures. Laslo Moholy-Nagy (1895–1946) combined several picture components in the production of a new work and termed his approach 'photolastics'. Malik of Berlin were the first publishers to use photomontage for book jackets. Most extensively, the process has been employed in ADVERTISING, though the British artist Peter Kennard has created many unforgettable – and satirical – images using photomontage. See PICTURE POSTCARDS.

Phototypesetting Method that bypassed the traditional metal type stage of print production by PRINTING type photographically from an optical or electric store of individual characters. Though the first photocomposing machine was created as early as 1894, it was not until it could be 'manned' by computers, in the 1960s, that the process became widespread. Modern typesetting allows operators to lay out pages on VDUs. This means that the same person can enter copy, make up the pages, check errors; then, one touch of a button and a high-quality proof is produced. See *TOPIC GUIDE* under MEDIA: TECHNOLOGIES.

Picture postcards German Heinrich von Stephan is generally considered to have thought up the idea of the postcard, in 1865, though Emmanuel Hermann ran him close, persuading the director-general of the Austrian Post to issue the first government postcard, in 1869. It was called a 'correspondence card'. In 1870 the first government postcard was issued in the UK; 70 million such cards were sold in the first year. The US government followed suit in 1872.

Since then the picture postcard has provided a treasure house for the analysis of contemporary interests and attitudes: art, fashion, new technology, warfare, royalty, exploration, history, travel; ideas of patriotism and Empire, of family, entertainment, comedy, etc. The title Mail Art has been given to a practice widespread in the late 1970s and 1980s of artists exchanging visual ideas by postcard.

During the same period the postcard became popular in a propagandist role, especially among protest groups of the Left. A classic piece of photomontage in postcard form is Peter Kennard's version of the painting by the nineteenth-century British painter, John Constable, *The Haywain*. Kennard superimposed cruise missiles on the horse-drawn wagon as it passes through a tranquil Suffolk landscape. Such cards use cartoons, photographs, photograffiti and quotations.

Inevitably cards of past ages have become collectors' items; the word Deltiology (from the Greek, *deltion*, small picture) was coined by American Randall Rhoades for picture postcard collecting and study. See CIGARETTE CARDS: CULTURAL INDICATORS; POSTERS.

Pidgin See COMMUNICATION: INTERCULTURAL COMMUNICATION.

Pilkington Committee Report on Broadcasting (UK), 1962 Set up under the chairmanship of Sir Harry Pilkington in 1960, the Committee's chief concern in a 297-page strongly worded deposition, was the nation's cultural and intellectual life, and the effect upon these of broadcasting now that commercial television had been on the scene since 1954: 'Our conclusion,' declared the Committee, 'is that where it prevails it operates to lower general standards of enjoyment and understanding.'

The BBC emerged unscathed, and not a little praised, from the Committee Report: 'The BBC knows good broadcasting and by and large they are providing it.' The 'villain' of the scenario was ITV. So dissatisfied with ITV programmes was the Committee that one of its recommendations (never put into practice) was that the IBA take on responsibility for the planning of programmes.

Pilkington expressed disquiet at the portrayal of physical violence in TV programmes and of a 'comprehensive carelessness about moral standards generally'.

Most of the recommendations of Pilkington were ignored, yet the Report did have its effect. It gave the BBC, staggering from the impact of ITV competition, a shot in the arm; and it was through Pilkington that the BBC was the first to receive a second channel (BBC2, 1964). John Whale in *The Politics of the Media* (UK: Fontana, 1977) says Pilkington 'aimed at large effects and missed them'. Nevertheless, Pilkington established a set of judgmental criteria, albeit elitist-cultural, which have formed a rallying point ever since for broadcasting reformers. See *TOPIC GUIDE* under COMMISSIONS, COMMITTEES, LEGISLATION; MEDIA INSTITUTIONS.

Pilot study A preliminary testing or 'experimental experiment' in which the researcher seeks to try out a new idea, system or approach; to determine whether an intended study is feasible, to clarify assumptions and improve instruments of measurement.

Pirate radio The monopoly of RADIO BROADCASTING held in the UK by the BBC was colourfully challenged in the 1960s by 'pirate' stations broadcasting from ancient forts and ships anchored in the North Sea. They played non-stop popular music, collected ADVERTISING revenues, paid no royalties on the music they played and thus made substantial profits.

In 1964, Radio Caroline, broadcasting from a ship called *Caroline*, took the air on 28 March, one of a long line of pirates. Ronan O'Rahilly, founder of Radio Caroline, received over 20,000 letters in the first ten days of broadcasting. The Duke of Bedford was the first advertiser, for Woburn Abbey – an advertisement that brought in 4500 people the next day.

War on the pirates was initially conducted in the Council of Europe. The European Agreement for the Prevention of Broadcasts transmitted outside National Territories, signed by member states in Strasbourg in 1965, sought to outlaw pirate broadcasting throughout the countries of the Common Market.

This was followed, in the UK, with the Labour government's Marine, etc. Broadcasting (Offences) Act that became law in 1967. Among sections of the broadcasting and political establishment there was fear that the pirates might not only undermine existing systems of broadcasting but have an 'undesirable' cultural and even political impact. The 1967 Act made it an offence to direct unlicensed broadcasts into the UK and to buy advertising time on illegal channels.

With the apparent defeat of the pirates, and the dismantling of their stations, there was clearly a gap to be filled in the pattern of official broadcasting services. At the end of 1966 the Labour government issued a White Paper containing proposals that opened the way for the creation of Radio 1.

That was not the end of pirate radio. A widespread enthusiasm for radio broadcasting independent of the duopoly was sustained through the 1970s, and in the 1980s pirates began popping up all over – making illegal broadcasts from unlicensed transmitters in woodlands, on hilltops, in back bedrooms, in garages and even on the move. See COMMERCIAL RADIO; COMMUNITY RADIO. See also *TOPIC GUIDE* under BROADCASTING.

Pistolgraph See CAMERA, ORIGINS.

Pixel Short for 'picture element', a pixel is one dot on a computer screen. Today's least expensive monitors are typically 640 pixels wide and 480 pixels high. Larger and more expensive monitors range up to 1600 x 1200 pixels and special purposes monitors may go much higher than that.

Plagiarism From the Latin, 'plagiarius', kidnapper; the act of stealing from others their thoughts or their writings and claiming them for one's own.

Play theory of mass communication In *The Play Theory of Mass Communication* (US: University of Chicago Press, 1967), William Stephenson counters those who speak of the harmful effects of the mass media by arguing that first and foremost the media serve audiences as play-experiences. Even newspapers, says Stephenson, are read for pleasure rather than information and enlightenment. He sees the media as 'a buffer against conditions which would otherwise be anxiety producing'. The media provide communication-pleasure.

Stephenson argues that what is most required by people within a national culture is something for everyone to talk about. For him mass communication 'should serve two purposes. It should suggest how best to maximize the communication-pleasure in the world. It should also show how far autonomy for the individual can be achieved in spite of the weight of social controls against him.' See *TOPIC GUIDE* under COMMUNICATION THEORY.

Pleasure: active and reactive Mary Ellen Brown in *Soap Opera and Women's Talk* (UK: Sage, 1994) speaks of the active and reactive pleasure of women viewers of soap operas. She argues that 'active pleasure for women in soap opera groups affirms their connection to a woman's culture that operates in subtle opposition to dominant culture'. It is this 'cult of the home and of women's concerns,' says Brown, 'recognized but devalued in patriarchal terms, that provides a notion of identity that values women's traditional expertise'.

On the other hand, reactive pleasure, 'while not rejecting the connection women often feel towards women's cultural networks and concerns, also recognizes that these concerns often arise out of women's inability to completely control their own lives'. Consequently they are able to 'recognize and to feel at an emotional level the price of oppression'.

Key to resistive soap opera groups is talking, the very act of which 'indicates the importance of connectedness to others'. Brown acknowledges that soaps are a genre 'designed and developed to appeal to women's place in society' and largely to keep her in that place, yet 'Although soap operas work at isolating women in their homes and keeping them busy buying household products, in fact many observations indicate that they actually bring women together'; thus, it would seem, paradoxically undermining HEGEMONY while aiming to underpin it.

Pluralism The view that modern industrial societies have populations that are increasingly *heterogeneous* that is, different in kind – divided by such factors as ethnic, religious, regional and CLASS differences. Such heterogeneity, it is argued, produces a diversity of NORMS, VALUES interests and personal perspectives within such societies. Technological developments, such as those fostered by the digital revolution, make it increasingly possible for the media and cultural industries to address and access the heterogeneous nature of audiences – niche advertising being but one example of this.

It can also be argued that a plurality of groups compete for power and influence within society. Power is seen, therefore, as being increasingly diffuse in terms of its distribution within these societies. This perspective is not without its critics. Some GROUPS are likely to have more power than others and will be in a better position to impose their values upon other groups. As far as the field of Media Studies is concerned, recent concentrations in media ownership throw some doubt on the degree to which power is becoming more diffuse in its distribution.

The proliferation of media outlets has not, in the view of some commentators, guaranteed for audiences a broader choice of programmes; indeed in the 'age of digitization' there is the fear that more may prove to be less, and that consumerist criteria may reduce pluralism rather than extend it. See DIGITIZATION; ELITE; SOCIAL ACTION (MODE OF ANALYSIS).

Pluralist Many modes, many alternatives; in media terms, *diversity* – of ownership, style, content and standpoint. A pluralist society is one in which there are many choices and many interpretations of MEANING.

Polarization Refers to the tendency to think and speak in terms of opposites (see WEDOM, THEYDOM) or what have been termed *binary oppositions.* The English language abounds with terms denoting opposition. Reality, however, is more complex, and arguably few things can be seen meaningfully in terms of polar opposites. Our language then may tempt us into misleadingly simple perspectives.

As Gail Myers and Michele Myers in *The Dynamics of Human Communication* (US: McGraw-Hill, 1985) argue, 'Our language supports dividing the world into false opposites. Polarization consists of evaluating what you perceive by placing it at one end of a two-pole continuum and making the two poles appear to be mutually exclusive. ... If you are honest, you cannot be dishonest.'

Whilst there are situations in which genuine opposites are found, what we should be wary of is applying this perspective when it is not appropriate and in so doing denying the complexities of a situation, or debate, and the range of alternatives that can or may exist. See VISIONS OF ORDER.

Politics of accommodation (in the media) Potential conflict between various individuals and GROUPS within media corporations, and between these corporations and a central social authority is seen by some commentators to be mediated by what Tom Burns in *The BBC: Public Institution and Private World* (UK: Macmillan, 1977) calls a 'politics of accommodation'. This is a negotiated compromise in which notions such as professional standards and the public interest are used as trading pieces. Negotiations of this type can be conducted at several levels: between the professionals and the management, between one corporation and another and between a corporation and the government.

Even between rival media empires there can exist, temporarily at least, what might be termed *reciprocal silence,* an agreement to censor information that may be, if publicized, damaging to one or other sides. A case in point is the silence exercised by the UK *Daily Mail* and its sister paper the *Mail on Sunday* over the controversial take-over of the *Mail*'s rival, Express Newspapers by porn king Richard Desmond, chief of the Northern and Shell company. The Labour government's approval in 2002 of this takeover was explained by some commentators – though not in the *Mail,* among Labour's harshest critics – as being linked with Desmond's £100,000 contribution to Labour Party funds.

Associated Newspapers (AN), owners of the *Mail* and *Sunday Mail,* turned out to have a legal agreement with Northern and Shell – a pact of reciprocal silence – not to report the controversy in return for the Express Group's silence concerning allegations about the Rothermere family, owners of AN. Margaret McDonagh, the then Labour Party general secretary who banked the £100,000 for Labour, shortly afterwards joined Northern and Shell. See CONSENSUS; ELITE; ESTABLISHMENT; HEGEMONY; MEDIA CONTROL; MEDIATION; REGULATORY FAVOURS; STRATEGIC BARGAINING. See also *TOPIC GUIDE* under MEDIA INSTITUTIONS; MEDIA: POLITICS AND ECONOMICS.

Polysemy Many meanings; broadly used, the term describes the potential for many interpretations in media TEXTS, or the capacity of AUDIENCE to read into such texts their own meanings rather than merely the PREFERRED READING of the communicators. For some commentators, audience is the 'victim' of media messages; for others, it is perceived as being capable of making its own diverse responses (see AUDIENCE: ACTIVE AUDIENCE; DOMINANT, SUBORDINATE, RADICAL). There is CONSENSUS among researchers that the extent of polysemy is to be viewed with caution.

As Celeste Michelle Condit writes in 'The rhetorical limits of polysemy', in *Television: The Critical View* (US: Oxford University Press, 1994), edited by Horace Newcomb, 'It is clear that there are substantial limits to the polysemic potential of texts and of decodings.' She recommends that we differentiate between the polysemy of texts and their interpretation by audience and suggests the term 'polyvalence' to describe the meanings ascribed to texts by audience.

'Polyvalence occurs,' says Condit, 'when audience members share understandings of the denotation of a text but disagree about the evaluation of those denotations to such a degree that they produce notably different interpretations.' It is different from polysemy in that it reflects 'not a multiplicity or instability of textual meanings but rather a difference in audience evaluations of shared denotations'.

Condit describes her research findings based upon the response of two students to an episode of the American TV cop series *Cagney & Lacey* (11 November 1985) in which the issue of abortion is dealt with. 'Jack', a pro-lifer, and 'Jill', pro-choice, had no difficulty understanding the *denotational* aspects of the episode. Where they took diametrically opposite viewpoints was in their response to the programme, which had a pro-choice message; their *connotational* reading. See OPEN, CLOSED TEXTS; OPINION LEADER; SIGNIFICANT OTHERS.

Polyvalence See POLYSEMY.

Pool system Practice, particularly in wartime, of governments chanelling media access to NEWS events through a regulated 'pool' of reporters; and consequently the 'pooling' of information for publication or broadcasting. This strategy of NEWS MANAGEMENT effectively censors journalists by corralling them, while at the same time claiming to offer prompt and reliable information on events. The first Gulf War (1991) offered a classic example of control through pooling.

Poor Man's Guardian Title of perhaps the most influential radical newspaper in Britain during the nineteenth century, edited by Bronterre O'Brien, published by Henry Hetherington. It appeared between 1831 and 1835, and was described by George Jacob Holyoake, a campaigner against the Taxes on Knowledge levied by government on the press, as 'the first messenger of popular and political intelligence which reached the working classes'. Other radical papers of this turbulent period were Richard Carlile's *Gauntlet* (1833–34), Robert Owen's *Crisis* (1832–34), James Watson's *Working Man's Friend* (1832–33) and Fergus O'Connor's *Northern Star* (1837–52), principal organ of the Chartist movement. See STAMP DUTY; UNDERGROUND PRESS. See also *TOPIC GUIDE* under MEDIA HISTORY.

Popular culture See CULTURE: POPULAR CULTURE.

Populism According to some theorists one of the distinguishing features of a mass society is its populist nature. Legitimacy is given to those persons, ideas or actions that are thought to best express the popular will or meet the most widely shared expectations. One result, such theorists claim, is that a premium is placed upon the capacity of those in leadership positions, to both create and placate popular opinion. The mass media tend to be seen as the agents through which such leaders control and exploit the masses.

Pornography Term originating from the Greek, 'writing of harlots'. Two sorts of pornography are usually differentiated: *erotica* – concentrating on physical aspects of heterosexual activity; and *exotica* – focusing on abnormal or deviationist sexual activity. Attitudes to pornography reflect a society's permissiveness, its current 'tolerance threshold' and also cast a light on prevailing social values.

Tolerance of pornography only makes sense if there is no felt risk; if pornography is thought to be linked with the abuse of women and children, and the degradation of human relationships and family life, pornography will be fought against whether the link is proved or not. In any case, pornography itself often makes the link between sexuality and violence: hard porn is, by general definition, a DISCOURSE in dominance expressed through violence which, at the very least, poses examples of possible behaviour.

Of interest and concern is the indisputable fact that in many countries pornography is big business. Civic concern about the possible link between porn and violence was registered by the Minneapolis City Council in 1983. Exhaustive public hearings took place to provide a basis of information for a decision whether or not to add pornography as a 'discrimination against women' to existing civil rights legislation. The transcript of the Minneapolis hearings was published in 1988. Quoting evidence from academic and clinical research on the effect of pornography on ordinary men, the report stated that, exposed to pornography, men become desensitized; they see themselves more likely to commit rape, less likely to respond sympathetically to women who are victims of rape or more likely to be lenient in their response to men who commit rape. According to the Minneapolis transcript, pornography that portrays women enjoying rape or violence or humiliation is most damaging.

As a result of the hearings the City Council passed a civil rights law enabling women victims of pornography to bring civil rights actions against the pornographers. However, the law was vetoed by the mayor and never implemented. A similar situation arose in Indianapolis where pornographers claimed they were being denied their constitutional right to free speech (under the First Amendment). Thus, in the courts, free speech took precedence over women's equality and safety from physical abuse.

In a UK *New Scientist* article, 'Flesh and blood' (5 May 1990), on the effects on men of pornography, Mike Baxter writes, 'The weight of evidence is accumulating that intensive exposure to soft-core pornography desensitizes men's attitudes to rape, increases sexual callousness and shifts their preferences towards hard-core pornography. Similarly, the evidence is now strong that exposure to violent pornography increases men's acceptance of rape myths and of violence against women. … Many sex offenders claim they used pornography to stimulate themselves before committing their crimes.'

The arrival and expansion of the INTERNET, with its relative freedom from control and overview, have offered global opportunities for pornography, along with the pornography of race hatred (see CYBERSPACE). Any system that combines the privacy of output and input with potentially universal access will be abused. It has been argued that for women exercising their right to explore the net there is as much danger from predators as there is on the streets at night. See CENSORSHIP; DESENSITIZA-TION; REGULATION OF INVESTIGATORY POWERS ACT (RIPA) (UK), 2000; STEREOTYPE; WILLIAMS COMMITTEE REPORT ON OBSCENITY AND FILM CENSORSHIP, 1979.

* Andrea Dworkin, *Pornography: Men Possessing Women* (UK: Women's Press, 1981); N.M. Malamud and E.M. Donnerstein (eds), *Pornography and Sexual Aggression* (US: Academic Press, 1984); D. Zillman and J. Bryant, 'Pornography, sexual callousness and the trivialization of rape', in *Journal of Communication*, Autumn 1982; Catherine Itzin, 'Pornography and civil liberties', in *Index on Censorship* 9, 1990; and Itzin's book, *The Case Against Pornography: Sex Discrimination, Sexual Violence and Civil Discrimination* (UK: Grafton, 1991); Pamela Church Gibson and Roma Gibson (eds), *Women, Pornography, Power* (UK: BFI, 1993).

Postcards See PICTURE POSTCARDS.

Posters Printed posters have had a short but vivid history, dating from the 1870s when the perfection of techniques in colour LITHOGRAPHY first made mass production possible. Posters have been described as the art gallery of the street and indeed the form has appealed to many artists, such as Henri Toulouse-Lautrec (1864–1901), members of the Art Nouveau movement and the graphic designers of the Bauhaus and the De Stijl group. Posters have served every mode of PROPAGANDA – social, political, religious, commercial. The arresting clarity of their images, combined with words used dramatically, emotively, humorously have often continued to impress long after the ideas, events or products they relate to have faded from attention.

So immediate and memorable are posters, and so widely recognized, that they have formed a regular inspiration for image-makers: imitated, reproduced, turned into cult objects, transmuted into other meanings. For example, many different uses have been made of Alfred Leete's famour poster (1914) 'Your Country Needs You', in which Lord Kitchener, with sweeping moustache, points out towards the audience, offering a formidable challenge to all those who have not yet volunteered for the First World War.

In peacetime, between elections, ADVERTISING dominates the poster contents of the billboards – sometimes with bold, witty and memorable images such as the Guinness adverts or Benetton's striking socio-political images. Posters come into their own in time of protest or revolution. Some of the finest posters were designed and printed during and after the Russian Revolution of 1917, while the Spanish Civil War (1936–38) stimulated the production of hundreds of hard-hitting, passionate and often tragic images. See *TOPIC GUIDE* under MEDIA HISTORY.

Postmodernism Term referring to cultural, social and political attitudes and expression characteristic of the 1980s and 1990s, following the modernist period of psychoanalysis, functional, clean-line, machine-inspired architecture, abstract art and stream-of-consciousness fiction. Wendy Griswold in *Cultures and Societies in a Changing World* (US: Pine Forge Press, 1994) writes, 'Many people believe that society has entered this new stage beyond modernity, a postindustrial stage of social development dominated by media images, in which people are connected with other places and times through proliferating channels of information.'

If hope and anxiety were features of modernism, says Griswold, 'the postmodern person is characterized by a cool absence of illusion. Modern minds were sceptical, Postmodern minds are cynical.' The prevailing cynicism is wary of traditional attempts at explaining the evolution of society. It discards the affirming or 'grand narratives' (*metanarratives*) of the past that subscribed to the view of the inevitability of human progress – what might be described as the Enlightenment position. Reality itself is an uncertainty: being a creation of language and existing in socially produced DISCOURSE, it represents an infinitely movable feast.

Marxism has been rejected by postmodernist thinkers such as Michel Foucault, Jacques Derrida, Jean-François Lyotard and Jean Baudrillard as having 'totalizing ambitions', that is, offering grandiose explanations of reality that cannot be sustained. They therefore reject the central tenet of Marxism, its belief in the emancipation of humanity.

The postmodernist position derives much of its vision from the German philosopher Friedrich Nietzsche (1844–1900), in particular his profound antipathy to any system and his rejection of the view expressed by an earlier German thinker, Georg Wilhelm Friedrich Hegel (1770–1831), of history as progress. Instead of such totalizing, postmodernism embraces *fragmentation* (and this includes views on the fragmentation of time itself, and therefore of concepts of the past and present). It homes in on micro-situations. The stress is on the local. Taking a deeply Rightist position, postmodernists declare that progress is a MYTH. If there are no unities, then nothing figures; if nothing figures, nothing matters and if nothing matters then anything goes.

Thus in architecture postmodernism scorns traditional forms while unapologetically plagiarizing them. It has varyingly been described as a culture of surfaces, of self-aware superficiality characterized by the ephemeral and discontinuity. In the postmodernist approach, writes Norman K. Denzen in a review, 'Messy methods of communication research', in the *Journal of Communication* (Spring 1995), all 'criteria are doubted, no position is privileged'.

Taken to a logical conclusion such a standpoint facilitates cultural freedom and unshackled PLURALISM; it could also unhinge freedom from responsibility on the ground that a definition of responsibility could only be arrived at on a personal, micro-level, hence the accusation made in some quarters that postmodernism is the cultural arm of the COMMODITIZATION of information and knowledge.

Madan Sarup in *An Introductory Guide to Post-Structuralism and Postmodernism* (UK: Harvester Wheatsheaf, 1993) says of Baudrillard, 'Personally I find many of his insights stimulating and provocative but, generally, his position is deplorable. In Baudrillard's world truth and falsity are wholly indistinguishable, a position which I find leads to moral and political nihilism.' The danger for a postmodernist world resides in a view expressed by Lyotard, that power has increasingly become the criterion of – the *synonym* for – truth. See DECONSTRUCTION; MEDIASPHERE. See also *TOPIC GUIDE* under COMMUNICATION THEORY.

* David Harvey, *The Condition of Postmodernity: An Inquiry into the Origins of Cultural Change* (UK: Blackwell, 1990); J.-F. Lyotard, *The Postmodern Condition* (UK: Manchester University Press, 1984); Frederic Jameson, *Postmodernism, or, The Cultural Logic of Late Capitalism* (UK: Verso, 1991); Christopher Norris, *Uncritical Theory: Postmodernism, Intellectuals and the Gulf War* (UK: Lawrence & Wishart, 1992); Angela McRobbie, *Postmodernism and Popular Culture* (UK; Routledge, 1994); John Hartley, *Popular Reality: Journalism, Modernity, Popular Culture* (UK: Arnold, 1996); George Myerson, *Heidegger, Habermas and the Mobile Phone* (UK: Icon Books, 2001).

Post-synchronization Or *dubbing*. In film-making, the process of adding new or altered dialogue in the original language to the soundtrack of a film after it has been shot. See SYNCHRONOUS SOUND.

Postulates of communication ·To define the fundamental attributes of the communication process is possibly a more fruitful area of analysis than struggling for an all-embracing and acceptable definition of communication. C.D. Mortensen in *Communication: The Study of Human Interaction* (US: McGraw-Hill, 1972), poses a single, basic postulate, that 'Communication occurs whenever persons attribute significance to message-related behaviour'; and then follows this up with five secondary postulates. These are as follows. (1) Communication is dynamic. (2) Communication is irreversible. (3) Communication is proactive (as opposed to *reactive*). Mortensen says here, 'The notion of man as a detached bystander, an objective and dispassionate reader of the environment, is nothing more than a convenient artefact. Among living creatures man is the most spectacular example of an agent who amplifies his environment.' We are shapers, not mere recipients. (4) Communication is interactive. (5) Communication is contextual. See *TOPIC GUIDE* under COMMUNICATION MODELS.

Postural echo Occurs when people – friends, lovers, etc. – unconsciously imitate or 'echo' each other's GESTURES and postures; this Desmond Morris in *Manwatching: A Field Guide to Human Behaviour* (UK: Jonathan Cape, 1977) describes as 'part of a natural body display of companionship'. He writes, 'Because acting in unison spells equal-status friendship, it can be used by dominant individuals to put subordinates at their ease.' See TIE-SIGNS.

Posture An element of non-verbal communication, a person's posture can be used or taken to indicate a range of aspects of behaviour. For instance, people often make judgements about others' states of mind from their body posture, and certain postures do seem to communicate something of the way a person feels. Optimism, confidence and dominance, for example, are often associated with an upright posture, whereas depression tends to be associated with a slouching, shrinking posture. Posture can be used to provide a variety of messages in feedback and can also be used to communicate our attitude to others.

Positive feelings towards others are often shown, in part, by a leaning forward posture in conversation, and by POSTURAL ECHO. Conversely, negative feelings can be indicated by leaning back from others. High status can be signalled by an upright posture. Aggressive attitudes towards others can be demonstrated by a progressively more exaggerated exhibition of high status or dominant behaviour. Shifts in posture can be used to mark stages in a conversation. See COMMUNICATION, NON-VERBAL.

Power This has been defined, and written about at length, by many theorists in many different disciplines, but a useful working definition is that provided by John B. Thompson in *The Media and Modernity: A Social Theory of the Media* (UK: Polity Press, 1995): power is 'the ability to act in pursuit of one's aims and interests, the ability to intervene in the course of events and to affect their outcome. In exercising power, individuals employ the resources available to them; resources are the means which enable them to pursue their aims and interests effectively.' Whilst the individual may be the basic building block of the power structure of any society, some blocks are arguably a lot bigger than others as some individuals have personally considerably more resources than others.

Further, as Thompson argues, 'While resources can be built up personally, they are also commonly accumulated within the framework of institutions, which are important bases for the exercise of power. Individuals who occupy dominant positions within large institutions may have vast resources at their disposal, enabling them to make decisions and pursue objectives which have far-reaching consequences.'

A concept closely related to that of power is *influence*. Charles B. Handy in *Understanding Organizations* (UK: Penguin, 1993) describes the relationship between power and influence thus: 'Influence is the process whereby A modifies the attitudes and behaviour of B. Power is that which enables him to do it.' The exercise of power and influence, in addition to resources requires what French and Raven term a 'power base' (quoted in B. Raven and J. Rubin, *Social Psychology*, US: John Wiley, 1983) and at the same time the selection of appropriate methods of influence. In turn this is predicated to a considerable extent on the acceptance of, or acquiescence in, the exercise of power by those subjected to it.

John B. Thompson offers a distinction between the differing *sources* of power and categorizing these into four main types: *economic, political, coercive* and *symbolic*. Of course these often overlap, and the way in which they do so is in itself an indication of the often complex and at times mutually supportive relationships that exist within the overall power structure. Varying forms of power are often concentrated in institutions. *Economic power* is based in ownership or control of those resources required for the productive activity involved in transforming human, material and financial resources into goods and services, for sale or exchange in a market in order to generate a means of subsistence. This might also be described as *corporate power.*

Political power stems from the authority – usually of governments and those bodies invested with *authority* – to organize the activities of individuals, GROUPS or organizations and to control and direct, to varying extents, these activities. These might include parliament, the civil service and local authorities. *Coercive power* expresses itself through the use of force and can be found in a diverse range of power relationships. Most states, for example, whatever their form of government, have resources that underscore their political power with the ability to employ physical force when the exercise of power by persuasion seems likely to fail.

Very different but not necessarily less effective is *symbolic power*, which Thompson defines as stemming from 'the activity of producing, transmitting and receiving meaningful symbolic forms'. He sees such activity as being 'a fundamental feature of social life. … Individuals are constantly engaged in the activity of expressing themselves in symbolic forms and in interpreting the expressions of others; they are constantly involved in communicating with one another and exchanging information and symbolic content.' To do so, individuals draw upon the various 'means of information and communication' such as access to the channels of communications, communicative competence, knowledge and acknowledged expertise in areas of symbolic exchange. The mass media serve as key operators of symbolic power.

The pivotal role that the media play in transmitting information about politics and politicians to a wide audience – in *power-broking* – has resulted in their being referred to as the FOURTH ESTATE; that is, they rank alongside the judiciary, the Church and government as exercisers of power and influence. Indeed it is the media that play an essential role in communicating to the public the nature, location and distribution of power in the community and the power relationships operating within it; hence the central interest among media analysts and researchers in the media's capacity to influence, shape, reinforce or undermine the exercise of power at all levels of society and the degree to which people may be influenced. See DEMOCRACY AND THE MEDIA; EFFECTS OF THE MASS MEDIA. See also *TOPIC GUIDE* under MEDIA: POWER, EFFECTS, INFLUENCE; MEDIA: POLITICS AND ECONOMICS; MEDIA; VALUES AND IDEOLOGY.

Power elite Term used by C. Wright Mills in his seminal analysis *Power, Politics and People* (US: Oxford University Press, 1963) to describe those members of a society who combine social and political privilege with power and influence. See CULTURAL APPARATUS; ELITE; HEGEMONY.

PR See PR: PUBLIC RELATIONS.

Predatory pricing In relation to the PRESS, reduction in the price of a newspaper in order to undercut the competition, and in the long run put the competition out of business.

Preferred reading Stuart Hall poses this concept in 'The determination of news photographs', in Stanley Cohen and Jock Young (eds), *The Manufacture of News* (UK: Constable, 1973). Here the preferred reading of a photograph – preferred, that is, by the transmitter of the photograph – is one, Hall believes, that guides us to an interpretation that lies within the traditional social, political and cultural VALUES of the time, symbolizing and reinforced by the interests of the dominant HIERARCHY. The framing, cropping, captioning and juxtaposition of the photograph with TEXT all serve to close off the reader from lateral, or independent, interpretations of the photography; from ABERRANT DECODING of the MESSAGE. Thus *closure* is achieved. The term has come to be applied to message systems generally. See DOMINANT, SUBORDINATE, RADICAL; MEDIATION; POLYSEMY. See also *TOPIC GUIDE* under AUDIENCES/CONSUMPTION AND RECEPTION OF MEDIA.

Prejudice Ernest R. Hilgard, Richard C. Hilgard and Rita L. Hilgard in *Introduction to Psychology* (US:

Harcourt Brace Jovanovich, 1975) define prejudice as 'an attitude that is firmly fixed, not open to free and rational discussion and resistant to change'. Such an attitude may be directed towards ideas, objects, situations or people, and may be positive or negative. Prejudice is arguably of greatest concern when it is negative and directed towards other people. In this instance prejudice is often accompanied by negative STEREOTYPES of its targets.

The targets of prejudice tend to be those who are the relatively powerless members of GROUPS, organizations or societies, as well as those who are perceived as being deviant. It is of course possible to be both. The term *discrimination* is normally used to describe the acting out of prejudice, which often shows itself in communicative behaviour.

Gordon Allport in *The Nature of Prejudice* (UK: Addison-Wesley, 1954) identifies five stages in the behavioural component of prejudice: *anti-locution, avoidance, discrimination, physical attack* and *extermination*. Examples of anti-locution include insults and so-called jokes (in which the intention is to denigrate the subject). Avoidance of communication, though a more passive demonstration of prejudice, will tend to ensure that negative beliefs and attitudes are unchallenged by contact. Rejection shown in communicative behaviour may, however, be a precursor to much more damaging actions. See DEVIANCE; LABELLING PROCESS (AND THE MEDIA); NORMS.

Press See *TOPIC GUIDE* under AUDIENCES/CONSUMPTION AND RECEPTION; MEDIA HISTORY; MEDIA INSTITUTIONS; MEDIA ISSUES AND DEBATES; MEDIA: POWER, EFFECTS, INFLUENCE; NEWS MEDIA.

Press barons As early as 1884 Scots-American steel magnate Andrew Carnegie headed a syndicate that controlled eight daily papers and ten weeklies. In the UK Edward Lloyd owned the mass circulation *Daily Chronicle* and the blockbuster Sunday paper *Lloyd's Weekly*, the first periodical to sell a million copies. As the costs of founding and running newspapers grew, leaving ownership a privilege of none but the very rich or joint stock companies, the trend towards chain ownership accelerated.

In *The Life and Death of the Press Barons* (UK: Secker and Warburg, 1982), Piers Brendon points out that 'the press barons of the New World, stimulated by the tradition of freedom and protected by constitutional guarantees, were wilder beasts than their Old World counterparts'; but they shared characteristics with UK press barons, being 'vicious, unstable, despotic ...' sharing a 'ruthless quest for wealth, power and independence'. However, in Brendon's view, 'their refusal to endure restraints on journalistic freedom was a real boon', despite their being 'armour-plated sabre-toothed behemoths'.

James Gordon Bennett (1795–1872), perhaps the first press baron, compared himself to Moses, Seneca, Socrates and Martin Luther, and ranked his own genius as a newspaper baron with Shakespeare, Scott, Milton and Byron. He handed over the New York *Tribune* in 1868 to his son of the same name: James Gordon Bennett Jr matched his father's outrageous eccentricity as well as demonstrating, in Brendon's words, 'flair, enterprise and decision'.

Then came the heavyweight contestants Joseph Pulitzer (1847–1911), proprietor of the New York *World*, referred to as His Majesty by his staff, and William Randoph Hearst (1863–1932) whose *Journal* and other newspapers, spreading as they did throughout America, made their owner 'the most vilified press baron in history'.

Across the Atlantic, egotism, eccentricity and paranoia were to be found in generous supply in the UK press barons, such as Alfred Harmsworth, later Lord Northcliffe (1865–1922) whose admiration for Pulitzer was reciprocated to the point where Pulitzer offered Harmsworth editorship of the *World* for one day, 1 January 1900. Harmsworth produced a twelve-page four-column 'tabloid', about half the *World's* normal size. Of this publication, William Randolph Hearst confessed, 'We all thought it was a clever stunt, but few of us realized the vital importance of the principle'; and this was, by any means, to provide reading material that would attract and hold the interest of the masses.

In 1888 Harmsworth had launched a weekly journal, *Answers*, modelled on George Newnes' *Tit-Bits*, comprising jokes, puzzles, 'sound-bites' of odd news and information but, advancing on *Tit-Bits*, encouraging reader involvement, in particular, with competitions for prizes.

In 1890, *Answers*, which had now reached a circulation of over 200,000, was supplemented by *Comic Cuts*, followed by *Illustrated Chips, Home Chat, The Marvel, Wonder* and *Union Jack*. Harmsworth bought, and rejuvenated the *Evening News* in 1898 and in 1896 he founded the *Daily Mail*, following the 'Harmsworth way', containing condensed news, gossip, sports reports and striving to prove through rising circulation Harmsworth's dictum that 'Most of the ordinary man's prejudices are my prejudices.'

Harmsworth was a publicist of genius but he owed much to the business acumen of his brother Harold, later Lord Rothermere, who eventually inherited and continued the Northcliffe media stable. For his services to the Conservative Party, in particular the support offered the Tories by the *Daily Mail*, Harmsworth was offered a peerage (1905), becoming Lord Northcliffe.

By 1921, he controlled *The Times*, the *Daily Mail*, the *Weekly Despatch* (later a Sunday paper) and the *London Evening News*. Brother Harold controlled the *Daily Mirror*, the *Sunday Pictorial*, the *Daily Record* and several other papers. Together they owned the large magazine group Amalgamated Press while brother number three, Sir Lester Harmsworth, owned a string of papers in the south-west of England. Between them these baronial brothers owned papers with an aggregate circulation of over six million. Their dominance was rivalled by another larger-than-life press baron, Lord Beaverbrook (1879–1964). His *Daily Express* led all its competitors in the late 1930s. His four papers reached a joint circulation of 4.1 million by 1937.

Regional newspaper chains displayed similar baronialist tendencies. The Berry brothers, Lords Camrose and Kemsley, pushed their tally from four daily and Sunday papers in 1921 to twenty daily and Sunday papers by the outbreak of the Second World War in 1939. As newspapers fell into fewer hands, circulation expanded dramatically. Between 1920 and 1939 the circulation of national dailies went from 5.4m to 10.6m while Sunday paper circulations rose from 13.5m to 16m. In the US Hearst, by 1942, ran 17 daily and 12 Sunday papers, at the time the biggest media business in the world.

Although in the UK the leading Sunday paper owners, Kemsley, Beaverbrook and Camrose, controlled 59 per cent of national sales in 1937, it was 8 per cent less than the control exercised in 1910 by lesser-known barons, Dalzil, Riddell and Lloyd. Equally the control exercised over daily circulation in 1937 by Rothermere, Beaverbrook and Cadbury fell 7 per cent below that exercised by Pearson, Cadbury and Northcliffe in 1910. As James Curran and Jean Seaton point out in *Power Without Responsibility* (UK: Routledge, 5th edition, 1997), 'The press magnates' hegemony over the press was, in fact, waning during the period celebrated for their ascendancy.'

Almost to a man, the press barons were autocratic, eccentric and immensely ambitious, exerting far-reaching editorial control and involving themselves minutely in the day-to-day running of a newspaper business. Competition was savage and unrelenting. It was necessary for the press barons to attract readership with special offers, life insurance, attention-catching competitions, and to fill their pages with stories their readers were interested in – which meant, as a *News Chronicle* survey of readers' responses in 1933 indicated, more stories about accidents, crime, divorce and human interest (and less 'serious' matters such as politics and world events).

Politics was important, but profits came first. In fact the British political establishment viewed the press barons with dislike and suspicion, for they were not so easily 'bought' or persuaded as their predecessors had been. Of course this did not stop them meddling in politics.

Between 1919 and 1922 Rothermere and Northcliffe put all their press backing behind policies advocating public spending cuts. Their Anti-Waste League won three parliamentary by-elections in 1921. Beaverbrook and Rothermere formed the United Empire Party in 1930 aimed at creating a tariff wall around the British Empire, and an election victory was achieved on the issue at Paddington in October 1930. Prime Minister Stanley Baldwin fought back – on the issue of who rules: government or press? – and won the Westminster St George's by-election comfortably.

During the 1930s Rothermere's papers the *Daily Mirror* and *Daily Mail* supported the British Union of Fascists for a brief period and were rabidly anti-red. The record of press persuasion on single issues is, however, less significant than the longer-term influence the popular press had at this time. According to Curran and Seaton, this demonstrated itself in 'the consolidation of public opinion, particularly amongst the middle class, against change': 'The papers controlled by the press barons conjured up imaginary folk devils that served to strengthen commitment to dominant political norms and to unite the centre and the right against a common enemy', that is, socialism and Marxism; the so-called 'red peril'. Patriotism, a deep emotional attachment to Empire, ill-concealed racialism, hatred of foreigners, these – along with their inveterate anti-socialism – characterized the 'voice' of press baronage in the inter-war years.

The post-war period saw new styles of press leadership as the one-product newspaper tycoons gave way to multi-marketing trends, conglomerate ownership and more self-effacing, though no less far-reaching, control. Today, 'baronialism' is more powerful because it is more global in reach and influence, and barons such as Rupert Murdoch think and act globally, aiming for greater and greater media diversity. In addition to owning newspapers worldwide, the Murdoch empire counts among its portfolio of ownership film studios, publishing houses, TV stations and SATELLITE broadcasting. Compared to Murdoch's holdings in 175 newspapers worldwide, nine TV networks and an estimation that has been made that his media reach one in three of the world's population, the imperialism of Hearst and Northcliffe (with whom Murdoch developed a close friendship) pale in comparison. See BERLUSCONI PHENOMENON; COMMANDERS OF THE SOCIAL ORDER; CONGLOM-ERATES: MEDIA CONGLOMERATES; GLOBAL MEDIA SYSTEM: THE MAIN PLAYERS; MEDIA CONTROL; NEWSPAPERS, ORIGINS. See also *TOPIC GUIDE* under MEDIA HISTORY.

* Nicholas Coleridge, *Paper Tigers* (UK: Heinemann, 1993); Roy Greenslade, *Maxwell's Fall* (US: Simon & Schuster, 1992); Tom Bowyer, *Maxwell: The Final Verdict* (UK: HarperCollins, 1996); Gillian Doyle, *Media Ownership: Concentration, Convergence and Public Policy* (UK: Sage, 2002).

Press commissions See *TOPIC GUIDE* under COMMISSIONS, COMMITTEES, LEGISLATION.

Press Complaints Commission (UK) Body created by the UK newspaper industry, beginning its duties on 1 January 1991, and replacing the Press Council; Lord McGregor being appointed the Commission's first chairman. The PCC operates on the basis of a Code of Practice, the 'five com-mandments' of which concern privacy, opportunity for reply, prompt correction and appropriate prominence, the conduct of journalists and the treatment of race. The Code warns newspapers against publishing 'inaccurate, misleading or distorting material' as well as recommending them 'to distinguish clearly between comment, conjecture and fact'. See CALCUTT COMMITTEE REPORTS ON PRIVACY AND RELATED MATTERS, 1990 AND 1993.

Press, four theories of Classification by F.S. Sibert, T. Peterson and W. Schramm in *Four Theories of the Press* (US: University of Illinois Press, 1956), these are the *libertarian, communist, authoritarian* and *social responsibility* traditions. See NORMATIVE THEORIES OF MASS MEDIA.

Pressure groups Also known as interest groups or lobbies, pressure groups aim to influence central and local government and its actions in certain, limited areas of policy. They do not usually seek formal political office although some pressure groups do sponsor elected individuals. Pressure groups can usefully be divided into two main types: those that act to protect their members' interests and those that are concerned to promote a cause that they believe will be in the general interests of society.

Pressure groups vary not only in the focus of their concern but more crucially in the degree of influence they have. In some cases a government may consult relevant pressure groups before introducing or amending legislation or policies, and some groups enjoy relatively easy access to government.

To be successful, pressure groups need well-planned strategies of communication, or campaigns. The methods used here vary but include letter-writing, gaining interviews on local or national radio, using radio phone-in slots, the distribution of literature, advertisements, demonstrations and gaining television coverage. The INTERNET has proved to be a key means of disseminating information by pressure groups. Its capacity for *interactivity* has in particular facilitated planning and organization across national borders, often bypassing traditional channels of mass communication.

Pretty Good Privacy (PGP) Title of a computer software program designed to protect computer data from intrusion; an encrypting process created by American Phil Zimmerman, who in 1998 received the Life Achievement Award from *Secure Computing Magazine*. Governments have proved less welcoming to PGP, seeing it as a barrier to their systems of SURVEILLANCE.

Primacy, the law of The view that whichever side of a case or argument is presented first will have greater impact on an AUDIENCE than anything that follows. F.H. Lund is considered to have been the first to advance this theory in 'The psychology of belief', in the *Journal of Abnormal and Social Psychology* (1925). There are those, however, who espouse the law of *recency*, asserting that that which is most recent is the more likely to have greatest impact and retention.

Primacy puts its faith in first impressions, recency in last impressions; both are marginal factors in the real context of debate where who goes first or last, and what is said first or last, in what situation and by what means, are more fundamental criteria.

Primary groups See GROUPS.

Primary, secondary definers In relation to events, primary definers are those such as the police who are in a position to speak authoritatively in matters of crime and public order; who are structurally dominant in terms of their potential for defining reality. The media are secondary definers, either re-presenting, interpreting or rejecting the dominant definition. The position becomes complicated when the field of definition is occupied by rival definers – such as when employers and unions are in conflict.

Primary, secondary texts See TEXT: TERTIARY TEXT; TEXT.

Primetime US term to describe the peak viewing period of TV viewing: generally between 8p.m. and 11p.m.

Printing John of Gutenberg introduced printing using movable type in 1450, though the Chinese had developed print technology centuries before. Printing made the mass production and dissemination of knowledge and information possible for the first time and had a revolutionary impact on the conduct of business, commerce, government, learning, literature, politics, the recording of history, the advance of technology and the sciences.

Gutenberg's system, still widely practised today despite sophisticated advances in computer-generated texts, worked by the application of ink, and subsequently paper, to a raised surface, a process called *relief printing*. Other methods are *planographic* and *intaglio* or *gravure*. With the former, the design to be printed and its background are in one flat surface; in intaglio printing the part to be printed is etched or cut into the plate – the exact reverse of relief printing.

Bavarian actor/playwright Alois Senefelder in 1798 found that some kinds of stone absorb both oil and water. He drew on the stone with a greasy crayon and then dampened the stone that absorbed the water only where there was no crayon design. He then made an ink of wax, soap and lamp black which stuck to the crayon and came off on paper, producing a print. *Lithography* from the Greek 'lithos', stone, was born. Today zinc or aluminium sheets are used and the design to be printed is applied to the plates by a photographic process.

Offset lithography, the main process of planographic printing employed today, came about as a result of an accident by American printer Ira W. Rubel who had allowed the rubber covering of the impress cylinder to become inked. He discovered that the perfect impression it transferred to the sheet of paper was of better quality than that produced by direct contact with the plate. The first patent for a system of printing using *photocomposition* was taken out by William Friese-Greene in 1895, though typesetting by photography was not in commercial use until the early 1950s.

Despite regular claims that the 'age of print' of the book-in-the-hand rather than the book-on-the-screen, is coming to an end, the printed book as an artefact shows few signs of ever becoming the dinosaur of communications; and though the statistical profile of newspapers is less assertive in many countries than in the past, the *habit* of newspaper reading is likely to continue, regardless of the ongoing failure to stop printer's ink transferring to readers' fingers. See CYLINDER OR ROTARY PRESS; LINOTYPE PRINTING; MONOTYPE PRINTING; NEWSPAPERS (UK), ORIGINS; UNDERGROUND PRESS. See also *TOPIC GUIDE* under MEDIA HISTORY.

---

* Asa Briggs and Peter Burke, *A Social History of the Media: From Gutenberg to the Internet* (UK: Polity, 2002).

Prior restraint Legal term describing the rights in some countries for CENSORSHIP to be exercised before publication. In the United States, where the Second Amendment of the Constitution protects freedom of speech, there is no such thing as prior restraint. In the UK, however, it was prior restraint, on the grounds of confidentiality, that prevented the publication of Peter Wright's book, *Spycatcher* (see SPYCATCHER CASE).

The *Guardian, Observer* and *Sunday Times* newspapers challenged the action of the United Kingdom government at the European Court of Human Rights in Strasbourg. In November 1991 the court, while unanimously holding that the papers had been denied their right to freedom of expression when they were prevented from publishing extracts from *Spycatcher* after the book had been published widely elsewhere, nevertheless affirmed, by a vote of 14 to 10, the right to prior restraint.

The dissenting minority of the Euro-judges struck a more encouraging note for civil liberties, declaring that, 'in a free and democratic society there can be no room, in time of peace, for restrictions of that kind, and particularly not if these are resorted to, as they were in the present case, for governmental suppression of embarrassing information'.

In February 1999 Labour's Home Secretary Jack Straw attempted to impose prior restraint on the *Sunday Telegraph* when he received information that the paper intended to publish extracts, three days before its official release, of the Macpherson Report into police conduct in the case of the murdered teenager, Stephen Lawrence. Justice Rix at first imposed a court order, then 24 hours later removed it. A *Guardian* leader, headed 'A very British farce', declared prior restraint 'as fundamentally inimical to free speech'. See *TOPIC GUIDE* under MEDIA: FREEDOM, CENSORSHIP.

Privacy A keenly debated issue of our time is the perceived threat to, or indeed loss of, individual privacy. Our privacy is at risk from those in authority who hold information on us, and from the media, part of whose mission is to make the private public, to uncover dark secrets, to bring illumination to facts held from view. The right to privacy obviously clashes with the right to know; where there is debate is on just how much is rightly private, and how much of public interest.

Should, for example, the President of the United States have a right to protection in matters that, on the face of it, are not connected with 'public virtues' or the qualities for which the president was elected? On the other hand, is the separation between public and private personas viable – if a president deceives his wife, will he not also deceive his nation?

This issue can affect all of us at some time or another if we do something newsworthy, which will invite the interest of the media; but for the most part the privacy of ordinary citizens is more at risk from surveillance on the part of those who hold data on us (see SURVEILLANCE SOCIETY).

The French philosopher Michel Foucault, in *Discipline and Punish* (US: Pantheon, 1990), refers to 'technologies of power' that reach into the very hearts of our lives; while Mark Poster in *The Mode of Information: Poststructuralism and Social Context* (UK: Polity, 1990) fears that the 'populace has been disciplined to surveillance and to participating in the process' willingly, without coercion: 'Social security cards, drivers' licences, credit cards, library cards and the like – the individual must apply for them, have them ready at all times, use them continuously. Each transaction is recorded, encoded and added to databases. Individuals themselves in many cases fill out the forms; they are at once the source of information and the recorder of the information.'

Home networking constitutes 'the streamlined culmination of this phenomenon: the consumer, by ordering products through a modem connected to the producer's database, enters data about himself or herself directly into the producer's database in the very act of purchase'. In this sense, the population participates in 'the disciplining and surveillance of themselves as consumers'.

Less discussed than computer access to our private lives, but no less intrusive, is the practice, worldwide, with ever-increasing sophistication, of phone-tapping, and the inadequate legal protection against this form of surveillance.

It must be acknowledged that surveillance and the loss of privacy are not entirely one-way. The performance of a nation's leaders, civil servants, business people – whose activities have traditionally been shielded from public gaze – are now more *visible* to the public than ever before. John B. Thompson in *The Media and Modernity: A Social Theory of the Media* (UK: Polity, 1995) says that 'the development of communication media provides a means by which many people can gather information about a few and, at the same time, a few can appear before many; thanks to the media, it is primarily those who exercise power, rather than those over whom power is exercised, who are subjected to a certain kind of visibility'.

We as the public may, through the computer data systems that threaten our privacy, feel vulnerable, but, Thompson believes, the visibility made possible by communication media makes it 'more difficult for those who exercise political power to do so secretively, furtively, behind closed doors'.

The power of intrusion remains, however, with those in authority. The results of a survey of conditions of privacy conducted by Privacy International and the Electronic Privacy Information Centre, US, and published in 2002, cited UK government and authorities as one of the most ineffective of 50 countries in protecting rights to privacy. The UK government in recent years has not only increased practices of surveillance in Britain but has been instrumental in pushing the European Community in the same direction. According to Simon Davies, director of Privacy International, government ministers in the UK have mounted a 'systematic attack' on the right to privacy by introducing laws extending mass surveillance. His belief is that 'The UK demonstrates a pathology of antagonism towards privacy', declaring that, for example, the UK Data Protection Act 'is almost useless in limiting the growth of surveillance'. See CALCUTT COMMITTEE REPORTS ON PRIVACY AND RELATED MATTERS, 1990 AND 1993; DATA PROTECTION ACT (UK), 1984; PRIVACY: PRESS COMPLAINTS COMMISSION CODE OF PRACTICE (UK), 1997; FREEDOM OF INFORMATION; HUMAN RIGHTS ACT (UK), 2000; REGULATION OF INVESTIGATORY POWERS ACT (RIPA) (UK), 2000; USA – PATRIOT ACT, 2001. See also *TOPIC GUIDE* under MEDIA FREEDOM, CENSORSHIP; MEDIA ISSUES AND DEBATES.

Privacy: Press Complaints Commission Code of Practice (UK), 1997 Following the death of Diana, Princess of Wales, in a car crash in Paris, and the widespread belief that this had been caused in part by the hounding of her by paparazzi (see PAPARAZZO), the UK Press Complaints Commission issued in December 1997 a Code of Practice concerning privacy and PRESS harassment. Clause 3 of the Code declares that 'Everyone is entitled to respect for his or her privacy and family life, home, health and correspondence. A publication will be expected to justify intrusion into any individual's life without consent.' Taking pictures of people 'in private places without their consent is wholly unacceptable', a private place being 'public or private property where there is a reasonable expectation of privacy'.

On harassment, Clause 4 urges that journalists and photographers 'must neither obtain nor seek to obtain information or pictures through intimidation, harassment or persistent pursuit' and this extends to 'telephoning, questioning, pursuing or photographing individuals after having been asked to desist'. The Code also sets out rules concerning intrusion into the lives of children, banning press payment to minors.

The Code is self-regulatory, without the power of law, being the creation of the newspaper industry. It draws upon the European Convention for the Protection of Human Rights and Fundamental Freedoms, Article 8 of which, having asserted the right of the citizen to respect for his or her privacy and family, home and correspondence, then lists the exceptions to the rule of personal privacy: 'There shall be no interference by a public authority with the exercise of this right except such as is in accordance with the law or is necessary … in the interests of national security, public safety or the economic well-being of the country, for the prevention of disorder or crime, for the protection of health or morals, or for the protection of the rights and freedoms of others.'

Privatization Dominant trend in media organization throughout the 1980s and 1990s, in which public-owned media utilities were sold off into private hands; specifically into those of the great transnational companies (TNCs); and with it the privatization of information itself; or as some commentators have put it, the *commoditization* of information. In fact the process commenced with the expansionism of multinational, multi-product corporations after the Second World War.

It was soon perceived that in the developing Age of Information, information was profitable. Corporations that were not already owners of media, bought into media. Private ownership and its dominance of cultural and social expression – whether in the arts, education, the museums service, libraries, sport or entertainment generally – came up against a major competitor: the public sector. In this domain, information was treated as a public right available to all rather than essentially a saleable commodity.

Such rivalry in an increasingly competitive world was considered bad for private business. It became, then, corporate policy to pressurize governments into dismantling the public sector. Rightist governments in the 1980s and 1990s (the US under Ronald Reagan and George Bush Senior, the UK under Margaret Thatcher and John Major) made privatization the driving force of political and cultural change. Notions of 'public good' or 'public interest' were to become conditional upon the requirements of 'market forces'; as was social responsibility.

At a global level, privatization has been linked with financial and technical aid. The World Bank and the International Monetary Fund (IMF), for example, have refused economic assistance to developing nations wishing to update their telecommunications systems unless these have first been privatized. Telmex, the Mexican state-owned telecommunications system, privatized in 1990, increased the local telephone rate by over a thousand per cent in the next decade.

The chief beneficiaries of cross-world privatization of previously state-run systems have been American-owned tele-corporations. These hold substantial and increasing investments in operations in over 36 countries. In an article, 'Pedaling the e-ticket to the development train: Washington's global e-commerce agenda', posted on the CorpWatch website (8 May 2002), Sarah Anderson states that 'The US government has taken advantage of the world love affair with the internet to advance an agenda that has obvious benefits for large corporations, but raises serious concerns for the environment, workers, and communities, particularly in the development world.'

The new millennium saw no diminution of the pressures to privatize, though popular support for PUBLIC SERVICE BROADCASTING (PSB), and indeed the competitive edge PSB services had developed in competition with the commercial sector stayed the hand of privatization. See COMMANDERS OF THE SOCIAL ORDER; COMMUNICATIONS BILL (UK), 2002; CROSS-MEDIA OWNERSHIP; DEMOCRACY AND THE MEDIA; DEREGULATION; PUBLIC SPHERE; REGULATORY FAVOURS. See also *TOPIC GUIDE* under GLOBAL PERSPECTIVES; MEDIA INSTITUTIONS; MEDIA ISSUES AND DEBATES; MEDIA: OWNERSHIP AND CONTROL.

Pro-con, con-pro In capturing the attention of an AUDIENCE, is it best to put good news, or good points (*pro*) before the bad (*con*), or after them? Researchers have indicated that pro-con generally works best. See PRIMACY, THE LAW OF.

Producer choice The term used to describe the operation of an internal market system within, for example, the BBC for the purchase of the services and facilities needed in programme-making. Since 1993 producers have had control over their budgets and have been free to buy the services and facilities they need, such as post-production, from the most cost-effective provider. The BBC's previous in-house providers of such services and facilities thus have had to compete with other providers for contracts from programme-makers. The designer of the scheme, Sir John Birt, argued that the system would create a more cost-effective and less bureaucratic organization and thus enable more resources to be channelled into creative areas.

Criticisms of the system are that it has contributed to a reduction in staffing levels; that it has accelerated the trend, partly attributable to the increasing use of independent producers, towards freelancing and CASUALIZATION of employment in the TV industry; that it threatens the long-term prospects of in-house providers and thus ultimately of the BBC itself as an organization concerned with making programmes as opposed to commissioning them; and that it may eventually result in a considerable loss of expertise within the organization, thus a lowering of standards in programme-making. See CAMPAIGN FOR QUALITY TELEVISION REPORT (UK), 1999; INDEPENDENT PRODUCERS.

Product placement A branch of modern ADVERTISING, especially in the US, where agencies place, in films and TV programmes, the products of clients – brightly lit, facing camera and in clear focus – and pay programme-makers considerable sums for the privilege of doing so. In the movie *Days of Thunder* (1990), Tom Cruise wore black Levi 501s throughout and sales of the garment went up considerably. Perhaps the classic *coup* in terms of product placement in movies occurred when, in *Independence Day* (1996), Jeff Goldblum saves the world, threatened by an invasion of aliens – using his Apple Powerbook.

Once an artefact is featured 'in shot', the company then draws further publicity by advertising the fact in its commercials. As the worlds of big business and entertainment grow closer and interlock – *synergize*

– and as budgets for films and TV grow tighter, product placement threatens to become more assertive throughout the media.

The position of the UK's Independent Television Commission (ITC) concerning product placement is clear: it is not allowed. The Commission's *Code of Programme Sponsorship* (see SPONSORSHIP: ITC CODE OF PROGRAMME SPONSORSHIP) defines product placement as '… the inclusion of, or reference to, a product or service within the programme-maker or ITC licensee (or any representative of either). This is prohibited.' However, 'When a product or service is an essential element within a programme, the programme-maker may, exceptionally, acquire a product or service at no, or less than full, cost. This is not product placement. It is acceptable providing no undue prominence is given to the product or service in question.' This is conditional upon Rule 11 being fulfilled: 'There must be no promotional reference within the programme itself to the sponsor or to any of his products or services.' See *TOPIC GUIDE* under ADVERTISING/MARKETING.

Profane language The Latin derivation of profane is *pro fana*, meaning outside the temple. Profanity referred to anyone refusing to be initiated into the ways of the temple, thus showing a contempt for that which is sacred. Profane language takes three main forms: religious, excretory or sexual; and the questions asked about such language are, why do people use profanities and what are the effects upon listeners – upon AUDIENCE – of the use of profanity?

J.D. Rothwell in 'Verbal obscenity: time for second thoughts', in *Western Speech* 35 (1971) listed five reasons for using profane language: (1) to create attention; (2) to discredit someone or something; (3) to provoke confrontations; (4) to provide a type of *catharsis* or emotional release for the user; and (5) to establish interpersonal identification. Profanity depends for its impact on who is actually using it and in what circumstances.

In 'The effects of three type of profane language in persuasion messages?', in the *Journal of Communication*, December 1973, Robert N. Bostrom, John R. Baseheart and Charles M. Rossiter Jr write of research which indicates that where profanity is used, greater attitude change can be expected to occur if the communicator is female, in any of the three categories (religious, excretory, sexual). Bostrom *et al.* also reach the general conclusion that profanity has a detrimental effect on the perceived credibility of the communicator.

Professionalization (of political communication) Describes the ways in which governments and political parties have adopted the practices of professionals in media communication, indeed employing such professionals, in the transmission of policies, the nurturing of favourable images in the minds of the public and of putting a 'spin' on aspects of news. In short, NEWS MANAGEMENT – slick presentation, use of the latest communication technologies; not just at times of elections but as elements of a permanent, ongoing campaign. Such professionalization of communication risks public cynicism, a factor that inevitably leads to fraught re-examinations of current strategies of persuasion and a hunt for new ways to win public trust. See *TOPIC GUIDE* under MEDIA: POLITICS AND ECONOMICS.

* Ralph Negrine and Darren G. Lilleker, 'The professionalization of political communication: continuities and change in media practices', *European Journal of Communication*, September 2002.

Programme codes (UK) See ITC PROGRAMME CODE; RADIO AUTHORITY (UK) PROGRAMME CODES; SPONSORSHIP: ITC CODE OF PROGRAMME SPONSORSHIP.

Programme flow 'In all developed broadcasting systems,' writes Raymond Williams in *Television: Technology and Cultural Form* (UK: Fontana, 1974), 'the characteristic organization, and therefore the characteristic experience, is one of sequence or flow.' Williams believes that flow is a chief principle of programming; the process of organizing a pattern of programmes, each one leading on to the next; each one being a 'tempter' for the AUDIENCE to stay tuned to a particular channel. Programme boundaries, says Williams, are constantly being obscured by advertisements and/or trailers for other programmes, to counteract the itchy finger on the remote control button, and the much-feared viewer indulgence in zapping (see ZAPPING, ZIPPING).

Programme sponsorship See SPONSORSHIP: ITC CODE OF PROGRAMME SPONSORSHIP.

Proiaretic code See CODES OF NARRATIVE.

Projection A throwing outwards or forwards; term commonly used within several areas of communication and media studies. The ability to *project* oneself is an important communication skill. Here projection has been achieved when a person, in giving a talk, making a speech or acting a part on stage has reached the whole AUDIENCE both with words and his/her personality. Voice, posture, eye contact, facial expression, GESTURE combine in creating effective projection.

The term can be used in a psychological sense: when people tend to project on others – *transfer* to others – their own motives for behaviour, in particular those that cannot be gratified or that are regarded as unacceptable; in other words, to assume in others the same motives. We may be more inclined to make such assumptions about those we like and perceive as being similar to ourselves. Clearly projection can lead to errors in PERCEPTION and to misunderstandings in the communication process.

Projection of pictures A German Jesuit, Athanasius Kircher (1601–80), professor of mathematics at the Collegio Romano in Rome, is generally thought to be the first person to project a picture on to a screen. His apparatus was crude but effective, containing all the essentials – a source of light with a reflector behind it and a lens in front, a painted glass slide and a screen. Kircher's astonished audience spoke of black magic. Undaunted, the inventor published a description of his findings.

The projection of moving pictures was first demonstrated by Baron Von Uchatius (1811–81) in 1853. He used a rotating glass slide, a rotating shutter and a fixed lens. An improved version contained a rotating light source, fixed slides and a series of slightly inclined lenses whose optical axes met on the centre of the screen. See CINEMATOGRAPHY, ORIGINS.

Project of self See SELF-IDENTITY.

Prolefeed The rubbishy entertainment and spurious news piped to the proletariat by the Party in George Orwell's novel *Nineteen Eighty-Four* (1949).

Propaganda Usually deliberate manipulation by means of symbols (words, gestures, images, flags, monuments, music, etc.) of other people's thoughts, behaviour, attitudes and beliefs. The word originates with the Roman Catholic Congregation for the Propagation of the Faith, a committee of cardinals in charge of missionary activities of the church since 1622. Propaganda works through emphasizing some factors and excluding others, often emotively appealing to anxieties, fears, prejudices and ignorance of the true facts. Propaganda can be blatant (see RADIO DEATH) or work by stealth, often using entertainment as a means of 'sugar-coating' messages.

 In the world of contemporary politics, propaganda takes the form of NEWS MANAGEMENT or *spin*; and a profession of *spin-doctors* now 'doctor' facts in ways intended to favourably propagate to the public the ideas, policies and performance of government. Propaganda, whether it is that of governments, companies, institutions, charitable organizations or the world of sport aims to create in the public mind a favourable impression. This might be termed *white* propaganda. In contrast, propaganda that sets out to create in the public mind a bad impression – of other countries, for example, other ethnic groups, foreigners, asylum-seekers, minorities, that is, defining them as 'enemy' – might be termed *black* propaganda.

Garth J. Jowett and Victoria O'Donnell in *Propaganda and Persuasion* (US: Sage, 1999) identify three forms of propaganda: *white, black* and *grey*: 'White propaganda comes from a source that is identified correctly, and the information in the message tends to be accurate ... Although what listeners hear is reasonably close to the truth, it is presented in a manner that attempts to convince the audience that the sender is the "good guy".

'Black propaganda on the other hand,' explain the authors, '... is credited to a false source and spreads lies, fabrications and deceptions. Black propaganda is the "big lie", including all types of creative deceit.' DISINFORMATION would be an example of black propaganda. Grey propaganda lies 'somewhere between white and black. The source may not be correctly identified, and the accuracy of the information is uncertain.' See ADVERTISING; BRAINWASHING; CONSENT, MANUFACTURE OF; EFFECTS OF THE MASS MEDIA; LOBBYING; PUBLIC RELATIONS (PR); RHETORIC. See also *TOPIC GUIDE* under LANGUAGE/DISCOURSE/NARRATIVE.

Propaganda model of mass communication See CONSENT, MANUFACTURE OF.

Property: intellectual property See CULTURE: COPYRIGHTING CULTURE.

Propinquity A significant determinant of group membership, propinquity is liking through *proximity*; when people are close together physically there is a strain towards amicability that aids group formation, more reliably than with physically distant persons. See GROUPS.

Propp's people In a study of Russian folk tales, Vladimir Propp classified a range of stock characters identifiable in most NARRATIVES (see his *Morphology of the Folk Tale*, published in 1968 by the University of Texas Press). These may be individualized by being given distinguishing character traits but they are essentially functionaries enabling the story to unfold. Propp describes a number of archetypal story features: the *hero/subject* whose function is to seek; the *object* that is sought; the *donor* of the object; the *receiver*, where it is sent; the *helper* who aids the action and the *villain* who blocks the action.

Thus in one of the world's best-known folk tales, Red Riding Hood (heroine) is sent by her mother (donor) with a basket of provisions (object) to her sick granny (receiver) who lives in the forest. She encounters the wolf (villain) and is rescued from his clutches – and his teeth – by the woodman (helper).

This formula can be added to and manipulated in line with the requirements of the GENRE, but it does allow us to differentiate between *story level* and *meaning level*, between the denotive and the connotive, between the so-termed *mimetic plane* (the plane of representation) and the *semiosic plane* (the plane of MEANING production). See CODES OF NARRATIVE.

Prosodic signals Timing, pitch and stress of utterances to convey MEANING.

Proxemics The study of the way people approach others or keep their distance from others: the analysis of what we do with space as a dimension of non-verbal communication (see COMMUNI-CATION, NON-VERBAL). There appear to be definite features that mark the distance people observe between each other in communication situations. Within three feet is intimate; up to about eight feet is personal; over that distance is semi-public or social. The proximity between communicators differs, obviously, according to the nature of the MESSAGE and varies between cultures, classes and nations.

The personal but not intimate distance of Arabs, for example, can be as little as 18 inches – intimidating for an English listener. Middle-class distances tend, it has been found, to be slightly greater than those maintained between working-class communicators. Proxemics extends to the way we allocate space to those extensions of ourselves – rooms, houses, towns, cities – and the manner in which we occupy those extensions. See PARAPROXEMICS.

* Edward T. Hall, *The Hidden Dimension: Man's Use of Space in Public and Private* (UK: Bodley Head, 1966).

PR: Public relations See PUBLIC RELATIONS (PR).

PSB (Public Service Broadcasting) See PUBLIC SERVICE BROADCASTING (PSB).

Pseudo-context In his sharply critical assessment of the impact of TV on society, in *Amusing Ourselves to Death* (UK: Methuen, 1986), American author and communications professor Neil Postman says of a pseudo-context that it is 'a structure invented to give fragmented and irrelevant information a seeming use'. However, the pseudo-context offers us no useful function for the information in terms of action, problem-solving or change. TV is the culprit in this fragmenting process. All that is left for what Postman calls the 'decontextualization of fact' by the non-print media, particularly TV, is to amuse. All knowledge, having been fragmented, is reduced to a trivial pursuit. See EFFECTS OF THE MASS MEDIA.

PSI Para-social identification; that is, members of an AUDIENCE associate with fictitious characters as portrayed in the media, or with well-known personalities whom they regularly 'meet' through the mediation of radio, TV, etc. See PARASOCIAL INTERACTION.

Psycholinguistics The study of the interplay between language acquisition, development and use, and other aspects of the human mind.

Psychology This discipline seeks to explore the way in which individual behaviours are linked together to form a 'personality'. Its focus is upon the experience and behaviour of the individual, upon the individual's reaction to certain physiological and/or social conditions. Some areas of social psychology are concerned with the behaviour of individuals in small groups or crowds; here there is some overlap between this discipline and that of SOCIOLOGY.

---

* Valerie Walkerdine and Lisa Blackman, *Psychology and the Media* (UK: Macmillan, 1999).

Public communication Alternative term to *mass media* or *mass communication*, and one preferred by some writers – among them, Raymond Williams.

Public communication values See NORMATIVE THEORIES OF MASS MEDIA.

Public cues See BARNLUND'S TRANSACTIONAL MODEL OF COMMUNICATION, 1970.

Public data access See TELEDEMOCRACY.

Public Interest Disclosure Act (UK), 1999 See WHISTLE-BLOWING.

Public Occurrences Both Foreign and Domestic Title of the first American newspaper, founded in Boston on 25 September 1690 by Benjamin Harris. The paper survived one issue only, being immediately suppressed by the Governor and Council of the then British colony.

Public opinion The Greek AGORA is traditionally seen as the birthplace and location of public opinion. It was an open space where free citizens gathered to discuss and ideally shape the affairs of state. By its nature public opinion lacks the structure of, for example, ELITE opinion and there are difficulties both of definition and identification. The modern-day OPINION POLL tests samples of the whole public; market and audience research have pursued increasingly sophisticated, technology-aided modes of opinion measurement. For such research, measurement is of TASTES, expectations, needs, VALUES and behaviour as well as opinions. For the student of media, the public is examined from the point of view of how the media *represent* public opinion, purport to speak for it, indeed, to define it; and to shape it especially in the light of perhaps the most important and specific expression of public opinion – voting.

Susan Herbst and James R. Beniger in 'The changing infrastructure of public opinion', published in *Audiencemaking: How the Media Create the Audience* (US: Sage, 1994), edited by James S. Ettema and D. Charles Whitney, explore the connections between the concept of public opinion and the means by which public opinion is measured, the one being influenced by the other; thus what public opinion is in any situation is to a degree defined by how it is defined and measured. The authors say that 'both polling and voting embrace a conception of public opinion as the aggregation of individual opinions and both provide means for elite management of those opinions'.

They identify three phases in the evolution of public opinion infrastructures. The first was located in the salons of mid-eighteenth-century France (see SALON DISCOURSE). Here the political and intellectual elite gathered socially to discuss all matters from art to philosophy, not least the affairs of state and the nature of government. This elite model of public opinion found a modestly downmarket parallel in the coffee houses of London presided over by such 'agorans' as Dr Samuel Johnson (1709–84). These 'spaces' for DISCOURSE were only one aspect of the infrastructure; what formed an extension of them were the writings of those novelists, poets, scientists and philosophers who attended the salons or met in the coffee houses.

Towards the middle of the nineteenth century the press became the dominant residence of public opinion, but the newspapers were increasingly reflecting, both in the UK and USA, the development of political parties. Herbst and Beniger believe that 'In concert with the newspapers that shared their ideologies, political parties were a critical component of the late-nineteenth century American infrastructure of public opinion expression and assessment.' In fact PRESSURE GROUPS of all kinds, including trades unions, contributed to the group-based model of public opinion.

New media technology such as RADIO and more efficient measurement practices contributed to what Herbst and Beniger term 'a shift from publics to audiences'. What had, until the emergence of audience-measurement techniques (such as the Audimeter-based NIELSEN RATINGS in the States), been an aggregate of opinions, was now a profile of *differences* – leading to what in ADVERTISING terms was to become SEGMENTATION. The ability to discriminate between shades of opinion as far as this audience model is concerned indicates advancing degrees of rationalization, and this, state Herbst and Beniger, 'works best for those at the top of a given system'. See INFORMATION COMMONS; MEDIASPHERE.

Public radio Term used in Australia to refer to COMMUNITY RADIO.

Public relations (PR) In *Advertising as Communication* (UK: Methuen, 1982), Gillian Dyer cites the aim of PR as being 'to promote positive and favourable images of people or firms in public life, without actually appearing to do so'. Many companies and institutions in both the public and private sectors have PR departments dedicated to creating and sustaining their good image and reputation with a variety of publics: for example, shareholders, taxpayers, clients, customers and employees.

Dyer comments, 'The "publicity boys" rehearse politicians before they go in front of the camera … they stage-manage walkabouts … kissing babies all for the benefit of the mass media.' Public relations personnel may work alongside those in ADVERTISING and marketing but their role is essentially focused on building relationships and fostering the two-way communication channels required to achieve this aim.

Shirley Harrison in *Public Relations: An Introduction* (US/UK: Routledge, 1995) writes that 'The most common public relations activities undertaken by practitioners are media relations, publicity and publications, corporate public relations and provision of information.' See NEWS MANAGEMENT. See also *TOPIC GUIDE* under ADVERTISING AND MARKETING.

* Quentin Bell, *The PR Business* (UK: Kogan Page, 1991).

Public service broadcasting (PSB) This term refers to any BROADCASTING system whose first duty is to a public within a DEMOCRACY, serving to inform, educate and entertain, and to regard AUDIENCE as constituting citizens, members of communities and individuals rather than merely consumers. PSB is essentially the creation of government in the first instance though for this reason safeguards are built in to the system so that its operation is (relatively) free of government control and influence. Financing of PSB is usually through some form of taxation or licence, subject to periodic revision by government; or in the case of COMMERCIAL TELEVISION, by means of ADVERTISING.

The BBC, in the UK, represents for many the classic example of public service broadcasting (see BBC, ORIGINS). It was created by Act of Parliament and is subject to *regulation* laid down by Parliament. Commercial TV in the UK is equally subject to regulation: the governors of the BBC and the Independent Broadcasting Authority (IBA) – succeeded by the ITC (Independent Television Commission) in 1991 – are answerable to Parliament. Regulation aims, for example, to achieve BALANCED PROGRAMMING, that is, balance between information and entertainment, preserving the one against the possible encroachment of the other. Regulation serves to guarantee a balance between the serious and the popular, between programmes that appeal to minorities and programming designed to attract mass viewing.

Throughout world broadcasting in the 1990s PSB suffered diminishment in the face of commercial competition, greater diversity of provision brought about by new technology and dominant ideologies working towards the PRIVATIZATION of the airways – to the point when some commentators expressed the view that PSB would not survive long into the new century.

Pressure on governments by multinational corporations seeking to extend their media portfolios, and seeing PSB as an obstacle to their ambitions has been unrelenting (see BRITISH MEDIA INDUSTRY GROUP (BMIG)). As long ago as 1991, Peter Golding and Graham Murdock in 'Culture, communications, and political economy', in *Mass Media and Society* (UK: Edward Arnold, 1991), edited by James Curran and Michael Gurevitch, were writing that assaults on PSB are 'part of a wider historical process whereby the state in capitalist societies has increasingly assumed a greater role in managing communicative activity'. This process, the authors point out, has occurred hand in glove with big business: modern communication media are significant for their 'growing incorporation into a capitalist economic system'.

That PSB continues to be defined as an issue rather than a crisis lies in part a result of a determination to maintain a central place in AUDIENCE use of broadcasting, and this has meant matching the commercial sector in terms of programme popularity and thus of *ratings* (see AUDIENCE MEASUREMENT). The fear is that *quality* programming (a vital principle of PSB) will be sacrificed in the pursuit of *quantity*. Debate over what has been termed the *dumbing-down* of PSB has been welcome, lively but generally inconclusive.

What might be seen as the greatest opportunity and at the same time the greatest hazard facing PSB is the advent of DIGITIZATION. The degree to which governments support PSB in future, and the degree to which governments concede to the demands of media corporations, will continue to dominate the scenarios of broadcasting as well as those of newspaper and book publishing, the music and film industries and network communication. See AUDIENCE FRAGMENTATION; COMMU-NICATIONS BILL (UK), 2002; DEMOCRACY AND THE MEDIA; DEREGULATION, FIVE MYTHS OF; McQUAIL'S ACCOUNTABILITY OF MEDIA MODEL, 1997; MEDIASPHERE; PUBLIC SPHERE; RADIO BROADCASTING. See also *TOPIC GUIDE* under BROADCASTING.

* Denis McQuail, *Media Performance: Mass Communication and the Public Interest* (UK: Sage, 1992); John Keane, *The Media and Democracy* (UK: Polity Press, 1991).

Public sphere With the development of capitalism in the mid-seventeenth century, argues Jürgen Habermas, a public sphere of debate and communicative interchange was opened up – mainly among the bourgeoisie – in western society. Economic independence provided by private property, the expansion of published literature such as novels that encouraged critical reflection, and the growth of a market-based press created a new public awareness of politics and involvement in public debate.

The public sphere existed between the economy and the state, and represented a nascent form of supervision of government. However, Habermas believed that from the middle of the nineteenth century the public sphere came to be dominated by the expanded state and organized economic interests. The media ceased to be an agency of EMPOWERMENT, surrendered much of its role as a WATCHDOG, and became a further means by which the public were sidelined and PUBLIC OPINION manipulated. According to Habermas, the public sphere ceased to be a 'neutral zone'.

Today, commentators see the INTERNET as a welcome extension of the public sphere while at the same time expressing doubts as to how long this AGORA will remain a space of free exchange for communities of interest in the face of corporate ambitions to oocupy – to commercialize – that space. At the same time that space is seen as being increasingly subject to government surveillance. See INFORMATION COMMONS; MEDIASPHERE; SURVEILLANCE SOCIETY.

*Jürgen Habermas, *Communication and the Evolution of Society* (US: Beacon, 1979); Habermas, *The Structural Transformation of the Public Sphere* (UK: Polity, 1989); Peter Dahlgren and Colin Sparks (eds), *Communication and Citizenship: Journalism and the Public Sphere* (UK: Routledge, 1993); John Hartley, *Popular Reality: Journalism, Modernity, Popular Culture* (UK: Arnold, 1996); Michael Bromley (ed.), *No News is Bad News: Radio, Television and the Public* (UK: Longman, 2001); Bob Franklin (ed.), *British Television Policy: A Reader* (UK: Routledge, 2001).

Pulitzer Prize for Journalism American award created by Joseph Pulitzer, Hungarian-born newspaper proprietor and rival of William Randolph Hearst (model for Orson Welles' film *Citizen Kane*, 1943). Along with Pulitzers for JOURNALISM, there are prizes for music and literature. Originating in 1947, the Pulitzer Prizes are awarded annually.

Q

Quadrophony See GRAMOPHONE.

Qube See INTERACTIVE TELEVISION.

Questionnaires A popular method of data collection, a questionnaire basically consists of a series of questions designed to obtain factual information and/or information about people's attitudes, VALUES, opinions or beliefs about a particular subject or issue. A questionnaire can also be constructed so as to contain questions about a *range* of topics or issues. They are regularly used as a tool of market research and are central to AUDIENCE MEASUREMENT.

It is not usually possible to give a questionnaire to all those who make up the group in which you are interested and so questionnaires are normally given to a sample (see SAMPLING); care needs to be taken to ensure that the sample represents the total population, that is the total number of people in that group, in all significant respects.

Questionnaires are useful for gathering large amounts of data but may be less useful for investigating an issue in depth; here PARTICIPANT OBSERVATION or INTERVIEWS may be more useful. Further, constructing an unambiguous, unbiased and productive questionnaire is not easy – nor is the impartial analysis of the responses collected. See *TOPIC GUIDE* under RESEARCH METHODS.

Quotas Limits placed upon the import of foreign printing, film and broadcast material to protect indigenous, home-grown media products. Quotas are immensely difficult to establish and sustain, and, with the modern shift of emphasis from producers to consumers (through the availability of video, DVD, cable transmission and satellite transmission), import controls will be even less effective. For quotas to work, it would be necessary to rival the attraction value of the materials available – cheap, packaged, of proven success with audiences. See MEDIA IMPERIALISM.

Quota sample See SAMPLING.

QWERTY Arrangement of letters on the traditional TYPEWRITER keyboard, devised in 1873 to overcome jamming problems on the world's first production machine, a Remington.

R

Racism Discrimination against individuals or GROUPS of people on the basis of assumed racial differences. The term is problematic in that there is some argument as to whether the concept of race is useful anyway in describing biological differences between people. Racism, though, rests on the belief that different races with specific characteristics can be meaningfully identified. At an individual level such discrimination takes the form of PREJUDICE, whereas the term racism is often used to describe the way in which such discrimination is embedded into the structure of a society.

Cultural racism refers to the perpetuation, consciously or unconsciously, of such discrimination and the beliefs and VALUES on which it rests through the cultural institutions of a society – for example, education and the mass media. As Stuart Hall notes in 'The whites of their eyes: racist ideologies and the media', in *The Media Reader* (UK: BFI Publishing, 1990), edited by Manuel Alvarado and John O. Thompson, 'the media are ... part of the dominant means of ideological production. What they "produce" is precisely representations of the social world, images, descriptions, explanations and frames for understanding how the world is and why it works as it is said and shown to work. And, amongst other kinds of ideological labour, the media construct for us a definition of what race is, what meaning the imagery of race carries, and what the "problem of race" is understood to be. They help to classify out the world in terms of the categories of race.'

One important focus of current media research is the role that the media play in shaping and perpetuating racism and racist STEREOTYPES. Research suggests that negative and stereotypical images of ethnic minorities abound and present an image of them as inferior, marginal and a potential source of social problems. Simon Cottle in *Ethnic Minorities and the Media* (UK: Open University Press, 2000), edited by Cottle, argues that 'Over recent decades a considerable body of research conducted in both the UK and the US has examined the media's representations of ethnic minorities.

'The collective findings of this research effort generally make depressing reading. Under-representation and stereotypical characterization within entertainment genres and negative problem-orientated portrayal within factuality and news forms, and a tendency to ignore structural inequalities and lived racism experienced by ethnic minorities in both, are recurring research findings.'

Manuel Alvarado, Robin Gutch and Tana Wollen argue in *Learning the Media* (UK: Macmillan, 1987) that the portrayal of black people on television largely falls into four main categories: the *exotic*, for example coverage of tribal dancing used to welcome members of the UK royal family when visiting various Commonwealth countries; the *dangerous*, for example coverage of immigration as an issue that presents coloured immigrants and asylum-seekers as a threat; the *humorous*, where humour may well serve to reinforce notions of racial difference to the detriment of coloured people; and the *pitied*, for example media coverage of famines in Africa and of western attempts to provide aid, which tend to represent famine as resulting from the inadequacies of the people and their governments rather than as a legacy of western colonialism.

Tuen A. Van Dijk in 'New(s) racism: a discourse analysis approach', published in Cottle's *Ethnic Minorities and the Media*, analyses the contribution news coverage in the press makes to *new racism*, which opts for a more subtle negative portrayal of ethnic groups rather than the more obvious and open racism of the past. Van Dijk writes that 'most mentions of "terrorists" (especially also in the US press) will stereotypically refer to Arabs. Violent men who are our friends or allies will seldom get that label.

'For the same reason, "drug barons" are always Latin men in South America, never the white men who are in the drugs business within the US itself.' News racism extends to the selection of stories for news coverage and Van Dijk argues that as regards news about immigrants and ethnic minorities, there is 'a preference for those topics that emphasize Their bad actions and Our good ones'. The consequence, he concludes, is that 'Systematic negative portrayal of the Others, thus vitally contributed to negative mental models, stereotypes, prejudices and ideologies about the Others, and hence indirectly the enactment and reproduction of racism.' See BIGOTRY; COMPASSION FATIGUE; ETHNOCENTRISM; MEDIA IMPERIALISM; NEWS AID?; OTHER. See also *TOPIC GUIDE* under MEDIA ISSUES AND DEBATES.

---

* John Twitham (ed.), *The Black and White Media Book* (UK: Trentham Books, 1990); Tuen van Dijk, *Racism and the Press* (UK: Routledge, 1992); Karen Ross, *Black and White Media: Black Imagery in Popular Films and Television* (UK: Polity, 1996); Oscar H. Gandy Jr, *Communication and Race: A Structural Perspective* (UK: Arnold, 1998); Steve Fenton, *Racism, Class and Culture* (UK: Macmillan, 1999); Sarita Malik, *Representing Black Britain: Black and Asian Images on Television* (UK: Sage, 2001); Norman K. Denzin, *Reading Race* (UK/US: Sage, 2002).

Radical press See MEDIA: ALTERNATIVE (OR RADICAL) MEDIA; UNDERGROUND PRESS.

Radical suppression of potential (technology) See SUPERVENING SOCIAL NECESSITY.

Radio See RADIO BROADCASTING.

Radio Authority See COMMERCIAL RADIO.

Radio Authority (UK) Programme Codes 1 The Radio Authority took over supervision of independent COMMERCIAL RADIO from the IBA on 1 January 1991. As well as being empowered to assign frequencies and appoint licensees, the Authority was required to publish codes to which licensees must adhere. Code 1 on *News Programmes and Coverage of Matters of Political or Industrial Controversy or Relating to Current Public Policy* is based on the requirements of sections 90 and 107 of the BROADCASTING ACT (UK), 1990. The Code insists on IMPARTIALITY in NEWS, current affairs and DOCUMENTARY programmes. Notes on the Code state that the rules 'do not mean that "balance" is required in any simple mathematical sense of equal time or an equal number of lines being given to each relevant viewpoint'.

'Personal view' programmes or features on political matters must not be scheduled at times when UK and European Parliamentary or local government elections are pending. Corrections of factual errors should be broadcast, states the Code, 'as soon as is sensibly possible after the original error'. 'Licence Holders must not broadcast fiction or drama designed to commend one side or the other in a matter of political or industrial controversy unless a further drama or fictional broadcast is planned to occur within three months which commends an opposing view.' The Code acknowledges that the 'due impartiality required of a piece of fiction or drama by an independent writer is not identical to that required of a current affairs programme produced by a Licence Holder'.

Code 2 Deals with *Violence, Sex, Taste and Decency, Children and Young People, Appeals for Donations, Religion and Other Matters*, and is based on the requirements of sections 90 and 91 of the Broadcasting Act, 1990. Bad language is dealt with in the first paragraph of the code, sex in the second and bad taste in humour in the third. 'The gratuitous use of language likely to offend'; 'Smut, titillation, crudity and sexual stereotyping must be avoided'; and jokes about disability or based on different racial characteristics must be 'considered with great care on every occasion'.

The guide notes on paragraph 1.2, *Sex*, acknowledge that much of the world's greatest drama, music and fiction 'has been concerned with love and passion, and it would be wrong (if not impossible) to require writers or lyricists to renounce all intention to shock and disturb: but the aim should be to move, not offend'.

On violence the Code states 'Licence Holders should note that there is no evidence that the portrayal of violence which is shown to have good or "legitimate" ends is less likely to be harmful to the individual, or to society, than the portrayal of violence for evil ends.' They must ensure that 'the degree of violence portrayed and described is essential to the integrity and completeness of the programme'.

The utmost care is to be taken concerning the young and the vulnerable. The Code is of the opinion that insecurity 'is less tolerable for a child – particularly an emotionally unstable child – than for a mature adult. Violence, menace and threats can take many forms – emotional, physical and verbal … Research evidence shows that those who are socially or emotionally insecure, particularly if adolescent, are especially vulnerable.' The Code declares that while imagination, creativity or realism on radio 'cannot be constrained to such an extent that the legitimate service to the majority is always subordinated to the constraints for a minority', nevertheless 'a civilized society pays special attention to its weaker members'.

The Code deals with a very wide range of matters – hypnotism, horoscopes, accuracy of news, PRIVACY and information gathering, crime, terrorists, defamation, smoking and drinking, drug-taking and solvent abuse, D-NOTICES and the OFFICIAL SECRETS ACT (UK).

Radio ballads Form or GENRE of musical DOCUMENTARY inspired in the UK by radio producer Charles Parker, and compiled by folk singers Ewan McColl and Peggy Seeger, beginning in 1958 with *The Ballad of John Axon*. The introduction of high-quality portable tape-recorders to the BBC enabled Parker and his team to create new patterns of vocal sound, interlaced with sound-effects (real, not studio-simulated), which served as an 'impressionistic' means of describing the lives and work of ordinary people. John Axon was a train driver, killed in a crash, and the nature of his life was recreated in ballad and recollection. *Singing the Fishing* (1960), taking for its theme the hard life of the North Sea fisherman, won the Italia Press award. The BBC withdrew financial support from this pioneering team in 1964. See RADIO DRAMA.

Radio broadcasting The First World War (1914–18) had given impetus to the development of radio for military purposes, and the training of wireless operators. Visionaries of the age saw the possibility of wireless programmes as an exciting extension of wireless messages – a 'household utility' that would create a world of sound, of voices and music; that would annihilate distance and offer undreamed-of opportunities for CULTURE, entertainment and information. With the ending of the war, crystal sets tuned in by their 'cat's whisker' became immensely popular. The valve, called the 'magic lantern of radio', developed between 1904 and 1914, soon usurped the place of the crystal.

The first 'broadcast' of music and speech was made by an American, R.A. Fissenden, in 1906. The American Radio and Research Company was broadcasting concerts twice and three times a week as early as 1916, though KDKA of Pittsburgh won the earliest renown as a pioneer in the field (on air, 1920).

A ban imposed on 'amateur' radio in Britain at the outbreak of the First World War was not lifted until 1919, but in February 1920 the Marconi Company in the UK began broadcasting from Writtle/Chelmsford, though later in the year the Post Office withdrew permission for these broadcasts. However, on 14 February 1922 the first regular broadcasting service in Britain was again beamed from Writtle, organized by the Experimental Section of the Designs Department of Marconi. Their London station, 2LO, began broadcasting on 11 May of the same year.

The Post Office, faced with nearly 100 applications from manufacturers who wanted to set up broadcasting stations, and realizing the need to have some sort of control of the airwaves, proposed a consortium of companies to centralize broadcasting activity: the British Broadcasting Company was born, and John Reith appointed its managing director (see BBC, ORIGINS). The BBC, set up by Royal Charter, came into existence on 1 January 1927. It was to hold a monopoly of broadcasting in the UK until commercial radio was legalized in the SOUND BROADCASTING (UK) ACT, 1972.

From its beginning, radio broadcasting in the US was financed by ADVERTISING; from its beginning, radio broadcasting in the UK was free of advertising; the one was predominantly local, the other a national public service and eventually a national institution. No study of the evolution of broadcasting in the UK can avoid also being an analysis of the philosophy, vision and practices of the BBC's managing director and later director general John (later Sir John) Reith. Varyingly called the Napoleon of Broadcasting, and Prospero, the all-powerful magician, Reith disliked politics and politicians, viewed commerce with disdain (and commercialism with contempt). He forged a definition of PUBLIC SERVICE BROADCASTING (PSB) that dominated broadcasting – both radio and TV – for generations and, even in the age of the dispersal of control, affects us still.

Radio newsreaders wore dinner jackets and bow ties to read the NEWS, a symbol of the aloofness and distancing characteristic of Reith and much of the output of the BBC. There was even a Pronunciation Committee. Yet the Corporation resisted criticisms from the popular press that its tastes were too elitist. It was to give drama and classical music – as well as many other forms of music – a new structure and a new popularity. Equally, there was room for developing the special potentials of radio – in outside broadcasts, drama documentary, discussion programmes and fireside talks.

The greatest fear of the broadcasters was – and continues to be – government interference. Reith's caution was as monumental as the extent of his control. His desire to render the BBC beyond political reproach led to the Corporation often censoring itself so as to be one step ahead of being censored. The risks to the BBC were not imagined. During the General Strike of 1926 Winston Churchill wanted the government to commandeer the Corporation, a move Reith managed to resist – but at a price: during the strike no representative of organized labour was permitted to broadcast, and the leader of the Opposition, Ramsay MacDonald, was also banned. See WIRELESS TELEGRAPHY. See also *TOPIC GUIDE* under BROADCASTING.

---

* Asa Briggs, *The History of Broadcasting in the United Kingdom* (UK: Oxford University Press, four volumes, 1961, 1965, and, Volumes 3 and 4, 1979); P.M. Lewis and J. Booth, *The Invisible Medium: Public Commercial and Community Radio* (UK: Macmillan, 1989); Paddy Scannell and David Cardiff, *A Social History of British Broadcasting: Vol. 1 1922–1939: Serving the Nation* (UK: Blackwell, 1991); Andrew Crissell, *Understanding Radio* (UK: Routledge, 1994) and *An Introductory History of British Broadcasting* (UK: Routledge, 1997); Stephen Barnard, *Studying Radio* (UK: Arnold, 2000); Caroline Mitchell (ed.), *Women and Radio* (UK: Routledge, 2000); Michele Hilmes (ed.), *Radio Reader: Essays in the Cultural History of Radio* (US/UK: Routledge, 2001); Asa Briggs and Peter Burke, *A Social History of the Media: From Gutenberg to the Internet* (UK: Polity, 2002).

Radio Cracker See COMMERCIAL RADIO.

Radio Death Or Hate Radio; nickname given to Rwanda's Radio Television Libre des Milles Collines (Thousand Hills Television Radio) which, following the assassination of President Juvenal Habyarimana, conducted an intensive campaign of hatred against the minority tribe, the Tutsis (9 per cent of the population as against 90 per cent Hutu). RTLM proved the power of radio in a land almost without TV and with an illiteracy rate of over 50 per cent of the population. A broadcast in April 1994 claimed that 'by the 5th May the elimination of the Tutsis should be finished'. In the first week of the killing spree upwards of 200,000 people were murdered as Hutu militia combed the countryside.

In 1995 Reporters Sans Frontières, a Montpellier-based group of journalists, set up in 1987 to defend press freedom worldwide, and journalists in trouble, initiated a civil lawsuit in Paris against the founders and organizers of Radio Death, alleging their responsibility for genocide, violation of humanitarian law and crimes against humanity.

In response to the torrents of hatred emerging from RTLM, Radio Gatashya was formed and appeared on air for the first time in August 1994 in Goma, its own nickname, Humanitarian Radio, providing an information service of help and support for the thousands of refugees. In a BBC Radio 4 documentary, *War Radio*, broadcast in December 1998 journalist Micha Glenny compares the propagandist radio of Rwanda with that of local stations in Bosnia during the late 1990s, emphasizing that as language is the *essence* of radio's power, so it is the essence of ethnic and other differences.

Listeners learn how ethnic groups previously sharing a common language began – through radio – to introduce words and terms that served as markers of difference. The antidote to a MEDIUM that lies as it dominates is not, Glenny concludes, to shut it down but to match it with rival radio that is professional and a respecter of the truth. It is argued that all United Nations peacekeeping enterprises should be supported by a radio service that, from the beginning of UN activity, is 'on air' in the battle for hearts and minds.

In June 2000 a Belgian-born announcer on Radio Death, Georges Ruggiu, was sentenced by an international criminal tribunal to 12 years' imprisonment on two counts of inciting the Hutu massacres of Tutsis in Rwanda.

Radio drama The first ever radio play was Richard Hughes' *Danger* (1923), about a couple trapped in a mine, but the play that appears to have had the most substantial impact as a work in a new MEDIUM was Reginald Berkeley's *The White Chateau*, broadcast by the BBC to an audience of over 12m on Armistice Day, 1925, and telling an extremely harrowing story of the trench war.

Since that time hundreds of writers have been given a start in their professional lives by radio, one of whose many virtues is cheapness: today, a 30-minute radio play requires one day's studio time; an hour-long play, two days. The radio playwright need not concern him/herself with the massive costs of scene changes; there is little need to keep costs down by writing plays for two people and an armchair. The whole world of time and space is at the writer's command.

Most importantly, there is the awaiting imagination of the listener. The best radio plays take the listener on a journey into his/her imagination, where the play is given its own unique setting, the characters a unique appearance – all with the help of voices, sound-effects and silence; an art form, as the poet W.H. Auden once said, that is 'not spoiled by any collision with visual reality'.

Radio drama possesses the characteristic of intimacy – it has made the interior monologue, the soliloquy, a dramatic device perhaps more convincingly acceptable than on the stage; at the same time, because its stage is contained by no proscenium arch or screen-frame, because its 'stage set' is actually the mind of the listener, radio also lends itself successfully to epic drama: Shakespeare can be marvellous on radio.

Among writers who took an early interest in radio as a serious art form was the Irish poet Louis MacNeice (1907–65). His verse plays, broadcast during and after the Second World War, such as *The Story of My Death* (1943) and *The Dark Tower* (1946), impressively explored the potential of radio, while in 1953 another poet, Welshman Dylan Thomas (1914–53), gave to the world one of the best-known and most loved plays for radio, *Under Milk Wood*. The play was first broadcast on 25 January 1954, with a distinguished all-Welsh cast and produced by Douglas Cleverdon.

For 30 years Val Gielgud as Head of Radio Drama at the BBC guided the evolution of the radio play, himself producing and writing. Throughout its history, radio drama has witnessed a strong tradition of able producers – such as Cleverdon, Lancelot Sieveking, Donald McWinnie and Alfred Bradley – nurturing writers who later became famous: Harold Pinter, Stan Barstow, Giles Cooper, Allan Prior, Alun Owen, William Trevor, Henry Livings, Peter Terson, Alan Plater, David Rudkin and Tom Stoppard.

Despite its creative potential, radio as a dramatic medium has acquired less status, and been paid less attention than other – more glamorous – media; and less than it deserves. However, the BBC continues to broadcast between 200 and 300 radio plays a year, classical drama as well as new works. See TELEVISION DRAMA; 'WAR OF THE WORLDS'.

Radio: independent radio; Radio Luxembourg; Radio Normandy See COMMERCIAL RADIO.

Radio Northsea PIRATE RADIO station that began broadcasting off the coast of Essex immediately prior to the general election of 1970. Mindful of the Labour government's antipathy to COMMERCIAL RADIO and the Conservatives' support for it, Radio Northsea broadcast pro-Tory propaganda at an election in which the 18–21 age group was voting for the first time.

Many constituencies in London and the south-east were marginal seats. Labour lost the election; in the constituencies nearest Radio Northsea, the swing against Labour was greatest. At the Royal Opening of Parliament on 2 July 1970, the Queen's speech confirmed that legislation would be introduced for local radio stations 'under the general supervision of an independent broadcasting authority'.

Radio 1, Radio 2, Radio 3, Radio 4, Radio 5 Live (BBC) Radios 1 to 4 have broadcast in their present form from 1967; Radio 5 took to the air in August 1990, to be revamped into Radio 5 Live in March 1994. Prior to 1967 there was the Home Service, catering for news, plays, talks, comedy shows and magazine programmes – the Talk Channel; the Light Programme, largely for popular music and entertainment; and the Third Programme serving the world of classical music and drama. During the 1960s PIRATE RADIO invaded the airwaves with pop music, which attracted large audiences. The Marine Broadcasting (Offenders) Act, 1967, made such stations illegal. BBC Radio 1 was created to meet the new demand and successfully competes with COMMERCIAL RADIO stations for the attention of popular music fans.

Radio 2 took on a similar if not identical role to that of the Light Programme, Radio 3 that of the Third Programme, and Radio 4 became Britain's premier talk radio channel. For its richness, diversity and sheer quality of output, Radio 4 must rank among the world's finest radio services. Faced with competition from CLASSIC FM, Radio 3 has proved itself responsive to audience needs without sacrificing (too much) quality.

Radio 5 was to be a speech-led service catering for the needs of children and young people, sharing airtime with news and sport. Just when this pioneering new channel was beginning to win listeners and to produce programmes of originality, the BBC abandoned the adventure of, in the words of the Controller of Radio 5, Pat Ewing, introducing 'a new generation to speech radio', and opted for Radio 5 Live, more general in orientation, often crossing lines with Radio 4 but in terms of its sports coverage, unexcelled. See BBC DIGITAL. See also *TOPIC GUIDE* under BROADCASTING.

RAJAR Radio Joint Audience Research; research body of both the commercial radio and PUBLIC SERVICE BROADCASTING sectors in the UK. RAJAR contracts out its radio research work to an independent company, Ipsos-RSL. Areas of audience research reported by RAJAR are 'weekly reach', 'average hours' listening on the part of audience and 'share of listening' between public and private stations. Weekly reach and share listening figures comprise RATINGS.

---

* Jo Tacchi, 'Who listens to radio? The role of industrial audience research', in Michael Bromley (ed.), *No News is Bad News: Radio, Television and the Public* (UK: Longman, 2001).

Random sample See SAMPLING.

Ratings See AUDIENCE MEASUREMENT.

Reaction shot When a person is being interviewed on television there are regular *in-cuts* where the viewer is offered a glimpse of the reactions of the reporter or interviewer – nodding, smiling, acknowledging. When interviews take place on location rather than in the studio, such reaction shots are usually filmed separately and edited in later. See SHOT.

Readership See MEDIASPHERE.

Reading Just as, in modern usage, we refer to TEXT as any human-made artefact, rather than merely a printed text, so we refer to reading as a process that is a response to all texts. Use of this term suggests a more positive, attentive and interpretative reaction to a text rather than merely looking. We read critically; we analyse, while at the same time modern usage accepts the more open nature of 'readings' – their POLYSEMY (or many-meaningness). A *work*, as Roland Barthes has defined it, emanates from a creator, an encoder – writer, artist, composer, for example – but the *text* belongs in the sphere of reading and thus becomes, as it were, the property of the decoder.

It does not necessarily follow that all readings are of equal value, for inevitably there are informed as contrasted with uninformed readings. Recognition of *competence* has to be considered, and this would involve what Noam Chomsky has termed 'linguistic competence', as well as knowledge, experience, training and a degree of EMPATHY. The study of media communication is largely about learning to read competently, with PERCEPTION and understanding. See *TOPIC GUIDE* under TEXTUAL ANALYSIS.

Realism That which is portrayed as 'reality' in art, literature, theatre, film fiction or documentary and photography. It constitutes an imitation of *perceived* reality, a simulation. Because it is the result of a range of choices concerning subject matter and aesthetics, realism is a *construct* of reality rather than a reproduction of it, influenced by VALUE, IDEOLOGY and convention. Socialist realism in Russian cinema, for instance, focused on the realities of the lives of workers, on the land or in factories, but such portraits of reality were highly charged with the ideology of the Soviet system in the ways that labour was idealized rather than portrayed by means of a critical READING of the system.

Susan Strehle in *Fiction in the Quantum Universe* (US/UK: University of Carolina Press, 1992) suggests the use of the term 'actualism' rather than 'the old mechanistic reality' because it has 'its roots not in things [or facts] but in acts, relations and motions'. The term corresponds to ACTUALITY, an approach pioneered by early radio DOCUMENTARY-makers to allow real situations to be communicated with a minimum of intervention from the programme-maker. Yet however absent seems to be the hand of MEDIATION, it is (in actuality) ever-present.

Peter Dahlgren in *Television and the Public Sphere: Citizenship, Democracy and the Media* (UK: Sage, 1995) says of TV texts that 'realism' (his inverted commas) is a 'very central feature' but one that is highly problematical. We should constantly remind ourselves, Dahlgren believes, that 'all representation involves construction'. In discussing TV the author talks of the 'pleasure of verisimilitude'. Essentially TV is 'mimetic', it imitates reality rather more than it interprets it. In Dahlgren's view this limits the potential TV has for POLYSEMY and thus in this context, the representation of alternative realities. See *TOPIC GUIDE* under REPRESENTATION.

Reality TV Perhaps best described as 'live documentary'; a prime example being, in the UK, Channel 4's *Big Brother*, versions of which have been produced in many other countries worldwide. While participants in reality TV are real people (rather than actors), and while the story of their interactions is unscripted and not known in advance, such programmes are essentially *contrivances* of reality; highly mediated by the TV production team; and highly manipulated from start to finish.

The participants are painstakingly vetted (indeed as though there were a script). Once selected, though they are 'real' people they are placed into a situation that requires *performance*. They become actors in front of cameras and millions of viewers, knowing full well that the performance of the realities of self-presentation will be judged by a 'participatory' audience.

Such programmes as *Big Brother*, the BBC's *Castaway* or ITV's *Pop Idol* and *Popstars: The Rivals* have been described as docu-soaps with gameshow appeal, and they chiefly target younger-generation audiences. Their popularity, the unscripted sensation-seeking of many participants, and the encouragement of such sensationalism on the part of the popular press, have provoked criticism and a degree of righteous indignation.

France's near-equivalent to *Big Brother*, entitled *Loft Story* (in which men and women are housed together in a loft under 24-hour TV surveillance) prompted street riots, protest marches and an Anti-*Loft Story* day of action. Screened on M6, the pay-per-view channel, *Loft Story* threatened to knock TFI, the main state broadcaster from its number one slot in the viewer ratings. TFI reported *Loft Story* to the Audiovisual High Council. In a UK *Guardian* article, 'In search of loft principles' (21 May 2001), Emily Bell wrote, 'What *Loft Story* has highlighted for the French, and maybe for the rest of us, is the issue of ratings versus responsibility and trash versus culture.'

In 2002 there were even stirrings of protest from tabloid commentators. Gary Bushell ('King of Telly!') in a piece 'Why British telly is going down the pan', in the *News of the World* (2 June) reported that the most thrilling thing that happened in the *Big Brother* house was that 'one of the assembled mutants soiled the toilet seat. For pity's sake, enough!' Across the red-tops, Charlie Catchpole of the *Daily Star* (3 June) under a headline, 'Bruv's enough to drive you mental', declared, 'Yup. Watching paint dry is now a recognized pastime for almost six million people …'.

Perhaps the *Daily Mirror's* Kevin O'Sullivan ('Anti-Big Brother Correspondent') summed up what is the kernel of 'reality' TV: its fascination for audiences and for the popular press, when he wrote, on 3 June, 'Put any group of dumb animals in an enclosed environment and before long their thoughts will turn to breeding.' Despite such comments, Channel 4, desperate to boost its audience share, programmed *Big Brother* seven nights a week in 2002, incurring accusations that its special text-messaging service could lead to soaring phone bills, especially among children.

Reassurance, structure of See NEWS.

Received pronunciation (RP) That mode of pronunciation in English that is free of regional

ACCENT and aspires to a generally accepted standard; derives from the speech of the court and of public schools; traditionally the 'vocal sign' of the educated person, adopted as the norm for BBC broadcasters, and eventually being termed 'BBC English'. RP no longer has the prestigious status or the dominance it once had. Regional accents have been 'in' since the 1960s, though RP has retained a substantial foothold in national broadcasting.

Receiver See SENDER/RECEIVER.

Recency effect See FIRST IMPRESSIONS; PRIMACY, LAW OF.

Reception studies In recent years particular research emphasis has been placed upon the ways that AUDIENCES receive media messages; how they react to their reading, listening and viewing; and what audiences do with that experience, what MEANINGS they make of it. Such reception studies have, as far as television is concerned, shifted from a prime focus on audience response to news and current affairs to the investigation of audience reception of popular GENRES, such as SOAP OPERAS. See AUDIENCE MEASUREMENT. See also *TOPIC GUIDE* under AUDIENCES/CONSUMPTION AND RECEPTION OF MEDIA.

---

* Tony Wilson, *Watching Television: Hermeneutics, Reception and Popular Culture* (UK: Polity Press, 1995); Sonia Livingstone, *Making Sense of Television: The Psychology of Audience Interpretation* (UK: Routledge paperback, 1998); Pertii Alasuutari (ed.), *Rethinking the Media Audience* (UK: Sage, 1999).

Record player See GRAMOPHONE.

Redundancy In communication terms, redundancy refers to that which is conventional or predictable in any message. Its opposite is *entropy*, that which is unexpected and surprising, of low predictability. John Fiske in *Introduction to Communication Studies* (UK: Methuen, 1982) says 'The English language is about 50% redundant. This means we can delete about 50% of any utterance and still have a usable language capable of transmitting understandable messages.'

Redundancy is established through frequent use until it becomes a convention, both technical, in terms of correctness, and social, in terms of general acceptability. It is essential if the MEANING of messages is to have wide currency and be 'on wave-length' with the codes and reference tables of the receiver.

The entropic challenges these codes and reference tables with novelty – new expression, new thought, overturning predictability and probability. The art of the avant-garde is entropic; at least in its initial phase, it speaks in a language the general public find difficult to understand, and often provocative. Of course the shock of the new passes: yesterday's outrage is today's fashion, yesterday's entropy is today's redundancy.

A scan of the popular arts reveals their reliance on the conventional forms and practices that make up redundancy – the predictable rhymes and metres of pop songs, for example, the repetitive refrains of folk songs. Fiske writes, 'Redundancy is generally a force for the status quo and against change. Entropy is less comfortable, more stimulating, more shocking perhaps, but harder to communicate effectively.' See PHATIC LANGUAGE.

Referent The actual object, entity in the external world to which a SIGN or linguistic expression refers. The referent of the word table is the object 'table'.

Referential code See CODES OF NARRATIVE.

Reflective-projective theory of broadcasting and mass communication Posed by Lee Loevinger in 'The ambiguous mirror: the reflective-projective theory of broadcasting and mass communication', in G. Gumpert and R. Cathcart (eds), *Inter/Media: Interpersonal Communication in a Media World* (US/UK: Oxford University Press, 1979). Loevinger states, 'that mass communications are best understood as mirrors of society that reflect an ambiguous image in which each observer projects or sees his own vision of himself and society'. The media reflect images of society but not of the individual.

'While the mirror can pick out points and aspects of society, it cannot create a culture or project an image that does not reflect something already existing in some form in society.' BROADCASTING can clarify or distort images of society; it can focus broadly or narrowly. According to the theory, the media 'are most unlikely to become instruments of social reform or great public enlightenment'. Thus violence on TV reflects the existence of and tolerance of violence in society. See *TOPIC GUIDE* under COMMUNICATION THEORY.

Reflexivity Self-monitoring in terms of COGNITIVE practice; but more significantly for the analysis of the individual's self-positioning within a fast-changing society in which NORMS, VALUES and practices are rendered less certain, less distinct. Reflexivity is central to the construction of identity. It operates intuitively and aesthetically as well as cognitively and mass communication is seen to be an agency in the control of or liberation of self-interpretation in relation to the READING of and reaction to media TEXTS. Reflexivity makes critical use of NARRATIVES, personal and collective, through which sense is forged out of experience. See SELF-IDENTITY.

Reformers See ADVERTISING: MAINSTREAMERS, ASPIRERS, SUCCEEDERS AND REFORMERS.

Refutation The employment of counter-arguments, evidence and proof to dispute the arguments of another person. Strictly speaking, to disprove allegations.

Register Term describing the compass of a voice or instrument, the range of sound tones produced in a particular manner. The soprano and the bass sing in different registers. The word also describes the structures of language used in varying social contexts: its levels of vocabulary, sentence construction, tones and inflexions. Thus the register adopted by an infant school teacher in his/her class will differ from the register selected for the staff room, just as a scientist will adjust his/her register between conversations held with scientific colleagues and with casual acquaintances in the local pub. In printing, register refers to the exact adjustment of position, as of colours in a picture, or letterpress on opposite sides of the page.

Regulation of Investigatory Powers Act (RIPA) (UK), 2000 One of the most far-reaching pieces of government SURVEILLANCE legislation, RIPA extends blanket powers of interception on TELEPHONE and INTERNET traffic to not only the police and security agencies such as MI5 but to a broad spectrum of government departments as well as local government. In 2002 what had initially been claimed to be a means of tracking online crime was suddenly opened out to be what a UK *Guardian* leader, 'British Liberty RIP' (11 June 2002), called 'a mockery of the right to privacy that the Human Rights Act is supposed to protect'. RIPA was seen to 'have profound civil liberty implications'.

The Act opens up all telephone messages and e-mails to official scrutiny. In addition it empowers employers to monitor the e-mail exchanges of their employees. It obliges Internet Service Providers (ISPs) to install 'black boxes' that record all server traffic. It makes illegal any ENCRYPTION that might deny access by the authorities. Refusal on the part of individuals or GROUPS to declare keys to encryption is punishable by up to two years' imprisonment. Unwittingly, ISPs become the snouts of government and its agencies.

In future, the 'spy-in-the-wire' will know who you talk to, when, what you talk about and where you having been talking from. It can accumulate vast amounts of information about you that will be made available to people you have never met, never heard of, about whom you know nothing; and that information – the fact that information has been gathered and stored – is secret to you but not to them; and you will not know how that information is to be used and for what purpose.

Roy Greenslade in an article 'I arrest you for e-mailing' (*Guardian*, 31 July 2000), believes that 'The passing of the RIP act denies everyone the freedom, and the privacy, we thought the internet had provided. It robs journalists and their sources – including that most potent and essential of tipsters, the whistleblower – of their rights, and quite possibly, threatens their liberty.' The issue of interception warrants by those in authority has to be kept secret; and it is a criminal offence to publicize that a demand for an encryption key has been made.

Sections 21 to 25 of the Act grant the state powers to gather data from Internet traffic where the following might be considered to be at risk: national security, the detecting or preventing of crime, matters of disorder, traffic that may be deemed to be in the interests of the UK's economic well-being, public safety, public health, the levying/collecting of taxes, and for any purposes – subject to parliamentary approval – the Secretary of State specifies.

Caspar Bowen, Director of the Foundation for Policy Research, declared in a UK *Tribune* article (26 June 2001), 'that Britain now has the most draconian snooping laws in the world and the law infringed basic human rights'.

The opportunity, grasped by the Labour government in 2002, of tightening the screw of surveillance, was offered by the events of 11 September 2001 and the terrorist attack on the US Pentagon and New York's World Trade Center. It also resulted in the UK government influencing the rest of the European Union to fall into line. Welcoming the EU's ready embrace of this new tranche of data-spying, the UK Home Office issued the following statement: 'The UK is very pleased that the [European] council and parliament have reached agreement on a text that will ensure that the fight against terrorism and other crime will be given the appropriate weight', conceding that 'It is, of course, important to protect people's fundamental rights and freedoms, but, as the tragic events of September 11 show, this must be balanced with the need to ensure that the law enforcement community can do its job.'

John Wadham, director of Liberty, condemned the Act and its European extension: 'This violates,' he believed, 'a fundamental principle of privacy, which is that data collected for one purpose should not be used for another.' The editor of *StateWatch*, Tony Bunyan, summed up the Act, and official attempts at CENSORSHIP generally, with the comment, 'The problem with wanting to monitor a few people is that you end up having to keep data on everyone.'

The question, widely asked, has been – human rights apart – will RIPA succeed in its stated aim of catching criminals? The *Guardian* leader of 11 June 2002 doubted it: 'Ironically, such Orwellian sur-veillance will be of little help in tracking terrorists or organized crime cells. They can avoid identifica-tion by using pre-paid mobile phones or web-based e-mail from public terminals.' See *TOPIC GUIDE* under MEDIA: FREEDOM, CENSORSHIP.

Regulatory favours In an age when multinational corporations have acquired local, national and global voice by investing in media, it comes as no surprise to observe them using that voice to promote corporate interests, to employ those media to pressurize government to grant them favours. Jeremy Tunstall and Michael Parker in *Media Moguls* (UK: Routledge, 1991) use the term *regulatory favours*, which governments cede to big media-owning companies in return for a 'good press'. These favours principally constitute the abolition or waiving of media regulations that might hinder expansionist interests.

When, in May 2002, the UK government announced plans for the further DEREGULATION of BROADCASTING, a *Guardian* leader carried the headline 'Murdoch gets his way: New Labour rolls over for Rupert', referring to the decision that the way was to be made clear for Rupert Murdoch to expand into terrestrial TV in Britain. In an article in the same issue, media correspondent Emily Bell, under a headline 'Murdoch must have done a deal', talks of an 'unexpected act of munificence' and suggests that 'someone in the cabinet office checked the calendar and realized they had missed Rupert's birthday by six weeks, and they just happened to have a spare channel [Channel 5] kicking around in the cupboard'. See CONGLOMERATES; GLOBAL MEDIA SYSTEM: THE MAIN PLAYERS; POLITICS OF ACCOMMODATION (IN THE MEDIA); PRIVATIZATION; STRATEGIC BARGAINING. See also *TOPIC GUIDE* under MEDIA: POLITICS AND ECONOMICS.

Reinforcement There has been much argument over the role of the mass media in reinforcing, in underpinning, certain social and political VALUES and structures. Considerable attention has been given to two areas: the media's portrayal of violence and the role of the mass media in political com-munications.

There are those who claim that the frequent incidence of violence in the media has contributed to an increase in acts of violence in society. Research evidence, however, gives few clear pointers as to the nature or extent of any media influence. One school of thought rejects the notion that the media directly encourage violent behaviour in all viewers but argues that media violence may reinforce already existing tendencies to violence in some viewers.

This position is open to question. As Sonia Livingstone in an article, 'On the continuing problem of media effects', published in *Mass Media and Society* (UK/US: Arnold, 1996), edited by James Curran and Michael Gurevitch, comments, 'It is difficult to know what beliefs people might have espoused but for the media's construction of a normative reality, and difficult to know what role the media plays in the construction of those needs and desires which in turn motivate viewers to engage with the media as they are rather than as they might be.'

P.F. Lazarsfeld, B. Berelson and H. Gaudet, in a classic study of the effects of political communication by the mass media on voting behaviour, *The People's Choice* (US: Columbia University Press, 1948), were of the opinion that the media's main effect is to reinforce *existing* political preferences. The notions of *selective perception*, SELECTIVE EXPOSURE and *selective recall* are used to explain how the same output can reinforce the diverse views, values and beliefs of a mass audience. It is suggested that the audiences, rather than being passive receptacles for media output, select from the output those messages that are in accordance with their own prior dispositions and give attention to these, a point confirmed by Garth J. Jowett and Victoria O'Donnell reviewing research into the effects of persuasion and propaganda in their work *Propaganda and Persuasion* (US: Sage, 1999). They state: 'Selectivity in the perception of messages is generally guided by preexisting interests and behaviour patterns of the receivers … mass communication effects tend to take the form of reinforcement rather than change.'

Whilst in recent years there has been a tendency to adopt a more multiculturalist perspective in many areas of broadcasting this may result in the inadvertent reinforcement of more subtle negative attitudes. For example, Simon Cottle in *Ethnic Minorities and the Media* (US/UK: Oxford University Press, 2000), edited by Cottle, concludes from his study of regional TV news programmes in the UK that despite attempts to present a multiculturalist perspective, 'such "multiculturalist" representations … may actually serve to reinforce culturally sedimented views of ethnic miniorities as "Other" and simultaneously appear to give the lie to ideas of structural disadvantage and continuing inequality'. See AUDIENCE: ACTIVE AUDIENCE; EFFECTS OF THE MASS MEDIA; POLITICS OF ACCOMMODATION (IN THE MEDIA); RESONANCE.

Reithian Attitudes to BROADCASTING as typified by the first Director General of the BBC, Sir John Reith (1889–1971), who dominated the rise of broadcasting in the UK like a colossus. Dour, high-principled, autocratic, paternalist and a Scottish Presbyterian to boot, Reith was appointed General Manager of the newly formed British Broadcasting Company in December 1922. His philosophy was that broadcasting was a heaven-sent opportunity to educate and enlighten the people in the ways of quality, and that 'giving the people what they wanted' was the way to perdition.

This 'Tsar of Savoy Hill', as the press called him, believed – in the words of the *New Statesman* on Armistice Day 1933 – 'in the medicinal effects of education – a cultural dictatorship'. Though George Lansbury MP said of Reith, 'I have always felt that Sir John Reith would have made a very excellent Hitler for this country', Clement Attlee saw advantages: 'He puts up a splendid resistance to vested interests of all kinds.'

Elitist, imperious and sabbatarian, Reith nevertheless created in the BBC an organization resistant to commercialism, favouring the arts, serious debate and notions of public responsibility. Reith strove for IMPARTIALITY but never achieved *balance*: coverage of royal activities in the 1920s and 1930s was not in any way matched by coverage of the activities of the Labour movement and the unions and, during the General Strike of 1926, the BBC remained strictly 'neutral': it stayed silent. Reith, the Napoleon of Broadcasting, as Colonel Moore Brabazon called him, resigned as 'DG' (Director General), as his own staff spoke of him, in 1937. See BBC, ORIGINS. See also *TOPIC GUIDE* under MEDIA HISTORY; MEDIA INSTITUTIONS.

Relic gestures Those physical gestures that have outlived their original situation, yet continue to be used to effect even though their derivation is no longer obvious or explicable. Such gestures survive not only from historical past but from a human's infantile past. For example, the rocking to and fro of disaster victims in the face of intolerable grief.

Repertoire of non-verbal behaviour See NON-VERBAL BEHAVIOUR: REPERTOIRE.

Repetitive strain injury (RSI) Brought on by regular and intensive use of computer keyboards and thus the 'disease of journalists' as well as secretaries; resulting in severe pain in the hands, arm, neck and back. Once RSI has taken hold it is difficult and sometimes impossible for the sufferer to carry on working. It was reported in 1991 that a third of the journalists on the *Financial Times* were affected by RSI.

Reporters Sans Frontières Montpellier-based group of journalists set up in 1987 to defend press freedom worldwide, and journalists in trouble.

Report-talk, rapport-talk This is one way in which men and women's conversational style differs according to Deborah Tannen in her *You Just Don't Understand Me: Women and Men in Conversation* (UK: Virago Press, 1992). Men, she argues, are confident with public speech or what she calls *report-talk*, whether this be in a formal or an informal situation where several people are in conversation.

In these situations, when the company is mixed, men typically participate more in conversation than women and, in part, their performance may be a way of establishing status and control. In a more private setting though, this difference in the participation rate between men and women may change or even reverse. Here *rapport-talk* with which women, Tannen argues, are more comfortable is appropriate. Rapport-talk is used for establishing and reinforcing intimacy. These differences reflect the different GENDERLECTS that Tannen argues men and women use, which in turn reflect one main difference in their use of conversation: men using conversation to establish *status* and control, women to establish *intimacy*. See *TOPIC GUIDE* under GENDER MATTERS.

Representation A core function of media is to re-present to AUDIENCES the realities of 'the world out there'. Most of our knowledge of that world is brought to us via the media; and our perception of reality is mediated (see MEDIATION) by newspapers, TV, advertisements, films, etc. The media *image* the world for us. They do this by means of selection and interpretation, which operate through GATEKEEPING and according to AGENDAS that are suffused by IDEOLOGY. The media represent to us the past as well as the present, and representations – or interpretations – of the past affect our perceptions of the present. Out of such representations arise issues – concerning the representation of women, for example, of race, poverty, minorities.

What we as audience know of Africa and Africans, of Serbs and Albanians, of Israelis and Arabs is what we have experienced through the reports and pictures brought to us by the media. The study of media representation, therefore, is central to cultural, media and communication studies. Because it is impossible to represent the world in all its massive complexity, media representation has to be viewed as a 'version' of reality, in which FRAMING has taken place according to criteria such as NEWS VALUES or pressures to propagandize, sensationalize, binarize (that is, divide 'Us' from 'Them' – see WEDOM, THEYDOM) or seek to impose MEANING upon webs of complexity. Representation is essentially about *definition*, and media representation tends to be about imposing certain definitions, and therefore meanings, over others; thus endeavouring to affect the preferences of the public. See DISCOURSE. See also *TOPIC GUIDE* under REPRESENTATION.

---

* Richard Butt, *Rethinking Media Representations* (UK: Arnold, 2001).

Representation, machinery of See MACHINERY OF REPRESENTATION.

Representation of crime on screen See CRIME: TYPES OF CRIME ON SCREEN.

Representative sample See SAMPLING.

Repressive state apparatus See IDEOLOGICAL STATE APPARATUSES.

Repressive use of the media See EMANCIPATORY USE OF THE MEDIA.

Re-regulation The notion that DEREGULATION of media – essentially BROADCASTING – has actually meant fewer regulations and more freedom is challenged by Karen Siune and Wolfgang Truetzschler in *Dynamics of Media Politics* (UK: Sage, 1992). The authors write 'What has frequently been referred to as deregulation has turned out to be regulation in another form, and the concept of "re-regulation" is much more appropriate.' The more systems are fragmented, the authors argue, the more detailed rules are created concerning minor – but still significant – aspects of media structure; in contrast to the former overall framework 'that provides only vague outlines'.

Research centres (into the media) In the UK there are centres of research into culture and the media at the universities of Birmingham, Cardiff, Glasgow, Leeds, Leicester, London, Loughborough, Portsmouth, Sheffield and Stirling. At Birmingham there is the Centre for Contemporary Cultural Studies; in Cardiff the Tom Hopkinson Centre; in Glasgow the GLASGOW UNIVERSITY MEDIA

GROUP; in Leeds the Centre for Television Research; in Leicester the Centre for Mass Communication; in Loughborough the Communication Research Centre; in Portsmouth, the Media Research Group; in Sheffield the Centre for English Cultural Tradition; and in London the Media Research Groups at Goldsmith's College and the London School of Economics and Political Science.

Resistance (of audience to media)   See DOMINANT, SUBORDINATE, RADICAL; POLYSEMY.

Resistive reading   Occurs when AUDIENCE chooses not to accept without question the PREFERRED READING of media messages. Considerable research has been conducted into the capacity of audiences, and of segments of audiences such as women, to react independently to DOMINANT DISCOURSES: hence the *active audience* thesis. See AUDIENCE: ACTIVE AUDIENCE; DOMINANT, SUBORDINATE, RADICAL; EMPOWERMENT.

Resonance   Term used by George Gerbner and fellow researchers at the Annenberg School of Communications, University of Pennsylvania, Philadelphia, to describe a condition experienced by television viewers when what they see matches their expectations. If what they see confirms their vision of the world, of reality, that vision *resonates*. It is reinforced. More, for in 'The "mainstreaming" of America: violence profile no. 11' (*Journal of Communication*, Summer 1980), Gerbner, Larry Gross, Michael Morgan and Nancy Signorielli state that where TV reality and a person's experience or PERCEPTION of reality are in alignment, 'the combination may result in a coherent and powerful "double dose" of the television message'.

For example, city dwellers living in centres of high crime will find TV's violent imagery congruent with their experience. 'These people receive a "double dose" of messages that the world is violent, and consequently show the strongest associations between viewing and fear.' See EFFECTS OF THE MASS MEDIA; MAINSTREAMING; MEAN WORLD SYNDROME.

Response codes   See DOMINANT, SUBORDINATE, RADICAL; POLYSEMY.

Restricted code   See ELABORATED AND RESTRICTED CODES.

Reterritorialization   According to James Lull in *Media, Communication and Culture* (UK: Polity Press, 1995), reterritorialization means '... first that the foundations of cultural territory – ways of life, artefacts, symbols and contexts – are all open to new interpretations and understandings' and, second, 'implies that culture is constantly reconstituted through social interaction, sometimes by creative uses of personal communications technology and the mass media'. Thus *cultural territory* is potentially dynamic and changing, so reshaping is constantly possible.

Rhetoric   Traditionally, the theory and practice of eloquence, whether spoken or written; the use of language so as to persuade others. The word is almost always used today as a term of criticism: rhetoric is the style in which bare-faced persuasion – politicking – is used. It is emotive; it belongs to speeches, and while it is very often resounding it is rarely eloquent because it trades in empty phrases and endless repetitions. It is essentially redundant in that it tells supporters what they already know and antagonists what they know and don't want to hear.

Rhetoric is the stock-in-trade of the press, and of the popular press in particular. Practically every front-page headline is rhetorical in that it is soaked through with the ideological attitudes of the newspaper, not the least the belief in what sells newspapers, what commands attention, what readers want to be told. Indeed it might be said that one of the prime functions the popular press sets itself is to translate actuality into rhetoric: complex issues are translated into the simplifying mode of MYTH, of WEDOM, THEYDOM, Militant and Moderate, Order and Disorder, Black and White, Management and Unions, Dries and Wets. See NEWS VALUES; OTHER.   See also *TOPIC GUIDE* under LANGUAGE/DISCOURSE/NARRATIVE.

Rhetoric of the image   See IMAGE, RHETORIC OF.

Rhetoric of numbers   Phrase used by Itzhak Roeh and Saul F. Feldman to describe how the press, the popular press in particular, use numbers and amounts for *rhetorical* rather than *factual* purposes. The authors' analysis of the headlines of two Hebrew dailies, one ELITE, one popular, is reported on in 'The rhetoric of numbers in front-page journalism: how numbers contribute to the melodramatic in the popular press', published in *Text* 4(4) (1984).

Right of reply A long-established practice in continental countries, the right of reply in the UK press has been argued for long, hard and generally unsuccessfully. Such a right would require newspaper editors to publish within a given time the replies of individuals or organizations who allege serious press misrepresentation, or face a special court and a fine if found to be in error. It is argued that such a right would act as a deterrent to editorial bias and unethical practices. Newspapers do publish apologies but these are usually for printing factual errors that might land them with libel actions.

On the UK's Channel 4, for almost 20 years, the *Right to Reply* programme offered viewers the opportunity to have their say about BROADCASTING and other issues. It was taken off the air in the spring of 2001. Roger Bolton, the presenter of the programme, was of the opinion that 'There is now an accountability gap at Channel 4 and on British television.' See CAMPAIGN FOR PRESS AND BROADCASTING FREEDOM; PEOPLE'S COMMUNICATION CHARTER.

Rights and the media See CULTURAL OR CITIZEN RIGHTS AND THE MEDIA.

Riley and Riley's model of mass communication, 1959 John W. Riley Jr and Matilda White Riley in 'Mass communication and the social system', in *Sociology Today: Problems and Prospects* (US: Basic Books, 1959; Harper Torch Books, Vol. 2, 1965), edited by R.K. Merton, L. Broom and L.S. Cottrell Jr, pose a model in which the process of communication is an integral part of the social system. For Riley and Riley, both the Communicator (C) and the Recipient (R) are affected in the message process of sending, receiving, reciprocating, by the three social orders: the *primary group* or groups of which C and R are members; the larger *social structure*, that is the immediate community – social, cultural, industrial – to which they belong, and the *overall social system*. All of these are in dynamic interaction, with messages flowing multi-directionally.

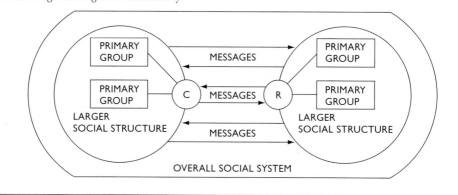

Riley and Riley's model of mass communication, 1959

The mass media audience Riley and Riley perceive as being neither impassive nor isolated but 'a composite of recipients who are related to one another, and whose responses are patterned in terms of these relationships'. See *TOPIC GUIDE* under COMMUNICATION MODELS.

RIPA See REGULATION OF INVESTIGATORY POWERS ACT (RIPA (UK), 2000.

Ritual, rites of passage A ritual can be seen as a carefully constructed act of communication, a focused organization of symbols, loaded with a range of meanings significant for the individuals or social GROUPS concerned. Some rituals involve a great deal of ceremonial activity whilst those of everyday life may be fairly simple. Rituals can be religious or secular. They operate to give individuals or groups a sense of collective identity and security.

Rites of passage is a term used to refer to those rituals that mark the transition from one status, stage or state to another either by the whole community or, more commonly, by individuals. The ceremonies that mark such changes provide a symbolic confirmation of the change of social identity involved: a wedding ceremony would be an example of one such ceremony, redolent with symbols reflecting socio-cultural VALUES and expectations.

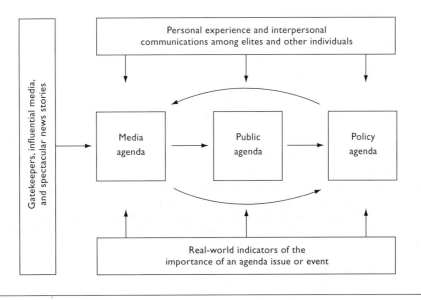

Rogers and Dearing's agenda-setting model, 1987

Rogers and Dearing's agenda-setting model, 1987 Published in the *Communication Yearbook* 11 (US: Sage, 1987) and examined in *Communication Models for the Study of Mass Communication*, McQuail and Windahl (eds), (UK: Longman, 5th impression, 1998), this development by E.M. Rogers and J.W. Dearing of previous AGENDA-SETTING models is a welcome acknowledgement of the competing agendas in the public sphere. In their *Yearbook* article, 'Agenda-setting, where has it been, where is it going?' the authors see the public agenda as existing separately, though locked between, the policy agenda, of the state, of government, and the media, each subject to influence by the others.

The triad of agendas is itself influenced by a number of contextual factors 'out there' – for example, spectacular news stories. There are substantial factors that shape one, two or all agendas but that may also temper, or restrict, the effectiveness of those agendas, such as personal experience or what Rogers

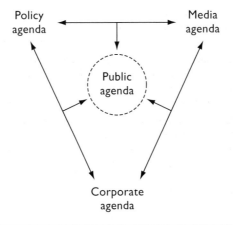

Tripolar model of competing agendas

and Dearing call 'real world indicators' of the importance of an agenda issue. In this sense, reality remains something other than what is constructed in the media, or 'fed to' the public as reality by those who forge the policy agenda.

One problem with the model is its linearity in that it does not sufficiently indicate the interactive nature of competing agendas. It also presents the public agenda as being in the same league, in terms of power, as the other agendas. Lastly, the model could arguably have a fourth agenda added to it, the *corporate* agenda, in order to reflect the increasingly dominant role in all aspects of policy, public debate and media operation, played by transnational companies on the global stage.

The Dictionary's authors would pose here a modest alternative to Rogers and Dearing, which emphasizes the *interactive* nature of the dominant agendas while shifting the public agenda into no less central a position, but one that is by its nature less defined, inevitably more diffuse and thus more open to influence. See REGULATORY FAVOURS. See also *TOPIC GUIDE* under COMMUNICATION MODELS.

Roles A social role consists of the expected behaviour associated with a particular social position. Thus the social position of a 'journalist' identifies a body of behaviours expected of a journalist, that is the role of the journalist in society. Role is a relational term. People play roles within a context in which other people are also playing roles. Roles within society or a social group carry with them responsibilities, obligations and rights.

There is some evidence that the role a person or group occupies within a given social context can influence the pattern of communication adopted. Basil Bernstein, for example, argues in 'Social class, language and socialization', in *Language and Social Context* (UK: Penguin, 1972), edited by P.P. Giglioli, that selective access to the elaborated language code may well result from the fact that there is selective access to the social roles that require its use (see ELABORATED AND RESTRICTED CODES).

Behaviour identified with a role is not necessarily rigidly prescribed. Through interaction with others, individuals can change the expectations that determine a particular role. To some extent roles can be negotiated within a social context; within small, informal groups roles are often arrived at through interaction alone. An individual usually performs several roles, such as teacher, wife, daughter, mother, friend and neighbour.

This multiplicity of roles tends to generate problems of conflicting demands, known as *role strain*. The individual may often have to adjust his/her communication pattern – non-verbal as well as verbal – to suit each particular role. Role strain occurs when our communication patterns cut across each other; when unexpected encounters take place between people from different role situations or, more seriously, when the role is deeply unnatural to us – an apparent denial of 'true' self.

The concept of role is used not only to describe the position of individuals within a social structure but also that of groups or organizations. In this sense commentators write of the role – or roles – of the mass media in society; hence the so-claimed role of the press as WATCHDOGS, defenders of the public good. Roles played by media in society vary according to who is defining such roles, but regular classifications include definers of reality, a nation's conscience, public entertainers, policers of deviance, defenders of tradition and guard dogs of HEGEMONY.

Roll film The first roll film for use in cameras was introduced by A.J. Melhuish and J.B. Spencer in 1854, though roll film cameras were not marketed until the Kodak of 1888.

Rostrum camera In TV, a film camera fixed in position over a table and used to take still photographs.

Rotary press See CYLINDER OR ROTARY PRESS.

Royal Commissions on the media See *TOPIC GUIDE* under COMMISSIONS, COMMITTEES, LEGLISLATION.

Rumour Indirect and unsubstantiated information; *hearsay*; transmitted along informal channels by word of mouth. Rumour has the following characteristic features: it can rarely if ever be traced back to its origin; it can spread (almost) at the speed of light; it will only spread if the rumour has the momentum of credibility (even if this credibility is only the size of a pinch of salt), and it thrives in close-knit communities that have either no regular or formal channels of communication or channels that are inefficient or not recognized as important.

A process of MEDIATION occurs at most or all points of telling, the original narrative being exaggerated and usually decorated with envy, spite or resentment. Good news rarely travels as quickly as bad news. In organizations, rumour often circulates most strongly in subcultures of those people generally well down in the HIERARCHY and who tend to be last in the queue when information is passed through formal channels.

The only antidote to rumour is efficient, full and open, participative communication, with strong lines of horizontal as well as vertical communication. The impact of rumour is rarely beneficial; in the main, rumour is corrosive of relationships, and fuels suspicion and bad feeling. Its favourite habitat is a communication vacuum. One dubious compensation is that the subjects, or 'victims', of rumour are generally the last to hear of it; unless, of course, they started the rumour themselves. See INTER-PERSONAL COMMUNICATION; LOONY LEFTISM.

Running story See SPOT NEWS.

Rushdie affair See FATWA.

Rushes In film-making, prints of 'takes' that are made immediately after a day's shooting; these are examined by the film team, led by the director, before the next day's shooting. Produced at a 'rush' from negative, they are also known as 'dailies'.

S

Salience All messages are not given equal attention by the receiver; some messages, or parts of a message, appear more prominent, more *salient*, to the receiver. This predisposition towards certain messages, or parts of a MESSAGE, can be the result of a complex of factors such as life experience, attitudes, VALUES and interests. There has been considerable research into the role of the media in the formation of salience, particularly in the field of current affairs.

The focus of investigation here is the extent to which extensive media coverage of certain issues leads the AUDIENCE to perceive those issues as being politically significant. See AGENDA-SETTING; ATTRIBUTE DIMENSION; McCOMBS AND SHAW'S AGENDA-SETTING MODEL OF MEDIA EFFECTS, 1978.

Salon discourse According to Susan Herbst and James R. Beniger in 'The changing infrastructure of public opinion', in *Audiencemaking: How Media Create the Audience* (US: Sage, 1994), edited by James S. Ettema and D. Charles Whitney, the first use of the term public opinion was made by Jacques Necker, the finance minister to the French King Louis XIV (1638–1715). Necker was referring specifically to the salons of the day, generally if not always presided over by women of high birth and attended by intellectuals, poets, statesmen and philosophers.

Here, among many things, matters of state were freely discussed and later diffused by the writings of those who attended the salons. Herbst and Beniger refer to this as the *elite model* of public opinion infrastructure: 'The public in the model is composed only of the most highly educated and influential members of society, while the bulk of the people are purposely excluded because their opinion is thought to be uninformed, and are in any case irrelevant – most people have no political power.' The authors argue that this model of public opinion held sway until the American and French Revolutions.

Salutation display Means by which we demonstrate that we wish someone well, or at the very least do not ostensibly wish them harm – greeting them when we meet and when we part company. Salutation display varies according to such factors as the nature of our relationship with the greeted person, the context of the encounter and the length of prior separation. See GESTURE; SHORTFALL SIGNALS.

Samizdat Russian, meaning 'self-published', a secret publication during the Soviet Communist era, circulated by hand, usually printed on a duplicator or simply on a typewriter with carbon copies, by dissident writers, at great personal risk of reprisals by the authorities. *The First Circle* (1968) by Russian novelist Alexander Solzhenitsyn began life in Samizdat. The word *Tamizdat* described work produced by Russians in the West, published there and then smuggled into the Soviet Union. *Dr Zhivago* (1957) by Boris Pasternak (1890–1960) is an example of this. See GLASNOST.

Sampling A statistical method of selecting a group for analysis, from a larger social group known as the *population*, the statistical term for all those persons, events or entities that are relevant to the subject of the enquiry. The aim of sampling is to be able to use what is discovered about the sample group as a basis for inference about the behaviour of the population. The reliability of such inferences depends upon how far the sample is representative of the population. A *representative sample* is constructed in such a way that it contains members of various significant categories and classifications in the same proportion as they appear in the population.

Not all samples are representative, or quota samples: *random sampling* techniques are also used. A random sample is selected in such a way that every member of the population has an equal chance of being chosen. Such a sample is used when it is felt that the population is not divided into particularly significant categories or classifications. See *TOPIC GUIDE* under RESEARCH METHODS.

Sapir–Whorf linguistic relativity hypothesis Developed by two notable linguists, Edward Sapir (1884–1939) and Benjamin Lee Whorf (1897–1941). Succinctly stated, the hypothesis proposes that ways of thinking and patterns of CULTURE (and also to some extent social structure) are determined by the structure of the language used in a particular culture. An individual's or group's thought and DISCOURSE about life generally can only be expressed in language and are thus constrained by the language structure available.

Satellite transmission There are three main types of satellite: (1) weather and observational satellites; (2) communications satellites; and (3) space probes. Sputnik in 1957 was the first observational satellite; Telstar, in 1962, the first communications satellite. Working off solar-powered batteries, satellites have equipment for monitoring the conditions in and around themselves and sending data back to earth for control purposes. Also, they carry reception equipment for control signals from earth for correction of orbital travel etc. Satellites orbiting the earth have generally given way to geo-stationary operation, that is satellites stationed some 23,000 miles out in space at a constant altitude and keeping pace with the revolutions of the earth.

Signals from ground stations are beamed to the geo-stationary communications satellites and reflected by them to receiving stations that then relay the signals by cable for recording or transmission, or to receiving 'dishes' or antennae. Most communication satellites receive and transmit simultaneously from a number of earth stations.

TV pictures were first transmitted via satellite on 10 July 1962 when Telstar was launched at Cape Canaveral, US, and circled the earth every 157.8 minutes, enabling live TV pictures transmitted from Andover, Maine, to be received at Goonhilly Down, Cornwall and in Brittany (11 July). In 1964 the unmanned Syncom relayed pictures of the Olympic Games from Tokyo. The first commercial communications satellite was Early Bird, which marked the beginning of regular TV transmission via satellite (2 May 1965).

The UK franchise for a three-transponder direct-broadcast satellite (DBS) was granted in 1986, with a start date of 1990. After financial and investment doubts, which led to early backers – such as the BBC – withdrawing from DBS plans, the contract for Britain's first two DBS channels was awarded to British Satellite Broadcasting (BSB). Rupert Murdoch's Sky Satellite arrived ahead of BSB, beginning programme transmission in the UK in March 1989.

Between them, the rival companies estimated to have spent £1.25 billion, yet by October 1990, such were the colossal start-up expenses, that British Satellite Broadcasting was forced into a merger with Sky. The 'squarial' dish, created to bring BSB programmes into the home suddenly became scrap. The founding principle of the free market – that competition is the basic dynamic of success – was itself 'squarialized'. Sky took on the initials of BSB, becoming British Sky Broadcasting. Corporate monopoly of satellite transmission joined that of those other 'free enterprise' industries in the UK, rail transport, gas, water and electricity.

Murdoch's ambition to make News Corp a global provider of TV programming was marked in the 1990s with the acquisition of Star Television in Asia. In November 1995 News Corp joined with the Globo Organization of Brazil, Grupo Televisa of Mexico and Telecommunications, Inc. of the US to set up a satellite TV service for Latin American and Caribbean markets with estimated total launch costs of US$500m. See COMMUNICATIONS BILL (UK), 2002; CROSS-MEDIA OWNERSHIP.

See also *TOPIC GUIDE* under MEDIA: TECHNOLOGIES.

Scanner Mobile control room used in outside TV broadcasts.

Scheduling Process by which programmes or types of programme are 'timetabled' in order to attract maximum audiences, and to keep them attracted in the face of competition from rival programmes. The aim of the programme scheduler is to minimize the danger of audiences switching off or, even worse, over. Low-appeal programmes are usually placed against weak opposition, or they are 'hammocked', that is, placed in between 'bankers', trusting to the INHERITANCE FACTOR. Conversely there is the so-called 'pre-echo' effect where anticipation of a really popular programme can induce viewers to switch on earlier – and thus watch a programme with less popular appeal.

Scheduling techniques assume a high degree of passivity on the part of an audience, and might be said seriously to underestimate audience potential for variety and challenge. Competitive scheduling above all reduces the range of choice open to the viewer simply by making risk-taking more difficult.

Schema (plural, schemata) A schema is basically a framework or pattern, stored in the memory, which preserves and organizes information about some event or concept. The framework may be expanded as new information about the event or concept is acquired. It is argued by several researchers concerned with learning and memory that existing schemata affect our PERCEPTION of new information and that there is a tendency for us to try and fit new information into our existing frameworks – at least initially.

Schemata themselves can form cross-linkages to provide a wider mental or conceptual map of an area of knowledge or experience. This perspective on the way in which we receive and process information has important implications for the analysis of the way in which we send and receive messages in the communication process.

Schramm's models of communication, 1954 Wilbur Schramm built on SHANNON AND WEAVER'S MODEL OF COMMUNICATION, 1949 (the Mathematical Theory of Communication), but was more interested in mass communication than in the technology of commu-nication transmission. In 'How communication works', in W. Schramm (ed.), *The Process and Effects of*

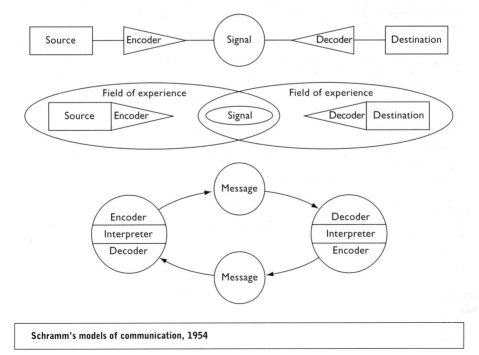

Schramm's models of communication, 1954

Mass Communication (US: University of Illinois Press, 1954) the author poses three models (see figure).

Shannon and Weaver's 'Transmitter' and 'Receiver' become 'Encoder' and 'Decoder', and their essentially linear model is restructured in Schramm's second model to demonstrate the overlapping, interactive nature of the communication process and the importance of what the Encoder and Decoder bring with them to the communication situation, their 'field of experience'; where that field of experience overlaps is the signal, Schramm's third model emphasizes FEEDBACK, and in doing so points up the circularity of the communication process. See *TOPIC GUIDE* under COMMUNICATION MODELS.

Scripts These are described by Eric Berne in *What Do You Say After You Say Hello?* (UK: Corgi Books, 1975) as 'a preconscious life plan' by which an individual structures 'longer periods of time – months, years or his whole life'. Scripts are developed in our early years but then have the capacity to influence and shape our transactions with others. A script contains within it an individual's self-concept and his/her general perception of and orientation towards other people and the world. It thus forms a basis for action. Berne identifies a number of possible scripts individuals may have as a result of their early experiences.

One example is the 'You Can't Trust Anybody' script. An individual with this script would obviously be suspicious and distrustful of others and act accordingly; such a script has obvious implications for communication with others. Berne argues that individuals tend to seek proof that their scripts are valid, by behaving in a way or interpreting behaviour in a manner that will reinforce them. So to a greater or lesser extent behaviour might be script-driven. Scripts can obviously be limiting but can, of course, be changed.

In *TA Today* (UK: Lifespace, 1987) Ian Stewart and Vann Joines discuss three main types of script: Winning, Losing (or *hamartic* – from the Greek, meaning basic flaw) and Non-winning (or *banal* scripts). A 'winner' is an individual who achieves the goals he/she has set for him/herself. It is also implied that these are met, 'comfortably, happily and smoothly'. A loser does not achieve set goals or does but is unhappy or damaged as a result. The losing script may resemble Ancient Greek drama when the basic flaw seems to lead inexorably to a tragic finale. A non-winning or banal script is one focused on playing safe and not taking risks. It may result in small gains and losses but the individual will remain a 'non-winner'. It seems that many people have a mixture of scripts, winning in some aspects of life whilst losing in others. See TRANSACTIONAL ANALYSIS.

Secondary viewing Term describing the circumstances in which TV viewing forms an accompaniment to other activities such as homework and reading.

Segmentation Term generally used to describe the constituent nature of TV – chopped up into segments, of NEWS, comedy, drama, commercial, DOCUMENTARY, quiz shows etc. John Fiske in 'Moments of television', in Ellen Seiter *et al.*, *Remote Control: Television, Audience and Cultural Power* (UK: Routledge, 1989), writes, 'Segmented texts are marked by abrupt transformations from segment to segment that require active, experienced, televisionally literate viewers to negotiate.'

In a wider sense and in relation to ADVERTISING and the targeting of AUDIENCES for the sale of goods and services (not to mention the marketing of images, ideas, ideologies, political parties, etc.), segmentation relates to current practices dividing consumers into lifestyle categories. Segmentation indicates a recognition that audiences are heterogeneous rather than homogeneous. Classification of audience into socio-economic groupings has become an industry in its own right. See ADVERTISING: MAINSTREAMERS, ASPIRERS, SUCCEEDERS AND REFORMERS; VALS TYPOLOGY. See also *TOPIC GUIDE* under ADVERTISING/MARKETING.

Selective exposure Individuals have a tendency to attend to, expose themselves to, messages that are consistent with their existing attitudes and beliefs. Equally they practise *selective perception* – reading messages in accordance with their existing attitudes. Thus they may either ignore or misinterpret those messages, or parts of a message, that conflict with or are dissimilar to held attitudes and expectations. Sometimes also referred to as *selective negligence*. See DISSONANCE; REINFORCEMENT.

Self-actualization See MASLOW'S HIERARCHY OF NEEDS.

Self-concept A person's self-concept is the total view that person has of him or herself. It includes such elements as an individual's view of his or her character, body image, abilities, emotions, qualities and relationships with others. The self-concept is commonly seen as being composed of the self-image and self-esteem. The self-image can be seen as the descriptive part of the self-concept. It is the picture we have of ourselves. Self-esteem, on the other hand is the evaluative part – it is how we feel about ourselves.

The self-image can further be divided into three elements: the self as I think I am, the self as I think others see me and the self I would like to be (the ideal self-image). Discrepancies between the ideal self-image and the self as I think I am can result in a low level of self-esteem as our self-esteem is usually based on our perceived successes and failures in life. Other people are clearly very influential in shaping any individual's conception of self, as in part an individual's self-concept depends upon his/her perception of the ideas others have about him/her. Individuals also attempt to influence the ideas others have, through controlling the impressions they create in self-presentation.

The feedback received from self-presentation enables the individual both to evaluate and shape his/her self-image. Paul Watzlawick, Janet Helmick Beavin and Don. D. Jackson have suggested in *Pragmatics of Human Communication: A Study of Interactional Patterns, Pathologies and Paradoxes* (US: W.W. Norton, 1967), that others respond to us in three distinct ways, by *confirmation*, *rejection* and *disconfirmation*. Confirmation takes place when others affirm our self-view; rejection when others do not treat us in a manner consistent with our self-view and disconfirmation when others fail to respond to our view of self or when others respond in a neutral manner.

Messages concerning the self abound in the content of INTERPERSONAL COMMUNICATION, whilst INTRAPERSONAL COMMUNICATION also plays a vital role not only in the generation of ideas about ourselves, some of which we may incorporate into the self which we present to others for feedback, but also in the decoding and evaluating of messages which we receive from others and in deciding whether to or how to act on them.

How we see ourselves affects the way we communicate. If, for example, we see ourselves as popular and sociable we are likely to be confident and outgoing in our communication with others. Excessive concern over self-esteem can lead to self-consciousness. People who are self-conscious are often shy, easily embarrassed and anxious in the presence of other people.

It should be remembered that the self-concept is not fixed but subject to continuing modification and change; it can alter according to the situations we are in, the people we are with and over time, and may also be found in mass communication, for example in images of ideal women found in advertisements. See ASSERTIVENESS; CONFIRMATION/DISCOMFIRMATION; DEVIANCE; IMPRESSION MANAGEMENT; JOHARI WINDOW; LABELLING PROCESS (AND THE MEDIA); SELF-FULFILLING PROPHECY; SELF-MONITORING; SELF-PRESENTATION.

* Brian Morris, *Anthropology of the Self: The Individual in Cultural Perspective* (UK: Pluto, 1994).

Self-disclosure Process by which – through statements verbal and non-verbal – we transmit new information about ourselves to others (see JOHARI WINDOW). Self-disclosure is based on honest, open interaction between people. Usually when we self-disclose to others, they reciprocate, and in this way a deeper understanding and relationship may develop. Of course we have to make careful choices in the first place about those to whom we will self-disclose, at what rate, to what extent, on what topics and in what situations. Self-disclosure involves an element of risk; an error of choice, for example if we self-disclose too much too soon in a relationship, it may result in a rebuff.

Through self-disclosure we not only learn more about others but also more about ourselves in that others' disclosures can contain views about ourselves. It is also a means by which we can come to terms with the positive and negative aspects of our self-image.

Self-fulfilling prophecy This effect occurs when the act of predicting that certain behaviour will take place helps cause that behaviour to occur and the prediction or prophecy is fulfilled. The expectations people have of an individual's behaviour can, if communicated to the individual, help create a situation in which the individual conforms to the expectations and fulfils the prophecy. There is a clear link between LABELLING and the self-fulfilling prophecy effect in that the act of applying a label can be the first step in ensuring a self-fulfilling prophecy.

The effect may be found particularly in situations where individuals have differing amounts of power and where one or more individuals are involved in the evaluating of others. Clearly the message contained in interpersonal and mass communication may often carry labels and thus have the potential for triggering self-fulfilling prophecy effects, but it is largely through INTRAPERSONAL COMMU-NICATION that an individual decides whether or not to conform to the expectations of others. Further, the self-fulfilling prophecy effect is only one of many influences on our behaviour and it may not be relevant in all cases. See DEVIANCE; LABELLING PROCESS (AND THE MEDIA); SELF-CONCEPT. See also *TOPIC GUIDE* under COMMUNICATION THEORY.

Self-identity In his book *Modernity and Self-Identity* (UK: Polity Press, 1991), Anthony Giddens defines self-identity in the conditions of late modernity as 'the self as reflexively understood by the person in terms of his or her biography'. Whilst self-identity is seen as normally having a degree of continuity it is 'such continuity as interpreted reflexively by the agent'. Self-identity also involves cognitive awareness of the self: 'To be a "person" is not just to be a reflexive actor, but to have a concept of a person.' Self-identity is an integral element of the SELF-CONCEPT.

Giddens further argues that although concepts of what a 'person' is may vary across cultures, 'The capacity to use "I" in shifting contexts, characteristic of every known culture, is the most elemental feature of reflexive conceptions of personhood.' Self-identity, Giddens argues, requires self-conscious thought and action; it is not 'something that is just given … but something that has to be routinely created and sustained in the reflexive activities of the individual'. It is an ongoing project, for in the conditions of late modernity self-identity has to be explored, developed and modified against a background of changing circumstances.

Giddens identifies four influences evident in the structure of post-traditional societies, which create the plurality of choices that make difficult the struggle of maintaining a coherent self-identity and which make necessary a *project of self*. Identities can only be achieved through choice – 'we have no choice but to choose' – given that much of the tradition that allowed them to be ascribed or indicated has lost its hold. Individuals inhabit a 'pluralization of lifeworlds' in which they have to present a number of different identities as they move from one social sphere to another, often negotiating differing expectations of their behaviour as they do so. What Giddens terms 'methodological doubt' is yet another feature of late modernity; certainty is seen as fragile as truth is seen as contextual and authority and reason provisional. 'Mediated experience' is seen to be at the heart of social life. Through the mass media and travel a vast range of 'lifeworlds' are presented to audiences, thus increasing the range of options available in the construction of identities.

Further, such identities have to be adjusted to cope with the range of changes that an individual is likely to encounter in such a society; the change to self-identity that usually accompanies a divorce being but one example. Giddens argues that little help is available to individuals in making such choices, although artefacts within consumer CULTURE may promise guidance – self-help manuals, for example. The ability to control SELF-PRESENTATION and in doing this to actively construct and reconstruct bodily appearance is seen by Giddens as essential to maintaining a coherent self-identity.

Don Slater notes in *Consumer Culture and Modernity* (UK: Polity Press, 1997) that another influence on late modernity – 'commercialization' – has resulted in 'a greater fluidity in the use of goods to construct identities and lifestyles'. It has also resulted, arguably, in individuals perceiving themselves, in part, as consumers – a perception which would reinforce the notion that individuals must make choices.

There are, of course, innumerable attempts to appeal to aspects of the self in ADVERTISING and marketing. The danger, warns Giddens, is that 'the project of self becomes translated into one of possession of desired goods and the pursuit of artificially framed styles of life … The consumption of ever-novel goods becomes a substitute for the genuine development of self.'

For Slater, 'Consumer culture "technicizes" the project of self by treating all problems as solvable through various commodities'. Further, 'identity can be seen as a saleable commodity'. Individuals may feel under pressure to 'sell' themselves in various social situations. Arguably many commodities are promoted on the grounds of their value to the individual in his/her task of constructing and maintaining self-identity. See IMPRESSION MANAGEMENT; MASLOW'S HIERARCHY OF NEEDS; SELF-CONCEPT; SELF-MONITORING.

Self-image See SELF-CONCEPT.

Self-monitoring This term refers to the degree to which people are sensitive to and able to respond to the demands of social situations with regard to their own behaviour. Richard D. Gross in *Psychology: The Science of Mind and Behaviour* (UK: Hodder & Stoughton, 1986) identifies high and low self-monitors. High self-monitors are motivated to and able to assess the demands of different situations, and adjust their SELF-PRESENTATION and general behaviour accordingly.

Low self-monitors on the other hand tend to behave in a similar fashion regardless of the situation, and their behaviour is more likely to be influenced by their own internal states. High self-monitors appear much more able to conceal their own moods, feelings and so on. Evidence suggests that high self-monitors have better social skills; for example, they can interpret non-verbal communication more accurately than low self-monitors.

Self-presentation Term used to describe the way in which we behave and communicate in differing social situations. It carries with it the implication that to some degree we consciously present ourselves to others in any given situation. The feedback we gain from self-presentation plays a role in shaping and changing our self-concept. Erving Goffman in *The Presentation of Self in Everyday Life* (US: Anchor, 1959; UK: Penguin, 1971) employs the dramaturgical perspective to analyse social interaction. Goffman writes, 'life itself is a dramatically enacted thing. All the world is not, of course a stage, but the crucial ways in which it is not are not easy to specify ... In short, we all act better than we know how.'

Goffman puts forward several useful concepts that have become influential in analysing self-presentation. A key concept is that of *persona*. The persona is the character we take on to play a part in a particular social situation. Different situations will usually require us to play different parts and therefore adopt different personas. So, for example, the persona an individual would adopt when visiting a folk festival with friends might be very different from the persona he/she would adopt in carrying out his/her work role as a High Court judge or an attorney.

The persona is part of our way of dealing with different people and the demands of different social situations. Once chosen for a particular situation it influences how we communicate in that situation. The ability to choose an appropriate persona for a situation and communicate accordingly can be seen as an important communication skill, as can the ability to shift from one persona to another as situations demand. Also, it is likely that the role a person is playing may dictate the kinds of persona it would be appropriate to adopt in any given situation.

Goffman uses the term *performance* to describe the act of self-presentation and in many cases these performances can be seen as staged. In staging a performance in everyday life we would use props just as actors would on a theatre stage; obvious examples here are dress, cars and furnishings. A well-established pattern of action that may be used as part of a performance is known as a *routine*. An example here would be a characteristic display of temper.

According to Goffman we also perform from behind a *front*, which he defines as 'that part of the individual's performance which regularly functions in a general and fixed fashion to define the situation for those who observe the performance'. Standard parts of the front are the setting, for example one's home and the personal front – age, dress, sex. See CONFIRMATION/DISCONFIRMATION; IMPRESSION MANAGEMENT; SELF-MONITORING. See also *TOPIC GUIDE* under INTERPERSONAL COMMUNICATION.

Self-regulation Although BROADCASTING in the UK has traditionally been regulated by acts of Parliament and governing charters, the press has been self-regulating. The Press Council was an advisory body, set up by the newspaper industry; its successor, the PRESS COMPLAINTS COMMISSION, which started work 1 January 1991, has similarly no statutory powers. The question often asked is whether the press, dominated by a handful of media barons, can be left to regulate itself – that is, be the judge of its own malpractices. A negative view of self-regulation has been taken by the CAMPAIGN FOR PRESS AND BROADCASTING FREEDOM in its publication, *Free Press.* The June 1991 issue declared 'The CPBF is sceptical that the PCC will take any meaningful steps to redress press abuses.'

In the wake of the death of Diana, Princess of Wales, in 1997, issues of self-regulation were widely discussed and the UK newspaper industry responded to public concern by agreeing to abide by criteria for respecting PRIVACY and curtailing media intrusion. In any event, the UK Labour government's incorporation into British law of the European Convention on Human Rights (see HUMAN RIGHTS ACT, 2000) made the privacy of the individual a legal right in Britain for the first time. See CALCUTT COMMITTEE REPORTS ON PRIVACY AND RELATED MATTERS, 1990 AND 1993. See also *TOPIC GUIDE* under BROADCASTING.

Selsdon Committee Report on Television (UK), 1935 The task of Lord Selsdon's Committee was 'to consider the development of Television and advise the Postmaster-General on the relative merits of several systems and on the conditions under which any public television should be provided'. The Report recommended that the BBC be made the initiating body, and that the cost of TV broadcasting be borne from the revenue derived from the existing 10-shilling radio licence fee. See *TOPIC GUIDE* under COMMISSIONS, COMMITTEES, LEGISLATION.

Semantic code See CODES OF NARRATIVE.

Semantic differential The analysis of semantic differential is one of three traditional empirical methods of measuring AUDIENCE response to the media, the others being CONTENT ANALYSIS and the investigation of uses and gratifications (see USES AND GRATIFICATIONS THEORY). In exploring semantic – or MEANING – differentials, analysts concentrate on people's attitudes, feelings and emotions towards certain concepts and VALUES as actuated by media performance. The values under scrutiny are presented in preliminary form by words or statements.

These are then selected and expressed as binarily opposed concepts (Offensive – Not Offensive, for example) on a five- or seven-point scale. Binary opposition is the most extreme form of significant difference possible. A sample audience, or selected group, is tested on the scale or scales, and the results averaged. The method was given currency by Charles Osgood in *The Measurement of Meaning* (US: University of Illinois Press, 1967). See *TOPIC GUIDE* under RESEARCH METHODS.

Semantics A major branch of linguistics in which the MEANING of language is analysed. The study of the origins of the form and meaning of words is etymology, a branch of semantics. The crucial point about the study of semantics is that it is an exploration of change – how the context of usage, historical, social, cultural, etc. – alters the meanings of words and expressions used. When King James II observed that the new St Paul's Cathedral was 'amusing, awful and artificial' he did not intend to be derogatory about Sir Christopher Wren's masterpiece; rather he meant that it was 'pleasing, awe-inspiring, and skilfully achieved'.

The differences are, of course, far from merely evolutionary. What, for example, is the meaning of the word equality? Its definition is modified by the perceptions and VALUES of all those who use it, and the situation in which it is used. As Simeon Potter points out in *Our Language* (UK: Penguin, 1950), 'Men frequently find themselves at cross-purposes with one another because they persist in using words in different senses. Their long arguments emit more heat than light because their conceptions of the point at issue, whether Marxism, democracy, capitalism, the good life, western civilization, culture, art, internationalism, freedom of the individual, equality of opportunity, redistribution of wealth, social security, progress, or what not, are by no means identical. From heedless sloth, or sheer lack of intelligence men do not trouble to clarify their conceptions.' Semantics, therefore, must lie at the heart of any serious study of communication processes. See *TOPIC GUIDE* under LANGUAGE/DISCOURSE/NARRATIVE.

Semiology/semiotics Word deriving from the Greek, *semeion*, sign; semiology is the general science of sign systems and their role in the construction and reconstruction of MEANING. All social life, indeed every facet of social practice, is *mediated* by language – conceived as a system of signs and representations, arranged by codes and articulated through various discourses. Sign systems, believes the semiologist, have no fixed meaning. The perception of the sign system rests upon the social context of the participants and the interaction between them.

Semiology examines the SIGN itself, the CODES or systems into which the signs are organized, and the CULTURE within which these codes and signs operate. The primary focus of semiology is upon the TEXT, thus differentiating such an approach from the *process* models of communication that regard the text – the message – as only one element of several in the communication process. For example, the semiologist prefers the term *reader* (even of a painting, photograph or film) to receiver because it implies a greater degree of activity, and that the process of reading is socially and culturally conditioned. The reader helps to create the meaning and significance of the text by bringing to it his/her experience, values and emotional responses.

There is special emphasis on the link between the reading and the IDEOLOGY of the reader. 'Wherever a sign is present,' writes V.N. Volosinov in *Marxism and the Philosophy of Language* (US: Seminar, 1973), 'ideology is present too. Everything ideological possesses a semiotic value'; or as Umberto Eco says, 'Semiology shows us the universe of ideologies arranged in codes and sub-codes within the universe of signs' (in 'Articulations of the cinematic code', in *Cinematics* 1, undated).

The theories of Swiss linguist Ferdinand de Saussure (1857–1913) provided the foundation stone of semiology. His lectures, *Cours de Linguistique Générale* (1916) were published after his death by two pupils, Charles Bally and Albert Sechehaye. De Saussure set out to demonstrate that speech is not merely a linear sequence like beads on a string but a system and structure where points on the string relate to other points on the string in various ways (the so-called *syntagmic* structure) and operate in a network of relationships with other possible points that could substitute for it (the *paradigmic* structure).

The American logician and philosopher C.S. Peirce (1834–1914) approached the structure of language with a wider-angle lens, conceiving semiotics (the term preferred in the US) as being an interdisciplinary science in which sign systems manifested in structures and levels could be analysed from philosophical, psychological and sociological as well as linguistic points of view. Peirce and other philosophers, such as Charles Morris and Rudolph Carnap, saw the field as divisible into three areas: *semantics*, the study of the links between linguistic expressions and the objects in the world to which they refer or which they describe; *syntactics*, the study of the relation of these expressions to each other; and *pragmatics*, the study of the dependence of the meaning of these expressions on their users (including the social context in which they are used).

The terminology of semiology/semiotics is complex and daunting, but the names Peirce gave to his categories are worth quoting here: the sign he called an *icon* resembles the object it wishes to describe, like a photograph; an *index* establishes a direct link between the sign and its object (smoke is an index to fire); finally, the *symbol* where there is neither connection nor resemblance between sign and object. A symbol communicates only because there is agreement among people that it shall stand for what it does (letters combined into words are symbols).

Semiology has come to apply, as a system of analysis, to every aspect of communication. There is practically nothing that is not a sign capable of meaning, or signification. The work of the French philosopher Roland Barthes (1915–80) has exercised particular influence on our understanding of areas such as music, eating, clothes and dance as well as language. See PARADIGM; MYTH. See also *TOPIC GUIDE* under COMMUNICATION THEORY; LANGUAGE/DISCOURSE/NARRATIVE.

Semiosic plane See MIMETIC/SEMIOSIC PLANES.

Semiotic power The power of members of the public – AUDIENCE, consumers – to turn the consumerist signs and symbols that dominate contemporary life to their own uses. The case is put by John Fiske who, while acknowledging the power of ADVERTISING and consumerist PROPAGANDA generally, gives substantial credit to individuals to exercise a 'semiotic power' – resistance – of their own. Our initial impression of the public flocking, for example, to an enticing new shopping mall might be to see it as a clear indicator of corporate influence at work.

However, Fiske argues in his chapter 'Shopping for pleasure', in *Reading the Popular* (US: Unwin Hyman, 1989) that 'the department store was the first public space legitimately available to women' and the 'fashionable commodities it offers provide a legitimated public identity and a means of participating in the ideology of progress'.

For Fiske 'the meanings of commodities do not lie in themselves as objects, and are not determined by their conditions of production and distribution, but are produced finally by the way they are consumed'. While he readily agrees that resistance from the bottom up in society is difficult and rarely likely to be effective beyond the micro-level of everyday life, this is not a reason to deny its existence. He writes, 'Scholarship that neglects or devalues these practices seems to me to be guilty of a disrespect for the weak that is politically reprehensible.'

Big companies may make style, in clothes or more broadly in lifestyle, but such styles are not followed slavishly. Rather they are appropriated: 'Women, despite the wide variety of social formations to which they belong, all share the experience of subordination under patriarchy and have evolved a variety of tactical responses that enable them to deal with it on a day-to-day level. So, too, other subordinated groups, however defined – by class, race, age, religion, or whatever – have evolved everyday practices that enable them to live within and against the forces that subordinate them.'

Fiske refers to people as forging their own meanings out of the signifiers available to them, exerting semiotic power, and though working only at the micro-level of society 'may well act as a constant erosive force upon the macro, weakening the system from within so that it is more amenable to change at the structural level'. See AUDIENCE: ACTIVE AUDIENCE.

Sender/receiver In early transmission models of the communication process, a message was seen to be conveyed, simply, from a sender to a receiver. *Transmitter* was also used, while the linguist Roman Jakobson preferred *Addresser* and *Addressee* (see JAKOBSON'S MODEL OF COMMUNICATION, 1958). The terms *author/reader* and *encoder/decoder* recognized both the complexity and the interactive nature of communication and the role of CODES and encoding in that process. In these cases due weight was given to the TEXT, which was encoded and decoded as well as the *context* in which the encoding/decoding takes places. Such terms acknowledge the critical nature of the reception of messages and the diverse ways in which such messages are interpreted.

At the same time they reflect the shift of emphasis away from a preoccupation with *sending* to a fuller recognition of the *power* that rests in reception; hence the importance of research into audience uses of media. See DECODE; ENCODE; SEMIOLOGY/SEMIOTICS.

Sensitization The process by which the media can alert the public, and specific social groups, to the fact that certain social actions are taking place, or to the possibility that certain social actions might take place. Stanley Cohen, for example, concludes in 'Sensitization: the case of the Mods and Rockers', in *The Manufacture of News: Deviance, Social Problems and the Mass Media* (UK: Constable, 1973 and subsequent editions), edited by Cohen and Jock Young, that media coverage of the bank holiday activities of the Mods and Rockers gangs, at certain southern-British holiday resorts in the mid-1960s, played a significant role in 'Reinforcing and magnifying a predisposition to expect trouble: "Something's going to happen".'

Cohen argues that once this perception had been established there was a tendency to interpret new, similar incidents in the same manner and fairly trivial events, normally overlooked, received media attention. Thus, 'Through the process of sensitization, incidents which would not have been defined as unusual or worthy of attention … acquired a new meaning.' In this particular case sensitization was the first step in a process of media coverage which, Cohen argues, significantly affected the course of real events.

A more recent example is provided by Kenneth Thompson in *Moral Panics* (US/UK: Routledge, 1998) in discussion of the moral panic aroused in the mid-1990s about female violence and girl gangs. Thompson argues that the well-publicized attack on actress, model and celebrity Elizabeth Hurley by four teenage girls served as a catalyst for considerable subsequent media coverage about the so-called rise in violent behaviour among girls and in the increase in the number of violent girl gangs. See LOONY LEFTISM; MEDIA IMAGES.

Sentence meaning, utterance meaning In his two-volume work, *Semantics* (UK: Cambridge University Press, 1977), John Lyons makes a useful distinction in the matter of 'meaning' versus 'use' in our employment of language. Sentence meaning is directly related to the grammatical and lexical (choice of words) meaning of a sentence, while utterance meaning includes all 'secondary' aspects of meaning, particularly those related to the context in which a linguistic exchange takes place. It is this distinction, between sentence and utterance meaning that allows a person to say one thing and actually mean something else.

Set A state of mental expectancy that is grounded in pre-formed ideas about some future event. The impact of a message is always influenced, to some extent, by the mental set of the receiver. See SCHEMA (PLURAL, SCHEMATA).

Seven characteristics of mass communications See MASS COMMUNICATIONS: SEVEN CHARACTERISTICS.

Sexism Discrimination against people on the grounds of assumed differences in their qualities, behaviours and characteristics resulting from their sex. Such discrimination may be targeted against men as well as women, but generally women are seen as its main victims. Sexism may manifest itself in an individual as a form of prejudice or bigotry, but more fundamentally concern focuses on the degree to which such discrimination is embedded within the structure and language of a society. In this respect the role that the media may play in generating or perpetuating this discrimination has been a theme of considerable recent research. See FEMINISM; GENDER; MALE-AS-NORM; STEREOTYPE. See also *TOPIC GUIDE* under GENDER MATTERS; MEDIA ISSUES AND DEBATES.

S4C The Welsh counterpart of CHANNEL 4 (UK) – Saniel Pedwar Cymru. Approximately half the channel's output is in Welsh to serve the 500,000 Welsh-speakers in Wales.

Shadowing See COCKTAIL PARTY PROBLEM.

Shannon and Weaver's model of communication, 1949 Developed by C.E. Shannon and W. Weaver to assist the construction of a mathematical theory of communication that could be applied in a wide variety of information transfer situations, whether by humans, machines or other systems. It is essentially a linear, process-centred model.

Shannon and Weaver were engineers working for the Bell Telephone Laboratories in the US and their objective was to ensure maximum efficiency of the channels of communication, in their case telephone cable and radio wave. However, in *Mathematical Theory of Communication* (US: University of Illinois Press, 1949), they claim for their theory a much wider application to human communication than solely the technical one. Within the framework of their model of transmission, the authors identify three levels of problem in the analysis of communication: Level A (technical), Level B (semantic – the meaning as emanating from the Transmitter's mode of address) and Level C (effectiveness in terms of reception or understanding on the part of the Receiver). Shannon and Weaver's model was constructed mainly to tackle Level A problems, and the assumption seems to be that to sort out the technical problems by improving encoding will, almost automatically, lead to improvements at Levels B and C.

In the Shannon and Weaver model, no provision has been made for feedback, and the fact that feedback modifies both the message and the communication situation; nor is there any acknowledgement of the importance of context – social, political, cultural – in influencing all stages of the communication process. Nevertheless, the Shannon and Weaver model arguably gave birth to what has come to be termed Communication Studies. See CHANNEL CAPACITY; CYBERNETICS; REDUNDANCY. See also *TOPIC GUIDE* under COMMUNICATION MODELS.

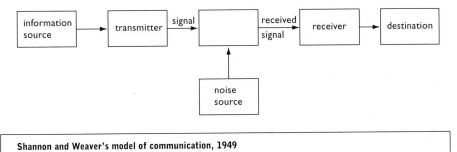

Shannon and Weaver's model of communication, 1949

Shawcross Commission Report on the Press (UK), 1962 The five-member Commission chaired by Lord Shawcross, lawyer and former Labour minister, declared that the real enemy of good-quality newspapers was competition; and competition threatened diversity. 'Within any class of competitive newspapers,' said the Report, 'the economies of large-scale operation provide a natural tendency for a newspaper which already has a large circulation to flourish, and to attract still more readers, whilst a newspaper which has a small circulation is likely to be in difficulties.'

Shawcross offered no radical solution to the problems his committee had delineated, trusting in the free market, albeit reluctantly: 'there is no acceptable legislative or fiscal way of regulating the competitive and economic forces so as to ensure a sufficient diversity of newspapers.'

The Report put forward an idea for a press amalgamations court that should scrutinize proposed mergers of all daily or Sunday papers with sales over three million, and to give the go-ahead only if the court considered such mergers to be no threat to public interest. In 1965 the Monopolies Commission was created by the Labour government under Harold Wilson, by means of the Monopolies and Mergers Act, which ruled that issues were to be decided by government, not the courts. See *TOPIC GUIDE* under COMMISSIONS, COMMITTEES, LEGISLATION.

Shortfall signals In interpersonal contact, a shortfall signal is, for example, a smile of greeting that disappears too soon; in other words, it fails to carry conviction as a true smile of greeting. In the main, shortfall signals consist of simulated warmth in salutation. The evasive glance, the pulled-away glance, the frozen smile, the smile of mouth without eyes – all of these and many more are INDICATORS of personal unease about the encounter.

The explanation may be because the person you greet is someone you dislike or fear, though the shortfall signal may have as much to do with personal mood – and preoccupation – as anything else. Conversely, there is the so-called *overkill signal*, where the greeting is too friendly, too effusive, the handshake too forcible. The overkill signal may be a simulation of sincere greeting; on the other hand, when people of different cultures or nations meet, one person's shortfall may be another's overkill. See GESTURE; PROXEMICS.

Shot In film-making, the shot is the equivalent, in writerly terms, of a word, a phrase, a sentence or a paragraph. The director of a movie shoots film; each shot is the length at which a camera works continuously from a still or moving position. A 'take' may constitute a series of shots or a continuous shot. It is visually defined by the use of the clapperboard held in front of the camera.

The board has the title of the film written on it, and the number of the take; the clapper is extended and then closed at the moment of the take. A correspondent on the function of the clapperboard, Peter Heinze, writing from the European Institute for the Media, says its prime function is to give the editor 'a synchronous point both on the picture and the sound track, without which it is difficult – sometimes impossible – to match the picture to the sound, and thus have words mouthed "in sync".' Heinze adds that it is true that on optical tracks (both variable area and variable density) it is possible to match the two by sight, the standard way is to listen for the 'clap'.

There are many types of shot: low and high angle, tilted; tracking, where the camera rests on a crab and track device and follows the action into or across the picture. The zoom lens allows the CU (close-up), MCU (medium close-up) and the BCU (big close-up). There is the wide-angle shot and the pan where the camera swings across the scene; there is the still shot and the slow-motion shot. Final decisions about how long a shot will be, which shots will be used and in what order come at the editing stage of film-making. See MONTAGE.

Showbusiness, Age of The present age of advancing communications technology has been given many titles – the Age of Information, the Telecommunications Age, the Age of the Global Village. Neil Postman in *Amusing Ourselves to Death* (UK: Methuen, 1986), calls it the Age of Showbusiness, a period in which TV dominates the lives of the community, turning people – in his view – into a population 'amusing ourselves to death'. In the Age of Showbusiness, Postman argues, all DISCOURSES are rewritten in terms of entertainment; substance is translated into IMAGE and the present is emphasized to the detriment of historical perspectives.

Postman's criticism is targeted upon the COMMERCIAL TELEVISION of his native America but his points are worth examining in wider contexts at a time when PUBLIC SERVICE BROAD-CASTING (PSB) looks nervously to its own future. According to Postman, TV 'does everything possible to encourage us to watch continuously. But what we watch is a medium which presents information in a form that renders it simplistic, non-substantive, non-historical and non-contextual; that is to say, information packaged as entertainment.' See CONSUMER SOVEREIGNTY; EFFECTS OF THE MASS MEDIA; MAINSTREAMING; PILKINGTON COMMITTEE REPORT ON BROADCASTING (UK), 1962; PSEUDO-CONTEXT.

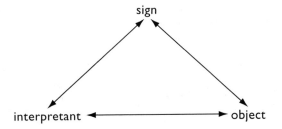

Sign In Communication Studies, a little word that triggers complex explanations. Father of semiology/semiotics, Swiss linguist Ferdinand de Saussure (1857–1913) regarded language as a 'deposit of signs'; he viewed the sign as a phenomenon comprising an 'acoustic image' and a concept (the thing signified). A word or combination of words in a language refers to, is an indicator of, some externally existing object or idea. Charles Peirce (1834–1914), the American philosopher and logician, posed a triangular relationship involving the activation of the sign (see figure).

The object is that which is described by the sign, but the sign only signifies – has MEANING – in the process of it becoming a mental concept (*interpretant*), or what de Saussure named the *signified*. The point to emphasize here is that the sign depends for its meaning on the context in which it is communicated. Edmund Leach in *Culture and Communication* (UK: Cambridge University Press, 1976) says signs do not occur in isolation; 'a sign is always a member of a set of contrasting signs which function within a specific cultural context'. Also, a sign only conveys information when it is combined with other signs and symbols from the same context. 'Signs signal,' writes Donis A. Dondis in *Contact: Human Communication and its History* (UK: Thames & Hudson, 1981), edited by Raymond Williams, 'they are specific to a task or circumstance.'

Of course there are not only different kinds or levels of meaning (or signification), there are many different kinds of sign. Peirce divided signs into three categories: the *icon*, *index* and *symbol*. These, like the triangular sign-object-interpretant are interactive, and they are overlapping. The icon is a resemblance or a representation of the object – a photograph or a map would constitute an iconic sign. An index is a sign connected or associated with its object – an indicator: smoke is an index of fire, for example.

The symbol may have no resemblance whatever to the object or idea. It is arbitrary. It comes about by choice, it exists by convention, rule or assent. It means something beyond itself. As Dondis neatly points out, 'Signs can be understood by animals as well as humans; symbols cannot.' They 'are broader in meaning, less concrete'.

Raymond Firth, in *Symbols, Public and Private* (UK: Allen & Unwin, 1973), adds a fourth sign type to Peirce's three – *signal*, a sign with an emphasis on 'consequential action', a stimulus requiring some response.

Signs combine to form systems, or codes, from the basic MORSE CODE or Highway Code to, for example, the complex codes of musical notation. See LANGUE AND PAROLE; JAKOBSON'S MODEL OF COMMUNICATION, 1958; TRIGGER EVENTS. See also *TOPIC GUIDE* under LANGUAGE/DISCOURSE/NARRATIVE.

Signal The physical manifestation of a message that allows it to be conveyed. See SHANNON AND WEAVER'S MODEL OF COMMUNICATION, 1949.

Significant others The analysis of the effects of a media message, of its impact, relies on the response not only of the direct respondent, but of those persons close to, influential upon, the respondent – relatives, friends, work colleagues. These are 'significant others'. In the case of a child watching TV commercials, his/her response may be conditioned and modified by parents, brothers and sisters, friends. See INTERVENING VARIABLES (IVs); OPINION LEADER; OTHER.

Significant symbolizers G.H. Mead in *Mind, Self and Society* (US: University of Chicago Press, 1934), uses this term to indicate how the social organization of a society, human or animal, needs the support of reliable, regular and predictable patterns or signs if it is not to be destroyed by accumulating discrepancy and misinformation. The symbol or symbolizer, whether vocal sound, GESTURE or SIGN, achieves meaningful definition only when it has the 'same effect on the individual making it as on the individual to whom it is addressed'. Thus, according to Mead, a person defines him/herself by 'talking to himself in terms of the community to which he belongs'. Through contact with 'significant' (meaningful) objects of the social world a person develops a coherent view of him/herself and of his/her relations with others. See INTERPERSONAL COMMUNICATION; INTRAPERSONAL COMMUNICATION.

Signification One of the most valuable contributions made by Swiss linguist Ferdinand de Saussure (1857–1913) to the study of language was his idea of differentiating between the name, the naming and the MEANING of what has been named. This process enabled the linguist more effectively to examine the *structural* elements of communication. Saussure contrasted the *significant* (or signifier) with *signifié* (or that which is signified).

The relationship between these, the physical existence of the sign, and the mental concept it represents, becomes signification which, for Saussure, is the manifestation of external reality or meaning. Signification, it is important to realize, is culture-specific as is the linguistic form of the signifier in each language. Saussure terms the relationship of signs to others in the sign system, *valeur*, and it is valeur that primarily determines meaning. Thus meaning is an active force, subject to constant change, the result of dynamic interaction. See SEMIOLOGY/SEMIOTICS.

Signification spiral Stuart Hall and co-authors in *Policing the Crisis: Mugging, the State and Law and Order* (UK: Macmillan, 1978) use this term for the process by which discrete, local problems and occurrences are pulled together by the media into a framework of NEWS coverage that links these together in such a way as to suggest the existence of a more widespread and serious social problem.

They argue that, for example, during the 1970s there emerged a signification spiral in which problems previously presented as atypical or parochial – such as student protest, industrial unrest and mugging – were presented by the media as part of a wider concern: the breakdown in law and order. See FOLK DEVILS; DEMONIZATION; SENSITIZATION.

Significs Enquiry into questions of meaning, expression and interpretation, and the influence of language upon thought.

Silence In certain circumstances silence is as effective a means of communication as speech. In *The Dynamics of Human Communication* (US: McGraw-Hill, 1985), Gail Myers and Michele Myers state: 'Silences … are not to be equated with the absence of communication. Silences are a natural and fundamental aspect of communication, often ignored because misunderstood.' Silences are used to give meaning to verbal communication but can also communicate a range of information in their own right such as feelings of anger, a state of mourning or preoccupation with one's own thoughts. There are many kinds of silence and we often need other non-verbal or verbal cues to help us identify what is meant when someone is silent.

Being aware of the range of meanings that silence may convey, and the ability to accurately interpret them and react sensitively to them, are an important communicative skill as in the ability to fill an embarrassing gap in a conversation. There is a tendency in our culture to perceive silence caused by lapses during a conversation as awkward. Myers and Myers point out that masking behaviours, which include coughing, whistling and sighing, are often employed to cover up such lapses until someone thinks of something to say. The use and acceptability of silence vary from one culture to another. See APACHE SILENCE; COMMUNICATION, NON-VERBAL; SILENCE: STRATEGIC SILENCE.

Silence, spiral of See NOELLE-NEUMAN'S SPIRAL OF SILENCE MODEL OF PUBLIC OPINION, 1974.

Silence: strategic silence In NEWS selection, that which is omitted. R. Lenz in 'The search for strategic silence: discovering what journalism leaves out', in *American Journalism* 8(1) (1991), perceives the working of ideology in reportorial omission and that such omission often says more about the selection process, and those who do the selecting, than what is included in news bulletins. That version of reality constructed by journalists, writes Lentz, 'relies upon the production of meanings based not only upon published content but upon ways in which some things are not "seen", or if seen, not recorded, as part of the social transaction between readers and creators of editorial matter'. The term *absence* is often used in this context.

Silent majority In the briefcase of every OPINION LEADER – be he/she politician, editor or TV guru – lies a hidden weapon, the 'silent majority'. The opinion leader claims access to the thoughts, attitudes and beliefs of those who, having no voice of their own, so the story goes – are grateful to the politicians or the press for putting words and opinions into their silent mouths. They are invariably moderates; they have bags of common sense; what is more, they are impossible to identify. If it were possible to locate them in person (no research has yet elicited the degree to which the silent are a majority or the majority silent) they might be perceived as, above all things, upholders of the status quo, inalienably opposed to activists, do-gooders and change agents of every type and hue.

Sincerity test (by the media) Some commentators claim that a by-product of political BROAD-CASTING is the way TV appearances by influential public figures are assessed by audiences for honesty and sincerity. Equally, the skilled public figure can use TV to project the desired image of honesty and sincerity in order to gain public support.

Sit-com Situation comedy on TV – the comedy growing out of context and recurringly generated or fuelled by amiable antagonism of one kind or another. Where the SOAP OPERA demands a substantial range of characters the sit-com generally focuses upon narrow circles of acquaintance and relationship such as families or groups of friends. Rarely does the narrative of one instalment of a sit-com continue from the previous one or continue to the next, again contrasting with the soap whose narrative key is balancing a number of ongoing stories and spinning these along over days and weeks.

Each instalment of a sit-com begins with a situation that is resolved within a single time-scale. Characters may be rounded, even complex, but rarely do they, or the situations they are involved in, develop or change. This does not mean that they are sealed against the events of the real world; indeed they often reflect real-world conditions and make use of current issues and trends. For example the UK sit-com *Men Behaving Badly* explored, amusingly and wittily, the 'gender war' of the 1990s in which men had to adjust to the threat to their traditional dominance by women confident that the future is theirs. Writers of sit-coms have succeeded in creating diverse themes, from comedy in prison – *Porridge* – to comedy in space – *Red Dwarf* – to aliens on earth – *Third Rock from the Sun.* The Korean War was the setting for one of the best and most incisive sit-coms, *MASH*, starring Alan Alda, while the zany antics of New York's thirtysomethings in *Friends* has proved a worldwide success.

The best sit-coms prove to have a long, and recurring, screen life – *The Phil Silvers Show* and *Dad's Army* have been introduced and reintroduced to succeeding generations of audience. Notable sit-coms from the UK stable have been *Till Death Us Do Part, Steptoe and Son, The Likely Lads, Rising Damp, The Good Life, Fawlty Towers, Last of the Summer Wine, Birds of a Feather, Father Ted* and *Goodness Gracious Me*; from the US, a few of many notable sit-coms have been *Bewitched, Rhoda, Taxi, Cheers!, Cybill, Roseanne* and *Frazier.*

Site The theoretical or physical space where a struggle over MEANING and the power to reinforce a particular meaning occurs.

Situational proprieties Erving Goffman in *Behaviour in Public Places* (US: Free Press, 1963) employed this phrase to describe rules of behaviour common to interpersonal and group situations, which oblige participants to 'fit in', to accept the particular normative behaviour suitable for a successful, dissonance-free interaction. Such properties might be to avoid making a scene or causing a disturbance; refrain from talking too loudly or too assertively; hold back from attempting to dominate proceedings or, in contrast, to check oneself from withdrawing from what is going on.

S-IV-R model of communication Derives from general theories of learning/communication, where the relationship between stimulus (S) and response (R) is regarded as providing the key to both learning and communication. Actually it is a teaching-orientated model rather than learner-centred, and implies a predominantly one-way traffic of information from teacher to pupil. The IV stands for INTERVENING VARIABLES, those factors in the communication situation that help, hinder or modify the response to the intended message. These variables are innumerable: NOISE (technical or semantic), lack of motivation or concentration, personal problems and, very importantly, the influence of other people – peer groups, friends, parents, etc. See MEDIATION; OTHER; SIGNIFICANT OTHERS. See also *TOPIC GUIDE* under COMMUNICATION MODELS.

Slander A false or malicious report by the spoken word or by SIGN or GESTURE. In law, slander may constitute DEFAMATION – of character or reputation – and may be subject to heavy fines.

However, no legal aid is granted in the UK for defamation cases. LIBEL is the written or printed equivalent of slander.

Slang Colloquial language, whose words and usages are not generally acceptable within formal modes of expression. The word was not used until about 1756. Prior to that it was called *cant*, and referred to the secret language of the underworld, of thieves and rogues; also termed *argot*. Slang usually begins as in-group language, then moves into popular use. For example, the criminal world's slang nouns for policeman (coppers, rozzers, bluebottles, the fuzz), for magistrates (beaks), for prison (stir, time, bird and porridge) have achieved broad currency.

Rhyming slang, associated with London cockneys and subsequently Australians, uses slang words that rhyme with the intended word. Thus apples and pears means stairs, trouble and strife means wife. The point of rhyming slang is to conceal the MEANING of the language used from unwanted listeners. See COLLOQUIALISM; DIALECT; JARGON.

SLAPPS Strategic Lawsuits against Public Participation, a practice originating in the US but spreading globally, in which big corporations put legal frighteners on critics of their activities. Wherever corporate interests – whether in the environment, in foodstuffs, in publicizing information – are deemed at risk, out come the lawsuits, focusing on accusations of DEFAMATION, invasion of PRIVACY and interference with business.

Julian Petley in an article 'SLAPPS and chills', in *Index on Censorship* 1 (1999) writes, 'These cases … are a form of strategic legal intimidation or gamesmanship, designed to frighten, harass and distract actual critics, and to discourage potential ones from even voicing their views in the first place.' Most cases do not reach court, and they are not intended to do.

However, for Helen Steel and Dave Morris, distributors of a leaflet entitled 'What's wrong with McDonald's?', there was to be no escape from LIBEL proceedings. Their trial was the longest in British history. It took every penny the defendants possessed (defendants are ineligible for legal aid in defamation cases). They squared up to a company that spends an estimated US$2bn dollars a year on advertising (see John Vidal's *McLibel: Burger Culture on Trial*, UK: Macmillan, 1997).

In June 1997 it was revealed that a TV documentary made by Franny Armstrong, *McLibel: Two Worlds Collide,* had been rejected by both the BBC and Channel 4 – because of the risk of libel action. Existing, well-established programmes such as the BBC's *Newsnight, Panorama* and *Watchdog* have stirred up snarling choruses of protest (to the Programme Complaints Unit and the BROADCASTING STANDARDS COMMISSION) from multinationals such as British Aerospace, Ford, Dixons, Hotpoint and Procter & Gamble. See CENSORSHIP; McDONALDIZATION. See also *TOPIC GUIDE* under MEDIA: FREEDOM, CENSORSHIP; MEDIA ISSUES AND DEBATES.

Sleeper effect Researchers into the responses of audiences to messages have noted how these responses can be delayed and only become manifest some time after exposure. This is the 'sleeper effect'. See EFFECTS OF THE MASS MEDIA.

Slider Many experiments have been conducted to investigate the effect of group pressure upon the individual and the manner in which such pressure manifests itself in the INTERPERSONAL COMMU-NICATION of the group. In a typical experiment one member of the group may take on the role of slider, that is he/she will initially disagree with the majority of the group on a matter but is persuaded to agree with them. The member of the group who takes on the role of *deviant*, however, consistently disagrees with the majority. Of those in the experimental situation some may be *naive*, that is, unaware of what is to take place in the experiment and some members may be *confederates*, that is, in league with the experimenters.

Slow-drip Term sometimes used to describe the regular, long-term coverage of certain issues by the media with a view to influencing the formation of opinion; a softening-up process that builds evidence and feelings in preferred directions. See EFFECTS OF THE MASS MEDIA.

Slow motion Has been used varyingly in the cinema to convey dream-like or fantasy situations, to emphasize reactions such as grief, bewilderment or to concentrate attention upon happenings that, in real life, would be here and gone before the full visual impact has been made. In contrast, accelerated motion has generally been used for comic effect, especially by the early silent movie comedians whose own actors' timing was rendered even more remarkable by the speeded-up action.

Reverse motion is another technique by which the cinema defies time: that which can happen can unhappen. In *October* (1927), for instance, Sergei Eisenstein (1898–1948) uses the magic of reverse motion to show a statue of the Tzar, previously smashed to pieces, miraculously restored, thus showing with impressive symbolism the restoration of the old order.

Lastly, there is stopped motion, using either still photographs or stopping the action of an otherwise moving sequence by repeating the same frame when editing the film. The freezing of action may signal transition from one time zone to another, or may be used for special emphasis or sometimes to underscore comic effects or impressions. See SHOT.

Small World Media Founded in 1993; UK-based, non-profitmaking alternative media operation, originally producing under the general title *Undercurrents*. The news-videos were aimed at bringing about social change. *Time Out* called the series, 'the news you don't see on the news'. Campaigning by video ended after ten editions of *Undercurrents* (No. 7 was a Tokyo Video Festival Winner) and a revamped umbrella organization (February 2000) re-emerged with *Undercurrents* as its title, with global aims and a switch to chiefly INTERNET operations. The organization manages a substantial archive of direct action images as well as having available a training manual, *The Video Activist Handbook* (published by Pluto Press). See www.undercurrents.org.

SMCR model of communication See BERLO'S SMC MODEL OF COMMUNICATION, 1960.

Smiling professions Namely, the media; at least those parts of them dedicated to smiling and keeping audiences smiling. John Hartley in *The Politics of Pictures: The Creation of the Public in the Age of Popular Media* (UK: Routledge, 1992) writes that smiling 'has become one of the most public virtues of our times, a uniform that must be worn on the lips of those whose social function is to create, sustain, tutor, represent and make images of the public'. Hartley asserts that 'Smiling, in fact, is now the "dominant ideology" of the "public domain", the mouthpiece of the politics of pictures.'

Snapshot Term invented by astronomer Sir John Herschel (1792–1871), writing in 1860 of 'the possibility of taking a photograph as it were a snap shot'. He may well have been referring to Thomas Skaife's PISTOLGRAPH of 1858. See CAMERA; PHOTOGRAPHY, ORIGINS.

Soap opera RADIO or TV domestic drama series; the term emanates from the US where such programmes were initially sponsored by big soap companies who had the housewife viewer in mind. Of the longest-running TV soap opera in the UK, *Coronation Street*, poet laureate John Betjeman once announced, 'At half-past seven tonight I shall be in paradise.' TV's appetite for soap opera is insatiable. The TV audience for the shooting of JR in the American series *Dallas* exceeded that for the FA Cup Final in the UK.

Traditionally soaps have been characterized by an immediately identifiable set-up, a stereotypical cast of characters, and a distancing from contemporary reality and anxieties. However, the end of the 1980s saw the arrival of soaps exploiting social problems for all they were worth. From the BBC, *EastEnders*, featuring abortion, rape, illegitimacy, murder, robbery, incest and unemployment; from Channel 4, *Brookside*, demonstrating that Merseyside can vie problem for problem with London's East End, featuring rape, stabbings, euthanasia, homosexuality and, of course, unemployment. The BBC's import from Australia, *Neighbours*, proved it could do more than hold its own – with beatings-up, meningitis, divorce *et al.*

In a sense, soaps have become a paradigm for television itself. In terms of TEXTS they take up a staggeringly large amount of viewing time and occupy centre stage in the minds of vast and international audiences. Critical theory has located in soaps rich seams for investigation, especially in an age when the way MEANING is read into texts by AUDIENCE, and the ways audiences *use* media, have come to dominate critical thinking and much media research.

Generally soaps are less concerned with action than with INTERACTION, primarily between the characters on the broad socio-cultural canvas but also, in a proactive way, between the characters and the viewers (see PARASOCIAL INTERACTION). That is, the gap between one episode of a soap and the next may be used by members of the audience to mull over the latest developments, talk about these to members of the family, fellow workers, friends, thus heightening anticipation and enjoyment, and making the viewer a more active 'reader' of the text.

Because most soaps distribute interest among numerous characters, no single character is indispensable. Of key importance is the *community* of characters in their situation. As Robert C. Allen writes in 'Reader-orientated criticism', in *Channels of Discourse: Television and Contemporary Criticism* (UK: Methuen, 1987; Routledge, 1990), edited by Allen, 'Anything might happen to an individual character, but, in the long run, it will not affect the community of characters as a whole.'

In a *European Journal of Communication* article, June 1998, 'European soap operas: the diversification of the genre', Tamar Liebes and Sonia Livingstone identify three types, or models, of soap opera – the *Dynastic,* the *Community* and the *Dyadic.* The first focuses on one powerful family with a number of satellite outsiders. The American soap *Dynasty* was an example of this model, while the UK soaps *Coronation Street* and *EastEnders* typify the community model. These are characterized by a number of interconnecting and interrelating families 'all living within one geographical neighbourhood and belonging to one community'.

The Dyadic model concerns a 'destabilized network of a number of young people, densely interconnected, mostly unigenerational, interchanging couples, with past, present and future romantic ties, continually absorbed in the process of reinventing kinship relations'. The authors cite the American soap *The Young and the Restless* as a prime example of the Dyadic model; to this we might add *This Life*, which won something of a cult status in the UK until in 1998 the BBC decided not to commission further episodes.

Community soaps, Liebes and Livingstone say, 'have been produced in the spirit of public broadcasting, indicating certain pedagogic aims' and 'constitute a type of public for debating social issues'. A notable example of a soap that has proved both pedagogic and a source of public debate is the highly popular Spanish drama, *Cuentame Como* (Tell Me How It Happened), first produced in 2002. The soap revisits – and retrieves – Spanish history, its characters and situations being cast in the dark days of Fascist rule under General Franco. An era that, to a modern generation had seemed a closed book, curtained off by official reluctance to examine a past of terror following the Spanish Civil War, had the curtains of forgetfulness drawn back; and all at once, the nation focuses on its past as never before.

Elizabeth Nash, writing from Madrid, in a news report entitled 'Spain gripped by soap set in dark years of Franco's rule' (UK *Independent*, 9 August 2002), says, 'The series has caught the imagination of all generations of Spaniards: those who remember Franco relish the authenticity of every detail; youngsters who never knew him are fascinated by this window on their otherwise silent and invisible history.' See FEMINISM; GENDER; GENDERED GENRE; GOSSIP NETWORKS; NARRATIVE.

---

* David Morley, *Family Television: Cultural Power and Domestic Leisure* (UK: Comedia, 1986); Yvonne Tasker, 'Having it all: feminism and the pleasures of the popular', in Sarah Franklin, Celia Lury and Jackie Stacey (eds), *Off-Centre: Feminism and Cultural Studies* (UK: HarperCollins Academic, 1991). Ien Ang, *Watching Dallas: Soap Operas and the Melodramatic Imagination* (UK: Methuen, 1985); David Buckingham, *Public Secrets: 'EastEnders' and its Audience* (UK: BFI, 1987); Mary Ellen Brown, *Soap Opera and Women's Talk* (UK: Sage, 1994); Robert C. Allen, *To Be Continued: Soap Operas Around the World* (UK: Routledge, 1995); Charlotte Brunsdon, *Screen Tastes: Soap Opera to Satellite Dish* (UK: Routledge, 1997).

Soaps: docu-soaps Popular variant of the fictional soap, presenting documentary series in the fashion of soaps – with the same emphasis on characters the audience can readily identify with, real-life situations intercut with parallel situations in the typical manner of soaps. Examples in the UK have been *Airport, Driving School* and *Hotel.*

Such programmes have tended to supplant serious, probing documentaries and are largely the result of the intense pressures of competition. Their fascination lies in the actuality of the mini-dramas and their sense of immediacy. Where docu-soaps are different from fictional soaps is in the freedom the 'characters' are given to comment on the mini-dramas that fill their working days. See REALITY TV.

Social action (mode of media analysis) Stresses the role of the individual as a potent force within a dynamic social system. It sees conflict as central to the process of change, in particular conflict between GROUPS seeking influence, power and status. Social action analysis concentrates on the media as a special group both reflecting and involved in the conflicts that concern social change, or resistance to it. A pluralist society, of competing ideologies and varying, changing definitions of truth and meaning, is acknowledged by social action analysis as are the complex influences at work upon media and media audiences, and the interaction between them. See FUNCTIONALIST (MODE OF MEDIA ANALYSIS); MARXIST (MODE OF MEDIA ANALYSIS); PLURALISM. See also *TOPIC GUIDE* under RESEARCH METHODS.

Social action broadcasting A broad term describing RADIO and TV programming that sets out not only to analyse current social problems and issues, and bring them to public attention, but to encourage people to take action in response to what they have heard or seen. In the UK such programmes range from the BBC's adult literacy series *On the Move* or *Crimewatch UK* to Capital Radio's *Helpline*. Information on social action broadcasting is disseminated by the National Volunteer Centre in its publication *Media Project News*, which produces a twice-yearly Directory of Social Action Programmes.

Social anthropology The study of the evolution of human communities and cultures.

Social class See CLASS.

Social influence theory See IDENTIFICATION.

Socialization The shaping of human behaviour through experience in and knowledge of certain social situations: the process by which individuals are made aware of the EXPECTATIONS others have of their behaviour; by which they acquire the NORMS, MORES, VALUES and beliefs of a social group or society; and by which the CULTURE of a social group or society is transmitted. Socialization continues throughout life as individuals change their ROLES and membership of social GROUPS.

There exist what are commonly known as *agents of socialization*. In modern industrial societies, the family, school and friendship groups are thought to be the most significant agents in shaping the behaviour of the individual. The mass media are also agents of socialization, and are considered to be particularly influential in transmitting awareness and expectations concerning a wide range of societal behaviour.

Individuals and societies may undergo radical change; if so, *re-socialization* may occur – the peeling away of learned patterns of behaviour and their replacement with quite different ones. There is interest as to the media's potential role in this process – its capacity as a disseminator of PROPAGANDA, for example, could be of significance. Additionally, media organizations are themselves social institutions and as such have their own patterns of behaviour, attitudes and beliefs into which their members are socialized. The degree to which the culture of media organizations affects their output is a considerable source of interest. See *TOPIC GUIDE* under MEDIA: VALUES AND IDEOLOGY.

Social lubricators Richard Hoggart in *Speaking to Each Other* (UK: Chatto & Windus, 1970), uses this term to describe those people involved in the research, design and presentation of material aimed at aiding the smooth running of a technologically advanced society: communications experts, public relations officers and advertising executives, for example. See PR; PUBLIC RELATIONS.

Socially unattached intelligentsia See IMPARTIALITY.

Social perception See PERCEPTION.

Social system Consists of a collective of people who undertake different types of task in order to achieve common goals and solve common problems. The term can be applied to a group of two or more individuals, complex organizations or whole societies. For the members of a social system to cooperate, there must be a shared language and some cultural similarities between them, although within the overall system there may be a variety of subcultures and language CODES, as well as other individual differences.

All social systems are liable to undergo social change: a process by which the structures and functions are altered. One focus for research has been the role of the communication of innovation in the process of social change. See SOCIALIZATION.

Societally conscious See VALS TYPOLOGY.

Sociolinguistics The study of the way in which an individual's linguistic behaviour might be influenced by the society to which he/she belongs. It investigates also the linguistic variations found between groups and their identification through language.

Sociology French philosopher Auguste Comte (1798–1857) was the first to use the word. The discipline attempts a scientific and systematic study of society, employing precise and controlled methods of enquiry. It is concerned with social structure; social systems; social action; the various GROUPS, institutions, categories and classes that go to make up a society or social system; the CULTURE and lifestyle of a society and the groups of which it is composed; the processes of socialization by which such cultures are communicated and maintained; and the types and allocation of social roles.

Social groups, their inter-relationships and INTERACTION, and their conditioning of individual behaviour could be seen as the building blocks of the discipline.

Sociometrics (and media analysis) Sociometrics is the analysis of small GROUPS, their coherence, and the interpersonal relationships and communication within them. This mode of analysis has been extended and applied within Media Studies to ascertain the nature of the relationships between owners of media organizations and owners of other industrial or commercial concerns, and the degree to which they are interlocking. The purpose of such a sociometric map of capitalism is to discover whether or not shared positions in and patterns of social and economic life produce recognized shared interests and a common cluster of beliefs, VALUES and perspectives that feed back into and influence media organizations and their products.

Increasingly, owners of communications concerns are also owners of other businesses, and these contacts are reinforced by overlapping directorships. Board members of top media corporations have been found to hold membership of elite London clubs also favoured by directors of leading financial institutions and some business corporations. Of course evidence of points of contact does not necessarily constitute evidence of shared values, beliefs and perspectives, or deliberate influence of media products. See CONVERGENCE. See also *TOPIC GUIDE* under RESEARCH METHODS.

'Somme, The Battle of the' First-ever film DOCUMENTARY of war; records the first day of the Battle of the Somme, 1 July 1916, during which the British Army suffered 57,000 casualties, almost a third of these killed. *The Battle of the Somme* was not filmed secretly but was produced with permission of the Secretary of State for War, David Lloyd George, whose words were read out at the first screening of the film on 10 August 1916 – scarcely more than a month after the events the film so tellingly describes. Lloyd George's breathtaking openness (to us now) was based upon a belief that to tell the public the truth would reinforce support for the war: 'You are invited,' he wrote, 'to witness by far the most imposing picture of the war that our staff has yet procured.'

It was true that the film was popular. Shot by Geoffrey Malins and J.B. McDowell, *The Battle of the Somme* was seen by over 20 million people in the UK, practically half the population. Perceived as PROPAGANDA by the British Army, the film had the opposite effect to that intended. People were horrified by what they saw, and government immediately learnt that in times of war truth is better concealed than revealed.

Rarely again did countries at war permit such frank revelations of the harrowing experiences of conflict to be shown, uncensored, to the public. The exception was the Vietnam War in which film and reports of carnage eventually turned public opinion in the US against the war. In succeeding 20th and 21st century wars – the Falklands and Gulf Wars in particular – censorship was resolutely applied.

Where censorship has proved less easy to impose, as in the wars in Bosnia and Kosovo, documentary footage has had a profound effect on public opinion worldwide.

A video, *The Battle of the Somme: Official Pictures of the Army in France* is available from the Imperial War Museum. See *TOPIC GUIDE* under MEDIA HISTORY.

Sound-bite Term originally derived from RADIO but which has come to apply equally to TV; describes a film or tape segment within a NEWS story, in which a reporter talks to a source – such as a politician or an eyewitness. With the advent of more sophisticated technology for handling news reports, the use of jump-cutting has added to the complexity and drama of the sound-bite. The *ellipsis* jump-cut splices two or more segments of the same person speaking in the same setting: these are classified as single sound-bites. The *juxtaposition* jump-cut places together contrasting segments, usually from different settings, in such a way as to make evident the discontinuity. These tend to be treated as separate sound-bites.

Research into the nature and degree of sound-bites in news broadcasting in the US indicates that contemporary news employs far more, and far shorter, sound-bites than in the past. In 'Sound-bite news: television coverage of elections, 1968–1988', in *Journal of Communication*, Spring 1992, Daniel C. Hallin reports that the average sound-bite has been shrinking, from more than 40 seconds in length in 1968 to under 10 seconds in the 1980s. The conclusion Hallin draws from this is that the news is much more *mediated* than the TV news of the 1960s and 1970s. He writes, 'Today's television journalist displays a sharply different attitude towards the words of candidates and other newsmakers. Today, those words, rather than simply being reproduced and transmitted to the audiences, are treated as raw material to be taken apart, combined with other sounds and images, and reintegrated into a new narrative.'

Hallin cites three reasons for the sound-bite revolution, as apposite in the twenty-first century as when he was writing: the technological one already mentioned, the weakening in political consensus and authority following Vietnam and WATERGATE, and the discovery by the TV industry in the US that news was big business if, that is, presentation was 'punchy' enough to attract and retain audience attention. Ironically, the approach derives from the very people journalists often accuse of manipulating the media – political campaign managers – so-called 'spin doctors' whose techniques of packaging candidates have centred around sound-biting images, one-liners, the use of triumphalist music etc.

Dan Hallin acknowledges that modern news is far more 'professional', far more varied, slicker than in the past, but he identifies serious worries. 'First and simplest, it is disturbing that the public never has the chance to hear a candidate – or anyone else – speak for more than 20 seconds', especially as showing 'humans speaking is something television does very effectively'. Also the modern pace of exposition raises questions concerning audience comprehension – the ability of viewers to understand what is coming at them at such speed. Not the least concern is that sound-bite journalism emphasizes techniques over substance: the very sin the journalist accuses the spin doctor of committing. See JOURNALISM; NEWS MANAGEMENT. See also *TOPIC GUIDE* under NEWS MEDIA.

* David Stayden and Rita Kirk Whillock (eds), *Soundbite Culture: The Death of Discourse in a Wired World* (US/UK: Sage, 1999).

Sound broadcasting See RADIO BROADCASTING.

Sound Broadcasting Act (UK), 1972 Gave the go-ahead to COMMERCIAL RADIO in the UK. The name Independent Television Authority (ITA) was changed to Independent Broadcasting Authority (IBA), and the IBA was empowered to create a new group of contractors in up to 50 British cities to run local commercial radio stations and collect advertising revenue in a manner similar to that of the TV programme companies. The first commercial radio stations went on the air in October 1973.

Sound, synchronous See SYNCHRONOUS SOUND.

Source An individual, group or institution that originates a message. See EVENT.

Source domination See PRIMARY, SECONDARY DEFINERS.

Spatial behaviour See ORIENTATION; PROXEMICS.

Spatial zones Those areas and distances that individuals maintain between each other, depending on the nature of the relationship between them. Edward T. Hall, 'inventor' of PROXEMICS (see his book, *The Silent Language*, US: Anchor Books, 1973), has specified four of these spatial zones: *intimate*, *personal*, *social* and *public* (each with a near and far phase). See INTERPERSONAL COMMUNICATION.

Special effects The 'real' gorilla in *King Kong* (1933) was just 18 inches high – that is special effects. Simulations of earthquakes, explosions, floods, fires, storms, of the interior of hell, of war in space or 40 fathoms deep is the job of the special effects wizards who today command fees as large as film stars. Special effects can, by dazzling defiance of the possible, make the success of a film. *Star Wars* (1977), directed by George Lucas, was raised from the humdrum and the banal to the spectacular by special effects; and computer graphics have provided an exciting new dimension to the art, with, first in the field, Walt Disney's US$18 million *Tron* (1982). The financial success of such movies as *Jurassic Park* (1993) and *Titanic* (1997) owed much to their special effects. The problem with effects is that they frequently became the main player in the NARRATIVE, a case of style dominating over content, as some critics pointed out in reviewing *Star Wars: Episode II: Attack of the Clones* (2002).

Speed photography See HIGH-SPEED PHOTOGRAPHY.

Spin doctor See NEWS MANAGEMENT; SOUND-BITE.

Spiral of silence See NOELLE-NEUMANN'S SPIRAL OF SILENCE MODEL OF PUBLIC OPINION, 1974.

Spiral model of communication See DANCE'S HELICAL MODEL OF COMMUNICATION, 1967.

Spoiler Device used by one or more newspapers to detract from a rival paper's scoop story; usually by running a different version of the story as told by lesser characters.

Sponsorship There is scarcely any field of the arts, sport, entertainment or media that is not to a greater or lesser extent dependent on sponsorship; and this sponsorship originates for the most part from industry, business and commerce. However, it could be said that sponsorship is as old as the pyramids; indeed, the pyramids constitute one of the most impactful examples of state sponsorship. Tombs, yes, but also symbols of the pharaohs' will to dominate the lives of their subjects. The pyramids were a constant reminder to the Egyptians that 'We are here.' Similarly, sponsorship of the arts by monarchs and the Church was at base born of a desire to enthrone the sponsor in the minds of the people.

Some powers of monarchy and the Church have been inherited by big business, as well as certain duties within the community. A company or corporation will sponsor a major art exhibition designed to give pleasure and illumination to thousands. And those thousands will in turn, so it is hoped, acknowledge the communal benefit made possible by the sponsoring company. Thus culture comes to us through the arch of sponsorship. At the same time the company will benefit by association.

To sponsor Mozart or Rembrandt is somehow to be touched by their greatness. Their quality rubs off on the sponsor. The danger is for Mozart to be hijacked from the public domain and transformed into yet another device for selling goods – processed, packaged and 'profitized'. Such is the awareness in public bodies of this danger that codes are written to regulate the degree of sponsorship and its nature. See the next entry.

Sponsorship: ITC Code of Programme Sponsorship The Independent Television Commission in the UK was required by the BROADCASTING ACT, 1990, to draw up and from time to time review a code that sets standards and practice in the sponsoring of programmes and identifies criteria for sponsorship. Compliance with the Code is a condition of an ITC licence. The Code makes this definition: 'A programme is deemed to be sponsored if any part of its costs of production or transmission is met by an organization or person other than a broadcaster or television producer, with a view to promoting its own or another's name, trademark, image, activities, or other direct or indirect commercial interests.'

The Code permits any programme to be sponsored, with the exception of news and current affairs programmes. Thus, 'Programmes and news flashes, comprising local, national or international news items must not be sponsored', and 'Current affairs programmes containing explanation or analysis of current events must not be sponsored.'

The following principles form the basis of the Code: no sponsor is permitted any influence on either the content or the scheduling of a programme; any sponsorship must be clearly identified at the beginning and/or end of the programme; no promotional reference to the sponsor, or to his product or service, is permitted within the programme he has sponsored; no sponsored programme may contain within it any promotional reference to any other product or service; no programme may, without the previous approval of the Commission, be sponsored by any person whose business consists, wholly or mainly, in the manufacture or supply of a product, or in the provision of a service, which is not acceptable for television advertising under the CODE OF ADVERTISING STANDARDS AND PRACTICE (ITC).

The Code of Programme Sponsorship prohibits PRODUCT PLACEMENT. The Code does not permit sponsorship of credits within programmes, with the exception of game shows, where there may be two factual aural references to the sponsor's provision of the prize(s) only. Credits must not suggest that a programme has been made by the sponsor and on-screen presenters as part of the sponsor credit are not acceptable. In trailers there may be only one reference to the programme's sponsor, which can be aural and/or visual, lasting not more than five seconds.

Sponsorship is denied to political parties or pressure groups whose aim may be defined as largely political. It is also denied to manufacturers of tobacco and pharmaceuticals only available on prescription. Though product placement is prohibited, 'When a product or service is an essential element within a programme, the programme-maker may, exceptionally, acquire that product or service at no, or less than full, cost. This is not product placement. It is acceptable providing no undue prominence is given to the product or service in question.'

Spot news Term used to describe unexpected or unplanned news events, such as natural disasters, air crashes, murders or assassinations, often referred to as *breaking* news, and to be distinguished from *diary stories*, which are known well in advance and can be planned for by the newspaper, RADIO or TV news team – such as news conferences, state visits, elections or budgets. The *running story* is that which is ongoing and may stretch over several days or weeks, such as strikes, wars and famines; all stories that transcend the newsday cycle.

Sputnik First artificial satellite launched into space, by the Russians in 1957. See SATELLITE TRANSMISSION.

Spycatcher case A book by former British secret service employee Peter Wright, first published in the US in 1987, and banned from publication in the UK, became the centre of the most celebrated case of attempted government censorship in the 1980s. *Spycatcher: The Candid Autobiography of a Senior Intelligence Officer* (US: Viking/Penguin, 1987) was not dissimilar in its revelations about the activities of MI5 to other books that had been permitted to appear, but Wright, having signed the OFFICIAL SECRETS ACT (UK), was deemed to have breached confidence and arguably set a precedent for other secret agents to 'spill the beans' on security.

The Conservative government was determined not only to prevent publication of *Spycatcher* in the UK but to block the intentions of newspapers such as the *Guardian,* the *Observer,* the *Independent* and *The Sunday Times* to publish extracts from Wright's book. At the same time, government law officers pursued the book across the world to the courts in Australia and Hong Kong stirring publicity and interest that made it a world best-seller. Only the British people were to remain in the dark about Wright's revelations.

The government did not prosecute under the Official Secrets Act but pushed their case on the grounds of *confidentiality,* that members of the secret service, having sworn never to divulge information about their work, must – in law – be held for ever to that allegiance.

Eventually the Law Lords deliberated on the saga of *Spycatcher* and in October 1988 rejected government demands for a blanket injunction against the publishing in the UK of extracts from Wright's book. 'In a free society,' said Lord Goff, one of the five Law Lords, 'there is a continuing public interest that the workings of government should be open to scrutiny and criticism.' The Law Lords attacked the government's conduct of the litigation and its claims that it is for government alone to judge what information must remain confidential. An estimated £3m was spent by the government on court proceedings.

This triumph for free speech was followed by government measures to revise the Official Secrets Act in order to achieve the kind of CENSORSHIP that had been so conspicuously rejected in the Lords' judgement. See *TOPIC GUIDE* under MEDIA: FREEDOM, CENSORSHIP; MEDIA HISTORY; MEDIA: POLITICS AND ECONOMICS.

Stages in audience fragmentation See AUDIENCE: FRAGMENTATION.

Stamp Duty A government tax in late eighteenth- and nineteenth-century Britain on newspapers, with the express intention of controlling the numbers of papers and access to them by the general public. With news of the French Revolution (1789) across the water, Stamp Duty was raised to two pence per newspaper copy, with an additional Advertising Tax at three shillings per advertisement. In 1797 Stamp Duty was raised to three and a half pence, and the hiring out of papers was forbidden. In the year of the Battle of Waterloo, 1815, the duty went up to four pence and the Advertising Tax was also raised.

These *Taxes on Knowledge* as they were described eventually provoked the 'War of the Unstamped', the struggle of papers unable or unwilling to pay the duties. William Cobbett (1763–1835) in his *Political Register* dropped news so as to evade tax, and concentrated on opinion. Unstamped, and costing two pence, Cobbett's periodical achieved a sale of 44,000. 'Here, in these critical years,' writes Raymond Williams in *The Long Revolution* (UK: Penguin, 1965), 'a popular press of a new kind was emerging, wholly independent in spirit, and reaching new classes of readers.'

Two of the Six Acts of 1819 were directed against the press, and the 1820s and early 1830s featured clashes, fines, imprisonments and heroic defiance. In 1836 Stamp Duty was reduced from four pence to one penny, three years after the Advertisement Tax had been reduced from three shillings and sixpence to one shilling and sixpence per insertion. In 1853 the Advertising Tax was finally abolished; in 1855 the last penny of the Stamp Duty was removed, and in 1860 the duty imposed on paper was abandoned. 'The era of democratic journalism had formally arrived,' writes Joel H. Wiener in *The War of the Unstamped* (US: Cornell, 1969), 'and the daily newspaper became the cultural staple of the social classes.' See NEWSPAPERS, ORIGINS; PRESS BARONS; UNDERGROUND PRESS. See also *TOPIC GUIDE* under MEDIA HISTORY.

Standards and practice in advertising See CODE OF ADVERTISING STANDARDS AND PRACTICE (ITC).

Status The concept of status derives from the work of the sociologist Max Weber, who argued that status, though linked to CLASS, is a distinct dimension of social stratification. Status is the social evaluation of an individual or group, the degree of prestige or honour that society accords him, her or it. Wealth and high income may confer status but do not necessarily do so. The reasons why individuals or GROUPS may enjoy considerable status within a community or society are complex, subject to change and derive from many sources: such as the degree of power or authority a person or group may have, the perceived social usefulness of the abilities of an individual or group, or the level of education an individual has (see CULTURAL CAPITAL).

Occupation or the ownership of property may bestow status or require attributes such as a high level of education, hence the link between status and class. Status may be *ascribed*, that is based on fixed criteria over which a person may have no control – such as ancestry, ethnic affiliation, sex – or *achieved*, that is gained by endeavour or luck. Status given may not coincide with an individual's perception of his or her status.

Status must normally be endorsed by behaviour: such as the possession of objects (status symbols), accent, manners and social skills consistent with the status position. Much communicative behaviour is involved in the display of status, the use of accent and dress, for example. The mass media carry many images of status. Advertisers in particular appeal to status-consciousness as a way of selling a wide range of products and services.

Status quo As things are: the way in which things are done or were done in a period of time under discussion. Within the social science disciplines the term is often used to mean the prevailing or recent social, economic or political system – the way it works, usually by tradition, and who in the community work it (see HEGEMONY).

There is some controversy within Media Studies as to whether or not the mass media generally play an important role in reinforcing the status quo by presenting it as the 'natural' or 'real' state of things, and by rarely, in their presentation of aspects of human life, calling it into question. Richard Hoggart in *Speaking to Each Other* (UK: Chatto & Windus, 1970) argues that the tendency to accept the status quo results in the mass media concentrating on entertaining people at the expense of exploring the nature of human existence – an exploration that might disturb the status quo. See COMMON SENSE; CONSENSUS; ESTABLISHMENT; POWER ELITE.

Stereophonic sound See GRAMOPHONE.

Stereoscopy The creation of the visual illusion of relief or three-dimensions. The stereoscope was invented by Sir Charles Wheatstone (1802–75) in 1838. The process has had many applications. In photography, two separate photographs, taken from minimally different angles corresponding to the position of two human eyes, are mounted side by side on a card. Viewed through the angled prisms of the stereoscope, they interact to give the appearance of depth or solidity.

In the cinema, experimental processes of stereoscopy were demonstrated as early as the 1930s. It was developed as Natural Vision, or 3-D, in the early 1950s but never caught on, mainly perhaps because members of the audience had to wear special glasses. Only in Russia has a stereoscopic process that does not require the wearing of glasses been developed, yet even there it does not appear to have been widely adopted. However, 3-D (with glasses) was brought experimentally to UK TV screens by ITV in 1982–83. See HOLOGRAPHY.

Stereotype Oversimplified definition of a person or type of person, institution, style or event; to stereotype is to pigeon-hole, to thrust into tight slots of definition that allow little adjustment or change. Stereotyping is widespread because it is convenient – unions are like this, Arabs are like this, Jews are like this, teenagers, women, gays, asylum-seekers are like this. Stereotyping is often – though not always – the result of or accompaniment to PREJUDICE. It serves the media well because they are in the business of instant recognition and ready cues. It is very rare that we actually know any stereotypes: we only read of them, hear of them or have them 'framed' for us on TV. See HALO EFFECT; LABELLING PROCESS (AND THE MEDIA); SELF-FULFILLING PROPHECY. See also *TOPIC GUIDE* under MEDIA ISSUES AND DEBATES.

---

* Michael Pickering, *Stereotyping: The Politics of Representation* (UK: Palgrave, 2001).

Stopwatch culture See IMMEDIACY.

Storyboard Sequence of sketches or photographs used by the director or the producer of a film to sketch out, scene by scene, and sometimes frame by frame, the film's progression, its sight and sound.

Storyness See NARRATIVE.

Strategic bargaining Between the subject of media interest, for example politicians, and the media, there is an interaction in which one gives to the other in return for a service: the media get a story, the politician gets publicity, preferably favourable. As Ralph Negrine says in *Politics and the Mass Media in Britain* (UK: Routledge, 1989), 'Each feeds off the other, each informs the other and the subsequent reactions are reciprocal and continuous … The product of the interaction or bargaining is the media content to which the public at large attend.' See CULTURE OF DEFERENCE; REGULATORY FAVOURS. See also *TOPIC GUIDE* under MEDIA: POLITICS AND ECONOMICS.

Strategic silence See SILENCE: STRATEGIC SILENCE.

Strategy A term sometimes used to describe a communicative act that has been planned to some extent beforehand, which is deliberate and which has a clear purpose. Strategies can become a matter of habit. An example here might be the strategy used by a door-to-door salesperson. There are many different kinds of strategies used in INTERPERSONAL COMMUNICATION and we learn to use them through experience. Some, like the greetings strategy, are commonly used by many people, some we invent for ourselves to deal with particular situations, and some may be specific to certain groups or circumstances.

Stringer Name given in the NEWS reporting business to a non-staff reporter.

Structuralism A twentieth-century term of wide definition to describe certain traditions of analysing a range of studies – linguistics, literary criticism, psychoanalysis, social anthropology, Marxist theory and social history. Swiss scholar Ferdinand de Saussure's *Cours de Linguistique Générale* (1916), translated as *Course in General Linguistics* (1954), is probably the initial key work in this movement, later developed and diversified by Claude Lévi-Strauss and Roland Barthes. Structuralism is something of an umbrella term linked with the study of SIGN systems or SEMIOLOGY/SEMIOTICS.

Structuralists would argue that language has both a natural and a cultural source. The natural source refers to language as a genetic endowment of the human race, and this is framed within a network of meanings derived from the CULTURE of society. Structuralism explores the deep and often unconscious assumptions about social reality that underlie language and its use. In particular, it examines the way language is employed to construct MEANING from social events. However, assumptions about social reality are themselves also a product of social conditioning. Thus different cultures and subcultures – and indeed individuals – may generate different patterns of meaning from the same objective event or situation. See POSTMODERNISM. See also *TOPIC GUIDE* under COMMUNICATION THEORY.

Style A means by which the individual or group expresses identity (see IDENTIFICATION; SELF-IDENTITY), attitudes and VALUES, about self, about others and about society. Style takes many forms – hair style, dress style, aesthetic style, or a complete pattern of living: lifestyle. A teenager may adopt the style of a teenage subculture, in dress, language, behaviour for several linked reasons: to secure a sense of personal identity, to acquire a sense of belonging, of being 'in' with a favoured group, as a gesture of rebellion (against the conventional style of parents, for example, or the older generation in all shapes and forms) and to achieve STATUS – that is, a status awarded him/her by others in the favoured group, and peers generally.

Defiance of society at large is often cited as a reason why certain styles are adopted; this may or may not be true in all cases, but what is certain is that society often interprets such styles as acts of defiance or rejection, and the arbiters in this process of interpretation (or MEDIATION) are the mass media. Coverage by the media, researchers have found, tends to overdramatize the significance of style, to create STEREOTYPES and summon up exaggerated fears in the community.

In the world of the arts style is that particular set of characteristics – of approach and treatment – which gives a work its identity. As with styles in hair or dress, styles are first created, then imitated. In painting, the style of Paul Cézanne (1839–1906) is highly distinctive and instantly recognizable by anyone with a particular interest in art. However, it took Cézanne many years to develop that style, which was a visible manifestation of everything he believed about visual art; thus style represents the outer part of a whole structure that is made up of personality, experience, learning, theory, belief – and fused, if the style is successful. Those coming after may slavishly imitate the style of the master or, like the Cubists in the case of Cézanne, assimilate the style and then recreate it, thrusting it in new directions. See CULTURE; FOLK DEVILS; LABEL LIBEL; LABELLING PROCESS (AND THE MEDIA); YOUTH CULTURE. See also *TOPIC GUIDE* under REPRESENTATION.

Subculture Alternatives to the dominant CULTURE in society, subcultures have their own systems of NORMS, VALUES and beliefs, and in some cases their own language CODES. Such systems are often expressions of rejection of or resistance to the dominant culture. Members of subcultures are often those to whom the dominant culture awards low, subordinate and/or dependent status: youth, for example. Each subculture represents the reactions of a particular social group to its experience of society.

Some subcultures and their members may be labelled *deviant* by others in society.

It has been argued that because of the fragmented social nature of modern society, the mass media play an increasingly important role in relaying images of such subcultures both to their own members and to members of the dominant culture. Dick Hebdige in *Subculture: The Meaning of Style* (UK: Methuen, 1979; reissued 2002) writes that in doing so the media tend to accommodate the subcultures within the framework of the dominant culture, thus preserving the CONSENSUS – a procedure he calls the 'process of recuperation'.

Subliminal Signals that act below the threshold of conscious reception. Most familiarly we use the word in reference to subliminal ADVERTISING, the trick of flashing up on the screen, or recording on tape, messages so rapid they are not consciously recorded but that may subsequently affect future attitudes or behaviour.

In the UK subliminal advertising is illegal and its use in other media is banned by the Institute of Practitioners in Advertising. In the US there is no such control. Many department stores use subliminal seduction to counteract shop-lifting. Messages such as 'I am honest, I will not steal' are mixed with background music and continually repeated. One retail chain reported a drop of a third in thefts in nine months as a result of its subliminal conscience coaxing.

Computer games escape rules concerning subliminal messages. The UK *Sunday Times* published a major story 'Children "drugged" by computer games' (8 October 1995), concerning the Time Warner game *Endorfun*. The messages are there, admit the manufacturers, but they are positive, one message being 'I forgive myself completely.' Randeep Ramesh, author of the article, quotes the opinion of Howard Shevrin, Professor of Psychology at the University of Michigan: 'It does not pay to fool around with subliminal messages. The results may not be good if you are the wrong person for the wrong message.' See CODE OF ADVERTISING STANDARDS AND PRACTICE (ITC); SLEEPER EFFECT. See also *TOPIC GUIDE* under MEDIA: PROCESSES AND PRODUCTION.

Subtitle Or striptitle, a text near the bottom of the projected image, usually providing a translation of foreign language dialogue. These days it is possible with foreign language films screened on TV to generate subtitles electronically so that the words are not actually on the film itself. In some multilingual areas, such as Cairo, where three or more titles in different languages and scripts are required, subtitles are projected on to separate screens at the sides and bottom of the main screen.

Succeeders See ADVERTISING: MAINSTREAMERS, ASPIRERS, SUCCEEDERS AND REFORMERS.

Super density (SD) discs Successors to the compact disc (CD), with more than 25 times the capacity of current CD-ROMs. As with the old rivalry between different video systems (VHS and Betamax) there is global rivalry between the SD format (SDI-DVD – Digital Video Disc) favoured by Time Warner and MGM/UA, and that of the co-inventors of the CD, Sony and Philips, called the MultiMedia Compact Disc. Both systems are in most respects identical without being compatible.

Supervening social necessity Notion that social or cultural pressures give the impetus to technological development, serving as *accelerators* in the process of change. Brian Winston suggests this feature in 'How are media born?', in *Questioning the Media: A Critical Introduction* (UK: Sage, 1990), edited by John Downing, Ali Mohammadi and Annabelle Sreberny-Mohammadi. He cites the arrival of TV in the US as being accelerated by the 'rise of the home, the dominance of the nuclear family, and the political and economic need to maintain full employment' after the Second World War. Winston argues that 'Supervening social necessities are at the interface between society and technology'. They may operate as a result of the needs of corporations or because of new or rival technologies.

As well as accelerators, social necessities may serve as *brakes* upon technological developments, which 'work to slow the disruptive impact of new technology. I describe the operation of these brakes as the "law" of the suppression of radical potential, using "law" in the standard social science sense to denote a regular and powerful general tendency.' In this case, new technology, though available, is resisted, checked or even suppressed. Says Winston, 'The brakes ensure that a technology's introduction does not disrupt the social or corporate status quo.'

Winston is of the view that while TV had been 'accelerated' after 1945, it had been 'braked' prior to the war: 'Thus in the case of TV, the existence of facsimile systems, the rise of radio … and the need not to destroy the film industry all acted to suppress the speed at which the new medium was introduced, to minimize disruption.' Winston returns to, and expands on, his analysis of the development of media technologies in his book *Media Technology and Society: A History from the Telegraph to the Internet* (UK: Routledge, 1998). See TECHNOLOGICAL DETERMINISM. See also *TOPIC GUIDE* under MEDIA: TECHNOLOGIES.

Surveillance Keeping watch; used in a media sense, the word indicates the way that listeners, viewers or readers employ the media with the aim of gleaning information from them: 'TV news provides food for thought' or 'I like to see how big issues are sorted out.' Equally surveillance implies the process of authority and its agencies keeping watch on the public. See USES AND GRATIFICATIONS THEORY.

Surveillance society New technology has vastly increased and speeded up access to personal data by those in authority or those individuals or organizations involved in financial, administrative or commercial transactions with members of the public. Each time we use a Switch card; each time we dial a telephone number we offer notification of our activities, our whereabouts and our lifestyle. David Lyon in *The Electronic Eye: The Rise of Surveillance Society* (US: University of Minnesota Press, 1994) identifies four domains of surveillance in contemporary life – government administration, policing and security, the workplace and the consumer marketplace; and for Lyon a key characteristic of surveillance is that it operates *across* boundaries.

The concept of a surveillance society is not new. The English philosopher, social and legal reformer, Jeremy Bentham (1748–1832), in a proposal for the humanitarian treatment of prisoners, suggested the construction of what he called a *Panopticon.* This was a circular building of cells with a central watchtower from which constant surveillance of the prisoners would take place, without their being certain at any given time that they were being directly observed. They would be well aware, of course, of the presence of surveillance and this knowledge would, without coercion, rule their behaviour until, so Bentham theorized, their good behaviour would become self-regulating.

For several commentators the Panopticon has become a metaphor for our own times. In particular, the French philosopher Michel Foucault (1926–84) has focused on the 'all-seeing' Panopticon. In *Discipline and Punish* (UK: Penguin, 1977) he likens the Panopticon to the Christian God's infinite knowledge and with computer monitoring of individuals in advanced capitalism. He argues that surveillance as represented by the contemporary Panopticon creates subjects responsible for their own subjection (see PRIVACY).

We are subject to surveillance not only as citizens but as AUDIENCE for media. In an article entitled 'Tracking the audience', in *Questioning Media: A Critical Introduction* (US: Sage, 1990), edited by John Downing, Ali Mohammadi and Annabelle Sreberny-Mohammadi, Oscar Gandy Jr remarks how the fragmentation of audience for media, rendered possible by new technology, has resulted in a desperation among programme-makers that has led to two strategies aimed at survival. These Gandy identifies as *rationalization,* that is 'the pursuit of efficiency in the production, distribution, and sale of goods and services', and *surveillance,* which 'provides the information necessary for greater control'. Increasingly, says Gandy, 'the surveillance of audiences resembles police surveillance of suspected criminals' and people are less and less aware that their behaviour as audience is being measured.

Gandy argues that 'Perhaps the greatest threat these computer-based systems for audience assessment represent is their potential to worsen the balance of power between individuals and bureaucratic organizations. Personal information streams out of the lives of individuals much like blood out of an open wound, and it collects in pools in the computers of corporations and government bureacracies.' Resistance to such powers is, in Gandy's view, 'almost nonexistent, and what little there is may be seen as passive and defeatist'.

While recognizing that a 'nearly invisible minority simply refuses to enter the system of records, giving up the convenience of credit cards and acquiring goods and services under assumed names or aliases', Gandy fears that 'to escape the information net means to become a nonperson'. It is a high risk, for one 'maintains privacy through the loss of all else'. See CCTV: CLOSED-CIRCUIT TELEVISION; ECHELON; INTERNET: MONITORING OF CONTENT; REGULATION OF INVESTIGATORY POWERS ACT (RIPA) (UK), 2000; USA – PATRIOT ACT, 2001. See also *TOPIC GUIDE* under MEDIA: FREEDOM, CENSORSHIP; MEDIA ISSUES AND DEBATES.

Survivors and the media A research report by Ann Shearer, 'Survivors of the media' (UK: John Libbey, 1991), commissioned by the BROADCASTING STANDARDS COUNCIL of the UK, found that insensitive media coverage adds to the distress of survivors of disasters and their bereaved relatives. Intrusions by media into PRIVACY, harassment, distortion and distasteful detail in what was reported, were identified by a sample of 54 people who had lost loved ones, as damaging and hurtful. Many comments placed the worst blame at the door of the press.

Sweetheart deals Term used to describe the informal practice by commissioning editors of BROADCASTING organizations, of awarding ex-employees with a favoured status when commissioning programmes from the independent production sector. A significant number of those formerly employed in broadcasting organizations entered the independent production sector when broadcasting organizations progressively downsized their labour force from the late 1980s to the mid-1990s. See CASUALIZATION; INDEPENDENT PRODUCERS.

Sykes Committee Report on Broadcasting, 1923 See BBC, ORIGINS.

Symbol Any object, person, or EVENT to which a generally agreed, shared MEANING has been given and which individuals have learned to accept as representing something other than itself: a national flag represents feelings of patriotism and national unity, for example. Symbols are almost always culture-bound. See ICONIC; METAPHOR; MYTH; SEMIOLOGY/SEMIOTICS; SIGN; SIGNIFICATION.

'Symbolic annihilation of women' (by the media) See NORMS.

Symbolic code See CODES OF NARRATIVE.

Symbolic convergence theory Professor Ernest G. Bormann in his article 'Symbolic convergence theory: a communication formulation', in the *Journal of Communication*, Autumn 1985, writes of 'shared fantasies' that 'provide group members with comprehensible forms for explaining the past and thinking about the future – a basis for communal and group consciousness' (see NARRATIVE PARADIGM).

Bormann posits a three-part structure to the theory: (1) the part that deals with the discovery and arrangement of recurring communicative forms and patterns that indicate the evolution and presence of a shared group consciousness; (2) the part that consists of a description of the dynamic tendencies within communication systems 'that explain why group consensuses arise, continue, decline, and disappear' and the effects such group CONSENSUS has in terms of meanings, motives and communication within the group – the basic communication process is the dynamic of people sharing group fantasies; (3) that part of the theory which consists of the factors that explain why people share the fantasies they do and when they do.

By 'fantasy' Bormann means the creative and imaginative shared interpretation of events 'that fulfil a group psychological or rhetorical need'. What the author terms 'rhetorical fantasies' are the result of '*homo narrans* in collectives sharing narratives that account for their experiences and their hopes and fears'. Such rhetorical fantasies may include 'fanciful and fictitious scripts of imaginary characters, but they often deal with things that have actually happened to members of the group or that are reported in authenticated works of history, in the news media, or in the oral history and folklore of other groups and communities'.

The sharing of fantasies brings a 'convergence of appropriate feelings among participants ... when members of a mass audience share a fantasy they jointly experience the same emotions, develop common heroes and villains, celebrate certain actions as laudable, and interpret some aspect of their common experience in the same way'.

This Bormann names *symbolic convergence*. While the 'rational world paradigm' claims that there is an objective truth that speakers can mirror in their communication, and against which its logic and argument can be tested and evaluated (and therefore regards myth and fantasy as untrue, as the recounting of falsehoods), for those giving credence to shared fantasies, 'the stories of myths or fantasy themes are central'.

An underlying assumption of the theory seems to be that fantasies are not only creative but benign. It would be interesting to apply symbolic convergence theory, the notion of *homo narrans*, to fantasies entertained about racial superiority, where fantasy becomes a nightmare. See *TOPIC GUIDE* under COMMUNICATION THEORY.

* E.G. Bormann, *Communicative Theory* (US: Holt, Rinehart & Winston, 1980); *The Force of Fantasy: Restoring the American Dream* (US: Illinois University Press, 1985).

Symbolic interactionism Term associated with the ideas of American scholar Herbert Blumer and crystallized in his book *Symbolic Interactionism: Perspective and Method* (US: University of California Press, 1969; first paperback edition, 1986). Blumer sees 'meaning as arising in a process of interaction between people'. The meaning of an object or a phenomenon for one person 'grows out of the ways in which other persons act towards the person with regard to the thing', that is the thing's *symbolic value*. Symbolic interactionism sees MEANING as a social product, as a creation 'formed in and through the defining activities of people as they interact'. All meanings, emphasizes Blumer, are subject to a constant and recurring 'interpretative process'; and this is a 'formative process in which meanings are used and revised as instruments for the guidance and formation of action'. See SEMIOLOGY/SEMIOTICS; SEMIOTIC POWER.

Symmetry, strain towards Concept posed by Theodore Newcomb in 'An approach to the study of communicative acts', *Psychological Review* 63 (1953). The act of communication is characterized, believes Newcomb, by a 'strain towards symmetry', that is towards balance and consistency. See CONGRUENCE THEORY; INTERPERSONAL COMMUNICATION; NEWCOMB'S ABX MODEL OF COMMUNICATION, 1953.

Synchronic linguistics See LINGUISTICS.

Synchronous sound In film, sound-effects synchronized with the visual image were first used commercially in 1926, in *Don Juan*, but it was *The Jazz Singer* in November 1927 that caused a sensation among audiences and marked the birth of the talkies. Warner Brothers had been heading for oblivion in the cut-throat world of the HOLLYWOOD studios when the company adopted a system developed by the Bell Telephones Laboratories, which reproduced sound from large discs, matching sound and picture by mechanical linkage. Nothing in the cinema was ever the same again.

The talkies marked the end of many careers made in the silent era but created new opportunities for actors from the theatre, writers, musicians, vaudeville and RADIO stars. As a technical possibility, synchronous sound had been inviting interest from movie-makers from as early as 1902. In that year Monsieur Gaumont gave an address to the Société Française de la Photographie, on film and employing synchronous sound. Indeed, two years earlier Herr Ruhmer demonstrated what he called 'light telephony' to record sound directly on to the film itself – the first soundtrack.

Following the inventions of the thermionic valve by John Fleming in 1904 and the audion vacuum tube by Lee De Forest in 1907, amplification of sound by comparatively simple electric methods was feasible: the studios were simply not interested, fearing, perhaps, the impact language differences might have on the universal appeal of film as mime, whose only verbal language was easily translatable titling (see reference to *suppression of radical potential* in SUPERVENING SOCIAL NECESSITY).

Though Lee De Forest's Phonofilm of 1923 demonstrated how light waves could synchronize sound and image, and though the Germans had developed the finest early sound system of all, Tri-Ergon, the continuing profitability of the silent movie blinded the studios to two significant facts: the potential of silent film had practically been exhausted; and audiences were becoming bored.

Lights of New York (1928) was the first all-talking picture and within a year thousands of cinemas had been equipped for sound. Warner's VITAPHONE disc was soon replaced by optical sound systems where images and sound were put together on the same film, to make the married print where sound synchronization with the picture could not be lost. As sound-recording techniques developed, dialogue, sound-effects and music were recorded separately, using a magnetic sound process, and then mixed at a later stage, thus allowing latitude for changes and creative editing.

The introduction of sound did not rescue the cinema from the general economic slump that followed the Wall Street Crash of 1929. During 1931, cinema attendances in the US dropped by 40 per cent and in 1932 the movie business lost between four and five million dollars. However, it was probably the new dimension of sound in the cinema that enabled the industry to rally so quickly.

The talkies interacted substantially with RADIO, the one drawing technical and creative ideas as well as talented personnel from the other. By 1937, 90 per cent of US-sponsored national radio programmes in the US were transmitted from Hollywood. See *TOPIC GUIDE* under MEDIA HISTORY; MEDIA TECHNOLOGIES.

Synergy The establishment of relationships between differing areas and/or organizations within the cultural and media industries that allow for greater efficiency in the production and promotion of two or more cultural/media artefacts. An example of synergy is when the launching of a new film is accompanied by the promotion of a wide range of related merchandise. Conglomerates (see CONGLOMERATES: MEDIA CONGLOMERATES) are in an enviable position to take advantage of the benefits of synergies.

Examples of synergic partnerships have multiplied until they become a NORM, and involve a range of sponsors and beneficiaries, thus McDonald's has synergized with Disney to promote *Monsters, Inc.* (2002) while Harry Potter, books and movies, benefit from and benefit Coca-Cola. Perhaps the classic synergic relationship is between sport and big business.

Syntactics A branch of SEMIOLOGY/SEMIOTICS; the study of the SIGNS and rules relating to signs, without reference to MEANING.

Syntagm See PARADIGM.

Syntax The combination of words into significant patterns; the grammatical structure in sentences.

T

Tabloid, tabloidese, tabloidization In '"Tabloidization" of news: a comparative analysis of Anglo-American and German press journalism' (*European Journal of Communication*, September 1999), Frank Esser writes that the term 'tabloid' orginally referred to a pharmaceutical trademark for the concentrated form of medicines as pill or tablet: 'This narcotic tabloid effect and the fact that it is easy to swallow have been readily transferred to the media.'

The term, in the UK, is used to refer to the size of a newspaper (in comparison with the *broadsheet* format) but, in general, 'tabloidese' describes the nature of news content and style. Esser quotes Marvin Kalb, director of the Shorenstein Center on the Press, Politics and Public Affairs at Harvard University: tabloidese is characterized by 'a downgrading of hard news and upgrading of sex, scandal and infotainment'. At the micro level, states Esser, tabloidization 'can be seen as a media phenomenon involving the revision of traditional newspaper and other media formats driven by reader preferences and commercial requirements' while on the macro level it 'can be seen as a social phenomenon both instigating and symbolizing major changes to the constitution of society'.

Esser's study focuses on the micro level of the tabloidization process, meaning 'a change in the range of topics being covered (more entertainment, less information), in the form of presentation (fewer longer stories, more shorter ones with pictures and illustrations) and a change in the mode of address (more street talk when addressing readers)'. He argues that the nature, evolution and relative predominance of tabloidization varies between America, the UK and Germany; thus it is an 'extremely problematic term' and can 'therefore only be analysed with reference to the respective media cultures and journalistic traditions' of the countries in question.

For example, tabloidization has never taken hold in Germany to the extent that it has in the UK; in part because – as far as sex scandals are concerned – Germany has a strong PRIVACY law that 'also protects public figures'. He cites research evidence showing that extensive coverage of scandals can increase public disillusionment with public life, hence the fears many commentators have 'that a shift towards sensation, emotion and scandal may have some negative effects on democracy'.

Currently the term tabloidization is used specifically to describe what many critics see happening both to the serious, broadsheet newspaper, and to TV NEWS, in the sense that they are 'getting more and more like the tabloids', matching them for populist content and design, and demonstrating the same fascination for covering the lives and antics of celebrities. In other words, the accusation is that while the tabloids – in the UK referred to as the red-tops – are already dumbed down, dumbing down is also what is happening to traditionally serious media. See *TOPIC GUIDE* under LANGUAGE/DISCOURSE/NARRATIVE.

Tactics and strategies Term used by Michel de Certeau in *The Practice of Everyday Life* (US: University of California Press, 1984) when analysing everyday cultural consumption, to draw the distinction between the strategies of the powerful controllers of the cultural industries and the tactics of the relatively powerless ordinary consumers in finding their own space for creating MEANING by adapting to their own use mass-produced cultural artefacts.

Some of these tactics subvert or resist the intentions and intended messages of the powerful. De Certeau's distinction, whilst acknowledging that audiences/consumers may be active in their consumption, does not imply that they have by any means the degree of power over cultural consumption exercised by those who own and control the cultural industries. See AUDIENCE: ACTIVE AUDIENCE; SEMIOTIC POWER.

Tag questions The addition of phrases such as 'Isn't it?' or 'Don't you think?' at the end of a statement as tag questions, according to some linguists, suggests tentativeness on the part of the speaker, and weakens the impact of what is said. However, there is some debate here. Tag questions can serve a range of functions, some relating to the content of speech, others relating to the facilitation of interaction, and the relationships and attitudes of the participants to one another.

When used to facilitate interaction, tag questions do not seem to be associated with tentativeness, indeed, the tendency here is for tags to be associated with powerful speakers. Several studies suggest that women use more tag questions than men when acting as facilitators in an interaction.

Take See SHOT.

Talkies See SYNCHRONOUS SOUND.

Talloires Declaration, 1981 Concerned at the attempts by the United Nations Educational, Scientific and Cultural Organization (UNESCO) seemingly to impose upon world information systems a 'New Order' that would be characterized by far-reaching controls, representatives from the news organizations of 20 countries met in the French village of Talloires in May 1981. They issued a declaration which insisted that journalists sought no special protected status – as it was planning to create – and that they were united in a 'joint declaration to the freest, most accurate and impartial information that is within our professional capacity to produce'. The declaration asserted that there could be no double standards of freedom for rich and poor countries. See MACBRIDE COMMISSION; MEDIA IMPERIALISM; NEW WORLD INFORMATION ORDER. See also *TOPIC GUIDE* under GLOBAL PERSPECTIVES.

Tamizdat See SAMIZDAT.

Taste In a media sense, the notion of good or bad taste relates less to aesthetic judgement than to decisions about how much and how far; the answers to these questions depend upon AUDIENCE expectations and readiness, and the degree of access and immediacy. A photograph of an execution, reproduced in a newspaper or magazine, is sufficiently controlled by the frame of print and the fact that the event took place in the past, to escape the accusation of bad taste.

However, there were vigorous protests when, on TV news, a Vietcong prisoner had a pistol put to his head, and pulled the trigger. This was bringing, as it were, too much reality into the sitting room. It may have been the truth, ran the argument, but somehow the reproduction and presentation turned reality into theatre, indeed into macabre entertainment. As such it appeared an insult to human dignity, to that of the victim and to that of the audience cast in the role of voyeurs. See CENSORSHIP; COMPASSION FATIGUE.

Taxes on knowledge See STAMP DUTY.

Taxonomic conquistadors Term used by Bill Nicholls in *Blurred Boundaries: Questions of Meaning in Contemporary Culture* (US: University of Indiana Press, 1994) to describe the agencies, sociological and marketing, that subject humans to classification or SEGMENTATION. Nicholls admits the dangers inherent in placing people into (often stereotypical) slots but concedes that 'with no categories at all culture itself would disappear'. The use of the term conquistadors suggests that such taxonomies – lists of classification – have an enforcing and shaping capacity through powers of persuasion and of inclusion/exclusion. See ADVERTISING: MAINSTREAMERS, ASPIRERS, SUCCEEDERS AND REFORMERS; AUDIENCE DIFFERENTIATION; AUDIENCE MEASUREMENT; VALS TYPOLOGY.

Technique: Ellul's theory of technique In a number of books written between the 1950s and 1990, Jacques Ellul saw contemporary society as being dominated by technological advances each aiding the MEDIATING power of mass communication; and together leading to a society in which efficiency and consequently conformity become the key determinants of human affairs. Ellul uses the term technique to suggest the generality of attitudes to, and uses of, machines in everyday life, applying equally to social production as to material production.

His view is a bleak one, seeing efficiency, brought about by the wholesale adoption by those who rule and those who are ruled, as being both authoritarian in tendency and beyond the control of governments: 'Technical advance,' says Ellul in *The Technological Society* (US: Knopf, 1964), 'gradually invades the state, which in turn is compelled to assume forms favourable to this advance.' Politicians Ellul sees as 'impotent satellites of the machine, which with all its parts and techniques, apparently functions as well without them'. However, the politicians do not step down. Instead they create an illusion of politics and political leadership.

Ellul anticipates the response that the information age has brought about a more involved public in the political process. For him the sheer volume of information works to reinforce the technological society by overwhelming the citizen. In a detailed analysis of Ellul's theory of technique in 'Hegemony, agency, and dialectical tension in Ellul's technological society', in the *Journal of Communication*, Summer

1998, Rick Clifton Moore writes, 'This is not to say that all of the blame for the political illusion must be laid at the feet of the state and the media. Ellul's orientation suggests the complicity of the citizens themselves … The modern citizen is much too willing to accept the comfortable route of technique, rather than make difficult choices that would require humanness.'

The public, in Ellul's view, is subject to, and in thrall to, the 'spectacle-orientated society' in which everything is 'subordinated to visualization' and 'nothing has meaning out of it'. In today's society, Ellul says, there are many, and powerful, deterrents of human freedom, and a key question is, in societies where 'covetousness and the desire for power' are human constants across all cultural boundaries, whether there is sufficient agency among citizens to achieve freedom. See HEGEMONY; IDEOLOGICAL STATE APPARATUSES; IDEOLOGY; McDONALDIZATION; SEMIOTIC POWER; SURVEILLANCE SOCIETY. See also *TOPIC GUIDE* under MEDIA: TECHNOLO-GIES.

Technological determinism The view that if something is technically feasible then it is both desirable and bound to be realized in practice. Evidence points to the fact that such determinism is only partly convincing. Much technology usage is a by-product of technology devised for other purposes. RADIO became an 'inevitability', for example, largely because its determinant was radar, required to fulfil military needs, while satellites had a long record of military/political functions before they began to beam sporting events to the peoples of the world.

Set against notions of technological determinism is a second theory, *symptomatic technology*, which argues that technology is a by-product of a social process which itself has been otherwise determined. In *Television: Technology and Cultural Form* (UK: Fontana, 1974), Raymond Williams says that basically both theories are in error because in different ways they have 'abstracted technology from society' instead of examining the crucial interaction between them. Of course part of that interaction is the belief in technological determinism, and the risk of it becoming a SELF-FULFILLING PROPHECY.

Dwayne Winseck in 'Pursuing the holy grail: information highways and media reconvergence in Britain and Canada', in the *European Journal of Communication*, September 1998, argues that contrary to 'the belief that technological factors determine how media are organized', the primary drivers of media evolution 'are machinations between governments and industries, visions of how markets should evolve, and ideas about whether communication constitutes just another commodity or is something more imbued with cultural consideration and public service values'. See INTERNET; SUPERVENING SOCIAL NECESSITY. See also *TOPIC GUIDE* under MEDIA ISSUES AND DEBATES.

Technology of the media See *TOPIC GUIDE* under MEDIA: TECHNOLOGIES.

Teenagers and media use See CHILDREN, YOUNG PEOPLE AND THE CHANGING MEDIA ENVIRONMENT.

Telecommunication *Tele* means far off, at a distance; a telecommunication is communication by TELEGRAPHY or TELEPHONE, with or without wires or cables. In telephony and telegraphy signals are transmitted as electric impulses along wires. In RADIO and TV the signals are transmitted through space as modulations of carrier waves of electromagnetic radiation. See TELETEXT; WIRELESS TELEGRAPHY; WORLD TRADE ORGANIZATION (WTO) TELECOMMUNICA-TIONS AGREEMENT, 1997.

Teledemocracy Term used to describe theories that telecommunications serve to advance democracy by extending information and widening access to information; by counteracting through the use of computers and modems, the advantages of the information-rich over the information-poor. Local networks, using computers whose capacities have advanced as the prices have dropped, demonstrate the potential to link up nationally and internationally, favouring access to individuals and communities.

As evidence of teledemocracy the work of such alliances as PeaceNet, founded in San Francisco in 1986, EcoNet, London's GreenNet and the computer-communication project Public Data Access (PDA) is cited. PDA was responsible in the US for the dissemination of research into the exceptional-ly high correlation between toxic waste sites and the location of minority communities. Sceptics, however, hold to the view that in an age when information has become increasingly *commoditized*, it is the all-powerful agencies of information – governments, multinational corporations – who control the 'electronic highways' and that such highways are less public and free, and increasingly private and subject to tolls.

A true gauge of teledemocracy is the health of NEWS coverage, and whether that news coverage receives sufficient and increasing investment (in comparison with programme money going into entertainment). In a specific sense, the teledemocracy infers closer links between electorates and governments, encouraging greater interactivity through consultations (seeking out public opinion expressed electronically in various ways). Governments, however, have been slow to institute referendums via telecommunications, despite the success of TV in particular in seeking out and receiving public FEEDBACK, via correspondence, telephone and e-mail. See DEMOCRACY AND THE MEDIA. See also *TOPIC GUIDE under* MEDIA: POLITICS AND ECONOMICS

Telegenic Looking good on TV – a factor that has had particular significance in the domain of politics. There is no proof that it does not help to be handsome. See LOOKISM.

Telegraphy Only after the discovery of the magnetic effect of electric current was telegraphy possible. The first telegraph consisted of a compass needle that was deflected by the magnetic field produced by electric currents that flowed through the circuit whenever the transmitting key was depressed and contact established. The first patent for an electric telegraph was taken out by William Fothergill Cooke and Charles Wheatstone in June 1837, and later in the same year they demonstrated a five-needle telegraph to the directors of the London and Birmingham railway.

A year later the Great Western Railway connected Paddington and West Drayton by telegraph line, which soon gave a considerable boost of publicity to telegraphy: in 1845 a suspected murderer was spotted boarding a London-bound train at Slough; the news was telegraphed to Paddington, the man was arrested on arrival, and later found guilty and hanged.

In the US, Samuel Morse's first working telegraph of 1837 depended on the making and breaking of an electric current: an electromagnetically operated stylus recorded the long and short dashes of MORSE CODE on a moving strip of paper. After much persuasion, the US Congress, in 1843, voted to pay Morse (1791–1872) to build the first telegraph line in America, from Baltimore to Washington. It was in the following year, using the Morse Code, that Morse transmitted his famous message – 'What hath God wrought!' – on this line.

Development of telegraphy was swift. By 1862 the world's telegraph system covered some 150,000 miles, including 15,000 in the UK. A method of printing the coded telegraph messages had been invented in 1845 and was developed in the US as 'House's Printing Telegraph'. In 1850 a telegraph cable had been laid across the English Channel. In 1858 the Atlantic was spanned by telegraph cable. The duplex telegraphy of Thomas Alva Edison (1847–1931) made it possible to transmit two messages simultaneously over the same line. Soon, four- and five-message systems followed, and ultimately the teleprinter. Picture transmission by telegraphy resulted from the development work of English physicist Shelford Bidwell, the first such transmissions taking place in 1881. See TELEX.

'The significance of telegraphy,' writes James W. Carey in *Communication as Culture* (UK: Routledge, 1992), 'is that it led to the selective control and transmission of information. The telegraph operator was able to monopolize knowledge, if only for a few moments, along a route; and this brought a selective advantage in trading and speculation.' It also ushered in a new language of JOURNALISM, what Ernest Hemingway called 'the lingo of the cable' – terse, precise; as Carey puts it, 'a form of language stripped of the local, the regional, and colloquial ... something closer to a "scientific" language, a language of strict denotation in which the connotative featurers of utterance were under rigid control'.

Telegraphy continues to be widely used – by news services, the Stock Exchange telex service, public message services, certain police and fire alarm systems and private-line companies for data transmission. See TELEPHONE; WIRELESS TELEGRAPHY. See *TOPIC GUIDE* under MEDIA HISTORY.

---

* Brian Winston, *Media, Technology and Society: A History: From the Telegraph to the Internet* (UK: Routledge, 1998).

Telematics Term referring to the merging of telecommunications and computers, brought about by DIGITIZATION. The 1s and 0s of the computer are converted into tones relayed over telephone lines and then reconverted at the other end of the line by another computer. Thus information can be held centrally, despatched rapidly, updated easily and networked internationally. This trans-border data flow (TBDF) is enhanced by SATELLITES, the advantage of whose use is that transmission costs do not rise in relation to the distance being covered (as is the case with microwaves and cables); so long, that is, as the communication falls within the 'footprint' of the same satellite.

Telephone In his early years, a Scotsman Alexander Graham Bell (1857–1922) knew Charles Wheatstone (1802–75), co-inventor of TELEGRAPHY, and also Alexander John Ellis, an expert in sound. Ellis showed Bell that the vibration of a tuning fork could be influenced by an electric current. He was able to produce sounds very like those of a human voice. Bell, teaching deaf-mutes in Boston, Massachusetts, experimented on a musical telegraph (1872). He produced artificial 'eardrums' from sheets of metal and linked these with electric wire.

In 1876 Bell succeeded in passing a vocal message along a wire to an assistant in another room. The first telephone switching system was installed in New Haven, Connecticut, in 1878. However, while claiming credit for 'his' invention, and being acknowledged down the years as the inventor of the telephone, Bell must surrender the accolade to an unknown (and, until now, uncelebrated) Italian, Antonio Meucci (1808–89), who demonstrated his 'teletrofono' in New York in 1860. Alas, Meucci's poverty (he could not afford the $250 needed to patent his 'talking telegraph') and his failure to secure financial backing left the way open for Bell – who had shared a laboratory with Meucci and thus had access to his findings – to file a patent and pursue a lucrative deal with Western Union.

A century later, the US telephone system, largely the monopoly of the company Bell founded, was handling an average of over 240m phone conversations a day and, as Maurice Richards points out in *The World Communicates* (UK: Longman, 1972), the telephone system had 'developed into a communications network infinitely more versatile than could have been envisaged by the pioneers'.

Now telephone lines serve complex computer data systems; documents are transmitted via telephone – a scanning head records the light and shade of the document as it turns on a rotating drum, translating intensity of tone into electrical impulses for transmission over the wire to be re-translated at the receiving end. Telephone lines also carry telex services.

Microwave transmission techniques now allow telephone calls through air, free of wires, poles or underground conduits. Transmitting from point to point, tall towers now beam as many as 1500 calls on a single carrier wave. London's Post Office Tower has potential load capacity of 150,000 telephone calls and capacity to transmit 100 TV channels.

Mobile phones (see MOBILIZATION) can be said to be the technological advance that more swiftly than any other became a means of communication on a mass scale, to the point where their use began to be seen as a public nuisance. Their increasing sophistication (and the fact that they had become a STYLE accessory) created a new crime – mobile mugging, setting the manufacturers the challenge of making the devices inoperable except by the legitimate owner. Today, in addition to phoning in the traditional way, and text-messaging, users of mobiles can tune into the INTERNET as well as RADIO and TV broadcasts.

Belatedly, in the summer of 2002, justice was done to the memory of the Florentine, Antonio Meucci. The US House of Representatives voted in favour of recognizing Meucci as the true father of telecommunications, 113 years after his death. See *TOPIC GUIDE* under MEDIA HISTORY; MEDIA: TECHNOLOGIES.

Telephone tapping See PRIVACY.

Telerecording Introduced in 1947, the first telerecording equipment consisted of a special 35mm film camera pointed at the screen. Picture quality was poor as a result of incompatibility between the camera shutter and TV's scanning process. The Ampex Corporation of America produced a definitive answer using a 'quadruplex' technique: a two-inch-wide tape travelled at normal speed while a rapidly spinning drum carrying four heads recorded tracks across the tape rather than along it, thus achieving the high and constant speed required.

The Ampex machine was in service in the US in 1956 and in May of the following year Associated Rediffusion in the UK installed the first pair of recording machines in Europe. The BBC followed suit shortly afterwards. Helical scan recorders were an advance upon the quadruplex machines. Instead of recording across the tapes, the spinning head-drum laid down tracks almost parallel to its length. Gradually, in the late 1970s, these machines took over from quadruplex though there were problems over product compatibility. Ampex and Sony agreed a common standard, known as C-format, and helical scan became the norm.

Teletext Data in textual or graphic form transmitted via the TV screen; the BROADCASTING version of viewdata which is telephone-linked. In the UK, the BBC provides its CEEFAX information service; the COMMERCIAL TELEVISION equivalent was, until 1993, the Oracle service. In the auction for such services, empowered by the BROADCASTING ACT (UK), 1990, the licence-winner was Teletext UK, a consortium headed by Associated Newspapers and Philips, the electronics company. The name of the new service from 1993 is Teleview.

Telethon A live TV discussion or entertainment programme, often lasting for several hours, during which the public may ring in with questions and comments, and to make donations, and guest stars appear – all in aid of charity.

Television See *TOPIC GUIDE* under BROADCASTING.

Television: access television Term describing alternative, generally grassroots media; and exemplified in the US by PAPER TIGER TELEVISION and its offshoot, Deep Dish TV (DDTV), funded through grants, bequests and donations; operating with minimal staffs backed by teams of helpers and targeting public access channels.

Access TV aims to cover ISSUES and events perceived to be neglected or marginalized by mainstream, commercial media. John D.H. Downing (with Tamara Villareal Ford, Geneve Gil and Laura Stein) in *Radical Media: Rebellious Communication and Social Movements* (US/UK: Sage, 2001), writes that 'access television may be understood as an institution that provides citizens with some of the necessary tools for self-governance' within the framework of democratic practices.

Downing *et al.* see this happening in three ways. (1) Access TV 'enables its users to reinterpret, reframe, and refute the artefacts, messages, and ideologies of commercial culture from within a dominant forum for political communication'. (2) It creates for users 'a space in which to represent themselves and their interests to the larger community'. (3) It 'permits the exercise of democratic functions of speech that are largely absent from commercial media'.

In these ways, access (or radical) TV proves to be a 'feasible and appropriate forum in which to respond to the hegemonic position of the larger medium'. However, standing in the way of the greater democratic potential of access television is 'its predominantly local orientation, and its marginalization as a sphere of public debate'. What advocates and participants should work for, believe the authors of *Radical Media*, is 'a policy environment more conducive to democratic communication'. See CULTURAL OR CITIZEN RIGHTS AND THE MEDIA; DEMOCRACY AND THE MEDIA.

Television Act (UK), 1954 Gave birth to COMMERCIAL TELEVISION in the UK; the Act set up the Independent Television Authority (later to be named the Independent Broadcasting Authority with the coming of COMMERCIAL RADIO). A rigorous set of controlling rules was imposed on the Authority, which required 'that nothing is included in the programmes which offends against good taste or decency or is likely to encourage or incite to crime or to lead to disorder or to be offensive to public feelings or which contains any offensive representation of or reference to a living person'.

A proper balance was required in subject matter and a high general standard of quality. Due 'accuracy and impartiality' were required for the presentation of any news given in programmes, in whatever form. There were also to be 'proper proportions' in terms of British productions and performance in order to safeguard against the dumping of American material.

Of vital significance in the Act were the elaborate precautions that were taken to prevent advertisers gaining control of programme content. The governing body of ITV set up by the Act was similar in size and function to that of the BBC, with seven to ten governors each serving for five years and dismissible at the behest of the Postmaster-General. Like the BBC, the ITA was to have a limited period of existence, followed by parliamentary review and renewal. See SOUND BROADCASTING ACT (UK), 1972.

Television broadcasting Technical developments in the UK, the Soviet Union and the US combined to make TV a feasibility by 1931 when a research group was set up in Britain under Isaac Shoenberg, who had had considerable experience in radio transmission technology in the Soviet Union. He furthered the evolution of a practical system of TV broadcasting based on a camera tube known as the Emitrion and an improved cathode-ray tube for the receiver. Shoenberg elected to develop a system of electronic scanning that proved far superior to the mechanical scanning method pioneered by Scotsman John Logie Baird (1889–1946), who had first demonstrated his system publicly in 1926.

The BBC was authorized by government to adopt Shoenberg's standards (405 lines) for the world's first high-definition service, which was launched in 1936 – a system that proved sufficiently successful to continue in the UK until 1962, when the European continental 625-line system was introduced. In the US, TV was slower to develop. It was not until 30 April 1939, at the opening of the New York World's Fair, that a public demonstration was made by the National Broadcasting Company (NBC).

The BBC's nascent TV service closed down during the Second World War (1939–45), which also hampered TV development in America, though by 1949, there were a million receivers in the US and, by 1951, 10 million. In the UK, TV transmission resumed in June 1946. Swiftly TV became, in terms of reach, diversity and popularity of content, the most influential and most powerful form of mass communication. The arrival of colour, transmission by cable and satellite, the possibilities of VIDEO recording and eventually DIGITIZATION confirmed and carried forward the Age of Information while at the same time turning it into the Age of the Image.

While TV has displaced, and sometimes marginalized other forms of communication, it has also proved their willing customer, borrowing and adapting forms from print, RADIO and cinema, in turn proving for them a constant source of material: how, for example, would popular newspapers survive without 'stories' from TV dramas such as SOAPS? TV fact and fiction have become so much a part of the culture of the modern age that they have become its benchmarks and its reality.

What's real, is what is on TV; who appears on TV is deemed real. If an event does not appear on TV it is argued (at a metaphysical level) that the EVENT has really not taken place. Because of the nature of the medium, TV accentuates the image over the word, the dramatic over the analytical, and critics such as Neil Postman, in *Amusing Ourselves to Death* (UK: Methuen, 1986), claim that TV transforms all things into pure entertainment.

TV delivers audiences to advertisers; in turn advertisers use TV to reinforce the dominance of the image, in their case the image arising from imperatives of consumerism. TV news is seen to be a window on the world, a view attracting critical attention from media analysts who see in its underlying intentions frameworks essentially western in orientation, highly selective and thus offering a skewed vision of the world.

TV is where partnerships are forged, between sport and business. It is the venue of lifestyle, the route to celebrity, and for these and many other reasons it is a battleground between those who are ambitious to control it, the axis of the ongoing struggle between public and private ownership. The study of the effects, influence, impact and power of the media largely centres on TV and the questions prompting answers are legion: does TV and its blizzard of images confuse rather than clarify; does it distract rather than aid attention; does it fulfil the fears of those who (subscribing to the notion of a so-termed three-minute culture) rob viewers of the ability to concentrate for more than a few moments at a time; does its constant plethora of images of violence desensitize audiences to examples of violence in the real world? In brief, what *cultural differences* has TV brought about? See *TOPIC GUIDE* under BROAD-CASTING; MEDIA INSTITUTIONS; MEDIA: POLITICS AND ECONOMICS; MEDIA: POWER, EFFECTS, INFLUENCE.

* Anthony Smith (ed.), and Richard Patterson (associate ed.), *Television: An International History* (UK: Oxford University Press, 1998); Asa Briggs and Peter Burke, *A Social History of the Media: From Gutenberg to the Internet* (UK: Polity, 2002).

Television drama In an interview printed in *The New Priesthood: British Television Today* (UK: Allen Lane, 1970) edited by J. Bakewell and N. Garnham, TV playwright Dennis Potter (1935–95) said of TV, 'It's the biggest platform in the world's history and writers who don't want to kick and elbow their way on to it must be disowning something in themselves.' While the PILKINGTON COMMITTEE REPORT ON BROADCASTING (UK), 1962, found that the chief 'crime' of TV was triviality, much of TV drama (from the very first drama production on experimental TV, the BBC's *The Man with a Flower in his Mouth* by Luigi Pirandello, on 14 July 1930) has been a striking exception to that judgement. In fact few might argue with the claim that TV's most substantial achievement has been to encourage generations of quality dramatists working specially for the medium, and a canon of plays, from both the BBC and commercial TV companies, to rival anything produced in the live theatre during the same post-Second World War period.

In the early days of TV drama, plays were stage-bound or, more accurately, studio-bound, both in concept and execution, taking for their model the theatre rather than the cinema, but the ideas of young directors making their mark during the 1960s, excited by the possibility of film drama, prevailed. Nell Dunn's *Up the Junction* (BBC, 1965) marked the first occasion when virtually the whole story was done on film. The camera was seen to be as important as the pen; indeed the camera in many ways became the pen. The social – and sometimes political – themes favoured by many writers and directors took the cameras more and more out of the studio and into 'real life', and many plays looked like, and had the impact of, documentary.

Produced by Tony Garnett, written by Jeremy Sandford and directed by Ken Loach, *Cathy Come Home* (BBC, 1966) detailed the decline into tragedy of a homeless family in affluent Britain. The sense of reality was almost unbearable: the camera was often hand-held, the scenes staged so realistically that the audience was tempted to forget it was watching something constructed, not something happening before their very eyes.

The intimacy, the close scrutiny of humans under stress at which film and TV can excel, has rarely been used to more disturbing effect than with John Hopkin's quartet of plays *Talking to a Stranger* (BBC, 1966), described as the first authentic masterpiece of television. The immediacy of the medium was stunningly demonstrated in Colin Welland's epic *Leeds United!* (BBC, 1974) about Leeds clothing workers who went on strike spontaneously in 1970 for an extra 10 pence an hour: the camera became part of the ongoing action to such an extent that it was impossible to detect what had been scripted and what was happening for real.

Much of this kind of drama obviously grew from the opportunities of the moment, and from improvisation – a method used most notably by Mike Leigh, who works with actors for long periods before filming, encouraging them to 'become' the characters, and eventually invent or improvise their speech and actions.

Such experimental screen drama was soon to hit the buffers of economic necessity. In a 1982 publication for the IBA, *Television and Radio,* David Cunliffe, then Head of Drama at Yorkshire TV, wrote: 'The inescapable fact is that over the last few years the television single play has spiralled in production costs and plummeted in popularity.' Having moved from the studio to location, plays had become 'nearly Hollywood-size movies'. Cunliffe cited dramas such as Potter's LWT series, *Rain on the Roof, Blade on the Feather* and *Cream in My Coffee* as works that, despite their quality as drama, appealed to 'relatively small sections of viewers'. The death knell had more or less been sounded for the one-off play and increasingly in the following years dramatists turned to writing TV serials, which have more over-time impact and are more saleable commodities on the international programme market, and adapting classics such as novels by Jane Austen and Charles Dickens.

Today crime dominates TV drama, in mini- or long-running series: cops, prosecutors, forensic scientists, psychologists specializing in crime are in, the recipes for the GENRE being tweaked here and there – by reaching for greater and greater actuality or by reversing traditional NARRATIVES (by putting women in charge of men for a change) or by abandoning the good guys/bad guys format in preference for closer examination of criminals as individuals. Much contemporary crime drama on TV seeks to explore the pressures on personal relationships, on marriages, on families, resulting from the dedication of those employed to protect the law and apprehend the lawbreakers.

In a rare case of cross-channel cooperation, the BBC and Channel 4 in 1996, combined in the production of Dennis Potter's two last plays for TV, *Karaoke* and *Cold Lazarus*. They proved Potter's epitaph, but also closed the chapter in TV drama of which he was the most outstanding exemplar. See CAMPAIGN FOR QUALITY TELEVISION REPORT (UK), 1999.

---

* John Tulloch, *Television Drama: Agency, Audience and Myth* (UK: Routledge, 1990); David Paget, *No Other Way to Tell It: Dramadoc/Docudrama on Television* (UK: Manchester University Press, 1998).

Television news: inherent limitations In analysing the degree of 'informedness' between viewers of TV news and readers of newspapers, two American researchers found that TV makes for less effective *retention* than the printed page. John P. Robinson and Dennis K. Davis in 'Television news and the informed public: an information-processing approach', *Journal of Communication*, Summer 1990, found that in none of their studies 'do viewers of TV news programs emerge as more informed than newspaper readers'.

They identify seven inherent limitations of TV as an information medium: (1) a TV newscast has fewer words and ideas per news story than appear in a front-page story in a quality newspaper; (2) attention to a newscast is distracted and fragmented compared to attention when reading; (3) TV newscasts provide little of the repetition of information, or redundancy, necessary for comprehension; (4) TV viewers cannot 'turn back' to, or review, information they do not understand or that they need to know to understand subsequent information; (5) print news stories are more clearly delineated, with headlines, columns etc.; (6) TV news programmes fail to coordinate pictures and text; and (7) TV has more limited opportunity to review and develop an entire story. It is the authors' view that 'while TV has the power to evoke empathy and interest, time and other constraints prevent this power from being exercised'. See *TOPIC GUIDE* under NEWS MEDIA.

'Television without frontiers' See EUROPEAN COMMUNITY AND MEDIA: TELEVISION WITHOUT FRONTIERS.

Telex Worldwide link-up system providing a rapid means of communicating written messages, via teleprinter among subscribers, combining the speed of the telephone with the accuracy and authority of the printed word. A printed copy of the message is available at both the sending and receiving teleprinters. Calls can be made to any telex subscriber in the UK and overseas 24 hours a day, and messages may be transmitted to a subscriber even though his/her machine is unattached, provided it remains switched on. A telemessage (inland) and a telegram (overseas) can also be sent from a telex teleprinter to a Post Office telegraph office or to Cable & Wireless Telegraph offices for onward transmission at normal telephone rates, and incoming telemessages can be accepted directly on the teleprinter.

Telstar Communications satellite launched on 10 July 1962; transmitted the first live TV pictures between the US and Europe. See SATELLITE TRANSMISSION.

Ten commandments for media consumers In 'Ethics for media users', published in the *European Journal of Communication*, December 1995, Cees J. Hamelink discusses the role the viewer, reader and listener should adopt in relation to the 'quest for freedom, quality and responsibility in media performance', arguing that the consumer must not only beware of the nature of media messages but be proactive in responding to them. The ten 'commandments' Hamelink suggests in order to assist the consumer with moral choices concerning the media are as follows. Thou shalt: (1) be an alert and discriminating media consumer; (2) actively fight all forms of censorship; (3) not unduly interfere with editorial independence; (4) guard against racism and sexist stereotyping in the media; (5) seek alternative sources of information; (6) demand a pluralist supply of information; (7) protect thine own privacy; (8) be a reliable source of information; (9) not participate in chequebook journalism; and (10) demand accountability from media producers.

The author, however, cautions against over-reliance on such a code of user response, for moral issues and dilemmas ought to be addressed according to situation and context, a point well made when we take a global view of the 'commandments'. A pre-existing code must not be imposed on a situation, rather, the situation must be examined in the light of evolving and changing approaches to moral dilemmas. See *TOPIC GUIDE* under MEDIA ISSUES AND DEBATES; MEDIA: VALUES AND IDEOLOGY.

Tenth art See VIDEO GAMES.

Terrestrial broadcasting That which is transmitted from the ground and not via SATELLITE.

Territoriality The need in humans and animals to establish and maintain private territory. Several elements of SPATIAL BEHAVIOUR may be employed by both individuals and groups to mark and defend territory. For example, the use of furniture and belongings to signify claim to a particular space.

Terrorism: Anti-Terrorism, Crime and Security Act (UK), 2001 Following the destruction of New York's World Trade Center twin towers on 11 September 2001, the UK government hastened to tighten the law on a whole range of matters, some of them directly affecting media communication. The 125-clause Terrorism Act allows for the arrest and internment for up to six months of suspected terrorists. It permits confidential information about an individual helped by any government agency to be disclosed to the intelligence services and the police – for any criminal investigation, not just for investigations of alleged terrorist offences.

A new offence, incitement to religious hatred, is introduced; a blanket provision that, arguably, could criminalize criticism of, or humour about, religions and religious practices. Liberal-Democrat MP Simon Hughes said of the Act that it was 'a mixture of the welcome, the reasonable, the worrying and the completely unacceptable'. Clause 93 makes it a punishable offence for anyone to refuse a police request to remove a disguise, such as a mask or face paint. See REGULATION OF INVESTIGATORY POWERS ACT (RIPA) (UK), 2000.

Terrorism as communication The main aim of terrorist activity in liberal democracies is publicity. The existence of a free press, and TV and radio companies independent of government authority within societies that subscribe to the sanctity of the individual's right to life, provides fertile ground for headline-seeking by acts of terror such as hijacks and abductions. 'The modern terrorist makes maximum use of mass media,' writes Dan van der Vat in *Index on Censorship* 2 (1982). 'Little more than a century ago, before the invention of the rotary press, he would have been inconceivable; he came into his own only in the last 15 years or even less, when television became an instantaneous medium, capable of sending live pictures round the globe by satellite.'

On 11 September 2001 the United States became victim of the most dramatic, daring and devastating act of terrorism with the destruction of the twin towers of New York's World Trade Center by means of hijacked passenger aircraft, and a similar onslaught on the country's military HQ, the Pentagon. In the case of New York, cameras recorded the tragedy as it happened. Millions of people across the world witnessed the vulnerability of even the most powerful nation in the world, and varyingly read messages into that sudden vulnerability.

The events of '9/11' could be seen as a publicity triumph, at least in the sense that the acts of terror drew attention to a number of issues. However, there can have been little satisfaction felt by the perpetrators of the carnage when American military wrath was felt by Afghanistan, accused of acting as host to the terrorists responsible. Terror, in this case, was answered by terror, leaving resolution of many issues as distant as ever. See *TOPIC GUIDE* under MEDIA ISSUES AND DEBATES; MEDIA: POWER, EFFECTS, INFLUENCE.

Text According to Tim O'Sullivan, John Hartley, Danny Saunders, and John Fiske in *Key Concepts in Communication* (UK: Methuen, 1983), text refers to '… a signifying structure composed of signs and codes which is essential to communication'. This structure can take a variety of forms: film, speech, writing, painting, records, for example. O'Sullivan *et al.* argue that the word text usually '… refers to a message that has a physical existence of its own, independent of its sender and receiver and thus composed of representational codes'.

Text is the focal point of study in SEMIOLOGY/SEMIOTICS. Texts are not normally seen as being unproblematic but as capable of being interpreted in a variety of ways, depending on the socio-cultural background and experience of the reader. The central concern of semiology is to discover the ways in which given texts can generate a range of meanings.

Occupying the special attention of analysts in recent years is the relationship between texts, the way they interconnect, interweave and interact upon one another. *Intertextuality* operates essentially in the perception and experience of AUDIENCE; a TV movie tells the story of a serial killer; TV news reports carnage caused by a madman loose with a machine-gun; on the way to work the viewer sees a massive poster advertising *Silence of the Lambs: The Sequel.* What does he or she make of all this, and how does one text influence another in the mind's eye?

Of course intertextuality works at the level of simple publicity and promotion. A film may be writ large in our consciousness, but perhaps not only because of the power of the individual text: there will have been trailers, publicity material, interviews with the stars on TV; there will have been conversation about it.

The power of intertextuality is to blur the boundaries between individual texts. For example, which is the text in a promo-video – the chart-busting song of the rock group, the video of the performance, the presentation of that video on *Top of the Pops* or all of these as a package of texts that themselves link in with previous songs/videos by the group and by other groups, and features in fan magazines or celebrity appearances in support of AIDS research? Roland Barthes, the French media philosopher, was of the view that culture is a web of intertextuality and that texts tend to refer essentially to one another rather than anchor their referral in reality. See CODES; DECODER; ENCODER; MESSAGE; NARRATIVE. See also *TOPIC GUIDE* under LANGUAGE/DISCOURSE/NARRATIVE; TEXTUAL ANALYSIS.

Text: integrity of the text With the coming of the INTERNET, two major issues concern the producers of texts – books, articles, scripts, photographs, music, etc. – the questions of *integrity* of the text and of *paternity.* Copyright laws have until now protected the work of an author. While a book can be quoted from, it cannot be reprinted, reproduced in any way or altered without due permission. The net, as yet an open space for the communication of items of all kinds, uncontrolled by traditional regulation and so far evasive of what controls, legal and technical, might be applied, threatens to rob texts of integrity and to ignore their paternity (that is, the right of the author, composer, artist or performer to command 'ownership' of the text).

In short, networking is open to the abuse of SOURCE; indeed, texts often soar through CYBERSPACE with little or no acknowledgement of source. Released from the tie of ownership – possibly doctored in whole or in part for whatever reason – are texts reliable any more? Does authorship continue to have any meaning?

The *moral rights* of paternity and integrity are enshrined in the Berne Convention. They are central to the UK's Copyright Designs and Patents Act (1988). The right of paternity is the right to be identified as the author of a copyright work, and that includes adaptations, film rights, etc. The major exception in the Berne Convention is authorship of the 'news of the day'. The UK Copyright Act also excludes from protection all work made for the reporting of current events, and this includes articles in newspapers and journals. See *TOPIC GUIDE* under MEDIA ISSUES AND DEBATES.

Texts See OPEN, CLOSED TEXTS.

Text: tertiary text The primary TEXT is that which is produced and transmitted – the painting, the poem, the poster, the film; the secondary text is that which members of an AUDIENCE receive, what is perceived as the text. The tertiary text results when the first two texts are translated into conversation between members of the audience, their families and friends. John Fiske uses the term in *Television Culture* (UK: Methuen, 1987) to denote the many uses media messages can be put to, interpretative, analytical, affirmative or rejective. The existence of the tertiary text indicates that audience has within its capacity the potential to be independent of the PREFERRED READING residing in the primary text (see AUDIENCE: ACTIVE AUDIENCE; EMPOWERMENT; RESPONSE CODES).

A more general use of the terms primary and secondary is current. The primary text is that which is produced – the novel, the film, the TV soap. Secondary texts arise out of the first, and these may take many forms – publicity, trailers, critiques, interviews with the author or director, documentaries, translations into other creative forms (a novel into a movie or a TV series). Secondary texts at least begin as dependants upon the primary text; they are its satellites. However, these may become more and more divorced from connection with the original until, arguably, they become primary texts in their own right. Where texts interact, interconnect and are interdependent we have what is termed *intertextuality* (see TEXT).

Thaumatrope Or 'wonder-turner'; a small cardboard disc, having different images on each surface, threaded on two pieces of silk or string which, when twisted, creates a joining of images, thus illustrating the phenomenon of PERSISTENCE OF VISION. The device was first produced by the English doctor J.A. Paris in 1826. See ZOETROPE.

Theatre censorship See LORD CHAMBERLAIN.

Theories and concepts of communication See *TOPIC GUIDE* under AUDIENCES/CONSUMPTION AND RECEPTION OF MEDIA; COMMUNICATION THEORY; COMMUNICATION MODELS; LANGUAGE/DISCOURSE/NARRATIVE; MEDIA: POWER, EFFECTS, INFLUENCE; MEDIA: VALUES AND IDEOLOGY; REPRESENTATION.

3-D The technique of filming and projecting movie pictures that gives the illusion of their being three-dimensional. See STEREOSCOPY.

Third-person effect Where we judge the impact/influence of the media to be stronger on others than ourselves; this effect is countenanced largely when the media message is negative or when persuasion by the MESSAGE is perceived to be less than desirable. In other words, *we* might not be affected, but others – usually at a social distance – are more likely to be.

Tie-signs Any action – GESTURE or posture – that indicates the existence of a personal relationship is termed a tie-sign: linked arms, held hands, body closeness (or proximity), comfortable silence between two people, instinctive reciprocal movements. *Symbolic* tie-signs are wedding rings, lovers' tree engravings, etc. See COMMUNICATION, NON-VERBAL; PROXEMICS.

Time-lapse photography See HIGH-SPEED PHOTOGRAPHY.

Time-shift viewing Made possible by the introduction of the video-recorder. By recording TV programmes, the viewer is released from the schedules of the broadcasting companies to watch his/her programmes whenever and as often as desired.

Touch Not the least important of the five senses, though often the most neglected. H.F. Harlow in *Learning to Love* (US: Albion, 1971) writes of his now famous experiments with baby monkeys. He had found that the deprivation of physical contact resulted in a failure to learn necessary responses to their own society. They became non-sociable, were unable to mate successfully or to rear their young.

Touch is an important ingredient in the transmitting of information, especially in the young when other channels of communication such as speech are undeveloped. In western society the incidence of touching between people begins to diminish when a child reaches the age of five or six, with males being touched less than females; it increases again in the teenage period, where touching and sex become equated to such an extent that touch becomes a sexual indicator unless applied by validated 'touchers' such as doctors, tailors or hairdressers.

CLASS, STATUS and ROLES are inextricably involved in touch-permission or touch-prohibition: a nurse may touch a patient, but it is not usual for a patient to touch the nurse, where it constitutes a trespass. Self-touching is acceptable, unless it becomes socially offensive (like nose-picking), as a form of substitution for the touch of others – face- and head-touching, hair-stroking or hand-wringing, for example.

Where we cannot touch other humans we substitute pets, stroking them and cuddling them, receiving (and perhaps giving) sensations of comfort. In illness and stress, in times of grief or great happiness, touching becomes more necessary and more acceptable. Touching can communicate reassurance, affection, friendship, courage-giving, support, sharing, understanding, invitation, desire, etc., as well as on occasions, hostility and aggression. The practice varies considerably from class to class, CULTURE to culture and country to country, and from hemisphere to hemisphere. See COMMUNICATION, NON-VERBAL; EYE CONTACT; GESTURE; INTERPERSONAL COMMUNICATION; NON-VERBAL BEHAVIOUR: REPERTOIRE; PROXEMICS.

Tracks In film-making, tracks are the portable 'railway lines' along which the camera, mounted on a dolly, moves. The term is also used to identify separate sound reels accompanying a film. These are harmonized into one at the dubbing stage of film production.

Traditional transmission US linguist Charles Hockett defined 16 design features characteristic of human language, of which traditional transmission is one, described in Hockett's 'The origin of speech',

Scientific American 203 (1960). This design feature refers to the passing on of language from one generation to the next. 'Human genes,' Hockett writes, 'carry the capacity to acquire a language, and probably also a strong drive towards its acquisition, the detailed conventions of any one language are transmitted extra-genetically by learning and teaching.'

Traffic data Information about a message sent electronically – by whom, to whom, when (excluding contents of the message itself). Refers to e-mails, websites and TELEPHONE calls. Phone bills include all traffic data, time, destination and length of call. In the case of mobiles the data includes the base station used.

Transactional analysis Originally an approach to psychotherapy introduced by Eric Berne, transactional analysis is now more widely used as a technique for improving INTERPERSONAL COMMUNICATION and social skills. In essence it aims to increase the individual's awareness of the intent behind both his or her own and others' communication, and to expose and eliminate, or deal with, subterfuge and dishonesty.

The details of the framework are fairly complex and readers are referred to the works recommended below for an introduction to this area. Basically, however, transactional analysis investigates any act of interpersonal communication by considering what are called the 'ego states' of the communicators.

The hypothesis is that we are all able to function out of three 'ego states', which Berne identified as the Parent, the Adult and the Child. The states are produced by a playback of recorded data of events in the past involving real people; real times, places and decisions; and real feelings. Everyone is seen as carrying these voices inside them. We interact out of these 'ego states'.

The Parent is much influenced by the pronouncements of and examples set by our own parents and other authority figures, early in our life. It is concerned with our responsibility towards ourselves and others. It can be critical and set standards but it can also be protective and caring. The Adult within us is the part of us that rationally analyses reality. It collects information and thinks it through in order to solve problems, reach conclusions and judgements, and make decisions. The Adult develops throughout life and can arbitrate between the Parent and the Child. The Child is one of our most powerful states; it contains our feelings and carries our ability to play and act creatively. It can be spontaneous and risk-taking. It can also be rebellious or alternatively compliant or servile.

A *transaction* is a two-person interaction in which an ego state of one person stimulates an ego state of another. Transactions are analysed by assessing out of which 'ego state' people are speaking. We can distinguish these states in ourselves and others by such non-verbal cues as tone of voice or facial expression, as well as by the verbal content of the transactions. One of the chief values of transactional analysis (TA) is that it has the capacity to help clarify communication problems.

Other concepts commonly emplyed in TA are *Games*, LIFE POSITIONS and SCRIPTS. Eric Berne in *Games People Play* (UK: Penguin, 1964) describes a game as 'an ongoing series of complementary ulterior transactions progressing to a well-defined, predictable outcome'. Games are recurring sets of transactions, identifiable by their hidden motivations and the promise of psychological payoffs or gains for the game players.

The victim of the game is call a *mark*, and it is the known weakness of the mark, known as the *gimmick*, that allows the game player to hook his victim and achieve his/her desired *payoff*. Every game, Berne believes, whether played consciously or unconsciously, is essentially dishonest; generally taking the form of a defensive strategy in communication as far as the manipulator is concerned. Examples of such games played in everyday life, identified by Berne, are 'If it weren't for you' and 'See what you made me do'.

* Eric Berne, *What Do You Say After You Say Hello?* (UK: Corgi Books, 1975); T.A. Harris, *I'm O.K. You're O.K.* (US: Harper & Row, 1969); Ian Stewart and Vann Joines, *TA Today* (UK: Lifespace, 1987); Amy and Thomas Harris, *Staying O.K.* (UK: Arrow Books, 1995).

Transculturation The movement of cultural forms across geographical boundaries and periods of time resulting in cross-cultural interaction that may give rise to new cultural forms. See HYBRIDIZATION.

Transmission model of mass communication See ATTENTION MODEL OF MASS COMMU-NICATION.

Trigger events See AGENDA-SETTING: TRIGGER EVENTS.

Truth, visualization of See VISIONS OF ORDER.

TV: independent producers See TELEVISION: INDEPENDENT PRODUCERS.

Two-step flow model of communication See ONE-STEP, TWO-STEP, MULTI-STEP FLOW MODELS OF COMMUNICATION.

Typewriter A patent for an 'Artificial Machine or Method for Impressing or Transcribing of Letters Singly or Progressively one after another, as in Writing, whereby all Writing Whatever may be Engrossed in Paper or Parchment so Neat and Exact as not to be distinguished from Print' was taken out in the UK as early as 1714, but the first practical typewriter working faster than handwriting was probably that of American Christopher Latham Sholes (1868) who, after several improvements to his machine, signed up with E. Remington & Sons, gunsmiths of New York. The first Remington machines were marketed in 1874.

1878 saw the introduction of the shift-key typewriter, followed by machines that for the first time allowed the typist to actually see what he/she was typing (1883). That jack-of-all-trades among inventors, Thomas Alva Edison (1847–1931), produced an electrically operated machine containing a printing wheel, in 1872, though it was many years before a commercially viable electric machine was produced (by James Smathes in 1920).

IBM introduced the famous 'golf ball' electric typewriter in 1961, allowing for different typefaces and type sizes to be used with the same machine. Today electronic typewriters – or word-processors – possess the mind and memory of a computer; they self-correct, they work silently, they can bank text, which is recalled at the press of a button and they can print out at considerable speed. See *TOPIC GUIDE* under MEDIA HISTORY; MEDIA: TECHNOLOGIES.

U

U-certificate See CERTIFICATION OF FILMS.

UK Gold Launched on 1 November 1992, UK Gold is a satellite and cable channel run jointly by BBC Enterprises and Thames Television based on their combined programme libraries.

Ullswater Committee Report on Broadcasting, 1936 This government-appointed committee under the chairmanship of Viscount Ullswater was given the task of making recommendations on the future of the BBC once its first charter expired on 31 December 1936. The report praised the BBC for its impartiality and catholicity but chided it for the heaviness of its Sunday entertainment. The Charter of the BBC was renewed following the report for another ten years; the number of governors was increased from five to seven and the ban on advertisements was to continue – though sponsorship was to be permitted in the case of TV (a right the BBC only seldom exploited).

Like reports before and after it, Ullswater made clear the very serious public responsibility of BROADCASTING: 'The influence of broadcasting upon the mind and speech of the nation' made it an 'urgent necessity in the national interest that the broadcasting service should at all times be conducted in the best possible manner and to the best possible advantage of the people.' Two other matters elicited concern. The first related to criticisms of the monolithic nature of the BBC (under the rigorous direction of Lord Reith – see REITHIAN) and the Committee recommended more internal decentralization of control, especially towards the national regions.

The second concern, published in a Reservation written by Clement Attlee (1883–1967), future Labour Prime Minister, called into question the BBC's 'impartiality' at the time of the General Strike (1926): 'I think,' wrote Attlee, 'that even in war-time the BBC must be allowed to broadcast opinions other than those of the Government.' See PUBLIC SERVICE BROADCASTING (PSB). See also *TOPIC GUIDE* under COMMISSIONS, COMMITTEES, LEGISLATION.

Ultra-violet/fluorescent photography Used in the examination of forged or altered documents, identifying certain chemical compounds, and in the examination of bacterial colonies. See HOLOGRAPHY; INFRA-RED PHOTOGRAPHY.

Underground press Or radical, alternative or SAMIZDAT; those newspapers that are committedly anti-establishment, opposing in part or entirely the political and cultural conventions of the time; often publishing information or views seen as threatening by those in authority, and likely to incur CENSORSHIP.

In the UK the so-called 'pauper press' of the nineteenth century, finding its readership in the increasingly literate working class, was subject to harshly repressive measures by government. Editors such as William Cobbett, Henry Hetherington, William Sherwin, Richard Carlile and James Watson courted arrest and imprisonment, and the shutting-down of their presses as a routine professional hazard. Wooler's *Black Dwarf* stirred the government to wrath with its criticism of the authorities in their handling of the Peterloo Massacre (1819). Wooler escaped libel action on the plea that he could not be said to have written articles that he set up in type without the interventions of a pen.

Cobbett's *Weekly Political Register* had a substantial circulation despite the crippling STAMP DUTY that forced him to charge one shilling and a halfpenny per copy. Carlile's *Republican* was both republican and atheist; the Chartist *Oracle of Reason* incurred blasphemy prosecutions while Bradlaugh's *National Reformer* declared itself 'Published in Defiance of Her Majesty's Government'. So long as radical newspapers could fight off the need to win ADVERTISING, they could survive, despite prosecutions. Edited by people close to the working class, they reflected the chief perspectives of the vanguard of the working-class movement and directed themselves to its increased politicization. They were dependent, however, paying their way through circulation and subscription alone.

The costs of publishing and the reliance upon advertising proved increasingly formidable barriers to underground, radical or alternative newspapers and periodicals in the post-Second World War period (from 1945). In the 1960s they abounded – *Oz, IT, Frendz* and *Ink* – all in one way or another getting up the nose of authority, the *Oz School Kids Issue* earning for itself the longest-ever obscenity trial (see OZ TRIAL).

Distribution has proved yet another hazard for the small radical press. In the UK this is practically a duopoly of W.H.Smith and Menzies, whose hesitancy over providing the radical press with distribution outlets has been rather more to do with a view that radicals are just not good business rather than for ideological reasons.

In the March/April 1994 edition of *Free Press*, the news sheet of the CAMPAIGN FOR PRESS AND BROADCASTING FREEDOM, Tony Harcup mourned the decline in the Thatcher–Major years of the radical regional press. In '*Northern Star* silenced', an obituary for the *Leeds Other Paper/Northern Star*, he points out that where in 1980 there had been more than 70 local alternative papers covering towns and cities in the UK, there were now only two, *Peninsula Voice* covering Cornwall west of Truro and Penzance, and the *West Highland Free Press*. The *LOP/Northern Star*, having survived 20 years, went into liquidation after 820 issues on 20 January 1994. It had been, in Harcup's words, 'a beacon of radical journalism … a thorn in the side of the local establishment'.

Ironically the paper had made as many enemies on the Left as the Right in local politics: 'The paper was too anarchistic for some Labour party members; too rank and filist for some union officials; too male dominated for some feminists; too pro-feminist for many men.'

Perhaps the future for radical JOURNALISM lies not in print and paper but in the relatively cost-free 'pages' of the INTERNET, where the political readership is both local and global. See *TOPIC GUIDE* under MEDIA HISTORY.

---

* Stanley Harrison, *Poor Men's Guardians: A Survey of the Struggles for a Democratic Newspaper Press, 1763–1973* (UK: Lawrence & Wishart, 1974); Patricia Hollis, *The Pauper Press* (UK: Oxford University Press, 1970); Stephen Koss, *The Rise and Fall of the Political Press in Britain* (UK: Collins, 1990); Kevin Williams, *Get Me a Murder a Day! A History of Mass Communication in Britain* (UK: Arnold, 1997); Elisabeth Eisenstein, *The Printing Press as an Agent of Change* (UK: Cambridge University Press, 1999); Chris Atton, *Alternative Media* (UK: Sage, 2001); John D.H. Downing (with Tamara Vallareal Ford, Geneve Gil and Laura Stern), *Radical Media: Rebellious Communication and Social Movements* (US/UK: Sage, 2001).

Unitary, pluralist, core-periphery, breakup models of audience fragmentation See AUDIENCE: FRAGMENTATION OF.

Universality Principle that public services such as education, health and justice must be available to all within a society; applies equally to the notion of PUBLIC SERVICE BROADCASTING (PSB).

USA – Patriot Act, 2001 Surveillance measure that became law within a month of the terrorist attacks on New York and the Pentagon, 11 September 2001. Under its full title, Strengthening America by Providing Appropriate Tools Required to Intercept and Obstruct Terrorism, the Patriot Act – all 342 pages of it – provides the US government and its agencies with a formidable armoury of new powers to rein in civil liberties. Basically security agencies are granted extended powers to intercept wire, oral and electronic communications relating to terrorism; to share criminal investigation information; to seize voice-mail messages pursuant to warrants; to use DNA identification of terrorists and other violent offenders; to demand disclosure of educational records; and to confiscate the assets of organizations suspected of planning or carrying out terrorism.

In its analysis of the Act, the Electronic Frontier Foundation talks of a 'rush job'; of 'sweeping new powers' that eliminate 'the checks and balances that previously gave courts the opportunity to ensure that these powers were not abused'. The EEF is of the view that 'The civil liberties of ordinary Americans have taken a tremendous blow with this law, especially the right to privacy in our online communications and activities', believing that 'there is no evidence that our previous civil liberties posed a barrier to the effective tracking or persecution of terrorists … the opportunities for abuse of these broad new powers are immense'.

Nancy Chang, Senior Litigation Attorney at the Centre for Constitutional Rights, New York, calls the Act 'a blatant power grab'. In *Silencing Political Dissent: How Post-September 11 Antiterrorism Measures Threaten Our Civil Liberties* (US: Seven Stories Press, 2002), she states that the Act 'grants the executive unprecedented, and largely unchecked, surveillance powers including the enhanced ability to track e-mail and Internet usage, conduct sneak-and-peek searches, obtain sensitive personal records, monitor financial transactions and conduct nationwide wiretaps'.

The author believes the Act 'sacrifices our political freedoms in the name of national security and upsets the democratic values that define the nation by consolidating vast new powers in the executive branch of government'. Chang sees terrorism status being conflated with immigration status in the Act. Its power, however, might be seen to embrace the potential activities of all forms of protesters – environmental or anti-globalization activists, for example – virtually outlawing direct action.

Use of media by the young See CHILDREN, YOUNG PEOPLE AND THE CHANGING MEDIA ENVIRONMENT.

Uses and gratifications theory View that mass media audiences make active use of what the media have to offer arising from a complex set of needs that the media in one form or another gratify. Broadly similar uses have been categorized by researchers based on questionnaires or interviews. An example is the *compensatory use* of the media – to make up for lack of education, perhaps, lack of STATUS or social success. Where the media have a *supplementing use*, the AUDIENCE may be applying what they see, hear and read in social situations – as subject-matter for conversation, for example.

In 'The television audience: a revised perspective', in Dennis McQuail (ed.), *Sociology of the Mass Media* (UK: Penguin, 1972) McQuail, Jay G. Blumler and J.R. Brown define four major categories of need which the media serve to gratify. (1) *Diversion* (escape from constraints of routine; escape from the burdens of problems; emotional release). (2) *Personal relationships* (companionship; social utility). (3) *Personal identity* (personal reference; reality exploration; value reinforcement). (4) *Surveillance* (need for information in our complex world – 'Television news helps me to make up my mind about things').

Blumler and Elihu Katz in the book of which they are editors, *The Uses of Mass Communication* (US: Sage, 1974), emphasize the social origin of the needs that the media purport to gratify. Thus where a social situation causes tension and conflict, the media may provide easement, or where the social situation gives rise to questions about VALUES, the media provide affirmation and REINFORCEMENT.

Uses and gratifications theory has been subjected to criticism by a number of commentators. In *The Export of Meaning: Cross-Cultural Readings of 'Dallas'* (US: Oxford University Press; UK: Polity Press, 1993), Tamar Liebes and Elihu Katz state, 'The idea that readers, listeners, and viewers can bend the mass media to serve their own needs had gone so far [with gratificationists] that almost any text – or indeed no text at all – was found to serve functions such as social learning, reinforcing identity, lubricating interaction, providing escape, etc. But it gradually became clear that these functions were too unspecified.' In other words, theorizing about use needs to be based, specifically, upon the TEXTS that are judged to fulfil audience needs; and no less importantly, *how* such texts gratify needs. See COGNITIVE (AND AFFECTIVE); IDENTIFICATION; MASLOW'S HIERARCHY OF NEEDS. See also *TOPIC GUIDE* under COMMUNICATION THEORY.

Utterance meaning See SENTENCE MEANING, UTTERANCE MEANING.

V

Validity effect Carole Wade and Carol Tavris in *Psychology* (US: HarperCollins, 1993) discuss the findings of studies conducted by Hal Arkes (1991) in which he demonstrated that people had a tendency to believe a statement was true, was valid, if it were repeated frequently enough; no other means of persuasion was necessary. This phenomenon is known as the *validity effect*.

VALS typology Arnold Mitchell's *Nine American Lifestyles: Who We Are and Where We're Going* (US: Macmillan, 1983) describes a landmark in the documentation of human needs – a massive research project funded and carried out in America in 1980 by SRI International. The principle on which the research was based and which Mitchell's influential book articulates is that humans demonstrate their needs in their lifestyle and that both needs and lifestyle fluctuate according to circumstance and 'drive'. VALS stands for Values and Lifestyle.

The VALS approach, and its typology of categories of lifestyle, pigeon-hole people on an all-embracing scale. It has given a significant boost to marketing trends that have increasingly been preoccupied with *segmenting* people into consumer categories. VALS links the pursuit of lifestyle with personal growth: 'With this growth comes change, so that new goals emerge, and in support of these new goals come new beliefs, new dreams, and a new constellation of values,' writes Mitchell.

Though the main focus of research – ongoing rather than a one-off exercise – was upon the population of the United States, what Mitchell terms 'side spurs' of research explored VALS in five European countries – France, Sweden, Italy, West Germany and Britain. The VALS typology to a considerable degree reflects Abraham Maslow's notion of hierarchy (see MASLOW'S HIERARCHY OF NEEDS) and gives support to his categorization. There are those for example at the bottom of the social pile, called *Survivors*, 'whose existence has shrivelled to the bleak reality of the moment and the fantasy world of television'. Higher up the pecking order of lifestyle are the *Achievers*. They 'are at the top ... the driving and the driven people who have built "the system" and are now at the helm'. More than anything else 'Achievers have learned to live the comfortable, affluent, affable, outer-directed life, and in so doing they have set the standard for much of the nation.'

The typology identifies lifestyles as they are, or are becoming, and consequently has offered a model for change. Arnold Mitchell claims that VALS aids the 'eminently worthwhile' endeavour of choosing the kind of lifestyle 'a person, or a society of persons, would like in future'. At the same time he warns that the future holds a number of possible 'scenarios', some of brighter promise than others. The Hard Times scenario, for example, would produce a very different VALS typology to the one Mitchell terms 'Bouncy Prosperity'.

Each scenario would favour lifestyle types in different ways, advantaging some, disadvantaging others. The Need-Driven in the scenario of bouncy prosperity would rise up the hierarchy of opportunity, adding to the ranks of the *Belongers* (usually the comfortably-off, middle-of-the-roaders with conservative tastes to match). On the other hand, VALS research seems to indicate that 'the Societally Conscious segment would shrink', for many of their causes would have been addressed because there had been resources to deal with them.

With the Hard Times scenario 'There would be an increase in basic fear, insecurity, anxiety, dependence, rigidity, compulsiveness, and the desire for forceful leadership and for law and order'. A view from the twenty-first century might confirm the modern age as one veering more towards hard times than bouncy castles, especially following the events of 11 September 2001 when hijacked aircraft smashed into the American dream; one fallout from that event being serious downturns in a number of world industries, in particular air travel. For a period at least, a new category seemed to have joined the typography of lifestyles – the *Stay-at-homer.* See ADVERTISING: MAINSTREAMERS, ASPIRERS AND REFORMERS; MEDIA SPECIES. See also *TOPIC GUIDE* under ADVERTISING/MARKETING.

Values Each society, social group or individual has certain ideas, beliefs, ways of behaving, upon which is placed a value. A collection of these values, the criteria for judgement of one often acting as REINFORCEMENT for others, may amount to a *system* of values. Such a system, if it is not to cause DISSONANCE in a person, has either to be generally consistent, or be perceived as generally consistent.

Values are not merely systems of personal belief: they represent shared attitudes within social GROUPS and society at large, of approval and disapproval, of judgements favourable and unfavourable, towards other individuals, ideas, objects (such as the value placed on property), social action and events. Like NORMS, values vary from one social group or society to another; and they change over time and in different circumstances.

An individual's perception and interpretation of reality will be influenced by the values of the social groups or society to which he/she belongs. The pervasiveness of such values ensures that they are enmeshed in all aspects of communication processes. The images and codes that are the stock-in-trade of the mass media are shaped by value systems; and their intention is to support and reinforce the value systems that shape them. Jeremy Tunstall in his 'Introduction' to *Mass Sociology* (UK: Constable, 1970), edited by Tunstall, remarks that 'The media are saturated with social values of every kind.' These values come to the fore, achieve clearest definition, at times of crisis and conflict. See CULTURE; IDEOLOGY; MYTH; NEWS VALUES.

Vamp Early word for sex-star in the movies. In 1914 producer William Fox (1879–1952) created a star by going to the farthest extreme away from screen idol Mary Pickford, symbol of purity and innocence, by imposing a parody of sensuality and eroticism on Theda Bara in the film adaptation of the Kipling poem *A Fool There Was.* The word 'vamp' was used in the publicity for the film, whose financial success helped Fox set up his own studio, among the most important of the 1920s.

V-chip See CLIPPER CHIP.

V-discs In 1943, during the Second World War (1939–45), record companies and musicians agreed to waive fees and contractual rights to a series of very high-quality musical offerings to the US forces. Such recordings, many of them by giants of the jazz world – Benny Goodman, Louis Armstrong, Duke Ellington – are now prized by collectors.

Verbal devices in speech-making Max Atkinson in his illuminating study of the speech-making techniques of politicians and other well-known contemporary orators, *Our Masters' Voices: The Language and Body Language of Politics* (UK: Methuen, 1984), analyses various forms of what *The Shorter Oxford English Dictionary* terms *claptraps* – linguistic or non-verbal devices to catch applause. Particularly successful, says the author, is the list of three, which stimulates audience response, reinforces that stimulus and then pushes it to the climax. Antithesis is also an effective claptrap ('I come to bury Caesar, not to praise him'). Atkinson cautions the would-be orator that these devices require skill, timing and judgement to be effective, and claptrap 'always involves the use of more than one technique at a time'. See *TOPIC GUIDE* under LANGUAGE/DISCOURSE/NARRATIVE.

Victim funds These were organized by the UNDERGROUND PRESS in the nineteenth century to help out fellow papers subjected to heavy government fines for evading the taxes on knowledge – STAMP DUTY, Advertising Tax, Paper Duty and State Security System Tax. Between 1830 and 1836, at least 1130 cases of selling 'unstamped' papers were prosecuted in London alone. See NEWSPAPERS, ORIGINS.

Video The process of recoding TV programmes on cassette tape proved to be one of the most popular technical developments in the late 1970s and the 1980s. Video permitted time-shift viewing, liberating the viewer from the restrictions imposed by television schedules. At the same time, films and TV programmes on video became commercially available, creating a situation in which it was possible to escape altogether TV as it was traditionally experienced.

With the arrival of video began a fast-accelerating process of audience *fragmentation* (see AUDIENCE: FRAGMENTATION OF); and this trend was given further impetus with the availability of DVD in the 1990s. On the other hand, sales of video recordings proved – and continue to prove – a profitable supplement to media business.

Video, because it is reusable, and considerably cheaper than traditional film stock, has opened opportunities for film production, and indeed video soon became for aspiring film-makers the key medium of production. Video cameras are smaller and cheaper than film cameras, allowing for immediate playback.

What was once a means of communication restricted to professionals and largely to the film industry, enabled individuals, cooperatives, pressure GROUPS, clubs, schools, Media Studies students in particular – anyone with a case to urge, beliefs or feelings to express – to counter, at least at the level of a local community, the dominant voices of the national broadcasters or mass media communicators generally. Where recordable DVD scores and will inevitably triumph, is in the quality of picture and sound, permitting the work of professionals and amateurs alike parity with the standards expected 'in the trade'. See *TOPIC GUIDE* under MEDIA: TECHNOLOGIES.

* Sean Cubbitt, *Timeshift: On Video Culture* (UK: Comedia/Routledge, 1992).

Video games Like so many examples of popular CULTURE, the video game has incurred condemnation for being anti-social, a threat to the minds and mentality of the young – who are seen to be the main players – and loaded with harmful features. However, games have also achieved cultural status and have been claimed by some critics as amounting to an important art form, while 'cult status' is awarded to some of the protagonists of such games, the formidable Lara Croft, star of the *Tomb Raider* series, being the most notable. In *L'Univers Des Jeux Video/The Universe of Video Games* (France: Editions La Decouverte, 1998), Alain and Frederic Le Diberder see video games as 'the 10th art' (cinema being the seventh, TV the eighth and cartoons or 'graphic novels' the ninth).

The authors point to the following distinctive pleasures derived from video-game playing: competition, accomplishment, mastery of a system and spectacle. General concern is expressed about the long-term impact of playing games in which the central actions generally focus on violence and the destruction of enemies, and the subliminal *enculturalization* into what might be described as 'samurai mode', arising from the Japanese origin of most games.

Some 'classics' of the history of video games have been *Spacewar* (1962), *Space Invaders* (1978), *Tetris* (1989), *Mortal Kombat* (1992), *Doom* (1993), *WipEout 2097* (1996) and *Rainbow Six* (1998) in which the player employs six SAS warriors to save the world from deadly international terrorists. In the same year the UK's BAFTA award for best electronic entertainment went to Nintendo's *Goldeneye*, based on the James Bond film of the same title. This cross-pollination between films and games has become a key trend in marketing, while players of some new games can also read 'the novel of the game'.

A highly readable commentator on the game scene, Steven Poole, in a UK *Guardian* article 'The new game plan' (27 November 1998), spotlights the worrying ideologies that lurk behind so many video games. He refers to 'the increasingly subterranean political messages of video games', citing Sid Meier's city-building game *Civilization*, 'in which capitalism is king and no matter how hard the player tries, it is impossible to run a hippy commune'.

* Steven Poole, *The Prometheus Engine* (UK: Fourth Estate, 1999).

Video nasties A market that developed in the 1980s of specially-made-for-video films of a singularly nasty, brutal and sexist nature. Court action in the UK in 1982 against several of these films led to their enforced withdrawal from circulation but, to the considerable disgust of the late Mary Whitehouse and the National Viewers' and Listeners' Association – among many others – there was no order made for their destruction. However, the Conservative government brought in rigorous controls of video nasties with the VIDEO RECORDING ACT, 1984 (see next entry).

In 1994 there was dramatically renewed interest in the possible effects of video nasties on behaviour following the Jamie Bulger trial in which two 11-year-old boys were convicted of murdering the small boy they had abducted. The judge in the trial, Mr Justice Morland, conjectured that the boys may have been influenced by seeing *Child's Play 3*, whose plot paralleled, to a degree, the real actions of the killers. Though this connection was dismissed by many in the TV and film industry, there was support from child psychologists, in particular from Elizabeth Newson, Professor of Development Psychology at the University of Nottingham, who spoke of the need for special concern when children – or, indeed, adults – are repeatedly exposed to images of cruelty in the context of entertainment.

Video Recording Act (UK), 1984 Passed through Parliament in the UK with all-Party support, MP Graham Bright's measure was designed to restrict the access of young persons to VIDEO NASTIES, many of which eluded the usual vetting process of the BRITISH BOARD OF FILM CENSORS.

The Act established by statute an Authority (initially the BBFC) whose purpose was to classify video cassettes as suitable for home viewing and to censor those deemed unsuitable. Fines of up to £20,000 are liable for dealers and distributors breaking the law. All video works must be submitted for scrutiny, classification and certification unless they are educational or concerned with sport, religion or music.

However, if such videos 'to any extent' portray 'Human sexual activity' or 'Mutilation, torture or other acts of gross violence' or show 'human genital organs' they also have to be submitted to the censors. See CENSORSHIP; MORAL PANIC.

Viewers: light, medium and heavy Research into the amount and nature of TV viewing discriminates between the light viewer, generally classified as watching TV for two hours or less a day, the medium viewer, watching for between two and three hours a day, and the heavy viewer watching for four hours or more a day. In the analysis of viewer response, special attention has been paid to the differences of attitude to issues and controversies that can be detected between light and heavy viewers, and thus the influence TV programmes may have on attitude formation and attitude change. See CULTIVATION; MAINSTREAMING; MEAN WORLD SYNDROME; RESONANCE.

Violence and the media See VIOLENCE ON TV: CODES OF PRACTICE; VIOLENCE ON TV: THE DEFENCE. See also *TOPIC GUIDE* under AUDIENCES/CONSUMPTION AND RECEPTION OF MEDIA; MEDIA: FREEDOM, CENSORSHIP; MEDIA ISSUES AND DEBATES; MEDIA: POWER, EFFECTS, INFLUENCE; REPRESENTATION.

Violence on TV: codes of practice Although the BROADCASTING ACT (UK), 1990, purported to exchange the 'firm' hand of regulation as represented by the Independent Broadcasting Authority (IBA) for a 'lighter touch' regulatory body, the Independent Television Commission (ITC), the code of practice concerning screen violence remains rigorous (see ITC: PROGRAMME CODE). Indeed the tradition of British broadcasting indicates a greater caution over the amount and degree of violence permitted on our screens than many other countries. 1980 saw the publication of *The Portrayal of Violence on Television: BBC and IBA Guidelines.* They offered the following criteria for programme-makers. (1) They must ask themselves, is violent action essential to the story? (2) If essential, how much detail is necessary for the sake of clarity? (3) Is a violent act being shown in a way that may encourage dangerous imitation by the young and immature? (4) Is violence being used to create excitement and to hold attention?

The ITC Code included in part two of *The Portrayal of Violence on Television* declares 'Violence is not only physical: it can be verbal, psychological and even metaphysical or super-natural. Whatever form the violence in a programme may take its inclusion can only be justified by the dramatic or informational context in which it is seen, and the skill, insight and sensitivity of the portrayal.' Programme-makers are reminded that people seldom view just one programme and 'An acceptable minimum of violence in each individual programme may add to an intolerable level over a period.' A substantial amount of this Code reappears in the ITC Programme Code and the RADIO AUTHORITY (UK) PROGRAMME CODES, operating from 1991.

A report by the Department of Journalism Studies at Sheffield University brought comfort to both the BBC and commercial channels in 1995. Report authors Barrie Gunter and Jackie Harrison summarized research findings based upon the monitoring of 4715 hours of programmes. They identified a drop in the featuring of violence on the terrestrial channels, BBC1, BBC2, ITV and Channel 4, from 1.1 per cent of total output in 1966 to 0.61 per cent in 1994/95. There was marginally more violence (1.53 per cent) on satellite channels, Sky One, Sky Movies, the Movie Channel and UK Gold. Of the programmes sampled, a third contained some violence, with 21,000 separate violent acts catalogued, though most of this occurred after the 9pm watershed.

The authors of the Sheffield study, costing £93,000 and jointly commissioned by the BBC and the ITC, believed that it 'would be very easy to misconstrue the level of violence on television by reference only to the gross figures ... Violence represents only a tiny proportion of the total programme output.' See BROADCASTING STANDARDS COUNCIL (UK).

* Barrie Gunter and Jackie Harrison, *Violence on Television: An Analysis of Amount, Nature, Location and Origin of Violence in British Programmes* (UK: Routledge, 1998).

Violence on TV: the defence The portrayal of violence on screen, whether in the cinema or on TV has long attracted controversy and is an ongoing ISSUE of our time. The dominent tendency among commentators is to deplore it, its nature, its extent and its amount. Simulated violence is seen to prompt some members of the AUDIENCE to re-enact that violence in real life; and violence is judged to desensitize viewers to the real thing.

Taking issue with these perspectives is Jib Fowles. In *The Case for Television Violence* (US: Sage, 1999), Fowles argues that contrary to the notion that screen violence breeds real violence, it is more likely to inhibit or reduce it: 'Television violence is good for people.' Recognizing in human beings an in-built violent impulse, Fowles says that society requires 'outlets' for this impulse. Violence is ever-present and has to be managed: 'In isolation, television violence may seem reproachable and occupy the foreground with a menacing intensity, but with a longer perspective it can seem comparatively like an improvement – a purer distillation of the age-old processes for containing and redirecting violence.'

We have to remember, says Fowles, 'that television violence is symbolic only ... Nobody actually suffers for our pleasure.' For the author, 'the assault on television violence is absolutely unwarranted'. It is 'simply the most recent and least damaging venue for the routinized working out of innate aggressiveness and fear'. The fuss TV violence causes Fowles describes as a variant on the MORAL PANIC, which is usually accompanied by the fervour and 'extreme righteousness of the condemners as they lash out at conjured or magnified transgressions'; and the response 'is always out of proportion to whatever instigates it'. Fowles concludes: 'Perhaps, to give television violence its due, we need first to respect ourselves more fully, to have greater regard for the complex, semiviolent creatures that we are.'

As in addressing all theories, a cautionary note is perhaps required here, for cases occur from time to time in which the enactment of real violence echoes and sometimes directly simulates screen violence. The UK *Observer* (9 June 2002) reported under a headline, 'Murder linked to horror trilogy', that French authorities were blaming the savage stabbing in Saint-Sebastien-sur-Loire by a teenager of a girl he had invited for a walk on the youth's seeming obsession with the *Scream* series of movies.

Two similar murders, by teenagers, had alerted the authorities to the possible influence the films exerted on impressionable young people. An *Observer* listing of what seemed to be copycat offences between 1999 and 2002 indicated that it was not only teenagers working out fantasies of violence on real-world victims, but older men too, or in the case of a murder in Massachussetts in 2000, a woman and two men wearing *Scream* masks.

In his *Observer* report, Paul Webster quoted psychiatrists worried 'about the inability of some young people to distinguish between reality and fiction'. Dave Grossman, American expert on the psychology and physiology of killing would plainly challenge Jib Fowles' assertions. His belief, reported by Webster, was that 'repetition, desensitization and escalation reduced the normal human unwillingness to kill'.

Virtual reality Simulation of the real by technological means, using multi-media inputs – head-mounted display, data gloves, three-dimensional audio system and magnetic position tracker (to name the basics); what has been termed a 'technological cluster'. Generally, the simulation of the real exists in that 'window of realities', the TV monitor.

In a paper 'The ultimate display' for the Proceedings of the IFIPS Congress 2, published as early as 1965, Ivan Sutherland defined the VR dream: 'The screen is a window through which one sees a virtual world. The challenge is to make that world look real, act real, sound real and feel real.'

Virtual reality technology is three-dimensional and interactive. It is extensively used in engineering and architectural design, in medicine and telecommunications. It is potentially a vital component in reconstructing the past. At the first Virtual Reality Heritage conference in Bath, UK, November 1995, IBM's Brian Collins described the VR reconstruction of a church that no longer exists, the Frauenkirche in Dresden 50 years after its destruction by bombing. Using the few drawings, plans and colour photographs taken by the Nazis, VR technology provides a detailed reconstruction enabling the original to be rebuilt.

A more general application of the term virtual reality centres on the worlds 'out there' as brought to users of the computer, the INTERNET and the myriad experiences available online. It has become a matter of widespread concern that so many users seem to prefer life online to life beyond the monitor. Mark Slouka in *War of the Worlds: Cyberspace and the High-Tech Assault on Reality* (US: Basic Books, 1995; UK: Abacus, 1996) talks of a 'culture of simulation' that blurs 'fiction and reality'; and this in his view risks creating in the public a fear 'of unmediated reality', especially considering our willingness to buy in to the virtual – that is, 'we're buying in to a fake'. It follows that reality itself 'is beginning to lose its authority'. See CYBERSPACE. See also *TOPIC GUIDE* under MEDIA ISSUES AND DEBATES.

Virus: computer virus See COMPUTERS IN COMMUNICATION.

Visibility See GLOBAL SCRUTINY; PRIVACY.

Visions of order A notion long associated with the role and function of the journalist is that of 'bringer-of-light', of enlightenment. The French writer Jacques Derrida in *Writing and Difference* (UK: Routledge & Kegan Paul, 1978) poses the 'heliological metaphor', describing the journalist as a human version of the heliograph, recorder and transmitter of light – of revelation to AUDIENCE. The process is one of *envisioning*, that is, offering a vision of the world: light for others to see by. In *The Politics of Pictures: The Creation of the Public in the Age of Popular Media* (UK: Routledge, 1992) John Hartley takes up this theme in a chapter entitled 'Heliography: journalism, and the visualization of truth'. What journalism brings to light, what it renders visible are, Hartley argues, 'distant visions of order'. It is not so much the actual truth that is brought to light as the *vision* of truth as visualized in terms of order.

The reader might raise the objection that journalism is really all about disorder rather than order; and this is exactly Hartley's point: what he calls 'a process of photographic negativization' takes place, 'where the image of order is actually recorded as its negative, in stories of disorder'. The 'distant vision of order' is not, however, of 'oneness'; rather, Hartley believes, ordering works on a basis of what the author terms WEDOM, THEYDOM – Us (good) and Them (bad). See JOURNALISM.

---

* Richard V. Ericson, Patricia M. Baraneh and Janet B.L. Chan, *Representing Order: Crime, Law and Justice in the News Media* (UK: Open University, 1991).

Vistavision Paramount's response to 20th Century Fox's CINEMASCOPE in the 1950s. The negative was made on 70mm stock and reduced to 35mm during printing, to reduce graininess.

Vitaphone Trade name of the first successful synchronous movie sound, introduced in 1926 by Warner Brothers. On 6 August at the Warner Theatre in New York, John Barrymore starred in *Don Juan*, to the accompaniment of a Vitaphone 16-inch 33⅓rpm disc recording of voice and music. Curiously *Don Juan* caused less audience excitement than the Vitaphone shorts that accompanied it, such as the New York Philharmonic playing Wagner's Tannhauser Overture. The real sensation of the talkies was Warners' next picture, *The Jazz Singer* (1927) starring Al Jolson. There were, in fact, only 281 words spoken in the film, all of them ad-libbed by Jolson. See SYNCHRONOUS SOUND. See *TOPIC GUIDE* under MEDIA HISTORY.

Vocal cues All the oral aspects of speech except the words themselves; pitch – the highness or lowness of voice; rate – rapidity of expression; volume; quality – the pleasantness or unpleasantness of voice tone or delivery; and enunciation – pronunciation and articulation. See PARALANGUAGE.

Voiceover In film and TV film production, voiceover accompanies what the AUDIENCE is seeing with comment – explanation and analysis – without the commentator being on view. In feature films voiceover is often that of the chief character in a story, though the DOCUMENTARY approach of an unidentified narrator is also common. Voiceover plays a significant role in shaping the MEANING of a film TEXT. It signals the way that audience is expected to read what is seen and heard in a programme. In this sense, voiceover closes down a text to a prescribed meaning, allowing the viewer little room for interpretation. See NARRATIVE; OPEN, CLOSED TEXTS.

Vox popping Collecting the opinions of large numbers of the general public (*vox populi* is Latin for 'voice of the people') in order to broadcast public reaction to a current issue or topic.

W

'War of the Worlds' Title of the American CBS network radio adaptation by Howard Koch, produced and narrated by Orson Welles (1938), of H.G. Wells' famous story. Conveying the immediacy of a combat report from a war correspondent, the production actually convinced many listeners that an interplanetary war had broken out. However, reports to the effect that Orson Welles' radio 'hype' had caused panic in the streets have taken on the magic of legend, and become somewhat exaggerated in the telling. See IDENTIFICATION; PARASOCIAL INTERACTION.

War: four stages of war reporting According to Philip Knightley, author of the classic analysis of war reporting, *The First Casualty: A History of War Reporting* (UK: revised edition, Prion, 2000; first published in 1975), western coverage of military conflicts is highly predictable, and passes through four stages. These he discusses in a UK *Guardian* article, 'The disinformation campaign' (4 October 2001), following the terrorist attack on New York's World Trade Center (11 September).

Knightley calls stage 1, the crisis; in stage 2, the enemy leader is DEMONIZED; in stage 3, the enemy as a whole is demonized. Stage 4 focuses on atrocities. 'Comparing the leader with Hitler,' writes Knightley, 'is a good start because of the instant images that Hitler's name provokes' (see HISTORICAL ALLUSION): 'The crudest approach is to suggest that the leader is insane', and those who publicly question any of this 'can expect an even stronger burst of abuse'.

The simplest way of demonizing a whole people, says Knightley, is the atrocity story: 'Take the Kuwaiti babies story. Its origin goes back to the first world war when British propaganda accused the Germans of tossing Belgian babies into the air and catching them on their bayonets.

'Dusted off and updated for the Gulf War [1991] this version had Iraqi soldiers bursting into a modern Kuwaiti hospital, finding the premature babies ward and then tossing the babies out of incubators so that the incubators could be sent back to Iraq.' This story, as well as others, was a fabrication, but it had served its propagandist function. See *TOPIC GUIDE* under NEWS MEDIA.

War of the Unstamped See STAMP DUTY; UNDERGROUND PRESS; VICTIM FUNDS.

Watchdogs The media pride themselves on their role as watchdogs of injustice, abuse and corruption; champions of public interest. The watchdog barks on behalf of the people, in their defence against the powerful, whether these are in government, business, industry or any walk of life where the interests of the public can be affected. The role of the watchdog may be seen as key to media functions and a guiding principle.

Research tends to point to the media being rather less than wholly effective in this capacity; generally to follow rather than initiate the investigation of abuse; indeed to be guilty of *omission* as much as commission (see GUARD DOG METAPHOR).

True 'watchdoggery' can only come about through genuine media independence – from ADVERTISING and sales revenue, from the influence of capital or institutional control. Fulfilling the role of watchdog becomes problematic when that role is seen to trespass upon the vested interests of those who own and control the watchdogs in question.

An arms manufacturing company with a portfolio that includes newspapers, radio and TV stations is unlikely to smile benignly on these media if, in the interests of the public, they wish to challenge arms manufacture and export. The result, usually, is not overt CENSORSHIP, but *self-censorship*. With the trend in recent years of CONVERGENCE of ownership, the risks of self-censorship, of failing to fulfil the role of public watchdog, have inevitably increased.

It is for this reason, among others, that media commentators express concern about convergences of media ownership worldwide, fearing that watchdogs will be 'seen off' by guard dogs. See CONGLOMERATES; DEMOCRACY AND THE MEDIA; HEGEMONY; NEWS VALUES; WATERGATE.

Watergate Scene of one of history's most famous break-ins, and source of one of modern history's most dramatic scandals, which eventually led to the resignation of the US president. The apartment block called Watergate in Washington DC was the 1972 election campaign headquarters of the National Committee of the Democratic Party. It was broken into in June by agents of the rival Republican Party's Committee to Re-elect President Richard Nixon. They were caught in the act as they were removing electronic bugging devices.

The ensuing cover-up was penetrated and revealed by two reporters on the *Washington Post*, Bob Woodward and Carl Bernstein, fed with significant information by a mysterious DEEP THROAT within government, possibly close to the president. A Senate investigation committee pushed fearlessly against presidential closed doors. Eventually the Supreme Court forced the White House to give access to tape-recordings made, at Nixon's command, over a long period in the president's office. The tapes proved Nixon's complicity in the Watergate Affair.

He was the first president of the US to resign; if he had not resigned, he would have been impeached by Congress. His successor, President Ford, extended a blanket pardon to Nixon, but not to his associates, several of whom ended up in jail (and most of whom wrote successful books on their experiences). Watergate is varyingly cited as a supreme example of investigative JOURNALISM; a classic case study of official corruption and an alarming illustration of the paranoia that sometimes comes with power and authority.

However, it is perhaps most importantly a breathtaking glimpse of the nature of open government and the potential of the democratic process. No Watergate revelations could possibly take place in the UK: the OFFICIAL SECRETS ACT would have brought down the steel curtain of CENSORSHIP long before the tide of proof of corruption swirled around the feet of a British prime minister. See SPYCATCHER CASE.

Web radio See COMMUNITY RADIO.

Web: World Wide Web (www) Formed in 1992 by Tim Berners-Lee at the European Nuclear Research Centre as a computer network capable of delivering information more swiftly and comprehensively than any previous delivery system. Darin Barney in *Prometheus Wired: The Hope for Democracy in the Age of Network Technology* (US: University of Chicago Press, 2002) writes, 'Information on the Web is organized as a massive, searchable database of "pages" existing, not in just a single computer somewhere, but in all the computers linked to the network via servers.' Thus the Web is a network that 'is itself a giant expanding database' capable of linking documents etc. to any number of other Web documents, brought about by *hypertexting.*

The Web, Barney points out, 'accentuates the capacity of networks to enmesh with one another and become networks of networks in an exponentially increasing matrix of connectivity'.

Wedom, Theydom Version of 'Them-and-Us'. John Hartley uses the term in *The Politics of Pictures: The Creation of the Public in the Age of Popular Media* (UK: Routledge, 1992) to describe the *binary* nature of popular JOURNALISM and image-creation in the turn-of-the-century press and beyond. Hartley sees the practices of popular journalism as being determinedly *adversarial* in nature, defining the world in terms of opposites – private and public, reality and illusion, allies and enemies – and arising out of a process in which media is integrated into social policy. Wedom incorporated not only the British but the Empire while excluding foreigners, though Theydom was soon conferred upon those elements of Wedom that stepped out of line – trades unions, pacifists or communist sympathizers.

Hartley speaks of a tradition of 'foe creation', which is related to notions of order – the upholding of it. What the press does, he argues, is operate a 'process of photographic negativization, where the image of order is actually recorded as its own negative, in stories of disorder'. In *Visualizing Deviance: A Study of News Organizations* (UK: Open University Press, 1989) Richard Ericson, Patricia Baraneh and Janet Chan had come to the same conclusion, but with regard to the modern journalist. 'In sum,' they argue, 'journalists are central agents in the reproduction of order.'

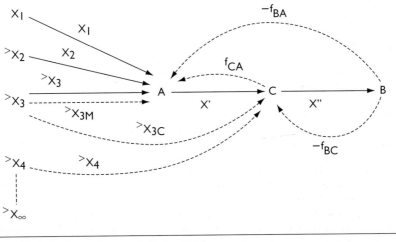

Wesley and MacLean's model of communication, 1957 In their article 'A conceptual model for communications research', in *Journalism Quarterly* 34, B.H. Wesley and M.S. MacLean develop NEWCOMB'S ABX MODEL OF COMMUNICATION, 1953, with the aim of encapsulating the overall mass communication process. To Newcomb's A (communicator) B (communicator) X (any event or object in the environment of A, B, which is the subject of communication), Wesley and MacLean added a fourth element, C. This represents the editorial communicating functions – the process of deciding what and how to communicate.

Newcomb's model represented chiefly interpersonal communication; it was a triangular formation, with A, B and X interacting equilaterally. Wesley and MacLean indicate that the mass media process crucially shifts the balance, bringing A (in this case the would-be communicator) and C (the mass communication organization and its agents who control the channel) closer together. C is both channel and mediator of A's transmission of X to B (now classifiable as audience), and B's contact with X is more remote than in the Newcomb model, if it exists at all save through the combined 'processing' of AC. FEEDBACK is represented by f.

It can be seen from the model that X need not go through to B via A and C, but via C alone. The role of C as intermediary has a dual character, purposive when the process involves conveying a message through C from an 'advocate' – a politician, for example, and non-purposive when it is a matter of conveying the unplanned events of the world to an audience.

The main thrust of the model appears to be emphasizing the *dependency* of B upon A and C. What is missing from the model, and what later thinking about mass media processes insists upon, are the numerous message sources and influences that work upon B other than AC, and counter-balance the influence of AC – such as the family, friends, members of peer groups, workmates, colleagues, or wider influences such as school, church, trades unions, etc. See INTERVENING VARIABLES (IVs); SIGNIFICANT OTHERS. See also *TOPIC GUIDE* under COMMUNICATION MODELS.

Western Hollywood's most popularly successful transformation of the past into MYTH, with the enshrining of heroic VALUES – self-help, individualism, the legitimization of violence in the name of timeless (though rarely analysed) notions of law and order, and of human rights equated with access to and possession of the earth. The western has held a firm grip on the imagination of every generation of film-goer since 1903 when Edwin S. Porter's *The Great Train Robbery* set the GENRE off to a brisk gallop.

Much of the fascination in studying the genre of the western lies in relating its ideological changes to cultural and political changes taking place in America. Several commentators see the western as a metaphor for American VALUES, or 'Americanness': configurations of the lone hero, the community threatened by lawlessness, the appeal of the frontier, and the sense of old values and lifestyles being overtaken by the urban and the corporate, continue to prompt serious research and analysis. Writing in *Westerns: Aspects of Movie Genre* (UK: Secker & Warburg, 1973), Philip French says of the western that it is among the most didactic of film genres; as he memorably puts it, 'For every Showdown at Wichita there's a little teach-in in Dodge City.'

Westerstähl and Johansson's model of news factors in foreign news, 1994 A useful complement to GALTUNG AND RUGE'S MODEL OF SELECTIVE GATEKEEPING, 1965, and ROGERS AND DEARING'S AGENDA-SETTING MODEL, 1987, this model is featured in an article 'Foreign news: news values and ideologies', by Jorgen Westerstähl and Folke Johansson, published in the *European Journal of Communication*, March 1994. Just as the environment or context is the centre and axis from which communicative action springs in ANDERSCH, STAATS AND BOSTROM'S MODEL OF COMMUNICATION, 1969, IDEOLOGY is the central 'generator' of news coverage according to Westerstähl and Johansson.

As reporting of news is coloured by a prevailing ideology of national interest, *proximity* and *importance* constitute two of four major criteria for news selection; proximity in the sense of geographic, cultural, political, linguistic or cultural closeness, affecting and being affected by another country's importance to 'us'. While the US is distant geographically from the UK it is nevertheless important – an ELITE nation. The Netherlands, in contrast, while being geographically close, is less 'important'. Events occurring in the US are therefore more likely to be reported than events in The Netherlands, unless those events have a direct relevance to the UK.

We recognize the NEWS VALUES as identified by Galtung and Ruge here – ethno-centrism and elitism in particular. The notion of *drama* is obvious enough but *access* is a welcome criterion: where reporting is possible, where reporters have access, there is greater likelihood that foreign events will be covered. The nature of that access is also critical. There was massive coverage of the Gulf Wars of 1991 and 2003, but access to the kind of information reporters wanted if a full picture of events was to be transmitted was severely curtailed by NEWS MANAGEMENT on the part of the military authorities and by ideological pressures requiring the activities of the 'home team' to be presented in the best light.

Westerstähl and Johansson use their model to illustrate how coverage might run counter to traditional news values. They cite the case of the West's interest in Poland during strikes and protests mounted by

News factors in foreign news

the Polish trade union Solidarity in the 1980s. The events were dramatic, yet Poland was neither near nor 'important'. The key to this special attention was, in the view of the authors, ideology. Solidarity's actions threatened the chief ideological rival to capitalism – Communism.

If performed in the West, Solidarity's actions would have incurred critical media attention: strikes are bad for business. However, such strike action taking place in an Iron Curtain country, and in the context of the Cold War, led to Solidarity's trades unionists being cast as heroes fighting for freedom against Soviet socialist totalitarianism.

'In our view,' write Westerståhl and Johansson, 'ideologies are the main source of deviation in news reporting from a standard based on more or less objectified news values.' See DISCOURSE OF POWER. See also *TOPIC GUIDE* under COMMUNICATION MODELS.

Westminster view Opinion that the media in the UK take their cue from and align their perspectives to the standpoint of the activities of parliament. This produces the simplistic equation – politics equals parliament, and can result in a less than adequate coverage of political events that take place away from Westminster. See POLITICS OF ACCOMMODATION (IN THE MEDIA).

Whistle-blowing A whistle-blower is usually an individual within an organization – industrial, commercial, governmental, etc. – who can no longer keep silent about practices in that organization; perhaps because he/she perceives them as unsafe, corrupt, dishonest or misleading. Almost invariably whistle-blowers act out of conscience. Their need for security is outweighed by a higher-order need, to square behaviour with a sense of VALUES (see MASLOW'S HIERARCHY OF NEEDS): they must speak out against the perceived abuse, even though their 'going public', by leaking information to the media, may result in dismissal. In the UK a degree of protection is offered to whistle-blowers in the Public Interest Disclosure Act of 1999. Substantial compensation may be granted to whistle-blowers who have suffered victimization, or dismissal, raising concerns about financial malpractice, breaches of contract or cover-ups generally.

White's gatekeeper model, 1950 The existence of 'gate areas' along channels of communication was identified by Kurt Lewin in 'Channels of group life' in *Human Relations* 1 (1947). At such points, decisions are made to select out information passing through the gate areas. Lewin's particular study was concerned with decisions about household food purchases, but he drew a comparison with the flow of NEWS in mass communication. David M. White in an article entitled 'The "gatekeepers": a case study in the selection of news', in *Journalism Quarterly* 27 (1950), applied Lewin's idea in a study of the telegraph wire editor of an American non-metropolitan newspaper.

Today the model is only acceptable as a starting point for analysis of the GATEKEEPING process; indeed it is a useful exercise for the student to build on the model by adding important factors that White does not include – such as the organizational elements of the mass communication process that constrain and direct it. The model also indicates only a single gate and a single gatekeeper, where in practice news passes through many gatekeepers, official and unofficial, direct and indirect. White's model should be studied in relation to McNELLY'S MODEL OF NEWS FLOW, 1959, and GALTUNG AND RUGE'S MODEL OF SELECTIVE GATEKEEPING, 1965. See also *TOPIC GUIDE* under COMMUNICATION MODELS.

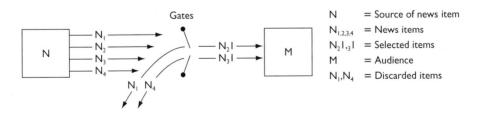

White's gatekeeper model, 1950

Wi-fi See INTERNET: WIRELESS INTERNET.

Williams Committee Report on Obscenity and Film Censorship (UK), 1979 Under the chairmanship of Bernard Williams, philosopher and then Provost of King's College, Cambridge, the Committee was set up in July 1977 by the Labour Home Secretary Merlyn Rees and reported in October 1979. The task of the Committee was 'to review the laws concerning obscenity, indecency and violence in publications, displays and entertainments in England and Wales, except in the field of broadcasting, and to review the arrangements for film censorship in England and Wales; and to make recommendations'.

After exhaustive analysis of often conflicting data, evidence and opinion on the effects of PORNOGRAPHY, the Report concluded that 'the role of pornography in influencing the state of society is a minor one. To think anything else, and in particular to regard pornography as having a crucial or even a significant effect on essential social values, is to get the problem of pornography out of proportion with the many other problems that face our society today.' The publication of the Williams Committee recommendations coincided with a change of government in the UK. No direct or immediate legislation resulted from the Report. See *TOPIC GUIDE* under COMMISSIONS, COMMITTEES, LEGISLATION.

---

* Bernard Williams (ed.), *Obscenity and Film Censorship: An Abridgement of the Williams Report* (UK: Cambridge University Press, 1981).

Wired world Or wired society; term used to describe the new, post-industrial economy – a telecommunications network bringing to the home multi-channel cable and satellite TV, electronic mail, push-button business transactions, all, theoretically, on a universal scale. See CYBERSPACE; INTERNET; VIRTUAL REALITY; WEB: WORLD WIDE WEB (WWW).

Wireless network See INTERNET: WIRELESS INTERNET.

Wireless telegraphy In the 1870s, James Clark Maxwell (1831–79), first professor of experimental physics at the University of Cambridge, argued that wireless telegraphy would be possible by employing electro-magnetic waves. In 1885, Welsh electrical engineer Sir William Preece (1834–1913) sent currents between two insulated squares of wire a quarter of a mile apart. Two years later Heinrich Rudolf Hertz (1857–94), German physicist, proved the existence of radio waves, and in 1894 English physicist Sir Oliver Lodge demonstrated how messages could be transmitted and received without wires.

Similar pioneer work had been conducted by Italian Guglielmo Marconi (1874–1937) who arrived in England to further his ideas. Supported by Preece – then engineer-in-chief of the Post Office telegraphs – Marconi filed an application for a wireless patent (1896) and was soon sending long-distance messages by MORSE CODE, first across the Bristol Channel and then the English Channel. His telegraph was used to save a ship in distress in the North Sea and it was rapidly accepted that radio equipment was essential on board all ships. The British Admiralty paid Marconi £20,000 a year for the use of his system in the Royal Navy.

By 1901, wireless messages were being transmitted from Cornwall to Newfoundland, tapped out in Morse. A year later R.A. Fissenden of the University of Pittsburgh transmitted the sound of a human voice over a distance of a mile. Further progress was made possible by the invention of the thermionic valve or electron tube, by English electrical engineer John Ambrose Fleming (1904). This device served to change the minute alternating current of a radio signal into a direct current, capable of actuating a TELEPHONE receiver or the needle of a meter. American physicist Lee De Forest improved the valve by making amplification possible. In 1910 De Forest fitted what he named a 'radio-phone' on the roof of the Metropolitan Opera House in New York, enabling listeners to hear the voices of the singers 100 miles away.

The First World War (1914–18) accelerated developments in radio, where it received baptism as a weapon of PROPAGANDA – by the Germans. The future possibilities for radio were encapsulated by American engineer David Sarnoff when, in 1916, he declared, 'I have in mind a plan of development which would make a radio a "household utility" like the piano or electricity. The idea is to bring music into the house by wireless.' See RADIO BROADCASTING. See also *TOPIC GUIDE* under BROAD-CASTING; MEDIA HISTORY; MEDIA: TECHNOLOGIES.

Wireless Telegraphy Act (UK), 1904 The result of a meeting of the major international powers held in Berlin in 1903 to prepare an international plan for the regulation of wireless telegraphy at sea. The UK government required legislation in order to sign the ensuing agreements that enforced uniform rules of working. The Act established universal wireless licensing in Britain, shore and sea, granted by the Postmaster-General with the consent of the Admiralty and Army Council, and the Board of Trade.

World Press Freedom Committee Formed in May 1976 to 'unify the free world media for major threats that develop'; consists of over 30 journalistic organizations ranging from the American Newspaper Publishers Association (ANPA), and international press agencies to the INTER-NATIONAL FEDERATION OF JOURNALISTS (IFJ). See MACBRIDE COMMISSION; MEDIA IMPERIALISM; NEW WORLD INFORMATION ORDER; TALLOIRES DECLARATION, 1981; YAMOUSOUKRU DECLARATION. See also *TOPIC GUIDE* under MEDIA: FREEDOM, CENSORSHIP.

World Trade Organization (WTO) Telecommunications Agreement, 1997 Signed by 68 countries, this agreement to abolish national and regional barriers to free trade in telecommunication services was, as the WTO believed, 'an important step towards fully competitive markets'. This radical move towards DEREGULATION was widely challenged by critics, who argued that more freedom actually meant more American dominance; and that fully competitive markets were likely to reward the strong and punish the weak.

Edward Herman and Robert McChesney write, in *The Global Media: The New Missionaries of Corporate Capitalism* (US/UK: Continuum, 1997), 'It may be worth noting that the United States is home of ten of the sixteen largest telecommunications firms in the world, and these are the firms that are the major ben-eficiaries of free trade.' The authors believe that while this and other liberalizing measures in global markets have 'improved services for business and the affluent in the developing world, the principle of universal access has been compromised, if not abandoned'. Also, such measures have 'led to numerous episodes of large-scale graft and corruption'.

The liberalization (meaning PRIVATIZATION) of telecommunications has encouraged mergers, part-nerships and joint ventures among the decreasing number of giant players, leading to what the UK *Financial Times* (2 April 1996) termed 'a handful of giants, straddling the world market'. See GLOBAL MEDIA SYSTEM: THE MAIN PLAYERS. See also *TOPIC GUIDE* under GLOBAL PERSPEC-TIVES; MEDIA ISSUES AND DEBATES.

X

X-certificate See CERTIFICATION OF FILMS.

Xerography Reprographic process using a photo-electric surface that converts light into an electronic charge. Documents can be reproduced in black and white and in colour to a very high standard, reduced in size or enlarged. The electrostatic image of a document attracts charged ink powder, which in turn is attracted to charged paper. A visible image is formed and fixed permanently by heating.

Xenophobia Fear of foreigners; from *xeno* – strange, foreign, guest – and *phobos*, fear. The media's role in cultivating xenophobic tendencies in the public has a long, and often tragic, history. The speed at which such tendencies can be provoked and manipulated is a vital area of media research. See DEMO-NIZATION; EFFECTS OF THE MASS MEDIA; FOLK DEVILS; MORAL PANIC; RADIO DEATH; STEREOTYPE; WEDOM, THEYDOM.

Y

Yamousoukrou declaration Issued by African leaders in 1985, the declaration states 'One of the main keys to solving Africa's development problems lies in mastering the national management of information in all its forms.' The text of the declaration that appeared in an International Bureau of Information Report (1986) argued that information management and control are 'not only a positive force for regional and continental integration but also an essential condition for the survival of Africa within the community of nations in the 21st century'. See CORE NATIONS, PERIPHERAL NATIONS; DEVELOPMENT NEWS; INFORMATION GAPS; MACBRIDE COMMISSION; MEDIA IMPERIALISM; NEW WORLD INFORMATION ORDER.

Yellow journalism Phrase used in the US to describe newspapers involved in the internecine (dog-eat-dog) warfare of the popular metropolitan press empires of the late nineteenth century; a battle that has continued to the present day with mass-circulation tabloids competing for readership with all sorts of exploitative offers, lurid revelations and blockbuster bingo.

Yellow Kid Newspaper cartoon character, the possession of whose widely popular image – and the use of that image – was fought over by New York's press barons, Joseph Pulitzer (1847–1911) and William Randolph Hearst (1863–1951). The pictorial image was fast dominating the pages of newspapers at the beginning of the twentieth century, proving a circulation-booster and a marketing device. Pulitzer's *New York World* first featured Richard B. Outcault's cartoon, *Shantytown* (renamed *Hogan's Alley*). Hearst 'raided' the *World*'s Sunday edition, buying in the entire production team of the paper for his own, newly purchased *Journal*. The gap-toothed Kid in his yellow smock, whose grin was recognized throughout the city on billboards and sandwich boards, joined the *Journal* as cartoon and promotional image. Soon Hearst was organizing the Yellow Fellow Transcontinental Bicycle Relay followed by a bike carnival in New York's Central Park.

In response, Pulitzer hired Richard Buks to continue the original cartoon strip and in 1895 two Yellow Kids were in competition. 'For contemporaries,' writes Andrew Wernick in *Promotional Culture: Advertising, Ideology and Symbolic Expression* (UK: Sage, 1991), 'the Kid's colour became emblematic of the effects of intensified consumerization on the whole character of the popular press.'

Visual appeal had become central to the process of promotion. When Hearst followed Pulitzer in issuing a full-colour Sunday supplement, the *Journal* announced its own 'eight pages of irridescent poly-chromous effulgence that makes the rainbow look like a lead pipe'. It is perhaps more than a coincidence that the most popular TV comic strip, *The Simpsons*, continued with the effulgence of yellow. See *TOPIC GUIDE* under MEDIA HISTORY.

Youth and media See CHILDREN, YOUNG PEOPLE AND THE CHANGING MEDIA ENVIRONMENT.

Youth culture Since the Second World War (1939–45) considerable attention has been paid to the cultures and subcultures of young people – to their symbols, SIGNS, philosophies, MORES, NORMS, language and music. Music is an essential part of all youth cultures and subcultures, a mode of self-identification (see SELF-IDENTITY) and different GROUPS favour different musical styles, and use music in different ways.

Youth cultures and subcultures differ not only over time but also between CLASS, sex and racial groups. Whilst they manifest significant differences there are some links between them and individuals may move from one to another. They adopt and adapt aspects of each other's cultural style and those of past youth cultures and subcultures. The more dramatic subcultures have attracted attention from the media and academics. Their often spectacular modes of expression offer contrast and challenge to society, usually communicated by STYLE – the mohican hairstyle of the punks for example.

The media have been a notable mediator of society's reaction to such challenges, and this role has been a focus of media research. Essentially youth culture is seen as deviant, or potentially deviant, and as a function of media is to patrol the boundaries between the norm and the deviant, particular interest is expressed in youth culture, often leading to DEMONIZATION and a tendency to work up concern that threatens to constitute a MORAL PANIC. See FOLK DEVILS; SENSITIZATION.

Z

Zapping, zipping The practice of TV channel-switching, especially when the commercials come on is referred to as zapping; made worryingly easy – as far as advertisers are concerned – with the arrival of remote control. In France, an anti-zapping strategy designed to keep viewers glued to the commercials was introduced in the late 1980s: individual numbers placed in the corner of the screen offer viewers a bingo-style competition. A full line of numbers wins a cash prize. Zipping is fast-forwarding through recorded programmes, again most generally to escape the commercials.

Zinoviev letter, 1924 Probably forged by Russian émigrés and used as a 'Red scare' tactic by the *Daily Mail* to put the frighteners on the electorate immediately before the 1924 election. Labour lost the election and the Zinoviev letter probably made some difference if not a substantial one. It was a 1200-word document marked 'Very Secret', bearing the address of the 3rd Communist International, the organization in Moscow responsible for international Communist tactics.

The letter was addressed to the Central Committee of the British Communist Party and its tenor was the need to stir the British proletariat to revolutionary action against their capitalist masters. Among other recommendations, the letter urged the formation of cells in the armed forces – the 'future directors of the British Red Army'.

The impact of the forged letter was due to its timing. It was 'intercepted' by the Conservative *Daily Mail* just a few days before the election of October 1924 and published four days before polling day. The *Mail* used a seven-deck (or lines) headline, topping the deck with 'Civil War Plot By Socialists' Masters'. With the exception of the *Daily Herald*, the entire British press swallowed and regurgitated the story. *The Times* discovered 'Another Red Plot in Germany' and on voting day the *Daily Express* warned, in red ink, 'Do Not Vote Red Today'. Labour lost 50 seats – but gained more than a million votes.

Eventually (but always too late) the truth will out; and in February 1999 Gill Bennett, chief historian at the UK Foreign Office, produced a 126-page report, commissioned by then Foreign Secretary Robin Cook, pointing a sure finger of accusation at Desmond Morton, an MI6 officer and friend of Winston Churchill, as the official who supplied the *Mail* with its sensational disclosure. Also named is Major Joseph Ball, an MI5 officer who joined the Conservative Central Office in 1926. Bennett reported that the forged letter was 'probably leaked from SIS [the Secret Intelligence Service, alias MI6] by somebody to the Conservative Party Central Office'.

MI6 was at the centre of the scandal but Bennett could not be sure at this distance in time whether Admiral Hugh Sinclair, head of MI6, was party to the conspiracy. In a UK *Guardian* article 'The hidden hand' (4 February 1999), Robin Cook took the fullest opportunity to celebrate a 'remarkable exercise in openness' 75 years after the event, at the same time exonerating the Foreign Office from any blame, insisting that there was no institutional conspiracy and admitting that important questions remain unanswered, 'such as who forged the letter'. See DISINFORMATION; FREEDOM OF INFORMATION. See also *TOPIC GUIDE* under MEDIA: FREEDOM, CENSORSHIP; MEDIA: POWER, EFFECTS, INFLUENCE.

Zircon affair UK *New Statesman* journalist Duncan Campbell in 1986, made a series of six TV programmes for the BBC entitled *Secret Society*. The first of these was about a Ministry of Defence project – Zircon – to put a spy satellite into space, at an estimated cost of £5m. On 15 January 1987, Alisdair Milne, the BBC's soon-to-be-dismissed director-general, banned the Zircon programme on grounds of national security, a decision the *Observer* made public on 18 January.

The most notorious aspect of the Zircon affair was the police raids. Special Branch descended upon the *New Statesman* offices; upon Campbell's home as well as the homes of two other *Statesman* journalists and finally there was a raid on the Glasgow offices of BBC Scotland, where all six of the *Secret Society* films were seized. Two days before, Milne had been sacked as the BBC's director-general.

The irony of the case is that Zircon was not really a closely guarded state secret; indeed the position of the proposed satellite was filed by the Ministry of Defence at the International Communications Union, an institution of which the former USSR was a member. Eventually the Zircon programme was transmitted by the BBC in September 1988, by which time the Zircon project had been cancelled. See *TOPIC GUIDE* under MEDIA: FREEDOM, CENSORSHIP; MEDIA: POLITICS AND ECONOMICS; MEDIA: POWER, EFFECTS, INFLUENCE.

Zoetrope Or 'wheel of life'. Early nineteenth-century 'toy' in which pictures inside a spinning drum, viewed from the outside through slits, appear to be in motion. Invented in 1834 by Englishman W.G. Horner, the zoetrope simply but effectively demonstrated the phenomenon of PERSISTENCE OF VISION, the realization of which opened the way for the birth of cinema.

Zones In *The Hidden Dimension: Man's Use of Space in Public and Private* (UK: Bodley Head, 1966) Edward T. Hall identifies four distinct zones, or territorial spaces, in which most men and women operate. These are *intimate* distance; *personal* distance; *social* distance and *public* distance, each with its close and far phases. See PROXEMICS.

Zoom lens On a movie camera, a lens that can be adjusted automatically to give the effect of movement away from or towards the stationary camera.

Zoopraxography Pioneer photographer Eadward Muybridge (1830–1904) was not the inventor of cine-film but he made the first photographic moving pictures – a process he called Zoopraxography – 15 years before the Lumières' first films. Muybridge described his Zoopraxiscope as being 'the first apparatus ever used, or constructed, for synthetically demonstrating movements analytically photographed from life'. In 1878 he set up an experiment at Palo Alto, California, to ascertain by photography, whether all four hooves of a galloping horse were ever simultaneously clear of the ground; 24 cameras were aligned along a running track, each triggered off by the horse as it galloped past.

The Zoopraxiscope consisted basically of a spinning glass disc bearing the photographs in sequence of movement. The disc, when attached to a central shaft, revolved in front of the condensing lens of a projecting lantern parallel to and close to another disc fixed to a tubular shaft that encircled the other, and around which it rotated in the opposite direction.

By 1885 Muybridge had produced an encyclopaedia of motion: men and women, clothed and unclothed, performed simple actions such as running, drinking cups of tea or shoeing horses; and a massive and varied study of animals and birds in movement. His carefully catalogued work was published in 1887. See *TOPIC GUIDE* under MEDIA HISTORY.

APPENDIX: A CHRONOLOGY OF MEDIA EVENTS

This Chronology is drawn from many sources but our best thanks go to Patrick Robertson whose *The New Shell Book of Firsts* (UK: Headline, 1994), a remarkable piece of historical detective work, has been immensely helpful. *UK* is used in a generalized sense as a composite reference to England, Britain and the United Kingdom.

AD 105   Paper produced from pulp; invention attributed to Ts'ai Lun, China.

AD 704   First printed book, the *Dharani Sutra*, created in Korea from woodblocks on a scroll, and discovered in the foundations of the Pulguk Sa pagoda in Kyongju, South Korea, October 1966.

1174   First evidence of woodblock printing in Europe, by Benedictine monks at Engelberg, Switzerland, used to print capital letters in illuminated manuscripts.

1234   *Compendium of Rites and Rituals*, first book printed using movable type comprising 50 chapters, 28 copies of which were published in Korea. The type was made using a sand-moulding technique developed in 1102 for casting coins.

1451   *Donatis Latin Grammar*, two leaves of a 27-line publication, the first evidence of the use of movable type in Europe, possibly the same type as that used by John of Gutenberg in his 42-line Bible believed to have been printed at Mainz between 1451 and 1454, 48 copies of which survive, 36 printed on paper, 12 on vellum.

1454   Gutenberg prints the first calendar.

1461   Albrecht Pfister of Bamberg publishes the first books in the vernacular: Ulrich Boner's *Edelstein* and Johann von Tepl's *Ackermann aus Böhmen*.

1474   In Bruges, the Englishman William Caxton publishes *The Recuyell of the Histories of Troye*, a translation from original French text. Caxton moved to London where he printed in 1477 *The Dictes and Sayengis of the Philosophres*, a work of 74 leaves 'drawn out of frensche into our Englisshe tonge' by Anthony Earl Rivers.

1475   Jodocus Pflanzmann of Augsburg prints the first illustrated Bible.

1484   Caxton prints *Morte D'Arthur*.

1494   John Tate of Stevenage is the first to manufacture paper in England. Tate produced the first-known watermark in the UK – a star and circle.

1517   Martin Luther nails his 95 Theses, protesting against the sale of indulgences, on the church door at Wittenberg. The printing and distribution of his works ignites the Reformation, and the division of Europe between Roman Catholic and Protestant faiths.

1526   William Tyndale's translation of the New Testament into English is published by Peter Schoeffer in Worms, Germany.

1527   Leipzig: printer Hanz Hergot executed for twice publishing *On the New Direction of Christian Life,* a pamphlet advocating common ownership of land and goods.

1536   Myles Coverdale's complete translation of the Bible into English published, probably in Cologne. This was printed in London by James Nicholson the following year.

1559   Roman Catholic church promulgates the Index Librorum Prohibitorum, a list of prohibited books; and in 1571 the Index Expurgatoris, of books permitted after censorship.

1588   Dr Timothy Bright introduces the first recorded system of shorthand. His system appeared under the title *Characterie; the art of short, swift, and secret writing.*

1608   The civil authorities of Norwich open the first municipal public library, chiefly for 'the use of preachers'. In 1656 Chetham's Library in Manchester became the first to employ a librarian. Chetham's was open to all. As late as 1849 it remained the only substantial collection of books fully accessible to the public. Manchester also took the lead with the lending of books. In 1852 the Manchester Free Library instituted a lending system, issuing over 70,000 books in its first year. This followed the Public Libraries Act of 1850.

1611   Issue in the UK of the Authorized Version of the Bible, the composite work of 46 translators and revisers.

1619   State of Weimar becomes the first to introduce compulsory education for all between the ages of 6 and 13. In the UK similar legislation had to wait until 1870.

1621   First *Corantos* published in London, followed in same year by first Proclamation against Corantos.

1637   Star Chamber Decree regulating printing, followed in 1643 with Ordinance for regulating printing, and in 1649 the first Printing Act.

1642   The *Mayflower* arrives in America from Plymouth, England, with a printing press on board.

1644   Publication of John Milton's *Areopagitica* presenting the case for the freedom of the press.

1649   UK: Charles I beheaded. During the period in power of the Lord Protector, Oliver Cromwell, and until the restoration of the monarchy in 1660, under Charles II, England becomes a hotbed of radical, chiefly religious, publications. John Lilburne issues *England's New Chaines Discovered.*

1650   At Leipzig, the first daily newspaper, the *Einkommenden Zeitungen,* is published by Timotheus Ritzsch. In the UK the *Perfect Diurnall* was published daily, except Sunday, between February and March 1660, though British readers had to wait till 1702 for the first successful daily, the *Daily Courant.*

1651	Publication of Thomas Hobbes' *Leviathan*.
1657	First classified advertisement in a UK paper printed in Thomas Newcombe's *Publick Advertiser*, the first English paper devoted entirely to advertising.
1660–1	Parliament prohibits publication of its proceedings.
1680	Royal Proclamation suppressing all newsbooks except those under licence from the authorities.
1693	In UK, the *City Mercury* is the first giveaway newspaper.
	London bookseller John Dunton issues the first women's magazine, the *Ladies' Mercury*.
1695	Parliament does not renew the Licensing Act.
1701	First provincial newspaper in the UK, the *Norwich Post*, a weekly, with an approximate circulation of 400-500 copies.
1702	First daily newspaper in Britain, the *Daily Courant*, is published in London.
1704	John Campbell publishes *Boston Newsletter*, the first newspaper in the US not to be a one-issue failure.
1709	English Copyright Act, the first enactment to secure the rights of authors and publishers by offering legal protection against 'pirating' of texts. A similar act was passed in France in 1793 and in the Grand Duchy of Saxe-Weimar in 1839 (the first to employ the 30-year term of protection after an author's death). The principle of international reciprocity of rights was established in the Berne Convention of 1886.
1712	In Britain, first 'Taxes on Knowledge' introduced – duties on newspapers and advertising and excise duty on paper.
1720s	Benjamin Franklin begins successful publishing career with *Pennsylvania Gazette*.
1725	Stamp Act in Britain applies 1712 regulations to all newspapers, whatever their size or format.
1739	Scotsman William Ged devises method of preserving pages of type for future reprints, using a mould made from plaster of Paris from which metal plates were made. In fear of their livelihoods, Scottish printers wrecked the invention; 60 years later it was revived by Firmin Didot who reversed the process by creating the metal plate from sunken surfaces. Eventually stereotyping, as the process came to be known, was made a commercial proposition by amateur inventor Lord Stanhope, in 1805, at the Clarendon Press, Oxford.
	In 1829 the plaster and metal plates gave way to papier mâché, reducing time, weight and bulk – innovations happening at virtually the same time in Italy, France and England. Stanhope also improved the printing press by replacing the wooden press with an iron structure and by increasing the bed of the machine in order to produce one-pull larger-scale sheets.

1741	First magazines, in US, Andrew Bradford's *American Magazine*, followed by Benjamin Franklin's *General Magazine*.
1757	UK: increases in taxes on newspapers; increased again in 1776, 1780, 1789 (the year of the French Revolution), 1797 and 1815.
1764	London: prosecution of firebrand editor/journalist John Wilkes for seditious libel published in the *North Briton*.
1770s	Thomas Paine in America. His *Common Sense* (1776), arguing powerfully for the separation of the States from English rule, will prove an immensely influential bestseller.
1771	Press permitted to report the proceedings of the House of Commons, followed by those of the House of Lords (in 1775).
	The *Morning Post* published in London.
1776	Publication of Adam Smith's *An Inquiry into the Nature and Causes of the Wealth of Nations.*
	Publication of Tom Paine's *Common Sense: Addressed to the Inhabitants of America,* a summons to the people of America to rise up in battle and overthrow British rule. As one English historian believed: 'It would be difficult to name any human composition which had an effect at once so instant, so extended, and so lasting.' 120,000 copies *of Common Sense* were sold within three months of publication.
1780	UK: first Sunday newspaper published – the *British Gazette and Sunday Monitor*.
1785	Founding of *The Times* newspaper followed by the *Observer* in 1791.
	Paris: fortnightly *Le Cabinet des Modes* is published, the first fashion magazine.
1787	First recorded advertising agency formed in London by William Tayler, who for a handling fee booked advertisements in the provincial press.
1788	UK: publication of first daily evening newspaper – *Star and Evening Advertiser*.
1789	Revolution in France: the Declaration of the Rights of Man and Citizens is promulgated 27 July; the key to this being the notion of popular sovereignty. The principles of the Revolution were to be an inspiration to radicalism in Britain and a guiding light of the Radical press.
	In turn events in France provoked the authorities in Britain to take repressive measures against the Radicals and the causes they advocated.
1790	Orator and conservative theorist Edmund Burke publishes *Reflections on the Revolution in France* condemning the uprising of the common people.
1791	Tom Paine's *The Rights of Man* Part 1 published, a stirringly eloquent riposte to Burke's *Reflections*.
	English philosopher Jeremy Bentham designs a 'panopticon', (the all-seeing one) for the central inspection of convicts; an idea given new life in the twentieth century in an age of electronic surveillance.
	First Amendment to the American Bill of Rights guarantees the freedom of the press.

1792   First Libel Act becomes law in Britain.

            Part 2 of Tom Paine's *Rights of Man* published. Also Mary Wollstonecraft's *Vindication of the Rights of Women*, demanding equal educational opportunities for women.

1793   John Bell, Yorkshire-born founder of the *Oracle or Bell's New World* becomes the first-ever foreign correspondent, reporting to his own paper the fighting between the British and French in the Low Countries. He chose to march with the French rather than with the forces of the Duke of York. He reported on the British victories at Le Cateau-Cambrésis, Villiers-en-Cauche and Troixelle as well as the defeat at Tournay. His example was emulated by *The Times* in 1808 when Henry Crabb Robinson was commissioned to cover the Peninsular War.

1798   France, at the Essonne mill: Nicolas Robert introduces the first paper manufacturing machine; the first in England established at Frogmore, Hertfordshire, in 1805 by brothers Henry and Sealy Fourdriner, and at St Neots, Huntingdonshire, by John Gamble. Paper output increased tenfold.

            Prime Minister William Pitt increases the tax on British newspapers from $1\frac{1}{2}$ pence to $2\frac{1}{2}$ pence and bans the import into the UK of foreign newspapers.

1800   Bavarian Alois Senefelder takes out English patent for lithographic process, printing from the surface of a specially prepared stone. Photography is incorporated into the printed page, using lithography, from 1840.

1802   Founding of the *Weekly Political Register* by William Cobbett, one of the outstanding journalist/editors of the nineteenth century. Paper survives until 1835.

1805   Lord Stanhope's improved stereotyping machine set up at Oxford's Clarendon Press.

1811   Thomas Bensley makes first use in the UK of the Frederick Koenig steam-driven press to print in London 3000 sheets of the *Annual Register*.

1814   *The Times* installs the Koenig press, the most significant technological advance in printing since the age of Gutenberg. The steam-driven press made mass production of newspapers a reality and, in the company of other inventions in paper manufacture and stereotyping, ushered in the first age of mass communication. The initial run was 1100 sheets per hour. The first book to be printed on the power press in the UK was Johann Blumenbach's *Physiology*, in 1817.

1821   In Britain, the Six Acts passed, including two targeting the radical press.

            Manchester Guardian founded.

1822   Invention of the camera by Frenchman Joseph Nièpce who produced the first photograph (1826). Also in 1822, William Church's letter-founding machine makes for reductions in production costs. Hand-assembly could cast between 3000 and 7000 letters a day, Church's machine between 12,000 and 20,000.

            Sunday Times founded.

1826   Leipzig publisher F.A. Brockhaus applies Koenig's steam press to the printing of books.

First permanently fixed photograph created by Nicéphore Nièpce. This was taken from an upper storey at Nièpce's home at Gras, Chalon-sur-Saône.

1829 Four-cylinder steam press, invented by Augustus Applegarth and Edward Cowper for *The Times*, speeds the delivery of print, allowing 4000 sheets per hour. The same inventors follow this up in 1848 with the rotary press, which printed 8000 sheets per hour.

1830s UK: the 'War of the Unstamped' waged by the radical, unstamped press against the Taxes on Knowledge.

1831-5 Publication of Henry Hetherington's *Poor Man's Guardian*, one of the outstanding radical papers of the nineteenth century.

1832 W.E. Weber and K.F. Gauss construct the needle telegraph in Grottingen.

The *Penny Magazine* of London becomes the first mass-circulation paper selling over 100,000 copies.

1833 Advertising Duty reduced, followed in 1836 with the reduction of Stamp Duty and Excise Duty on paper. It was not until 1853 that Advertising Duty was abolished. 1855 saw the abolition of Stamp Duty and 1861 Paper Duties.

US: *New York Sun*, concentrating on stories of sex and violence, published by Benjamin Day. This was followed in 1835 by the *New York Herald*, published by John Gordon Bennett, with specific pages dedicated to sport and finance.

1835 Henry Fox-Talbot, British pioneer in the development of photography, publishes a description in the February edition of the *Literary Gazette* of the positive–negative process, which would enable the reproduction of photographs in any number.

Fox-Talbot's work coincided with that of the Frenchman Louis Daguerre who was the first to commercially exploit photography. The Daguerrotype used only the one-off positive, but it advanced exposure time from eight hours to only 15 to 30 minutes. The French government acquired the rights from Daguerre and Isidor Nièpce, heir of Nicéphore Nièpce (died 1833) who had gone into business with Daguerre. Thus the process became public property for all to use. Daguerre's own cameras were on sale before the end of the year.

1836 US: Samuel Morse builds his first telegraph.

1838 *The Times of India* founded.

Publication of the radical *Northern Star* (until 1852).

1839 In Paris, Alphonse Giroux manufactures for sale the first Daguerrotype camera.

1842 *Illustrated London News* is founded.

Samuel Morse lays first submarine telegraph cable, New York Harbour.

1843 Giuseppe Mazzini obtains patent for a composing machine, though the idea had originated as early as 1682 with Johann Joachim Becher, a political economist.

Though some 1500 patents had by 1900 been registered in the US for composing machines those invented by Robert Hattersley and Charles Kastenbein dominated. With each, the chief problem was the need to justify the lines by hand, a problem resolved by Linotype and Monotype machines, and the punch-cutting machine of Linn Boyd Benton of Milwaukee in 1885.

A Saxon weaver, Friedrich Gottleb Keller, produces paper from wood pulp, another innovation suggested much earlier but not developed or taken up.

The first public telegraph service is introduced following the completion of the Great Western Railway telegraph line from Paddington to Slough. William Cooke who had patented the system transferred the licence, for an annual fee, to Thomas Home and the first paid telegrams were sent by Cooke's double-needle electro-magnetic telegraph along a 20-mile wire. Eventually the Electric Telegraph Company took up the licence and pioneered nationwide telegraphy. By 1847 two systems, north and south, were in operation, linking major towns and cities. Unification of the regions took place in November.

Foundation of the *News of the World,* the *Economist* and, in Newcastle, the *Miners' Journal.*

1844	Transmission of the first press telegram, from a Congress reporter in Washington DC to the editor of the *Baltimore Patriot,* by Morse telegraph. In the UK the first press telegraph was sent in the same year, from Windsor Castle to *The Times* via the Slough-Paddington telegraph, announcing the birth of Prince Alfred to Queen Victoria.

William Fox-Talbot's *The Pencil of Nature* is the first book in the UK to be published with photographs. This was issued by Longman in six parts.

Society of Women Journalists founded in London.

1846	London: *Daily News* founded, with Charles Dickens (briefly) as editor.

1847–8	Karl Marx and Frederick Engels produce *The Communist Manifesto.* Having settled in the UK Marx produced his monumental work, *Das Kapital* (*Capital*) in 1859.

Paris: the photographic journal *Le Daguerrotype* published.

1848	In Havana, Cuba, Italian Antonio Meucci creates instrument with which he communicates between apartment floors with his invalid wife. However, it is 1860 before there is a public demonstration of the telephone, by Johann Philipp Reis of Germany, using a violin-case for a resonator, a hollowed-out beer-barrel bung for a mouthpiece and a stretched sausage skin for a diaphragm. In 1861 Reis demonstrated an improved version to the Frankfurt Physical Society, transmitting verses and songs – albeit with very poor clarity – over a 300-foot line.

The editor of the UK *Morning Chronicle* employs Eliza Lyn Linton to write features and reviews. She later became the paper's Paris correspondent. On her return to the UK she became Fleet Street's first-ever full-time woman journalist. She became known for her antipathy to women's suffrage.

1850	UK: Public Libraries Act.

Philadelphia: Frederick Langenheim patents first photographic slides.

1852	J.W. Brett lays first submarine telegraph cable between Dover and Calais.
	UK: House of Commons Press Gallery opens.
	Surgeon John MacCosh is first British war photographer; 47 studies survive of his photo-coverage of the Second Burma War.
1853	Liverpool: the *Northern Daily Times* becomes England's first daily provincial paper.
1854	Paris: *Le Figaro* founded.
1855	Englishman Alexander Parkes invents celluloid.
	Foundation of the *Daily Telegraph*.
	In UK, newspaper tax abolished.
1858	First transatlantic telegram sent by John Cash, American name-tape manufacturer, from London to his New York representative. At £1 a word, it read: 'Go to Chicago'.
1860	Antonio Meucci demonstrates, in New York, his 'telefono' but has insufficient funds to patent his invention. Only in 2002 was he acknowledged, by the US House of Representatives, as the true originator of the telephone (rather than Alexander Graham Bell who had access to Meucci's materials and had shared a laboratory with him). However, it was Bell who patented a version of Meucci's device in 1876.
1865	Father Giovanni Caselli developed the first fax machine between 1857 and 1864. It was introduced for public service over the Paris-Lyons telegraph line in May 1865. However, the first office fax did not become commercially available until the Xerox LDX was demonstrated in the company's showroom in New York, May 1964. The Japanese firm Sharp introduced the first colour fax in 1984.
1866	Mahloon Loomis of Washington DC, having described a system of radio signalling in a paper of July 1866, succeeds in October in broadcasting messages over a 14-mile distance. He was granted the world's first wireless patent in 1872. Lack of funds in a period of recession prevented Loomis developing radio commercially before his death in 1886. In the UK David Edward Hughes proved a significant pioneer into the phenomenon of radio waves, but he met with little encouragement. It was left to Heinrich Hertz, the German electrical scientist, to convince the scientific community of the existence and significance of radio waves, thus making possible the development of radio telegraphy and broadcasting.
1867	Invention of the typewriter by American Christopher Sholes.
1868	London, Press Association founded.
	New York: *Staats Zeitung* first newspaper to be printed on wood-pulp paper.
1870	UK: Education Act inaugurates systematic primary school education for all.
1870–1	Jessie White Mario becomes world's first woman war correspondent, covering the Franco-Prussian War for several US and British papers.

1872   Issue of first illustrated daily newspaper, the *New York Daily Graphic.*

1873   The *New York Daily Graphic* is first to publish a half-tone photograph, 2 December – an illustration of the city's Steinway Hall appeared on the back page.

1874   American writer Mark Twain becomes the first author to possess a typewriter – made by Remington. By 1890 in the US there were 30 manufacturers producing typewriters. In the UK none were on sale until 1889, from the Maskelyne British Typewriter & Manufacturing Company.

              In the same year George C. Blickensderfer's Connecticut company produced the first portable, the Blick. The introduction of the typewriter into business created new employment opportunities for women.

1876   Scotsman Alexander Graham Bell successfully initiates telephonic communication. Bell, of Edinburgh, patented the telephone on 9 March, and on 10 March, in Boston, US, the first truly coherent transmission took place – a message from Bell to his assistant, Thomas Watson: 'Come here, Watson, I want you.' The speaking telephone was demonstrated by Bell at the Centennial Exhibition, Philadelphia, 25 June. In July of the following year the first telephone line between two separate buildings was laid, in London, between the Queen's Theatre and Canterbury Hall. In the same year the first telephone exchange was created on behalf of the New England Telephone Company by Isaac D. Smith.

1877   Thomas Alva Edison of America patents the Phonograph, the first sound-recording system. The prototype being completed by Edison's mechanic, John Kruesi at West Orange, New Jersey, on 6 December, Edison proceeded to make history by reciting into the recording apparatus, 'Mary had a little lamb'. The Edison Speaking Phonograph Company began production in April 1879. The tin-foil cylinder provided so short a duration that public interest in the Phonograph declined.

              The wax-cylinder Graphaphone developed by Chichester Bell and Charles Sumner Tainter was patented in 1886, to be countered by Edison, his interest in recording renewed, with the Improved Phonograph. Edison Laboratories were the first to record music by an accredited musician, the boy pianist Josef Hofman, in 1888. There was no means of duplicating wax discs before 1892.

1878   The microphone, demonstrated in London by Professor David Edward Hughes.

1880   The Radiophone, devised by Charles Sumner Tainter and Alexander Graham Bell, successfully transmits speech between the top of Franklin School, Washington DC, and Bell's laboratory on 14th Street.

              Telephony without wires had been the invention of A.C. Brown of the Eastern Telegraph Company two years earlier. Reginald Fessenden produced the first conventional system of radio telephony capable of transmitting speech across distances regardless of obstacles between transmitter and receiver. He demonstrated his system for the first time, over a distance of a mile, 23 December 1900. His words were addressed to his assistant, 'Is it snowing where you are, Mr Thiessen?'

              In UK *Titbits* founded, followed in 1888 by *Answers* – two immensely popular weeklies.

1883   In US, Joseph Pulitzer starts up the *New York World.*

1884   Lewis Waterman in the US creates the first fountain pen.

1885   Louis Aimé Augustin Le Prince, French-born but living in the US, projects the first moving pictures – on to a wall at the Institute for the Deaf, New York, applying in November 1996 for an American patent for an 'Apparatus for producing Animated Pictures'. This was granted in January 1888 but reference to cameras and projectors was disallowed because of Dumont's British patent of 1861 (though this involved an arrangement of glass plates to form the facets of a prismatic drum and had nothing to do with the reproduction of moving images on a screen).

On the point of going into commercial production in 1890, Le Prince boarded a train in Dijon, bound for Paris where it was his intention to demonstrate his invention to the secretary of the Paris Opera. He – and his apparatus – disappeared; a mystery that remains unsolved.

1886   *New York Herald Tribune* installs the first Linotype machine, the invention of Ottmar Margenthaler.

Paris: *Le Petit Journal* becomes first paper to reach 1 million circulation.

1887   German Emile Berliner working in the US applies for a patent for the first gramophone or disc-recorder player. He demonstrated his invention at the Franklin Institute in Philadelphia in the following year. The hand-cranked gramophone was initially produced as a toy by Kammerer & Rheinhardt, Germany, using a five-inch vulcanized rubber disc at an approximate speed of 70rpm. Electrically operated machines were marketed by the United States Gramophone Company in Washington in 1894, using seven-inch records.

First overseas edition of a newspaper – *New York Herald* in Paris.

The Berliner Gramophone Company of Philadelphia produced the first shellac records in 1897. This company was also the first to create a recording studio and record shop. Double-sided discs were first manufactured in 1904 by the International Talking Machine Company, Germany, under the imprint Odeon Records.

San Francisco: William Randoph Hearst takes command of his father's paper, the *Examiner,* initiating a career as press baron to out-rival and out-live all his contemporaries. In 1895 he bought the *New York Journal,* which became the star and exemplar of Yellow Journalism.

Also in 1887, monotype printing invented in the US by Tolbert Lanston. Commercially established by 1897, the Monotype had the advantage over Linotype in that it cast each letter separately instead of in a compact line, thus making it easier to correct the text.

1888   George Eastman of Rochester, New York, produced first snapshot camera – the Kodak – for use by the general public. This used pre-loaded paper-roll film. It took 100 circular pictures 2.5 inches in diameter. Mass produced by the Eastman Company, Kodak No. 1 proved an immediate success in the US and worldwide.

In the same year John Carbutt of Philadelphia introduced celluoid film. This was made from celluloid sheets one-hundredth of an inch thick, and obtained from the Celluloid

Manufacturing Company. However, the first celluloid roll film to be manufactured commercially was another Eastman coup. The Eastman Dry Plate Company produced roll film for its Kodak cameras, beginning in August 1889. The first colour roll film came much later, and was invented by Robert Krayn in Germany in 1910. Amateurs had a longer wait – until Kodrachrome produced three-colour roll film in 1936.

UK: *Financial Times* founded.

1889   UK's first Official Secrets Act.

Kansas City undertaker Almon B. Stowger patents the first automatic telephone exchange. The first exchange was opened at La Porte, Indiana, in November 1892. Dial telephones were introduced in 1896.

1890   Alfred Harmsworth, later Lord Northcliffe, publishes the first comic, the eight-page *Comic Cuts*, edited by Houghton Townley. Nearly 120,000 copies of the first edition were sold and this rose to 300,000 within a month. In October 1890 a rival to *Comic Cuts*, *Funny Cuts* appeared with the first-ever front-page strip cartoon.

Telephoto lens invented by New Zealand geologist Alexander McKay.

London evening *Star* prints the first front-page newspaper headline, 16 July. This read: many happy returns of the day – wedding of professor stuart mp.

1891   Peep-show projector, the Kinetoscope, developed by William Dickson at the instigation of his employer, Thomas Alva Edison, has first public showing in Edison's workshops in West Orange, New Jersey, to 147 representatives of the National Federation of Women's Clubs.

The first commercial showing took place at Holland Bros' Kinetoscope Parlor, Broadway, in April 1894. The films were produced by the Edison Co., which was thus the first-ever film production company. In the same year Greek showman George Trajedis installed six kinetoscopes in a converted Old Bond Street store in London, October, charging 2 pence per film.

1893   UK: first issue of the *Sketch*.

1894   The first commercially viable radio communication was the work of the Italian Guglielmo Marconi of Bologna. Experiments conducted in 1894 and 1895 led Marconi to offer his invention to the Italian Ministry of Posts and Telegraphs. Failing to elicit interest, the inventor moved to England where customs officials broke open his equipment, suspecting him of being an anarchist. Undaunted, Marconi settled in London and in 1896 applied for a patent for a method by which 'electrical actions or manifestations are transmitted through air, earth or water by means of electrical oscillations of high frequency'.

The first public demonstration of Marconi's wireless took place on 12 December 1896. In the following year the Marconi Wireless Telegraph & Signal Company was formed.

1895   Brothers Auguste and Louis Lumière project the first-ever film on to a screen – *Workers Leaving the Lumière Factory*, 22 March, to members of the Société d'Encouragement a L'Industrie Nationale, at 44 rue de Rennes, Paris. On 28 December the Lumières entertained a paying audience at the Grand Café on the Boulevard des Capuchines: cinema was born.

William Randolph Hearst buys up the *New York Journal* having built up the *San Francisco Examiner*, given to him by his father, with sensational stories of gangsters and Hollywood sex scandals.

1896   First permanent cinema, the 400-seater Vitascope Hall, opened in New Orleans, 26 June, by William T. Rock. Admission was 10 cents, plus another 10 to view the Edison Vitascope projector. The 5000-seater Gaumont-Palace, formerly the Hippodrome Theatre, opened in Paris in 1910. The largest cinema ever built was the Roxy Theater in New York, with 6200 seats. In Berlin 300 cinemas were opened during 1908. In the UK by 1912 there were 4000 cinemas.

J.H. Rigg of Leeds manufactures the first motorized cinema projector. An electrically powered model was demonstrated at the Royal Aquarium, London, 6 April.

UK *Daily Mail* founded by Alfred Harmsworth, later Lord Northcliffe.

1897   First wide-screen film on 70mm stock introduced by Enoch J. Rector of the Veriscope Co., New York.

1898   The Telegraphone, the first magnetic recorder, is patented by Danish engineer Valdemar Poulsen employed by the Copenhagen Telephone Company. Demonstrated in public for the first time at the Paris Exposition of 1900, the Telegraphone used magnetized piano wire running between spools at 7 feet per second.

Commercial production began in America in 1903. An improved model was used by Lee de Forest for experiments in talking film. The use of metal tape instead of wire came in 1929 with the Blattnerphone, again used in film production, at Elstree Studios.

The use of plastic tape originated in Berlin with the Magnetophon produced by the firm AEG. This proved the archetype for all recorder developments from that time.

1900   Film: sound on disc demonstrated to a paying audience at the Paris Exposition. The first sound-on-film process was patented by French-born Eugene Lauste of Brixton in 1906. His first successful experiment in recording and reproducing speech on film came in 1910. He was ready to exploit his system commercially, only to be interrupted by the outbreak of war in 1914. He crossed the Atlantic with his idea but met with the same lack of interest as America itself entered the war.

1901   Marconi transmits messages by wireless telegraph from Cornwall to Newfoundland.

1902   Canadian-born Reginald Fessenden of the US introduces the first radio-telephone; makes the first transmission of speech by wireless.

UK: Arthur Pearson founds the *Daily Express*.

Alfred Harmsworth founds the *Daily Mirror*.

1906   Fessenden makes the first radio broadcast, using the 420-foot-high radio mast of the National Electric Signalling Company's radio station at Brant Rock, Massachusetts. On

24 December the programme began with Fessenden playing Gounod's 'O, Holy Night' on the violin, followed by him singing and reciting from St Luke's Gospel. The first gramophone record to be broadcast came next, a recording of Handel's 'Largo'. The transmission ended with Fessenden wishing his listeners a happy Christmas. The audience for the broadcast turned out to be ships' operators within a five-mile radius. Fessenden's second broadcast, on New Year's Eve, in better atmospheric conditions, was received as far away as the West Indies.

In the UK the first radio broadcast came in the following year – from the radio room of HMS *Andromeda*. It was initiated by Lieutenant Quentin Crauford RN and transmitted to other ships at Chatham. News of the broadcast was not made known, for the Admiralty saw the possibilities of radio in military use, in particular as aiding communication between submarines and shore and other vessels.

1907	First regular experimental broadcasts conducted by Lee De Forest's Radio Telephone Company from the Parker Building, New York. Two years later De Forest introduced his mother-in-law Harriet Stanton Black to listeners. She gave the world's first broadcast talk; her theme was women's suffrage.
	Lord Northcliffe purchases *The Times*.
	In UK foundation of National Union of Journalists (NUJ).
	First patent, in London, Berlin and St Petersburg of all-electric television cathode-ray tube receiver, by Russian Boris Rozing. On 9 May 1911 Rozing succeeded in transmitting by wireless over distance 'a distinct image … consisting of four luminous bands'.
1909	In US, National Board of Censorship of Motion Pictures established.
1911	UK Copyright Act requires copies of all British publications to be supplied to the British Museum and to five other copyright libraries.
	First Hollywood studio, the Nestor Studio, opened on Sunset Boulevard by David Horsley.
1912	Foundation, initially as the *Herald*, of the *Daily Herald*.
1913	The British Board of Film Censors, formed in 1912 by the Kinematograph Manufacturers' Association, begins operation.
1914	Price of *The Times* reduced to one penny.
	First full-length feature film in colour, *The World, the Flesh and the Devil*, shown to the trade in February, and opened at the Holborn Empire in April. Kinemacolor was a two-colour system. Gaumont Chronochrome (1914) produced three colours, but three-colour processing was costly and slow in development.
	Technicolor successfully produced, in 1932, the Disney cartoon *Flowers and Trees*, while the first feature-length film in Technicolor was Rouben Mamoulian's *Becky Sharp*, released in 1935.
1914–18	First World War.

1915	UK: *Daily Express* bought by Max Aitken, Lord Beaverbrook, for £17,500.
1916	Film, *The Battle of the Somme* – first-ever war documentary.
	Clydeside workers are supported in their refusal to make munitions by the Labour paper *Forward*. It is suppressed.
1918	UK: first Film Society, the Stoll Picture Theatre Club, opens with a presentation by Baroness Orczy of *The Laughing Cavalier*.
1919	UK: Arthur Mee founds the *Children's Newspaper*.
1920	The Marconi Company begins radio transmission from its Chelmsford works on 19 January. On 15 June Dame Nellie Melba gives a 30-minute recital, from Chelmsford, sponsored by Lord Northcliffe. Her fee was £1000. In November transmissions from Chelmsford were suspended on the grounds that they interfered with radio communication to aircraft and ships. Broadcasts resumed from Marconi's Station 2MT at Writtle, February 1922. 2MT was the first regular broadcasting station in the UK.
1922	Marconi's new station 2LO broadcasts from Marconi House in the Strand, London. Along with three other radio stations, 2LO was merged into what was to become the British Broadcasting Company. Broadcasting from Writtle remained independent until it closed down on 17 January 1923. The first BBC programme was broadcast on 14 November 1922 from 2LO – a news bulletin put out at 6pm.
	First play on radio, *The Wolf* by Eugene Walter, is broadcast by WGY Schenectady of New York, 3 August. In the UK *Cyrano de Bergerac* was presented by engineering staff at Marconi's experimental station 2MT Writtle, 17 October. The first play specially written for radio was Phyllis M. Twigg's *The Truth about Father Christmas*, a children's story, broadcast by the BBC 24 December.
	First programme of sound-on-film production at Berlin's Alhambra cinema using the Tri-Ergon process developed by Joseph Engl, Joseph Massolle and Hans Voght. In the US Lee De Forest's Phonofilm process is demonstrated to the first paying audience, at the Rialto Theater in New York in April 1923.
1924	UK: Sykes Committee Report on Broadcasting, followed in 1925 with the setting up of the Crawford Committee from which emerged the prime principles governing broadcasting in the UK until the coming of commercial TV – monopoly, funding by licence, administration by an independent public corporation.
	Publication in the *Daily Mail* of the notorious Zinoviev Letter, a fake, now considered to have emanated from the UK's own secret service, MI6.
	Felix the Cat becomes the first film character to be merchandized. Licences issued on behalf of Felix's creator Pat Sullivan for Felix to 'feature' on packaging and later as a soft toy.
1925	Using a mechanical scanner for transmitting and receiving, Scotsman John Logie Baird (with others) creates the first television pictures on 30 October. Baird transmitted an image with gradations of light and shade using a primitive amalgam of parts, including an empty biscuit-box for the lamphouse. For test purposes a dummy's head was used,

to be replaced shortly afterwards by 15-year-old office boy William Taynton, who consented to be the first star of TV for the fee of half a crown.

Baird demonstrated his invention to the press on 7 January 1926, and gave a public demonstration on 27 January for members of the Royal Institution. Baird's mechanical system was soon to be overtaken by electronic TV transmission, first developed in Los Angeles by Philo T. Farnsworth in July 1929, though a more practical system developed by Russian-born Vladimir Zworykin of Westinghouse showed the way ahead. All modern TV systems derive from Zworykin's Kinescope and the Ionoscope, the camera tube he developed in 1933.

Lionel Guest and H.O. Merriman of London apply their electrical recording process to record the burial service of the Unknown Warrior at Westminster Abbey, proving that it was possible to substitute a microphone for the studio horn, thus location recording was born. The process was not pursued commercially, but location recording was set in progress in both the US and the UK in the same year. The all-electric record player, with loudspeaker amplification instead of the usual horn, was the Brunswick Panatrope, made by the Brunswick Company of Iowa. This year also saw the introduction of the automatic record-changer, built by 20-year-old Eric Waterworth of Hobart, Tasmania.

First issue of the *New Yorker*.

BBC broadcast first full-length play for radio, Reginald Berkeley's *The White Chateau*, 11 November.

1927   *The Jazz Singer*, using the Vitaphone synchronized disc system, opens at the Warner Theater on Broadway, 6 October. Directed by Alan Crosland and starring Al Jolson, the film is generally acknowledged to have inaugurated the age of sound cinema and marked the death knell of silent movies. There are only two talking sequences in the film and 281 words spoken, but the reception the film received on both sides of the Atlantic was phenomenal.

The Lights of New York, also from Warner Bros, was the first all-talking feature film. It was premiered at New York's Strand Theater, 6 July 1928. Fox Movietone's *In Old Arizona*, a Western directed by Raoul Walsh, screened in December 1928 in Los Angeles, was the first all-talking sound-on-film feature. The first all-talking colour film was Warner Bros' *On With the Show*, screened at New York's Wintergardens, 1929.

1928   On 9 February John Logie Baird makes the first international TV transmission, sending 30-line images of his own face from London by land-line to the transmitting station G2KZ at Coulsdon, Surrey, and then across the Atlantic to a receiving set manned by his assistant, Ben Clapp, at Hartsdale, New York State. On 3 July Baird became the first to transmit television in colour. Employing a Nikow scanning-disc with red, blue and green filters he screened red and blue scarves, a lighted cigarette and red roses. Baird was to be the first to demonstrate high-definition colour – at the Dominion Theatre, London, on 4 February 1938.

Walt Disney release *Steam Boat Willie*, the first animated film using synchronous sound.

1929   Radar invented, by Scotsman Robert Watson-Watt.

UK: first issue of the Communist *Daily Worker*.

1931	Experiments in electronic high-definition TV transmission are carried out by an EMI research team at Hayes, Middlesex, under the direction of Russian-born Isaac Shoenberg. The EMI system was demonstrated to the BBC in the following year – a film of the Changing of the Guard at Buckingham Palace, viewed on a 130-line cathode ray receiver with a five-inch square screen.
	RCA Victor launches the 33⅓rpm long-playing record. The first recording was of Beethoven's Fifth Symphony. However, the radiograms required to play the long-player were expensive in a time of acute recession and the venture was not a success. The LP did not come into its own until 1948 when Columbia issued microgroove records developed by Peter Goldmark – vinylite discs with a playing time of 23 minutes per side, and 224-300 grooves to the inch.
1932	Stereophonic cinema sound patented by French film-makers Abel Gance and André Debrie. Gance's eight-hour silent 1927 epic *Napoléon Bonaparte* was re-edited with added dialogue and sound-effects, and screened at the Paramount Cinema, Paris, in 1935. Warner Bros' *House of Wax* (1953) was the first feature film with complete stereo sound.
	The first stereophonic disc recordings are made by Arthur Keller of the Bell Telephone Laboratories. Made on wax masters at 78rpm, they were not produced commercially but were demonstrated at the Chicago World's Fair, 1933. The first stereo discs to be manufactured for sale were produced by Emory Cork of Stamford, US, in 1957.
1933	Chief of the German Navy's Signals Research Department, Dr Rudoph Kühnold produces the first working radar system. Radar in the UK was the brainchild of Robert Watson-Watt, superintendent of the radio research laboratory at Ditton Park. Experiments with radar in February 1935 led to the establishment of a number of air-defence radar stations which were to prove critical in the Second World War (1939–45).
1934	The Emitron electronic camera is an advance on the system developed by Shoenberg in 1931. In the following year Shoenberg inaugurated the 405-line system and on 1 November 1936 the EMI–Marconi system became standard as the BBC television service began operation from Alexander Palace.
1935	Berlin: first television mobile unit comes into operation, employed at the opening of the Berlin TV station of the Reichs Rundfunk, 22 March. The first mobile units in the UK, designed by T.C. Macnamara, were used in the BBC's first major outside broadcast, of the Coronation, May 1937.
1936	First full-length animated film, *Snow White and the Seven Dwarfs* from the Disney Studios.
1938	Russian hypnotist, sculptor and journalist Lazlo Biró constructed a prototype ball-point pen with quick-drying ink. Having acquired British rights, Biró began manufacture in a disused RAF hangar in 1944. In 1953 Baron Bic, in France, introduced the first 'throwaway' ball-point. In the UK priced at 1 shilling, sales during 1959 totalled 53 million.
1939–45	Second World War.
1939	US: William C. Huebner introduces photosetting of type.
	Premiere of *Gone with the Wind.*

1940   UK: statutory newsprint rationing introduced; ended 1956.

1941   Release of Orson Welles' film masterpiece *Citizen Kane*, based on the life and lifestyle of American media baron William Randoph Hearst.

USSR: Tamara Lobova becomes first woman to shoot a feature film, *Suvarov*, released in January.

John Logie Baird demonstrates 3-D television in colour, a 500-line system, 18 December, at Sydenham.

The Communist *Daily Worker* is suppressed.

1944   Automatic digital computer, by American Howard Aiken, is followed in the next year by the electronic computer invented in the US by J. Presper Eckert and John W. Mauchly.

1945   BBC launches the Light Programme, now Radio 2; and the following year, the Third Programme, now Radio 3.

1946   The Southwestern Bell Telephone Company of St Louis, US, offers the first commercial car phone service.

1947   Polaroid camera, by Edwin Land, US.

Soviet Union: first 3-D colour feature film, *Robinson Crusoe*, directed by A.N. Andreyevsky. Special spectacles were not required.

US: Private Commission on Freedom of the Press, founded by publisher Henry Luce and chaired by the chancellor of the University of Chicago, Robert Hutchens, to 'examine areas and circumstances under which the press of the United States is succeeding or failing; to discover where freedom of expression is or is not limited, whether by government censorship, pressure from readers or advertisers or the unwisdom of its proprietors or the timidity of its management'. The Commission report broached, formally for the first time, the concept of *social responsibility* and listed criteria for the fulfilment of those critena.

1947–9   First UK Royal Commission on the Press – the Ross Commission.

1948   The Universal Declaration of Human Rights is adopted by the United Nations Assembly in Paris, 10 December.

NBC of America screens first TV Western series, *Hopalong Cassidy*, starring Bill Boyd.

1948   Bell Telephone Company scientists John Bardeen, Walter Brattain and William Shockley introduce the first transistor.

1949   Xerography invented by Chester Carlson, US, the same year as Peter Goldmark of the US introduces the first long-playing record.

CBS launches first TV thriller series, *Suspense*.

1950	Yoshiro Nakamats of the Imperial University, Tokyo, develops the floppy disc.
1952	First video recorder demonstration conducted in the US by John Mullin and Wayne Johnson at the Bing Crosby Enterprise laboratories in Beverly Hills, California, 11 November. A colour video was demonstrated by the same company in September of the following year. Neither was developed commercially. Ampex was the first to go into production, its initial production model being acquired by CBS.
	In the UK the BBC's VERA came into operation in April 1958 with a recording of *Panorama*. Sony brought out a transistorized video recorder in 1961, while the first domestic video recorder, also from Sony, was launched in the US in July 1965. It was not until 1972 that Sony launched, in Japan, its first video cassette recorder.
	In Europe Philips introduced the first domestic video cassette recorder in 1974. The VHS format was introduced in 1976 by JVC of Japan; and in the same year JVC produced the first camcorders for amateur use.
1953	Inauguration of the British Press Council.
	BBC demonstrates colour TV. An outside broadcast of the Coronation procession was relayed by closed circuit at Great Ormond Street Hospital for Sick Children.
	The first movie in Cinemascope, 20th Century Fox's *The Robe*, is premiered at Grauman's Chinese Theater, Hollywood, and in the same month, September, *This is Cinerama* opened in New York.
1954	In the UK in July, the Television Bill is given royal assent, creating the Independent Television Authority. Commercial TV began broadcasting in Britain in September 1955.
	Eurovision is inaugurated on 6 June when TV services in eight European countries linked together with a 4000-mile chain of relays. The first programme to be screened was the Festival of Flowers from Montreux, Switzerland.
1955–6	First daily TV soap broadcast in Britain – *Sixpenny Corner*, running for 15 minutes daily. It failed even though it was transferred by ITV to an evening slot.
1959	The *Manchester Guardian* becomes the *Guardian*.
1960	Bell Telephone's Touch-Tone telephone is successfully tested and becomes commercially available in 1963.
	ITVs *Coronation Street* opens its record-breaking run.
	The American Telephone & Telegraph Company makes the first transatlantic satellite transmission on 11 July, from Andover, Maine, to Goonhilly Downs, Cornwall, via Telstar.
	America launches first communications satellite, Echo 1.
	UK: death of the *News Chronicle*; first issue of the *Sunday Telegraph*.

1962 UK: Pilkington Committee Report on Broadcasting and the Shawcross Commission Report on the Press.

    First nights on UK TV for *Z Cars*, *Steptoe and Son* and the satirical series *That Was The Week That Was*. In the following year, *Dr Who* and *World in Action*.

1963 Founding of International Publishing Corporation (IPC); following year, IPC launches the *Sun*, replacing the *Daily Herald*.

    UK: BBC ends its ban on the mention of religion, politics, royalty or sex in comedy programmes.

    University of Michigan scientists Emmett Leith and Juris Upatnicks develop the first hologram.

1964 BBC launches new channel, BBC2, in April.

    UK starters: *Match of the Day* and *Crossroads*.

1965 Via the Early Bird satellite on 2 May 300 million viewers in nine countries sample the first transatlantic programme relay; 15 days later America's NBC was first with a colour transatlantic satellite programme transmission.

    Influential drama-documentary, *Cathy Come Home*, about Britain's homeless is broadcast by the BBC.

    Smoking advertisements are banned from UK television.

1966 Lord Thomson buys *The Times*.

    China: Chairman Mao launches the Cultural Revolution against 'reactionary bourgeois ideas in the sphere of academic work, education, art and theatre and publishing'.

1967 First colour TV broadcast in the UK, BBC2, 1 July.

    BBC Radio 1 is launched, 30 September.

    The Postmaster-General, Edward Short MP, opens Radio Leicester, the first local radio station in the UK.

1968 In UK first broadcast of comedy series *Dad's Army*.

1969 First commercially produced microprocessor developed by Edward Hoff of the Intel Corporation of California.

    Australian Rupert Murdoch buys the *Sun* and the *News of the World*.

    Denmark: film censorship is abolished.

    UK: York University launches first university radio station.

1972   US: first pre-recorded video tapes offered for hire by Sears, Roebuck. Pre-recorded tapes were not available in the UK until 1979, supplied initially by Intervision who acquired 200 film titles from United Artists for £250,000. By the end of the year they had franchised some 150 outlets. Such was the immediate competition that Intervision soon went under despite the increase in the sales of VCRs and rental outlets.

     The UK *Sunday Times* is banned on 17 November from publishing a series of articles on Thalidomide, a drug taken by expectant mothers and causing horrific deformities in babies.

     Cable TV transmission starts in UK.

1973   London Broadcasting (LBC) is the first commercial radio station in mainland UK, on air 8 October.

1974   UK: BBC inaugurates Ceefax, the UK's first teletext service.

1977   UK: Annan Commission Report on Broadcasting and the McGregor Commission Report on the Press.

1978   UK: first series of the comprehensive school-set series *Grange Hill.*

     First video cassette recorder introduced in the UK.

     Japan: the Sony Walkman is launched.

1979   UK: Williams Committee Report on Obscenity and Film Censorship.

     First digital recording, by Decca, of a New Year's Day concert in Vienna; recorded live by the Vienna Philharmonic Orchestra and issued in April.

1980   The compact disc (CD), developed by Philips over several years, is demonstrated at the Salzburg Festival in April. By agreement with Philips, the Japanese firm Sony launched the first CD in 1982. With a playing time of 75 minutes, the CD used a grooveless miniature 12cm disc using a laser beam to read digitally encoded information.

     MacBride Commission Report for UNESCO.

     UK: ITV documentary *Death of a Princess* causes offence to the government of Saudi Arabia; millions of pounds in trade orders are lost as a result. The British government apologizes to the Saudis, 22 April.

1981   UK: Australian media baron Rupert Murdoch acquires the British newspapers, *The Times* and *Sunday Times,* having been exempted from a monopolies enquiry by the Conservative government, led by Margaret Thatcher.

1982   UK: Hunt Committee on Cable Expansion and Broadcasting Policy.

     UK: Channel 4 television begins transmission.

1983   Breakfast TV starts on the BBC; the CD player, the pocket TV and the first cordless telephone are introduced to the UK.

1984   UK: first satellite TV channel – Rupert Murdoch's Sky – begins transmission, 16 January.

Civil servant Clive Ponting is acquitted by a jury of breaking the Official Secrets Act. His relevation to the press of details concerning the British sinking of the Argentine battleship *The Belgrano* were justified in court as being in the public interest. Later the Act was redrafted to exclude public interest as a defence. The advent of a Labour government has not led to the return of the public interest clause.

Robert Maxwell takes over the *Daily Mirror* group.

1985   Rupert Murdoch buys American film company 20th Century Fox.

Panasonic of Japan introduces to the UK the first VHS camcorder in January, and in May Sony launches the digital video-recorder.

British Board of Film Censors issues age classification for videos, following the passing of the Video Recordings Act.

1986   Eddy Shah's *Today* newspaper, published in the UK, is the first to use on-the-run colour. Launched on 4 March the 44-page paper carried 16 pages in colour.

Australian TV soap *Neighbours* is introduced to UK on BBC.

USSR: Michail Gorbachev announces new policy of Glasnost, 'openness'.

Wapping, London: thousands of print workers picket Murdoch's new premises, protesting about computerization and the loss of jobs.

Czechoslovakia: the Jazz Union is closed down for urging the freedom of the arts.

1987   Sydney, Australia, September: British government is rebuffed in its courtroom appeal against the decision to permit the publication of *Spycatcher*.

1988   The first transatlantic optical fibre cable is laid, costing £220 million, between the US and UK/France, able to carry simultaneously 40,000 telephone calls.

1989   The Iron Curtain that divided eastern European nations – Poland, Hungary, Czechoslovakia and East Germany etc. – from the West, is drawn aside. The trades union Solidarity is permitted to contest elections in Poland; in Hungary border troops tear down the barbed-wire frontier with Austria. Most significantly, the Berlin Wall is dismantled. However, in June, freedom protests in Beijing are crushed in Tiananmen Square. The rest of the world watches events on TV.

In Iran, the Ayatollah Khomeini condemns as blasphemous the novel *The Satanic Verses* by British writer Salman Rushdie and issues a fatwa, or edict, calling on all Muslims to strike down the offender. Despite worldwide protests, the death sentence remained active until September 1998 when the government of Iran distanced itself from, without rescinding, the Khomeini edict.

1990   UK: Broadcasting Act separates control of commercial television (ITC, Independent Television Commission) and radio (the Radio Authority).

The *Northern Echo* edited in Darlington becomes the first UK newspaper on CD-ROM.

The first tapeless answering machine, the ADAM (All-Digital Answering Machine), storing messages on a silicon chip, launched in the US by PhoneMate.

Iraq: Farzad Barzoft, journalist on the UK *Observer*, is executed in Baghdad after 'confessing' to spying.

UK: Calcutt Committee reports on its deliberations concerning 'a wide public aversion to newspaper intrusion', and recommends 'reform by self-regulation' and a Code of Practice. The Press Complaints Commission emerged from Calcutt recommendations.

1991	Robert Maxwell dies in a drowning accident.
1992	Los Angeles: street riots after screening of police beating up a black motorist, Rodney King.

UK: first land-based national commercial radio station – Classic FM – launched 7 September.

Canada: government Bill C-128 bans the depiction of under-18s engaging in any form of 'explicit sexual activity', including kissing.

1993   UK: carried via London Interconnect cable network, the first black TV service – Identity TV – begins, 13 July, with estimated audience of 150,000, and on 1 September BSkyB launches first women's TV channel.

Transmitting from coaches driving round London, the BBC begins first experiments in DAB (Digital Audio Broadcasting).

1994   BBC converts generalist service, Radio 5, which featured programmes for young listeners, to Radio 5 Live dedicated to sports, news and chat.

1998   UK: Sky TV launches digital television service, 1 October.

1999   A jury in Oregon, US, fines anti-abortionist campaigners \$107mn for publishing on their Internet website a 'wanted' list of abortion doctors, their clinics and addresses, seeing it as a thinly veiled death threat.

During the war for Kosovo, NATO bombers target TV stations in Serbia's capital, Belgrade.

UK: Greg Dyke is appointed new director-general of the BBC in succession to Sir John Birt.

2000   UK: Regulation of Investigatory Powers Act (RIPA), extending official surveillance to Internet communication.

US: merger of the world's biggest media giant, Time Warner, with AOL (America On Line).

2001   11 September: TV viewers across the world witness the terrorist destruction of the twin towers of New York's World Trade Center.

Italy: Silvio Berlusconi, media magnate, becomes Italy's prime minister for the second time.

2002   Labour government issues Communications Bill proposing the loosening of broadcasting regulations and abandoning rules concerning cross-media ownership. With modifications, becomes Act of Parliament, 2003.

ITV Digital services go bust, but a consortium led by the BBC steps in to offer over 20 digital channels (freeview). New digital services from the BBC: CBBC (for children, aged 6-13), Cheebies (for under 6s) BBC Four (art, history, current affairs), BBC Three (drama, entertainment, music). At the same time, BBC radio goes digital (BBC Digital, Asian Network, 6Music, 1Xtra, Five Live Sports Extra and BBC7 (comedy, drama and children's programmes).

China: analysts estimate that the state employs 30,000 people to monitor and control information.

Gulf Cooperation Council, meeting in Oman, warns satellite TV station al-Jazeer to make programmes 'more respectful'.

Poland: Church-run Radio Maryja is shut down on the orders of the Catholic primate, Cardinal Josef Glemp.

US: Iranian film-maker Abbas Kiarostami is denied a visa permitting him to enter the country at the invitation of the New York Film Festival to lecture at Harvard University.

UK: David Shayler, former M15 officer, is jailed for six months for breaking the Official Secrets Act by leaking documents concerning alleged malpractice in the UK secret service.

Announcement of plans for a £2.6b merger between Granada (7 ITV licences) and Carlton Communications (5 ITV licenses), subject to approval by the UK office of Fair Trading. The merger leaves only three independent UK franchises – Grampian, Scottish and Ulster TV.

Report on human rights in 50 countries by the Electronic Privacy Information Center and Privacy International declares that post-11 September 2001 'many new anti-terrorist laws adopted by national governments . . . threaten political freedom'.

2003   Federal Communications Commission (USA) initiates major shift towards loosening regulations concerning the delivery of TV and radio news, considering that many in-place rules are 'antiquated'; that is, standing in the way of futher media mergers.

Global publics find their voice in protesting against war in Iraq, but million-strong marches do not prevent US and UK forces going into battle despite the failure to obtain a United Nations mandate for military action.